Entrepreneurial Teams and New Business Creation

The International Library of Entrepreneurship

Series Editor: David B. Audretsch
Max Planck Institute of Economics, Jena, Germany
and Ameritech Chair of Economic Development
Indiana University, USA

Wherever possible, the articles in these volumes have been reproduced as originally published using facsimile reproduction, inclusive of footnotes and pagination to facilitate ease of reference.

For a list of all Edward Elgar published titles visit our site on the World Wide Web at
www.e-elgar.com

Entrepreneurial Teams and New Business Creation

WITHDRAWN

Edited by

Mike Wright

Professor of Financial Studies
and Director of the Centre for Management Buy-out Research
Nottingham University Business School, UK

and

Iris Vanaelst

Assistant Professor
Vlerick Leuven Gent Management School
Belgium

THE INTERNATIONAL LIBRARY OF ENTREPRENEURSHIP

An Elgar Reference Collection
Cheltenham, UK • Northampton, MA, USA

Published by
Edward Elgar Publishing Limited
The Lypiatts
15 Lansdown Road
Cheltenham
Glos GL50 2JA
UK

Edward Elgar Publishing, Inc.
William Pratt House
9 Dewey Court
Northampton
Massachusetts 01060
USA

A catalogue record for this book is available from the British Library

Library of Congress Control Number: 2008943841

Mixed Sources
Product group from well-managed forests and other controlled sources
www.fsc.org Cert no. SA-COC-1565
© 1996 Forest Stewardship Council
FSC

ISBN 978 184 844 480 5

Printed and bound in Great Britain by MPG Books Ltd, Bodmin, Cornwall

Contents

Acknowledgements

The editors and publishers wish to thank the authors and the following publishers who have kindly given permission for the use of copyright material.

Academy of Management via Copyright Clearance Centre for articles: Warren Boeker and Rushi Karichalil (2002), 'Entrepreneurial Transitions: Factors Influencing Founder Departure', *Academy of Management Journal*, **45** (3), 818–26; Christine M. Beckman (2006), 'The Influence of Founding Team Company Affiliations on Firm Behavior', *Academy of Management Journal*, **49** (4), 741–58.

American Sociological Association for article: Martin Ruef, Howard E. Aldrich and Nancy M. Carter (2003), 'The Structure of Founding Teams: Homophily, Strong Ties, and Isolation Among U.S. Entrepreneurs', *American Sociological Review*, **68** (2), April, 195–222.

Blackwell Publishing Ltd for articles: Judith B. Kamm and Aaron J. Nurick (1993), 'The Stages of Team Venture Formation: A Decision-Making Model', *Entrepreneurship Theory and Practice*, **17**, Winter, 17–27; Deborah H. Francis and William R. Sandberg (2000), 'Friendship Within Entrepreneurial Teams and its Association with Team and Venture Performance', *Entrepreneurship Theory and Practice*, **25** (2), Winter, 5–25; Deniz Ucbasaran, Andy Lockett, Mike Wright and Paul Westhead (2003), 'Entrepreneurial Founder Teams: Factors Associated with Member Entry and Exit', *Entrepreneurship Theory and Practice*, **28** (2), Winter, 107–27; Iris Vanaelst, Bart Clarysse, Mike Wright, Andy Lockett, Nathalie Moray and Rosette S'Jegers (2006), 'Entrepreneurial Team Development in Academic Spinouts: An Examination of Team Heterogeneity', *Entrepreneurship Theory and Practice*, **30** (2), March, 249–71; G. Page West III (2007), 'Collective Cognition: When Entrepreneurial Teams, Not Individuals, Make Decisions', *Entrepreneurship Theory and Practice*, **31** (1), January, 77–102; Nikolaus Franke, Marc Gruber, Dietmar Harhoff and Joachim Henkel (2008), 'Venture Capitalists' Evaluations of Start-Up Teams: Trade-Offs, Knock-Out Criteria, and the Impact of VC Experience', *Entrepreneurship Theory and Practice*, **32** (3), May, 459–83.

Cornell University for article: Kathleen M. Eisenhardt and Claudia Bird Schoonhoven (1990), 'Organizational Growth: Linking Founding Team, Strategy, Environment, and Growth among U.S. Semiconductor Ventures, 1978–1988', *Administrative Science Quarterly*, **35** (3), September, 504–29.

Elsevier for articles: Juan B. Roure and Modesto A. Maidique (1986), 'Linking Prefunding Factors and High-Technology Venture Success: An Exploratory Study', *Journal of Business Venturing*, **1** (3), 295–306; Michael D. Ensley, Allison W. Pearson and Allen C. Amason (2002), 'Understanding the Dynamics of New Venture Top Management Teams: Cohesion, Conflict, and New Venture Performance', *Journal of Business Venturing*, **17** (2), July, 365–86; Sanjib Chowdhury (2005), 'Demographic Diversity for Building an Effective Entrepreneurial Team: Is it Important?', *Journal of Business Venturing*, **20** (6), November, 727–46; Aegean Leung, Jing Zhang, Poh Kam Wong and Maw Der Foo (2006), 'The Use of Networks in Human Resource Acquisition for Entrepreneurial Firms: Multiple "fit" Considerations', *Journal of Business Venturing*, **21** (5), September, 664–86.

INFORMS (Institute for Operations Research and the Management Sciences) for articles: Warren Boeker and Robert Wiltbank (2005), 'New Venture Evolution and Managerial Capabilities', *Organization Science*, **16** (2), March/April, 123–33; Christine M. Beckman and M. Diane Burton (2008), 'Founding the Future: Path Dependence in the Evolution of Top Management Teams from Founding to IPO', *Organization Science*, **19** (1), 3–24.

Sage Publications for article: Frédéric Delmar and Scott Shane (2006), 'Does Experience Matter? The Effect of Founding Team Experience on the Survival and Sales of Newly Founded Ventures', *Strategic Organization*, **4** (3), 215–47.

Springer Science and Business Media for article: Thomas Lechler (2001), 'Social Interaction: A Determinant of Entrepreneurial Team Venture Success', *Small Business Economics*, **16** (4), June, 263–78.

Every effort has been made to trace all the copyright holders but if any have been inadvertently overlooked the publishers will be pleased to make the necessary arrangement at the first opportunity.

In addition the publishers wish to thank the Library of Indiana University at Bloomington, USA, for their assistance in obtaining these articles.

Introduction

Mike Wright and Iris Vanaelst

Introduction

There is growing interest in the diversity and complexity of entrepreneurial teams because of their potential to shape new business growth. In particular, curiosity surrounds the question of what entrepreneurial teams should look like in order to allow new businesses to be created and to ensure their growth. This focus makes sense since, in comparison to other determinants of new business performance, such as market conditions and competitors' (re)actions, a venture's management has much more control of the composition of its entrepreneurial team.

Studies on entrepreneurial teams build on the argument by Gartner *et al.* (1994) that *the entrepreneur in entrepreneurship* is typically plural, instead of singular. Rather than one single heroic entrepreneur, an entrepreneurial team seems better suited to deal with the volatilities and uncertainties associated with new businesses that demand flexibility and complexity in decision making. The argument that the entrepreneurial activity of initiating, establishing and growing a new venture is more often a collective than a singular one is now widely acknowledged (Reich, 1987; Kamm *et al.*, 1990; Gartner *et al.*, 1994; Eisenhardt and Schoonhoven, 1996; Ensley *et al.*, 1999).

In focusing on the critical issues and events in the life of an entrepreneurial team, it is useful to consider the team's formation and composition, the social interaction and interpersonal processes within teams, team turnover and the potential links between the team and new business outcome. The importance of each of these topics in studying entrepreneurial teams is reflected in the parts of this book devoted to each of these subjects and depicted in Figure 1. Prior to any consideration of the different factors associated with entrepreneurial teams and their potential to create and grow new businesses, it is necessary to delineate the term entrepreneurial team.

There has been considerable debate as to what exactly is understood by the term 'entrepreneurial team'. Kamm *et al.* (1990) define entrepreneurial teams as 'two or more individuals who jointly establish a firm in which they have a financial interest' (Kamm *et al.*, 1990, p. 7). Gartner *et al.* (1994) broadened this definition to cover those individuals who have direct influence on strategic choice. Ensley *et al.* (1998) combine both delineations by stating that an individual has to fulfil three criteria in order to be considered a member of the entrepreneurial team: (1) jointly establish a firm; (2) have a financial interest; and (3) have a direct influence on the strategic choice of the firm. Other researchers have made the equity stake condition stricter and impose a minimum equity stake before some one can be considered a member of the entrepreneurial team (Ucbasaran *et al.*, Chapter 13).

This debate is related to the fact that entrepreneurial teams are frequently investigated within a static framework. Often entrepreneurial teams are studied around the time of formal incorporation of the new venture. However, there is abundant evidence in the new technology

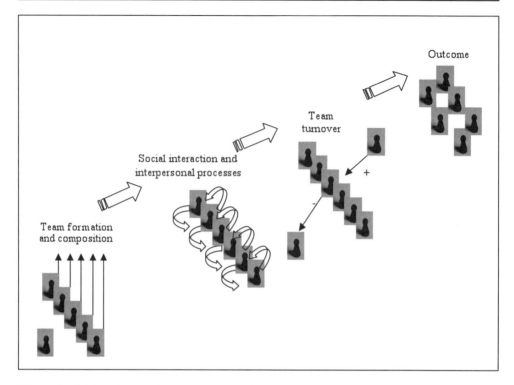

Figure 1   Main subjects of "Entrepreneurial Teams in New Business Creation"

based firms and spin-out literature that the date of legal founding is already the outcome of a long process of search and selection of team members, and team formation (Clarysse and Moray, 2004; Vohora *et al.*, 2004; Forbes *et al.*, 2006). Before a venture is legally founded, a team formation process has already taken place (Gartner, 1985; Katz and Gartner, 1988). Even when teams are considered around and after the time of formal incorporation of the new ventures, the evolutionary aspects of entrepreneurial team formation and development are most often implicitly neglected. Recent research has attempted to tackle this problem and has studied team entry and exit (Ucbasaran *et al.*, Chapter 13; Chandler *et al.*, 2005, Vanaelst *et al.*, Chapter 5). This research suggests that, over the life of the organization, the composition of the team is likely to vary: some members are added to the team while others leave. The dynamics associated with team entry are distinct from those associated with team exit (Ucbasaran *et al.*, Chapter 13; Chandler *et al.*, 2005, Vanaelst *et al.*, Chapter 5).

Moreover, some researchers suggest that changes in the composition of the team result from the fact that teams face different challenges in different stages of their life and that these changes are translated in team turnover, as an adaptive mechanism (Boeker, 1997; Chandler *et al.*, 2005). Some evolutionary theories suggest that this adaptive mechanism is a path-dependent process. This path-dependent process implies that the configuration of the founding team shapes subsequent executive teams (Boeker, 1989; Beckman and Burton, 2005). This adaptive mechanism builds on the premise that as the venture evolves through the different stages of its life, its needs towards different kinds of resources may change in order to meet the changing environment in which it is active. Since different members of the team may provide a venture with access to an array of human, social and financial resources (Kor and Mahoney, 2000), its composition is likely to alter in response to these changing needs. This book brings the different insights together on how team members come together to form a team and create a new business, and how the team evolves over the life of the new business and sets a research agenda for future research on entrepreneurial teams.

The team concept is related to the different stages in the venture creation process (Kamm and Nurick, Chapter 1; Clarysse and Moray, 2004; Vanaelst *et al.*, Chapter 5). This has resulted in several team concepts that can be found in the literature: entrepreneurial team (Kamm *et al.*, 1990; Ensley *et al.*, 1998; Ucbasaran *et al.*, Chapter 13), founding teams (Chandler and Hanks, 1998a; Delmar and Shane, 2003), and founding top management teams (Eisenhardt and Schoonhoven, Chapter 16; Boeker and Karichalil, Chapter 12). The distinctions between these terms are often unclear and more research is needed to understand these differences.

Founding teams are distinct from top management teams (TMTs) (Beckman and Burton, Chapter 18). Founding teams are made up of people who create the new business, irrespective of whether they hold executive titles. TMTs are made up of people who hold executive titles, regardless of when they join the new business. Although there is overlap between these teams at founding if all founders hold executive titles, the teams are conceptually and empirically distinct. Founders are not added as the new business grows, and, as TMT members join the firm and founders leave, the teams continue to diverge.

The distinction between founder and entrepreneurial teams depends greatly on perceptions of the nature of entrepreneurship. A view that entrepreneurship involves the creation of a venture would imply that founding teams are entrepreneurial. This perspective would also suggest that teams developed following the creation of a venture are not entrepreneurial as the entrepreneurial act has passed. However, if entrepreneurship is held to involve the identification and pursuit of new opportunities, teams in existing ventures that identify and pursue new opportunities would be entrepreneurial.

Delineation of the team concept has important implications for the nature of the research questions under study. For example, using founding teams to study the nature of teams in entrepreneurial firms may be problematical as this takes a static view on a dynamic process. The use of founding teams does not capture processes prior to and after the legal founding of the venture, like research on team entry and exit (Ucbasaran *et al.*, Chapter 13). Research on founding teams may imply that entrepreneurial teams only exist in start-ups, which would exclude corporate entrepreneurship and management buy-outs (MBOs) for instance. A focus on TMT as teams involved in running and managing existing businesses may not necessarily capture teams that are entrepreneurial in the sense of identifying and pursuing opportunities. The identification and pursuit of opportunities is at the very core of entrepreneurial teams. These activities can occur within both start-up businesses and existing organizations, leading to academic or corporate spin-outs for instance.

Clarification of the team concept also has implications for policy. If the aim of policy intervention is to strengthen and increase societal entrepreneurship, the concept of the founding team does not fully capture the dynamics of infusing entrepreneurship in different contexts. Support for entrepreneurial teams may need to include MBOs, management buy-ins (MBIs), family firms, and academic and corporate spin-outs as well as start-ups.

Entrepreneurial teams are often studied in an innovative high-tech environment. The complexity and dynamic character of an innovative high-tech environment are expected to bring about more dramatic team dynamics. Moreover, the success of high-tech entrepreneurial teams is attributed to the reasoning that 'high technology industries might require more skills than an individual would be likely to have, necessitating that individuals combine their abilities in teams in order to start an organization successfully' (Gartner, 1985, p. 703). Therefore entrepreneurial teams are often studied in innovative high-tech start-ups (Vanaelst, 2006). Innovative high-tech start-ups are new ventures that develop and commercialize new products or services. In these innovative high-tech start-ups a distinction can be made between independent innovative ventures and ventures with a link with a university or public research institution, like academic spin-outs that are a particular group of innovative high-tech start-ups (Clarysse, 2004). In order to study the new business creation process, academic spin-outs have received particular recent attention (Vanaelst, 2006; Vanaelst *et al.*, Chapter 5; Forbes *et al.*, 2006; Clarysse and Moray, 2004; Vohora *et al.*, 2004; Wright *et al.*, 2007a). This focus on academic spin-outs in order to study the process of new business creation can be explained by two reasons. The first is that academic spin-outs are a substantial group of innovative high-tech start-ups (Moray, 2004). The second reason is that an in-depth study of the entrepreneurial team formation process over the different stages of the venture's life calls for the identification of individuals in the first stage of the venture creation process. Academic spin-outs originate out of a parent organization, either a university or a research institute (Clarysse *et al.*, 2005). As a consequence of the fact that the population of the parent organization is delineated, those individuals that are potentially involved in the very early stage of development of a venture are identifiable and key insights on entrepreneurial team formation and composition can be developed.

Team Formation and Composition

The creation of a new business entails a decision regarding who will participate and what they will contribute. Some entrepreneurs begin entirely on their own, but turn to others for support on various aspects of the new business creation process. Others start with a team, making the creation of a new business a collective effort. At the extreme, a founding team comes together without a clear idea of what the potential venture will do (Beckman, Chapter 2). The idea generation can not be separated from the experiences of the founders of the new business. In many cases, individuals' experiences shape the technological opportunities they recognise (Shane, 2000); thus, the characteristics, experiences, and affiliations of team members shape the ideas and opportunities that are eventually pursued. The team and initial idea for a business can emerge in a dynamic, reciprocal fashion in which the idea is embedded in the context and experience of the founders (Beckman, Chapter 2). Team formation decisions are mainly based on the mutual interests of potential team members or their common aspirations to create a new business (Chandler and Hanks, 1998b). Research indicates that how a new business comes into existence and whether others are recruited to join the effort can have lasting consequences for its survival and performance. Founding strategy does not only influence the resources of young firms but may also lock the new business into a particular strategic direction such that founding strategies persist long after the founding of the new business (Boeker, 1989); this underlines the importance of team composition in the early stages of new business creation.

Entrepreneurship scholars have suggested that the advantage of start-up teams comes from the composition of the team, especially in terms of the diversity of its characteristics, knowledge and skills (Gartner, 1985; Pelled *et al.*, 1999). Team composition, defined in terms of attributes such as gender, age and educational level (Bantel and Jackson, 1989; Foo *et al.* 2006) and functional level (Roure and Maidique, Chapter 15; Eisenhardt and Schoonhoven, Chapter 16; Ancona and Caldwell, 1992) is related to outcomes. Research relating TMT functional diversity to venture performance seems to suggest that diversity strengthens venture performance because broad functional representation ensures that the TMT has the full range of capabilities to manage the organization (Eisenhardt and Schoonhoven, Chapter 16; Ancona and Caldwell, 1992). Chowdhury (Chapter 6) examined the influence of demographic diversity variables relating to gender, age and functional background on entrepreneurial team effectiveness. These factors were found not to be important for entrepreneurial team effectiveness. Educational diversity leads to different cognitive styles and perspectives in the team (Wiersema and Bantel, 1992). Having different views is assumed to be beneficial as the team analyses problems from multiple approaches. It is assumed that diversity effects depend on the team's context. In an uncertain environment such as a new business, diversity is likely to benefit the team through improved problem-solving capabilities while cognitive benefits may outweigh potential costs of diversity (Foo *et al.*, 2006).

The underlying assumption seems to be that heterogeneous teams are more effective in solving complex issues, which are common during the creation of new businesses. This view arises because the diversity of perceptions, skills, abilities and knowledge that prevails in a heterogeneous team is assumed to increase the team's cognitive resources. These resources will contribute to team effectiveness in handling complex tasks and challenges and problem solving ability (Bantel and Jackson, 1989; Eisenhardt and Schoonhoven, Chapter 16), enabling the team to go into issues more deeply and develop a more complete understanding of problems and alternative solutions (Foo *et al.*, 2005; Pelled *et al.*, 1999). However, team diversity does not necessarily bring different demographic characteristics amongst the team members (Chowdhury, Chapter 6). Differences in personality traits and thinking styles can in their turn create diversity of cognitive attributes within a team that are important in making novel and creative decisions like in a new business creation process (Chowdhury, Chapter 6). To achieve team-level diverse cognitive capabilities, the team interaction process is at least as important as having members with a variety of cognitive attributes (Chowdhury, Chapter 6).

Heterogeneous teams are expected to be suited to the generation of new business performance because of their assumed benefits through improved creativity and innovativeness. However, diversity can lead to less effective teams (Ancona and Caldwell, 1992), as heterogeneity may also produce conflicts and emotions amongst the team members which have a negative impact on business performance (Amason and Sapienza, 1997). On the other hand, homogeneity within a group may lead to inferior decision making because of 'groupthink' and insufficient airing of conflict (Eisenhardt and Schoonhoven, Chapter 16).

Entrepreneurship and new business creation implies solving complex problems under time pressure. Therefore, research has looked into the potential effects of prior joint working experience on new business performance (Roure and Maidique, Chapter 15; Eisenhardt and Schoonhoven, Chapter 16). Prior joint working experience affects the speed of decision making. Executives who have a history together have learned how to get along and communicate with each other. They are also likely to have developed routines for making decisions quickly and are more likely to understand the idiosyncrasies and strengths of their colleagues in comparison to teams formed of strangers (Eisenhardt and Schoonhoven, Chapter 16). Founding teams with prior joint working experience can save valuable time in building coordination and trust (Stinchcombe, 1965) and can focus on venture problems, rather than on group-process issues. As a consequence, founding teams with prior joint working experience are involved in firms that have higher levels of growth than teams with less overlapping experience (Roure and Maidique, Chapter 15; Eisenhardt and Schoonhoven, Chapter 16). Prior joint working experience is discussed in relation to the cohesion stemming from managers' having worked together in the past, but Beckman (Chapter 2) added that this cohesion may result from shared affiliations as well as from direct experience with one another.

The discussion in this section has made clear that is important to study diversity because diversity affects how members interact with each other.

Social Integration and Interpersonal Processes Within Teams

The previous section indicated the importance of diversity in the composition of the entrepreneurial team. Interpersonal processes and intrateam dynamics should enable the translation of multiple perspectives in a founding team into the development of a cohesive point of view across the team. On the one hand, forces underlying the team composition tend towards a homogeneous group that can develop synergistic benefits that enhance the potential of the new business (Colombo and Grilli, 2005). On the other hand, this can limit the scope and newness of the perspectives infused into the new business creation process (Ruef *et al.*, Chapter 3). Building on Boeker (1989), this entails limits to the potential development of the newly created business. According to Boeker (1989), conditions at founding – including size of the team and the extent to which a business is owned by its founding managers – can imprint an initial strategy on the new business that resists change, and as a consequence the range of the perspectives considered by the team is limited. West (Chapter 10) refers to the tension between the propensity to surface new ideas in order to adapt the venture to changing circumstances and the inertia of the venture's initial direction.

Team formation means that individuals are brought together which implies interpersonal processes and relationships. The interpersonal relationships between team members are supposed to create dynamics that shape team boundaries. Moreover, previous research found that the nature of the interaction between the team members matters (e.g. Knight *et al.*, 1999). Entrepreneurial teams by their very nature take strategic decisions. By doing so, the team taps into its cognitive resources through its own process of interaction. The quality of the team's decisions, and as a consequence the business' strategy and performance, depends on those processes (Francis and Sandberg, Chapter 7). Interpersonal problems within entrepreneurial teams may have several causes such as a lack of heterogeneous experience and skills, the absence of leadership on account of a desire for equitable influence, and conflicting values and goals (Timmons, 1979; Francis and Sandberg, Chapter 7).

Amason (1996) identified a team's interaction process as antecedent to decisions and types of conflict. Conflict is a process that teams go through to make decisions, take action and create cognitive schema (Ensley and Pearce, 2001). A distinction is made between cognitive and affective conflict (Amason, 1996; Amason and Sapienza, 1997). Cognitive conflict is task-oriented disagreement arising from differences in perspective; it deals with judgemental differences about how to best achieve common goals. It may be beneficial as it has a positive effect on strategic decisions and performance (Amason and Sapienza, 1997; Ensley *et al.*, Chapter 8). Eisenhardt *et al.* (1997) also analyse the key elements of managing constructive conflict to create collaboration between top management teams. In contrast, affective conflict is individual-oriented disagreement arising from personal disaffection, it has to do with personal incompatibilities, and may be detrimental to the development of the venture. Research suggests that demographic diversity has the potential to create emotional conflicts within teams (Ancona and Caldwell, 1992; Eisenhardt *et al.*, 1997), which is found to influence team effectiveness negatively (Pelled *et al.*, 1999; Amason and Sapienza, 1997) and can lead to team exit (Vanaelst *et al.*, Chapter 5).

Debates amongst team members based on their different perspectives lead to increased decision comprehensiveness, and are particularly important in situations characterized by change and uncertainty (Eisenhardt, 1989), which is the case in the creation of a new business. Conflict within teams in making strategic decisions is beneficial to the decision quality but may be detrimental to the team's willingness to continue working together. Apparently, the key to grasping the benefits from conflicts without having to bear the costs is to encourage a give-and-take of cognitive conflict while avoiding the affective conflict that makes the disagreement more personal and corrodes the relations within a team (Amason, 1996; Amason and Sapienza, 1997).

Founding top management teams are likely to differ in their ability to exploit or enhance the amount of resources (Eisenhardt and Schoonhoven, Chapter 16). Successful executive teams combine high conflict between team members with fast decisions. Successful executives move quickly to keep pace with the resource opportunities that rapidly appear and disappear in technology-based industries. Conflict appears essential among team members for effective top management performance (Eisenhardt, 1989; Eisenhardt and Schoonhoven, Chapter 16).

In addition to research on conflict within teams and between team members, studies have developed insights on interorganizational conflict between entrepreneurial teams and key stakeholders such as venture capitalists. In particular, Higashide and Birley (2002) investigated the factors associated with the nature of conflict in the post-investment relationship between the venture capitalist (VC) and the entrepreneurial team in a newly created business that was funded by the venture capital firm. They examined both cognitive and affective conflict in two strategic areas – organizational goals and policy decisions – and relate them to the new business performance. Their results confirm that conflict as disagreement can be beneficial for the performance of the new business, although at the same time, conflict as personal friction is negatively associated with performance. Their research shows that past findings with respect to cognitive and affective conflict are replicated in the VC–entrepreneurial team relationship. In particular, goal conflict has a greater impact on the new business performance than policy conflict, and works independently of policy conflict. On the other hand, goal conflict seems to be a necessary condition to make policy conflict work. Getting the right entrepreneurial management team upfront in the investment process seems to have been more crucial for the satisfaction of the VC, compared with managing the risk after the deal. Besides, the reduction of ambiguity and uncertainty, which stems from the constructive conflict in the VC–entrepreneurial team relationship, seems to have had a limited impact on the eventual perceived new business performance. Higashide and Birley (2002) warn VCs to be careful not to interfere in the goals and policies of their investee companies since any resultant disagreement could wipe out any potential positive effects. On the other hand, they also warn the entrepreneurs to be aware of VCs who want to be involved in decision making since such involvement could be detrimental to the VCs perception of the new business performance.

The entrepreneurship literature has found that team process variables such as team comprehension and deftness are important contributors to team competency and ultimately new business performance (McGrath *et al.*, 1995; Chowdhury, Chapter 6). Team comprehension is defined as a team's collective understanding of the important drivers of its business and deftness is defined as the 'emergence of a collective mind' that creates effective relationships among team members and that allows effective execution of interrelated activities. A team with high comprehension and deftness would have a diverse team-level cognitive capability in terms of the team's ability to understand and draw on a variety of perspectives, ideas and alternatives in solving complex problems and executing plans. Team-level cognitive comprehensiveness is a team process that examines critical issues with a wide lens and formulates strategies by considering diverse approaches, decision criteria and courses of action (Miller *et al.*, 1998; Chowdhury, Chapter 6).

Interactions amongst team members generate intrateam processes. In new businesses, the tasks are often ill-defined if defined at all, which makes the influence of intrateam processes more important since these interactions will shape and determine what the team does (Foo *et al.*, 2006). Research (e.g. Ancona and Caldwell, 1992) has found significant effects of communication on team effectiveness. Intrateam processes of social integration and open communication were positively related to both perceived team viability and member satisfaction (Foo *et al.*, 2006).

Communication facilitates problem solving by improving information flow. Despite the apparent benefits of information exchange, the effects of communication on team effectiveness are equivocal (Foo *et al.*, 2006) as they are considered in relation to conflict. This links into the argument made by Foo *et al.* (2006) that it is not so much the frequency of the communication but more important is how it is being communicated. Open communication can be the seedbed of cognitive conflicts that are assumed to enhance team effectiveness, as stressed before.

At the same time, team processes that minimize emotional conflict and enhance cooperation among team members should play an important role in improving team effectiveness. Team commitment is an important team process variable (Watson *et al.*, 1995; Pettigrew, 1998; Chowdhury, Chapter 6). Team commitment is assumed to enhance cohesion, loyalty and synergy, and minimize emotional conflicts between team members, and as a consequence it should increase entrepreneurial team effectiveness.

The nascent stage of the new business is crucial since the team is still fragile and will not be able to survive unless it can establish membership, identity, process and commitment (Foo *et al.*, 2006). These findings suggest that entrepreneurs should build teams focusing more on highly committed members who will value each other's cognitive styles, perceptions and abilities rather than on members' demographic diversity. Members of an entrepreneurial team should focus on developing trust and loyalty toward the team. This may create team commitment and decrease emotional conflict and as a consequence team effectiveness will improve (Chowdhury, Chapter 6).

The interpersonal relationships between team members are supposed to create dynamics which shape team boundaries. Social network researchers classify relationships on the basis of their content (Balkundi and Harrison, 2006). Two common types of relationship content are instrumental or economic and non-instrumental or affective (Lincoln and Miller, 1979; Larson and Star, 1993; Francis and Sandberg, Chapter 7; Forbes *et al.*, 2006). In the instrumental perspective, team formation is seen as a rational process driven by economic, instrumental considerations. This is what Francis and Sandberg (Chapter 7) call *gesellschaft*. Gesellschaft features rationally conceived relationships or roles that exist to achieve instrumental objectives. Instrumental relationships are considered to be vital to effective task performance. The primary content exchanged is information or knowledge that is relevant to fulfil one's role within a group.

In the non-instrumental perspective, relationships are more affect-laden and team formation is a process driven by interpersonal attraction and social networks. This is what Francis and Sandberg (Chapter 7) refer to as *gemeinschaft*. The gemeinschaft view considers people in a group as being bound by ties of feelings, reacting to each other in social relationships as personalities and not merely as role incumbents. Despite the apparent contrast, instrumental and non-instrumental relationships are not mutually exclusive, and there tends to be an overlap. Non-instrumental relationships might come into existence as a result of instrumental relationships. On the other hand entrepreneurs might first turn to their family and friends to translate an idea into a business reality and as such will an affective interpersonal relationship be translated into an economic one. Still, the primary content of the two types of relationships remains theoretically distinct; not all colleagues are friends, and vice versa (Van de Bunt *et al.*, 2005; Balkundi and Harrison, 2006).

Team Turnover

Teams do not remain static over time but tend to change over the life of the venture (Ucbasaran *et al.*, Chapter 13; Vanaelst *et al.*, Chapter 5). Recent research has provided an evolutionary perspective on team formation and its development over the life of the venture (e.g. Ucbasaran *et al.*, Chapter 13; Boone *et al.*, 2004; Beckman and Burton, 2005; Forbes *et al.*, 2006; Vanaelst *et al.*, Chapter 5). Some evolutionary theories even highlight a path-dependent process in which the founding team shapes subsequent executive teams (Boeker, 1989; Beckman and Burton, 2005).

Previous research considered the metabolism of a team over a period of time and considered the entry and exit of (characteristics of) individuals into and out of these social aggregates (Cooper and Daily, 1997; Ucbasaran *et al.*, Chapter 13; Boone *et al.*, 2004; Forbes *et al.*, 2006). Factors associated with team entry were not the same as those associated with team exit (Ucbasaran *et al.*, Chapter 13; Vanaelst *et al.*, Chapter 5). Departures from the team may reflect the difficulty teams have in coming to an agreement when differing points of view are present (Ucbasaran *et al.*, Chapter 13; Vanaelst *et al.*, Chapter 5). On the other hand, mismatches between the competencies required by the venture and those possessed by the team may emerge over time. As a consequence, individuals with human capital not currently present in the team may be encouraged to join the team (Birley and Stockley, 2000). Moreover, additions to the team are expected to inject novel experience and new understandings into the teams' collective decision making process (Leung *et al.*, Chapter 11).

Some scholars in the entrepreneurship literature take a life-cycle perspective and attribute the business' adjustment to a changing context or environment. They suggest there is a need to capture different skills in the entrepreneurial team in order to be able to deal with these changes. There seems to be a broad consensus that successful businesses are led by professionals who bring a full range of skills to the business (Cooper *et al.*, 1994; Beckman and Burton, Chapter 18) and create an organization of functional structure with clear roles and accountability (Ancona and Caldwell, 1992; Beckman and Burton, Chapter 18). Therefore executives are replaced as the new business outgrows their capabilities in a process of professionalization (Rubenson and Gupta, 1996; Boeker and Karachalil, Chapter 12; Boeker and Wiltbank, Chapter 14). Rubenson and Gupta (1996) suggest a model examining three sets of variables that seem to influence this process of professionalization: those relating to the changing needs of the organization, those relating to the ability and desire of the founder to adapt to those changing needs, and those related to the ability of the founders to prevent their own succession. Beckman and Burton (Chapter 18) point to the fact that much of the organizational literature emphasizes homophily (Ruef *et al.*, Chapter 3), imprinting (Boeker, 1989) and inertia (Hannan *et al.*, 1996) and suggest that this kind of professionalization and organizational evolution would be both difficult and unlikely.

Although some research indicates founder departure (Boeker and Karichalil, Chapter 12), other studies emphasize the value of TMT tenure in new businesses (Ensley *et al.*, Chapter 8; Eisenhardt and Schoonhoven, Chapter 16; Roure and Maidique, Chapter 15). This seems to suggest that, as team members continue to work together, they grow closer and develop greater knowledge about each other's skills, abilities, and personal idiosyncrasies.

In newly created businesses, the addition of a new member is a critical moment in the life of the new venture. The decision to add a member is crucial for two reasons. First, it has an impact on the human resources available to the new business. Second, it may provide the new business with access to additional financial and social resources. As such, the addition of a new member to the team brings the potential to change the strategic direction of the new business dramatically, which may be needed in order to realize its goals (Vanaelst, 2006).

As the new business evolves through the different stages of its life, it should be able to unfold an adequate strategy as a response to changes in the environment surrounding the new business. The realization of this growth strategy may call upon a new way of deploying existing and/or accessing new resources. This may result in the introduction of new key stakeholders as a response. These stakeholders can provide access to human, social, financial and technological resources. The introduction of external resources and the associated institutions of governance introduce an exchange of power from the founder/CEO (chief executive officer) and founding team to other stakeholders. These stakeholders are represented in the board of directors, although it should be noted that not all stakeholders are represented on the board of directors. External stakeholders on the board of directors are provided with a source of power. Power tensions are likely to occur between different stakeholders represented in the board of directors. These power tensions likely vary over the new business' life (Lynall *et al.*, 2003; Vanaelst, 2006). TMT new member entry may be a reflection of the relative power of key stakeholders at different stages of the life of a new business. In their attempts to safeguard the interests they have in a business, key stakeholders are likely to exert power on those factors that are assumed to be easy to influence. Of these factors, team composition is more likely to be sensitive towards the power exerted by key stakeholders, than the market structure or reactions of competitors. In this perspective, team addition is a reflection of the power exerted by key stakeholders. Over the different stages of the venture's life the key stakeholders and the power tensions between them are likely to change, which may induce team turnover (Vanaelst, 2006).

Three strands of discussion seem relevant to the exploration of team member introductions: theoretical explanations for team member entry, the relative power of key stakeholders, and the life cycle of the venture (Vanaelst, 2006). Below we expand on these themes by exploring formal theoretical approaches that have been used to explain new team member entries namely, resource-dependence theory, interpersonal attraction and social network theory, agency theory, and institutional theory.

As one of the main motivators of team entry, Forbes *et al.* (2006) identified resource dependence. According to resource-dependence theory, team member addition is a rational process driven by economic, instrumental reasons. A resource-dependence view appears implicit in the competency-driven search model: the process is rational and focuses on identifying the candidate with the best access to resources critical to the new business (Forbes *et al.*, 2006). In this perspective there is a problematical search for a new team member: the team has identified a resource problem and then undertakes a search for a new member. This resource-dependence view is also supported by Ucbasaran *et al.* (Chapter 13), who propose that team members are added to fill gaps in skills and to provide necessary human capital to pursue the goals and strategies of the new business.

Moreover, according to resource-dependence theorists, a firm is an open system, dependent on external organizations and environmental contingencies (Pfeffer and Salancik, 1978). Resource-dependence theorists argue that the survival and success of a business is dependent on its abilities to link the business with its external environment (Pfeffer and Salancik, 1978). In this perspective, boards of directors are seen as a means of managing external dependency, environmental uncertainty and reducing transaction costs associated with environmental interdependency by linking the organization with its external environment. In the resource-dependence perspective, the role of the board is to serve as a resource provider (Lynall *et al.*, 2003).

An alternative primary motivation for team addition is interpersonal attraction and social networks (Forbes *et al.*, 2006). New team members are added as a consequence of social psychological needs of existing team members. In this view, the search for additional team members is an opportunistic search: the team adds a member with whom it is already in contact and without first identifying a (resource) problem or undertaking a search. In this perspective team formation is driven by relational and personal characteristics of team members, often leading to a reinforcement of existing homophily (Ruef *et al.*, Chapter 3).

These dynamics are related to the attraction–selection–attrition (ASA) cycle described by Schneider (1987) to explain how the attraction, selection and attrition of team members take place within a team. This cycle would predict that founding and future TMTs will share similar characteristics. Founders select managers like themselves, and managers are assumed to seek organizations where those in current management positions have similar characteristics, and managers who do not fit will leave. Boone *et al.* (2004) find that even when environmental conditions shifted dramatically, Dutch newspaper executives tended to hire new executives who were demographically similar to those already in place. There are indications that founders and managers are assumed to be attracted to one another when they share common experience and knowledge. As shown by scholars such as Ruef *et al.* (Chapter 3), this leads to team homophily. Team homophily involves the similarity of individuals, predisposing them toward a greater level of interpersonal attraction, trust and understanding. Founders tend to privilege and recruit executives who have characteristics and functional experiences similar to their own rather than executives with functional experience that may be more relevant of the position being filled. Beckman and Burton (Chapter 18) noted that these tendencies toward functional homophily within a position may result in team-level functional heterogeneity. Teams will be functionally diverse if, for instance, individual preferences for homophily exist in founding teams where members come from a variety of functional backgrounds. Alternatively, founders with diverse functional backgrounds may value that variety and seek TMT members who themselves have diverse experiences. Thus, at the team level, homophily and similarity attraction arguments imply similarity between the experiences of the founding team and the experiences of the TMT.

Social network theory (Westphal, 1999) deals with the influence of social networks on team formation and composition, and builds on resource dependence theory (Lynall *et al.*, 2003). In this perspective a venture's actions are embedded in social networks, where embeddedness refers to the extent that actions are informed, influenced, and enabled by the network of social relations (Granovetter, 1985). The social network perspective underlines the importance of network formation on reputation, trust, reciprocity, and mutual interdependence (Larson, 1992). These ideas have been further elaborated by Leung *et al.* (Chapter 11) who found that due to multiple considerations of fit, entrepreneurial firms adapt different network strategies in acquiring their core human resources at different developmental phases. It seems that these two perspectives, resource seeking and interpersonal attraction, introduced by Forbes *et al.* (2006), do not cover the entire picture of team entry. For instance, Lynall *et al.*'s (2003) theory adds to these perspectives insights from agency and institutional theory.

Agency theory (Jensen and Meckling, 1976) is related to the separation between ownership (shareholders) and control (management). This separation of ownership offers the opportunity for managers–agents to act in their own self-interest by maximizing their own wealth and power at the expense of the owners–principals. From the agency theory perspective, boards of directors are put in place in order to monitor managers on behalf of the shareholders (Eisenhardt, 1989). Independent boards are supposed to be the most effective at monitoring because their actions are not compromised by dependence on the CEO or organization. As a consequence, shareholders will opt for an independent board or will try to align the interests of directors with their own to ensure an effective monitoring of management. The managers on the other hand will opt for a board composition that safeguards their independence. Agency theory is restricted to the insider/outsider distinction, whereas resource dependence theorists consider the linkages with external organizations (Lynall *et al.*, 2003).

Institutional theorists see firms as consisting of cognitive, normative, and regulative structures and activities that give meaning to social behaviour (Scott, 1995). Over time, ventures reflect the enduring rules institutionalized and legitimized by their social environments (DiMaggio and Powell, 1983). Zajac and Westphal (1996) showed that societal norms influence CEO selection and executive compensation. While either agency theory or alternative theories of compensation could have been used to justify CEO incentive decisions, congruence with investor norms was more instrumental to this decision (Zajac and Westphal, 1996). Institutional theorists argue that team composition will be determined by prevailing institutionalized norms in the organizational field and society. Theories of institutional isomorphism (DiMaggio and Powell, 1983) suggest that teams in the same institutional set will tend to be more similar to each other than to those in organizations outside their set (Lynall *et al.*, 2003).

Lynall *et al.* (2003) contend that it is not a matter of choosing one theoretical perspective over another but of identifying the conditions under which each is more applicable. Vanaelst (2006) argued that there are two sets of conditions that need to be considered: the stages of a ventures life cycle and the power of key stakeholders throughout the lifetime of the venture. A central element of most life-cycle models is that the firm's challenges and opportunities vary across different stages. One of the most cited differences across life-cycle stages are changing resource needs, sophistication and complexity of systems and structures, and managerial capabilities (Jawahar and McLaughlin, 2001; Lynall *et al.*, 2003;). Quinn and Cameron's (1983) integrative model suggests a four stage life cycle comprising: (1) an entrepreneurial stage (early innovation, niche formation, creativity); (2) a collectivity stage (high cohesion, commitment); (3) a formalization and control stage (stability and institutionalization), and (4) an elaboration of structure stage (domain expansion and decentralization). As firms progress through the life cycle, they will increase in size but not at the same rate. Therefore Lynall *et al.* (2003) suggest that instead of looking at size, *complexity* is more salient to progression through the life cycle with respect to governance requirements. Transitions to different managerial and organizational systems, like for instance increased delegation of authority, centralization of administration and adoption of functional structures, are rather associated with the inability of the existing systems to cope with the complexities associated with venture growth and development, and not necessarily with venture size.

As intimated earlier, as the venture evolves, so does its resource requirements. Consequently, new stakeholders are introduced. The introduction of external resources and the associated governance structures that follow can result in a transfer of power from the founders to external stakeholders providing these external resources. Power indicates the capability of one social actor to overcome resistance in achieving a desired aim (Pfeffer, 1981; Lynall *et al.*, 2003). Previous research introduced several dimensions of power: structural, ownership, expert, and prestige (Finkelstein, 1992; Lynall *et al.*, 2003). Each of these dimensions shows some relevance to the relative influence of stakeholders over team formation. Structural power is related to the formal organization structure and hierarchical authority. Ownership power reflects position in the principle–agent relationship. Expert power is related to the ability to deal with environmental contingencies. Prestige power is based on reputation in the institutional environment and among other stakeholders.

As newly created businesses evolve and become more mature businesses, a separation of decision and risk-bearing functions is likely to be observed (Fama and Jensen, 1983). Moreover, an organization's decision process consists of decision management (initiation and implementation) and decision control (ratification and monitoring). The common apex of the decision control systems of organizations, in which decision agents do not bear a major share of the wealth effects of their decisions, is a board of directors that ratifies and monitors important decisions and chooses, dismisses, and rewards important decision agents. Larger companies can suffer from a divorce of share ownership and managerial control to the extent that those responsible for day-to-day management may have interests that differ from those of the shareholders. At some point in time shareholders may want to sell all or part of the firm and management is often an obvious purchaser, a so-called management buy-out (Wright *et al.*, 2000; Wright and Bruining, 2008). An important element of the restructuring that typically ensues is the adjustment of the management team to one more appropriate to an independent private existence, which often means both team entry and exit (Wright and Coyne, 1985).

According to Baruch and Gebbie (1998) management is by far the most important factor in the success of a buy-out. They confirm that team work is an essential element (Katzenbach and Smith, 1993) in a management buy-out. The buy-out process and the running of business in the future require the team to work closely together, and the blend of characteristics and personalities is a decisive factor in the success of the buy-out. If a weakness can be identified in one key position, this may reduce the credibility of the entire team and may have disastrous consequences. Baruch and Gebbie (1998) stress that the principal success factor is the commitment of the team, followed by other team-oriented qualifications. They acknowledge that team culture is a crucial element in the efficient development of an organization. According to Baruch and Gebbie (1998) the 'culture of success' is proactive, supportive, and group oriented. Besides, it can be moderately aggressive and is averse to complacency or static thinking. In their study it is clear that the greater the non-financial success of the business, the greater the profitability. Their study shows that success should not be measured purely by profits and losses, but should be seen as a combination of several factors including human characteristics and how they fit together to shape the culture and personality of an efficient organization.

Outcome

Stinchcombe (1965) argued that newly created businesses have a high propensity to fail. New organizations are likely to fail because their organization members cannot adjust quickly enough to new working relationships and roles, and they lack a track record with outside stakeholders. Moreover, underlying the failure of young organizations are their limited resources. Stinchcombe (1965) underlined the importance of two sets of founding factors. One set is organizational. Young organizations typically have key organization members in unfamiliar roles and new work relationships. This often results in inefficiencies that jeopardize the newly created business. The second set is environmental. Young businesses face risks because they lack the legitimacy and power of existing stakeholders. This 'liability of newness' has been supported in a number of studies (e.g. Freeman *et al.*, 1983). In stark contrast, however, some young businesses become very successful.

Research has included a variety of factors that would allow newly created businesses to overcome these liabilities of newness, and positively affect new business outcome. These factors include aspects of external environments, including founding conditions (Eisenhardt and Schoonhoven, Chapter 16), industry characteristics (Eisenhardt and Schoonhoven, Chapter 16), and aspects of firm strategy (Boeker, 1989). According to Delmar and Shane (2006) researchers have examined the effect of a variety of individual and team related factors, including venture team size (Cooper and Bruno, 1977; Eisenhardt and Schoonhoven, Chapter 16), the social capital of founders (Davidsson and Honig, 2003), founding team demography (Eisenhardt and Schoonhoven, Chapter 16; Chowdhury, Chapter 6), the functional background of the founders of new ventures (Roure and Maidique, Chapter 15; Eisenhardt and Schoonhoven, Chapter 16; Ancona and Caldwell, 1992), prior joint work experience of the team members (Roure and Maidique, Chapter 15; Eisenhardt and Schoonhoven, Chapter 16), with founding team experience recognized as a critical factor in the survival and growth of newly created businesses (Delmar and Shane, 2006).

Researchers seem to agree that teams favourably influence venture performance in comparison to solo entrepreneurs (Roure and Maidique, Chapter 15; Kamm *et al.*, 1990, Siegel *et al.*, 1993). An important antecedent of new venture outcome seems to be new businesses' ability to access different kinds of capital. Traditionally, access to financial capital has been a focus of interest (Cooper *et al.*, 1994; Carter *et al.*, 1997; Davila *et al.*, 2003); more recently scholars have argued that human capital is even more important (Chandler and Hanks, 1998a; Watson *et al.*, 2003). They have shown the influence of human capital on the viability of organizations (e.g. Watson *et al.*, 2003). Especially the impact of human capital on the viability of newly created business has been considered. In general, human capital comprises work experience, education, and other skills and perspectives that increase knowledge accumulation and business sagacity. More specifically, differences in human capital characteristics are argued to have an important impact on venture performance (Wright *et al.*, 2007b).

The relationship between teams and firm performance has been examined in the literature on the 'upper-echelon perspective' (Hambrick and Mason, 1984). Research conducted under the upper-echelon perspective has produced evidence of a relationship between top management team interaction and business performance. In particular, the performance of the TMT is assumed to be reflected in the performance of the firm itself (Hambrick and Mason, 1984). Under the 'upper-echelon' perspective the performance of entrepreneurial teams is examined based upon TMT characteristics that can affect team understanding and decisions (Busenitz *et al.*, 2003), using dimensions such as previous experience (Roure and Maidique, Chapter 15; Eisenhardt and Schoonhoven, Chapter 16; Delmar and Shane, Chapter 17), networking activity (Leung *et al.*, Chapter 11) and entrepreneurial orientation (Covin and Slevin, 1991; Lumpkin and Dess, 1996), or based upon differences among team members such as consensus and conflict (Ensley *et al.*, Chapter 8; Lechler, Chapter 9; Amason and Sapienza, 1997).

Prior work on new ventures has shown that founders and the founding team shape a firm's initial strategies, structures, actions, and performance (Boeker, 1988; Roure and Maidique, Chapter 15; Eisenhardt and Schoonhoven, Chapter 16; Beckman *et al.*, 2007). A firm's founding team creates the initial structures and processes that shape its future actions (e.g. Baron *et al.*, 1996). The founding team will have a lasting imprint, and a team with both common and diverse founder affiliations will leave an imprint that provides the basis for both exploration and exploitation (Beckman, Chapter 2). In addition, although other team members may eventually supplement or replace founding team members, evolutionary arguments of path dependence and inertia suggest that subsequent teams are shaped by founding teams (Beckman and Burton, Chapter 18). Through an attraction–selection–attrition cycle (Schneider, 1987) founders select other team members like themselves, while members who do not fit the existing organization leave. This path-dependent process implies that the configuration of the founding team shapes subsequent executive teams (Boeker, 1989; Beckman and Burton, 2005). It stresses the importance of team formation and composition when the new business is being created as, although the team composition is likely to alter over the life of the newly created business as an adaptive mechanism, it is assumed to follow a path-dependent process.

As Stincombe (1965) explained, new business managers must learn new roles while on the job and while working within new social networks. The result is often misunderstanding, confusion and inefficiency. While facing these difficulties, new business managers must also build up relationships with different stakeholders, like customers, suppliers and investors, a process made difficult by the new business' youth and unfamiliarity (Amason *et al.*, 2006). According to Amason *et al.* (2006), although all new businesses are in some way new, they are not all equally novel; and, just like novelty can distinguish one new business from another, so too does it affect the tasks of each new business TMT (Amason *et al.*, 2006). This has implications as the firm performance reflects the fit of the TMT to its task and the requirements of its strategy (Eisenhardt and Schoonhoven, Chapter 16; Amason *et al.*, 2006). Since the capabilities of a team are determined by its composition (Hambrick and Mason, 1984), different types of teams should be best suited to these different types of tasks (Amason *et al.*, 2006). Amason *et al.* (2006) take into consideration that while all new businesses face liabilities associated with their newness, the highly novel new business must contend with being simultaneously new and different. They believe that high novelty requires creativity, enactment, and the ability to build a shared understanding. This process can be enhanced by behavioural integration (Amason *et al.*, 2006). As a consequence, highly novel new business with more homogeneous teams may perform better because more homogeneous teams will find higher levels of behavioural integration easier to achieve. Creative and coordinated efforts are made more difficult by increasing heterogeneity among the TMT members (Amason *et al.*, 2006). Since novelty changes over time, the conditions that favour a homogeneous team could diminish over time. It may be that the speed with which the new business TMTs seek to add members and develop a broader skill set, should relate to the new business novelty (Amason *et al.*, 2006).

New venture outcome can be measured in a multitude of ways. Empirical studies exploring the outcomes of entrepreneurship have used various financial and non-financial yardsticks to measure firm-level performance and growth (Chandler and Hanks, 1993; Wright *et al.*, 2007b). Since receiving venture capital and initial public offering (IPO) are the most significant milestones in the life of a young start-up, these milestones are identified as new business outcomes (Shane and Stuart, 2002; Beckman *et al.*, 2007; Beckman and Burton, Chapter 18). Beckman *et al.* (2007) go beyond human capital explanations of teams and also consider group composition and turnover on teams as important predictors of new business outcome. They develop the concept of background affiliation – a new kind of team demographic characteristic – that may be particularly relevant for the success of young businesses. Managers bring tacit knowledge with them from their prior business about how to organize and manage work processes, and this knowledge is likely to differ even between two businesses in a similar industry. They examine affiliation diversity (i.e., how many unique businesses the team members have worked for) and affiliation overlap (i.e., proportion of prior past business experiences at the same company). Beckman *et al.* (2007) found that businesses whose top management teams have affiliation diversity are more likely to be successful than businesses with fewer business affiliations. Contrary to expectations, affiliation overlap only has a positive effect on going public for founding teams. In their study the key independent variables, functional diversity, background affiliations, and turnover, capture a team's ability to access new information and experience by virtue of having TMT members that have worked for many different employers (diverse prior company affiliations) and have diverse prior experiences (functional diversity), which tend to be associated with positive outcomes. Besides, they found that functional diversity and prior executive experience generally aids teams in securing venture capital and realizing an IPO. Prior start-up experience has a negative relationship with business outcome. Moreover, entrants to and founder exits from the TMT increase the chances that a business achieves an IPO. TMT exits reduce the chances if achieving an IPO. Besides, their results suggest that prior human capital experience is consistently associated with positive business outcomes. Their findings suggest that team experiences, composition and turnover are associated with the likelihood that a new business will succeed.

The Chapters in the Book

The chapters in this book examine entrepreneurial teams in different stages of the new business creation process. Part I covers five chapters that examine team formation and team composition. Part II deals with social interaction and interpersonal processes within teams in further detail and encompasses five chapters. Part III examines team turnover in four chapters. Part IV develops insights on entrepreneurial team impact on new business outcome in four chapters. These contributions are reviewed in the following sections.

Team Formation and Composition

In order to learn more about why and how teams of founders come together to create new organizations, Kamm and Nurick (Chapter 1) present a model that assumes that the founder's decision-making process is a key factor in understanding how they operate and succeed. Their model of multi-founder organizational formation assumes that organizations emerge in two main stages, following a sequence of transitions. The idea stage comes first: within the context of their social networks individuals or teams make decisions about the business concept and what is needed to implement it. The second stage encompasses implementation decisions, covering who will supply resources, what inducements will be used to attract more partners if necessary, and how the team will be kept together. Feedback loops indicate that the process may return to the concept and implementation needs decisions, depending on the choices made at certain critical junctions.

In the idea stage, the idea generation is key. Beckman (Chapter 2) argues that the idea generation can not be separated from the experiences of businesses' founders. Team executives' choices are driven by their past experiences. Beckman argues that founding team members' prior company affiliations shapes new firm behaviours. More in particular, their prior experiences predispose firms to engage in explorative or exploitative behaviours. Firms with founding teams whose members have worked at the same company engage in exploitation because they have shared understandings and can act quickly. On the other hand, founding teams whose members have worked at many different companies have unique ideas and contacts that encourage exploration. In addition, firms whose founding teams have both common and diverse prior company affiliations have advantages that allow them to grow. The results suggest that team composition is an important antecedent of explorative and exploitative behaviour and firm ambidexterity. In particular, the results suggest that founding team prior company affiliations predict whether a firm pursues exploratory and exploitative behaviour, and they also suggest that firms whose founding teams have both types of affiliations are more likely to grow over time. These results support a strong relationship between founding team affiliations and consistent patterns of firm behaviour. Moreover, differences in firm exploration and exploitation are built in at team formation.

Whether a new business simply copies an existing form of organization or opts for a novel territory can depend on the extent to which its founding team exhibits diverse capabilities and perspectives (Ruef, 2002). Ruef, Aldrich and Carter (Chapter 3) consider how achieved and ascribed characteristics of entrepreneurs affect the composition of founding teams and how these characteristics are mediated by the social context of the entrepreneurial effort. Based on the sociological literature on group formation they identify five general mechanisms that could influence team membership, covering considerations of homophily, functionality, status expectations, network constraint, and ecological constraint. Homophily refers to the selection of other team members on the basis of similar ascriptive characteristics, such as gender, nationality, ethnicity, appearance, and the like. Functional theory addresses the extent to which team members possess valuable and complementary achieved competences that help ensure the success of a collectivity. Theories of status variation consider the capacity of high-status individuals to attract other team members, compared with low-status individuals. Network perspectives put forward that team formation occurs within a pre-existing network of weak and strong ties that constrains the choice of team members by the members of the founding team. Ecological perspectives stress the importance of the spatial proximity and environmental distribution of potential team members. Ruef, Aldrich and Carter's findings in Chapter 3 suggest that homophily and network constraints based on strong ties have the most pronounced effect on group composition. Social isolation (i.e. exclusion from a group) is more likely to occur as a result of ecological constraints on the availability of similar alters in a locality than as a result of status-varying membership choices.

In the decision process to create a new business the identification and screening of the needed resources is crucial. When new businesses apply for early stage venture capital funds, the project proposal is evaluated. In fact, the evaluation of venture proposals is a key activity of venture capitalists (VCs). Prior research indicates that VCs use various criteria to assess the attractiveness of venture proposals, such as market size and growth, product, the expected rate of return, and the expected risk of a venture proposal (MacMillan *et al.*, 1985). Among the set of evaluation criteria, VCs place great importance on criteria related to the start-up team (e.g. MacMillan *et al.*, 1987; Muzyka *et al.*, 1996). Specifically, Franke, Gruber, Harfhoff and Henkel (Chapter 4) found that the start-up team plays a key role in VCs' evaluations of venture proposals. Their research provides a detailed exploration of VCs' team evaluation criteria and investigates the moderator variable of VC experience. Franke *et al.*'s research indicates that industry experience, educational background, and leadership experience are the most important team characteristics in evaluations of venture proposals by VCs. Moreover, their study provides insights on utility trade-offs between different team characteristics. For industry experience and leadership experience, they found that it may suffice when only some team members possess it. As for the educational background, heterogeneous teams are strongly preferred over teams where all team members have a similar background.

Drawing on cognitive theory Shepherd *et al.* (2003) found that the experience of VCs has a significant influence on the VCs' decision making. Since the assessment of team quality plays an important role in VCs' decision making, the evaluation of start-up teams may also be subject to experience effects. Franke *et al.* (Chapter 4) explored whether VCs' experience has a significant moderating effect on the evaluation of start-up teams. They found that novice and experienced VCs both see industry experience as the most important criterion. Both rank the field of education among the top three criteria, and the type of prior professional experience as the least important criterion. However, novice and experienced VCs also critically diverge in some of their preferences. Apart from the finding that novice and experienced VCs differ significantly in certain preferences, an interesting pattern was discovered with respect to the type of criteria valued differently by both groups. Franke *et al.*'s results suggest that team cohesion (as evidenced by mutual acquaintance among team members) is of high importance to experienced VCs, whereas novice VCs tend to emphasize individual level, more tangible characteristics such as university degrees and prior leadership experience in start-up teams. Franke *et al.* (2008) consider the rankings of experienced VCs more valid indicators of desirable team characteristics.

The characteristics, experiences, and affiliations of team members shape the ideas and opportunities that are pursued within the creation of a new business (Beckman, Chapter 2). Together an idea and founders evolve into a new business (Clarysse and Moray, 2004). This process was studied in-depth by Vanaelst, Clarysse, Wright, Lockett, Moray and S'Jegers (Chapter 5) who examine the dynamics of entrepreneurial teams as they evolve through the different stages of a spin-out process. Using a unique, hand-collected set of data covering all team members in ten cases, an in-depth analysis of the heterogeneity of team members' experience and perception of the strategic orientation needed to attain different milestones in the spin-out process was performed. Their findings suggest that teams evolve over time and change in composition, and therefore, they can not be studied as immutable entities. Van Muijen *et al.*'s (1999) types of orientation toward how a team should ideally work (support, innovation, rules and goals) was used to measure heterogeneity in the perceived strategic orientation need for new business success. An in-depth analysis of different spin-out teams was performed and led to several new insights on how entrepreneurship is infused into new businesses through the evolution of teams as they take the spin-out from research to an independent venture. At the start of the venture formation, they introduce a new team role, the privileged witness, potentially specific for spin-outs. Analysis of the teams indicates that the team's heterogeneity changes as it evolves through the different stages of the spin-out process. In particular, they found that new team members brought in different kinds of experience; however, they did not introduce a different view on doing business from the initial team members. Their insights seem to suggest that the evaluation of proposed additional team members is not based upon purely economic arguments, but more interpersonal aspects are taken into account such as their ability to get along with a person.

Social Interaction and Interpersonal Processes Within Teams

As discussed earlier, diversity is an important topic in studying team-level issues (e.g. Pelled *et al.*, 1999) as it is assumed to have an impact on business performance (Ensley *et al.*, 1998). Chowdhury (Chapter 6) examines the influences of demographic diversity variables in terms of age, gender, and functional background and team process variables in terms of team-level cognitive comprehensiveness and team commitment on entrepreneurial team effectiveness. This chapter argues that the diversity of team composition is not as important as team commitment and the process of cognitive comprehensiveness, which utilizes diverse decision criteria. With field interview data from 79 entrepreneurial teams this study suggests that demographic diversity is not important for entrepreneurial team effectiveness, whereas the team process variables of team commitment and cognitive comprehensiveness both positively influence team effectiveness. The findings also indicate that the diversity in terms of gender, age, and functional background does not significantly contribute to the team-level cognitive comprehensiveness and team commitment. The results show that effective entrepreneurial teams are those that have high member commitment and that develop a process using diverse perspectives on problems, a variety of potential solutions and a variety of criteria for evaluating solutions to make complex and innovative decisions, which are to be taken during the process of new business creation.

Making complex decisions under pressure, difficulties, and high professional and personal stakes, associated with the creation of a new business, lend themselves to study the interdependence amongst the team members. In particular, Francis and Sandberg (Chapter 7) explore friendship within the entrepreneurial team with particular attention to its association with the team's behaviour and the performance of the venture. Friendship is an interpersonal relationship that may affect team dynamics. It is assumed to hold teams together and stimulate heroic efforts during challenging times. According to their research, friendship facilitates the formation of (management) teams for new ventures, thereby improving their early performance. As the entrepreneurial team continues to function, friendship is conductive to decision-making processes that enhance the team's effectiveness in solving complex problems and ultimately improve the new business performance. Their study indicates that friendships, under different circumstances, may exert either positive or negative influences on turnover within the entrepreneurial team and those influences may improve or impair the new business' performance. Besides, behaviour within the team or events in the business' development may affect friendships within the team. The notion of interdependence in friendship offers a framework for understanding interpersonal processes. Interdependence brings experiences between interacting persons that influence one another's preferences, motives, behaviour and outcomes.

In their study on interdependence amongst team members in new business creation, Ensley, Pearson and Amason (Chapter 8) draw upon the research under the upper-echelon perspective to explain new venture performance as a function of cohesion and decision making conflict within the top management team (TMT). The success of the business is often regarded as a reflection of the team's ability to meld talent and abitily in a creative and coordinated way. Central to the effort to meld talent and ability is the use of conflict. They reasoned that cohesion increases constructive cognitive conflicts while simultaneously decreasing destructive affective conflicts. Cohesion refers to the degree to which members of a group are attracted to each other (Shaw, 1981). Cohesive teams are likely to have a stable and solid foundation of interpersonal relationships that allows them to interact in a flexible and effective manner. Cohesive teams are assumed to have interactive advantages that allow them to perform better than their less cohesive counterparts. One where such an interactive advantage is likely to occur is in the case of conflict. Due to the familiarity and comfort amongst their members, cohesive teams should experience lower levels of affective conflict and higher levels of cognitive conflict than their less cohesive counterparts. As a consequence, cohesiveness should relate positively to superior new business performance. Data were collected from a sample of 70 new businesses and results support their reasoning. TMT cohesion is an important characteristic of new business teams. Ensley, Pearson and Amason (Chapter 8) suggest that cohesion, when combined with efforts to promote open interaction, will lead to more decision-making conflict and as such to more effective teams and better performing new businesses.

Lechler (Chapter 9) stresses in his research that conflict is not a sufficient substitute measurement for social interaction. Lechler introduces the concept of social interaction in the study of entrepreneurial teams. The components of social interaction considered in his study on entrepreneurial teams are: communication, cohesion, work norms, mutual support, coordination and conflict resolution. Social interaction within entrepreneurial teams could be seen as an important yet not sufficient factor of new business success. His research shows that the quality of the social interaction within entrepreneurial teams is positively linked to new business success.

According to West (Chapter 10), new business success often depends on how the founding team collectively understands its world, estimates effects of possible actions, makes decisions, and allocates appropriate resources. Drawing on work in managerial cognition and entrepreneurship, West's chapter argues for the importance of examining cognition at the team level. While the different team members will have individual perspectives and cognitions about the new business, it is a collective perspective or a collective knowledge structure at the team level that guides the direction of the new business. Collective cognition refers to the content of the combination of individual perspectives and the structural characteristics of that combination. West uses new business strategy as a springboard to discuss collective cognition. Because strategy is perspective, multidimensional, and collective, it is proposed that entrepreneurial team collective cognition is a mediating variable between new business performance and both the environment and individual top managers, or, collective cognition mediates between individual cognitions and firm actions and performance. A method for assessing entrepreneurial top management team cognition is developed and then tested in an explanatory study of technology-based new businesses. The results show that two structural characteristics of collective cognition, differentiation and integration of strategic perspectives in top management team, are strongly related to new business performance. This is because these characteristics describe the extent to which entrepreneurial top management teams consider new strategic alternatives in an environment where strategic demands are continually shifting, and the extent to which these teams share a unified perspective of the relative importance of available strategy choices. Differentiation represents the extent to which each strategic construct is construed as different from every other strategic construct. Integration represents the degree to which top managers think in a similar way about a set of strategy constructs. Integration within a new business team suggest that members individually view both the relevance of strategic constructs and their relative importance in ways that are similar to other members on their top management team. New business strategy can be seen as a function of the composition of the top management team, and changes in the new business strategy may result from changes in the team composition. Additions to the team may inject new content into strategic discussions and may view existing content differently from others in the team, resulting in changing collective cognition of the team itself. New team members may also forestall change. West points out in Chapter 10 that, while CEOs often value new colleagues with whom they have previously worked or who have significant within-industry experience, these additions to the team tend to homogenize points of view rather than challenge conventional thinking. This may diminish new business performance, especially in dynamically changing environments where new ideas about the strategy are important. Leung *et al.* (Chapter 11) posit that strategic needs and interpersonal dynamics are the key drivers in human resource acquisition practices to strengthen the core team.

Team Turnover

In the development of the firm's strategy the quality of core human resources is key. Practices adopted by new businesses in acquiring their core talents may alter during the different developmental stages of the new business. The general proposition in the study of Leung, Zhang, Wong and Foo (Chapter 11) is that entrepreneurial businesses adopt different network strategies in acquiring their core human resources at different stages due to multiple considerations of 'fit'. More particularly, their chapter proposes a multidimension, multicontingent 'fit' perspective for examining different practices adapted by entrepreneurial firms in acquiring human resources. Bearing the smallness and liabilities of newness (Stinchcombe, 1965) in mind, 'what to buy' and 'how to buy' in terms of core human resources, taking their needs and constraints into account, are important and relevant questions for new businesses. By examining how environmental constraints, strategic needs and interpersonal dynamics in entrepreneurial businesses interact during different developmental phases, their study highlights unique features in human resource acquisition in their core team. Leung *et al.* defined core team members as people who hold key positions in the company involved in the company's management and strategic decision process. Data were collected from two cohorts of ten entrepreneurial firms each. With the first cohort they captured the recruitment of initial team members other than the founders. With the second cohort, they captured data on how they recruited their core team members during both the start-up and the growth phase. Their overarching theoretical framework is the 'system approach' of contingency theory which stresses the interactions among multiple contingencies and structural characteristics in an organization.

Leung *et al.* (Chapter 11) posit that while environmental constraints are important considerations for adapting recruitment practices through networks, strategic needs and interpersonal dynamics are the key drivers in human resource acquisition practices to strengthen the core team. In the transition from the start-up to the growth phase, entrepreneurial businesses utilize different network pools in search of diversity, yet cling to strong ties to find talents with common values and goals. Recruitment through networks seems to be the predominant practice to acquire core talents. The types of networks entrepreneurs tap into vary from a mixed pattern during the start-up phase to an overwhelming reliance on business networks during the growth phase, whereas the use of strong ties in acquiring talents for their core team persists during the different developmental phases. Their analysis indicated that the change in the network pattern may be attributed to the need for different types of talents due to the changing environmental conditions and strategic needs of the businesses. On the other hand, the stability in the tie strength may reflect the persistent emphasis on values and goal congruence when the core team members are chosen. In shifting from personal networks to business networks in search of talents with diverse competences, entrepreneurs cling to strong ties to find talents who are different from themselves, and yet still share certain common values.

According to Leung *et al.* (Chapter 11) drawing on different network pools to search for talents in accordance with varying strategic needs does not automatically translate into getting people with the 'right fit'. Rather than just having a clear business vision as a common ground, entrepreneurial team members are being drawn to each other based on similar beliefs, interests and personal chemistry (Bird, 1988). In the growth phase new businesses need to have members with diverse perspectives and complementary competences and members who share the vision of the organization.

According to the study by Boeker and Karichalil (Chapter 12) growth may create a need for new managers with different capabilities leading to founder departure. Their research in entrepreneurship and life cycle theories of the business have both suggested that new businesses may outgrow the managerial capabilities of their founding teams, at which point the founders may be replaced by professional managers. Boeker and Karichalil explore factors affecting founder departure among semiconductor start-ups from 1983 through 1999 to understand better the process by which new businesses manage the transition to established companies. Their investigation covers firm and individual characteristics that influence the likelihood of departure among founders rather than specific motivations, voluntary or not, of each founder. Their study examines how founder departure is influenced by the size and growth of a business and then examines the effects of firm governance, including the influence of ownership and board composition. Their results indicate that founder departure increases with firm size, decreases with founder ownership and board membership, and has a U-shaped relationship with firm growth. Besides, their research shows that founders who work in research and development or who are chief executives are also less likely to leave.

Ucbasaran, Lockett, Wright and Westhead's (Chapter 13) exploratory study provides a review of team turnover in the context of independent private businesses owned by entrepreneurial founder teams. A novel distinction is made between entrepreneurial founder team member entry and team member exit. Their study monitored 90 owner-managed businesses between 1990 and 2000. Presented hypotheses relating to an entrepreneurial team's human capital were explored using multivariate logistic regression analysis. Variables associated with entry were found not to be the same as those associated with exit. The size of the founding team was significantly negatively associated with subsequent team member entry. An important motive for the need to bring in new team members is to add to the total amount of human capital within a team. The link between team turnover and entrepreneurial team heterogeneity was mixed. Functional heterogeneity was weakly significantly positively associated with team member entry. Heterogeneity of prior entrepreneurial experience was significantly positively associated with team member exit. This suggests that where one or more entrepreneurs have prior entrepreneurial experience, they may try to dominate those who do not have entrepreneurial experience, thus reducing cohesion and creating conflict-induced team turnover. Prior entrepreneurial experience brings assets as well as liabilities. In addition, family firms were significantly negatively associated with team member exit. Finally, the average age of the team was not significantly associated with team entry or exit.

A significant amount of research has examined top management team transitions in established firms, but much less is known about the factors influencing the evolution of top management capabilities in new businesses, which was examined by Boeker and Wiltbank (Chapter 14). This study expands on the life-cycle arguments by including effects of top management team characteristics, governance and ownership. By examining changes in the top management of new businesses they obtain a more comprehensive picture of the factors driving changes in managerial talent. Boeker and Wiltbank study these issues in a sample of new businesses founded from 1983 through 1995, examining each firm for seven years after its founding to evaluate the conditions that influence a new business' changes in top management. Their study shows what factors motivate new businesses to change their top management, and how the ownership and oversight of the business can enhance or interfere with that process.

Boeker and Wiltbank's results demonstrate clear differences between new and established business. In addition, their results indicate that top management team changes occur in cases of very low or very high business growth, but are mitigated by a functionally diverse top management team. Their study indicates that low growth is leading to top management change. Growth and success is associated with a lack of change in top management, in the case of established businesses. Whereas, in successful new businesses it is precisely because of the success and rapid growth that different managerial capabilities are needed in order to be able to handle the increased complexity of managerial tasks.

Power and control of inside and outside constituencies also affect changes in top management, with venture capital ownership and board representation increasing change in top management, and managerial ownership decreasing, changes. The combination of concepts from life-cycle theory and power in executive succession depicts how new businesses come to make changes in their management. The development of the business presents a need for different managerial capabilities and changing leadership needs. In teams with greater diversity of experience these capabilities may already exist, but the power and influence represented by ownership and boards of directors directly influence the extent to with changes in top management team actually occur. Since the combination of the different members of the entrepreneurial team seems to evolve over the life of new businesses and lead to different new business outcomes, Part IV of this book is devoted to potential linkages between the entrepreneurial team and new business outcome.

Outcome

Roure and Maidique (Chapter 15) report on the prefounding factors influencing the success of high-technology start-up businesses. Information was obtained on those prefounding factors that were available for investor review prior to funding, such as the founders' track records, the characteristics of the founding team, the nature of the target market, the technological strategy of the business, the proposed composition of the board, and the deal structure. The study was done in collaboration with two major US West Coast venture capital firms. Their findings revealed differences between successful and unsuccessful businesses. The founders of the successful businesses had more prior experience working together. They found that successful businesses tend to form larger and more complete teams and had a higher percentage of critical functions filled at the time of first financing. Successful entrepreneurs had had prior experience in the same roles and had more extensive experience in the function they performed in the newly created business. Successful entrepreneurs had had fast-rising careers in high-growth units of medium to large companies. In addition, successful founders also had experience in rapid growth businesses that competed in the same industry as the new created business.

Moreover, successful businesses seemed to target product-market segments with high buyer concentration in which, through technological advantage, their products could attain and sustain a competitive edge. Often this advantage was achieved by careful management of the product-development process, which resulted in early market entry and reduced competition. Both successful and unsuccessful businesses targeted high growth markets, anticipated high gross margins, had founders with over five years of relevant experience, had experienced venture capitalists on their boards, and were characterized by a wide range of founder equity shares.

Roure and Maidique's research suggests that the likelihood of a start-up's success can be increased by having a management team with previous joint experience, thus avoiding the waste of resources associated with integrating the different members of the team. In addition, their results seem to suggest that a successful high growth technological start-up needs from the beginning an experienced, complete team that can manage the business throughout the development process.

Organizational growth in technology-based businesses is further explored by Eisenhardt and Schoonhoven (Chapter 16). According to Eisenhardt and Schoonhoven, founding conditions play a key role in shaping young businesses and affect organizational growth. They build on Stinchcombe's (1965) argument of liability of newness. Stinchcombe argued that founding conditions have a disproportionate effect on young organizations. At founding they are set on a trajectory that may be difficult or costly to alter (Boeker, 1989). Structures and processes become part of an integrated whole in which it is difficult to change one element without affecting the whole. Young organizations invest in people, technology, and assets that they may not be able to change because they are too myopic or lack the resources to do so (Eisenhardt and Schoonhoven, Chapter 16).

The purpose of their study was to link organizational growth with founding conditions, including the top-management team, technical strategy, and competitive environment. Therefore characteristics of the founding top management team, strategy, and environment were related to the sales growth of newly founded semiconductor businesses in the USA.

Their results indicate significant main and interaction effects for the founding top management team and market stage on firm growth. Particularly, the founding top management team and market-stage effects were increasingly large over time. Their results indicate that both environmental determinism and strategic choice operate on young businesses. Their findings also suggest chaos-theory linkages to positive-feedback models and sensitive dependence of organizational growth on founding conditions. In contrast, the technical innovation of business strategy and marketplace competition were not significant.

Previous research has argued that the start-up and industry experience of the founding team should have a positive effect on the performance of newly created businesses, however robust empirical support for these arguments has been lacking. Furthermore, theory seems to suggest that the relationship between founding team experience and the performance of newly created businesses may be more complex than previous empirical evidence suggests. Delmar and Shane (Chapter 17) point to the fact that previous research exploring the effect of founding team experience on new business performance posits a linear relationship that does not vary with venture age or with the amount of experience in the founding team. Delmar and Shane make use of a methodology that overcomes several limitations of previous research.

While previous research has examined the effect of a variety of individual factors, Delmar and Shane (Chapter 17) include prior founding team start-up and industry experience in their study on new venture survival and sales. Start-up experience is the previous creation of new organizations that provides information about activities such as opportunity identification and evaluation, resource acquisition and firm organizing. Industry experience refers to previous work in the industry in which the new business will operate, and provides information on the rules and norms prevailing in the industry, as well as on the customer and supplier networks, and employment practices. Their study develops from the idea that both these forms of experience help entrepreneurs to overcome liabilities of newness and enhance the performance of their new businesses because the activities in which the entrepreneurs engage are subject to learning curves. The more that entrepreneurs start up firms or work in an industry, the better they become at organizing businesses, acquiring resources, attracting customers and suppliers, and hiring people. Since this learning can be transferred from one setting to another, the position of a new business on the learning curve is determined, at least partly, by the prior start-up and industry experience the founding team. In Chapter 17, Delmar and Shane test specific hypotheses about the effect of founding start-up and industry experience on the survival and sales of 223 new businesses initiated by a representative sample of Swedish new ventures. Their results show that founding team experience enhances both new venture survival and sales, but that the effects are non-linear and vary with venture age. Their findings suggest that the effect of founding team start-up experience on new venture survival and new venture sales are not the same. Therefore, Delmar and Shane suggest that researchers need to explain the effects of founding team experience on new venture performance in nuanced ways that account for the differences in effects on venture survival and sales, the non-linear forms of these effects and their interaction with venture age.

Beckman and Burton (Chapter 18) contrast life-cycle and path-dependent views of entrepreneurial businesses by examining the evolution of top management teams. They show how initial conditions constrain subsequent outcomes by demonstrating that the founding team's prior functional experiences and initial organizational functional structures predict subsequent top manager backgrounds and later functional structures. Functional structure refers to the existence of functional roles or positions irrespective of any person who might occupy the role, but functional experience refers to the human capital characteristics of the individual incumbents. This distinction allowed them to consider team evolution from both a structural perspective and a human capital/social psychological perspective. Since receiving venture capital and achieving an IPO are the most significant milestones in the life of a young start-up (Shane and Stuart, 2002), these milestones were identified as new business outcomes, affected by the initial conditions at founding.

Beckman and Burton demonstrate in Chapter 18 that founding teams strongly influence the top management team through path dependence. Consistent with homophily expectations, founding teams that begin with broadly experienced team members are more likely to attract broadly experienced executives. Consistent with ecological perspectives, firms that begin with a range of functional structures are more likely to develop more complete structures. Thus, path dependence, where the founding team shapes the subsequent top management team, occurs through both homophily and imprinting.

In addition, they find that narrowly experienced teams have trouble adding functional expertise not already embodied in the team. They also find that businesses beginning with a limited range of functional positions are less likely to develop complete functional structures. Importantly, Beckman and Burton do not find functional structure and functional experience to be interchangeable. They find that firms beginning with more complete functional structures are likely to go public faster, and firms beginning with already experienced team members obtain venture capital more quickly regardless of the experience and structural composition of the top management team in place at the time of these outcomes. Besides, broadly experienced founding teams that build an early team with a full complement of functional positions achieve important milestones faster than firms that start with neither experience nor structure. This suggests that creating positions as 'placeholders' in new businesses, where positions are created and filled with the intent of bringing individuals with more relevant experience in later, appears to be detrimental to the firm's ability ultimately to attract broadly experienced executives. By examining the origins of top management team experience and functional structures, Beckman and Burton illustrate the lasting imprint of founders on top management team composition and firm outcomes. Their research suggests that, not only do founding teams directly impact firm outcomes, but, through a process of path dependence, the founding team shapes the top management team. According to Beckman and Burton much more needs to be understood about entrepreneurial teams. A qualitative assessment of how ideas, people, experiences, and structures come together to create a new business would be an important contribution of future work.

Future Research

This section presents some avenues for future research on entrepreneurial teams in new business creation and is summarized in Figure 2.

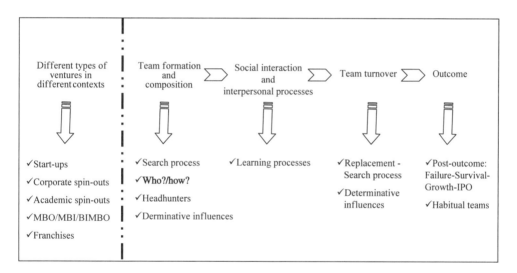

Figure 2   *Future research on entrepreneurial teams in new business creation.*

There is a clear need for more comparisons of the nature of entrepreneurial teams in different entrepreneurial contexts: start-ups, corporate entrepreneurship, academic entrepreneurship, MBOs, MBIs, BIMBOs (buy-in management buy-outs) and franchises (e.g. Wright *et al.*, 2007b; Amason *et al.*, 2006; Ensley and Hmieleski, 2005; Shepherd and Krueger, 2002). Amongst others, bearing the heterogeneity of technology-based entrepreneurship in mind, future research could study how entrepreneurial teams differ within the context of corporate spin-outs and academic spin-outs in terms of their formation and development over the life of the new business and taking the potential impact of the mother organizations into consideration. While we know entrepreneurship takes place in different entrepreneurial contexts, much research focuses on start-ups. There is a need to compare start-up team issues with MBOs, MIBs, franchises and the like. Moreover, as stressed by Amason *et al.* (2006) all new ventures are in some way new, but they are not all equally novel. New ventures can represent different degrees of novelty and so be significantly different from one another. Future research may build on these insights and include a multidimensional definition of newness, that includes both age and novelty, which can be linked to the fit between the teams and the new businesses they create and they manage.

Clarysse and Moray (2004) found that the development of the entrepreneurial team is interrelated with the life-cycle stages of the venture and indicate that it takes time for an entrepreneurial team to take form as experiential learning processes occur. On the other hand, Birley and Stockley (2000) believed that gaps between competences required by the new business and possessed by the team would emerge over time.

This underlines the need for more research relating the entrepreneurial team to the different stage of the new business life cycle. In particular, future research may be aimed at the identification of the specific life-cycle stages where team changes are critical, building on existing research (e.g. Vohora *et al.*, 2004; Vanaelst *et al.*, Chapter 5) and broadening the scope to IPO stage and trade-sale exits. At the same time, there is a clear need for research on entrepreneurial teams in the earliest stages of new business creation process.

Shane and Venkataraman (2000) emphasized the study of the existence, discovery, and exploitation of business opportunities. Therefore, future research may consider the relevance of teams in the process of opportunity recognition and how opportunity recognition occurs within teams. Next, the role of human capital of teams as they recognize and evaluate opportunities in comparison to individuals may be explored further.

Building on previous research (e.g. Lynall *et al.*, 2003; Vanaelst, 2006) we need to know more about who effects the team changes and under what circumstances. For instance, are these changes 'mutually agreed' or 'bad leavers' or forced by stakeholders such as financial institutions? Moreover, future research may look into *how* team changes occur, that is what are the search processes in finding replacement members and to what extent do these processes differ in the different stages of the new business. Future research could also look into the different agents (e.g. head hunters) involved in these search processes of team member replacement. Future entrepreneurship research that studies diversity could include personality and thinking styles in addition to demographics, since the effect of diversity seems to be mixed (e.g. Chowdhury, Chapter 6).

Bringing different team members together in different stages of the new business' life, implies social interaction and interpersonal processes. Where the human capital of individual team members is heterogeneous, this may lead to superior decisions and in turn venture performance due to team members being able to access and share diverse knowledge. This sharing of knowledge implies interaction between different team members. Previous research found that the nature of the interaction between the team members matters (e.g. Knight *et al.*, 1999). In particular, even if a team has what on the surface appears to be a set of complementary skills, there is no guarantee this will be translated into venture success. The fact that the knowledge and expertise embodied in the human capital of the individual team members is brought together does not guarantee that this knowledge will be shared and more importantly be understood and appreciated by other team members. Therefore, future research should focus on the nature of the interaction among the team members taking the team formation process and its evolution of the life of the newly created business into consideration.

Future research could focus on what happens to the teams after the outcome of the newly created business: to what extent are teams different in a new business that survives, fails, or realizes an IPO, MBO or MBI? In particular, little is known about the outcomes of different types of teams in MBOs and MBIs. Moreover, building on the work of Ucbasaran *et al.* (2008) future research could focus on the prevalence and evolution of habitual teams in these different post-outcomes.

This book is a step stone towards a richer understanding of entrepreneurial teams in new business creation and an invitation to future research endeavours on entrepreneurial teams in new business creation.

References

Amason, A.C. (1996), 'Distinguishing the effects of functional and dysfunctional conflict on strategic decision making: resolving a paradox for top management teams', *Academy of Management Journal*, **39**: 123–48.

Amason, A.C. and Sapienza, H.J. (1997), 'The effects of top management team size and interaction norms on cognitive and affective conflict', *Journal of Management*, **23**(4): 495–516.

Amason, A.C., Shrader, R.C. and Tompson, G.H. (2006), 'Newness and novelty: Relating top management team composition to new venture performance', *Journal of Business Venturing*, **21**: 125–48.

Ancona, D.G. and Caldwell, D.F. (1992), 'Bridging the boundary: external activity and performance in organisational teams', *Administrative Science Quarterly*, **37**(4): 634–66.

Balkundi, P. and Harrison, D.A. (2006), 'Ties, leaders, and time in teams: strong inference about network structure's effects on team viability and performance', *Academy of Management Journal*, **49**(1): 49–68.

Bantel, K.A. and Jackson, S.E. (1989), 'Top management and innovations in banking: does the composition of the top team make a difference?', *Strategic Management Journal*, **10**: 107–24.

Baron, J.N., Burton, M.D. and Hannan, M.T. (1996), 'The road taken: origins and evolution of employment systems in emerging companies', *Industrial and Corporate Change*, **5**: 239–75.

Baruch, Y. and Gebbie, D. (1998), 'Cultures of success: characteristics of the U.K.'s leading MBO teams and managers', *Journal of Business Venturing*, **13**: 423–39.

Beckman, C.M. and Burton, M.D. (2005). 'Founding the future. The evolution of top management teams from founding to IPO'. Working paper April 2005.

Beckman, C.M., Burton, M.D. and O'Reilly, C. (2007), 'Early teams: the impact of team demography on VC financing and going public', *Journal of Business Venturing*, **22**: 147–173.

Bird, B. (1988), 'Implementing entrepreneurial ideas: the case for intention', *Academy of Management Review*, **13**: 442–53.

Birley, S. and Stockley, S. (2000) 'Entrepreneurial Teams and Venture Growth', in D.L. Sexton and H. Landstrom (eds), *The Blackwell Handbook of Entrepreneurship*, Oxford: Blackwell, 287–307.

Boeker, W. (1988), 'Organizational origins: Entrepreneurial and environmental imprinting at time of founding', in G.R. Carroll (ed.), *Ecological Models of Organizations*, Cambridge, MA: Ballinger, 33–51.

Boeker, W. (1989), 'The development and institutionalization of subunit power in organization', *Administrative Science Quarterly*, **34**, 388–410.

Boeker, W. (1997), 'Executive migration and strategic change: the effect of top manager movement on product entry', *Administrative Science Quarterly*, **42**: 213–36.

Boone, C., van Olffen, W., van Witteloostuijn, A. and De Brabander, B. (2004), 'The genesis of top management team diversity: selective turnover among top management teams in Dutch newspaper publishing, 1970–94', *Academy of Management Journal*, **47**: 633–56.

Busenitz, L., West, G.P. III, Shepherd, D.A., Nelson, T., Chandler, G.N. and Zacharis, A.L. (2003), 'Entrepreneurship research in emergence: fifteen years of entrepreneurship research in management journals', *Journal of Management*, **29**(3): 285–308.

Carter, N.M., Williams, M. and Reynolds, P.D. (1997), 'Discontinuance among new firms in retail: the influence of initial resources, strategy, and gender', *Journal of Business Venturing*, **12**(2): 25–146.

Chandler, G. and Hanks, S.H. (1993), 'Measuring the performance of emerging businesses: a validation study', *Journal of Business Venturing*, **8**: 391–408.

Chandler, G.N. and Hanks, S.H. (1998a), 'An examination of the substitutability of founders' human and financial capital in emerging business ventures', *Journal of Business Venturing*, **13**: 353–69.

Chandler, G.N. and Hanks, S.H. (1998b), 'An investigation of new venture teams in emerging businesses', in P.D. Reynolds, W.D Bygrave, N.M. Carter, S. Manigart, C.M. Mason, G.D. Meyer and K.G. Shaver (eds), *Frontiers of Entrepreneurship Research*, Wellesley, MA: Babson College, 318–30.

Chandler, G.N., Honig, B. and Wiklund, J. (2005), 'Antecedents, moderators, and performance consequences of membership changes in new venture teams', *Journal of Business Venturing*, **20**: 705–25.

Clarysse, B. (ed.) (2004), *Eendagsvlieg of pionier: welke ondernemer redt de economie?* Leuven: Garant.

Clarysse, B. and Moray, N. (2004), 'A process study of entrepreneurial formation: The case of a research-based spin-off', *Journal of Business Venturing*, **19**: 55–79.

Clarysse, B., Wright, M., Lockett, A., Van de Velde, E. and Vohora, A. (2005), 'Spinning out new ventures: a typology of incubation strategies from European research institutions', *Journal of Business Venturing*, **20**(2): 183–216.

Colombo, M.G. and Grilli, L. (2005), 'Founders' human capital and the growth of new technology-based firms: a competence based view', *Research Policy*, **34**(6): 795–818.

Cooper, A.C. and Bruno, A.V. (1977), 'Success among high-technology firms', *Business Horizons*, **20**(2): 16–22.

Cooper, A.C. and Daily, C.M. (1997) 'Entrepreneurial Teams', in D.L. Sexton and R.W. Smilor (eds), *Entrepreneurship 2000*, Chicago, IL: Upstart Publishing Company, 127–50.

Cooper, A., Gimeno-Gascon, F.J. and Woo, C.Y. (1994), 'Initial human and financial capital as predictors of new venture performance', *Journal of Business Venturing*, **9**: 371–95.

Covin, J.G. and Slevin, D.P. (1991), 'A conceptual model of entrepreneurship as firm behavior', *Entrepreneurship Theory and Practice*, **16**(1): 7–25.

Davidsson, P. and Honig, B. (2003), 'The role of social and human capital among nascent entrepreneurs', *Journal of Business Venturing*, **18**: 301–31.

Davila, A., Foster, G. and Gupta, M. (2003), 'Venture capital financing and the growth of startup firms', *Journal of Business Venturing*, **18**: 689–708.

Delmar, F. and Shane, S. (2003), 'Does business planning facilitate the development of new ventures?', *Strategic Management Journal*, **24**: 1165–85.

DiMaggio, P.J., and Powell, W.W. (1983), 'The iron cage revisited: institutional isomorphism and collective rationality in organizational fields', *American Sociological Review*, **48**: 147–60.

Eisenhardt, K.M. (1989), 'Making fast strategic decisions in high-velocity environments', *Academy of Management Journal*, **32**(3): 543–76.

Eisenhardt, K.M. and Schoonhoven, C.B. (1996), 'Resource-based view of strategic alliance formation: strategic and social explanations in entrepreneurial firms', *Organization Science*, **7**(2): 136–50.

Eisenhardt, K.M., Kahwajy, J.L. and Bourgeois, L.J. (1997), 'Conflict and strategic choice: how top management teams disagree', *California Management Review*, **39**(2): 42–62.

Ensley, M.D. and Hmieleski, K.M (2005), 'A comparative study of new venture top management team composition, dynamics and performance between university-based and independent start-ups', *Research Policy*, **34**(7): 1091–105.

Ensley, M.D. and Pearce, C.L. (2001), 'Shared cognition in top management teams: implications for new venture performance', *Journal of Organizational Behavior*, **22**: 145–60.

Ensley, M.D., Carland, J.C. and Carland, J.W. (1998), 'The effects of entrepreneurial team skill heterogeneity and functional diversity on new venture performance', *Journal of Business and Entrepreneurship*, **10**(1): 1–11.

Ensley, M.D., Carland, J.C., Carland, J.W. and Banks, M. (1999), 'Exploring the existence of entrepreneurial teams', *International Journal of Management*, **16**(2): 276–86.

Fama, E.F. and Jensen, M.C. (1983), 'Separation of ownership and control', *Journal of Law and Economics*, **26**: 301–25.

Finkelstein, S. (1992), 'Power in top management teams: dimensions, measurement, and validation', *Academy of Management Journal*, **35**: 505–38.

Foo, M.D., Wong, P.K. and Ong, A. (2005), 'Do others think you have a viable business idea? Team diversity and judges' evaluation of ideas in a business plan competition', *Journal of Business Venturing*, **20**(3): 385–402.

Foo, M.D., Sin, H.P. and Yiong, L.P. (2006), 'Effects of team inputs and intrateam processes on perceptions of team viability and member satisfaction in nascent ventures', *Strategic Management Journal*, **27**: 389–99.

Forbes, D.P., Borchert, P.S., Zellmer-Bruhn, M.E. and Sapienza, H. (2006), 'Entrepreneurial team formation: an exploration of new member addition', *Entrepreneurship Theory and Practice*, **30**(2): 225–48.

Freeman, J.H., Carroll, G.R. and Hannan, M. (1983), 'Liability of newness: Age dependence in organization death rates', *American Sociological Review*, **48**: 692–710.

Gartner, W.B. (1985), 'A conceptual framework for describing the phenomenon of new venture creation', *Academy of Management Review*, **10**(4): 696–706.

Gartner, W.B., Shaver, K.G., Gatewood, E. and Katz, J.A. (1994), 'Finding the entrepreneur in entrepreneurship', *Entrepreneurship Theory and Practice*, **18**(3): 5–10.

Granovetter, M. (1985), 'Economic action and social structure: a theory of embeddedness', *American Journal of Sociology*, **91**: 481–510.

Hambrick, D.C. and Mason, P.A. (1984), 'Upper-echelons: the organization as a reflection of its top managers', *Academy of Management Review,* **9**(2), 193–207.

Hannan, M.T., Burton M.D. and Baron, J.N. (1996), 'Inertia and change in the early years: Employment relations in young, high technology firms', *Industrial Corporate Change*, **5**: 503–36.

Higashide, H. and Birley, S. (2002) 'The consequences of conflict between the venture capitalist and the entrepreneurial team in the United Kingdom from the perspective of the venture capitalist', *Journal of Business Venturing*, **17**(1): 59–81.

Jawahar, I.M. and McLaughlin, G.L. (2001), 'Toward a descriptive stakeholder theory: an organizational life cycle approach', *Academy of Management Review*, **26**: 397–414.

Jensen, M.C. and Meckling, W.H. (1976), 'Theory of the firm: managerial behavior, agency costs, and ownership structure', *Journal of Financial Economics*, **3**: 305–60.

Kamm, J.B., Shuman, J.C., Seeger, J.A. and Nurick, A.J. (1990), 'Entrepreneurial teams in new venture creation : a research agenda', *Entrepreneurship Theory and Practice*, **14**: Summer, 7–17.

Katz, J. and Gartner, W.B. (1988), 'Properties of emerging organizations', *Academy of Management Review*, **13**(3): 429–41.

Katzenbach, J.R. and Smith, D.K. (1993). *The Wisdom of Teams*, Boston, MA: Harvard Business School Press.

Knight, D., Pearce, C.L., Smith, K.G., Olian, J.D., Sims, P.H., Smith, K.A. and Flood, P. (1999), 'Top management team diversity, group process and strategic consensus', *Strategic Management Journal*, **20**(5): 445–65.

Kor, Y.Y. and Mahoney, J.T. (2000), 'Penrose's resource-based approach: the process and product of research creativity', *Journal of Management Studies*, **37**(1): 109–39.

Larson, A. (1992), 'Network dyads in entrepreneurial settings: a study of the governance of exchange relationships', *Administrative Science Quarterly*, **37**: 76–104.

Larson, A. and Starr, J.A. (1993), 'A network model of organization formation', *Entrepreneurship Theory and Practice*, **17**: Winter, 5–15.

Lincoln, J.R. and Miller, J. (1979), 'Work and friendship ties in organizations: a comparative analysis of relation networks', *Administrative Science Quarterly*, **24**(2): 181–99.

Lumpkin, G.T. and Dess, G.G. (1996), 'Clarifying the entrepreneurial orientation construct and linking it to performance', *Academy of Management Review*, **21**(1): 135–72.

Lynall, M.D., Golden, B.R. and Hillman, A.M. (2003), 'Board composition from adolescence to maturity: a multitheoretic view', *Academy of Management Review*, **28**(3): 416–31.

MacMillan, I.C, Siegel, R. and Subbanarasimha, P.N. (1985), 'Criteria used by venture capitalists to evaluate new venture proposals', *Journal of Business Venturing*, **1**: 119–28.

MacMillan, I.C., Zemann, L. and Subbanarasimha, P.N. (1987), 'Criteria distinguishing successful from unsuccessful ventures in the venture screening process', *Journal of Business Venturing*, **2**: 123–37.

McGrath, R.G., MacMillan, I.C. and Venkataraman, S. (1995), 'Defining and developing competence: a strategic process paradigm', *Strategic Management Journal*, **16**(4): 251–75.

Miller, C.C, Burke, L. and Glick, W. (1998), 'Cognitive diversity among upper echelon executive: implications for strategic decision processes', *Strategic Management Journal*, **19**: 39–58.

Moray, N. (2004), 'Innovatief ondernemen aan onderzoeksinstellingen: wishful thinking of pure reality?', in B. Clarysse (ed.), *Eendagsvlieg of pionier: welke ondernemer redt de economie?* Leuven: Garant, 97–135.

Muzyka, D., Birley, S. and Leleux, B. (1996), 'Trade-offs in the investment decisions of European venture capitalists', *Journal of Business Venturing*, **11**(4): 273–88.

Pelled, L.H., Eisenhardt K.M., and Xin, K.R. (1999), 'Exploring the black box: an analysis of work group diversity, conflict, and performance', *Administrative Science Quarterly*, **44**(1): 1–28.

Pettigrew, T.F. (1998), 'Intergroup contact theory', *Annual Review of Psychology*, **49**: 65–85.

Pfeffer, J. and Salancik, G. (1978), *The External Control of Organizations: A Resource Dependence Perspective*, New York: Harper & Row.

Pfeffer, J. (1981). *Power in Organizations*, Marshfield, MA: Pitman.

Quinn, R.E. and Cameron, K. (1983), 'Organizational life cycles and shifting criteria of effectiveness: some preliminary evidence', *Management Science*, **29**: 33–51.

Reich, R.B. (1987), 'Entrepreneurship reconsidered: the team as hero', *Harvard Business Review*, **65**(3): 77–83.

Rubenson, G.C. and Gupta, A.K (1996), 'The initial succession: a contingency model of founder tenure', *Entrepreneurship Theory and* Practice, **21**: 21–36.

Ruef, M. (2002), 'Strong ties, weak ties, and islands: structural and cultural predicators of organisational innovation', *Industrial and Corporate Change*, **11**: 427–49.

Schneider, B. (1987), 'The people make the place', *Personnel Psychology*, **40**: 437–53.

Scott, W.R. (1995), 'Institutions and Organizations: Theory and Research', Thousand Oaks, Calif.: Sage Publications.

Shane, S. (2000), 'Prior knowledge and the discovery of entrepreneurial opportunities', *Organization Science*, **11**: 448–69.

Shane, S. and Stuart, T. (2002), 'Organizational endowments and the performance of university start-ups', *Management Science*, **48**(1): 154–70.

Shaw, M.E. (1981), *Group Dynamics: The Psychology of Small Group Behaviour*. New York: McGraw-Hill.

Shepherd, D. A. and Krueger, N. F. (2002) 'An intentions-based model of entrepreneurial teams' social cognition', *Entrepreneurship Theory and Practice* **27**(2): 167–86 .

Shepherd, D.A., Zacharis, A.L. and Baron, R.A. (2003), 'VCs' decision process: evidence suggesting more experience may not always be better', *Journal of Business Venturing*, **18**: 381–401.

Siegel, R., Siegel, E. and MacMillan, I.C. (1993), 'Characteristics distinguishing high-growth ventures', *Journal of Business Venturing*, **8**: 169–80.

Stinchcombe A. (1965), 'Social structure and organizations', in: J.G. March (ed.), *Handbook of Organizations*, Chicago: Rand McNally, 142–93.

Timmons, J.A. (1979), 'Careful self-analysis and team assessment can aid entrepreneurs', *Harvard Business Review*, **57**: Nov–Dec, 198–206.

Ucbasaran, D., Alsos, G., Westhead, P. and Wright, M. (2008)., 'Habitual entrepreneurs', *Foundations and Trends in Entrepreneurship Research*, 1–93.

Vanaelst, I. (2006), 'Essays on entrepreneurial teams in innovative high-tech start-ups', unpublished dissertation, Vrije Universiteit Brussel–Universiteit Gent.

Van de Bunt, G.G., Wittek, R.P.M. and de Klepper, M.C. (2005), 'The evolution of intra-organizational trust networks. The case of a German paper factory: An empirical test of six trust mechanisms', *International Sociology*, **20**(3): 339–69.

Van Muijen, J.J., Koopman, P., De Witte, K., De Cock, G., Susanj, Z., Lemoine, C., Bourantas, D., Papalexandris, N., Branyicski, I., Spaltro, E., Jesuino, J., Gonzalves Das Neves, J., Pitariu, H., Konrad, E., Pieró, J., González-Romá, V. and Turnipseed, D. (1999), 'Organizational culture: the focus questionnaire', *European Journal of Work and Organizational Psychology*, **8**(4): 551–68.

Vohora, A., Wright, M. and Lockett, A. (2004), 'Critical junctures in the development of university high-tech spin-out companies', *Research Policy*, **33**(1): 147–76.

Watson, W.E, Ponthieu, L. and Critelli, J.W. (1995), 'Team interpersonal process effectiveness in venture partnerships and its connection to perceived success', *Journal of Business Venturing*, **10**: 393–411.

Watson, W., Stewart, W.H. Jr. and BarNir, A. (2003), 'The effects of human capital, organizational demography, and interpersonal processes on venture partner perceptions of firm profit and growth', *Journal of Business Venturing*, **18**: 145–64.

Westphal, J.D. (1999), 'Collaboration in the boardroom: behavioural and performance consequences of CEO-board social ties', *Academy of Management Journal*, **42**: 7–25.

Wiersema, M.P. and Bantel, K.A. (1992), 'Top management team demography and corporate strategic change', *Academy of Management Journal*, **35**: 91–121.

Wright, M. and Bruining, H. (2008) (eds), *Private Equity and Management Buyouts*, Cheltenham, UK and Northampton, MA, USA: Edward Elgar.

Wright, M. and Coyne, J. (1985), *Management Buyouts*. Beckenham: Croom Helm.

Wright, M., Hoskisson, R., Busenitz, L. and Dial, J. (2000), 'Entrepreneurial growth through privatization: the upside of management buy-outs', *Academy of Management Review*, **25**: 591–601.

Wright, M., Clarysse, B., Mustar, P. and Lockett, A. (2007a). *Academic Entrepreneurship in Europe*, Cheltenham, UK and Northampton, MA, USA: Edward Elgar.

Wright, M., Hmieleski, K.M., Siegel, D.S. and Ensley, M.D. (2007b), 'The role of human capital in technological entrepreneurship', *Entrepreneurship Theory and Practice*, **31**(6): 791–806.

Zajac, E.J. and Westphal, J.D. (1996), 'Who shall succeed? How CEO/board preferences and power affect the choice of new CEOs', *Academy of Management Journal*, **39**: 64–90.

Part I
Team Formation and Composition

[1]

1042-2587-93-172$1.50
Copyright 1993 by
Baylor University

The Stages of Team Venture Formation: A Decision-making Model

Judith B. Kamm
Aaron J. Nurick

This model of multi-founder organizational formation assumes that organizations emerge in stages, following an *a priori* sequence of transitions. The idea stage comes first. In it, individuals or groups within the context of their social networks make decisions about the business concept and what is needed to implement it. The second stage consists of implementation decisions, including who will supply resources, what inducements will be used to attract more partners if necessary, and how the team will be kept together. Feedback loops indicate that the process may return to the concept and implementation needs decisions, depending upon choices made at certain critical points.

Organizations emerge from the coalescence of individuals with a "specific conscious *joint* purpose" (Bernard, 1962, p. 114). While some organizations are formally founded and owned by one person, many others are team ventures. That is, two or more people formally establish and share their ownership of the new organization (Kamm, Shuman, Seeger, & Nurick, 1990). While more work has been done recently to understand the pre-organizational stage of venture creation (Hansen & Wortman, 1989; Hansen, 1990), very little of it has focused specifically on how and why teams of founders come together to create new organizations.

In order to learn more about why and how successful team ventures form, the model presented here assumes that the founders' decision-making process is a key factor that deserves to be studied. Paraphrasing Herbert Simon, understanding the decisions made in starting team ventures is the key to understanding how they operate and how they succeed (Simon, 1976, p. xi).

Much of the existing literature about the conception and birth of organizations, regardless of whether or not they have multiple founders, may be grouped into three major schools of thought: the "state," the "population ecology," and the "stage" conceptual frameworks (Kamm, Nurick, & Edwards, 1987). The "organizational states" view is that organizations' existence at any given point in time can be described as a dynamic equilibrium (Starbuck, 1965; Hedberg, Nystrom, & Starbuck, 1976; Miller & Friesen, 1980a, 1980b; Tichy, 1980; Rhenman, 1973; Normann, 1977). The states are not, however, part of a life cycle. Instead they reflect the major activity occurring (Filley & Aldag, 1980; Romanelli & Tushman, 1983). In contrast, "population ecology" distinguishes itself by its focus on groups of organizations and their environments, which are more macro units of analysis (McKelvey, 1982; Stinchcombe, 1965; Pennings, 1982). Aldrich (1979), Aldrich and Mueller (1982), and Hannon and Freeman (1978), however, believe that this model's ideas also apply to individual organizations.

Unlike the "state" perspective, the "stages" school assumes that organizations develop in an evolutionary manner, following an *a priori* sequence of transitions rather than a random series of occurrences (Mintzberg, 1984; Lippitt & Schmidt, 1967; Greiner, 1972; Katz & Kahn, 1978; Vozikis & Glueck, 1980; Tibbits, 1979; Churchill & Lewis, 1983; McGivern, 1978). Additionally, "stage" theorists tend to use biological metaphors (Kimberly, Miles & Associates, 1980; Cafferata, 1982; Bartunek, 1983; Torbert, 1974; Lavoie & Culbert, 1978; Cameron, 1976; Quinn & Cameron, 1983; Kimberly, 1979; Neal, 1979). Bartunek notes, however, that such models usually begin with the firm's formal commencement, without considering that "prehistory experiences" affect later development (Bartunek, 1983, p. 5).

Kazanjian (1988) found that in the first stage of successful technology-based company growth, one of the two most important problems was the "people" factor, or "attracting capable personnel," and "achieving management depth and finding talent." His study, however, does not go beyond identifying this factor's importance at the start of the life cycle. Our team venture model represents Kazanjian's "people" factor in more detail, based upon our belief that the stage school of thought most realistically describes organizational development.

THE MODEL

Figure 1 presents a model of the sequence and types of decisions we expect to find individuals and groups making as they form team ventures. Like most innovations, the formation of a new organization can be conceptualized as occurring in two broad stages. First comes the idea, followed by action to implement it.

STAGE I: THE IDEA

At the idea stage of a team venture, one of two processes is assumed to occur. An individual may get an inspiration for a new venture by recognizing a market's unmet need (also known as an opportunity). This can be termed the "lead entrepreneur" approach, in which one person gets and processes information, often from members of his or her social network, as well as from personal experience at work, at school, or at home, or from the news media. Most other types of innovation also emerge from such an idea-generation phase (Kamm, 1987). The primary decision to be made at this first stage is whether or not to act on this idea for a new venture.

Alternatively, as Figure 1 indicates, two or more individuals may recognize an opportunity to work together, regardless of whether or not any of them have an idea for a particular new venture (Kamm et al., 1990). This "group approach," as contrasted to the "lead entrepreneur" approach, may be motivated more by the perception of the benefits to be derived from the relationship than from the benefits of task accomplishment. That is, the relationship may take top priority in the beginning, at least. The model also indicates the importance of the teammembers' social networks as a key factor influencing their perception of the opportunity to work together (Kamm & Aldrich, 1991). The primary decision to be made in this approach is whether or not to formalize the relationship and become business partners.

The Business Concept and Implementation Needs Decisions

Whether the lead entrepreneur or group approach is taken, if a decision is made to pursue further the initial opportunity, then more decisions follow. Specifically, how to

Figure 1
A Decision-making Model of Team Venture Formation

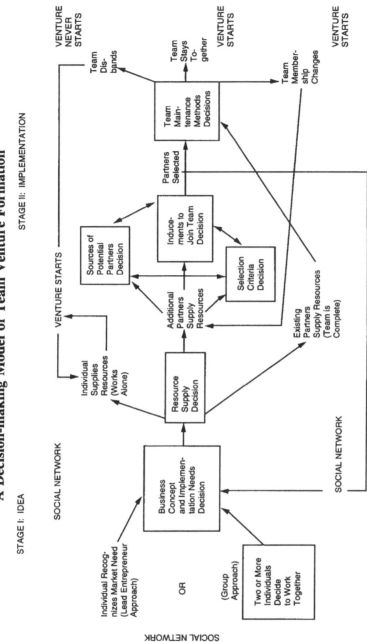

get more information about what is needed to make the opportunity more than just an idea must be determined. The process of getting more information may cause the nature of the opportunity itself to change. That is, the business concept (what the venture will make or provide, and in what way) or the relationship (who will be on the team and what roles will be played) may shift as more information is obtained.

The process by which the team generates the idea for its venture, makes decisions about it, starts to implement it, and then modifies it is represented by the feedback arrow in the model from the "Partners Selected" outcome to the "Business Concept" box. That is, as team members work together, they may modify and redefine the business concept and their decisions about the resources needed to implement it. We assume that this problem-solving process is what turns an informal social group into an entrepreneurial team. Yukl's (1989, pp. 249-261) synthesis of the literature on group decision making provides some theories to test about how effective groups generate new ideas and solve problems. For instance, groups tend to be most effective at problem solving when they: (1) take enough time to thoroughly consider alternatives; (2) include the participation of all members; (3) avoid polarization; and (4) carefully develop action plans.

STAGE II: IMPLEMENTATION

Resource Supply Decisions

As Scott notes (1981, p. 156), "Organizations do not spontaneously emerge but require the gathering and harnessing of . . . materials, energy, information, and personnel." The next major set of decisions to be made, therefore, is where these resources will be sought; labelled "Resource Supply Decision" in Figure 1. This is the first step in the implementation stage of a team venture. It addresses how individuals or groups decide to seek a partner or partners to help them supply resources.

The model proposes that there are three likely outcomes from this decision: (a) the individual entrepreneur will supply resources; (b) the existing group will supply them; or (c) partners will be sought. This is a pivotal decision for both individuals and groups. If individuals decide to supply resources themselves and believe for other reasons that partners are unnecessary, they remain solo entrepreneurs and no team is formed. As Figure 1 indicates, this represents an end-point on the model.

How and why groups decide not to increase their membership in order to implement the business concept could be a factor in the venture's future. This outcome by-passes the next set of decisions in our model. Rather than considering how to find and recruit new team members, they are concerned with maintaining themselves and launching their ventures. On Figure 1 the arrow leading from the "Existing Partners Supply Resources" outcome box goes right to the "Team Maintenance Methods Decision" box.

If a problem-solving view is adopted to explain team ventures, then it can be hypothesized that team members perceive a gap between needed resources or the likelihood of the venture's failure and their ability or willingness to assume these costs (Bass, 1983). This model permits testing of the notions of "bounded rationality" and "satisficing" (Simon, 1976) to learn more about the extent to which team builders adhere to the long-prescribed rule that entrepreneurs should undergo systematic self-assessment prior to starting new firms (Cossman, 1975; Osgood & Wetzel, 1976; Swayne & Tucker, 1973; Timmons, 1979; Webster, 1976). Risk-assessment theories about factors influencing the degree of risk individuals and groups perceive and are willing to take could also be used in testing our hypothesis that groups are formed to share perceived risk when individuals are unwilling or unable to do so (Slovic, Fischhoff, & Lichtenstein, 1977; Kogan & Wallach, 1965, 1967).

On the other hand, starting a team venture may be less a matter of problem solving and more a matter of preference for individuals or groups whose members either (1) personally value working as a team; or (2) belong to professions (science and engineering, especially), cultures, or some other socializing force where working with one or more partners is highly valued (Katz & Kahn, 1966; Scott, 1981).

Partner Recruitment Decisions

Once it has been determined that partners are needed in order to start a new firm, a constellation of decisions follows: where to find partners; how to choose the best one(s); and how to convince them to participate. As the double-headed arrows in Figure 1 indicate, these decisions are likely to be related to each other. The kind of people sought (criteria used) may be located in certain places (sources) and may have certain motivational patterns (inducements). Alternatively, ready access to certain people (sources) or to the amount or types of rewards that can be offered (inducements) may determine the kind of people available (criteria).

Sources. Many entrepreneurial teams consist of friends, relatives, or associates from former employers or educational institutions, indicating that they emerge from existing relationships, often without consideration of members' capabilities to successfully launch a new business (Kamm et al., 1990). Consequently, Cyert and March's (1963, pp. 120-123) concept of "problemistic search" appears to be relevant. Nonetheless, we have observed team builders who want to move beyond familiar sources to find partners. We also know from our experience and the entrepreneurship literature that the venture capital industry is a source of "unfamiliar" partners (Gorman & Sahlman, 1986; Hay & Walker, 1986; MacMillan, Kulow, & Khoylian, 1988) as well as financing (Ronstadt, 1984), although some entrepreneurs decide not to use this source (Kamm, 1990).

Criteria. When we have informally asked entrepreneurs how they decided who would make a good new venture partner or teammember, their unprompted response has been, "It's like a marriage." We believe, therefore, that the "chemistry" of forming entrepreneurial teams may be a practical application of interpersonal attraction theory (Bird, 1989; Berscheid & Walster, 1969; Duck, 1977; Duck & Gilmour, 1981; Byrne, 1971).

Attraction has been cast as an exchange with rewards and costs (Homans, 1961; Thibaut & Kelley, 1959). People are drawn to others who have similar beliefs and interests, possess particular abilities and competencies, have qualities that are deemed admirable, and return the sentiment of liking (Aronson, 1984). Berscheid and Walster (1969) identified other rewards, such as the reduction of anxiety and stress, ease of access to information by proximity, and the ability to cooperate in a task, thereby enabling the attainment of some mutual goal. In the entrepreneurial context, possession of money to invest and experience and expertise needed for success in the venture also attract potential teammembers to each other (Bird, 1989, p. 221). Attraction, therefore, is a multidimensional phenomenon that goes beyond simple liking.

A common prescription for creating effective teams is to insure that they are well balanced in terms of members' functional expertise (MacMillan, Siegel, & Subbanari-simha, 1985) and "management skills, decision-making styles and experience" (Timmons, 1979, p. 198). This prescription is related to attraction theory; if entrepreneurs follow it, they are attracted to others who possess qualities and competencies very different from their own, but which are needed for starting the envisioned new firm.

However, it is possible for homogeneous teams to be successful, and the concept of balance may be problematic to use as a criterion for selecting partners (Kamm, Shuman, Seeger, & Nurick, 1989). Instead, we believe that a more important decision criterion may be the mutuality of teammembers' compelling interests'' or the "primary driving personal force behind their wanting to start the venture.'' Alignment of these interests with the start-up's mission or reason for being is also thought to be crucial for success (Ronstadt & Shuman, 1988, p. 23). The importance of common interests extends beyond initial recruitment (Barnard, 1938; Simon, 1976), as it has been theorized that "interest, irrespective of trust, could make cooperation more likely simply by making action more pressing . . .'' (Gambetta, 1988, p. 226).

Inducements. The model assumes that in some instances prospective partners must be convinced to join entrepreneurial teams. For a variety of reasons, including prior career commitments, family responsibilities, or negative attitudes toward uncertainty, attractive prospects may be hesitant to take the obvious risks of starting a new venture. The promise of future rewards from joint ownership as a way to motivate candidates has received most attention in the entrepreneurship literature (Mamis, 1983, p. 60). Ownership can be initially divided in many different ways. Shares may be equal or unequal. If unequal, they may be distributed in any number of combinations (*Venture,* 1989). Nonetheless, there are risks inherent in using ownership as an incentive to join an entrepreneurial team. Not only can the value of the shares be diluted by creating more shares, but also the decision-making control of the venture can dissipate. Entrepreneurs' willingness to share decision-making control may be a primary factor in whether or not they decide to use ownership as an incentive to recruit partners.

It is likely, therefore, that entrepreneurs seeking partners decide to use inducements either in addition to or instead of ownership in order to get people to join them in their venture. Organizational theorists classify inducements in a variety of ways. For example, Barnard's (1962) "specific inducements'' that can be directly offered to individuals are material (money, goods, pleasant physical conditions); non-material opportunities for "distinction, prestige, personal power and the attainment of dominating position . . .'' (p. 145); desirable physical conditions of work; and "ideal benefactions'' (satisfying "personal ideals usually relating to non-material, future, or altruistic relations. They include pride of workmanship, sense of adequacy, altruistic service . . . patriotism . . . aesthetic and religious feeling'') (p. 146).

In our research on why people join entrepreneurial teams, we have either been told about or have inferred the following "specific inducements'': the ability to structure the new venture so as to avoid or correct perceived faults in previous employers' firms; the ability to become an instant president or executive; an opportunity for an inexperienced outsider to "get his/her ticket punched'' in a rapidly growing industry in which more established firms only hire experienced people; an opportunity to become employed; the opportunity to have a credible, attractive office in a prestigious location; the opportunity to gain practice for a future solo venture; and the opportunity to be acquired by a larger firm, thereby "coming in at the top'' of a wealthier, better-established organization.

Scott's (1981) typology of incentives, like Barnard's, extends beyond material rewards for organizational cooperation to include social and "purposive'' rewards ("intangible rewards related to the goals of the organization . . .'' (p. 160). Barnard (1962, p. 146) calls these "general incentives,'' which cannot necessarily be directly offered to an individual. Among these are "associational attractiveness'' (social/personal compatibility) and "opportunities for enlarged participating.'' In our studies of new firms we have found that people also join founding teams in order to work with people they know, admire, and trust. In one case two academic colleagues with complementary talents and styles decided to work together as partners. As the business began to grow they brought in family members to assist in specific roles. In another case the lead entrepreneur recruited former co-workers whose talents he respected. In turn, one vice president reported that she joined his start-up firm because he was one of the best bosses she had ever had.

Team Maintenance Decisions

We believe that a new venture's success is facilitated by its founding team's cohesiveness and longevity. The next set of decisions, therefore, is about how to maintain the group long enough to at least launch the venture. Much of what has been written about entrepreneurial teams appears to focus upon their difficulties (Bird, 1989; Thurston, 1986; Timmons, 1979; *Inc.*, 1983; Kamm & Nurick, 1985). The model in Figure 1 assumes that at least one member of an entrepreneurial team is sufficiently aware of the importance of human relationships to actually make decisions about how to keep the group together.

Group maintenance does not necessarily mean that all members are retained, however. We have observed that it may be necessary to remove or replace a member in order for the team to continue functioning effectively. Figure 1 depicts the replacement process with the "Team Membership Changes" outcome box and loop back to the "Additional Partners Supply Resources" point on the model.

Based upon the group dynamics theories of Wilfred Bion (1961), and the open systems theories of Miller and Rice (1967), as well as the work of the Tavistock Institute of Human Relations (Colman & Bexton, 1975; Colman & Geller, 1985), the model assumes that decision-making authority is a major team maintenance issue, which successful teams address by consciously defining and agreeing upon each member's role not only on the team but also in the emerging organization. Furthermore, effective teams use their common goal as a primary criterion in making decisions about how to resolve conflicts, such as over the amount of equity to offer as an inducement to a prospective partner. Finally, team boundaries (who is in the group and what requirements differentiate this group from others that members may belong to) are a maintenance issue that successful teams address by permitting all members some degree of participation in recruitment, termination, and reward decisions. For instance, bringing in partners' family members or co-workers from partners' current workplaces can raise boundary issues that cause groups to disband.

The model's last set of outcomes represents the possible link between the team and the venture. One possibility is that the team disbands and the venture never officially starts. An alternative here, however, is that a solo founder remains and the venture does start. This is depicted by the arrow returning to the "Individual Supplies Resources" box on the model. Another possibility is that the team stays together and the venture begins. The third outcome is that the organization starts, but the founding team's membership changes.

CONCLUSION

We believe that what this model helps us to discover about assembling team ventures will have a number of important effects upon management science in the areas of entrepreneurship and organizational theory, especially decision making and development. It could provide the field of organizational theory with insights about the conception, gestation, and birth of new business firms. Use of this conceptual framework should also contribute to theory building about selection and recruitment decisions as a special case of managerial decision making under conditions of extreme uncertainty. This model may also serve as a foundation for much needed further theory building on entrepreneurial teams.

REFERENCES

Aldrich, H. E. (1979). *Organizations and environments*. Englewood Cliffs, NJ: Prentice Hall.

Aldrich, H. E., & Mueller, S. (1982). The evolution of organizational forms: Technology, coordination, and control. In B. M. Staw, & L. L. Cummings (Eds.), *Research in organizational behavior*, vol. 4, pp. 33-87.Greenwich, CT: JAI Press.

Aronson, E. (1984). *The social animal*. New York: Freeman.

Barnard, C. I. (1962). *The functions of the executive*. Cambridge, MA: Harvard University Press.

Bartunek, J. M. (1983). The stages of organizational creation. Paper presented at the Academy of Management Meeting, Dallas.

Bass, B. L. (1983). *Organizational decision making*. Homewood, IL: Richard D. Irwin, Inc.

Berscheid, E., & Walster, E. (1969). *Interpersonal attraction*. Reading, MA: Addison-Wesley.

Bion, W. R. (1961). *Experiences in groups*. London: Tavistock Publications.

Bird, B. J. (1989). *Entrepreneurial behavior*. Glenview, IL: Scott, Foresman.

Byrne, D. (1971). *The attraction paradigm*. New York: Academic Press.

Cafferata, G. L. (1982). The building of democratic organizations: An embryological metaphor. *Administrative Science Quarterly*, 27(2), 280-303.

Cameron, K. S. (1976). Organizational diagnosis and group stage development. Discussion paper, Yale University.

Churchill, N. C., & Lewis, V. L. (1983). The five stages of small business growth. *Harvard Business Review*, May-June, 30-44, 48-50.

Colman, A. D., & Bexton, W. H. (Eds.). (1975). *Group relations reader*. Sausalito, CA: GREX.

Colman, A. D., & Geller, M. H. (Eds.). (1985). *Group relations reader 2*. Washington, DC: A. K. Rice Institute.

Cossman, E. J. (1975). *Entrepreneurial flow charts*. Los Angeles: Pepperdine University.

Cyert, R. M., & March, J. G. (1963). *A behavioral theory of the firm*. Englewood Cliffs, NJ: Prentice Hall.

Duck, S. (1977). *Theory and practice in interpersonal attraction*. New York: Academic Press.

Duck, S., & Gilmour, R. (1981). *Personal relationships, 2: Developing personal relationships*. London: Academic Press.

Filley, A. C., & Aldag, R. J. (1980). Organizational growth and types: Lessons from small institutions. In B. M. Staw, & L. L. Cummings, *Research in organizational behavior*, vol. 2, pp. 279-320. Greenwich, CT: JAI Press.

Gambetta, D. (Ed.). (1988). *Trust: Making and breaking cooperative relationships*. New York: Basil Blackwell.

Gorman, M., & Sahlman, W. A. (1986). "What do venture capitalists do?" In R. Ronstadt, J. A. Hornaday, R. Peterson, & K. H. Vesper (Eds.), *Frontiers of entrepreneurial research*, pp. 414-436. Wellesley, MA: Babson College.

Greiner, L. (1972). Evolution and revolution as organizations grow. *Harvard Business Review*, 49, 37-46.

Hannan, M. T., & Freeman, J. H. (1978). The population ecology of organizations. In M. W. Meyer & Associates (Eds.), *Environments and organizations: Theoretical and empirical perspectives*. San Francisco: Jossey-Bass.

Hansen, E. L. (1991). Structure and process in entrepreneurial networks as partial determinants of initial new venture growth. Paper presented at Babson College Entrepreneurship Research Conference, Pittsburgh.

Hansen, E. L., & Wortman, M. S. (1989). Entrepreneurial networks: The organization *in vitro*. *Academy of Management Best Paper Proceedings*, 49th Annual Meeting, Washington, D.C., pp. 69-73.

Hay, R. K., & Walker, M. J. (1986). An assessment of the use of venture capitalists as mentors in entrepreneurial first ventures. In R. Ronstadt, J. A. Hornaday, R. Peterson, & K. H. Vesper (Eds.), *Frontiers of entrepreneurship research*, pp. 241-243. Wellesley, MA: Babson College.

Hedberg, B. L. T., Nystrom, P. C., & Starbuck, W. H. (1976). Camping on seesaws: Prescriptions for self-designing organization. *Administrative Science Quarterly, 21*, 41-65.

Homans, G. (1961). *Social behavior: Its elementary forms*. New York: Harcourt, Brace and World.

Inc. (1983). Inside the *Inc.* 500, December, 67-76.

Kamm, J. B. (1987). *An integrative approach to managing innovation*. Lexington, MA: Lexington Books.

Kamm, J. B. (1990). Vaporware containment: Software start-ups' methods for managing change. In L. R. Gomez-Mejia & M. Lawless (Eds.), *Managing the high technology firm*. Greenwich, CT: JAI Press.

Kamm, J. B., & Aldrich, H. E. (1991). Differences in network activity between entrepreneurial individuals and teams. Paper presented at Babson Entrepreneurship Research Conference, Pittsburgh.

Kamm, J. B., & Nurick, A. J. (1985). Software action team. A case study available from the authors.

Kamm, J. B., Nurick, A. J., & Edwards, K. (1987). *Building a theory of small organizations*. Working Paper: WP 87-056. Waltham, MA: Bentley College.

Kamm, J. B., Shuman, J. C., Seeger, J. A., & Nurick, A. J. (1989). Are well-balanced entrepreneurial teams more successful? Paper presented at the Babson Entrepreneurship Research Conference, St. Louis. Available from the authors.

Kamm, J. B., Shuman, J. C., Seeger, J. A., & Nurick, A. J. (1990). Entrepreneurial teams in new venture creation: A research agenda. *Entrepreneurship Theory & Practice, 14*(4), 7-17.

Katz, D., & Kahn, R. J. (1978). *The social psychology of organizations*. New York: John Wiley & Sons.

Kazanjian, R. K. (1988). Relation of dominant problems to stages of growth in technology-based new ventures. *Academy of Management Journal, 31*(2), 257-279.

Kimberly, J. R. (1979). Issues in the creation of organizations: Initiation, innovation, and institutionalization. *Academy of Management Journal, 22*, 437-457.

Kimberly, J. R., Miles, R. H., & Associates. (1980). *The organizational life cycle: Issues in the creation, transformation, and decline of organizations*. San Francisco: Jossey-Bass.

Kogan, N., & Wallach, M. A. (1964). *Risk taking. A study in cognition and personality*. New York: Holt, Rinehart & Winston.

Kogan, N., & Wallach, M. (1967). *New directions in psychology: Group decision making involving risk*. New York: Holt, Rinehart & Winston.

Lavoie, D., & Culbert, S. A. (1978). Stages of organization and development. *Human Relations, 31*(5), 417-438.

Lippitt, G. L., & Schmidt, W. H. (1967). Crises in a developing organization. *Harvard Business Review, 47,* 102-112.

MacMillan, I. C., Kulow, D. M., & Khoylian, R. (1988). Venture capitalists, involvement in their investments: Extent and performance. In B. A. Kirchhoff, W. A. Long, W. E. McMullen, K. H. Vesper & W. E. Wetzel, Jr. (Eds.), *Frontiers of entrepreneurship research,* pp. 303-323. Wellesley, MA: Babson College.

MacMillan, I. C., Siegel, R., & Subbanarasimha, P. N. (1985). Criteria used by venture capitalists to evaluate new venture proposals. *Journal of Business Venturing, 1,* 119-128.

Mamis, R. A. (1983). Golden handcuffs. *Inc.,* August, 59-69.

McGivern, C. (1978). The dynamics of management succession. *Management Decision, 16*(1), 32-42.

McKelvey, B. (1982). *Organizational systematics: Taxonomy, evolution, classification.* Berkeley: University of California Press.

Miller, D., & Friesen, P. (1980a). Archetypes of organizational transition. *Administrative Science Quarterly, 25,* 268-299.

Miller, D., & Friesen, P. H. (1980b). Momentum and revolution in organizational adaption. *Academy of Management Journal, 23*(4), 591-614.

Miller, E. J., & Rice, A. K. (1967). *Systems of organization: The control of task and sentient boundaries.* New York: Tavistock Publications.

Mintzberg, H. (1984). Power and organization life cycles. *Academy of Management Review, 9*(2), 207-224.

Neal, J. A. (1978). The life cycles of an alternative organization. Boston: Intercollegiate Case Clearinghouse.

Normann, R. (1977). *Management for growth.* New York: John Wiley & Sons.

Osgood, W. R., & Wetzel, W. E. (1976). Systems approach to venture initiation. Paper presented to Academy of Management.

Pennings, J. M. (1982). Organizational birth frequencies: An empirical investigation. *Administrative Science Quarterly, 27*(1), 120-144.

Quinn, R. E., & Cameron, K. S. (1983). Organizational life cycles and shifting criteria of effectiveness: Some preliminary evidence. *Management Science, 29,* 33-51.

Rhenman, E. (1973). *Organization theory for long-range planning.* New York: John Wiley & Sons.

Romanelli, E., & Tushman, M. L. (1983). Executive leadership and organizational outcomes: Changes over organizational life cycles. Paper presented at the Annual Meeting of the Academy of Management, Dallas.

Ronstadt, R. (1984). *Entrepreneurship: Text, cases and notes.* Dover, MA: Lord Publishing.

Ronstadt, R., & Shuman, J. C. (1988). *Venture feasibility planning guide.* Natick, MA: Lord Publishing.

Scott, W. R. (1981). *Organizations.* Englewood Cliffs, NJ: Prentice Hall.

Simon, H. A. (1976). *Administrative behavior. A study of decision making processes in administrative organizations,* third ed. New York: The Free Press.

Slovic, P., Fischhoff, B., & Lichenstien, S. (1977). Behavioral decision theory. *Annual Review of Psychology, 28,* 1-39.

Starbuck, W. H. (1965). Organizational growth and development. In J. G. March (Ed.), *Handbook of organizations,* pp. 451-533. Chicago: Rand McNally.

Stinchcombe, A. L. (1965). Social structure and organizations. In J. G. March (Ed.), *Handbook of organizations,* pp. 142-193. Chicago: Rand McNally.

Swayne, C., & Tucker, W. (1973). *The effective entrepreneur.* Morristown, NJ: General Learning Press.

Thibaut, J., & Kelley, H. (1959). *The social psychology of groups.* New York: Wiley.

Thurston, P. H. (1986). When partners fall out. *Harvard Business Review,* November-December, 24-26, 30, 32, 34.

Tibbits, G. E. (1979). Small business management: A normative approach. *MSU Business Topics,* Autumn, 5-12.

Tichy, N. (1981). Problem cycles in organizations and the management of change. In J. Kimberly & R. H. Miles (Eds.), *The organizational life cycle.* San Francisco: Jossey-Bass.

Timmons, J. A. (1979). Careful self-analysis and team assessment can aid entrepreneurs. *Harvard Business Review,* November-December, 198-206.

Venture (1989). The IPO fast-track, *Venture, 11*(4), 25-39.

Vozikis, G., & Glueck, W. F. (1980). Small business problems and stages of development. *Academy of Management Proceedings,* August, 373-377.

Webster, A. (1976). Model for new venture initiation. *Academy of Management Review, 1*(1), 26.

Yukl, G. A. (1989). *Leadership in organizations,* second ed. Englewood Cliffs, NJ: Prentice Hall.

Judith B. Kamm is Associate Professor of Management at Bentley College.

Aaron J. Nurick is Professor of Management at Bentley College.

[2]

° *Academy of Management Journal*
2006, Vol. 49, No. 4, 741–758.

THE INFLUENCE OF FOUNDING TEAM COMPANY
AFFILIATIONS ON FIRM BEHAVIOR

CHRISTINE M. BECKMAN
University of California, Irvine

This paper's argument is that founding team composition—in particular, members' prior company affiliations—shapes new firm behaviors. Firms with founding teams whose members have worked at the same company engage in exploitation because they have shared understandings and can act quickly. Conversely, founding teams whose members have worked at many different companies have unique ideas and contacts that encourage exploration. In addition, firms whose founding teams have both common and diverse prior company affiliations have advantages that allow them to grow. The results suggest team composition is an important antecedent of exploitative and explorative behavior and firm ambidexterity.

The terms "exploration" and "exploitation" have been used broadly to capture a wide array of firm actions and behaviors. The concepts are central to studies of adaptation, organizational learning, and technical innovation (Abernathy, 1978; Benner & Tushman, 2002, 2003; Katila & Ahuja, 2002; Levitt & March, 1988; March, 1991). Exploratory behaviors are those that increase variance and generate internal variety (McGrath, 2001; Tushman & Smith, 2002); exploration involves radical innovation, creating new markets and products, experimentation, broad search, frequent change, and discovery (Katila & Ahuja, 2002; Miner, Bassoff, & Moorman, 2001; Rosenkopf & Nerkar, 2001). Exploitative behaviors, in contrast, are variance-decreasing and efficiency-oriented (March, 1991); exploitation involves incremental innovation, implementation, refinement, routinization, local search, and efficiency (Beckman, Haunschild, & Phillips, 2004; Benner & Tushman, 2003; March, 1991). Although there are benefits to being able to do both (He & Wong, 2004), organizations that explore may have

processes, strategies, structures, and capabilities quite distinct from those of organizations engaging in exploitation (Benner & Tushman, 2002; Katila & Ahuja, 2002; McGrath, 2001; Rosenkopf & Almeida, 2003).

Existing research suggests an important antecedent to exploration and exploitation: managers who create the right structures or develop supportive contexts (Brown & Eisenhardt, 1997; Gibson & Birkenshaw, 2004; Smith & Tushman, 2005; Tushman & O'Reilly, 1996). How do managers decide which structures or processes to adopt? Rather than having a clear idea about what structures are appropriate in a given context, I argue executive choices are driven by their past experiences. Managers bring ideas with them when they move across firm boundaries, and an executive's career experiences shape the range of actions she or he will consider at a new firm (Baty, Evan, & Rothermel, 1971; Boeker, 1997; Kraatz & Moore, 2002; Sørensen, 1999). In this study, I examine groups of early executives that comprise firms' founding teams and argue that their prior experiences predispose firms to engage in explorative or exploitative behaviors. In a broader sense, this view suggests that team composition both informs and constrains later firm action.

A founding team's past company *affiliations* are an important and understudied component of team composition. Much of the existing research focuses on how the functional experience and key relationships among founding team members influence firm strategy and action (Beckman, Burton, & O'Reilly, 2006; Boeker, 1988; Roure & Maidique, 1986; Shane & Stuart, 2002). Yet affiliations are important because the past companies in which managers have worked offer employees models for

I am grateful to Diane Burton, Cristina Gibson, James G. March, Damon Phillips, and the seminar participants at UCLA, Emory University, and the University of Washington for helpful comments on earlier versions of this paper. I would like to thank Jon Reuter for his research assistance. I would also like to thank the guest coeditor for the special research forum, Christina Shalley, and three anonymous reviewers for their constructive feedback. This research was supported by the Stanford Project on Emerging Companies (SPEC) at the Graduate School of Business; the Harvard Business School Division of Research; the MIT Entrepreneurship Center; and the University of California, Irvine. The remaining errors are my own.

what an organization should look like and how it should act. Following Burton and colleagues (2002), this study focuses not on the *what* of the experience, but on the *where*. To take a simple example, compare a three-person team where everyone has had prior experience at Apple Computer and a three-person team with one member from Apple, one from Intel, and one from Hewlett-Packard. Regardless of any overlap in functional or industry experience, the two teams bring with them different company affiliations from their prior jobs. The all-Apple team shares a language and set of tacit understandings even if the managers were not at Apple at the same time, whereas the team from the three different firms has a variety of experiences and diverse sources of information. These affiliations are a critical source of ideas, frames of reference, and contacts that shape the behaviors in which a new firm is likely to engage. And, in contrast to the stark example above, teams can both share common affiliations and bring multiple unique affiliations to their firms, as would be the case if, for example, the people from Intel and Hewlett-Packard in the above example also had prior experience at Apple.

In general, I argue that prior affiliations of management team members shape firm exploration and exploitation behaviors. Teams with some common prior company affiliations share a language and vision (Nahapiet & Ghoshal, 1998) that allow them to easily implement and routinize activities. Thus, firms whose management team members have shared affiliations should be more likely to pursue exploitative behaviors such as improving on existing processes and moving new products or processes quickly to market. In contrast, founding teams whose members come from a wide array of past companies bring diverse knowledge and contacts to their firms, and a variety of perspectives stimulates innovation and the discovery of new alternatives (Amabile, Conti, Coon, Lazenby, & Herron, 1996). Thus, firms whose teams have diverse affiliations should be more likely to pursue explorative behaviors such as investigating multiple ideas and becoming technical pioneers. Furthermore, teams should benefit from diverse and common prior company affiliations because these firms engage in behaviors that support both implementation and innovation. Thus, having a mix of both diverse and common team affiliations should be a precursor to organizational ambidexterity. Overall, this study develops the concept of team affiliations as an important antecedent to firm exploration and exploitation.

THEORY AND HYPOTHESES

To understand how prior founding team affiliations shape firm behaviors, it is first important to discuss how new firms are created. What brings founders and ideas together? At the extreme, a founding team comes together without a clear idea of what the potential firm will do. For example, Bill Hewlett and Dave Packard decided they wanted to start a company together, then decided what type of firm to create (Collins & Porras, 1994: 24). Their prior experiences and affiliations informed the early activities pursued and ideas generated. Indeed, the idea generation cannot be separated from the experiences of a firm's founders. In many cases, individuals' experiences shape which technological opportunities they recognize (Shane, 2000); thus, the characteristics, experiences, and affiliations of team members shape the ideas and opportunities that are eventually pursued. Together an idea and founders evolve into a firm (Clarysse & Moray, 2004). Imagine two engineers from the same company deciding they should exploit an innovation that their current employer is not exploiting. Or imagine two sales representatives from different firms comparing notes and deciding to take advantage of a market opportunity that neither firm has acknowledged. The team and initial idea for a firm emerge in a dynamic, reciprocal fashion in which the idea is embedded in the context and experience of the founders—the firm and market experiences of founders are thus embedded in the new firm created.[1]

Indeed, prior work on new ventures has shown that founders and founding team shape a firm's initial strategies, structures, actions, and performance (e.g., Beckman et al., 2006; Boeker, 1988; Burton, Sorenson, & Beckman, 2002; Eisenhardt & Schoonhoven, 1990; Gompers, Lerner, & Scharfstein, 2005; Roure & Maidique, 1986). Routines and competencies are embedded in managerial experiences, and these routines are passed to new firms through employee mobility (McKelvey, 1982; Phillips, 2002, 2005). In keeping with this literature, the general argument of this paper is that shared understandings and unique knowledge are embedded in prior team affiliations that shape firm exploitation and exploration.

Common Company Affiliations and Exploitation

Distinct from the commonalities that come from a shared discipline or a prior relationship are com-

---

[1] Thanks to an anonymous reviewer for making this point.

2006   *Beckman*   743

monalities among the members of a new firm's founding team who have worked at the same company, commonalities based on a shared understanding of how organizational work should be managed and coordinated. Founding team members with common prior company affiliations have a shared language, culture, and narratives. A shared language suggests a common perspective and trustworthiness (Tsai & Ghoshal, 1998). A shared organizational culture provides a common frame of reference, a shared vision and set of goals, and a conceptual filter that helps generate expectations about work (Nahapiet & Ghoshal, 1998). A shared narrative suggests that people from the same company will have many of the same stories and examples of appropriate and inappropriate behaviors. In fact, common work experiences affect the development of shared beliefs and culture as well as firm performance (Baron, Burton, & Hannan, 1996; Chattopadhay, Glick, Miller, & George, 1999). Eisenhardt and Schoonhoven (1990) found that founding teams with joint prior work experience had higher levels of growth than teams with less overlapping experience. They discussed the cohesion stemming from managers' having worked together in the past, but I add that this cohesion may result from shared affiliations as well as from direct experience with one another.

When founding teams' members share some common prior company affiliations, they share routines that aid their firms in "the exploitation of old certainties" (March, 1991: 71). Commonality will help teams be efficient and improve incrementally on existing processes or practices. Routinization and implementation are faster and easier when team members have shared understandings because team members will quickly agree on what needs to be done and how to do it. Of course, people from different companies will have some shared understandings (e.g., if they are from companies with similar strategies), but the level of mutual understanding and shared tacit knowledge will be greater when teams have shared affiliations.

When two founders come from the same prior company, they are more likely to talk to each other about the firm-specific knowledge that they share. This idea is consistent with the common knowledge effect: people talk about what they have in common (Stasser, Taylor, & Hanna, 1989). Firm-specific shared knowledge among founders encourages local search because team members find discussion straightforward, disagreements minimal, and the appropriate actions relatively clear. Taken together, these points suggest common prior company affiliations among the members of a firm's founding team will encourage exploitation.

Exploitative behaviors are those that build upon existing products and technologies and are efforts to seek competitive advantage through technical enhancements or cost advantages. Exploitation requires the efficiency and consistent implementation that common understandings facilitate. If all of a firm's founders come from a similar starting point (e.g., the same company), their narrower range of experience and knowledge suggests the firm is relatively limited in its routines and competencies and thus less likely to discover an innovation that is not readily apparent (Levinthal, 1997).

Firms pursuing exploitation will bring a product to market more quickly because they have the required routinization and standardization to move swiftly. In addition, the trust that arises from shared understandings will increase the speed of strategic decision making (Talaulicar, Grundei, & Werder, 2005; Tsai & Ghoshal, 1998). Common understandings facilitate the execution and implementation of ideas (Williams & O'Reilly, 1998); indeed, Schoonhoven, Eisenhardt, and Lyman (1990) argued that joint work experience increases trust, common goals, and mutual understandings, thereby decreasing the time inefficiencies of learning new roles and expectations. This decrease, they argued, should translate into a shorter time to first product shipment. Similarly, Reagans, Zuckerman, and McEvily (2004) found that shared work experience resulted in shorter project duration. The argument of the current article is that a firm's founders' having worked at the same company, even if not together, will also result in faster time to market because of the language and understandings that they share from their prior company affiliation.

Counterexamples exist of spin-offs pursuing exploration strategies (such as some spin-offs from Fairchild Semiconductor), but these examples, as the analysis I will subsequently present demonstrates, are not typical. Generally, a group of founders breaks off from an employer to fill a particular competency niche. The innovativeness achieved by the founding team with common prior experiences may be quite high if the founding team spins off from parents that themselves have innovator strategies (Christensen, 1993), but spin-offs generally exploit existing technologies rather than introduce innovations (Klepper, 2001). A founding team from the same parent is more often involved in extending and utilizing knowledge that the parent company has little interest in pursuing than in pursuing a technology at the knowledge frontier. It is also important to point out that not all teams whose members have common prior company affiliations are spin-offs, because team members may

744   *Academy of Management Journal*   August

not come directly from that company, and they may not have been there at the same time.

Hypothesis 1. Founding teams with common prior company affiliations are likely to engage in exploitative behaviors.

Diverse Company Affiliations and Exploration

Although common company affiliations may give a team shared understandings, firms also need access to external social capital to improve the amount of available information. External social capital refers to the actual and potential resources, outside information, and new ideas obtained through external ties (Adler & Kwon, 2002). External social capital can have a wide range of sources, such as alliances, joint ventures, and professional associations, but the prior company affiliations of founding teams are likely to be an important source of such social capital at firm founding (Burton et al., 2002). Consider again the earlier example of an all-Apple team and a team from three different companies. The team from three different firms has access to significantly more external social capital. Although common prior affiliations build internal communication, diverse prior affiliations provide new insights and knowledge that allow firms to pursue explorative, innovative behavior. External social capital increases the heterogeneity of available information, encourages deeper deliberations and discussions about the reasons for variety, and can result in debate and the surfacing of new alternatives (Beckman & Haunschild, 2002).

Innovation often comes from bringing together knowledge from disparate places (Damanpour, 1991; Hargadon, 2003; Rodan & Galunic, 2004; Schumpeter, 1934). Katila (2002) found innovation came from old extraindustry knowledge. The creativity literature suggests that access to diverse information, ideas, and alternatives stimulates creativity and ground-breaking advancement (Amabile et al., 1996; Perry-Smith & Shalley, 2003). Thus, access to information, contacts, and perspectives from a diverse set of company affiliations should encourage and facilitate exploration and innovation. These firms will have the internal variety and external reach to develop new technologies and markets. As Kanter argued, "Contact with those who see the world differently is a logical prerequisite to seeing it differently ourselves" (1988: 175). This ability to gather information, adapt, and innovate is consistent with the pursuit of technical innovation. Explorative behaviors include efforts to win a technology race in a new niche or to gain competitive advantage by being the first to develop

new, hitherto unproven, technologies. Innovators develop routines and competencies that are different from those of other organizations (Aldrich & Martinez, 2001), and teams with diverse networks are more likely to engage in innovative activities (Ruef, 2002). When founders come from a range of prior companies, the common knowledge they share includes broader market issues. Sharing broadly based market knowledge will encourage innovation and the development of new technologies more than a discussion of narrow firm-specific knowledge because team members with a variety of former company affiliations have different understandings about technical procedures, customer requirements, productive organizational cultures, and appropriate routines and processes. In fact, unique knowledge is more likely to be shared and integrated in teams in which people are not familiar with one another (Phillips, 2003). Thus, founding teams that draw on diverse prior company affiliations are more likely to pursue explorative behaviors because they have the knowledge and capacity to innovate.

Founding teams with a broad range of prior company affiliations have, in addition to a wealth of collective internal knowledge, a wide range of potential contacts and diverse relationships on which to draw. Access to diverse contacts may increase the centrality of a firm, which further privileges it, giving it a variety of information. In fact, an "exploration trap" refers to the pattern of behavior in which firms continue to seek new and different ideas without fully exploiting earlier ideas (March, 1991). Entrepreneurial firms are often trapped in this type of exploration (Aldrich, 1999). This view suggests that firms with diverse affiliations will not be tied to a particular idea and will pursue different ideas. Diversity of affiliations will not only encourage new and innovative behaviors, but also, in keeping with the nature of innovation, frequent change. Thus:

Hypothesis 2. Founding teams with diverse prior company affiliations are likely to engage in explorative behaviors.

Managing Exploration and Exploitation

Thus far I have suggested that the prior company affiliations of a founding team shape exploitative and explorative firm behavior but have not addressed the outcomes of these behaviors. Research on organizational ambidexterity suggests that firms capable of both exploring and exploiting do better than firms rooted in either one (Gibson & Birkinshaw, 2004; Katila & Ahuja, 2002; Tushman &

O'Reilly, 1996). For example, He and Wong (2004) found firms that had both exploitative and explorative innovation strategies had higher growth rates than other firms.

Existing research focuses on the structural and cognitive requirements for a firm to both explore and exploit (Smith & Tushman, 2005; Tushman & O'Reilly, 1996). For example, Tushman and O'Reilly (1996) described organizations with ambidextrous organizational forms. Loosely coupled units maintain different selection and search criteria, which allow both exploration units and exploitation units to operate. It is the group or individual at the top that must "manage across" these subunits (Smith & Tushman, 2005). Within a larger ambidextrous organization, this parallel operation of both exploring and exploiting units can lead to exploration *and* exploitation at the organization level. Entrepreneurial firms, however, are more likely to exist as a single business units.

The question that surfaces, then, is whether the same team can engage in both explorative and exploitative behaviors. Brown and Eisenhardt (1997) observed entrepreneurial firms that used sequential attention or rhythmic pacing to shift from exploration to exploitation. Such shifting between exploration and exploitation is distinct from contextual ambidexterity (Gibson & Birkinshaw, 2004), in which organizations manage to simultaneously reinforce adaptation and alignment tendencies (akin to exploration and exploitation) within the same organizational subunit. Contextual ambidexterity and rhythmic pacing both suggest that the same organizational units, and thus the same organizational personnel, can engage in both explorative and exploitative behaviors either sequentially or simultaneously, given the right organizational context. Despite this possibility, in the studies cited above the numbers of ambidextrous business units and firms were small, which suggests that engaging in both exploration and exploitation may be particularly difficult. I argue the pattern of affiliations in a founding team may be important for understanding which firms are able to do both and, thus, this pattern may be important for understanding firm performance.

If founding team affiliations predict exploitation and exploration, firms should see performance benefits when their founding teams have both common and diverse prior company affiliations. Diversity of prior affiliations alone will not improve performance because diversity encourages innovation but not implementation. Common prior affiliations alone will not improve performance because shared affiliations promote efficiency but not new discoveries. Teams with both common and diverse prior company affiliations will have the shared understandings to efficiently transmit knowledge and the unique perspectives to support innovation and change.

This performance benefit should be maintained over time for several reasons. First, a firm's founding team creates the initial structures and processes that shape its future actions (e.g., Baron et al., 1996). The founding team will leave a lasting imprint, and a team with both common and diverse founder affiliations will leave an imprint that provides the basis for both exploration and exploitation. In addition, although other managers may eventually replace or supplement founding teams, evolutionary arguments of path dependence and inertia suggest that subsequent teams are shaped by founding teams (Aldrich, 1999; Beckman & Burton, 2005; Phillips, 2002, 2005). Through an attraction-selection-attrition cycle (Schneider, 1987), founders select managers like themselves, and managers who do not fit the existing organization leave. Thus, patterns of founding team affiliations will be perpetuated over time. As a result, firms whose founding teams have both types of affiliations will be more likely to recruit managers with both types of affiliations. Taken together, these points suggest that founding teams with both common and diverse affiliations will both explore and exploit over time. He and Wong (2004) pointed to performance benefits for those firms that explore and exploit; thus,

Hypothesis 3. Firms whose founding teams have both common and diverse prior company affiliations will have higher levels of performance.

DATA AND METHODS

Sample

Data for this study were drawn from a longitudinal study of more than 170 young high-technology firms in California's Silicon Valley (for sampling details, see Burton et al. [2002]). The sample focused on a subset of high-technology industries: computer hardware and/or software, telecommunications (including networking equipment), medical and biological technologies, manufacturing, research, and semiconductors. Focusing on firms within a single region and a narrow range of similar industries holds constant key labor market and environmental conditions. Sampled firms had at least ten employees and were no more than ten years old at the time of first contact in 1994–95 (Certo, Covin, Daily, and Dalton [2001] used a similar age cutoff). About half of the firms had been founded before 1989, and founding year ranged from 1982 to 1995.

Interview, survey, and archival data were collected to gather information on the founding and evolution of these companies. Trained MBA and doctoral students conducted semistructured interviews with a member of the founding team of each firm to gather information about firm formation and early practices. The interviews, which provided data on the background and experience of the founding teams, were supplemented with archival data on the firms and teams. Data were collected for all firms from founding until they were acquired, died, or disappeared, or until July 2001. At the point of the last observation, the median firm was 13 years old (the range was 4–21 years). Of the 173 firms in the initial sample, I dropped 14 firms from the analysis because of missing data on key variables and an additional 18 because they were founded by solo entrepreneurs. These exclusions left a final sample of 141 firms. I eliminated solo entrepreneurs because, although a solo entrepreneur can have narrow or diverse prior company affiliations, the notion of shared understandings can only exist (or not exist) in a team. Although a team of two may operate differently than a larger team, two founders were considered a team because they exhibit team characteristics: ongoing interaction, interdependence, shared responsibility, and identification as a social entity (Cohen & Bailey, 1997).[2] To account for differences in team dynamics resulting from team size, I included number of founders as a control in all analyses.

I constructed the key study variables from the career histories of individual team members. Career backgrounds were hand-collected for every founder and executive who held the role of vice president or higher from a variety of sources, including interviews, internal company documents, Securities and Exchange Commission (SEC) documents, Lexis/Nexis news searches, Dow Jones Interactive, Edgar Archives, the *San Jose Mercury News*, and extensive Web searches. For founders with no background experience, it was difficult to ascertain whether there were no data because the founders had no prior jobs, or because the experiences were simply not reported in available sources. For 50 percent of the firms, the founders' prior places of employment were confirmed with the human resources departments of the sampled firms. It was confirmed that at least 38 founders started companies directly after school, so their prior employment experience was nonexistent. The resulting data set contains 329 founders who had worked for a total of 1,300 prior employers (454 distinct prior employers).

To investigate the sequence of events leading to firm formation, I coded and analyzed interviews with founders in which stories of firm formation were recounted. The data are consistent with the idea that the founding team and initial idea evolve together in the early days of a firm's life. This scenario differs from that typical in established firms, where the needs and espoused strategy of the firms often drive managerial selection (Fligstein, 1987). The sequence of firm formation was coded from the interviews by two people blind to study conditions (K =.69, ICC = .78). For example, a firm could be coded as a spin-off, as a restart, as begun by a group of entrepreneurs, or as begun by a solo entrepreneur with a specific idea who sought out founding team members. In the 100 interviews providing enough data to code the sequence, 64 percent of the firms reported that their founding teams evolved before or with the idea for the firms. In the remaining firms, one founder often had a specific idea before bringing on other founders. As other founders were brought in, the ideas were fine-tuned and strategies developed. Again, ideas develop in the social contexts in which they operate. Rather than argue that firm strategy drives team selection, I emphasize the dynamic process of firm formation whereby these decisions coevolve.

A *t*-test indicated that sequence of events varied neither by the type of prior company affiliation nor by an exploration firm strategy. Interestingly, firms with exploitation strategies were more likely to have founding teams that were formed prior to the ideas of the firms. This finding points to the presence of a subset of firms in which a group of entrepreneurs came together first, and then decided what idea to exploit or pursue. I included the sequence variable as a control in supplementary analyses. The results, which are described below, remained significant, despite the significantly reduced number of observations (with the exception of firm growth, which became marginally significant [$p < .10$]). Taken together, these initial analyses supported my view of team formation and idea generation as dynamic and reciprocal.

Dependent Variables

Exploration and exploitation behavior. To predict whether founding team members' prior company affiliations were associated with explorative or exploitative behaviors (Hypotheses 1 and 2), I examined several outcomes. Maximum-likelihood logistic regression was used as a means to predict

---

[2] Similar results were obtained when I included the 18 firms with solo entrepreneurs and when I excluded the 52 two-person teams.

whether a firm pursued an exploration strategy and changed initial ideas (change is consistent with exploration). I also used maximum-likelihood logistic regression to predict the pursuit of an exploitation strategy and employed event history analysis to examine time to first product (rapid product shipment is consistent with exploitation).

To test Hypotheses 1 and 2, the strategic behaviors and intentions that comprised firm strategy were examined. Most of the organizational strategy typologies empirical scholars employ allow for a distinction between innovators and incrementalists (e.g., Miles & Snow, 1978; Porter, 1980). A theme in all of the typologies is the importance of differentiating firms that are exploiting existing markets from those that are exploring or creating new markets. In the interviews, founders reconstructed early firm actions. Each founder was asked to describe the core competence of his or her firm at founding. Open-ended responses (supplemented by early press reports, product announcements, business plans, and prospectuses) comprised the raw data that were used to categorize each firm as falling into one of four strategic archetypes: innovator, enhancer, marketer, or low-cost producer (see Hannan, Burton, & Baron, 1996). Innovators seek to gain first-mover advantages by winning technology races. Firms that explore may also pursue other strategies, but here the focus is on exploration through technical innovation. A firm was coded as having an exploration strategy (exploration = 1, otherwise = 0) if it had a technical innovator strategy (48 percent of the sample firms). Enhancer firms seek to produce products similar to those of other companies but develop general modifications or enhancements to gain competitive advantage. Low-cost producers seek cost advantages through efficient production techniques, relationships with low-cost suppliers, or economies of scale. Because the enhancer and cost strategies both revolve around extending existing products or services, an exploitation strategy was coded as present (exploitation = 1, otherwise = 0) if a firm had an enhancer or low-cost strategy (25 percent of the sample firms). Marketers seek competitive advantage through superior sales, marketing, or customer service, and this approach does not clearly constitute either exploration or exploitation. The remaining 27 percent of the sample firms had marketing or hybrid strategies.

There is reason to be confident that the strategy measures capture differences in firm behavior with a high degree of accuracy. Respondents were not asked to classify the strategies themselves; rather, two people independently coded strategies in an iterative fashion based on the interview and archi-

val research. A list of phrases and words were created to assist in coding. For instance, interviewees' use of words like "forefront," "pioneer," "first mover," and "innovation" when discussing their firms' activities was a basis for coding their firms as having exploration strategies. Words and phrases such as "clone," "low cost," "better design," and "feature-rich" signaled an exploitation strategy. Disagreements were reconciled through both coders discussing them with a third person. Hellmann and Puri (2000) performed a number of post hoc analyses of these same firms, linking patenting activity to the four firm strategies outlined above. They found that innovators accumulated larger patent portfolios, generating further confidence that the measure captured actual firm behaviors. These strategies describe the initial activities and behaviors of firms as recounted by their founders and early press releases. In later interviews, coders determined whether the initial firm strategies changed (e.g., from innovator to incremental). Although stability and change in strategy were not the focus of this study, these initial strategies were relatively stable in the early years of the sampled firms' lives (Hannan et al., 1996).

In addition to the above coding, I used two additional measures of exploitation and exploration. Firms with exploitation strategies are likely to ship products more quickly. The dates of product shipment came from a founder survey. Not all founders completed the survey, but interviews and other company data were used to supplement when possible. Firms with exploration strategies are likely to change ideas or direction more often than other firms. In fact, changing products or marketing channels is an important part of exploration. In order to measure whether a firm's founding idea changed, two independent coders examined the interview transcripts. The interviews did not contain enough information to adequately code this dependent variable for a sizeable number of firms. Thus, there are only 68 observations for model 3 in Table 4 (Hypothesis 2). The coders examined ten transcripts to develop and agree on a coding scheme and then independently coded the other transcripts. Differences were resolved through discussion, and the initial agreement was substantial (K =.76, ICC = .83). The coding scheme for the founding idea included "stable," "elaborated," "one major restart," "multiple ideas pursued," and "multiple ideas considered." The variable was coded 1 if an initial idea changed and 0 if the idea was stable or elaborated.

Firm performance. Hypothesis 3 predicts firm performance. In new ventures, firm growth is an important marker of success (Eisenhardt & Schoonhoven, 1990). Particularly in this time period and region, firms desired growth. Thus, new ventures founded with both types of affiliations (shared past employers and diverse past employers) should have grown more quickly because the resources, routines, and behaviors of these founding teams supported both exploitative and explorative behaviors. *Firm growth* was measured as growth in employees. A proportional firm growth measure was created:

$$Growth_{i,t} = \log(employees_{i,\,t+1}/employees_{i,\,t}),$$
(1)

where *employees* was the number of employees for firm *i* and *t* represented year. Number of employees was collected at the end of each year from survey and archival sources.

Independent Variables

Using the career histories described above, I identified the most recent three firms for which each founder had worked. Three past company affiliations were used, although results were similar when one prior company affiliation for each team member and all available data were used for each team member. *Diverse prior company affiliation* was a count of the number of discrete prior firms reported by all the members of a given founding team. *Common prior company affiliation* was a count of the number of firms at which more than one member of the founding team worked. For example, if one founder had worked at Apple, another founder at Global Village and Apple, and a third at Fairchild Semiconductor, Apple, and Applied Materials, the founding team was coded as having one common (Apple) and four diverse (Apple, Global Village, Fairchild, Applied Materials) prior company affiliations. Results were the same if diverse affiliations only included those firms where there was no overlap (three in the above example), but I included all discrete firms because ideas come from the full range of prior companies in which founders have worked. There was a .15 correlation between common prior company affiliation and diverse prior company affiliation at founding. These measures were calculated at founding and thus were not time-varying because "imprinting" arguments suggest that founders' impact lasts, even when they leave and new managers join their firm. This impact occurs through subsequent recruiting of similar others and established routines and practices that remain past the time of

a founder's employment at a firm (Beckman & Burton, 2005; Phillips, 2005).

Control Variables

Industry. Some industries may be more likely to adopt a particular strategy or develop a product quickly. For example, biotechnology firms are more likely to have exploration strategies and ship products late in their life cycles. Preliminary analyses revealed that medical (including medical devices and biotechnology), networking and telecommunications, and manufacturing were significantly different from other industries (results are available from the author). Those industry dummy variables that were significantly different from the other industries were included in each set of analyses.

Venture capital. An important external factor to consider when predicting firm growth and speed to product shipment is whether a firm has obtained venture capital (VC) backing. *VC financing* data were collected via a combination of public and proprietary databases, SEC-required filings and annual reports, internal company documents, and a survey instrument sent to the most senior finance executive at each firm (see Hellmann & Puri, 2000). The number of cumulative VC rounds obtained by a firm in each year is included in Tables 3 and 4.

Firm controls. I used the measures of exploration and exploitation strategies, which are described above, as control variables when examining firm growth and time to product shipment. Product shipment speed and growth may depend on firm size, so number of employees is included in Tables 3 and 4. Firm growth may also be a function of firm age, so firm age (in months) is included in Table 4.

Team controls. Larger founding teams have the potential for both more diverse and more common past company affiliations. *Founding team size* was coded as part of the interview process and corroborated with the career history data. Founding team size ranged from 2 to 12 members ($\bar{x} = 3.3$) and was included in all analyses. I included the *proportion of founders* currently employed by a firm for Tables 3 and 4 to account for changes in founding teams over time. Hypothesis 3 examines firms over time, so it was important to control for changes in top management teams after founding. I included *top management team size* and cumulative *executive entrances and exits* in Table 4, aggregated from the career history data. In so doing, I could be certain I was capturing lasting effects of founding teams over time, regardless of how these teams had changed over time.

TABLE 1
Descriptive Statistics and Correlations[a]

Variable	Mean	s.d.	Minimum	Maximum	1	2	3	4	5	6	7	8	9	10	11	12	13	14	15	16
1. Prior diverse company affiliations	3.33	1.99	0	11																
2. Prior common company affiliations	1.02	1.36	0	7	.15															
3. Exploration strategy	0.48	0.50	0	1	.07	−.07														
4. Exploitation strategy	0.25	0.43	0	1	−.11	.07	−.52													
5. Medical industry	0.16	0.36	0	1	−.10	−.18	.35	−.25												
6. Telecom industry	0.21	0.41	0	1	.17	−.08	−.16	.08	−.24											
7. Manufacturing industry	0.06	0.23	0	1	−.19	−.10	−.21	.14	−.10	−.12										
8. Founding team size	3.33	1.61	2	12	.02	.46	.11	−.08	.07	−.05	−.08									
9. Firm size	2.47	14.80	0	380	.05	.05	.03	−.02	−.04	.11	−.03	−.03								
10. Idea change	0.13	0.34	0	1	.22	.34	−.10	.17	−.10	.26	−.07	.33	.06							
11. Venture capital financing	2.62	2.62	0	11	.00	−.05	.19	−.06	.12	.02	−.22	.01	.04	−.09						
12. Executive exits	3.28	5.47	0	43	.03	.16	.05	.02	−.01	.06	−.13	.09	.43	.00	.30					
13. Executive entrances	6.74	6.25	0	44	.05	.20	.09	.02	−.02	.08	−.17	.08	.44	−.02	.34	.88				
14. Top management team size	4.29	3.38	0	29	.10	.17	.05	−.01	−.01	.10	−.16	.07	.19	−.02	.25	.29	.68			
15. Firm age	7.00	4.28	1	21	−.03	.04	−.09	.01	−.01	.07	−.05	−.01	.21	.13	.35	.60	.51	.20		
16. Firm growth	0.24	0.45	−4.03	3	.06	.02	.02	−.04	−.01	.03	−.01	−.03	−.04	−.05	−.09	−.20	−.12	−.01	−.01	
17. Proportion of founders in firm	0.69	0.38	0	1	−.04	−.00	−.04	.03	−.11	.02	.12	−.05	−.18	−.14	−.32	−.59	−.47	−.07	−.27	.17

[a] Correlations greater than .17 are significant at $p < .05$.

TABLE 2
Results of Logistic Regression Analysis Predicting Firm Strategy and Idea Change[a]

	Exploration Strategy			Exploitation Strategy			Idea Change		
Variable	Model 1	Model 2	Model 3	Model 4	Model 5	Model 6	Model 7	Model 8	Model 9
Medical industry	7.80** (5.13)	8.66** (5.78)	7.43** (5.04)				0.67 (0.84)	0.41 (0.61)	0.54 (0.80)
Telecom industry	0.56 (0.26)	0.51 (0.24)	0.44+ (0.21)	1.67 (0.78)	1.77 (0.85)	1.95 (0.95)	3.49 (3.14)	2.73 (2.58)	2.62 (2.54)
Manufacturing industry				3.62+ (2.72)	4.34+ (3.31)	3.61+ (2.82)			
Founding team size	1.08 (0.13)	1.08 (0.13)	1.22 (0.17)	0.95 (0.13)	0.84 (0.13)	0.83 (0.13)	1.60* (0.34)	1.65* (0.35)	1.45 (0.37)
Diverse prior company affiliation		1.17+ (0.11)	1.22* (0.13)			0.87 (0.10)		1.38* (0.26)	1.41* (0.29)
Common prior company affiliation			0.75+ (0.12)		1.35* (0.22)	1.41* (0.25)			1.39 (0.45)
Exploration strategy							0.64 (0.57)	0.54 (0.51)	0.66 (0.65)
Observations	141	141	141	141	141	141	68	68	68
Log-likelihood	−88.31	−87.00	−85.39	−77.10	−75.43	−74.75	−21.74	−20.29	−19.76
Pseudo-R^2	0.10	0.11	0.13	0.02	0.05	0.05	0.18	0.24	0.26

[a] Odds-ratios are reported, with standard errors in parentheses. One-tailed tests for hypothesized variables.

+ $p < .10$
* $p < .05$
** $p < .01$

RESULTS

Table 1 presents the descriptive statistics and correlations among the study variables. Although cumulative entrances and exits are highly correlated with firm age, firm size, and top management team size (correlations range from .4 to .8), the effects for team affiliations do not change with these variables in the model.

Table 2 reports the effects of founding team prior company affiliation on firm-level strategy. The Pearson chi-square goodness-of-fit test suggested a reasonable model fit for all models (not reported). Model 1 presents the control variables. The medical industry was 7.8 times more likely to have an exploration (i.e., innovator) strategy. As predicted, model 2 demonstrates that founding teams with diverse prior company affiliations were more likely to have an exploration strategy. Model 3 replicates the finding in model 2 and also indicates that the firms of founding teams with prior common company affiliations were less likely to have an exploration strategy (a relationship that was not hypothesized but is consistent with the theory). Odds-ratios are reported, so model 3 suggests teams with one more diverse prior company affiliation are 1.22 times more likely to have an exploration strategy. The variance explained in model 3 is 13 percent (pseudo-R^2 = .13), and the overall "hit rate" of the model is 67 percent. This rate suggests that although industry is the largest predictor of an exploration strategy, there is also strong support for Hypothesis 1.

Model 4, with the control variables, shows that manufacturing firms were significantly more likely

to have an exploitation (i.e., incremental) strategy.[3] Model 5 demonstrates that firms with teams with prior common company affiliations were more likely to have an exploitation strategy. In model 6, I added diverse prior company affiliations to be sure that the relationships were consistent with the theory (consistency required nonsignificance in this model). Model 6 confirms model 5 and thus, Hypothesis 2 is supported. The overall hit rate of the model is 75 percent, and the firms of teams with one additional common prior company affiliation were 1.41 times more likely to adopt an exploitation strategy. Although the explained variance is only 5 percent, results do show that common prior company affiliations predict exploitation rather than exploration strategies. This finding is consistent with prior work on spin-offs (Klepper, 2001), although not all teams in my sample with common prior company affiliations were spin-offs. In sum, founding teams whose members have worked for some of the same prior companies are more likely to pursue an exploitation strategy and less likely to pursue an exploration strategy, whereas founding team members from different prior companies are more likely to support an exploration strategy.

Models 7–9 concern the effects of team affiliations on the stability of the initial idea for a firm. Model 7 includes the control variables. Large founding teams were 60 percent more likely to change a basic firm concept. Findings reported under model 8 support Hypothesis 2, showing that

---

[3] The medical industry drops out because no firms in that industry pursued an incremental strategy.

TABLE 3
Results of Event History Analysis Predicting Speed of Product to Market[a]

Variable	Model 1		Model 2		Model 3	
Exploitation strategy	1.11	(0.19)	1.12	(0.19)	1.11	(0.18)
Medical industry	0.39**	(0.10)	0.41**	(0.10)	0.41**	(0.10)
Telecommunications industry	1.15	(0.15)	1.19	(0.15)	1.20	(0.16)
Venture capital financing	1.10†	(0.06)	1.09†	(0.06)	1.09†	(0.06)
Firm size	1.23**	(0.08)	1.25**	(0.08)	1.25**	(0.08)
Founding team size	0.93†	(0.04)	0.89*	(0.04)	0.89*	(0.04)
Proportion of founders in firm	1.52	(0.71)	1.43	(0.72)	1.44	(0.72)
Common prior company affiliations			1.09†	(0.06)	1.10†	(0.06)
Diverse prior company affiliations					0.99	(0.04)
Observations	417		417		417	
Log-likelihood	−547.66		−546.94		−546.90	

[a] Hazard ratios are reported, with robust standard errors in parentheses; n = 138; 129 failures. One-tailed tests for hypothesized variables.
† $p < .10$
* $p < .05$
** $p < .01$

TABLE 4
Results of Panel Regression Analysis Predicting Firm Growth[a]

	Model 1		Model 2		Model 3	
Medical industry	0.00	(0.04)	0.02	(0.03)	0.02	(0.03)
Manufacturing industry	−0.04	(0.03)	−0.02	(0.03)	−0.02	(0.03)
Telecom industry	0.05[†]	(0.03)	0.06*	(0.03)	0.05*	(0.03)
Exploration strategy	−0.01	(0.03)	−0.01	(0.03)	−0.01	(0.03)
Executive exits	−0.03*	(0.01)	−0.03*	(0.01)	−0.03*	(0.01)
Executive entrances	0.02	(0.01)	0.02	(0.01)	0.02	(0.01)
Top management team size	0.00	(0.01)	0.00	(0.01)	0.00	(0.01)
Venture capital financing	−0.00	(0.01)	−0.00	(0.01)	−0.00	(0.01)
Founding team size	−0.01	(0.01)	−0.01	(0.01)	−0.01	(0.01)
Proportion of founders	−0.00	(0.06)	−0.00	(0.06)	−0.00	(0.06)
Firm age	−0.03**	(0.00)	−0.03**	(0.00)	−0.03**	(0.00)
Firm size	0.00	(0.00)	0.00	(0.00)	0.00	(0.00)
Common and diverse prior company affiliations both high			0.05*	(0.02)	0.08*	(0.03)
Common prior company affiliations high, diverse prior company affiliations low					0.05	(0.03)
Common prior company affiliations low, diverse prior company affiliations high					0.03	(0.04)
Constant	0.40**	(0.07)	0.40**	(0.07)	0.36**	(0.07)
Observations	1,368		1,368		1,368	
Wald X^2	165.72		169.60		166.87	
R^2	0.10		0.10		0.10	

[a] Robust standard errors are in parentheses. Models are random-effects analyses clustered by firm; $n = 141$. One-tailed tests for hypothesized variables.
[†] $p < .10$
* $p < .05$
** $p < .01$

when a firm's founding team has an additional diverse prior company affiliation, the initial idea is 38 percent more likely to change, and the overall hit rate of the model is 88 percent. Although no control variables for industry were significant, I included industry to maintain consistency with earlier models.[4] Thus, founding teams with diverse prior affiliations were found to be more likely to explore and change ideas.

Table 3 reports the effect of founding team common prior company affiliation on time to first product shipment, another indicator of an exploitation strategy. Model 1 reports the control variables, indicating that the most important predictor of time to market is industry. Hazard ratios are reported; firms in the biotechnology/medical industry have a 61 percent lower hazard rate for product to market (biotech firms take much longer than other types of firms to bring a product to market). Firms with exploitation strategies and larger firms brought products to market more quickly, and large founding teams were slower to bring products to market. In support of Hypothesis 1, model 2 shows that

_____

[4] The manufacturing industry drops out of the model because the idea never changed for any firm in the manufacturing industry.

founding teams with members with prior common company affiliations bring products to market more quickly. The effects of common affiliation are not as large as those of the other variables in the model, but an additional common prior company affiliation increased the hazard rate by 9 percent. Model 3 demonstrates that it is common prior affiliations, not diverse prior affiliations, that increases speed to market.

Table 4 presents the results of a panel random-effects generalized least squares regression analysis with robust standard errors clustered by firm, which I conducted to examine whether founding team affiliations have a long-term impact on firms (Hypothesis 3). Model 1 presents the control variables alone. Telecommunications firms were more likely to grow, and teams with high levels of top manager exit were less likely to grow. In addition, older firms were less likely to grow. The next model examined whether founding teams with diverse and common prior company affiliations were more likely to grow. There are no effects for the continuous variables and no interaction effects between the continuous diverse and common prior company affiliation variables. I examined the distribution of the continuous variables and found that common prior company affiliations were often

2006   *Beckman*   753

zero. I then created variables using a median split for both affiliation variables. The median founding team in the sample had no common affiliations and had prior experience in three companies. Specifically, common prior company affiliation was coded 1 if any of the founders had worked at the same prior company. Diverse prior company affiliation was coded 1 if the founding team had worked at three or more unique prior companies. I then created four additional dummy variables: founding teams with diverse and common prior affiliations both high; those with high common and low diverse prior affiliations; those with high diverse and low common prior affiliations; and those with low diverse and low common prior affiliations. Twenty-two percent of the firms were coded into the category for high diverse and common prior company affiliations, and 32 percent were coded into the category for low diverse and low common prior company affiliations. By creating dummy variables, I was able to clarify that only firms with founding teams that had *both* diverse and common prior company affiliations received performance benefits.

Model 2 includes only the high diverse/common category, omitting all other founding team categories. Founding teams with high common and high diverse prior company affiliations were more likely to grow. This result offers support for Hypothesis 3. I calculated the growth rate from coefficients in model 2 and found that firms whose teams had high common and high diverse prior company affiliations had a 19 percent higher growth rate than other firms. Model 3 confirms that these effects hold when low diverse/common prior company affiliations is the omitted category. Despite the small change in explained variance (R^2), the hypothesized variables significantly increase model fit. These results offer some evidence that firms whose founders have both common and diverse prior affiliations (those teams that engage in explorative and exploitative behaviors at founding) are more likely to grow. It is important to note that these founding team variables are significant despite the presence of variables controlling for changes in teams over time. A founding team leaves a lasting impact that shapes firm growth. In supplementary analyses, I also controlled for functional diversity and later team affiliations. No additional variable changed the support for the hypothesized effects.

I also examined whether founding teams needed aligned experience and strategy (for instance, did founding teams with common prior affiliations do better when their firms also had an exploitation strategy?). Supplementary analyses provided no evidence that firms benefited from founding teams with prior company affiliations and a consistent strategy (e.g., an exploration strategy with diverse affiliations). This pattern of findings suggests that, although prior company affiliations shape the *likelihood* of a firm's engaging in one pattern of activities or another, an affiliation profile does not necessarily shape the *success* of those particular activities over time. Yet it is firms with both types of founding team affiliations that do best. The results in Table 4 suggest that initial team affiliation is linked to overall firm growth. Perhaps prior founding team affiliations that are both diverse and common allow a firm to hire the personnel most necessary for its success (Beckman & Burton, 2005) or for engaging in exploration and exploitation behaviors that are not examined here.

DISCUSSION

Overall, the results suggest that founding team prior company affiliations predict whether a firm pursues exploratory and exploitative behavior, and they also suggest that firms whose founding teams have both types of affiliations are more likely to grow over time. In general, these results support a strong relationship between founding team affiliations and consistent patterns of firm behavior. The mechanisms suggested for these linkages are the shared understandings that emerge from common prior company affiliations and the creativity associated with diverse prior company affiliations. Shared understanding suggests easier implementation and speed, whereas unique knowledge is associated with innovation and change.

Contributions

This study challenges and extends recent work on exploration and exploitation. I examined the antecedents of exploration, exploitation, and organizational ambidexterity and obtained results suggesting an alternative to a managerial "ability" to manage exploration and exploitation (Smith & Tushman, 2005). These results suggest that both exploring and exploiting may require management teams to draw on members' common and unique affiliations both, but to date research has seemed to advocate managerial insight and planning rather than choosing team members with the best set of experiences. This article indicates that teams are more constrained by history than current work suggests and that differences in firm exploration and exploitation are built in at team formation. Thus, ambidextrous firms may be those whose teams have significant common and diverse experience at founding.

For learning theories, these results confirm that initial starting positions shape the potential for change and growth (Levinthal, 1997). The link between firm growth and founding team affiliation is consistent with the path dependencies of learning. Furthermore, research indicating that founding teams are generally formed for reasons of convenience, not strategy (Ruef, Aldrich, & Carter, 2003) suggests a founding team's ability to support innovation and incremental learning may be an accident of founding.

These findings also contribute to network theory in important ways. The present arguments for the benefits of common and diverse company affiliations are similar to network arguments for cohesion and structural holes. In network theory, dense connections between team members may hinder exploration but aid exploitation (Coleman, 1988). In contrast, structural holes, where actors have access to disconnected others with nonredundant information, increase a firm's ability to explore and reach diverse information (Burt, 1992). However, past company affiliations do not align with network concepts in several important ways. First, networks may exist without an affiliation. Second, founding team members with an affiliation to a given organization may not have a prior relationship because they worked for the organization in different divisions or at different times. In fact, in these data the correlation between whether founding team members had known each other previously and whether they were from a common set of past companies was .17. The correlation was much higher when founders were coworkers (because by definition at least some of the founders simultaneously shared company experience), but including coworkers as a control did not change the pattern of reported results. This result demonstrates that, in addition to shared norms developing through close relationships, shared values and understandings develop through identification and experience with a common former organization. The way in which I examined affiliations is similar in concept to the study of affiliation or membership networks, where individuals are connected through events (Wasserman & Faust, 1994). But even in this work the focus is on direct ties formed through shared affiliations. Company affiliations offer an alternative means of developing cohesion or obtaining diverse knowledge without assuming prior dyadic relationships.

For managers, this research suggests that they might usefully spend more attention at founding creating a team with both common and unique prior company affiliations. This is not to say that,

without such initial team planning, history dictates firm outcomes. The multiple means by which shared understandings and diverse knowledge can be obtained should be acknowledged. However, rather than focusing solely on functional experience, race, or gender, this research suggests a more subtle experience that shapes perceptions and alters team dynamics: prior company affiliations. These affiliations are important for managers to consider, as are the more general benefits of accessing unique knowledge and having shared understandings.

Limitations and Future Research

To be certain, this analysis does not capture all exploration and exploitation behaviors. I focused on behaviors associated with exploitation and exploration strategies, but affiliations may lead to broader patterns of exploration and exploitation. For example, there is evidence that a key means by which firms engage in exploration is maintaining relationships with other firms (Brown & Eisenhardt, 1997; Rosenkopf & Almeida, 2003). Here, supplementary analyses showed that team-level affiliations were unrelated to the initial number and range of external advisors. However, it is beyond the scope of the data to predict whether prior company affiliations might be influential in predicting specific external relationships. A longitudinal study of external partnerships is a promising topic for future research.

Future research should examine these issues in other samples of firms. For two key reasons, the present sample is success-biased. First, the firms were observed during the 1980s and 1990s. The latter half of the 1990s was an extraordinary economic time in general, and in particular in Silicon Valley. Thus, some of the sampled firms might have survived longer than they would have in another period, buoyed by the optimistic financial markets. Second, the sampling frame (at least ten employees) meant that the firms under investigation had achieved some minimum scale. Despite this data limitation, the sample had some noteworthy advantages for the purposes of this study. It spanned a range of industries and included firms that did and did not receive venture capital, go public, and become successful. This variety in itself is quite unusual. Owing to data limitations, much of the research in a similar vein looks only at firms that receive VC or have gone public. Although many valuable things can be learned from that type of research, this sample offered a much broader range of firms.

It is important to acknowledge that firm strategy

2006 *Beckman* 755

may emerge with a founding team itself. I controlled for variables that might plausibly drive both founding team selection and firm strategy (i.e., industry and team size). Additionally, supplementary analyses suggested that firm strategy did not predict later top management team affiliation. This finding suggests the causality more often works in the direction hypothesized: founding teams shape firm strategy, and/or the strategy and team evolve together. By examining other behaviors that indicate explorative and exploitative behaviors that clearly happen after team formation (product shipment, changing the idea pursued by a firm), the analysis demonstrates a broad pattern consistent with the hypothesized causality. Yet future research on firm and team formation could further illuminate these causal processes.

The concept of common organizational affiliation net of direct contact among actors is an important contribution of this work. Future research should examine the influence of "connections" that are neither actual relationships nor between structurally equivalent actors. Network theory needs to expand the study of networks beyond strong ties (see Lawrence, 2006) and to consider affiliation networks as more than precursors to dyadic relationships. Take, for example, two individuals who went to the same college several decades apart. Although the two individuals did not meet at school, they share a language about people, places, and things, and perhaps a feeling about the cultural experience, shared experiences that give them a common bond. Thus, the shared understandings that develop through common past affiliations are similar but distinct from bonds that develop through direct relationships. These types of connections may be formed through common school or company affiliations or through intense professional training (e.g., advanced educational degrees). The relevance of these common past affiliations may vary depending on the other relationships and attributes salient in a team.

This study also informs research on spin-offs. Although not all founders with common prior company affiliations create spin-offs from the parent firms, all spin-offs have founders with common prior company affiliations. Although research has often suggested that spin-offs are the source of innovations (e.g., Christensen, 1993), more evidence is consistent with spin-offs as exploiters of existing technology (Klepper, 2001) than with spin-offs as innovators. The results of this study are consistent with Klepper's and raise the question of whether, in spin-offs, exploitation comes from the teams' shared understandings or from the technologies of the parent that are available to exploit. Here I found

that teams with common prior company affiliations were more likely to have exploitation strategies, and these teams were also likely to have been formed before their firms' central ideas were settled on. Future research could help better explain the mechanisms that lead spin-offs to exploit and examine details about parent firms. For example, does the innovativeness of a parent moderate the effects found here?

In conclusion, by examining the antecedents of explorative and exploitative behavior in organizations, this article develops links between the team and the firm levels of analysis. Team-level prior company affiliations, and experiences more generally, influence firm-level choices and behaviors. I find that common founding team affiliations are related to faster product shipment and use of an exploitation strategy, whereas diverse team affiliations predict an exploration strategy and change in founding ideas. Firms that have founding teams whose members have both diverse and common affiliations are more likely to grow over time, which suggests team composition is an important component of firm ambidexterity. By examining new ventures, I demonstrate this link without the confounding influence of prior firm actions and expectations. The study points to the importance of both people and the constraints people face in the creation and growth of organizations.

REFERENCES

Abernathy, W. J. 1978. *The productivity dilemma*. Baltimore: Johns Hopkins Press.

Adler, P. S., & Kwon, S. W. 2002. Social capital: Prospects for a new concept. *Academy of Management Review*, 27: 17–40.

Aldrich, H. E. 1999. *Organizations evolving*. Newbury Park, CA: Sage.

Aldrich, H. E., & Martinez, M. A. 2001. Many are called, but few are chosen: An evolutionary theory for the study of entrepreneurship. *Entrepreneurship Theory and Practice*, 25(summer): 41–56.

Amabile, T. M., Conti, R., Coon, H., Lazenby, J., & Herron, M. 1996. Assessing the work environment for creativity. *Academy of Management Journal*, 39: 1154–1184.

Baron, J. N., Burton, M. D., & Hannan, M. T. 1996. The road taken: Origins and evolution of employment systems in emerging companies. *Industrial and Corporate Change*, 5: 239–275.

Baty, G. B., Evan, W. M., & Rothermel, T. W. 1971. Personnel flows as interorganizational relations. *Administrative Science Quarterly*, 16: 430–443.

Beckman, C. M., & Burton, M. D. 2005. *Founding the*

future: The evolution of top management teams from founding to IPO. Working paper, Paul Merage School of Business, University of California, Irvine.

Beckman, C. M., Burton, M. D., & O'Reilly, C. 2006. Early teams: The impact of team demography on VC financing and going public. *Journal of Business Venturing:* In press.

Beckman, C. M., & Haunschild, P. 2002. Network learning: The effects of partners' heterogeneity of experience on corporate acquisitions. *Administrative Science Quarterly,* 47: 92–124.

Beckman, C. M., Haunschild, P., & Phillips, D. 2004. Friends or strangers? Firm-specific uncertainty, market uncertainty, and network partner selection. *Organization Science,* 15: 259–275.

Benner, M. J., & Tushman, M. 2002. Process management and technological innovation: A longitudinal study of the photography and paint industries. *Administrative Science Quarterly,* 47: 676–706.

Benner, M. J., & Tushman, M. L. 2003. Exploitation, exploration, and process management: The productivity dilemma revisited. *Academy of Management Review,* 28: 238.

Boeker, W. 1988. Organizational origins: Entrepreneurial and environmental imprinting at time of founding. In G. R. Carroll (Ed.), *Ecological models of organizations:* 33–51. Cambridge, MA: Ballinger.

Boeker, W. 1997. Executive migration and strategic change: The effect of top manager movement on product-market entry. *Administrative Science Quarterly,* 42: 213.

Brown, S. L., & Eisenhardt, K. M. 1997. The art of continuous change: Linking complexity theory and time-paced evolution in relentlessly shifting organizations. *Administrative Science Quarterly,* 42: 1–34.

Burt, R. 1992. *Structural holes: The social structure of competition.* Cambridge, MA: Harvard University Press.

Burton, D. M., Sorensen, J. B., & Beckman, C. 2002. Coming from good stock: Career histories and new venture formation. In M. Lounsbury & M. Ventresca (Eds.), *Research in the sociology of organizations,* vol. 19: 229–262. Greenwich, CT: JAI Press.

Certo, S. T., Covin, J. G., Daily, C. M., & Dalton, D. R. 2001. Wealth and the effects of founder management among IPO-stage new ventures. *Strategic Management Journal,* 22: 641–658.

Chattopadhay, P., Glick, W., Miller, C., & George, H. 1999. Determinants of executive beliefs: Comparing functional conditioning and social influence. *Strategic Management Journal,* 20: 763–789.

Christensen, C. M. 1993. The rigid disk drive industry: A history of commercial and technical turbulence. *Business History Review,* 67: 531–588.

Clarysse, B., & Moray, N. 2004. A process study of entre-preneurial formation: The case of a research-based spin-off. *Journal of Business Venturing,* 19: 55–79.

Cohen, S. G., & Bailey, D. E. 1997. What makes teams work: Group effectiveness research from the shop floor to the executive suite. *Journal of Management,* 23: 239–290.

Coleman, J. S. 1988. Social capital in the creation of human capital. *American Journal of Sociology,* 94(supplement): S95–S120.

Collins, J. C., & Porras, J. I. 1996. *Built to last: Successful habits of visionary companies.* New York: Harper-Collins.

Damanpour, F. 1991. Organizational innovation: A meta-analysis of effects of determinants and moderators. *Academy of Management Journal,* 34: 555–590.

Eisenhardt, K. M., & Schoonhoven, C. B. 1990. Organizational growth: Linking founding teams, strategy, environment and growth among U.S. semi-conductor ventures. *Administrative Science Quarterly,* 28: 274–291.

Fligstein, N. 1987. The intraorganizational power struggle: Rise of finance personnel to top leadership in large corporations, 1919–1979. *American Sociological Review,* 52: 44–58.

Gibson, C. B., & Birkinshaw, J. 2004. The antecedents, consequences and mediating role of organizational ambidexterity. *Academy of Management Journal,* 47: 209–226.

Gompers, P. A., Lerner, J., & Scharfstein, D. S. 2005. Entrepreneurial spawning: Public corporations and the genesis of new ventures, 1986–1999. *Journal of Finance,* 60: 577–614.

Hannan, M. T., Burton, M. D., & Baron, J. N. 1996. Inertia and change in the early years: Employment relations in young, high technology firms. *Industrial and Corporate Change,* 5: 503–536.

Hargadon, A. 2003. *How breakthroughs happen: The surprising truth about how companies innovate.* Boston: Harvard Business School.

He, Z. L., & Wong, P. K. 2004. Exploration vs. exploitation: An empirical test of the ambidexterity hypothesis. *Organization Science,* 15: 481–494.

Hellmann, T., & Puri, M. 2000. The interaction between product market and financing strategy: The role of venture capital. *Review of Financial Studies,* 13: 959–984.

Kanter, R. M. 1988. When a thousand flowers bloom: Structural, collective, and social conditions for innovation. In B. M. Staw & L. L. Cummings (Eds.), *Research in organizational behavior,* vol. 10: 169–211. Greenwich, CT: JAI Press.

Katila, R. 2002. New product search over time: Past ideas in their prime? *Academy of Management Journal,* 45: 995–1010.

Katila, R., & Ahuja, G. 2002. Something old, something

new: A longitudinal study of search behavior and new product introduction. *Academy of Management Journal*, 45: 1183–1194.

Klepper, S. 2001. Employee startups in high-tech industries. *Industrial and Corporate Change*, 10: 639–674.

Kraatz, M. S., & Moore, J. H. 2002. Executive migration and institutional change. *Academy of Management Journal*, 45: 120–143.

Lawrence, B. S. 2006. Organizational reference groups: A missing perspective on social context. *Organization Science*, 17: 80–100.

Levinthal, D. A. 1997. Adaptation on rugged landscapes. *Management Science*, 43: 934–950.

Levitt, B., & March, J. G. 1988. Organizational learning. In W. R. Scott (Ed.), *Annual review of sociology*, vol. 14: 319–340. Palo Alto, CA: Annual Reviews.

March, J. G. 1991. Exploration and exploitation in organizational learning. *Organization Science*, 2(1): 71–87.

McGrath, R. G. 2001. Exploratory learning, innovative capacity, and managerial oversight. *Academy of Management Journal*, 44: 118–131.

McKelvey, B. 1982. *Organizational systematics: Taxonomy, evolution, classification.* Berkeley: University of California Press.

Miles, R. E., & Snow, C. C. 1978. *Organizational strategy, structure and process.* New York: McGraw-Hill.

Miner, A. S., Bassoff, P., & Moorman, C. 2001. Organizational improvisation and learning: A field study. *Administrative Science Quarterly*, 46: 304–337.

Nahapiet, J., & Ghoshal, S. 1998. Social capital, intellectual capital, and the organizational advantage. *Academy of Management Review*, 23: 242–266.

Perry-Smith, J. E., & Shalley, C. E. 2003. The social side of creativity: A static and dynamic social network perspective. *Academy of Management Review*, 28: 89–106.

Phillips, D. J. 2002. A genealogical approach to organizational life chances: The parent-progeny transfer among Silicon Valley law firms, 1946–1996. *Administrative Science Quarterly*, 47: 474–506.

Phillips, D. J. 2005. Organizational genealogies and the persistence of gender inequality: The case of Silicon Valley law firms. *Administrative Science Quarterly*, 50: 440–472.

Phillips, K. W. 2003. The effects of categorically based expectations on minority influence: The importance of congruence. *Personality and Social Psychology Bulletin*, 29: 3–13.

Porter, M. E. 1998. *Competitive strategy* (1st ed.). New York: Free Press.

Reagans, R., Zuckerman, E., & McEvily, B. 2004. How to make the team: Social networks vs. demography as criteria for designing effective teams. *Administrative Science Quarterly*, 49: 101–133.

Rodan, S., & Galunic, C. 2004. More than network structure: How knowledge heterogeneity influences managerial performance and innovativeness. *Strategic Management Journal*, 25: 541–562.

Rosenkopf, L., & Almeida, P. 2003. Overcoming local search through alliances and mobility. *Management Science*, 49: 751.

Rosenkopf, L., & Nerkar, A. 2001. Beyond local search: Boundary-spanning, exploration, and impact in the optical disk industry. *Strategic Management Journal*, 22: 287–306.

Roure, J., & Maidique, M. 1986. Linking prefunding factors and high-technology venture success: An exploratory study. *Journal of Business Venturing*, 1: 295–306.

Ruef, M. 2002. Strong ties, weak ties and islands: Structural and cultural predictors of organizational innovation. *Industrial and Corporate Change*, 11: 427–449.

Ruef, M., Aldrich, H. E., & Carter, N. M. 2003. The structure of founding teams: Homophily, strong ties, and isolation among U.S. entrepreneurs. *American Sociological Review*, 68: 195–222.

Schneider, B. 1987. The people make the place. *Personnel Psychology*, 40: 437–453.

Schoonhoven, C. B., Eisenhardt, K. M., & Lyman, K. 1990. Speeding products to market: Waiting time to first product introduction in new firms. *Administrative Science Quarterly*, 35: 177–207.

Schumpeter, J. A. 1934. *Theory of economic development.* Cambridge, MA: Harvard University Press.

Shane, S. 2000. Prior knowledge and the discovery of entrepreneurial opportunities. *Organization Science*, 11: 448–469.

Shane, S., & Stuart, T. 2002. Organizational endowments and the performance of university start-ups. *Management Science*, 48: 154–170.

Smith, W. K., & Tushman, M. L. 2005. Managing strategic contradictions: A top management team model for managing innovation streams. *Organization Science*, 16: 522–536.

Sorensen, J. B. 1999. Executive migration and interorganizational competition. *Social Science Research*, 28: 289–315.

Stasser, G., Taylor, L. A., & Hanna, C. 1989. Information sampling in structured and unstructured discussions of three- and six-person groups. *Journal of Personality and Social Psychology*, 57: 67–78.

Talaulicar, T., Grundei, J., & Werder, A. V. 2005. Strategic decision making in start-ups: The effect of top management team organization and processes on speed and comprehensiveness. *Journal of Business Venturing,* 20: 519–541.

Tsai, W., & Ghoshal, S. 1998. Social capital and value creation: The role of intrafirm networks. *Academy of Management Journal,* 41: 464–476.

Tushman, M. L., & O Reilly, C. A. 1996. Ambidextrous organizations: Managing evolutionary and revolutionary change. *California Management Review,* 38(4): 8.

Tushman, M. L., & Smith, W. 2002.Organizational technology. In J. Baum (Ed.), *Companion to organizations:* 388–414. Malden, MA: Blackwell.

Wasserman, S., & Faust, K. 1994. *Social network analysis: Methods and applications.* Cambridge, U.K.: Cambridge University Press.

Williams, K., & O'Reilly, C. A. 1998. Demography and diversity in organizations: A review of 40 years of research. In B. M. Staw & R. I. Sutton (Eds.), *Research in organizational behavior,* vol. 20: 77–140: Greenwich, CT: JAI Press.

Christine M. Beckman *(cbeckman@uci.edu)* is an associate professor at The Paul Merage School of Business, University of California, Irvine. She received her Ph.D. from Stanford University. Her research focuses on the ways in which organizations learn through and are influenced by their networks, and the ways in which this influence in turn affects organizations' strategic decisions.

[3]

THE STRUCTURE OF FOUNDING TEAMS: HOMOPHILY, STRONG TIES, AND ISOLATION AMONG U.S. ENTREPRENEURS

MARTIN RUEF
Stanford University

HOWARD E. ALDRICH
University of North Carolina

NANCY M. CARTER
University of St. Thomas

The mechanisms governing the composition of formal social groups (e.g., task groups, organizational founding teams) remain poorly understood, owing to (1) a lack of representative sampling from groups found in the general population, (2) a "success" bias among researchers that leads them to consider only those groups that actually emerge and survive, and (3) a restrictive focus on some theorized mechanisms of group composition (e.g., homophily) to the exclusion of others. These shortcomings are addressed by analyzing a unique, representative data set of organizational founding teams sampled from the U.S. population. Rather than simply considering the properties of those founding teams that are empirically observed, a novel quantitative methodology generates the distribution of all possible teams, based on combinations of individual and relational characteristics. This methodology permits the exploration of five mechanisms of group composition—those based on homophily, functionality, status expectations, network constraint, and ecological constraint. Findings suggest that homophily and network constraints based on strong ties have the most pronounced effect on group composition. Social isolation (i.e., exclusion from a group) is more likely to occur as a result of ecological constraints on the availability of similar alters in a locality than as a result of status-varying membership choices.

SOCIOLOGISTS have made major strides toward understanding the conditions under which new organizations and new organizational forms are created, as well as the kinds of social locations that are most likely to spawn their creators. Beginning with Max Weber's ([1904–1905] 1992) analysis of ascetic Protestantism's contributions to the entrepreneurial spirit, sociologists have offered both macro- and microlevel interpretations of entrepreneurial phenomena (Carroll and Mosakowski 1987; Ruef 2000; Stinchcombe 1965). Today, sociologists conduct multilevel investigations, ranging from the personal networks of individual entrepreneurs to the transition of entire societies from socialism to capitalism (Aldrich forthcoming). Yet the mechanisms that may connect individual founders to one another remain poorly explicated.

The emergence of a new formal organization invariably entails a decision regarding who will participate and what they will contribute. Many entrepreneurs begin entirely on their own, although they may turn to oth-

Direct correspondence to Martin Ruef, Graduate School of Business, Stanford University, Stanford, CA 94305–5015 (ruef_martin@gsb.stanford.edu). We gratefully acknowledge the National Science Foundation for research support to Nancy Carter and Howard Aldrich under grant SBR-9809841, and the Center for Entrepreneurial Leadership at the Kauffman Foundation for their assistance in making this data available. We benefited from responses to presentations at Princeton, Harvard, Boston College, and the 2002 annual meeting of the American Sociological Association in Chicago. In particular, we thank Holly Arrow, Paul DiMaggio, Nancy DiTomaso, Elizabeth Mannix, Mark Mizruchi, Richard Moreland, Howard Stevenson, and anonymous *ASR* reviewers for their suggestions. All opinions and findings expressed are those of the author(s).

ers for help with various aspects of the founding process. Others begin with a team, making the enterprise a collective effort. Framed in this way, new organizations are clearly social entities from the beginning, as even solo founders implicitly make choices—or face constraints—that lead them *not* to cooperate with others in the founding process. How an organization begins and whether others are recruited to join the effort can have lasting consequences for its survival and performance. Why do some entrepreneurs go it alone, rather than join with others? On what basis do entrepreneurs in multimember teams choose other founders?

Our interest in entrepreneurial founding teams is linked with two broad themes in recent sociological theory and research. First, new organizations ensure the reproduction of existing populations of organizations and lay the foundation for the creation of new populations. Organizational ecologists have generally focused on dynamics within existing populations, noting that most founding attempts reproduce existing forms of organizations and are incremental rather than novel additions to the organizational landscape (Carroll and Hannan 2000). By contrast, evolutionary theorists have focused on the generation of new organizational populations, analyzing the conditions under which new forms of organizations carve out niches for themselves (Aldrich and Fiol 1994). Whether a new business simply copies an existing form or strikes off into novel territory can depend on the extent to which its founding team exhibits diverse capabilities and perspectives (Ruef 2002b). Investigating the forces that generate variation within founding teams thus carries the potential for explaining organizational innovation more generally.

Second, new organizations affect stratification and inequality in a society by shaping the life chances of entrepreneurs and their employees. Organizational foundings and disbandings generate a great deal of employment volatility through job creation and destruction. Between 1992 and 1996, about 28 million jobs were created in the United States by newly founded organizations (Birch 1997). For employees, organizational foundings create opportunities for advancement and facilitate the acquisition of addi-

tional human capital (Carroll and Mosakowski 1987; Haveman and Cohen 1994). For entrepreneurs, new business formation represents a potential for upward social mobility (Bates 1997; Nee and Sanders 1985). Many business owners employ family members in their business ventures, and some pass on their businesses—or the wealth gained from them—to their families (Keister and Moller 2000). To the extent that mobility and status considerations are taken into account by nascent entrepreneurs, these processes will tend to be reflected in mechanisms of inclusion and exclusion among organizational founding teams.

In this article, we consider how achieved and ascribed characteristics of entrepreneurs affect the composition of founding teams and how these characteristics are mediated by the social context of the entrepreneurial effort. From the sociological literature on group formation, we identify five general mechanisms that could influence team membership, including considerations of homophily, functionality, status expectations, network constraint, and ecological constraint. Homophily refers to the selection of other team members on the basis of similar ascriptive characteristics, such as gender, ethnicity, nationality, appearance, and the like (for a review, see McPherson, Smith-Lovin, and Cook 2001).[1] Functional theories consider the extent to which team members possess valuable and complementary achieved competencies that help ensure the success of a collectivity (e.g., Bales 1953; Slater 1955). Drawing on lines of research in expectation states (Fisek, Berger, and Norman 1991) and structuralism (Skvoretz and Fararo 1996), theories of status variation address the greater capacity of high-status individuals (with respect to ascribed *or* achieved characteristics) to attract other team members, compared with low-status individuals. Network perspectives posit that team formation occurs within a preexisting network of strong and weak ties that constrains the

---

[1] Most classical treatments of homophily (e.g., Lazarsfeld and Merton 1954) have not restricted it to ascriptive characteristics. For a purely homophilous mechanism to apply to achieved characteristics, however, the functional contributions of those characteristics must be ruled out.

founding team's choice of members. Finally, ecological perspectives emphasize the importance of the spatial proximity and environmental distribution of potential group members.

We examine these mechanisms of team composition using the Entrepreneurial Research Consortium's panel study of entrepreneurial dynamics (Reynolds 2000), a unique, nationally representative sample of nascent entrepreneurs. Previous studies of group formation have tended to analyze informal groups that happen to be observed in particular public spaces (James 1953; Mayhew et al. 1995), student project teams that are created in particular classrooms (Mannix, Goins, and Carroll 2002), or more formal teams that are observed in particular industries (for reviews and critique, see Cooper and Daily 1997; Lechler 2001). It is unclear to what extent these samples yield generalizable findings.[2] Another shortcoming of previous research on founding teams is that it has usually included only teams that have already achieved some level of success in organizational development. Such a "success bias" causes investigators to miss numerous founding teams that form but subsequently abandon their entrepreneurial effort and leads researchers to ignore the impact of changes in composition following initial team formation. We avoid such success bias by tracking entrepreneurs from the point when they first begin to take serious steps toward creating a new formal organization.

In addition to this empirical contribution, we also offer a methodological innovation that allows us to avoid success bias in analyzing the composition of entrepreneurial teams. As Goodman (1964) first noted in a path-breaking paper on systems of groups, proper estimation of size distributions and other mechanisms concerning group formation requires that an analyst consider all possible combinations of group members, not just those observed in a given sample. We employ *structural event analysis* (Ruef 2002a) to generate the distribution of possible entrepreneurial teams and compare chance expectations within that distribution to empirical counts of the 816 teams in the national panel study. Poisson regression models are applied to account for deviations from expectations of chance group membership, based on mechanisms of homophily, functionality, status expectations, network constraint, and ecological constraint. We conclude by drawing out the empirical implications of these mechanisms for the ostensible sociability of some entrepreneurs and the relative isolation of others.

MECHANISMS OF GROUP COMPOSITION

In analyzing the formation of entrepreneurial teams, we consider five general mechanisms of group composition (see Table 1), which yield a set of hypotheses (H), corollaries (C), and assumptions (A). The hypotheses follow from the claims associated with each mechanism and some basic empirical generalizations regarding American society; corollaries hold true as a consequence of empirical proof for particular hypotheses. Although our hypotheses are examined in the specific context of organizational foundings, we believe that they may apply more broadly to the formation of task groups within a variety of settings, including established formal organizations.

HOMOPHILY

The mechanism of homophily explains group composition in terms of the similarity of members' characteristics. In principle, these characteristics may refer to social identities that are attached externally to individuals (e.g., ascribed characteristics such as gender, race, or age) or to internal states concerning values, beliefs, or norms (Lazarsfeld and Merton 1954).[3] In either

---

[2] Arrow, McGrath, and Berdahl (2000, chap. 2) note that most small group research since the 1950s has emphasized experimental designs—with compositional properties manipulated in laboratory settings—rather than the study of naturally occurring groups. This trend has led scholars away from such issues as group formation and composition.

---

[3] Clearly, identity and cognitive orientation tend to be linked in this explanation. The mechanism of homophily implies that individuals sharing a common identity also tend to share values, beliefs, or norms.

Table 1. Five General Explanations of Task-Group Composition

Theory	General Claims	Empirical Hypotheses, Corollaries, and Assumptions [a]
Homophily	Task groups tend to be composed of members with similar ascriptive characteristics (e.g., gender, ethnicity).	H_1: All-male and all-female teams will be more common than will mixed-gender teams.
		H_2: Ethnically homogeneous teams will be more common than will mixed-ethnicity teams.
Functional	Task groups tend to be composed of members with diverse achieved characteristics (e.g., leadership, occupational competency).	H_3: Teams with occupational diversity will be more common than teams lacking diversity.
		H_4: Occupational diversity will increase as a function of team size.
Status expectations	Individuals with high-status characteristics are more likely to attract other task-group members than are individuals with low-status characteristics.	H_5: Teams composed only of high-status members will be more common than those composed entirely from lower statuses.
		C_1: Given H_5, low-status persons will be more likely to be isolated than those from other backgrounds.
Network	The presence of prior network ties in a task group affects the extent to which the group exhibits diversity in ascribed and achieved characteristics.	A_1: Teams including family ties will have less ethnic diversity than teams lacking such ties.
		A_2: Teams including partner pairs will have greater gender diversity than teams lacking such ties.
		H_6: Teams composed of prior business acquaintances will have less occupational diversity than teams lacking such ties.
Ecological	Task groups tend to be composed of members in the same geographic locale and/or industry.	H_7: Homogeneous teams become more likely under conditions of residential/industrial segregation.
		C_2: Given H_1 and H_2, individuals that represent the numerical minority in a region/industry will be more likely to be isolated than others.

[a] All hypotheses assume that the size distribution and marginal probability for each team are controlled for, under a model of statistical independence.

case, the similarity of individuals disposes them toward a greater level of interpersonal attraction, trust, and understanding—and, consequently, greater levels of social affiliation—than would be expected among dissimilar individuals. This tendency toward homophily should be especially noticeable in groups such as organizational founding teams, which require sizable investments of time and resources (Bird 1989).

Although homophily may be analyzed in terms of ascribed characteristics, achieved characteristics, or internal psychological states, we restrict our operational definition of homophily to ascribed characteristics for several reasons. First, by excluding achieved characteristics (education, occupation, income) we prevent arguments regarding homophily from slipping into functional arguments regarding the efficacy of a social group. This is especially pertinent for groups that are task-oriented, such as business founding teams. Second, the similarity of group members in terms of psychological states is often endogenous to the group-formation process itself. Moreover, homophily in this regard may result as much from the *misattribution* of shared understandings among affiliated individuals as from actual shared understandings, because individuals tend to assume that others with whom they have structural bonds think as they do (Jussim and Osgood 1989; McPherson et al. 2001).

One of the most widely studied ascriptive characteristics driving homophily is gender. Gender homophily has been identified in a variety of task-oriented settings, including work establishments (Kalleberg et al. 1996), voluntary organizations (McPherson and Smith-Lovin 1982, 1987), and managerial networks (Ibarra 1997). Although representative data for founding teams is sparse, researchers have found that men's business discussion networks contain few women and thus contribute to gender homogeneity (Aldrich 1999:85–86; Carter 1994). Women's business support groups, often formed as a reaction to male dominance in entrepreneurial activities (Aldrich 1989), may further enhance homophily. Insofar as gender is a highly visible ascribed characteristic driving attributions of similarity and difference in emergent organizations, we propose that:

Hypothesis 1: All-male and all-female organizational founding teams will be more common than will mixed gender teams.[4]

A second ascriptive dimension that generates strong network homophily is ethnicity (Marsden 1987; McPherson et al. 2001). Studies of many task-group settings—such as workplaces (Kalleberg et al. 1996; Reskin 1999) and classrooms (Schofeld 1995)—reveal substantial homogeneity in ethnic composition, especially among white ethnic majorities. For entrepreneurial founding teams, the literature has also tended to emphasize solidarity within ethnicities, but primarily

among minority and immigrant groups (e.g., Aldrich and Waldinger 1990; Wilson and Martin 1982). Variations of in-group preferences across ethnicities may result from a number of factors, including ecological constraints on the availability of other entrepreneurs sharing a common ethnicity, discriminatory status expectations, and unmeasured network effects. With respect to baseline expectations, however, the existing literature supports the proposition that:

Hypothesis 2: Ethnically homogeneous organizational founding teams will be more common than will mixed-ethnicity teams.

FUNCTIONALITY

In opposition to the principle of homophily, many functionalist theories of task-group composition argue for the importance of *diversity* among members, especially with respect to achieved characteristics, such as leadership skills and task expertise. Pioneering research by Bales (1953) and Slater (1955) on small-group settings emphasized the dual necessity of socio-emotional leadership and task leadership. Subsequent research and theorizing on organizational founding teams has explored the extent to which entrepreneurs draw on diverse, complementary skills that may lie beyond the abilities of any individual founder, especially in high technology industries (Gartner 1985:703; Vesper 1990). Eisenhardt and Schoonhoven (1990) linked team diversity to functional performance, noting that organizational growth among semiconductor firms was higher for organizations with heterogeneous founding teams. At a more microlevel, Ancona and Caldwell (1992) reported benefits of functional diversity for communication and innovation in their study of product teams.[5]

We anticipate that new formal organizations in general, rather than just those in high-tech environments, may benefit from having founders with a diverse set of work experiences and occupational backgrounds. Having a chef, a restaurant manager, and a

---

[4] All hypotheses are subject to the usual *ceteris paribus* conditions. In particular, this means that the marginal distribution of different groups (e.g., men and women) is controlled for, that the probability of joint occurrences from these groups is addressed, and that predictions are advanced net of group size.

[5] Ancona and Caldwell (1992) also identified a potential drawback in that functional diversity might impede successful collaboration.

marketing agent on the founding team, for instance, can enhance the success of a new restaurant. By the same token, a precision manufacturing facility may profit from the entrepreneurial skills of an industrial engineer, an experienced machine operator, and a shop-floor supervisor. Following a functionalist logic, if potential founders anticipate such benefits of skill diversity in advance, then we expect that:

Hypothesis 3: Teams with founders from diverse occupational backgrounds will be more common than will teams lacking functional diversity.

This hypothesis regarding diversity is subject to two important caveats. First, occupational attachments can be a source of homophily, as well as diversity, insofar as occupations provide a common basis of socialization and, possibly, interpersonal relationships. What predominates in a given situation may depend on contact opportunities among individuals from different occupations as well as on the functional salience of occupational diversity per se—as opposed, for example, to diversity in education, previous work roles, and nonoccupational skills. We address this issue in Hypothesis 6.

Second, the desire for a functional division of labor may be contingent on the size of an entrepreneurial team. As Durkheim ([1893] 1949) emphasized, functional specialization tends to increase with group size, largely as a mechanism for the reduction of interpersonal competition. In groups that are characterized by large numbers of members and intensive interaction, a lack of differentiation in functional competencies can lead members to engage in turf battles over resources or work responsibilities. Insofar as teams are subject to similar dilemmas resulting from overlapping competencies, a functionalist logic suggests that:

Hypothesis 4: The occupational diversity of founding team members will increase with team size.

STATUS EXPECTATIONS

Arguments about the mechanisms of homophily and functionality treat distinctions within task groups—based on ascribed or achieved characteristics—as simple nominal ones. However, an extensive literature in social psychology notes that such nominal distinctions tend to be translated into rank-ordered status relationships insofar as they become tied to performance expectations (Berger et al. 1977; Skvoretz and Fararo 1996).[6] Even those ascriptive characteristics that are logically irrelevant to task performance (e.g., gender and race in most task situations) become subject to a "burden of proof process" in which group members must demonstrate that those characteristics are, in fact, substantively irrelevant (Fisek et al. 1991). Consequently, widely held cultural biases regarding status (e.g., of men over women, of ethnic majorities over minorities, etc.) are likely to affect processes of task-group formation and composition.[7]

The principle impact of status expectations on group composition tends to involve differential homophily among status groups. Assuming that only two status groups (A and B) are salient, with A being high-status and B being low-status, we expect that A individuals will have a strong associative preference for other A individuals, while B individuals will also have an associative preference for A individuals (which may not always be fulfilled). One consequence of this pattern is that the observed level of homophily among the elite As will be high, while the observed level of homophily among the lower status Bs will be lower (or perhaps negligible, in the absence of a general homophily mechanism). Bs would rather associate with the higher status As than with one another. Operationally, such status-varying homophily may involve ascribed characteristics (e.g., gender) or achieved characteristics (e.g., occupation), leading to the following predictions for our sample of founding teams:

---

[6] Blau's (1977) theory of macrostructure likewise distinguishes between *nominal* and *graduated* parameters that may affect social interaction. Unlike the more micro-oriented theories in social psychology, however, he does not account for ways in which nominal parameters may be translated into graduated parameters (or vice versa).

[7] However, the gender effects found in early research on status expectations are probably weaker now in the general population than they were several decades ago.

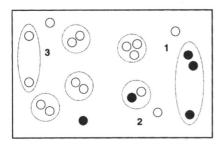

(a)
General Homophily
(No Differential Isolation)

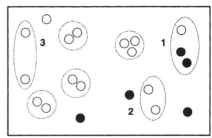

(b)
Status-Varying Homophily
(With Isolation of Low-Status Individuals)

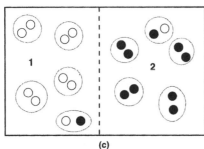

(c)
Ecological Homophily
(No Differential Isolation)

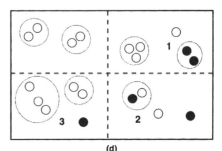

(d)
Ecological Constraint
(With Isolation of Numerical Minority)

Figure 1. Patterns of Homophily and Isolation

Hypothesis 5: Organizational founding teams composed only of high-status persons (e.g., males, members of the ethnic majority, professionals) will be more common than those created entirely from other statuses.

For some sociodemographic dimensions, this tendency toward high-status homophily appears to be widely institutionalized in contemporary society. For example, the term "old boys network" connotes homophily among male managers and entrepreneurs. Similarly, the legal recognition of a professional partnership or corporation (Burke and Zaloom 1970) increases the likelihood of homophily within professional occupations—though it is more typically described in the guise of professional autonomy and self-determination (Freidson 1986). For other sociodemographic dimensions, the direction of status-varying homophily is less clear. Thus, the literature on ethnic entrepre-

neurship implies a tendency *away* from high-status homophily, as minorities and immigrants, regardless of occupation, form stronger in-group bonds than do whites in the face of discrimination and lack of alternative career opportunities (Aldrich and Waldinger 1990).

Status-varying homophily has a second general consequence that bears analysis. If members of an elite status group, A, tend to attract other members of A as well as some upstarts from a lower status group, B, it follows that individuals in B will be at higher risk of social isolation than those in A. Bs who are unable to affiliate with As may even prefer going solo, rather than working with other Bs. Notably, this consequence cannot be derived from general homophily alone (see Figure 1a). Given a population of 15 individuals in group A (white circles), five individuals in group B (black circles), and no status differentiation between the two, a general homophily effect predicts proportionate isolation of A and B individuals, with a relatively high proportion of other individuals in homogeneous groups (1 and 3) and only a few in heterogeneous groups (2). But with the activation of status differences (see Figure 1b), homogeneous low-status groups will seek to incorporate proximate high-status individuals in lieu of low-status ones (1) and formerly heterogeneous groups will tend to drop low-status members to conform to a homogeneous, high-status ideal (2). As a result, low-status individuals become disproportionately isolated.[8]

For entrepreneurs, isolation can pose both functional and social psychological problems. Multimember teams enjoy several benefits over solo entrepreneurs (Kamm and Nurik 1993; Lechler 2001), including a more diverse skill set (Vesper 1990), improved capacity for innovation (Ruef 2002b), and higher levels of social and emotional support (Bird 1989). Consistent with a theory of status expectations, empirical evidence suggests that entrepreneurs with a lower ascribed or achieved status are less likely to be members of teams and enjoy these benefits. For instance, while longitudinal trends in the United States point to the increasing proportion of female entrepreneurs, they also suggest that women are disproportionately involved in founding solo proprietorships, rather than partnerships or corporations (U.S. Department of Commerce 1996). More generally, if status-varying homophily applies to sociodemographic dimensions such as gender, ethnicity, and occupation (Hypothesis 5), it follows that:

Corollary 1: Low-status entrepreneurs (women, minorities, blue-collar workers) will be more likely to be isolated than will those from other sociodemographic backgrounds.

NETWORK CONSTRAINT

During the process of group formation, the choice of members based on shared identities, functional considerations, or status expectations is inevitably constrained by struc-

tural opportunities for social contact. One conduit of structural opportunity involves prior network ties among group members. These ties can be characterized broadly in terms of three concentric circles of social relationships: family members (strong ties), acquaintances and friends (weak ties), and strangers (Aldrich, Elam, and Reese 1996; also see Granovetter 1973). The extent to which the relational composition of a group relies on one concentric circle rather than another has crucial implications for the operation of other mechanisms of group composition.

Family members, particularly spouses and domestic partners, fulfill many requisites of shared identity that are otherwise generated through homophily. They interact frequently and tend to share rewarding experiences. With respect to entrepreneurial activity, family members have many opportunities to discuss the possibility of starting a new organization together. Ideas that might be superficially discussed and dismissed in other contexts often lead, among kin, to more cumulative plans for action. These considerations suggest that a failure to control for the presence of kinship ties in founding teams may lead to inflated estimates of homophily along certain ascriptive dimensions, particularly ethnicity.

For one ascriptive characteristic, however, the reverse is true. The substantial number of heterosexual spouse pairs that attempt to start business or nonprofit organizations together will deflate estimates of gender homophily (Aldrich, Carter, and Ruef forthcoming). To separate choice homophily from the gender heterogeneity induced by spouse pairs, we recognize that teams including spouse pairs will have greater gender diversity than teams lacking such ties. As with kinship ties, we treat this effect not as a hypothesis, but instead as an assumption about the gender composition of spousal pairs.

Among individuals who are not related but who know each other fairly well—such as work associates working for the same employer or in the same industry—some of the same interpersonal dynamics apply as with family members, but with less intensity. Work associates also have opportunities to develop trust and observe one another's strengths and weaknesses. Nevertheless,

---

[8] Note that a dynamic consequence of Bs' preferences for affiliations with As and their difficulty of doing so is to further raise the already high status of As.

such functional benefits may be offset to some extent when work associates share overlapping competencies. If many work associates have similar work experiences or occupational backgrounds, the principle of functional diversity (Hypothesis 3) is compromised. Functional complementarity depends, in part, on team members having diverse occupations because they come from different organizations with distinctive divisions of labor. On the other hand, when entrepreneurial teams are developed on the basis of collegial ties, we expect that:

Hypothesis 6: Teams including prior business acquaintances will have less occupational diversity than teams lacking such ties.

ECOLOGICAL CONSTRAINT

Aside from network constraint, the sheer numbers and spatial distribution of individuals having distinctive characteristics will influence what associations are likely to form. The importance of geographic proximity in group formation has long been recognized in both the microsociological (Goffman 1963) and macrosociological (Hawley 1950) literatures. Blau's (1977, 1980) program of macrostructural research develops theorems explicitly on the basis of which nominal or rank-ordered characteristics tend to be more common among the population of a region, leading to ecological constraints on patterns of association. Similar ecological constraints operate at a microlevel, but many are so fundamental to processes of group formation that they constitute baseline expectations about which individuals are expected to be found together in a group, rather than predictions of theoretical interest.

Several implications of ecological constraints on association merit further analysis. Organizational ecologists have emphasized the impact of industrial, as well as spatial, context on founding processes (Carroll and Hannan 2000). With respect to individual entrepreneurs, both industry and spatial constraints can generate aggregate tendencies toward homophily or isolation, independently of the group membership choices being made by the entrepreneurs. For purposes of explication in our hypothetical system of 20 individuals in Figure 1, we now assume

that group formation is feasible only within two local "quadrants," which may be geographic or industry-based (Figure 1c). Because of residential or industrial segregation, one quadrant (1) is heavily dominated by individuals in group A (white circles), while the other (2) is dominated by individuals in group B (black circles). If we think of the two quadrants as representing car repair shops and beauty salons, for example, then this pattern might be observed for industry sex segregation, with entrepreneurs in the car repair industry having a 90/10 male-female ratio and entrepreneurs in the beauty salon industry having a 10/90 male-female ratio.[9]

Such extreme cases of industrial segregation can lead to pronounced levels of homophily at an aggregate level, even when teams are constituted by random mixing within industries. Eighty percent of the two-person dyads shown in the figure are homophilous, although we would only expect 50 percent to be homophilous given the marginal gender distribution across industries.[10] When the industries are analyzed separately, however, the number of homophilous dyads in each quadrant reproduce statistical expectations, calculated as $.9 \times .9 \times 1$ combination $= 81$ percent of dyads composed of dominant group members. This reasoning leads to the proposition that homophily—at an aggregate level—can be induced by ecological constraints, as well as network and social psychological mechanisms:

Hypothesis 7: Homogeneous founding teams become more likely under conditions of strong residential and/or industrial segregation among entrepreneurs.

Ecological constraint may have implications for isolation as well as team homo-

---

[9] We assume that entrepreneurs choose from a restricted range of options when considering which industries to enter. Thus, in the short run, they succumb to the constraints we have identified.

[10] The overall gender distribution is a 50/50 mix. Under a model of random mixing, we would expect 25 percent ($.5 \times .5 \times 1$ combination) of the dyads to involve two males, 25 percent ($.5 \times .5 \times 1$) to involve two females, and 50 percent ($.5 \times .5 \times 2$ combinations) to involve a mixed gender dyad.

phily. In his macrostructural theory, Blau (1977) notes that a population representing the numerical minority along some sociodemographic characteristic would be forced into greater levels of association with a population representing the numerical majority, as the minority population becomes proportionately smaller. In an elaboration on this model, Blau (1980) considers the possibility that members of a numerical minority may be at disproportionate risk of isolation, given the effects of homophily and propinquity (see Figure 1d). The likelihood that members of different groups will associate with one another is affected not only by their relative proportions in the population, but also by their degree of geographical dispersion or segregation. Group formation may only be feasible within local geographic "quadrants." In contrast to a system lacking ecological constraints (see Figure 1a), some geographically dispersed groups that are members of a numerical minority may not be able to find one another, leaving their solo members isolated. Naturally, the problem of ecological constraint also affects groups composed of members from the numerical majority (quadrant 3 in Figure 1d), but in those cases it is easier for the resulting isolates to reorganize themselves with proximate and similar alters. These considerations suggest that:

Corollary 2: Individuals who represent the numerical minority along any sociodemographic dimension will be more likely to be isolated than will those in the numerical majority.[11]

For many ascribed and achieved characteristics, Corollary 2 produces consequences similar to those anticipated because of status-varying homophily (Corollary 1). Our nationally representative sample suggests that female nascent entrepreneurs in the United States are only half as common as

---

[11] In contrast to Hypothesis 7, Corollary 2 assumes a relatively low level of residential or industrial segregation. High levels of segregation can reduce isolation among members of a numerical minority, while the random dispersion of a minority group among the majority necessarily leads to the former's isolation under conditions of general homophily and ecological constraints on association.

male entrepreneurs. Corollary 2 predicts, therefore, that female nascent entrepreneurs will be less likely to find associates with whom to found a new organization, given conditions of general homophily and ecological constraint. The same result, however, could be derived from a status-varying pattern of group formation in which women are less willing to associate with other women, even when geographic proximity is not a significant issue. Distinguishing between the two causes of isolation thus requires careful attention to the salience of general homophily and status-induced differential homophily.

DATA, MEASURES, AND METHOD

DATA

We use data from the Panel Study of Entrepreneurial Dynamics (PSED) to analyze the compositional properties of organizational founding teams. Between July 1998 and January 2000 a total of 64,622 individuals in the United States were contacted by telephone using a random-digit dialing process to identify those in the process of starting a business ("nascent entrepreneurs"). The data employed here are organized into three subsamples, which correspond to different funding sources and different data collection periods. The Entrepreneurial Research Consortium (ERC), which consisted primarily of academic institutions, financed data collection for a mixed-gender sample of nascent entrepreneurs. Another subsample was limited to an oversample of women entrepreneurs and funded by the National Science Foundation (NSF). Subsequently, the National Science Foundation provided funding for a third subsample—an oversample of minorities engaged in business start-up activities.

The research design for the PSED specified two phases for data collection. In the first phase, a marketing research firm telephoned households as part of a national survey that involved contacting 1,000 adults (500 females and 500 males 18 years of age or older) each week. Multiple phone calls (at least three) were made to contact each person. When an adult 18 years of age or older was identified and agreed to respond to the survey, a phone interview was administered. Two items were randomly inserted at different points in the survey and were used to determine whether the respondent qualified as a nascent entrepreneur: (1) "Are you, alone or with others, now trying to start a business?" and (2) "Are you, alone or with others, now starting a new business or new venture for your employer?" If the respondent answered yes to either of the questions, two additional questions were used to qualify whether the respondent was actively involved with the start-up process, and whether he or she would share ownership in the business. Affirmative responses to both additional questions were necessary for individuals to be considered "nascent entrepreneurs." Individuals who qualified as nascent entrepreneurs were invited to participate in a national study conducted through the University of Wisconsin and promised a cash payment.[12]

In the second phase of the data collection, the names, telephone numbers, and basic sociodemographic information of individuals who met the screening criteria were forwarded to the University of Wisconsin Survey Research Laboratory (UWSRL), where a detailed phone interview was conducted followed by a mailed questionnaire. More complete details about the sampling procedures can be found in Shaver et al. (2001).

SAMPLE AND WEIGHTS

The final sample of PSED respondents totals 830 nascent entrepreneurs. Of these, 7 respondents indicated that "nonpersons" expected to own more than 50 percent of the venture. We removed these cases from analyses, reasoning that they were influenced unduly by corporate interests rather than by the initiative of individual entrepreneurs. Six respondents indicated that their new venture had positive cash flow for more than 90 days before the initial interview by

UWSRL. We considered these efforts to be infant businesses and removed them from the analyses. Finally, one respondent indicated that their start-up involved a team, but failed to provide sociodemographic information that could be used to classify the respondent's gender or race/ethnicity. The case was disqualified. The elimination of these 14 cases reduced the sample size to 816 nascent entrepreneurs.

Because several of the subsamples described above involved oversampling of certain subgroups of the population, we employed post-stratification weights for each respondent based on estimates from the U.S. Census Bureau's Current Population Survey. The post-stratification scheme was based on gender, age, education, and race/ethnicity. More complete details about the computation of the weighting scheme can be found in Reynolds (2000).

MEASURES

The data of interest here come from items on the phone interview that were designed to collect information about: (1) characteristics of people who were helping to start the venture, and (2) relationships among the founding members (if applicable). During the UWSRL phone interview, respondents were asked, "How many people will legally own this new business—only you, only you and your spouse, or you and other people or businesses?" If the respondent indicated others would share ownership in the venture, they were asked to identify up to five who would have the highest level of ownership, and the ownership percentage to be held by each team member.[13] The respondent was then asked to provide information about each cofounder, including gender, ethnicity (white, African American, nonwhite Hispanic, Asian, other), primary occupation (open-ended response later classified into four categories: professional/technical; administrative/managerial; sales/service; operative/production), and the nature of the

---

[12] Offering incentives to gain participants, or to convert nonrespondents, has become a common practice in survey organizations (Singer, Van Hoewyk, and Maher 2000). A traditional method used to increase response rates in mail surveys, the practice has been expanded to telephone projects using random-digit dialing.

---

[13] Although this data collection procedure may truncate the team size distribution, less than 1 percent of the teams in the ERC sample involved more than six members (Reynolds 2002, personal communication).

206 AMERICAN SOCIOLOGICAL REVIEW

Table 2. Descriptive Statistics for Organizational Founding Teams: Panel Study of Entrepreneurial Dynamics, 1998 to 2000

Variable	Number of Cases	Response	Weighted Count/Proportion
Size of team	816	One member	395
		Two members	312
		Three members	55
		Four members	31
		Five+ members	23
Industry of team	800	Primary/manufacturing	.19
		Personal service	.17
		Retail/wholesale	.28
		Business/professional Service	.36
Gender of member	1,423	Male	.62
		Female	.38
Gender composition of multimember team	421	All male	.29
		All female	.07
		Mixed-gender	.64
Ethnicity of member	1,347 [a]	White	.72
		Black	.17
		Hispanic	.09
		Asian	.02
Ethnic composition of multimember team	399 [a]	Single ethnicity	.86
		Multiple ethnicities	.14
Occupation of member	1,089 [b]	Professional	.30
		Administrative	.28
		Sales/service	.21
		Operative/production	.21
Occupational composition of multimember team	303 [b]	Single occupation	.32
		Multiple occupations	.68
Relational composition of multimember team	421	With spouses/partners	.53
		With nonspouse family member	.18
		With business associates	.15

[a] Excludes multimember teams involving other ethnicities or with missing information.

[b] Excludes multimember teams with any missing information on occupational composition.

relationships among all team members (spouses/partners; relatives/family members; business associates/work colleagues; friends/acquaintances; strangers before joining the team; other).

The dependent variable in our analysis involves the number of founding teams conforming to a particular combination of sociodemographic and relational characteristics. In turn, those characteristics—and the design parameters that describe how they are combined—serve as the independent variables. Our methodological approach employs the 816 sampled founding teams as its units of analysis, while incorporating information on the 1,423 individual persons that make up the teams (see Table 2).[14]

The size distribution of the teams in our weighted sample follows the truncated Poisson distribution that has been noted more

---

[14] A few teams also involved institutional founding members; these members are ignored in the following analyses.

generally for free-forming groups (Coleman and James 1961; White 1962), with a substantial number of solo entrepreneurs (395) and relatively few large teams (e.g., 23 founding teams involving five or more entrepreneurs). The majority of the entrepreneurs in the sample are white (72 percent) males (62 percent) involved in professional (30 percent) or administrative (28 percent) occupations. We also report some aspects of team composition for the 421 multimember founding teams (i.e., excluding "solo" entrepreneurs). These statistics indicate that most multimember teams involve a mixture of men and women (64 percent), relatively few incorporate members from more than one ethnicity (14 percent), and over half include married couples or cohabitating partners (53 percent). The majority of multimember teams (68 percent) display some functional diversity, drawing on more than one occupational category.

STATISTICAL METHODOLOGY

We employ a structural event analysis (Ruef 2002a) to predict the number of entrepreneurial teams matching some set of compositional characteristics, considering all possible teams (not just those that actually form). The risk set of possible teams is enumerated using counting rules drawn from combinatorial analysis (see Appendix A). Each potential team is treated as a case for purposes of analysis, leading to a Poisson distribution of team counts (Goodman 1964). These counts can then be predicted via the following Poisson regression:

$$P[f(E_i) = y] = e^{-\lambda}(\lambda^y/y!), \qquad (1)$$

where λ is defined in terms of the conditional probability for structural event occurrence $\lambda = f(p[E|r], r)$, and r specifies the size of each team. A baseline probability for each group, under an assumption of random population mixing (see Appendix A), is included as a fixed parameter in every Poisson regression. All other design parameters reflect deviations from random mixing and are estimated using maximum-likelihood techniques.

Because the number of possible teams grows exponentially for analyses involving multiple sociodemographic dimensions,

bootstrap techniques are used to analyze large, sparse matrices. In these cases, we construct a sample by selecting all cells with a nonzero observed count of founding teams, all other cells involving solo entrepreneurs or dyads, and one percent of the cells with an expected team size of three or greater and no observed team counts.[15] Structural zeros—those cells where a marginal frequency is zero—are removed from the sample. Weighted maximum-likelihood techniques are used to derive the corresponding estimates.

RESULTS

We test the theoretical claims advanced in Table 1 via a series of analyses that address compositional properties among entrepreneurial founding teams, beginning with a simple descriptive analysis of gender homophily (see Table 3). Using rote enumeration, we see that there are 20 possible teams involving unrestricted combinations of the two gender roles ([M]ale and [F]emale). The same quantity can be derived from the respective counting rule (see Appendix A, equation A-1), which yields $2 + 3 + 4 + 5 + 6 = 20$ structural events for a system of two roles ($|N| = 2$) and no more than five participants per group ($r(H) = 5$). Categorizing teams further by the presence of spouse/partner ties, there are 20 possible gender combinations with no spouses or partners, 18 possible combinations with one spouse/partner pair (i.e., excluding solos), and 11 possible combinations with two spouse/partner pairs. The corresponding 49 structural events are shown in Table 3.

Inspection of the observed counts indicates that over a third (18) of the possible structural events are not actually realized for this sample; one gender combination (MFFFF) is not observed for any of the subsamples based on the presence of spouse/partner pairs. The expected counts in the table are derived using the multinomial formula (Appendix A, equation A-2) and knowledge of the marginal distributions.

---

[15] The sampling rate for the bootstrap methodology is based on the low sampling error anticipated for this sample size. The results are virtually identical when the rate is doubled or tripled.

Table 3. Observed and Expected Cell Counts for Gender Composition of Founding Teams: Panel Study of Entrepreneurial Dynamics, 1998 to 2000

Structural Event	Observed Count	Expected Count	Structural Event	Observed Count	Expected Count
Teams without Spouses/Partners			*Teams with One Spouse/Partner Dyad (Continued)*		
M	228	245.9	(MFF)	4	2.9
F	166	148.1	(FMM)	7	4.8
MM	73	46.7	(MMMM)	0	1.5
FF	27	17.0	(FFFF)	0	.2
MF	20	56.3	(MMFF)	1	3.3
MMM	28	10.7	(MFFF)	2	1.3
FFF	2	2.3	(FMMM)	7	3.7
MFF	3	11.7	(MMMMM)	0	.3
FMM	11	19.3	(FFFFF)	0	.0
MMMM	9	2.4	(MMFFF)	1	.6
FFFF	1	.3	(FFMMM)	1	1.0
MMFF	2	5.3	(MFFFF)	0	.2
MFFF	2	2.1	(FMMMM)	1	.9
FMMM	2	5.8			
MMMMM	10	1.6	*Teams with Two Spouse/Partner Dyads*		
FFFFF	1	.1	(MMMM)	0	.8
MMFFF	0	3.5	(FFFF)	0	.1
FFMMM	2	5.8	(MMFF)	5	1.7
MFFFF	0	1.1	(MFFF)	0	.7
FMMMM	4	4.8	(FMMM)	0	1.8
			(MMMMM)	0	.2
			(FFFFF)	0	.0
Teams with One Spouse/Partner Dyad			(MMFFF)	1	.4
(MM)	2	75.1	(FFMMM)	1	.7
(FF)	0	27.4	(MFFFF)	0	.1
(MF)	191	90.5	(FMMMM)	0	.6
(MMM)	0	2.7			
(FFF)	0	.6			

Note: The sum of observed counts may not equal marginal totals because of rounding errors. Parentheses indicate spouse/partner relationships; N = 816.

▨ Shaded areas indicate homogeneous multimember teams.

Men make up 62 percent of the entrepreneurs in the weighted sample, while women make up the remaining 38 percent. The distribution for the five size categories is: 395, 312, 55, 31, and 23. Finally, we note that 52 percent of the four-person founding teams do not include any spouse or partner pairs. Thus, to use one illustrative example, the expected number of founding teams without a spouse/partner pair composed of two men and two women is calculated as $[4!/(2! \times 2!)]$ $(.62^2 \times .38^2)(31)(.52) \approx 5.3$, more than twice

the observed cell count. In many cases, we find that observed counts of single-gender teams (see shaded areas in table) exceed expectations, while counts of mixed-gender teams are lower than expectations. Exceptions to the rule tend to occur when spouse/partner ties exist within the founding teams.

To further examine the interaction of gender homophily and network constraint, we conducted a structural event analysis using Poisson regression models (see Table 4, Models 1 through 3). Model 1 illustrates

Table 4. Coefficients from Poisson Regression Models Testing Gender Composition of Founding Teams: Panel Study of Entrepreneurial Dynamics, 1998 to 2000

Independent Variable	Baseline Models			Models Controlling for Network Ties	
	Model 1	Model 2	Model 3	Model 4	Model 5
Intercept	5.976***	6.894***	8.207***	6.714***	6.725***
	(.050)	(.069)	(.189)	(.244)	(.244)
Team size	—	−.782***	−1.188***	−1.052***	−1.056***
		(.034)	(.069)	(.068)	(.068)
Size Category					
1 member	—	—	−1.043***	.315	.232
			(.135)	(.201)	(.205)
2 members	−.230**	—	—	—	—
	(.076)				
3 members	−1.969***	—	—	—	—
	(.144)				
4 members	−2.542***	—	—	—	—
	(.187)				
5 members	−2.886***	—	—	—	—
	(.219)				
Homophily					
Gender homophily	—	—	−.355+++	1.611+++	1.457+++
			(.104)	(.171)	(.236)
Status-varying homophily	—	—	—	—	.195
					(.201)
Minority isolation [a]	—	—	—	—	.189+
					(.102)
Opportunity Structure					
Partners/spouses × Gender homophily	—	—	—	−6.258+++	−6.253+++
				(.730)	(.730)
Model fit (G^2)	438.94	517.43	458.90	78.72	74.34
Degrees of freedom (design/fixed)	5/7	2/7	4/7	5/8	7/8

Note: Numbers in parentheses are standard errors. Number of structural events = 49; number of teams = 816.

[a] Women represent the gender minority.

*p < .05   **p < .01   ***p < .001 (two-tailed tests)
+p < .05   ++p < .01   +++p < .001 (one-tailed tests)

how a structural event analysis can be used to recover the distribution of group sizes for a particular sample. The specification implicitly includes a fixed parameter log $p(E|r)$ with a coefficient constrained to 1.0, which accounts for the probability of observing a given gender composition under an assumption of random mixing (see Appendix A, equation A-2). The fixed parameter is calculated based on the marginal distributions of gender and of spouse/partnership ties across different team sizes (d.f. = 7).[16] The specification also includes an intercept and four design parameters for different team sizes.

[16] One degree of freedom is employed for the marginal gender distribution, four degrees of freedom are employed for the distribution of groups with a single spouse/partner dyad across team sizes two through five, and two degrees of freedom are employed for the distribution of groups with two spouse/partner dyads among team sizes four and five.

Adding the intercept (which corresponds to the number of founding "teams" with only a single member) to the respective coefficient estimates and taking the antilog allows us to recover the marginal size distribution (e.g., the number of four-member founding teams is $e^{5.976-2.542} = e^{3.434} = 31$).

Following the distributional implications of Goodman's (1964) model for group formation, Model 2 replaces the four size dummy variables with a single parameter for group size. Consistent with previous observations of free-forming groups (e.g. Coleman and James 1961; Mayhew et al. 1995), the parameter estimate reflects the fact that the observed frequency of founding teams varies inversely with size. This parsimonious model specification is then used as a baseline for a test of the homophily mechanism in Model 3, which adds two new design parameters. The parameter for homophily identifies whether a team is all-male or all-female (= 1) or of mixed composition (= 0). Surprisingly, the results suggest a strong *negative* effect for gender homophily ($p < .001$), with homogeneous groups appearing at a rate that is .70 ($e^{-.355}$) times that of comparable heterogeneous groups. This apparent tendency away from gender homophily seems to reflect the large number of heterosexual spouse and partner dyads on these entrepreneurial teams: 217 teams in the weighted sample included one spouse/partner pair and 7 teams included two.[17]

To what extent is gender heterogeneity induced by structural opportunity (e.g., selection of spouses as team members), and to what extent does it occur because of choice of dissimilar alters? Models 4 and 5 explore this issue by including a design parameter for single-gender teams with partner or spouse dyads. The results provide a more accurate picture of tendencies toward homophily (Model 4). Consistent with Hypothesis 1, there is now significant *positive* gender

homophily ($p < .001$), with homogeneous teams being five times ($e^{1.611}$) more likely than heterogeneous teams, net of romantic relationships. The specification in Model 4 illustrates the importance of separating the effect of the network constraint mechanism from the homophily mechanism.

Model 5 extends the analysis, considering whether there is substantial status-varying homophily—with all-male teams being more common than all-female teams—and whether female entrepreneurs tend to become disproportionately isolated. Contrary to status expectations theory (Hypothesis 5), there is no evidence that male entrepreneurs are more likely to band together than are female entrepreneurs. Nevertheless, there is disproportionate isolation of women in this sample, with solo female entrepreneurs appearing 1.21 times as often as expected based on the marginal distribution of gender. Given that entrepreneurial team formation is subject to general homophily but not status-varying homophily, we suggest (following Corollary 2) that the principal reason for the isolation of women may be ecological constraint. Because female entrepreneurs are far less common than male entrepreneurs, they may experience greater difficulty in finding other women with whom to start a business in their industry.

This explanation of gender homophily and differential isolation assumes that there is not a strong tendency toward gender segregation, particularly across industrial sectors. If gender segregation is high, then homophily may result as an artifact of ecological constraints on contact opportunities (Hypothesis 7). To explore this possibility, we split our founding team sample into subsamples based on industry categories—primary/manufacturing, retail/wholesale, personal services, business/professional services—and examined the gender distribution and level of homophily within each category (see Table 5).[18] There is some evidence of industrial sex segregation, with one sector—including primary and manufacturing industries—exhibiting a skewed gender distribution and no significant

---

[17] The other new parameter in Model 3 controls for "teams" composed of a single entrepreneur, which are tautologically homophilous. The corresponding parameter estimate is not substantively interesting in and of itself, but permits consistent estimation of the model independently of the way that gender homophily is coded for solo entrepreneurs.

[18] To eliminate the confounding influence of network constraint, this analysis excludes teams with spouse or partner dyads.

Table 5. Gender Composition and Coefficients for Gender Homophily of Founding Teams by Industrial Sector: Panel Study of Entrepreneurial Dynamics, 1998 to 2000

Industrial Sector	Gender Composition (Percent Male)	Gender Homophily Coefficients		Number of Events
		Coef.	(S.E.)	
Primary/manufacturing	88	.618	(.422)	105
Personal services	64	1.790***	(.438)	97
Retail/wholesale	61	1.323***	(.321)	163
Business/professional services	65	1.849***	(.304)	216
All sectors		1.570***	(.179)	581 [a]

Note: Numbers in parentheses are standard errors.

[a] Limited to teams reporting start-up industry (N = 800) and excluding teams with spouses/partners.

*p < .05   **p < .01   ***p < .001 (two-tailed tests)

intraindustry homophily. On the whole, however, estimates of intraindustry homophily tend to be similar to the level of homophily for the sample as a whole. This suggests that gender homogeneity is not generally an artifact of ecological constraints on team formation.

Table 6 presents a structural event analysis for a second major dimension of ascriptive homophily—ethnic composition. The basic risk set of structural events is again determined by counting rule (equation A-1 in Appendix A), calculated as 4 + 10 + 20 + 35 + 56 = 125 potential events for a system of four ethnic identities ($|N| = 4$) and maximum team size of 5. Differentiating between teams that contain kinship ties and those that do not, we obtain another 121 potential events (the basic risk set minus the four types of ethnicity for solo entrepreneurs), for a total of 246 structural events. Because of incomplete ethnic information among some founding teams, we restrict our sample to 778 teams for this analysis.

Models 1 and 2 again illustrate how the team size distribution can be modeled using nonparametric and parametric specifications, respectively. These models are substantively identical to the first two shown in Table 4, except they take account of data attrition owing to missing information on ethnicity. Model 3 addresses the prediction that ethnically homogeneous teams will be more common than heterogeneous teams (Hypothesis 2). We enter a parameter into the model based on the Shannon-Weaver entropy (H)

of ethnic composition in each team.[19] The estimated level of ethnic homophily is high, with homogeneous teams being 46 times as likely to occur as expected by chance. In particular, this finding reflects the fact that homogeneous minority teams are common, despite the relative rarity of minority entrepreneurs in the population as a whole. For instance, we observe four teams composed of four African American entrepreneurs, although only .02 team is expected under a model of random mixing.

To some extent, ethnic homogeneity may be generated through kinship ties in the entrepreneurial teams. Model 4 reveals that family networks do increase ethnic homophily, as we assumed, but are not the only source of it. Teams involving both familial networks and ethnic diversity are extremely rare—only one case in our weighted sample matches this pattern. However, even controlling for this opportunity structure, ethnically homogeneous teams occur at a rate that is 27 times expectations. Examining differential levels of homophily among ethnic groups (Model 5), we find that minorities have a significantly higher tendency toward homogeneity than do whites. White entrepreneurs

---

[19] The measure of diversity is computed as:

$$H = -\sum_{i=1}^{n} \left(\frac{\log y_i}{\log n} \right) y_i,$$

where n is the number of ethnic categories, and y_i is the proportion of team members within each category i (Shannon and Weaver [1949] 1963). Ethnic homophily is simply $1 - H$.

Table 6. Coefficients from Poisson Regression Models Testing the Ethnic Composition of Founding Teams: Panel Study of Entrepreneurial Dynamics, 1998 to 2000

Independent Variable	Baseline Models			Models Controlling for Network Ties	
	Model 1	Model 2	Model 3	Model 4	Model 5
Intercept	5.938***	6.864***	4.078***	4.533***	2.770***
	(.051)	(.071)	(.352)	(.351)	(.390)
Team size	—	−.791***	−.909***	−.887***	−.818***
		(.036)	(.070)	(.072)	(.072)
Size Category					
1 member	—	—	−1.064***	−1.005***	−2.448***
			(.122)	(.122)	(.153)
2 members	−.248**	—	—	—	—
	(.078)				
3 members	−1.946***	—	—	—	—
	(.145)				
4 members	−2.548***	—	—	—	—
	(.191)				
5 members	−2.997***	—	—	—	—
	(.235)				
Homophily					
Ethnic homophily	—	—	3.833+++	3.297+++	6.378+++
			(.297)	(.304)	(.382)
Status-varying homophily	—	—	—	—	−1.693+++
					(.133)
Minority isolation [a]	—	—	—	—	.184+
					(.111)
Opportunity Structure					
Family ties × Ethnic homophily	—	—	—	4.990+++	5.498+++
				(1.552)	(1.580)
Model fit (G²)	557.70	627.45	335.95	315.07	194.56
Degrees of freedom (design/fixed)	5/7	2/7	4/7	5/8	7/8

Note: Numbers in parentheses are standard errors. Number of structural events = 246; number of teams = 778. Ethnic information is missing for 38 teams.

[a] Blacks, Hispanics, and Asians represent ethnic minorities.

*$p < .05$ **$p < .01$ ***$p < .001$ (two-tailed tests)

+$p < .05$ ++$p < .01$ +++$p < .001$ (one-tailed tests)

are only .18 times as likely to develop mono-ethnic teams as are African Americans, Asians, and nonwhite Hispanics. Nevertheless, despite the propensity of many minority entrepreneurs to work within ethnic enclaves, they are still 1.20 times more likely to be isolated than white entrepreneurs, given ecological constraints on contact opportunities with other minority entrepreneurs (Corollary 2).

We turn next to the question of functional diversity, examining occupational composition within these founding teams (Table 7). Model 3 addresses the prediction that functionally diverse teams will be more common than expected under a model of random mixing (Hypothesis 3), again using an entropy measure of team composition (see footnote 19). The resulting coefficient estimate suggests a statistically nonsignificant effect for occupational diversity. Moreover, contrary to Hypothesis 4, there is a pronounced ten-

Table 7. Coefficients From Poisson Regression Models Testing the Occupational Composition of Founding Teams: Panel Study of Entrepreneurial Dynamics, 1998 to 2000

Independent Variable	Baseline Models			Models Controlling for Business Ties	
	Model 1	Model 2	Model 3	Model 4	Model 5
Intercept	5.892***	6.872***	6.846***	6.865***	6.907***
	(.053)	(.078)	(.418)	(.418)	(.427)
Team size	—	−.889***	−.537**	−.564**	−.568**
		(.041)	(.181)	(.183)	(.184)
Size Category					
1 member	—	—	−.418	−.409	−.498
			(.251)	(.251)	(.265)
2 members	−.447***	—	—	—	—
	(.084)				
3 members	−2.323***	—	—	—	—
	(.176)				
4 members	−2.826***	—	—	—	—
	(.222)				
5 members	−3.223***	—	—	—	—
	(.269)				
Functionality					
Occupational diversity	—	—	.466	.415	.323
			(.838)	(.836)	(.858)
Diversity × team size	—	—	−.850*	−.766*	−.754*
			(.337)	(.340)	(.342)
Status-varying homophily	—	—	—	—	−.103
					(.214)
Minority isolation [a]	—	—	—	—	.224+
					(.122)
Opportunity Structure					
Business ties × Occupational diversity	—	—	—	−.928	−.932
				(.607)	(.609)
Model fit (G^2)	245.76	294.47	225.71	223.28	219.78
Degrees of freedom (design/fixed)	5/7	2/7	5/7	6/8	8/8

Note: Numbers in parentheses are standard errors. Number of structural events = 246; number of teams = 665. Occupational information is missing for 151 teams.

[a] Operations/production workers represent the occupational minority.

*$p < .05$ **$p < .01$ ***$p < .001$ (two-tailed tests)
+$p < .05$ ++$p < .01$ +++$p < .001$ (one-tailed tests)

dency *away* from occupational specialization with increases in team size. Rather than emphasizing complementarities among different functions, larger founding teams seem to be characterized by homophily, even for achieved attributes such as occupation, once baseline interaction probabilities are taken into account.

Models 4 and 5 examine the extent to which this low level of occupational diver-

sity is induced by prior network relationships—in particular, the presence of former business associates on founding teams.[20] We

---

[20] Simple bivariate statistics suggest that the network density of business relationships in multimember teams has a slight (nonsignificant) negative correlation with the number of occupations represented ($r = -.04$). The lack of association between the two variables suggests that we

Table 8. Occupational Composition and Coefficients for Occupational Diversity of Founding Teams by Industrial Sector: Panel Study of Entrepreneurial Dynamics, 1998 to 2000

Industrial Sector	Occupational Composition				Occupational Diversity Coefficients	Number of Events
	Percent Production/ Operative	Percent Sales/ Service	Percent Adminis- trative	Percent Professional		
Primary/manufacturing	41	20	21	17	−.980 (.583)	110
Personal services	24	23	25	29	−1.513** (.549)	117
Retail/wholesale	21	22	28	29	−.540 (.506)	167
Business/professional services	14	22	31	33	−1.530** (.468)	218
All sectors					−1.312*** (.260)	613 [a]

Note: Numbers in parentheses are standard errors.

[a] Limited to teams reporting occupational composition and start-up industry (N = 654); excludes teams with business associates.

$^*p < .05$ $^{**}p < .01$ $^{***}p < .001$ (two-tailed tests)

constructed our measure of business ties within founding teams by counting any prior business-related association between two members of the team as an indication that the team's founding was influenced by business ties. As shown in Model 4, business ties do not decrease occupational diversity significantly (cf. Hypothesis 6). Inclusion of this effect only slightly attenuates the level of homogeneity from other structural and psychological mechanisms. The entrepreneurs in larger teams continue to show a pronounced tendency to congregate based on occupational similarity, rather than attention to functional diversity.

Model 5 completes the model specification, estimating parameters for the extent of disproportionate homophily among high-status occupations (professionals and paraprofessionals), as well as disproportionate isolation among low-status occupations (production and operations workers). Consistent with our findings for gender and ethnicity, there is no evidence of differential homophily among high-status entrepreneurs (contrary to Hypothesis 5), whereas there is evidence of a tendency toward differential isolation for blue-collar operatives

are not dealing with occupational subcultures. Network density is computed using the conventional formula for undirected graphs (Wasserman and Faust 1994).

and production workers. More specifically, entrepreneurs from a blue-collar background are 1.25 times more likely to be isolated than would be expected under a model of random mixing. Again, following Corollary 2, we suggest that this is a likely consequence of ecological constraint combined with a general tendency toward occupational homophily. Because organizational founders from a blue-collar background represent only 21 percent of all nascent entrepreneurs, they are slightly less likely to find other blue-collar workers with whom they can go into business.

As for the case of gender composition, occupational homophily may result from the segregation of occupations across industrial sectors or from the homogeneous selection of team members within sectors. A cross-tabulation of team member backgrounds and start-up industries reveals some segregation in this respect, with those founders having production or operative experience being more common among primary/manufacturing start-ups and those founders having administrative or professional experience being more common among business service/professional firms (see Table 8). Still, the sector-specific marginal distributions suggest that there is considerable potential for occupational diversity, even considering the ecological constraints imposed by industry.

Table 9. Coefficients from Poisson Regression Models Testing the Gender, Ethnic, and Occupational Composition of Founding Teams: Panel Study of Entrepreneurial Dynamics, 1998 to 2000

Independent Variable	Model 1		Model 2		Model 3	
	Coef.	(S.E.)	Coef.	(S.E.)	Coef.	(S.E.)
Intercept	3.082***	(.554)	2.602***	(.571)	.777	(.607)
Team size	−.269	(.193)	−.370	(.199)	−.306	(.197)
Size Category						
1 member	−1.017***	(.259)	.021	(.329)	−1.550***	(.358)
Homophily						
Gender homophily	−.580+++	(.125)	1.362+++	(.222)	1.263+++	(.273)
Status homophily (males)	—		—		.275	(.222)
Ethnic homophily	4.056+++	(.341)	3.599+++	(.337)	6.734+++	(.421)
Status homophily (whites)	—		—		−1.732+++	(.147)
Functionality						
Occupational diversity	.550	(.847)	.528	(.882)	.533	(.882)
Diversity × Team size	−.869*	(.359)	−.848*	(.378)	−.867*	(.367)
Status homophily (professionals)	—		—		−.126	(.220)
Isolation						
Women	—		—		.214+	(.115)
Ethnic minorities	—		—		.150	(.116)
Blue-collar workers	—		—		.289+	(.131)
Opportunity Structure						
Partners × Gender homophily	—		[F] [a]		[F] [a]	
Family Ties × Ethnic homophily	—		[F] [a]		[F] [a]	
Business ties × Occupational diversity	—		−.731	(.578)	−.699	(.585)
Model fit (G²)	1514.65		1274.63		1162.44	
Degrees of freedom (design/fixed)	7/33		8/38		14/38	

Note: Numbers in parentheses are standard errors. Number of structural events = 23,110; number of teams = 639. Occupational or ethnic information is missing for 177 teams.

[a] Indicates parameters that are fixed due to empirical zeros.

*p < .05   **p < .01   ***p < .001 (two-tailed tests)
+p < .05   ++p < .01   +++p < .001 (one-tailed tests)

Further evidence concerning the impact of ecological constraint can be found in the sector-specific estimates of occupational diversity. To simplify these analyses, we ignore interaction effects with team size and only estimate a single design parameter for occupational diversity. Founding teams in some industrial sectors—such as personal, business, and professional services—display the same trend away from occupational diversity observed in aggregate-level analyses. For other industrial sectors—including extractive, manufacturing, and retail/wholesale businesses—the tendency away from occupational diversity is not statistically significant. Although there is still no support for Hypothesis 3, the variability in sector-specific levels of occupational composition suggests that a small amount of the homogeneity observed among larger teams in the aggregate analysis is generated through ecological constraints (consistent with Hypothesis 7).

Given that occupation tends to be correlated with gender and ethnicity, the question remains whether the apparent occupational homophily within these teams is not simply derivative of homophily along ascriptive dimensions. We examine this issue using a combined structural event analysis of all three factors. Considering gender, occupation, and ethnicity together yields 32 role combinations at the individual level—white male professionals, white female professionals, black male professionals, black female professionals, etc. The basic risk set is therefore $s(H) = 32 + 528 + 5,984 + 52,360 + 376,992 = 435,896$ possible structural events (equation A-1). Because prior network ties may influence diversity and homogeneity in these groups, we parse multimember teams further into those that contain romantic, familial, and/or business ties and those that do not, leading to $2 \times 2 \times 2 \times 435,896 - 224 = 3,486,944$ structural events. After bootstrap sampling, 23,110 cases are considered in the analysis (see Table 9).

Controlling for structural opportunity, the impact of homophily and functional considerations on team composition can be seen in Model 2.[21] The tendencies toward ascriptive homophily and away from occupational diversity (in larger teams) are highly significant and comparable in magnitude to estimates from models that exclude other factors (see Tables 4, 6, and 7). As shown in Model 3, there is no evidence of differential homophily among males or professionals, while in-group preferences among whites are substantially lower than those observed for ethnic minorities. The variation of in-group preferences explains why ethnic minorities do not exhibit disproportionate levels of isolation, but women and blue-collar workers are likely to become solo entrepreneurs. The relative magnitude of isolation among the latter two social identities also provides additional support for the existence of ecological constraints on team formation, as isolation is predicted to be a function of the numerical prevalence of each identity under conditions of general homophily (Corollary 2). Accordingly, women, who repre-

sent 38 percent of the entrepreneurial population, should be less isolated than entrepreneurs from blue-collar backgrounds, who represent only 21 percent of the population. While our findings are consistent with this pattern of prevalence, it should be emphasized that the difference in the magnitude of the two estimates is quite small (an incidence rate ratio of 1.24 as opposed to 1.34, respectively).

As in previous analyses, strong network ties have a substantial impact on team composition, with ties among spouses/partners decreasing the gender homophily of entrepreneurial teams and ties among family members increasing ethnic homophily (cf. Models 1 and 2 in Table 9). Weak ties, on the other hand, do not play a statistically significant role in this analysis. Specifically, the presence of business acquaintances on the teams does not reduce occupational diversity markedly, once other factors are taken into account.

DISCUSSION

Using a nationally representative sample of organizational founding teams, we have tested for the operation of five mechanisms affecting the composition of entrepreneurial groups. We found strong support for one mechanism that influences group composition: homophily with respect to both ascriptive *and* achieved characteristics (in particular, gender, ethnicity, and occupation). We found mixed support for two other mechanisms—network and ecological constraint. The network constraint imposed by "strong" ties, such as romantic relationships and family ties, was quite pronounced, but "weak" ties, measured in our study by business acquaintances, imposed no significant network constraint. Our findings also suggest that ecological constraint contributes to the disproportionate isolation of numerical minorities—such as women and blue-collar workers—in the population of entrepreneurs. On the other hand, ecological segregation of these groups by industry does not appear to be a dominant factor driving team homophily.

We found little empirical support for two other mechanisms of group composition: functional diversification of achieved char-

---

[21] After removing cases with missing information on occupation and ethnicity, there are no founding teams with same-sex partners or with multi-ethnic family members. Consequently, the corresponding interaction effects are included as fixed, rather than empirical, parameters.

acteristics and differential homophily based on status expectations. Although baseline estimates of functional diversity were consistently insignificant, we found an unexpected tendency *away* from occupational specialization in larger teams. Contrary to Durkheim's ([1893] 1949) familiar argument, pressures for solidarity in these groups do not seem to favor the weak bonds of functional interdependence but instead contribute to functional homophily. Additional longitudinal research is required to identify how growth (or decline) in each team may lead to evolutionary changes in the mechanisms of group composition.

Our results concerning minority isolation are also provocative, suggesting that isolation in a founding team formation process can proceed without recourse to the stereotyped performance expectations associated with status-varying homophily. In short, social isolation can be produced largely by ecological, rather than psychological, mechanisms. However, as observed for the nonwhite ethnicities in our sample, *reverse* status homophily—particularly that producing greater in-group preferences among numerical minorities—may help combat the effects of ecological isolation.

IMPLICATIONS FOR THEORY

We studied naturally occurring groups involved in activities of fundamental importance to market-based economies: the emergence of new business start-ups. Our investigation thus goes beyond previous work on groups, which has mainly focused on concocted or well-established social units, such as work teams within established firms (Arrow et al. 2000). Within organizations, individuals usually have little choice in which teams to join or whom they will associate with on such teams. By contrast, the composition of entrepreneurial teams is likely to reflect the influence of patterns of association in which people are embedded within families, friendship circles, workplaces, and residential areas. As such, they provide an excellent context in which to observe the operation of basic social processes, such as homophily.

Our results represent a significant contribution to the accumulated set of empirical generalizations regarding homophily in social relations (McPherson et al. 2001). Even in a situation where we might reasonably expect stringent economic rationality to prevail—and thus lead to choices based on the functional diversification of achieved characteristics—we find that team composition is driven by similarity, not differences. Founders of organizations appear more concerned with trust and familiarity, at this early stage, than with functional competence, leading to a "competency discount" in founder recruitment. Just as in other areas of economic life, commercial exchanges involved in organizational foundings are strongly influenced by socially embedded patterns of associations (DiMaggio and Louch 1998; Zelizer 1994).

Our findings underscore a paradox of group formation that parallels similar structural dynamics identified in dyadic relationships (Burt 1992; Granovetter 1973). Granovetter (1992) described two aspects of network embeddedness that highlight the processes involved in team formation. Relational embeddedness refers to the depth of single dyadic ties, such as their degree of multiplexity and positive emotional investment. Structural embeddedness refers to the extent to which the mutual contacts of a dyad are themselves connected to one another. Our results show that relational embeddedness—prior ties along several dimensions—apparently dampen the functional diversity that Granovetter argued is achieved by weak ties or that Burt (1992) argued is achieved by structural holes.

During team composition, entrepreneurs seek out trusted alters, as well as those with whom they already have strong interpersonal relationships, while avoiding strangers who could bring fresh perspectives and ideas to the organizational founding process. Only 10 percent of the dyadic relationships within the PSED sample involve strangers (Aldrich et al. forthcoming). Interestingly, the number of distinctive occupational categories in teams involving strangers (mean = 2.1) is significantly higher than the number found in teams without strangers (mean = 1.3; t-statistic = 6.5; $p < .001$). Thus, entrepreneurs' tendency to avoid the inclusion of strangers on founding teams tends to decrease functional diversity and may, in the long run, inhibit the success of new formal organizations.[22]

At the outset, we noted that new organizations can reproduce and challenge the existing social order and that the kinds of organizations people construct are culturally embedded. The composition of entrepreneurial founding teams reflects the tendency toward gender, ethnic, and occupational homophily in the contemporary United States. Our results point to the emergence of social units that, if they persist, will exacerbate the already strong tendencies toward homophily in social relationships. Organizations are a significant sorting point along many dimensions of membership, especially gender and occupation. Our results confirm this tendency. Although McPherson et al. (2001) argue that organizations often create heterogeneity on the dimension of race, our results strongly suggest that, at least for organizational founders, teams are highly homogeneous by race and ethnicity. If homogeneous founding teams also hire employees similar to themselves, then new organizations represent a potent force for solidifying homophily within commercial relationships.

CAVEATS AND FUTURE CONSIDERATIONS

Our knowledge of organizational founding teams is still at a preliminary stage. A more complete description of compositional properties would consider additional characteristics, particularly other achieved characteristics that may be linked to functional diversity. It could be argued that our current occupational measure fails to capture more subtle functional properties of team member contributions. Thus far, we have also had little to say concerning the consequences of team composition and the evolution of compositional properties over time. Team composi-

tion may have a substantial impact on the problem of "collective action" in emergent formal organizations—that is, the problem of balancing the contributions of individual team members against the rewards they expect to receive from the collective enterprise (Simon 1945). Is the balance of contributions influenced only by the ascribed, achieved, and network characteristics of individual members? Or is the balance influenced by the composition of the organizational founding team as a whole, or by ecological properties of other teams in a given industry or geographic region? In turn, the balance of contributions and inducements—along with the initial composition of the teams—may influence the evolution of group composition. What members tend to stay and what members tend to leave organizational founding teams? Who is added to these groups? What mechanisms (homophily, functionality, status expectations, network or ecological constraint) govern this evolutionary process? Answering these questions represents an essential step in developing a more comprehensive understanding of the emergence of formal groups and organizations.

---

[22] Whether the benefits of recruiting trusted alters as team members outweigh the possible costs of excluding strangers can only be assessed via a longitudinal study. If emerging businesses benefit from strong, in-group–based ties among their members, then homophily should have a positive effect on survival. If, however, such ties reduce a team's ability to respond to unforeseen or radically changing circumstances, then homophily may be a handicap for teams.

Martin Ruef is Assistant Professor of Organizational Behavior and (by courtesy) of Sociology at Stanford University. His research considers processes affecting the origin of new organizations, organizational forms, and institutions. With W. Richard Scott, Peter Mendel, and Carol Caronna, he is the co-author of Institutional Change and Healthcare Organizations: From Professional Dominance to Managed Care *(University of Chicago Press, 2000), which won the ASA's Max Weber and Eliot Freidson Awards in 2001 and 2002, respectively. In addition to studying contemporary entrepreneurs, his current projects include historical analyses of U.S. medical schools and institutional transformation in the postbellum South.*

Howard E. Aldrich is Kenan Professor of Sociology at the University of North Carolina, Chapel Hill, where he won the Caryle Sitterson Award for Outstanding Teaching in 2002. In 2000, he received two honors: The Swedish Foundation of Small Business Research named him the Entrepreneurship Researcher of the Year, and the Organization and Management Division of the Academy of Management presented him with an award for a Distinguished Career of Scholarly Achievement. His latest book, Organizations Evolving *(Sage, 1999), won the Academy of Management George Terry Award as the best management book published in 1998–1999, and was co-winner of the Max Weber Award from the American Sociological Association's Section on Organizations, Occupations, and Work.*

Nancy M. Carter is the Richard M. Schulze Chair in Entrepreneurship at the University of St. Thomas, Minneapolis, Minnesota, where she directs the MBA entrepreneurship program. She also has worked professionally in advertising and marketing research. Her research interests include the emergence of organizations, with a special emphasis on women- and minority-owned initiatives, and the founding strategies of new businesses. She works closely with government and private-sector initiatives promoting women entrepreneurs.

APPENDIX A

Structural Event Analysis

COUNTING RULES

The risk set $s(H)$ of a structural event analysis enumerates all possible combinations over a set of roles (N), subject to group size (r) and restrictions on permissible role combinations (Ruef 2002a). When roles within a group can be repeated an indefinite number of times, the number of combinations for a multiset of N roles is calculated as:

$$s(H) = \sum_{r=1}^{r(H)} \binom{r + |N| - 1}{r}$$

$$= \sum_{r=1}^{r(H)} \frac{(r + |N| - 1)!}{r!(|N| - 1)!}, \quad \text{(A-1)}$$

where r varies over all observed group sizes—including singletons—up to $r(H)$ members (Brualdi 1992:71–73). Thus, a system of two gender roles N = {male, female} allows for three discrete forms of gender composition in structural dyads ($r = 2$): male-male dyads, male-female dyads, and female-female dyads. Using the counting rule, these combinations are calculated as ($r + |N| - 1$) choose r = ($2 + 2 - 1$) choose $2 = 3!/2! = 3$. To obtain arrangements for the two gender roles not exceeding three persons in size $r(H) = 3$, one simply sums the respective number of combinations for each possible size category: $s(H) = 2 + 3 + 4 = 9$ structural events.

Given multiple role dimensions, the role set should identify all possible combinations that may be held by any given group member. For two gender roles {[M]ale, [F]emale} and four occupational roles {[P]rofessional, [A]dministrative, [S]ervice, [O]perations}, there are eight unrestricted role combinations for each individual: N = {MP, MA, MS, MO, FP, FA, FS, FO}. If there are a priori restric-

tions imposed on role combinations (for instance, if women in a given society are not allowed to hold certain occupations), then the role set must be reduced accordingly.[a]

EVENT PROBABILITY

Probability theory provides the rules for calculating the expected chance of occurrence for any structural event under an assumption of random mixing. We designate the roles (or role combinations) in a set N as elementary events for purposes of statistical analysis and apply the rule of multiplication to determine the probability of joint events. Provided that the roles included in a particular structural event are events in N occurring with probability $p(n_1)$, $p(n_2)$, ... $p(n_k)$, the sampling distribution of joint structural events is given by the multinomial formula:

$$P(E|r) = \frac{r!}{|n_1|! |n_2|! K |n_k|!}$$

$$\times \left[p(n_1)^{|n_1|} \times p(n_2)^{|n_2|} \times K \; p(n_k)^{|n_k|} \right], \quad \text{(A-2)}$$

where $r = |n_1| + |n_2| + ... |n_k|$. It should be noted that the calculation of all joint event probabilities is conditional on structural events being of a particular size, r. For example, consider a structural analysis of organizational founding teams formed among three occupations: manual workers (n_1), service workers (n_2), and professionals (n_3). If structural events are drawn from a population of entrepreneurs that is 40 percent manual, 30 percent service, and 30 percent professional, then the expected probability of obtaining a three-member founding team with one manual worker and two service sector workers under an assumption of statistical independence is $p(E|3) = (3!/(2! \times 1!)) (.40^1 \times .30^2) = .108$. The event probability reflects the fact that there are three different ways to draw the participants. By comparison, the probability of obtaining a three-member team that consists only of manual workers is $p(E|3) = (3!/3!) (.40^3) = .064$.

For some analyses of structural events, joint event probabilities are not only conditional on group size but on other parameters as well. In analyzing the gender composition of groups, for instance, it may be important to control for the presence of romantic relationships that serve to deflate the observed level of gender homophily. Structural events involving these relationships can be separated from other events, and fixed effects can be introduced into models to control for the relationships present within each group-size category.

---

[a] Relational and group-level characteristics—and the restrictions imposed on them—can also be considered in generating the risk set of structural events. For instance, analyzing a set of two gender roles {M, F} and the presence or absence of a spousal/partner relationship (indicated by parentheses) yields six unrestricted combinations for a dyad: MM, FF, MF, (MM), (FF), (MF).

REFERENCES

Aldrich, Howard E. 1989. "Networking among Women Entrepreneurs." Pp. 103–32 in *Women-Owned Businesses*, edited by O. Hagan, C. Rivchun, and D. Sexton. New York: Praeger.

———. 1999. *Organizations Evolving*. Thousand Oaks, CA: Sage.

———. Forthcoming. "Entrepreneurship." In *Handbook of Economic Sociology*, 2d ed., edited by R. Swedberg and N. Smelser. Princeton, NJ: Princeton University Press.

Aldrich, Howard E., Nancy Carter, and Martin Ruef. Forthcoming. "With Very Little Help from Their Friends: Gender and Relational Composition of Nascent Entrepreneurs' Startup Teams." In *Frontiers of Entrepreneurship Research 2002*, edited by P. Reynolds et al. Wellesley, MA: Center for Entrepreneurial Studies, Babson College.

Aldrich, Howard E., Amanda Elam, and Pat Ray Reese. 1996. "Strong Ties, Weak Ties, and Strangers: Do Women Business Owners Differ from Men in Their Use of Networking to Obtain Assistance?" Pp. 1–25 in *Entrepreneurship in a Global Context*, edited by S. Birley and I. MacMillan. London, England: Routledge.

Aldrich, Howard E. and Marlene C. Fiol. 1994. "Fools Rush In? The Institutional Context of Industry Creation." *Academy of Management Review* 19:645–70.

Aldrich, Howard E. and Roger Waldinger. 1990. "Ethnicity and Entrepreneurship." *Annual Review of Sociology* 16:111–35.

Ancona, Deborah and David Caldwell. 1992. "Demography and Design: Predictors of New Product Team Performance." *Organization Science* 3:321–41.

Arrow, Holly, Joseph McGrath, and Jennifer Berdahl. 2000. *Small Groups as Complex Systems: Formation, Coordination, Development, and Adaptation*. Thousand Oaks, CA: Sage.

Bales, Robert. 1953. "The Equilibrium Problem in Small Groups." Pp. 111–61 in *Working Papers in the Theory of Action*, edited by T. Parsons, R. Bales, and E. Shils. Glencoe, IL: Free Press.

Bates, Timothy. 1997. *Race, Self-Employment, and Upward Mobility: An Illusive American Dream*. Baltimore, MD: Johns Hopkins University Press.

Berger, Joseph, M. Hamit Fisek, Robert Z. Norman, and Morris Zelditch. 1977. *Status Characteristics and Social Interaction: An Expectation States Approach*. New York: Elsevier.

Birch, David. 1997. *Small Business Research Summary*. RS Number 183. Washington, DC: U.S. Small Business Administration.

Bird, Barbara. 1989. *Entrepreneurial Behavior*. Glenview, IL: Scott, Foresman.

Blau, Peter. 1977. *Inequality and Heterogeneity*. New York: Free Press.

———. 1980. "A Fable about Social Structure." *Social Forces* 58:777–88.

Brualdi, Richard. 1992. *Introductory Combinatorics*. 2d ed. Englewood Cliffs, NJ: Prentice Hall.

Burke, William and Basil Zaloom. 1970. *Blueprint for Professional Service Corporations*. New York: Dun and Bradstreet.

Burt, Ronald. 1992. *Structural Holes: The Social Structure of Competition*. Cambridge, MA: Harvard University Press.

Carroll, Glenn and Michael Hannan. 2000. *The Demography of Corporations and Industries*. Princeton, NJ: Princeton University Press.

Carroll, Glenn and Elaine Mosakowski. 1987. "The Career Dynamics of Self-Employment." *Administrative Science Quarterly* 32:570–89.

Carter, Nancy. 1994. "Reducing Barriers between Genders: Differences in New Firm Startups." Presented at the annual meeting of the Academy of Management, August, Dallas, TX.

Coleman, James and John James. 1961. "The Equilibrium Size Distribution of Freely-Forming Groups." *Sociometry* 24:36–45.

Cooper, Arnold C. and Catherine M. Daily. 1997. "Entrepreneurial Teams." Pp. 127–50 in *Entrepreneurship 2000*, edited by D. Sexton and R. Smilor. Chicago, IL: Upstart Publishing.

DiMaggio, Paul and Hugh Louch. 1998. "Socially Embedded Consumer Transactions: For What Kinds of Purchases Do People Most Often Use Networks?" *American Sociological Review* 63:619–37.

Durkheim, Emile. [1893] 1949. *Division of Labor in Society*. Reprint, Glencoe, IL: Free Press.

Eisenhardt, Kathleen and Claudia Bird Schoonhoven. 1990. "Organizational Growth: Linking Founding Team, Strategy, Environment, and Growth among U.S. Semiconductor Ventures, 1978–1988." *Administrative Science Quarterly* 35:504–29.

Fisek, M. Hamit, Joseph Berger, and Robert Z. Norman. 1991. "Participation in Heterogeneous Groups: A Theoretical Integration." *American Journal of Sociology* 97:114–42.

Freidson, Eliot. 1986. *Professional Powers: A Study of the Institutionalization of Professional Knowledge*. Chicago, IL: University of Chicago Press.

Gartner, William. 1985. "A Conceptual Framework for Describing the Phenomenon of New Venture Creation." *Academy of Management Review* 10:696–706.

Goffman, Erving. 1963. *Behavior in Public Places: Notes on the Social Organization of Gatherings.* Glencoe, IL: Free Press.

Goodman, Leo. 1964. "Mathematical Methods for the Study of Systems of Groups." *American Journal of Sociology* 70:170–92.

Granovetter, Mark. 1973. "The Strength of Weak Ties." *American Journal of Sociology* 78: 1360–80.

———. 1992. "Problems of Explanation in Economic Sociology." Pp. 25–56 in *Networks and Organizations: Structure, Form, and Action,* edited by N. Nohria and R. Eccles. Boston, MA: Harvard Business School Press.

Haveman, Heather A. and Lisa E. Cohen. 1994. "The Ecological Dynamics of Careers: The Impact of Organizational Founding, Dissolution, and Merger on Job Mobility." *American Journal of Sociology* 100:104–52.

Hawley, Amos. 1950. *Human Ecology.* New York: Ronald.

Ibarra, Herminia. 1997. "Paving an Alternative Route: Gender Differences in Managerial Networks." *Social Psychology Quarterly* 60:91–102.

James, John. 1953. "The Distribution of Free-Forming Small Group Size." *American Sociological Review* 18:569–70.

Jussim, Lee and D. Wayne Osgood. 1989. "Influence and Similarity among Friends: An Integrative Model Applied to Incarcerated Adolescents." *Social Psychology Quarterly* 52:98–112.

Kalleberg, Arne, David Knoke, Peter Marsden, and Joe Spaeth. 1996. *Organizations in America: Analyzing Their Structures and Human Resource Practices.* Thousand Oaks, CA: Sage.

Kamm, Judy B. and Aaron J. Nurik. 1993. "The Stages of Team Venture Formation: A Decision Making Model." *Entrepreneurship Theory and Practice* 17:17–27.

Keister, Lisa A. and Stephanie Moller. 2000. "Wealth Inequality in the United States." *Annual Review of Sociology* 26:63–81.

Lazarsfeld, Paul and Robert K. Merton. 1954. "Friendship as Social Process: A Substantive and Methodological Analysis." Pp. 18–66 in *Freedom and Control in Modern Society,* edited by M. Berger, T. Abel, and C. Page. New York: Octagon Books.

Lechler, Thomas. 2001. "Social Interaction: A Determinant of Entrepreneurial Team Venture Success." *Small Business Economics* 16:263–78.

Mannix, Elizabeth, Sheila Goins, and Susan Carroll. 2002. "Starting at the Beginning: Team Formation, Composition, and Performance," Working Paper. Graduate School of Management, Cornell University, Ithaca, NY.

Marsden, Peter. 1987. "Core Discussion Networks of Americans." *American Sociological Review* 52:122–31.

Mayhew, Bruce, J. Miller McPherson, Thomas Rotolo, and Lynn Smith-Lovin. 1995. "Sex and Race Homogeneity in Naturally Occurring Groups." *Social Forces* 74:15–52.

McPherson, J. Miller and Lynn Smith-Lovin. 1987. "Homophily in Voluntary Organizations: Status Distance and the Composition of Face to Face Groups." *American Sociological Review* 52:370–9.

McPherson, Miller, Lynn Smith-Lovin, and James Cook. 2001. "Birds of a Feather: Homophily in Social Networks." *Annual Review of Sociology* 27:415–44.

Nee, Victor and Jimy M. Sanders. 1985. "The Road to Parity: Determinants of the Socioeconomic Achievements of Asian Americans." *Ethnic and Racial Studies* 8:75–93.

Reskin, Barbara. 1999. "The Determinants and Consequences of Workplace Sex and Race Composition." *Annual Review of Sociology* 25:335–61.

Reynolds, Paul D. 2000. "National Panel Study of U.S. Business Start-Ups: Background and Methodology." Pp. 153–227 in *Advances in Entrepreneurship, Firm Emergence, and Growth,* vol. 4, edited by J. Katz. Stanford, CT: JAI Press.

Ruef, Martin. 2000. "The Emergence of Organizational Forms: A Community Ecology Approach." *American Journal of Sociology* 106: 658–714.

———. 2002a. "A Structural Event Approach to the Analysis of Group Composition." *Social Networks* 24:135–60.

———. 2002b. "Strong Ties, Weak Ties, and Islands: Structural and Cultural Predictors of Organizational Innovation." *Industrial and Corporate Change* 11:427–49.

Schofeld, J. W. 1995. "Review of Research on School Desegregation's Impact on Elementary and Secondary School Students." Pp. 597–616 in *Handbook of Research on Multicultural Education,* edited by J. Banks and C. McGee. New York: Macmillan.

Shannon, Claude and Warren Weaver. [1949] 1963. *The Mathematical Theory of Communication.* Urbana, IL: University of Illinois Press.

Shaver, Kelly G., Nancy M. Carter, William Gartner, and Paul Reynolds. 2001. "Who Is a Nascent Entrepreneur? Decision Rules for Identifying and Selecting Entrepreneurs in the Panel Study of Entrepreneurial Dynamics (PSED)." Technical Paper. Jonköping International School of Business. Jonköping, Sweden.

Simon, Herbert. 1945. *Administrative Behavior.* New York: Macmillan.

Singer, Eleanor, John Van Hoewyk, and Mary P.

Maher. 2000. "Experiments With Incentives in Telephone Surveys." *Public Opinion Quarterly* 64:171–88.

Skvoretz, John and Thomas Fararo. 1996. "Status and Participation in Task Groups: A Dynamic Network Model." *American Journal of Sociology* 101:1366–1414.

Slater, Philip. 1955. "Role Differentiation in Small Groups." *American Sociological Review* 20:300–10.

Stinchcombe, Arthur L. 1965. "Social Structure and Organizations." Pp. 142–93 in *Handbook of Organizations,* edited by J. G. March. Chicago, IL: Rand McNally.

U.S. Department of Commerce. 1996. *Economic Census: Survey of Women-Owned Businesses.* Washington, DC: U.S. Government Printing Office.

Vesper, Karl. 1990. *New Venture Strategies.* Englewood Cliffs, NJ: Prentice Hall.

Wasserman, Stanley and Katherine Faust. 1994 *Social Network Analysis: Methods and Applications.* New York: Cambridge University Press.

Weber, Max. [1904–1905] 1992. *The Protestant Ethic and the Spirit of Capitalism.* Reprint, London: Routledge.

White, Harrison. 1962. "Chance Models of Systems of Casual Groups." *Sociometry* 25:153–72.

Wilson, Kenneth and W. Allen Martin. 1982. "Ethnic Enclaves: A Comparison of the Cuban and Black Economies in Miami." *American Journal of Sociology* 88:135–60.

Zelizer, Viviana A. 1994. *The Social Meaning of Money.* New York: Basic.

[4]

1042-2587
© 2008 by
Baylor University

Venture Capitalists' Evaluations of Start-Up Teams: Trade-Offs, Knock-Out Criteria, and the Impact of VC Experience

Nikolaus Franke
Marc Gruber
Dietmar Harhoff
Joachim Henkel

The start-up team plays a key role in venture capitalists' evaluations of venture proposals. Our findings go beyond existing research, first by providing a detailed exploration of VCs' team evaluation criteria, and second by investigating the moderator variable of VC experience. Our results reveal utility trade-offs between team characteristics and thus provide answers to questions such as "What strength does it take to compensate for a weakness in characteristic A?" Moreover, our analysis reveals that novice VCs tend to focus on the qualifications of individual team members, while experienced VCs focus more on team cohesion. Data were obtained in a conjoint experiment with 51 professionals in VC firms and analyzed using discrete choice econometric models.

Introduction

Research into the criteria venture capitalists use to assess venture proposals began in the 1970s and has been of constant interest to scholars until the present (Franke, Gruber, Harhoff, & Henkel, 2006; MacMillan, Siegel, & Subba Narasimha, 1985; MacMillan, Zemann, & Subbanarasimha, 1987; Muzyka, Birley, & Leleux, 1996; Poindexter, 1976; Shepherd, 1999; Tyebjee & Bruno, 1984; Wells, 1974). Three reasons seem to explain the strong interest that this field of research has attracted. First, knowledge on VC evaluation criteria helps those seeking funds to better judge their own venture project and to avoid potential flaws in their proposals. Second, the findings provide members of the VC community with an aggregate view of the evaluation criteria in use and with an empirical basis for comparing their own judgment to that of their peers. And third, as VCs are

Please send correspondence to: Joachim Henkel, tel.: +49-89-289-25741; fax: +49-89-289-25742; e-mail: henkel@wi.tum.de considered experts in identifying promising new ventures, their evaluation criteria are often interpreted as success factors for emerging firms (Riquelme & Rickards, 1992; Shepherd & Zacharakis, 2002).

The evaluation of venture proposals is one of the key activities of VCs. Previous studies indicate that VCs use various criteria to assess the attractiveness of venture projects, such as market growth and size, product offerings, the expected rate of return, and the expected risk of a venture project (MacMillan et al., 1985; Tyebjee & Bruno, 1981). Prior research also shows that among the set of evaluation criteria, VCs place particular importance on criteria related to the start-up team (Díaz de León & Guild, 2003; Gorman & Sahlman, 1989; Muzyka et al., 1996; Poindexter, 1976; Shepherd, 1999; Silva, 2004; Smart, 1999; Tyebjee & Bruno, 1981; Wells, 1974; Zopounidis, 1994). As a popular saying in the VC industry highlights, VCs would rather invest "in a grade A team with a grade B idea than in a grade B team with a grade A idea" (cf. Bygrave, 1997).

Although the qualifications of the start-up team play a major role in VCs' evaluations, knowledge of the criteria used in team evaluations remains on a fairly general level. This is largely due to the fact that most prior studies investigate the evaluation of *complete venture proposals* and thus provide aggregate criteria rankings such as (1) technical education, (2) new venture experience, and (3) focus strategy (e.g., Shrader et al., 1997). Whereas such results are important to obtain an overall understanding of VCs' evaluations of venture proposals, they are necessarily limited in the depth of insight they can offer on team evaluations. Specifically, the existing results do not yet provide information on the importance of different parameter values for particular team characteristics. For example, if new venture experience is an important criterion, is it desirable that all team members possess such experience? Moreover, the existing results cannot reveal utility trade-offs among different team characteristics. If a team lacks industry experience, which potential strengths may compensate for such a shortcoming? Can it be offset at all, or are short-comings in this regard a potential knock-out criterion? Hence, a more detailed under-standing of team evaluation criteria is required.

Recent research by Shepherd, Zacharakis, and Baron (2003) suggests a second impor-tant extension to prior scholarly work on VC evaluation criteria. Drawing on cognitive theory, these authors find that the *experience of VCs* has a significant influence on their decision making. Because the assessment of team quality plays an important role in VCs' decision making, the evaluation of start-up teams may also be subject to experience effects. Prior research has not yet addressed this question, although knowledge on the existence and direction of any experience effects would be crucial to theory development on VC decision making, to the design of future research studies, and also to VC practice and venture teams.

Against this backdrop, the purpose of this study is twofold: First, we seek to provide a more detailed exploration of VCs' evaluations of start-up team characteristics, and second, we explore whether novice and experienced VCs attach differing importance to these criteria. We apply a conjoint approach that allows an experimental variation of team characteristics. Prior research suggests that conjoint analysis is particularly suitable for research on VCs' decision making (Shepherd & Zacharakis, 1999) as it yields more valid results than the more frequently used *post hoc* methodologies (e.g., questionnaires using Likert-type scales). Our sample consists of 51 VCs who were asked to rank 20 teams described in terms of seven characteristics. We analyze the rankings with discrete choice econometric models.

This paper proceeds as follows: In the next section, we review prior studies on the criteria used by VCs when evaluating start-up teams and draw on cognitive theory to argue why VC experience could be an important moderator variable. We then provide an overview of the conjoint research design used in this study and present our empirical findings. We conclude by outlining the implications of our results for research and practice.

Review of Prior Research

Criteria Used by VCs to Evaluate Start-Up Teams

As mentioned in the previous section, research into the criteria VCs use to assess venture proposals has a relatively long tradition. Yet the more specific question of "How do VCs evaluate start-up teams?"—which could provide more detailed insights—has received only little attention to date, leading scholars to call for focused research on VCs' evaluations of start-up teams (Siegel, Siegel, & MacMillan, 1993; Timmons & Sapienza, 1992). We briefly discuss the results of key studies investigating VCs' evaluations of venture proposals and distill their findings on those criteria that are related to the evaluation of start-up teams.

Table 1 provides an overview of prior research into the criteria VCs employ when assessing venture proposals. In this context, two observations seem to be noteworthy. First, the table shows that a wide variety of evaluation criteria have been suggested by the literature. In essence, however, it seems that they can be collated into four major groups, namely evaluation criteria related to (1) the product/service offering; (2) the market/industry; (3) the start-up team; and (4) the financial returns to be expected from the new firm. This observation is mirrored in the findings of Tyebjee and Bruno (1984), one of the most widely cited works in this area, which identified five basic evaluation criteria used by VCs: market attractiveness, product differentiation, managerial capabilities, environmental threat resistance, and cash-out potential.

Second, we see that—although the existing results are somewhat heterogeneous—VCs consistently rank criteria related to the start-up team among the top three evaluation criteria. This result is already evident in the pioneering study by Wells (1974), who found that management commitment, products, and markets were the key evaluation criteria in the VC decision-making process. The results from the large number of studies that followed show that at least one, but often two or even all three of the top-ranked criteria pertained to characteristics of the start-up team. For example, Muzyka et al. (1996) find that (1) the leadership potential of the lead entrepreneur; (2) the leadership potential of the management team; and (3) the recognized industry expertise in the team were most important in VCs' evaluations of venture proposals. MacMillan et al. (1985) also investigated criteria that would disqualify a venture proposal. Again, the quality of the start-up team was key, as 5 of the 10 most frequently rated criteria were related to the human capital base of the venture. The most recent findings stem from a field study by Silva (2004), which did not provide an explicit ranking of criteria yet highlighted the fact that the attention of VCs is heavily focused on assessing the quality of the start-up team.

The available evidence thus indicates that evaluation criteria related to the start-up team are of major importance in VCs' decision making. More specifically, characteristics that are frequently mentioned by VCs as desirable features of start-up teams are industry experience, leadership experience, managerial skills, and engineering/technological skills. However, a consideration of existing findings also shows that current knowledge on VCs' evaluations is still rather general, a critique that has also been voiced by other scholars (Muzyka et al., 1996; Sandberg, Schweiger, & Hofer, 1988; Shepherd & Zacharakis, 1999). First, we still lack knowledge on the importance of different parameter values of particular team characteristics. For instance, relevant parameter values for the characteristic "educational background" might be (1) all team members have management

Table 1

Survey of the Literature

Author(s)	Sample	Method	Evaluation criteria by rank order of importance
Wells (1974)	8 VCs	Personal interviews	(1) Management commitment (2) Product (3) Market
Poindexter (1976)	97 VCs	Mail survey	(1) Quality of management (2) Expected rate of return (3) Expected risk
Johnson (1979)	49 VCs	Mail survey	(1) Management (2) Policy/strategy (3) Financial criteria
Tyebjee and Bruno (1981)	46 VCs	Phone interviews	(1) Management skills and history (2) Market size/growth (3) Rate of return
MacMillan et al. (1985)	102 VCs	Mail survey	(1) Capability for sustained intense effort (2) Familiarity with the target market (3) Expected rate of return
Goslin and Barge (1986)	30 VCs	Mail survey	(1) Management experience (2) Marketing experience (3) Complementary skills in team
Robinson (1987)	53 VCs	Mail survey	(1) Personal motivation (2) Organizational/managerial skills (3) Executive/managerial experience
Rea (1989)	18 VCs	Mail survey	(1) Market (2) Product (3) Team credibility
Dixon (1991)	30 VCs	Personal interviews	(1) Managerial experience in the sector (2) Market sector (3) Marketing skills of management team
Muzyka et al. (1996)	73 VCs	Personal, standardized interviews	(1) Leadership potential of lead entrepreneur (2) Leadership potential of management team (3) Recognized industry expertise in team
Bachher and Guild (1996)	40 VCs	Personal interviews	(1) General characteristics of the entrepreneur(s) (2) Target market (3) Offering (product/service)
Shrader, Steier, McDougall, and Oviatt (1997)	214 new ventures with IPO	Interviews, publicly available documents	(1) Technical education (2) New venture experience (3) Focus strategy
Shepherd (1999)	66 VCs	Conjoint experiment (personal/mail)	(1) Industry-related competence (2) Educational capability (3) Competitive rivalry

education; (2) some have management education/some have engineering education; and (3) all have engineering education. Similarly, relevant parameter values for "industry experience" might be (1) all team members have industry experience; (2) some have industry experience; and (3) none have industry experience. However, the available results do not reveal the relative preference VCs attach to these parameter values. Second, the existing results cannot reveal utility trade-offs between different team characteristics. For example, if a team lacks leadership experience, which potential strengths might compensate for such a shortcoming?

In summary, as knowledge on the *parameter values* of particular team characteristics and on *trade-offs* between different team characteristics is key to understanding VCs' evaluations of start-up teams but still lacking, the first goal of this paper is to provide a focused exploration of team evaluation criteria.

The Role of Experience in VC Decision Making

A recent study by Shepherd et al. (2003) suggests a second important extension to research on VCs' evaluations of venture proposals in general and the evaluation of start-up teams in particular. Drawing on cognitive theory, Shepherd et al. find that the experience of VCs has a significant impact on their decision making. As the evaluation of human capital "has to do with making projections of future behaviors that human capital is likely to perform" (Smart, 1999) and human capital is one of the most important but difficult areas to assess in venture proposals (Kozmetsky, Gill, & Smilor, 1985), novice and experienced VCs may differ in their evaluation of start-up teams.

Cognition research provides valuable insights into the development of expertise in decision making. To arrive at a judgment, decision makers select, combine, and evaluate information cues (Spence & Brucks, 1997). The way in which information cues are processed is influenced by an individual's cognitive structures (schemata). A schema is an organized network of knowledge that includes concepts, facts, skills, and action sequences (Gagné & Glaser, 1987). Schemata thus play an elemental role in all cognitive activities such as predicting, explaining, and developing opinions (Larkin, McDermott, Simon, & Simon, 1980; Matlin, 2005).

Prior research shows that individuals refine their schemata in various ways as they acquire experience in a particular domain. For example, Lurigio and Carroll (1985) suggest that experienced individuals possess more complete and detailed schemata than inexperienced individuals. Experienced individuals also group domain-specific knowledge in more meaningful ways than those with little experience, will draw on clearer concepts, create richer connections between concepts, and will be able to apply domain-specific problem-solving procedures they have developed over time (Adelson, 1981; Gobbo & Chi, 1986; Knowlton, 1997; Matlin, 2005). For instance, they will learn about the importance of different dimensions of a decision problem (Shepherd et al., 2003). With respect to the evaluation of start-up teams, this suggests that VCs will become increasingly knowledgeable about the question of which team characteristics are required for a successful new firm creation.

Research on VCs' decision making has not yet explored whether differences exist between the evaluation of start-up teams by novice VCs and by experienced VCs. However, knowledge on the existence and direction of such experience effects would be key for theory development on VC decision making and also for VC practice and start-up teams. In particular, if it turns out that experience effects play a considerable role in VCs' evaluations, future studies would need to control for that variable.

Against the backdrop of these observations, this paper seeks to contribute to the literature on entrepreneurship by (1) exploring in detail the criteria VCs use in the evaluation of start-up teams and (2) exploring how the decision-making experience of VCs influences the importance attributed to team evaluation criteria.

Method

Our study uses conjoint analysis. As this method allows researchers to *simulate* respondents' decision processes in real time, it is in several ways superior to commonly used *post-hoc* methods that collect data on VCs' self-reported decision policies (Shepherd & Zacharakis, 1999). In a conjoint experiment, respondents are asked to judge a series of profiles, that is, combinations of parameter values for several attributes. From the preferences revealed in this way, conclusions can be drawn about the contribution of the various parameter values of each attribute to the overall valuation a certain profile receives. In particular, trade-offs between different parameter values of the attributes under investigation are quantified. The application of this research method to our study is presented in the following paragraphs.

Focus on the Initial Stage of the Evaluation Process

VCs usually evaluate new venture proposals in a multistage process. An important early stage in this process is the appraisal of the business plan, where the decision is made whether to reject a venture proposal outright or to pursue it further by inviting the management team for a project presentation (Bagley & Dauchy, 1999; Dixon, 1991). Typically, 80% of all business plans submitted to a VC firm are rejected in this first round of evaluations, thus making it an important process for VCs and a crucial hurdle to pass for start-up teams (Roberts, 1991).

Our conjoint analysis focuses on this initial stage in the evaluation process of VCs and uses the team description given in the business plan as the basis for a decision experiment. Three arguments support the choice of this approach.

First, when studying team evaluation criteria it is important to define the stage in the decision process where these criteria are applied.[1] For example, whereas a team's educational background can be observed in the written business plan, the atmosphere within the team can only be observed during personal presentations, and qualities such as perseverance and stress resistance will only be observable in the long run.

Second, selecting the initial stage of the evaluation process is advantageous as the team characteristics given in a business plan are comparatively objective, unlike criteria such as personal fit within the team, which VCs can only observe in later stages. Hence, the characteristics of the hypothetical teams in our study could be communicated unambiguously to the participants.

Third, the evaluation of the start-up team's description in a business plan is well suited for a conjoint approach. Unlike in most other conjoint experiments, where the respondent has to imagine some real-world object based on a description on the conjoint card, the team description provided on our conjoint cards is of the same nature as the object itself (the team description given in the business plan). Thus, despite some necessary simplifications in team descriptions, the conjoint design employed here is relatively realistic, as the conjoint task closely resembles the task performed by the respondent in real life.

Construction of Team Descriptions

An important issue in conjoint analyses is to keep the thought-experiments manageable for the interviewees. As the literature review has shown, prior studies suggest

---

1. Although criteria related to the start-up team are consistently ranked among the most important criteria in VCs' decision making, there is also some scholarly debate on whether team criteria are of similar importance throughout the different stages of the evaluation process. To date, only a few studies have differentiated between various evaluation stages. For example, the findings of Hall and Hofer (1993) suggest that human capital characteristics do not play a major role during the screening stage of venture proposals; however, their study also indicates that VCs do evaluate team characteristics during this stage. More recent ethnographic findings by Silva (2004) suggest that the description of human capital is an important source of information in the screening stage.

Table 2

Percentage of Teams with a Given Parameter Value That Are Ranked in the Top Quintile

Variable	Parameter value 1	Parameter value 2	Parameter value 3
Relevant industry experience	0.8% none	25.5% some	35.9% all
Field of education	12.4% all management	38.9% some management, some engineering	11.5% all engineering
Experience in leading teams (5–10 people)	6.5% none	24.9% some	26.6% all
Acquaintance among team members	17.1% brief	16.8% for a longer time, privately	27.1% for a longer time, professionally
Level of education: university degree	7.5% none of the team members	27.2% some team members	23.5% all team members
Age of team members	12.4% 25–35 years	33.7% 35–45 years	15.4% 25–45 years
Prior job experience: type of firm	15.0% mostly large firms	24.5% some large firms, some start-up	22.2% mostly start-up

that VCs regard industry experience, leadership experience, managerial skills, and engineering/technological skills as key characteristics of start-up teams. Yet it would be problematic to include only these potentially important characteristics in a thought-experiment. Thus, to identify any additional team characteristics frequently used in team descriptions and thus subjected to VCs' evaluations, we conducted a pilot study that comprised seven exploratory interviews with VCs and a thorough analysis of two dozen real business plans. This led us to include four additional team characteristics—level of education, type of job experience (start-up vs. large firm), age, and mutual acquaintance within the team—to the criteria already mentioned earlier. Moreover, the pilot study provided information on the relevant parameter values for each of the seven team characteristics. For each characteristic, we included three different parameter values (Table 2).

The team size was fixed at four members. This was done for several reasons: First, our analysis of team descriptions in business plans showed that this is a common size for start-up teams. Second, as VCs usually provide support in finding individuals who could fill an open position in a management team, introducing varying team sizes into our conjoint design did not seem particularly important. Having an even number of team members also has the advantage that team attributes described as "some management, some engineering education" could be interpreted as an even split between the two subgroups. From these attributes and parameter values, we generated 20 profiles (a reduced set with two holdouts) using a full rank order method of conjoint analysis. These cards were pretested with five VCs, who confirmed that the team attributes and their parameter values given on the conjoint cards were adequately chosen and that the task of ranking 20 hypothetical team profiles was indeed manageable.

Figure 1

Description of the Venture as Presented to Interviewees

- Project is based on a *patented technical product*

- Considerable *cost savings* for users

- *Value proposition* is clearly visible

- Potential users are *small and medium-sized industrial firms*

- A working *prototype* exists

Venture Type

In conducting our conjoint experiment, we accounted for the fact that the evaluation of the start-up team is dependent on the type of venture project. For example, while new ventures in biotechnology usually need qualified scientists, new ventures in the software industry rely on founders who possess IT knowledge. As a result, it was necessary to specify the type of new venture that the start-up team under consideration wanted to pursue. On the other hand, an overly detailed description of the venture would have considerably raised the probability that individual respondents would identify the hypothetical start-up with a particular real investment experience, thus jeopardizing the generality of our analysis. So, after discussing several alternative descriptions with experts from the VC industry, we decided to employ a description that indicates several characteristics of the hypothetical venture but at the same time remains sufficiently general (see Figure 1).

Sample

Our sample consists of 51 conjoint experiments/interviews[2] that were conducted at 26 different VC firms located in Munich, Berlin, and Vienna. All of the respondents were actively involved in the evaluation of business plans. Apart from the conjoint experiments, background information on the respondents (age, education, professional experience, experience as a VC) and on the VC firms (size, volume of funds, specialization in industries or financing stages, evaluation process) was collected. As we used a convenience sample, our sample of VC firms cannot claim to be representative. A truly random sample of interviewees is difficult to obtain given the time constraints in the VC industry and the time required for interviews (Smart, 1999). However, we did make efforts to obtain a mix of different types of VC firms. The description in Table 3 shows that our sample contains VC firms of different sizes, different industry focus, and different degrees of internationalization. Since the VC firms were chosen to match our hypothetical venture project, obviously more of them invest in telecommunications, software, and e-commerce than in biotechnology. With regard to experience, our sample covers a sufficiently broad range in order to investigate the impact of different levels of experience. While the average

---

2. As Shepherd and Zacharakis (1999) suggest as a rule of thumb, a sample size greater than 50 is normally sufficient. Previous studies used sample sizes of 73 VCs (Muzyka et al., 1996), 53 VCs (Zacharakis & Meyer, 1998), and 66 VCs (Shepherd, Ettenson, & Crouch, 2000).

Table 3

Demographics of VC Firms and Individuals Surveyed

VC firms (N = 26)	
Firm age (years):	mean = 8.2, standard deviation (SD) = 12.6, median = 3, range: 1–56
Firm size (number of professionals):	mean = 75.4, SD = 202.8, median = 9, range: 1–800
Volume of funds (EUR):*	<10 m: 2; 26–100 m: 8; 101–250 m: 5; >250 m: 9; n.a.: 2
Investment stage:*·**	seed: 10; start-up: 17; first stage: 20; expansion: 17; later stages: 8
Industry focus:*·**	telecommunication: 23; software: 22; e-commerce: 19; electrical engineering: 13; biotechnology: 10; services: 5; other: 13
Location of interviews (offices):*	Munich: 40; Vienna: 7; Berlin: 4
Individuals (N = 51)	
Age:	mean = 35.0, SD = 6.7, median = 34, range: 24–57
Education level:*·**	apprenticeship: 4; university degree: 51; MBA: 15; doctorate: 11
Education type:*·**	business/economics: 39; engineering: 18; science: 6; law: 3; other: 2
VC experience (years):	mean = 3.9, SD = 5.2, median = 2, range: 0–30
Tenure with firm (years):	mean = 2.4, SD = 2.0, median = 2, range: 0–11
Number of business plans evaluated:	mean = 460, SD = 455, median = 300, range: 0–2000
Prior professional experience:	Type of firm:*·** start-up: 22; SME: 23; large firm: 35; no prior experience: 0
	Industry:*·** management consulting: 28; manufacturing: 25; financial services: 13; other: 9
Leadership experience:*	none: 9; 1–5 subordinates: 20; 6–20 subordinates: 16; >20 subordinates: 6

* For categorical variables, the number of respondents who chose the respective category is given; ** Multiple answers possible.

experience is almost 4 years of work as a VC, a substantial number of VCs interviewed had experience of 2 years or less (which is typical of the relatively young German VC industry).[3]

The conjoint experiments were conducted according to a fixed scheme by one interviewer who was present during the entire experiment. None of the participants encountered any problems in ranking the conjoint cards.

Analysis

We employ discrete choice methodology to identify the impact of various team characteristics on VCs' evaluations. Our model interprets the 20 rankings assigned to the simulated teams by each of our respondents as a rank ordering of choices from a given set. A suitable estimator to analyze such data has been proposed by Beggs, Cardell, and Hausman (1981). Following Marden (1995), the model is also known as the Plackett-Luce or as the "exploded logit" model. The marketing literature refers to the model as the choice-based conjoint analysis method.

---

3. Measuring experience by the number of years a decision maker has worked as a VC was suggested by Shepherd et al. (2003). We also used the alternative operationalization of experience as the logarithm of the number of years the rater had been working as a VC. While the explanatory variables that are significant in this specification are also significant in the basic one—hence, the results do not contradict each other—some other coefficients lose their significance in the log specification. The likely explanation of this finding is that the logarithmic function is too steep for small values of the argument and too flat around the median. We therefore chose the dummy operationalization as the most appropriate one.

To consider an example, an individual's ranking of A-C-B-D in a choice set (A, B, C, D) is taken to represent an observation in which A is chosen as the most preferred alternative from the full set (A, B, C, D); C is the preferred alternative from the restricted set (B, C, D); and B is chosen as the preferred alternative from the set (B, D).[4] The model thus extends McFadden's conditional logit to cases in which full ranking data are available.

Our model presumes that all alternatives are assessed by our subjects using a cardinal assessment function that reflects the quality of the team (and thus the likelihood of obtaining a favorable financing decision) as a linear additive function of team characteristics. Let the venture capitalist's assessment be denoted b_{ik} for the benefit that venture capitalist i would be able to draw from financing team k (out of a set of K alternatives). The ranking chosen by each venture capitalist emerges from a simple ordering of the K alternatives according to their b_{ik} values, which are functions of the team characteristics $b_{ik} = X_{ik}\beta + \varepsilon_{ik}$, where X_{ik} is a row vector of the characteristics of alternative k and (possibly) interaction terms between the characteristics of alternative k and of rater i, and β is a column vector of coefficients. Under the assumption that the error term ε_{ik} follows an independent identically distributed extreme value distribution, the probability that any alternative k is ranked as the best one by respondent i is given by

$$(1) \qquad \text{prob}\left\{b_{ik} > \max\left(b_{ij}\right)_{j \neq k}\right\} = \exp(X_{ik}\beta)/(\Sigma_j \exp(X_{ij}\beta)).$$

Returning to our earlier case in which the sequence of A-C-B-D is chosen from the choice set (A, B, C, D), the probability of observing this ranking from rater i would be given by[5]

$$(2) \qquad \text{prob}\{ranking\ A\text{-}C\text{-}B\text{-}D\} = \left[\exp(X_{iA}\beta)/(\Sigma_{j=A,B,C,D} \exp(X_{ij}\beta))\right] \cdot$$
$$\left[\exp(X_{iC}\beta)/(\Sigma_{j=B,C,D} \exp(X_{ij}\beta))\right] \cdot$$
$$\left[\exp(X_{iB}\beta)/(\Sigma_{j=B,D} \exp(X_{ij}\beta))\right]$$

In order to ensure convenient interpretation of our coefficient signs, we use the following parameter values as reference groups: age of team members between 25 and 35 years; no team member with a university degree; all team members have management education; team members have mostly large-firm experience; no team member with experience in the relevant industry; no team member with experience in leading teams of 5–10 individuals; and team members have known each other for a short period of time. This choice of reference parameter values is based on the descriptive data analysis (see Table 2, next section) and is made in such a way that the reference parameter value is presumably the one with the lowest benefit.

In our estimation, a team with these parameter values will automatically be assigned a benefit value of zero since the associated coefficient vector β is implicitly set to zero. In order to model parameter values deviating from the reference team, we employ a dummy variable technique where a separate dummy is used for the two other parameter values of each team variable. In addition, we interact, in the extended specification, all terms with a dummy variable Δ_i indicating that rater i's experience is above the median. Hence, our full specification of the benefit b_{ik} that rater i would expect to derive from team k can be written as follows:

---

4. We use the model implementation in STATA 8.0 (command rologit).
5. A more detailed derivation of the likelihood function for this model is given in Hausman and Ruud (1987, p. 86).

$$b_{ik} = \sum_{j=1}^{7} \left(\beta_{j1} D_{j1k} + \beta_{j2} D_{j2k} + \beta_{j3} \Delta_i D_{j1k} + \beta_{j4} \Delta_i D_{j2k} \right) + \varepsilon_{ik}$$

Empirical Results

Descriptive Analysis

Before turning to multivariate analysis, we briefly explore some simple associations between the ranking of the team, that is, the level of team success, and the variables that presumably have an impact on success in order to give some intuition on the findings and demonstrate their robustness. We measure the success of each team by computing the share of cases in which the team was ranked among the top four teams, the upper quintile. This share variable can be interpreted as the team's likelihood of reaching a certain cutoff level (the top 20%), which would (hypothetically) lead to an invitation to meet with a VC.[6]

Table 4 lists the teams and their characteristics in the order of the share of top quintile rankings achieved in our conjoint design. Since we use a reduced conjoint design, the "dream team" configuration, that is, the theoretically best profile, will not necessarily be among the 20 profiles presented to the interviewees. Team 10, which receives top quintile rankings in 96.1% of all cases, is therefore the most preferred team in the choice set according to our success variable, but not necessarily the theoretically optimal team configuration. While Table 4 shows that the top quintile share decreases quickly among the first 10 teams, it is difficult to extract clear information on the relative contribution of the various team characteristics from the simple ranking performed here. However, there appears to be a positive relationship between (favorable) ranking and industry experience, leadership experience, and the age of team members. It is more difficult to derive clear statements with respect to the other variables from the aggregate ranking information.

Whereas Table 4 shows complete team profiles, Table 2 presents the "success information" treating the parameter values of the team characteristics as fully independent. This table allows us to get a clearer impression of which team characteristics and which parameter values are likely to be important. For example, in 6 of our 20 team descriptions all team members have industry experience. Given 51 interviews, this yields 306 observations, of which 110 (35.9%) were ranked among the top four teams.

For the attributes "industry experience," "field of education," "acquaintance," and "age," we find a clear preference for a particular parameter value in that the distance from the respective next-best parameter value is larger than 10%. Preferred teams are those in which all members have industry experience, their educational background is mixed (some engineering, some management expertise), founders have known each other for a longer time professionally, and members are older (aged 35–45).

For the remaining three characteristics, a somewhat less transparent picture emerges: With regard to university training, prior job experience in corporate or start-up environments, and leadership experience, the best and second-best parameter values do not differ greatly when evaluated according to the share of top quintile rankings.

---

6. Obviously, taking the top quintile as our measure is an arbitrary choice. However, it does represent a reasonable compromise, as taking the share of top rankings (i.e., how often a team is considered the best one) would lead to an ambiguous result for many teams that never reach that position, while taking the top ten ranking would not discern very clearly between "above-average" teams of similar quality.

Table 4

Descriptive Statistics on Team Characteristics

Team number	Share of top quintile rankings (%)	Relevant industry experience	Field of education	Leadership experience	Acquaintance among team members	University degree	Age of team members	Prior job experience
10	96.1	All	Mixed	Some	Professional	Some	35–45	Start-up
3	60.8	Some	Mixed	All	Brief	Some	25–45	Mixed
13	58.8	Some	Mixed	All	Private	All	35–45	Corporate
16	47.1	All	All engineering	Some	Brief	All	35–45	Mixed
15	25.5	All	All management	All	Private	All	25–35	Start-up
8	25.5	All	All management	All	Professional	None	25–45	Mixed
6	23.5	Some	All management	Some	Professional	Some	25–35	Corporate
19	15.7	Some	All engineering	All	Professional	All	25–45	Corporate
5	11.8	Some	All engineering	None	Private	All	25–45	Start-up
7	11.8	All	Mixed	None	Brief	None	25–35	Corporate
12	9.8	All	All engineering	None	Private	Some	25–45	Corporate
2	7.8	Some	All engineering	Some	Private	None	25–35	Mixed
18	5.9	None	Mixed	None	Professional	All	25–35	Mixed
14	0.0	None	All engineering	All	Professional	None	35–45	Corporate
9	0.0	None	Mixed	Some	Private	None	25–45	Start-up
11	0.0	Some	All management	None	Brief	None	35–45	Start-up
4	0.0	None	All engineering	All	Brief	None	25–35	Start-up
1	0.0	None	All management	Some	Brief	Some	25–45	Corporate
20	0.0	None	All engineering	Some	Brief	All	25–45	Corporate
17	0.0	None	All management	None	Private	Some	35 to 45	Mixed

Note that Table 2 summarizes seven bivariate relationships—it is therefore not a substitute for a multivariate analysis. Nor does this table give us the opportunity to generate inference results. Hence, while Tables 2 and 4 provide some indication of which team characteristics are particularly important, a multivariate treatment of the data is required in order to arrive at a more structured response to our research questions.

Discrete Choice Analysis—Model Specification

The results of estimating the rank-ordered logit model are presented in Table 5. In specification (1), we use only the team characteristics as explanatory variables, while in specifications (2) to (5) we introduce interaction terms with the dummy variable Δ_i, which indicates whether the rater is an experienced VC. In essence, the upper half of columns (2) to (5) (i.e., those coefficients shown in the first part of Table 5) describe the choice behavior of less experienced VCs, while the lower half describes the difference between the preferences of more and less experienced raters.

Before interpreting the results, we need to discuss whether our findings are consistent with the assumption that our subjects have provided us with full rankings of the alternatives. There is considerable doubt in the literature that this assumption is always justified (Hausman & Ruud, 1987). What might have happened—and comments from our interviewees provide some evidence to this effect—is that subjects do spend effort on the upper ranks but pay less attention to the lower ones. In this case, heteroscedasticity will be introduced, which (in this model) will lead to inconsistent estimates if the full ranking information is used. For this reason, we present several specifications that differ with respect to the number of ranks taken into account. In columns (1) and (2) of Table 5, we present rank-ordered logit estimates which take the full rankings at face value. In specifications (3)/(4)/(5), in contrast, only the top 16/12/8 ranks are taken into account, while the residual ranks are treated as noninformative.

In essence, we discard information in columns (3) through (5) and should thus expect the precision of our estimates to decrease as more and more rankings are discarded. Indeed, even a cursory glance at the results shows that standard errors increase monotonically from column (2) to column (5). Moreover, the estimates show a second well-known pattern—the coefficients increase in size as we discard more of the lower ranks in our estimate. Hausman and Ruud (1987) argue that this phenomenon is consistent with the lower ranks being evaluated less carefully than the upper ones.[7] Still, while the coefficients increase overall, their relative size remains largely stable.

Discrete Choice Analysis—Pooled Results

We start by discussing the pooled results for all respondents (specification [1]) before addressing the differences due to the rater's level of experience. In discussing the pooled results, we first analyze the relative importance of the various team characteristics and then address the benefit contribution of the various parameter values for each characteristic. Finally, we consider trade-offs between different parameter values for different characteristics.

---

7. We did, in fact, estimate models for all possible specifications, both with and without interaction terms: using all ranks, the top 19 ranks, etc. down to using only the top 6 ranks (with even fewer ranks, convergence was not attained). With very few exceptions, the coefficients' signs and significance levels remain stable.

Table 5

Rank-Ordered Logit Results

Explanatory variables: Team characteristics. In spec. (2) to (5). coefficients refer only to inexperienced VCs	(1) No interactions, all 20 ranks	(2) With interactions, all 20 ranks	(3) With interactions, top 16 ranks	(4) With interactions, top 12 ranks	(5) With interactions, top 8 ranks
Experience in relevant industry—all team members	1.986*** (0.191)	1.980*** (0.241)	1.992*** (0.254)	2.278*** (0.253)	2.767*** (0.371)
Experience in relevant industry—some team members	1.614*** (0.165)	1.519*** (0.205)	1.476*** (0.218)	1.649*** (0.240)	1.706*** (0.281)
Field of education—all engineering	0.265** (0.120)	0.462** (0.201)	0.488** (0.201)	0.653** (0.288)	0.860** (0.354)
Field of education—some engineering, some mgmt.	1.113*** (0.127)	1.194*** (0.198)	1.269*** (0.213)	1.497*** (0.271)	2.031*** (0.346)
Leadership experience—all team members	0.725*** (0.116)	1.001*** (0.173)	1.029*** (0.195)	1.165*** (0.264)	1.498*** (0.341)
Leadership experience—some team members	0.704*** (0.111)	1.012*** (0.161)	1.078*** (0.175)	1.129*** (0.213)	1.650*** (0.320)
Acquaintance—for a long time, professionally	0.585*** (0.143)	0.300* (0.153)	0.321** (0.147)	0.408** (0.187)	0.831*** (0.240)
Acquaintance—for a long time, privately	0.247** (0.121)	-0.034 (0.134)	-0.033 (0.109)	-0.048 (0.148)	0.082 (0.236)
University degree—all team members	0.912*** (0.149)	1.505*** (0.236)	1.577*** (0.270)	1.432*** (0.296)	2.144*** (0.353)
University degree—some team members	1.003*** (0.110)	1.332*** (0.169)	1.363*** (0.214)	1.213*** (0.192)	1.530*** (0.208)
Age of team members between 25 and 45	0.191*** (0.070)	0.128 (0.079)	0.096 (0.080)	-0.011 (0.100)	0.148 (0.201)
Age of team members between 35 and 45	0.517*** (0.101)	0.517*** (0.166)	0.397*** (0.153)	0.237 (0.156)	-0.270 (0.265)
Prior job experience—some large firm, some start-up	0.221** (0.087)	0.176* (0.106)	0.181 (0.111)	0.084 (0.108)	0.053 (0.157)
Prior job experience—mostly start-up	0.246*** (0.083)	0.273** (0.117)	0.204 (0.134)	0.217 (0.140)	-0.090 (0.126)

(continued overleaf)

Explanatory variables: team characteristics interacted with dummy variable Δ, ($\Delta = 1$ if rater is experienced)					
Δ × experience in relevant industry—all team members		0.258 (0.391)	0.345 (0.420)	0.392 (0.400)	0.223 (0.478)
Δ × experience in relevant industry—some team members		0.326 (0.356)	0.436 (0.381)	0.470 (0.382)	0.624 (0.411)
Δ × field of education—all engineering		-0.397 (0.251)	-0.330 (0.292)	-0.289 (0.426)	-0.103 (0.539)
Δ × field of education—some engineering, some mgmt		-0.170 (0.257)	-0.098 (0.284)	-0.050 (0.375)	-0.084 (0.498)
Δ × leadership experience—all team members		-0.487** (0.224)	-0.456* (0.239)	-0.531* (0.299)	-0.538 (0.447)
Δ × leadership experience—some team members		-0.558*** (0.200)	-0.607*** (0.211)	-0.668** (0.264)	-0.885** (0.430)
Δ × acquaintance—for a long time, professionally		0.635** (0.308)	0.811** (0.327)	1.035** (0.417)	0.769 (0.474)
Δ × acquaintance—for a long time, privately		0.587** (0.265)	0.676** (0.278)	0.983*** (0.326)	0.582* (0.347)
Δ × university degree—all team members		-1.127*** (0.275)	-1.262*** (0.309)	-1.249*** (0.353)	-1.903*** (0.445)
Δ × university degree—some team members		-0.644*** (0.213)	-0.799*** (0.241)	-0.667*** (0.244)	-0.864*** (0.308)
Δ × age of team members between 25 and 45		0.187 (0.148)	0.172 (0.160)	0.206 (0.197)	-0.167 (0.320)
Δ × age of team members between 35 and 45		0.071 (0.206)	0.210 (0.199)	0.439** (0.212)	0.591 (0.396)
Δ × prior job experience—some large firm, some start-up		0.216 (0.165)	0.232 (0.175)	0.451** (0.209)	0.472* (0.246)
Δ × prior job experience—mostly start-up		-0.037 (0.258)	0.077 (0.345)	0.092 (0.392)	0.275 (0.223)
Observations	1,020	1,020	1,020	1,020	1,020
Log L	-1,834.9	-1,796.3	-1,632.3	-1,267.2	-836.2
Pseudo R²	0.150	0.168	0.183	0.217	0.266
Chi-squared	447.1	951.5	934.6	746.4	837.19
Df	14	28	28	28	28

Note: Robust standard errors in parentheses; * significant at 10%; ** significant at 5%; *** significant at 1%.

Figure 2

Benefit Contributions of Parameter Values of Team Characteristics
(Specification [1])

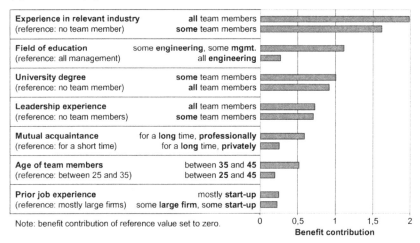

Note: benefit contribution of reference value set to zero.

We define the "importance" of a characteristic as the difference between the benefit contributions (i.e., the estimated coefficient) of the most and least preferred parameter values, normalized such that the sum of all importance values yields 100%. In other words, the importance of a characteristic is that share of the value difference between the best and the worst possible team that can be attributed to this characteristic.[8] Given that the reference parameter value, by construction, has a benefit contribution of zero for most characteristics, the importance is essentially the (normalized) benefit contribution of the most preferred parameter value.[9]

As Figure 2 illustrates, industry experience is by far the most important characteristic (32.2%). While this in itself is not a new insight, our approach allows a meaningful comparison of characteristics beyond a mere ordering of their relative importance. In

8. The importance of a characteristic obviously depends on the available parameter values. The more similar these are, the lower the characteristic's importance will turn out to be. Hence, "importance" must be interpreted with the underlying parameter values in mind. For this reason, a realistic choice of parameter values for our experiment was paramount. Note that by explicitly defining the parameter values we avoid another problem of surveys using rating scales: When asked about the importance of industry experience, for example, each respondent bases his or her assessment on personal experiences regarding this characteristic's typical parameter values. A VC who has never seen a team without industry experience will likely attribute lower importance to this characteristic than one who has.

9. In more detail, the importance values are calculated as follows. The contribution of industry experience to the overall score of the best team, compared to that of the worst team, equals 1.986 (see Figure 2 or the first column of Table 5), that of the field of education 1.113, that of leadership experience 0.725, etc. Normalization then yields the numbers given in the text following this footnote: 1.986/ (1.986 + 1.113 + 0.725 + . . .) = 0.322, etc.

particular, we find that industry experience is 1.8 times—i.e., almost twice—as important as the field of education, which ranks second in overall importance (18.0%). Third comes academic education with 16.2%, meaning that it is about half as important as industry experience. Less importance is attributed to leadership experience (11.7%), the team members' mutual acquaintance within the team (9.5%), and age (8.4%). The type of prior job experience ranks last at 4.0%.

We now delve deeper into the benefit contributions of each characteristic's parameter values. To begin with, we find that the marginal benefit contribution of having more team members with *industry experience* decreases strongly. When only some team members have relevant experience, the benefit contribution (1.61) is about 80% of that attained when all founders know the industry (1.99). Hence, while having no industry experience seems to be a *conditio sine qua non* (knock-out criterion) for a VC evaluating a venture team, it will often be sufficient to have some industry insiders on board.

For the *field of education*, the relative benefit contribution of the various parameter values confirms the insight that a heterogeneous team comprising technical and management skills is much desired (benefit contribution 1.11). A management-only team is clearly not *viable* (benefit contribution 0), which was to be expected given the technical nature of our business model. Despite the model's technical nature, however, teams consisting entirely of engineers also fare so badly that this parameter value (benefit contribution 0.27) seems like a disqualifier for advancing to further stages in the evaluation process.

For the team's *level of education*, we find that an academic background is essential, but that it hardly makes a difference whether some or all team members have an academic background. While a team with only some university graduates is slightly preferred, the difference between the two coefficients in Table 5 is insignificant. This could mean that VCs see the participation of founders with university degrees as a positive signal—which, however, does not improve further when the number of graduates in the team increases from "some" to "all"; in fact, it decreases. Alternatively, an "all university" team may mean a higher average level of human capital, while a mixed team offers (desirable) heterogeneity. When these two effects are of equal size, we should observe (as we do) equal benefit contributions for both parameter values.

For *leadership experience*, we find a pattern similar to the one identified for industry experience. Having no members with leadership experience (benefit contribution 0) is likely to be a knock-out criterion in the evaluation process. However, the benefit contribution of "some team members with leadership experience" (0.70) is nearly identical to that of "all team members" (0.73). This is a rather plausible finding since not all members in a venture team can assume a leadership role. Note, however, that this is only true in the early stages of the start-up, whereas after successful expansion all founders might find themselves in leading positions and thus need leadership experience.

With regard to *mutual acquaintance*, we find that the type of acquaintance is just as important as its duration. Being acquainted for a long time is less than half as valuable (benefit contribution 0.25) when based on private relationships than when it is based on professional collaboration (benefit contribution 0.59).

As for *age*, we find that having only young team members (aged 25–35) on board yields the lowest evaluation (zero). This result is consistent with anecdotal evidence from VCs who had negative experiences with "boy groups" during the e-commerce boom. What is surprising is that having some more senior people in addition to young members on the team only partly remedies the problem: A mixed team with members aged between 25 and 45 (benefit contribution 0.19) still fares much worse than a team consisting exclusively of older founders (35–45, benefit contribution 0.52).

Finally, for the *type of prior job experience*, we find similar positive benefit contributions for heterogeneous teams (i.e., those whose members have experience partly in large firms, partly in start-ups) (0.22) and teams in which members have only start-up experience (0.25). However, even though both coefficients are significant, their size shows that VCs seem to care comparatively little about this team characteristic.

Discrete Choice Analysis—Effects of VC Experience

We now explore whether VC experience has a significant moderating effect on the evaluation of start-up teams. Overall, we find that both more and less experienced raters attach the highest importance to industry experience and the lowest to the type of prior professional experience. However, our analysis also reveals some key differences. The level of academic education ranks second for less experienced VCs (importance: 22.1%) and only fourth for their more experienced colleagues (10.8%). Leadership experience is ranked fourth (14.8%) by novices and sixth (8.1%) by experienced raters. The latter, in turn, attach more importance to mutual acquaintance within the team (ranked third at 14.7%) than less experienced VCs (ranked sixth at 4.9%).

Table 5 provides more detailed insights into the ratings of novice and experienced VCs. As specifications (2) to (5) show, we consistently find significant differences between the preferences of novice and experienced VCs for each parameter value of the following three characteristics: leadership experience, mutual acquaintance, and academic education. In addition, heterogeneous prior job experience (some start-up, some large firm) receives significantly higher ratings from experienced raters in specifications (4) and (5), as does a higher age (35–45) in specification (4). As the results of specifications (2) to (5) are identical in qualitative terms, and as we seek comparability with the basic model (1), the following discussion will focus on specification (2).

Figure 3 displays the coefficients of the interaction terms as given in the second part of Table 5. Coefficients significantly different from zero on the 1% level are rendered as solid black bars, those significant on the 5% level as hatched bars. We find the largest and most significant differences between novice and experienced raters in the perceived benefit contribution of a university degree. All team members having a university degree leads to a benefit contribution of 1.51 for a novice VC and of only 0.38 (i.e., 1.51–1.13) for experienced VCs. While the latter value is still positive and significantly different from zero (1% level), it is only a quarter of the size of the value for novices. We obtain similar results for the benefit contribution of "*some* team members having a university degree": 0.69 for more vs. 1.33 (1% level) for less experienced VCs, a difference of −0.64 (see Figure 3). Furthermore, the preference order between purely academic and mixed teams is reversed for experienced raters: With a difference of 0.21, they significantly (1% level) prefer mixed teams, while their less experienced colleagues (insignificantly) prefer, by a margin of 0.17, teams in which all members have a university degree.

Leadership experience is also valued significantly less by experienced raters. Novices value leadership experience with a benefit contribution of 1.0 and attach little importance to whether all or some team members have such experience. In both cases, the benefit contributions perceived by experienced VCs are smaller by a value of roughly 0.5. While they are still highly significant (1% level), they are only about half as large as the values we obtained from less experienced raters.

The one characteristic for which we find a significantly *higher* valuation among experienced raters is mutual acquaintance within the team. If team members have known each other for a long time professionally, senior VCs perceive a benefit contribution that is 0.64 higher than their younger colleagues (0.94 vs. 0.30). Given a long-standing *private*

Figure 3

Difference in Benefit Contributions between Experienced and Novice Raters (Specification [2]). Reading Example: Experienced VCs Rate "Mutual Acquaintance for a Long Time, Professionally" 0.64 Points Higher

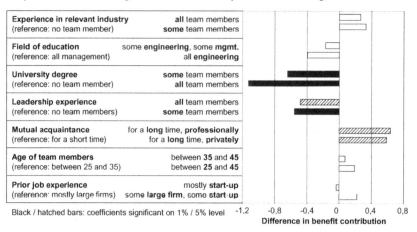

acquaintance, the difference is 0.59, with novices perceiving no benefit contribution at all (−0.03, not significant) in that parameter value.

Discussion

Criteria related to the start-up team are key in VCs' evaluation of venture proposals. We believe that this study makes two contributions to the literature. First, by focusing on VCs' evaluations of venture teams, we offer more detailed insights on desired team characteristics than previous research. Second, our study extends the research of Shepherd et al. (2003) comparing decision making by VCs with varying experience. Our analysis reveals significant differences between novice and experienced VCs' evaluations. We discuss these two contributions and their implications for research and practice in turn.

Team Characteristics and Trade-Offs

Our findings indicate that industry experience, educational background, and leadership experience are the three most important team characteristics. These general results are consistent with the findings of most prior studies (see "Review of Prior Research" and Table 1).

Our results go beyond the existing research by indicating the importance of different parameter values and by providing insights on utility trade-offs between different team characteristics. For industry experience as well as leadership experience, we find that it may suffice when only some team members possess it. Regarding the field of education, heterogeneous teams are strongly preferred over teams where all members have an engineering background or a management background.

As illustrative examples, consider the following *ceteris paribus* comparisons. A team whose members have known each other privately for a long time and are between 35 and 45 years old receives the same evaluation as a team whose members have a long-standing professional acquaintance and who are (all or some) between 25 and 35 years of age. That is, the bonus of a more senior team equals that of being acquainted for a long time through a professional (not a private) relationship. As a second example, consider team A, in which all members have industry experience, compared to team B, in which nobody knows the industry. We know from anecdotal evidence as well as our analysis that team B has hardly any chance of being considered for funding. However, despite its high level of industry experience, even team A is not guaranteed success if it performs badly in too many other dimensions. Hence the question: What other shortcomings have, in sum, the same effect as a lack of industry experience? According to our results, the two teams will receive roughly the same evaluation if the members of team B have a mixed educational background (some management, some engineering), some or all have a university degree, and they have known each other for a long time privately, while team A consists entirely of engineers with no university degree and only a short mutual acquaintance. In other words, the latter three parameter values lead to a penalty corresponding to that of having no industry experience—and will likely mean no funding for these founders.

Evaluations by Novice vs. Experienced VCs

Our results also go beyond existing research by exploring whether VCs' experience has a significant moderating effect on the evaluation of start-up teams. On the one hand, we find that novice and experienced VCs both see *industry experience* as the most important criterion. Both groups also rank the *field of education* among the top three criteria, and the type of prior professional experience as the least important criterion. On the other hand, however, novice and experienced VCs also critically diverge in some of their preferences. The most striking difference is *mutual acquaintance* among team members, which is ranked among the *top three* criteria by experienced VCs, whereas novice VCs rank it in the *second to last* spot.

In order to illustrate the size of the experience effect, consider a team in which no founder holds a university degree and whose members have known each other professionally for a long time. *Ceteris paribus*, this team's evaluation by an experienced VC would be 1.76 points higher than that of a novice—a utility difference nearly as large as the one between all team members vs. no team members having industry experience (1.99).

We view the rankings of experienced VCs to be more valid indicators of desirable team characteristics, although the beneficial effect of growing expertise has not remained unchallenged. The aforementioned empirical study by Shepherd et al. (2003) provides evidence of a curvilinear relationship between VC experience and decision performance, and suggests that decision effectiveness declines after approximately 14 years of experience in venture capital. Yet as most VCs in our "experienced" group are well below this 14-year threshold, we believe that their evaluations are indeed more valid indicators of desirable team characteristics than those made by novice VCs.

Apart from the important finding that novice and experienced VCs differ significantly in certain preferences, an interesting pattern emerges with respect to the type of criteria valued differently by both groups. Our results suggest that team cohesion (as evidenced by mutual acquaintance among team members) is of high importance to experienced VCs, whereas novice VCs tend to emphasize individual-level, more tangible characteristics such as university degrees and prior leadership experience in start-up teams. Using a somewhat clichéd yet still useful metaphor, it seems that experienced VCs attribute relatively more importance to the "forest" than to the "trees" when evaluating start-up teams. More research is needed to see whether this pattern holds in the evaluation of full venture proposals.

Implications for Start-Up Teams and VCs

For start-up teams seeking VC backing or consultants advising teams in early-stage venture development, our results offer an opportunity for team assessment. Provided with a more detailed understanding of the criteria VCs apply in their decision making, incomplete teams can try to find additional members to optimize their profile and their chances of obtaining VC financing. Faced with a choice between multiple potential new members, our results offer guidance as to who will make the best complement for a team. When a new firm has a high-quality team in place, our results will help team members make a clear and concise presentation of the team's quality in the business plan document.

Furthermore, at least two important implications for VCs are suggested by our findings. First, as novice VCs tend to be those employees in VC firms who are responsible for the initial screening of business plans, they are important gatekeepers whose decisions significantly impact the deal flow that more experienced VCs will evaluate at a later stage of the investment process. The divergence identified in team evaluations could prove problematic when novice VCs reject venture proposals on the basis of a negative assessment of criteria that experienced VCs would have evaluated more positively. As a result, VC firms may pass up interesting investment opportunities early on in the investment process. In this regard, our results also inform the VC community of the potential training needs of individuals entering the VC profession.

Second, individual VC firms can apply the method developed in this paper to develop a clearer understanding of their own decision processes. For example, deviations between agreed-upon investment policies and actual decisions can be uncovered and addressed. Furthermore, this method allows VCs to benchmark their own decision process (as regards teams) against that of other firms—a practice that could be particularly beneficial, as there seems to be room for improvement in the decision-making process of VCs (Shepherd & Zacharakis, 2002; Zacharakis & Meyer, 1998).

Implications for Future Research

Our results also offer several interesting insights for future research. First, as this study reveals significant differences in the team evaluations of novice and experienced VCs, it may be fruitful to extend this line of research by investigating whether experience also has a significant impact on the evaluation of other aspects of venture proposals. For example, it may well be that the assessment of business models (e.g., Amit & Zott, 2000) could be subject to experience effects. Whereas novice VCs may look at single components of business models (e.g., transaction efficiency), experienced VCs may place more weight on the fit of the various components, and thus may arrive at a better understanding of the overall value creation potential of the proposed venture.

Second, our findings reveal that future studies on VC decision making need to control for VC experience to avoid sample selection bias. Whereas biases arising from sample selection are troublesome in any kind of research, they seem to be particularly problematic in studies of VC decision making, as the findings of these studies are often interpreted as success factors in new firm creation.

Third, as our sample is comprised of a high share of less experienced VCs, future research could look more closely at VCs that have more than 10–14 years of experience and investigate whether this additional experience has an impact on team evaluations (or evaluations of other aspects of venture proposals, see earlier discussion). As noted previously, prior research indicates that decision effectiveness will decrease after a certain number of years in the VC profession.

Fourth, by exploring evaluation criteria this study focused on content issues in VC decision making. Smart (1999) investigated the methods VCs apply when assessing human capital (e.g., job analysis, work sample, reference interview) and thus complements our research with a tool-oriented process perspective. Future research could combine content- and process-oriented perspectives, and such research could also help in developing actuarial decision models (Zacharakis & Meyer, 2000).

Finally, this research was carried out in Germany and Austria, which might make the results specific to these countries. However, the maturing European VC scene in general is closely modeled on the U.S. example, and 36% of our interviewees work with U.S. venture capital firms. We tested whether the evaluation results differed between these respondents and the remainder of the sample but did not find any significant differences. Hence, we would not expect to see large differences between our results and a potential replication study conducted in the United States.

The perceived quality of the start-up team is of major importance in VCs' decision making. This paper adds to the growing literature on VCs' decision making by providing detailed evidence on their evaluation of start-up teams and by uncovering how the experience of VCs affects such evaluations.

REFERENCES

Adelson, B. (1981). Problem solving and the development of abstract categories in programming languages. *Memory and Cognition, 9,* 422–433.

Amit, R. & Zott, C. (2000). Value creation in e-business. *Strategic Management Journal, 22,* 493–520.

Bachher, J.S. & Guild, P.D. (1986) Financing early stage technology based companies: Investment criteria used by investors. In R. Ronstadt, J. Hornaday, R. Peterson, & K. Vesper (Eds.), *Frontiers of Entrepreneurship Research* (pp. 363–376). Wellesley, MA: Babson College.

Bagley, C. & Dauchy, C. (1999). Venture capital. In W. Sahlman, H.H. Stevenson, M.J. Roberts, & A. Bhidé (Eds.), *The entrepreneurial venture* (pp. 262–303). Cambridge, MA: Harvard Business School Press.

Beggs, S., Cardell, S., & Hausman, J. (1981). Assessing the potential demand for electric cars. *Journal of Econometrics, 16,* 1–19.

Bygrave, W.D. (1997). The entrepreneurial process. In W.D. Bygrave (Ed.), *The portable MBA in entrepreneurship* (pp. 1–26). New York: John Wiley.

Díaz de León, E.D. & Guild, P.D. (2003). Using repertory grid to identify intangibles in business plans. *Venture Capital, 5,* 135–160.

Dixon, R. (1991). Venture capitalists and the appraisal of investments. *OMEGA: International Journal of Management Science, 19,* 333–344.

Franke, N., Gruber, M., Harhoff, D., & Henkel, J. (2006). What you are is what you like—Similarity biases in venture capitalists' evaluations of start-up teams. *Journal of Business Venturing, 21*, 802–826.

Gagné, R.M. & Glaser, R. (1987). Foundations in learning research. In R.M. Gagné (Ed.), *Instructional technology: Foundations* (pp. 49–84). Hillsdale, NJ: Lawrence Erlbaum.

Gobbo, C. & Chi, M.T.H. (1986). How knowledge is structured and used by expert and novice children. *Cognitive Development, 1*, 221–237.

Gorman, M. & Sahlman, W.A. (1989). What do venture capitalists do? *Journal of Business Venturing, 4*, 231–248.

Goslin, L.N. & Barge, B. (1986). Entrepreneurial qualities considered in venture capital support. In R. Ronstadt, J.A. Hornaday, R. Petersen, & K.H. Vesper (Eds.), *Frontiers of entrepreneurship research* (pp. 366–377). Wellesley, MA: Babson College.

Hall, J. & Hofer, C. (1993). Venture capitalists' decision making criteria and new venture evaluation. *Journal of Business Venturing, 8*, 25–42.

Hausman, J.A. & Ruud, P.A. (1987). Specifying and testing econometric models for rank-ordered data. *Journal of Econometrics, 34*, 83–104.

Knowlton, B. (1997). Declarative and nondeclarative knowledge: Insights from cognitive neuroscience. In K. Lamberts & D. Shanks (Eds.), *Knowledge, concepts and categories* (pp. 215–246). Cambridge, MA: MIT Press.

Kozmetsky, G., Gill, M.D., Jr., & Smilor, R.W. (Eds.). (1985). *Financing and managing fast-growth companies: The venture capital process.* Lexington, MA: Lexington Books.

Larkin, J.H., McDermott, J., Simon, D.P., & Simon, H.A. (1980). Expert and novice performance in solving physics problems. *Science, 208*, 1335–1342.

Lurigio, A.J. & Carroll, J.S. (1985). Probation officers' schemata of offenders: Content, development, and impact on treatment decisions. *Journal of Personality and Social Psychology, 48*, 1112–1186.

MacMillan, I.C., Siegel, R., & Subba Narasimha, P.N. (1985). Criteria used by venture capitalists to evaluate new venture proposals. *Journal of Business Venturing, 1*, 119–128.

MacMillan, I.C., Zemann, L., & Subbanarasimha, P.N. (1987). Criteria distinguishing successful from unsuccessful ventures in the venture screening process. *Journal of Business Venturing, 2*, 123–137.

Marden, J.I. (1995). *Analyzing and modeling rank data.* London: Chapman & Hall.

Matlin, M.W. (2005). *Cognition* (6th ed.). New York: John Wiley & Sons.

Muzyka, D., Birley, S., & Leleux, B. (1996). Trade-offs in the investment decisions of European venture capitalists. *Journal of Business Venturing, 11*, 273–287.

Poindexter, J. (1976). *The efficiency of financial markets: The venture capital case.* Unpublished doctoral dissertation, New York University.

Rea, R.H. (1989). Factors affecting success and failure of seed capital/start-up negotiations. *Journal of Business Venturing, 4*, 149–158.

Riquelme, H. & Rickards, T. (1992). Hybrid conjoint analysis: An estimation probe in new venture decisions. *Journal of Business Venturing, 7*, 505–518.

Robinson, R. (1987). Emerging strategies in the venture capital industry. *Journal of Business Venturing, 2,* 53–77.

Roberts, E.B. (1991). *Entrepreneurs in high-technology—Lessons from MIT and beyond.* New York: Oxford University Press.

Sandberg, W.R., Schweiger, D.M., & Hofer, C.W. (1988). The use of verbal protocols in determining venture capitalists' decision processes. *Entrepreneurship Theory and Practice, 12*(Winter), 8–20.

Shepherd, D. (1999). Venture capitalists' introspection: A comparison of "in use" and "espoused" decision policies. *Journal of Small Business Management, 27,* 76–87.

Shepherd, D.A., Ettenson, R., & Crouch, A. (2000). New venture strategy and profitability: A venture capitalist's assessment. *Journal of Business Venturing, 15,* 449–467.

Shepherd, D.A. & Zacharakis, A. (1999). Conjoint analysis: A new methodological approach for researching the decision policies of venture capitalists. *Venture Capital, 1,* 197–217.

Shepherd, D.A. & Zacharakis, A.L. (2002). Venture capitalists' expertise: A call for research into decision aids and cognitive feedback. *Journal of Business Venturing, 17,* 1–20.

Shepherd, D.A., Zacharakis, A.L., & Baron. R.A. (2003). VCs' decision processes: Evidence suggesting more experience may not always be better. *Journal of Business Venturing, 18,* 381–401.

Shrader, R.C., Steier, L., McDougall, P.P., & Oviatt, B.M. (1997). Venture Capital and Characteristics of New Venture IPOs. In A.C. Cooper, J.A. Hornaday, & K.H. Vesper (Eds.), *Frontiers of Entrepreneurship Research* (pp. 513–524). Wellesley, MA: Babson College.

Siegel, R., Siegel, E., & MacMillan, I.C. (1993). Characteristics distinguishing high-growth ventures. *Journal of Business Venturing, 8,* 169–180.

Silva, J. (2004). Venture capitalists' decision-making in small equity markets: A case study using participant observation. *Venture Capital, 6,* 125–145.

Smart, G.H. (1999). Management assessment methods in venture capital: An empirical analysis of human capital valuation. *Venture Capital, 1,* 59–82.

Spence, M.T. & Brucks, M. (1997). The moderating effects of problem characteristics on experts' and novices judgments. *Journal of Marketing Research, 34,* 233–247.

Timmons, J.A. & Sapienza, H.J. (1992). Venture capital: The decade ahead. In D.L. Sexton & J.D. Kasarda (Eds.), *The state of the art of entrepreneurship* (pp. 402–437). Boston: PWS-Kent.

Tyebjee, T. & Bruno, A. (1981). Venture capital decision making: Preliminary results from three empirical studies. In K.H. Vesper (Ed.), *Frontiers of Entrepreneurial Research* (pp. 281–320). Wellesley, MA: Babson College.

Tyebjee, T.T. & Bruno, A.V. (1984). A model of venture capitalists investment activity. *Management Science, 30,* 1051–1066.

Wells, W.A. (1974). *Venture capital decision making.* Unpublished doctoral dissertation, Carnegie Mellon University, Pittsburgh, PA.

Zacharakis, A.L. & Meyer, D.G. (1998). A lack of insight: Do venture capitalists really understand their own decision process? *Journal of Business Venturing, 13,* 57–76.

Zacharakis, A.L. & Meyer, D.G. (2000). The potential of actuarial decision models: Can they improve the venture capital investment decision? *Journal of Business Venturing, 15,* 323–346.

Zopounidis, C. (1994). Venture capital modeling: Evaluation criteria for the appraisal of investments. *The Financier ACMT, 1*, 54–64.

Nikolaus Franke is Professor of Entrepreneurship and Innovation at Vienna University of Economics and Business Administration.

Marc Gruber is Assistant Professor of Entrepreneurship and Technology Commercialization at Ecole Polytechnique Fédérale de Lausanne (EPFL), College of Management of Technology.

Dietmar Harhoff is Professor of Innovation Research, Technology Management and Entrepreneurship at Ludwig-Maximilians University Munich and Research Fellow at the Centre for Economic Policy Research (CEPR), London.

Joachim Henkel is Professor of Technology and Innovation Management at Technical University of Munich and Affiliate at the Centre for Economic Policy Research (CEPR), London.

The authors thank Dr. Karin Hoisl and David Riessner for research assistance. Furthermore, the helpful suggestions of two anonymous reviewers and the Editor James J. Chrisman are gratefully acknowledged.

[5]

1042-2587
© 2006 by
Baylor University

Entrepreneurial Team Development in Academic Spinouts: An Examination of Team Heterogeneity

Iris Vanaelst
Bart Clarysse
Mike Wright
Andy Lockett
Nathalie Moray
Rosette S'Jegers

This article examines the dynamics of entrepreneurial teams as they evolve through the different stages of a spin-out process. Using a unique, hand-collected set of data covering all team members in 10 cases, an in-depth analysis of the heterogeneity of team members' experience and perception of the strategic orientation needed to attain different milestones in the spin-out process was performed. Our findings suggest that teams evolve over time and change in composition, and therefore, they cannot be studied as immutable entities. At the start of the venture formation, we introduced a new team role, the privileged witness, potentially specific for spinouts. Analysis of the teams indicates that the team's heterogeneity changes as it evolves through the different stages of the spin-out process. In particular, we found that new team members brought in different kinds of experience; however, they did not introduce a different view on doing business from the initial team members.

Introduction

Academic spinouts emerge out of a university or a research institute (Clarysse et al., 2005). At the core of every spinout lies research and know-how that can be commercialized through the creation of a new venture. The decision to create a spinout challenges the researchers since they have to enter a business community that is different from the scientific one in which they have been active. Many articles that deal with university–industry relations have already emphasized the different rules and norms that prevail in business and academic or research environments (Van Dierdonck, Debackere, & Engelen, 1990). A first step in the decision to startup a spinout is usually the screening of the

Please send correspondence to: Iris Vanaelst, e-mail: Iris.Vanaelst@vub.ac.be at Vrije Universiteit Brussel, Department of Business Economics and Strategic Management, Pleinlaan 2, 1050 Brussels.

different resources needed for a successful launch of the venture (Vohora, Wright, & Lockett, 2004; Clarysse & Moray, 2004). Financial and human resources often seem to be the most critical (Moray & Clarysse, 2005), while technological resources are usually in place. As shown by Heirman and Clarysse (2004), financial and human resources tend to be closely interrelated. When new ventures apply for early stage venture capital funds, the question of a well-balanced team with sufficient business experience is often raised by the potential investors to evaluate a project (MacMillan, Siegel, & Narasimha, 1985; MacMillan, Zemann, & Subbanarasimha, 1987; Muzyka, Birley, & Leleux, 1996). With the venture capital literature, we may therefore conclude that teams are an important factor in decisive entrepreneurial events such as raising venture capital. Venture capitalists place considerable emphasis on founding teams. But is there scientific support for a relationship between teams and firm performance?

The relationship between teams and firm performance has been examined in the literature on the "upper-echelon perspective" (Hambrick & Mason, 1984). We build on the upper-echelon perspective to analyze the effects of team dynamics on new venture performance of academic spinouts. A key difference between the large firms, where much of the upper-echelon research has been conducted, and spinouts is that the former are already established firms, whereas the latter are emerging ventures passing through the various stages to becoming an established entity. Although some have noted that in entrepreneurial team building, the founding core may have difficulties accommodating later arrivals, who often feel excluded from the founding group, (Ratcheva & Vyakarnam, 2001), little research has systematically examined the dynamics of new venture teams in general (Ucbasaran, Lockett, Wright, & Westhead, 2003), and there is an absence of such analysis in the context of academic spinouts. Filling this research gap is important in helping to address policy and research questions concerning the ability of academic spinouts to create wealth (Lambert, 2003). Therefore, our research question is: *how do entrepreneurial teams evolve over the different stages of a spin-out process?* The contribution of our research, therefore, lies in the fact that we take a dynamic team perspective, allowing for the identification of the effects of team heterogeneity on new venture performance, in the specific case of the development process of academic spinouts. In this article, venture performance is described in terms of reaching well-defined entrepreneurial events in the spin-out process and differs from research that considers venture performance as a static concept, defined in terms of "success" or "growth" at a certain moment in time.

This article proceeds along the following lines. First, we outline the theoretical background to the article in relation to teams, spin-out processes and shared cognition. Second, we discuss the research design data method of data collection that we employed in the study. Third, we present an analysis of the cases. Finally, we conclude and discuss our findings.

Theoretical Background

In this section, we present our definition of entrepreneurial teams and consider the link between team structure and performance.

Defining Entrepreneurial Teams

There has been considerable debate as to what exactly is meant by an "entrepreneurial team." Kamm, Schuman, Seeger, and Nurick (1990) define entrepreneurial teams as "two or more individuals who jointly establish a firm in which they have a financial interest" (Kamm et al., 1990, p. 7). Gartner, Shaver, Gatewood, and Katz (1994) broaden this definition to cover those individuals who have direct influence on strategic choice. Ensley, Carland, and Carland (1998) combine both delineations by stating that individuals have to fulfill three criteria in order to be considered members of the entrepreneurial team: they (1) have jointly establish a firm; (2) have a financial interest; and (3) have a direct influence on the strategic choice of the firm. Other researchers have made the equity stake condition stricter and have imposed a minimum equity stake before one can be considered a member of the entrepreneurial team (Ucbasaran et al., 2003).

Part of the definitional confusion is related to the fact that entrepreneurial teams are too often investigated within a static framework. Determining equity stakes and management positions is typically very much focused around the time of the formal incorporation of the venture. These studies therefore often implicitly neglect the evolutionary aspects of entrepreneurial team formation and development. Recent research has attempted to tackle this problem and has studied team entry and exit (Ucbasaran et al., 2003). Along the lines of this research, our study originates from the hypothesis that the concept "team" is evolving rather than static. In this respect, teams in spinouts differ markedly from those in established businesses.

To introduce the dynamic component in spin-out teams, we draw on the work of Vohora et al. (2004) and Clarysse and Moray (2004), who investigated the entrepreneurial events of the spin-out process in detail. In particular, these authors found that creating a spinout is a long process. Often, the legal startup of the spinout happens quite late in the development of the firm since parent institutes tend to incubate these companies over a considerable period. As this legal foundation is postponed until all elements such as external capital, customer identification, team, etc., are in place, the legal incorporation is often an important entrepreneurial event. We thus differentiate between the teams of spinouts that were not yet legally established, which we identify as pre-startup teams, and teams of spinouts that were already legally established, which we refer to as post-startup teams. Despite the differences in teams that we expect to find in these two phases of venture formation, we are interested in a common team denominator, which is the involvement of the team members in the core strategic decisions of the venture.

For the pre-startup teams, we operationalize the entrepreneurial team definition by asking the leading researcher to identify the individuals taking the core strategic decisions in the creation of the spinout. By definition, the core researchers are part of this strategic decision-making process. However, in addition to the researchers, representatives of the parent institute are involved in the creation of the spinout. In most cases, this role is performed by their technology transfer officers (TTO). In some cases, outsiders with no formal link to the parent institute can also be attracted to actively pursue the creation of the spinout. Often, these external parties are attracted to the creation of the spinout because they have business experience. Previous research (Franklin, Wright, & Lockett, 2001; Lockett, Wright, & Franklin, 2003) termed these external actors as "surrogate entrepreneurs." According to these authors, a surrogate entrepreneur is an outsider with commercial experience, who may be attracted to work together with the researchers to develop the venture. Usually, in our study, the entrepreneurial pre-startup teams consist of the key researchers and the surrogate entrepreneurs.

For the post-startup spinouts, we follow the argument of Fama and Jensen (1983) that the separation of decision and risk-bearing functions observed in large corporations is common to other organizations. Moreover, an organization's decision process consists of decision management (initiation and implementation) and decision control (ratification and monitoring). The common apex of the decision control systems of organizations, in which decision agents do not bear a major share of the wealth effects of their decisions, is a board of directors that ratifies and monitors important decisions and chooses, dismisses, and rewards important decision agents. Therefore, we operationalized the entrepreneurial team definition by asking the chief executive officer (CEO) or founder to identify the important decision agents. Usually, team members of the post-startup spinout, as indicated by the CEO as taking the core strategic decisions, were members of the management committee and the founders.

Team Structure and Performance

Existing research, as previously indicated, has linked teams to firm performance under the upper-echelon perspective. In the upper-echelon perspective, top management team characteristics, such as psychological characteristics, cognitive base, and observable characteristics, like age and functional expertise, determine strategic choices. The environmental factors surrounding the firm, upper-echelon characteristics, and the strategic choices made by the top management team interact to determine organizational performance levels (Hambrick & Mason, 1984). Translated to entrepreneurial teams, these findings suggest that changes in the composition and hence, characteristics of the team, may have an impact on the strategic choices made by the entrepreneurial team and ultimately, on the venture performance.

Ensley and Pearce (2001) build on this upper-echelon perspective to develop a theoretical framework that links shared strategic cognition in top management teams to group process and new venture performance. They define shared cognition in top management teams as the extent to which strategic mental models held in the hearts and minds of the top management team members overlap or agree. Their theoretical model suggests that cohesion impacts conflict, conflict impacts shared strategic cognition, and shared strategic cognition impacts firm performance. According to these authors, conflict is a process that teams go through to make decisions, to take action, and to create cognitive schema. They argue that conflict is the process of creating the overlap in strategic cognitive maps and is therefore a key group process in the development of shared strategic cognition. As group processes most directly relate to shared cognition, Ensley and Pearce (2001) examine cognitive and affective conflict in top management teams. According to Amason and Sapienza (1997) cognitive conflict is task-oriented disagreement arising from differences in perspective and may be beneficial. In contrast, affective conflict is individual-oriented disagreement arising from personal disaffection and may be detrimental to the development of the venture. Eisenhardt, Kahwajy, and Bourgeois (1997) also analyze the key elements of managing constructive conflict to create collaboration between top management teams. The results of Ensley and Pearce (2001) indicate that the group processes leading to the development of shared strategic cognition, cognitive, and affective conflict, are more important than the outcome of shared strategic cognition in terms of predicting organizational performance.

Another stream of research, positioned within the literature on organizational culture, has, in a parallel way, analyzed the underlying dimensions of what Ensley and Pearce (2001) have referred to as shared cognition. This work is based on Quinn's (1988) competing values model (1988). In particular, Van Muijen et al. (1999) identify four extreme types of orientation toward how a team should ideally work. Each team member individually has his own perception on how a team should ideally operate in order to realize its goals. The sum of each team member's individual orientation can be seen as the "organizational culture" of the entire team. The four different extremes are based upon two underlying dimensions: the opposite poles of flexibility versus control form the first dimension. The second dimension represents the internal versus external focus of the team members. (Van Muijen et al., 1999). A combination of these two dimensions results in four different types of orientation. Team members who are internal oriented but are very flexible are identified as mainly *support oriented*. They find concepts such as participation, cooperation, people based, mutual trust, team spirit, and individual growth very important. Communication is often verbal and informal. Employees are encouraged to bring ideas about their work and feelings about each other forward. Decisions are often made through informal contacts. Team loyalty is very much appreciated by these team members. However, team members who are internal oriented, but tend to focus on control, are *rules oriented*. They find respect for authority, rationality of procedures, and division of work important. Communication is often written and top-down. The structure is hierarchical and power is based on formal authority. Team members who tend to focus on control, but are external oriented are mainly *goal oriented*. They find concepts as rationality, performance indicators, accomplishment, accountability, and contingent reward very important. Team members who are external oriented but are flexible are considered to be mainly *innovation oriented*. Searching for new information in the environment, creativity, openness to change, experimentation and anticipation are much appreciated by these team members. Control is neither possible nor required, and management expects commitment and involvement of employees.

Research Design

The concepts outlined in the previous section provide the framework for the analysis of team dynamics in academic spin-out companies. Since entrepreneurial team formation and development remains a complex and largely underexplored area, we were unable to formulate clear-cut hypotheses *ex ante*. Instead, we adopt an inductive multiple-case research design. This enables a replication logic in which the cases are treated as a series of independent experiments (Yin, 1994). Multiple cases are generally regarded as more robust than single case studies in that comparisons across cases allow for a higher validity in the development of findings and a consideration of their context dependency (Yin, 1994). The level of analysis is the spin-out process and the unit of analysis is the entrepreneurial team, as people enter and exit the project/new venture at different stages.

Case Selection

The research comprises a detailed field study of 10 academic spin-out projects located in Flanders. Flanders is a small, export-intensive economy located in the northern part of Belgium. It is considered to be an emerging high-tech region, experiencing a fast process of convergence between old and new technologies and thereby improving its competitive position (Cantwell & Iammarino, 2001).

Flanders has a population of 6 million and about two researchers per 1,000 inhabitants (OECD, 2003). In total, there are nine public research organizations of which three are research institutes (IMEC, VIB and VITO)[1] and six are universities (UG, VUB, KUL,

---

1. IMEC, Inter University MicroElectronics Center; VIB, Flemish Institute for Biotechnology; VITO, Flemish Institute for Technological Research.

LUC, UA and KUB)[2]. In total, 93 companies emerged from Flemish Public Research Organizations from 1991 to 2002. The majority of the population of academic ventures are pure spinouts (56% or 52 companies), i.e., companies that started their activities on the basis of a formal transfer of technology from the parent institute. The academic startups that started their activities on the basis of university research, but without formal transfer of technology at the time of founding, represent almost 41% of the total (n = 38). Of the 93 starters, almost 70% emerged from the universities (Moray, 2004).

The commercialization of research through the creation of a spinout takes a long time (Vohora et al., 2004); (Clarysse & Moray, 2004). A longitudinal study of spin-out processes was, however, beyond the available resources of our study. Instead, a longitudinal-processual approach was adopted (Burgelman, 1983; Pettigrew, 1979). We selected 10 projects or new ventures that were stratified in particular stages of their development in the spin-out process to be included in our analysis. Vohora et al. (2004) identify five phases which spinouts encounter in their development: (1) research phase, (2) opportunity framing phase, (3) preorganization phase, (4) reorientation phase, and (5) sustainable returns phase. At the interstices between the different phases of development, they identify four critical junctures that spin-out companies need to overcome if they are to succeed: opportunity recognition, entrepreneurial commitment, credibility, and sustainability. Clarysse and Moray (2004) came to a similar classification of stages: a research phase, a phase during which the project prepares itself to formally incorporate into a spinout, and a stage during which external capitalization takes place. Vohora et al. (2004) add a phase, including the time frame during which second and third capital injections take place. We operationalized their delineation of the different stages in the spin-out process by taking their research phase and opportunity-framing phase together as the first phase in the spin-out process, while using a comparable delineation for the other successive developmental phases. More in particular, we identified the following four phases: (1) research commercialization and opportunity screening, (2) the organization-in-gestation phase, (3) proof of viability of the newly established venture, and (4) the maturity phase, as depicted in Figure 1. Following Vohora et al. (2004), we stress that each venture must pass through the previous phase in order to progress to the next one, but each phase involves an iterative, nonlinear process of development in which there may be a need to revisit some of the earlier decisions and activities. This is consistent with other recent research by Druilhe and Garnsey (2004) which suggests that the phases that a spinout passes through are characterized by the modification of business models in the light of the maturity of the entrepreneurs' initial resources and their improving knowledge of resources and opportunities.

Cases were selected on the basis of these four predefined stages, with at least two cases selected for each stage (Eisenhardt, 1989). The projects in the first two stages were selected based on contacts with technology transfer offices, which helped us to obtain some understanding of which projects seemed to be potential spin-out opportunities. The companies in the last two stages were selected based on a listing of spinouts in Flanders.[3] To discern whether the new ventures showed proof of viability or had reached maturity the founders/CEOs were contacted. Table 1 gives an overview of the sample used in our study.

For the first phase, we selected teams that were working on a research project and saw a market opportunity. Teams that had got in touch with the TTO in order to protect their intellectual property and that had recently filed or obtained a patent were selected. At the

---

2. UG, Ghent University; VUB, Vrije Universiteit Brussel; KUL, Katholieke Universiteit Leuven; LUC, Limburgs Universitair Centrum; UA, Universiteit Antwerpen; KUB, Katholieke Universiteit Brussel.
3. Steunpunt Ondernemingen, Ondernemerschap en Innovatie, 2004.

Figure 1

Phases in the Spin-Out Process

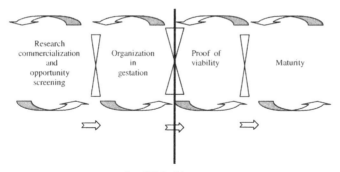

| Research commercialization and opportunity screening | Organization in gestation | Proof of viability | Maturity |

Legal birth of the new venture

time of the study, these teams were considering the options that they had to commercialize their intellectual property. Pursuing a spin-out trajectory was only one option being considered.

The cases used to analyze the second phase have identified a market opportunity and have decided to create a spinout. In the third phase, teams are considered that have legally founded a new venture and have brought together the necessary resources to develop it. Attracting financial resources is a central issue in this phase.

Ventures showing persistence were identified as cases in the maturity phase. The teams in this phase have proven their viability and have moved to building up maturity and sustainability. These ventures have built up credibility outside the scientific community and have been able to attract additional resources, among others financial ones, to carry out their growth.

Data Collection

Data were collected using different methods and tools. For each selected team, the contacts were highly personalized, leading to first-hand data on the team and ensuring a high response rate (Nicolaou & Birley, 2003). First, for the projects still located at the university, the head of the research team was contacted to provide data on the research and on the team involved. Our questionnaire was handed to the head of the research team and appointments were made to collect the questionnaires. For each selected formally incorporated venture, either the founder or CEO was asked about the startup history of the firm and particularly how the team evolved over time. This helped us to understand the context of how teams were formed and evolved. During these interviews we also asked for the exit/entry dates of individuals involved (Ucbasaran et al., 2003). The founder or CEO was handed the questionnaire and appointments were made to collect the questionnaires.

Second, for those teams still in the project stage, all members of the research team were asked to fill out the questionnaire. Each member of the management team of the

Table 1

Case Description Summary

Phase in spin-out process at present	Spin-out project/venture name	Startup	Technology	Starting capital	Parent organization	Link with parent
Research commercialization and opportunity screening	Project 1	Not yet	Fast fluids	Not available yet	VUB[1]	Still at university: Patent filed
	Project 2	Not yet	Snails	Not available yet	UG	Still at university: Patent filed
Organization in gestation	Project 3	Not yet	Plasma technology	Not available yet	UG	Still at university: Patent filed
	Project 4	Not yet	Chip-integrated circuit	Not available yet	VUB	Still at university: Patent filed
Proof of viability	Firm 1	2001	Toxins detection in food	375.000€	UG	Patent brought in
	Firm 2	2001	Inorganic phosphate cement production	62.000€	VUB	Exclusive license and royalties payment
	Firm 3	2002	In vitro bioassay systems	450.000€	VUB	Exclusive license
	Firm 4	2002	Identification of novel active molecules	600.000€	IMEC	Patents brought in
Maturity	Firm 5	1992	Simulations of streams of substances	62.000€	VUB	Royalties payment
	Firm 6	2000	Develops infrared image sensors	3.75mio€	IMEC	Exclusive license

VUB, Vrije Universiteit Brussel; UG, Ghent University; IMEC, Inter University MicroElectronics Center.

formally incorporated ventures was asked to fill out the questionnaire. This individual questionnaire consisted of two parts. The first part asked for background information, such as education and experience. The second part was aimed at the identification of the personal orientation required to realize venture success. This questionnaire was based on the Focus questionnaire of Van Muijen et al. (1999).

Third, we collected background information on all individuals entering and exiting the team in terms of age, gender, education, experience, etc. This allowed us to evaluate the experiential diversity of the team at the different stages during the spin-out process.

The number of persons filling out this survey ranged from two to eight, depending on the phase in which the project/venture was positioned (a venture that has reached maturity, is older and more prone to team turnover). It should be stressed, however, that instead of one representative responding on group features, all the members of the entrepreneurial team were involved in our study. In some cases, the researchers' patience was put to the test in their efforts to urge the team members to fill in the questionnaire.

For the mature projects, we followed Burgelman's approach (1983) and reconstructed the life histories of the companies, focusing on team formation, development, and turnover. For each phase, we combined both cross-sectional analysis (experiential and cultural diversity) and retrospective analysis (cultural diversity and turnover), resulting in a higher external validity.

As previously noted, the starting point of our research is that teams are not immutable entities but evolve over time and over the different stages of the spin-out process. Changes in the composition of the teams bring about changes in their characteristics. We conjecture that when individuals join a team at some stage in the spin-out process, they bring more heterogeneity to the team. Moreover, this increased heterogeneity occurs on two levels: the experience available in the team and the perception among the team members of the needed strategic orientation in order to realize new venture success.

Following Ucbasaran et al. (2003), Teachman's (1980) scale was used to measure heterogeneity of categorical variables: $(H) = -\Sigma P_i (\ln P_i)$. This measure takes into account how team members are distributed among the different categories of a variable. The total number of categories of a variable equals n, and P_i is the fraction of team members falling into each category. For experience heterogeneity, the categories taken into account were (1) research and development, (2) marketing, (3) management, (4) consulting and engineering, and (5) other experience (e.g., legal). In the case of heterogeneity of entrepreneurial experience, yes (1) and no (0) were used.

We assume that the further along the spin-out process a team is, the more heterogeneous the team's perceptions of the strategic orientation necessary to realize new venture success will be. It should, however, be stressed that we did not aim to identify the most optimal strategic orientation for venture success. For the identification of the heterogeneity in the perceived strategic orientation needed for new venture success, a questionnaire based on the research of Van Muijen et al. (1999) was used.

The literature previously cited has taken a very simplistic view of venture performance, defining it as "success" or "growth" at a certain point in time. As such, a snapshot is taken of the team composition at that point, and a link is made with performance. However, as noted earlier, teams are not a static concept (Ucbasaran et al., 2003). Also, success is not a static concept. Heirman and Clarysse (2004) describe success of a venture in terms of reaching a well-defined number of "entrepreneurial events." The success of a startup can, for instance, involve being able to attract venture capital, whereas the success of a three-year-old venture can mean reaching the break-even point. In this article, success of a venture is described in terms of reaching well-defined entrepreneurial events in the spin-out process, i.e., each of the four phases of development identified earlier.

Findings

This section analyzes how the entrepreneurial teams evolved over the different stages of the spin-out process. A detailed description of the different team features as they evolve through the different phases of the spin-out process can be found in Table 2. In taking a team focus in each phase in the development of a spinout, the team dynamics were identified. Our research found that the composition of the team evolves as the different phases in the development of the spinout are reached. Moreover, our study indicates that team turnover is linked with the different entrepreneurial events in the spin-out process. The dynamics of entry and exit are a result of the ambition of the team to attain the next milestone in the evolution of the venture. Before paying attention to the drivers of team entry and exit, we first consider the evolution of the team through the different phases of the spin-out process and its implications for the concept "team."

Team Evolution

In Figure 2, team evolution is identified for each of the different phases in the development of spinouts. Figure 2 shows that the concept "team" evolves through the different entrepreneurial events in the spin-out process.

Phase 1. At the core of every spinout lies research. Research activities are mostly performed within a department or a research team. In order to strengthen their research, researchers get in touch with peers in their scientific community. This may even result in joint research projects. At some point, researchers may find it necessary to protect their intellectual property when they want to bring their research results to society as a whole. In order to do, so they get in touch with the TTO who guides the researchers through the procedures for filing patents. These contacts with the TTO are often a way to get information on how to commercialize the intellectual property built up within the research team. As mentioned earlier, establishing a spinout is only one trajectory through which research can be commercialized. When a market opportunity is identified, the researchers are surrounded by peers, the TTO, and coaches. For the screening of the market opportunity and in order to map out potential market opportunities, the researchers may rely on coaches or consultants. At this stage, these people take on an advisory function in the spin-out trajectory. We call these people *privileged witnesses* because their involvement in the creation of the spinout implies a certain distance from the creation activities. The researchers and the privileged witnesses form together the *prefounding team.* However, in this phase of the spinout, the researchers play an active leading role in the team, while the privileged witnesses tend to perform a coaching role. In some cases, the TTO of the parent organization[4] initiates the screening of the market opportunity and opts for a commercialization trajectory through a spinout.

Phase 2. Once the decision is taken to go for the creation of a new venture, the prefounding team evolves to the second phase in the spinout's development. In this phase, the researchers have made the decision to pursue the creation of a spinout. However, not all researchers actively aspire to spin out a new venture and some will leave the prefounding team, typically opting to pursue a full academic career. In some cases, the researchers or the TTOs may find it necessary to attract a surrogate entrepreneur. This surrogate

---

4. For an in-depth analysis of IMEC, see Moray and Clarysse (2005).

Figure 2

Team Evolution

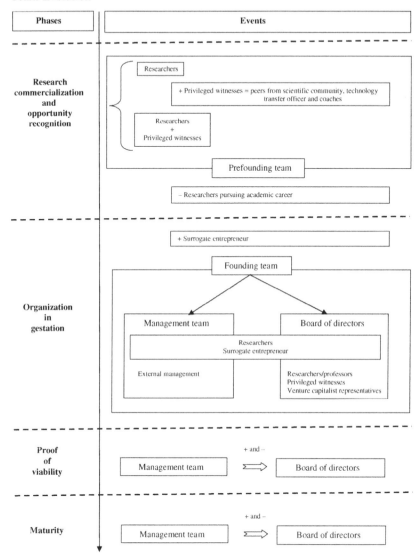

Table 2

Team Turnover Features in the Different Phases of the Spin-Out Process

Case study	Research commercialization and opportunity screening	Organization in gestation	Proof of viability	Maturity
Project 1	Team of eight researchers Privileged witness: TTO Contacts with potential industrial partners are positive, but main focus lies on strengthening research.	The spinout has not yet entered this phase.	The spinout has not yet entered this phase.	The spinout has not yet entered this phase.
Project 2	Team of three researchers Privileged witness: TTO and coach Research commercialization through the creation of a spinout was abandoned because of high perceived risk and limited market.	The spinout has not yet entered this phase.	The spinout has not yet entered this phase.	The spinout has not yet entered this phase.
Project 3	Team of two researchers Privileged witness: TTO and coach	A business developer has entered the team, who would become the manager of the spinout. The spinout is still in gestation, as it was decided to perform more research in cooperation with the textile industry.	The spinout has not yet entered this phase.	The spinout has not yet entered this phase.
Project 4	Team of three researchers Privileged witness: TTO	Two part-time business developers are attracted to screen the market opportunity and to prepare the business plan. Only one business developer has yet formally entered the team. He will become the CEO of the new venture.	The spinout has not yet entered this phase.	The spinout has not yet entered this phase.

Firm 1	Team of three researchers Privileged witness: TTO and coach	A surrogate entrepreneur enters the team and is the driving force behind the creation of the new venture. He becomes the CEO.	The CEO exits the new venture. The original leader of the research team becomes the interim CEO. Shortly afterwards, a new CEO enters the team. Besides, a business developer enters the team.	The spinout has not yet entered this phase.
Firm 2	Team of multiple researchers. Privileged witness: TTO	The head of the research department sees several market opportunities. He teams up with a colleague researcher. Besides, a surrogate entrepreneur and a business developer enter the team to pursue these opportunities.	One of the original founders exits the team shortly after the legal establishment of the new venture.	The spinout has not yet entered this phase.
Firm 3	Team of two researchers Privileged witness: TTO	A privileged witness, a coach, is attracted to advice on the creation of the new venture.	One of the researchers becomes the CEO. The other researcher stays at the university, is not a member of the management team, but is a member of the scientific advisory board. A business developer enters the team.	The spinout has not yet entered this phase.
Firm 4	Team of multiple researchers. Privileged witness: TTO and coach	Besides the main researcher, two more people are attracted by the parent institute to create an incubation venture. One team member exits before the spinout becomes established as the current legal entity.	An extra manager enters the team to enforce the remaining two founders in the management team.	The spinout has not yet entered this phase.
Firm 5	Head of research department takes the lead in the screen market opportunities.	Head of research department takes the lead in the creation of the new venture.	The attraction of venture capital is translated into external management entering the team. Besides, the head of the research department becomes the president. An employee becomes the general manager.	Members of the management team obtain shares in the venture.
Firm 6	Team of multiple researchers at the parent organization who are still working as researchers at the parent institute. Privileged witness: TTO and coach	Parent organization is the driving force behind spinout: attraction of four surrogate entrepreneurs to build spin-out organization	The four surrogate entrepreneurs form the management team.	One founder-surrogate entrepreneur exits the team, his tasks are taken over by one of the remaining managers.

TTO, technology transfer officer.

entrepreneur plays an active and leading role in the legal establishment of the new venture. The researchers and the surrogate entrepreneurs actively pursue the establishment of the new venture and are therefore considered as the *founding team*.

Once the new venture is legally established, two major teams come into existence: the management team and the board of directors. The researchers may be a member of the management team or the board of directors, or both. In most cases, the researchers are members of the management team and the board. This situation is comparable for the surrogate entrepreneur. The privileged witnesses from the first phase, the TTO and the peers from the scientific community, may have a seat on the board but are less likely to be in the management team. In this phase, their role is more formalized since the interests they protect are more pronounced. The TTO represents the research institute or university who brought in intellectual property, and the peers may continue their advisory function as a member of the board of directors or the scientific board. Other members of the board of directors can be the coaches from the previous phase in the development, who bring in counseling in exchange for equity. However, the board of directors may include representatives from financial partners like venture capitalists or seed funds from the university or research institute.

Phase 3. In the third phase, the management team and the board strive together to strengthen the viability of the new venture. In order to do so, it may be necessary to attract additional external financial resources through venture capitalists. This may imply a change in the composition of the board. Also, a change in the composition of the management team may take place, as the venture capitalists may appoint a CEO or a business developer. However, some financial partners may withdraw from the new venture and, accordingly, their representatives leave the board. Furthermore, members of the management may obtain shares and may even take their seat on the board. Usually, these members are external people attracted into the venture, who initially have options or warrants to become shareholders after a while and then eventually even take up a seat in the board.

Phase 4. In order to grow into maturity, the new venture may have to attract additional financial resources through several rounds of venture capital. This may have implications for the board as well as the management as previously described.

When the evolution of the teams over the different phases of the spin-out process is considered and the different roles performed by the team members are analyzed in depth, our cases indicate that for post-startups teams, the marking out of the different roles is more pronounced than for pre-startup teams. This is reinforced by the fact that in post-startups teams, more formal terms are used to indicate the roles that are performed within the team: the pre-startup researcher, who appeared to combine different roles at the same time, becomes the CEO, with (apparently) a clear-cut role. The role of the privileged witnesses maintains its advisory character throughout the spin-out process, but becomes formalized with the establishment of the board: TTOs take their seat on the board of directors, making their commitment to the spinout formal.

To summarize, our in-depth case analysis shows that the dynamics of the team taking the new venture from research to a mature growing firm call for clear distinctive team concepts. In our study, the prefounding team, being the researchers taking the lead in the spin-out process, guided by privileged witnesses (e.g., the TTO, peers, and coaches) identify together the market opportunity. Afterwards, surrogate entrepreneurs may be attracted. Together with the researchers, they form the founding team and actively pursue the legal establishment of the firm. Once the firm is legally created, the boundaries of the founding team disappear and evolve into two other teams which may overlap: the management team and the board. Mostly, the researchers leading the spin-out trajectory have a position in the management team and a seat on the board of directors. Others, such as the privileged witnesses, usually become members of the board of directors. The latter joins together representatives of suppliers of all human, technological, and financial resources brought together to establish the new venture, like for instance the TTO and the venture capitalists. Proving its viability and further growth into maturity is often brought back to the attraction of external financial resources, imposing a change in the composition of the board of directors and potentially the management team.

A key issue relating to team evolution is whether the people attracted into the new team bring a different experience and a way of looking at doing business to the startup. This analysis is the subject of the next section.

Changes in Team Composition

We focus on the pre-startup and the post-startup stages as the legal founding of the new venture appears to be the most important milestone in team evolution.

The size of the team does not change significantly before and after the legal founding of the new venture (Table 3). Detailed case analysis shows that some teams experience exit of team members, while other teams are reinforced by additional team members. Some teams startup with what appears to be too many founders, and some leave the team. Others startup with too few and attract some new members. Considering the impact of team changes on heterogeneity of team membership, we identify the following developments:

Experiential Heterogeneity. Teams active in the first phase of the spin-out process appear to be unbalanced in terms of experience. Their experience is highly concentrated in research and development. Teams having decided to actively pursue the creation of a spinout, however, show a broader range of experience. This is reinforced in later stages of the spin-out process. Moreover, we found that the experience of the team members is more balanced the further they move through the spin-out process, as expected.

Entrepreneurial Experience Heterogeneity. Teams in the first phase of the spin-out process, which are still deciding how to commercialize their knowledge, show a lack of entrepreneurial experience. Once the decision is taken to create a spinout, team members are attracted to the team that may have entrepreneurial experience. After the legal establishment of the firm, no clear finding on the nature of entrepreneurial experience was identified. Both extreme situations, of highly experienced and complete novice teams, were found. It is perhaps counter intuitive that complete novice teams do not attract entrepreneurial experienced people. Fully experienced startup teams more often make the choice to attract a manager who does not necessarily have entrepreneurial experience. However, the results remain inconclusive.

Cognitive Heterogeneity. We assumed that the further along the spin-out process a firm is, the larger would be cognitive heterogeneity of the team in terms of the perceived necessary strategic orientation.[5] Our assumption was that startup teams would be homogeneous, but new members would introduce another perspective on how to do business.

---

5. We examined the strategic orientation of individual team members versus the teams' strategic orientation, but no clear differences emerged; the results are therefore not reported here.

Table 3

Heterogeneity Analysis of the Team[†],[‡]

	Pre-startup Mean Median SD	Post-startup Mean Median SD
Size of team	4.5	3.5
	3.5	3
	2.3	1.2
Experiential heterogeneity	0.74	1.14
	0.74	1.17
	0.37	0.30
Entrepreneurial experience heterogeneity	0.33	0.31
	0.32	0.25
	0.38	0.35
Cognitive heterogeneity[‡]	1.24	1.27
	1.25	1.28*
	0.02	0.05
Innovation	28.13	30.04
	28.02	29.67**
	1.06	1.11
Support	28.77	28.33
	28.88	28.67
	0.63	1.79
Rules	19.45	21.23
	19.25	23.40
	2.01	4.68
Goals	27.45	29.14
	27.79	30
	1.83	2.52

$*p < 0.1$; $**p < 0.05$

[†] Mann–Whitney U test was used to identify differences between pre- and post-startup teams.

[‡] For entrepreneurial experience and cognitive heterogeneity, Teachman's scale (1980) was used.

[§] Detailed median data are included per orientation (min = 7; max = 35).

For instance, researchers tend to be support and innovation oriented, often lacking goal orientation and avoiding bureaucracy (rules orientation). We supposed, therefore, that when teams were formed further along in the process, the newly attracted members would bring in these different values. We did not, however, find that the team became more heterogeneous. Instead, post-startup teams seemed to show significantly less cognitive heterogeneity than pre-startup teams in contrast with what might be expected.

Looking at the individual orientation of the new members in the team after the legal startup of the new venture, we observe that the newcomers are also significantly innovation oriented and therefore reinforce the cognitive homogeneity of the team. This may be related to the fact that researchers usually prefer to recruit those people whose way of looking at a business is very close to theirs. As they are often leading people in their own domains, they may find it difficult to appreciate the values of people looking at the business in a totally different way. Another explanation for the reinforcement of the cognitive homogeneity of the team may be found in the involvement of the TTO in the attraction of new members to the team. These newcomers are often recruited from the TTOs' personal network of people whose way of looking at a business is likely very close to their own.

When looking in detail at the strategic orientation of the additions to the team at the different stages of the spin-out process, we expected that these people, who were mostly business developers, would show a more pronounced goal orientation for their strategic orientation than the other team members. This was not supported by our cases. In most cases, their goal orientation was similar to the other team members. Indeed, in one case, the business developed had even less goal orientation. We found that it is visionary people in particular who are attracted that get along well with the researchers at a cognitive and strategic level. However, cognitive conflict is assumed to have a positive effect on strategic decisions and performance (Amason & Sapienza, 1997; Ensley, Pearson, & Amanson, 2002). The lack of cognitive conflict in spin-out teams may explain their long incubation time and the difficulties experienced in changing their business model to obtain sustainable growth levels.

To conclude, our cases show that people attracted to the teams had different experience from the original team members, but they showed a comparable strategic orientation, leading to more cognitive homogeneity in the team.

Drivers of Team Turnover

Our research shows that irrespective of the specific phase considered, there is a clear distinction between the drivers leading to team exit and entry. The reasons why people leave the team are related to conflict. A distinction can be made between intrapersonal and interpersonal conflict as drivers leading to team exit. Intrapersonal conflict concerns one individual person. Interpersonal conflict implies different persons, in our cases, the different team members. A team exit caused by the fact that the personal ambition of a team member cannot be reconciled with the ambition of the venture is an example of an intrapersonal conflict. Conversely, a team exit caused by conflict over the strategy regarding how the firm should realize its ambition and the implementation of the strategy is an example of interpersonal conflict. Interpersonal conflict, in its turn, comprises cognitive and affective conflict. Although previous research (Amason & Sapienza, 1997); (Ensley et al., 2002) found cognitive and affective conflict to be positively related to one another, our case analysis suggests that affective conflict outweighed cognitive conflict and led to the decision to leave the team. Moreover, our case analysis indicated that when people left the team, negative aspects of conflict were a common denominator.

However, we do not suggest that the people remaining in the teams are free of any kind of conflict. Moreover, as indicated by Eisenhardt et al. (1997), conflict can be beneficial if effectively handled. We now highlight aspects of beneficial conflict in the teams. For instance, in the case of Firm 4, beneficial conflict in the team, expressed in several discussion rounds and disagreements as a result of differences in perspectives, has led to a major change in the firm's strategy. The original product was the delivery of tools that facilitate the research process in the pharmaceutical and biotech industries. However, the entrepreneurs learned that some pharmaceutical companies do not want to outsource their screening, so they decided to also sell the tool enabling firms to design their own experimental designs. Currently, Firm 4 adjusted its business plan since it became clear that also, the food industry and the chemical market can use their tool. A detailed analysis of conflict in entrepreneurial teams is an interesting research path; however, it lies beyond the scope of this study.

The drivers leading to team entry have a need for resources in common. Team entry can be the result of the attraction of additional human, technological, or financial resources. The ambition to reach the next step in a firm's life cycle may call for a reallocation of existing resources. However, the need to attract supplementary resources is far more common. For instance, when technological know-how is brought into the firm through a patent owned by the university, the TTO can become part of the team. The attraction of specific human resources, for instance, a surrogate entrepreneur, leads to addition to the team. Additional financial resources may be found internally in the firm. However, mostly they call upon external financing. This is often found by attracting venture capital. Attracting venture capital has implications for the team since the venture capitalist takes a seat on the board of directors and often appoints a new member of the management team, for instance, a CEO.

Changes in the composition of the team have an impact on the different roles performed by the team members. When people are added to the team, existing roles can be split up, refined and performed by more people or new roles were identified and filled in by the additional team member. On the other hand when people leave the team their role is transferred to one or more of the remaining team members.

Conclusions and Discussion

Using novel, hand-collected data comprising all venture team members, this article has built on the upper-echelon perspective to analyze the effects of team dynamics on new venture performance of academic spinouts. In the literature under the upper-echelon perspective, the relationship between teams and firm performance has been studied. Ensley and Pearce (2001) also build on this upper-echelon perspective to develop a theoretical framework that links shared strategic cognition in top management teams to group process and new venture performance. Another stream of research positioned within the literature on organizational culture has, in a parallel way, analyzed the underlying dimensions of what Ensley and Pearce (2001) referred to as shared strategic cognition. Based on Quinn's (1988) competing values model, Van Muijen et al. (1999) identify extreme types of orientation toward how a team should ideally work. Four different types of orientation were identified: the support, innovation, rules, and goal orientation. We used Van Muijen et al's. (1999) four orientations to measure heterogeneity in the perceived strategic orientation needed for new venture success.

We built upon these insights to perform an in-depth analysis of different spin-out teams. This analysis has led to several new insights on *how* entrepreneurship is infused into ventures through the evolution of teams as they take the spinout from research to an independent venture. At the start of the venture formation, we proposed that a new team role, which we describe as the *privileged witness*, is important in affecting the successful development of the venture. This role may be specific for spinouts, which are coached by dedicated persons at their parent organization. In line with previous studies, our research shows that not all researchers involved in the original research activities and identification of the market opportunity are actively involved in the spinout today. Indeed, the members of the team change as the spinout evolves. Our findings led us to propose that some researchers that are actively involved in the first phase of the spin-out process, where the market opportunity is identified, do not show the entrepreneurial commitment to create the spinout and leave this spin-out process before the formal creation of the spinout. That is, they make a career choice to stay with the parent organization. The decision to stay with the parent organization may be the result of the philosophy of the parent institute since the combination of full academic tenure and a position in a venture are restricted by the parent institute. Alternatively, our findings also led us to propose that researchers may leave the spinout during the phase in which the spinout has to prove its viability since they found it was taking too long. With our cases, we were able to propose that once the spinout has survived this third phase, the researchers stay and take the spinout to maturity. In other cases, surrogate entrepreneurs are attracted to set up the venture.

Second, we provide an important extension to previous research, which has tended to view team development in a static framework, in that different teams are considered in a certain moment in time, whereas we take into consideration the same teams at different moments in time, and by doing so, we take a dynamic perspective that covers different phases in the venture's development. Next to teams, success is not a static concept. We describe success in terms of reaching well-defined entrepreneurial events in the spin-out process. In particular, we analyze the team structure before and after formal startup of the venture. In line with expectations, we found that new team members brought in different kinds of experience. Especially, recruits with commercial background are appreciated. However, contrary to our expectations, these newcomers did not have a different view on doing business from the initial founders of the new venture. Hence, these findings lead us to propose that new entrants to spinouts reinforce shared cognition. This is surprising since the degree of shared cognition has been shown elsewhere in the literature to have mixed effects on performance. In other words, cognitive conflict is sometimes necessary to make strategic decisions and to increase venture performance.

This study suggests a number of areas for further research which derive from some of its limitations. The selection of the cases included in our study was based on the stage in which they are active in the spin-out process. Druilhe and Garnsey (2004) identify three types of spinouts which may evolve through a range of business models: (1) companies based on novel scientific breakthroughs where resource creation and opportunity recognition are interdependent, (2) product companies involving opportunity recognition that builds on the scientist's knowledge and connections, and (3) software companies. These different configurations and evolutionary paths may have implications for the evolution of the entrepreneurial teams involved. As we have noted, this study focused on the first category. Given the nature of the firms in our sample, our cases represent a continuum. The microelectronic firms (firms 4 and 6) and the technological test equipment firm (firm 1), which represent the two ends of this continuum, led us to conclude that the lead time is determined by the TTOs. They have the tendency to speed up the spin-out trajectory for complex projects. However, they seem to slow down the spin-out trajectory of less complex projects since they impose the same procedures as for complex projects. Further research may usefully perform a cross-sectoral analysis using both qualitative data and statistical analysis in a large sample of spinouts. A further potential feature of spin-out development concerns regression resulting from the "reinvention" or reorientation of the venture along the way, or the possibility of merger of two ventures into one organization. These aspects were not covered in this article but offer a further avenue for in-depth analysis.

We have focused on spin-out development in one geographical area. Different institutional environments that may be more or less munificent in terms of both the university context and the area surrounding a particular university may have different impacts on the availability of potential incoming team members as well as the alternative options available for academics. For example, Clarysse et al. (2005) identify different incubator models that may be applied in different contexts and may be associated with different types of spinout. Team dynamics differ between these incubator models. There is, therefore, a need for further research that examines the development of teams in different institutional contexts. With the small number of cases examined and the focus on a limited set of issues, we were also unable to examine the relationship between financial aspects and expertise and team size. Further case studies may be used to address this issue. By examining a small number of cases, we have emphasized conceptual development rather than general empirical testing. There would appear to be scope for more large-scale testing of the insights generated in this article.

The study examined different aspects of the spin-out development process, but the spinouts involved were at different stages in their development. Although we adopted an approach that addressed this issue, there is a need for longitudinal studies that trace the development of teams over time. However, obtaining access in such cases may present major barriers for research.

Finally, in terms of further research, our study has focused solely on academic spinouts. There is, therefore, a need for studies that compare directly the development of academic spinouts with the trajectory of similar nonacademic spinouts. To what extent do differences in heterogeneity occur in such cases? To what extent does the availability of different networks and social capital affect the changing nature of heterogeneity in the team?

With respect to managerial implications, the study provides a number of insights into optimizing the management of the spin-out process and the spin-out ventures themselves. Primarily, we have shown the existence of privileged witnesses. They are involved in the startup process of the company and have a very important stake in the subsequent composition of the founding team. They are often substitutes for the founder/entrepreneur and play an important role as sounding boards for the entrepreneurs involved in the startup process. Their presence and impact in the early stage of company development has both good and bad consequences. The good thing is that they make sure things happen. The bad thing is that by definition they are involved in starting up venture capital-backed startups. The privileged witness tends to look for a manager or business developer to introduce into the startup. However, this kind of top-down approach usually requires some form of starting capital to enable these individuals to be recruited. Moreover, the privileged witness also regulates the IP (intellectual property) involvement of the university, which again makes a valuation and external capital injection necessary. The emerging question is whether bottom-up stimulation of entrepreneurship associated with organizational and cultural changes may be a more appropriate alternative way of creating spinouts.

We also observe that in the early stages of spin-out formation, the composition of the founding team tends to undergo drastic changes. Surprisingly, while it may be expected that the changes embody team diversity, they do not. In terms of "attitude" in particular, the team newcomers tend to be similar to the surrogate entrepreneurs—practitioners that are already in place. This recruitment of similar personalities may be inspired by the consensus building that takes place between the surrogate entrepreneurs, who usually have some power over the technology that they have developed, and the privileged witnesses, who want to bring the technology onto the market. The privileged witnesses have to legitimize their own position and can seldom realistically propose somebody whom the entrepreneur does not like. The entrepreneur, however, does not evaluate the proposed person based upon purely economic arguments, but also takes more interpersonal aspects into account such as their ability to get along with the person or their personality. The latter seem to weigh more heavily than the economic arguments.

REFERENCES

Amason, A.C. & Sapienza, H.J. (1997). The effects of top management team size and interaction norms on cognitive and affective conflict. *Journal of Management, 23*(4), 495–516.

Burgelman, R. (1983). A process model of internal corporate venturing in the diversified major firm. *Administrative Science Quarterly, 28,* 223–244.

Cantwell, J. & Iammarino, S. (2001). EU regions and multinational corporations: Change, stability and strengthening of technological comparative advantages. *Industrial and Corporate Change, 10*(4), 1007–1037.

Clarysse, B. & Moray, N. (2004). A process study of entrepreneurial team formation: The case of a research based spin off. *Journal of Business Venturing, 19*(1), 55–79.

Clarysse, B., Wright, M., Lockett, A., Van de Velde, E., & Vohora, A. (2005). Spinning out new ventures: A typology of incubation strategies from European research institutions. *Journal of Business Venturing, 20*(2), 183–216.

Druilhe, C. & Garnsey, E. (2004). Do academic spin-outs differ and does it matter? *Journal of Technology Transfer, 29*(3/4), 269–285.

Eisenhardt, K. (1989). Building theories from case study research. *Academy of Management Review, 14*(4), 532–550.

Eisenhardt, K., Kahwajy, J., & Bourgeois, L. (1997). How management teams can have a good fight. *Harvard Business Review, 75*(4), 77–85.

Ensley, M.D., Carland, J.C., & Carland, J.W. (1998). The effects of entrepreneurial team skill heterogeneity and functional diversity on new venture performance. *Journal of Business and Entrepreneurship, 10*(1), 1–11.

Ensley, M.D. & Pearce, C.L. (2001). Shared cognition in top management teams: Implications for new venture performance. *Journal of Organizational Behavior, 22,* 145–160.

Ensley, M.D., Pearson, A.W., & Amanson, A.C. (2002). Understanding the dynamics of new venture top management teams. Cohesion, conflict, and new venture performance. *Journal of Business Venturing, 17,* 365–386.

Fama, E.F. & Jensen, M.C. (1983). Separation of ownership and control. *Journal of Law and Economics, 26,* 301–325.

Franklin, S., Wright, M., & Lockett, A. (2001). Academic and surrogate entrepreneurs in university spin-out companies. *Journal of Technology Transfer 26*(1–2), 127–141.

Gartner, W.B., Shaver, K.G., Gatewood, E., & Katz, J.A. (1994). Finding the entrepreneur in entrepreneurship. *Entrepreneurship Theory and Practice, 18*(3), 5–10.

Hambrick, D.C. & Mason, P.A. (1984). Upper echelons: The organization as a reflection of its top managers. *Academy of Management Review, 9*(2), 193–207.

Heirman, A. & Clarysse, B. (2004). How and why do research-based startups differ at founding? A resource-based configurational perspective. *Journal of Technology Transfer 29*(3–4), 247–268.

Kamm, J.B., Schuman, J.C., Seeger, J.A., & Nurick, A.J. (1990). Entrepreneurial teams in new venture creation: A research agenda. *Entrepreneurship Theory and Practice, 14*(4), 7–17.

Lambert, R. (2003). The lambert review of business–university collaboration. Final report. Crown Copyright, Norwich, UK. Published with the permission of HM treasury on behalf of the controller of Her Majesty's Stationary Office. Available at http://www.lambertreview.org.uk, accessed 7 June 2004.

Lockett, A., Wright, M., & Franklin, S. (2003). Technology transfer and universities' spin-out strategies. *Small Business Economics, 20,* 185–203.

MacMillan, I.C., Siegel, R., & Narasimha, P.N.S. (1985). Criteria used by venture capitalists to evaluate new venture proposals. *Journal of Business Venturing, 1,* 119–128.

MacMillan, I.C., Zemann, L., & Subbanarasimha, P.N. (1987). Criteria distinguishing successful from unsuccessful ventures in the venture screening process. *Journal of Business Venturing, 2,* 123–137.

Moray, N. (2004) Innovatief ondernemen aan onderzoeksinstellingen: Wishful thinking of pure reality? In B. Clarysse (Ed.), *Eendagsvlieg of pionier: Welke ondernemer redt de economie?* (pp. 97–135). Leuven: Garant.

Moray, N. & Clarysse, B. (2005). Institutional change and resource endowments to science-based entrepreneurial firms. *Research Policy, 34,* 1091–1105.

Muzyka, D., Birley, S., & Leleux, B. (1996). Trade-offs in the investment decisions of European venture capitalists. *Journal of Business Venturing, 11*(4), 273–288.

Nicolaou, N. & Birley, S. (2003). Social networks in organizational emergence: The university spin-out phenomenon. *Management Science, 49*(12), 1702–1725.

OECD. (2003). *Turning science into business: Patenting and licensing at public research organizations.* OECD: Paris.

Pettigrew, A. (1979). On studying organizational cultures. *Administrative Science Quarterly, 24,* 570–581.

Quinn, R.E. (1988). *Beyond rational management.* San Francisco: Jossey-Bass.

Ratcheva, V. & Vyakarnam, S. (2001). Exploring team formation process in virtual partnerships. *Integrated Manufacturing Systems, 12*(7), 512–523.

Teachman, J.D. (1980). Analysis of population diversity. *Sociological Methods and Research, 1,* 149–177.

Ucbasaran, D., Lockett, A., Wright, M., & Westhead, P. (2003). Entrepreneurial founder teams: Factors associated with members entry and exit. *Entrepreneurship Theory and Practice, 28*(2), 107–128.

Van Dierdonck, R., Debackere, K., & Engelen, B. (1990). University-industry relationships: How does the Belgian academic community feel about it? *Research Policy, 19,* 551–566.

Van Muijen, J.J., Koopman, P., De Witte, K., De Cock, G., Susanj, Z., Lemoine, C., et al. (1999). Organizational culture : The focus questionnaire. *European Journal of Work and Organizational Psychology, 8*(4), 551–568.

Vohora, A., Wright, M., & Lockett, A. (2004). Critical junctures in the development of university high-tech spin-out companies. *Research Policy, 33*(1), 147–176.

Yin, R.K. (1994). *Case study research: Design and methods.* Beverly Hills, CA: Sage Publications.

Iris Vanaelst is a research associate at the Department of Business Economics and Strategic Management, Vrije Universiteit Brussel, Brussels, Belgium.

Bart Clarysse is a professor at Vlerick Leuven Ghent Management School and at Ghent University, Ghent, Belgium.

Mike Wright is a professor of Financial Studies and director of Centre for Management Buy-out Research at Nottingham University Business School, Nottingham, England, United Kingdom.

Andy Lockett is an associate professor and reader in Strategy at Nottingham University Business School, Nottingham, England, United Kingdom.

Nathalie Moray is a postdoctoral researcher at Ghent University, Ghent, Belgium.

Rosette S'Jegers is the director of the Department of Business Economics and Strategic Management, Vrije Universiteit Brussel, Brussels, Belgium.

The authors would like to thank Johan Bruneel for his supporting efforts in collecting the data.

Part II
Social Interaction and
Interpersonal Processes Within Teams

[6]

Available online at www.sciencedirect.com

SCIENCE @ DIRECT·

ELSEVIER   Journal of Business Venturing 20 (2005) 727–746

JOURNAL
of BUSINESS
VENTURING

Demographic diversity for building an effective entrepreneurial team: is it important?

Sanjib Chowdhury[*]

466 Gary Owen Building, 300 W. Michigan Avenue, Department of Management, College of Business, Eastern Michigan University, Ypsilanti, MI 48197, USA

Received 1 February 2003; received in revised form 1 July 2004; accepted 1 July 2004

Abstract

Although traditional entrepreneurship literature often views entrepreneurship as an economic battle of a "lonely hero", the prevalence of entrepreneurial teams is an emerging economic reality. This study examines the influences of demographic diversity variables in terms of age, gender, and functional background and team process variables in terms of team-level cognitive comprehensiveness and team commitment on entrepreneurial team effectiveness. With field interview data from 174 entrepreneurs representing 79 entrepreneurial teams, this study suggests that demographic diversity is not important for entrepreneurial team effectiveness, whereas the team process variables positively influence team effectiveness. The findings also suggest that the diversity in terms of gender, age and functional background does not contribute to the team-level cognitive comprehensiveness and team commitment. Finally, the study explores implications of the findings for practice and future research.
© 2004 Elsevier Inc. All rights reserved.

Keywords: Entrepreneurial team; Diversity; Cognitive comprehensiveness; Commitment

* Tel.: +1 734 487 2215; fax: +1 734 487 4100.
  E-mail address: Sanjib.chowdhury@emich.edu.

0883-9026/$ - see front matter © 2004 Elsevier Inc. All rights reserved.
doi:10.1016/j.jbusvent.2004.07.001

1. Executive summary

Although relatively limited, an emerging body of entrepreneurship literature has started focusing on team-level issues (Frances and Sandberg, 2000; McGrath et al., 1994, 1995, 1996; Higashide and Birley, 2002; Lechler, 2001; Watson et al., 1995). This stream of research mainly examined team process and effectiveness. While scholars suggest that diversity is an important topic in both academic research and practice (Cox, 1993; Knouse and Dansby, 1999; Pelled et al., 1999) and team heterogeneity has important influence on firm performance (Ensley et al., 1998). However, research on demographic diversity in entrepreneurial teams is very limited (Lyon et al., 2000).

The present article focuses on demographic diversity in entrepreneurial teams and its influence on team effectiveness. With an extensive literature review this article argues that the diversity of composition is not as important as team commitment and the process of cognitive comprehensiveness that utilizes diverse decision criteria. Specifically, the article examines the influences of demographic diversity variables in terms of age, gender, and functional background and team process variables in terms of team-level cognitive comprehensiveness and team commitment on entrepreneurial team effectiveness.

The article tests these influences with field interview data from 174 entrepreneurs representing 79 entrepreneurial teams. The result shows that demographic diversity variables are not significantly related to entrepreneurial team effectiveness; whereas, team commitment and cognitive comprehensiveness are both positively and significantly related to entrepreneurial team effectiveness. Furthermore, the results show that demographic diversity in terms of gender, age and functional background does not significantly contribute to either cognitive comprehensiveness or team commitment.

The outcomes of the study have several important implications for research and practice. The findings suggest that scholars and practitioners should reconsider the effect of diversity in team effectiveness. Specific results of this study show that team diversity (gender, age, functional background) by itself does not positively influence entrepreneurial team effectiveness. The findings also suggest that scholars and practitioners must focus on team process that builds commitment and that promotes comprehensiveness in team decision-making. Specifically, results show that effective entrepreneurial teams are those that have high member commitment and that develop a process that uses diverse perspectives on problems, a variety of potential solutions and a variety of criteria for evaluating solutions to make complex and innovative decisions.

Hence, entrepreneurial teams must create an environment of trust and loyalty for improving team commitment. Additionally, entrepreneurs should collectively formulate an agreed-upon system of team interaction that not only would ensure that each member proposed different approaches, points of views, alternatives, etc., but would also encourage members to compare the diverse alternatives and approaches and weigh them against each other.

Future entrepreneurship research that studies diversity should focus on personality and thinking style in addition to demographics, since the effect of diversity seems to be a complex function of demographic and other individual traits (Tolbert et al., 1995). Hence, a

S. Chowdhury / Journal of Business Venturing 20 (2005) 727–746   729

comprehensive study of diversity and its influence on both entrepreneurial team dynamics and team effectiveness would be a promising direction for future research.

2. Introduction

High-tech entrepreneurial firms play a significant role in the Western economy because they account for a considerable portion of new product innovations. These ventures are continuously confronted with diverse challenges originating from uncertainties in terms of business processes, markets and technologies. An entrepreneurial team rather than a single entrepreneur seems better suited to deal with the uncertainties and volatilities associated with new ventures that require flexibility and complexity of decision making (Vesper, 1990). Accordingly, the existence of entrepreneurial teams is widespread and well documented in the Western economy. For instance, Charles Pfizer and Charles Erhart co-founded Pfizer in 1849, and Dr. Eugen Lucius, Carl Meister and Ludwig Miller founded Hoechst in 1863, and more recently David Filo and Jerry Yang co-founded YAHOO in 1995.

However, popular opinion generally characterized entrepreneurship as an economic battle of a "lonely hero" (Johannisson, 1998). In addition, traditional entrepreneurship literature that examined entrepreneurship characteristics often focused on individual characteristics (Kisfalvi, 2002; Lee, 2001; Low and MacMillan, 1988) as opposed to team-level variables (Davidsson, 2001). But, teams of entrepreneurs are more common than the entrepreneurship literature suggests (Lau, 2000; Lechler, 2001; Watson et al., 1995). In fact, the presence of entrepreneurial teams is a prominent economic reality especially in high-tech industry. Cooper et al. (1990) have found that entrepreneurial teams were founders of a vast majority of firms in the high-tech industry.

Although relatively limited, an emerging body of literature in entrepreneurship has started focusing on the team-level issues (Ensley et al., 2002; Frances and Sandberg, 2000; McGrath et al., 1994, 1995, 1996; Higashide and Birley, 2002; Lechler, 2001; Watson et al., 1995). While most of these studies have examined team process and effectiveness, they did not pay particular attention to the diversity of the team composition and its influence.

However, an important focus of team research has been the study of team composition, especially in terms of diversity (Pelled et al., 1999). Heterogeneous teams, with their suggested benefits of improved creativity and innovativeness (Sethi et al., 2002), should be well suited for entrepreneurial venture performance. On the other hand, heterogeneity might also produce conflicts and emotions among members of the entrepreneurial team resulting in poor performance.

Team composition may have been recognized as important for team effectiveness (Bantel and Jackson, 1989; Wanous and Youtz, 1986), but its role has not yet been widely investigated (Metzemaekers, 2000). In addition, research on team composition remains inconclusive since this research provided contradictory findings regarding effects of demographic diversity on team effectiveness (Pelled et al., 1999; Simons et al., 1999; Yu, 2002). Accordingly, diversity is often regarded as a "double-edged sword" (Milliken and

Martins, 1996) or a "mixed blessing" (Williams and O'Reilly, 1998) for its contradictory influence on team effectiveness.

Heterogeneous teams are regarded as more effective in solving complex, non-routine problems, which are common to entrepreneurial firms. This is because the diversity in perceptions, skills, abilities and knowledge that exists in a heterogeneous team is important for solving complex and ambiguous problems (Gladstein, 1984; Hackman, 1987; Pearce and Ravlin, 1987; Wanous and Youtz, 1986). Consequently, diversity is also perceived to link positively with cognitive task performance, which involves formulating plans, generating creative ideas, solving critical problems or making complex decisions (Bantel and Jackson, 1989; Eisenhardt and Schoonhoven, 1990; Murnighan and Conlon, 1991). The underlying assumption here seems to be that diversity improves the breadth of cognitive ability important for entrepreneurship.

While many scholars suggest that increased diversity provides a variety of benefits, others indicate that homogeneity may lead to better outcomes when considering satisfaction, communication, conflict (Pearce and Ravlin, 1987) and turnover (Jackson et al., 1991). Accordingly, it is unclear whether diversity in team composition always improves complex and/ or non-routine problem- solving ability. Additionally, diversity in a team merely brings together people with different perspectives, cognitive styles, skills and abilities, but it does not ensure that the team harnesses all these into extensive team-level cognitive attributes.

Moreover, a team can achieve diversity without having different demographic characteristics among its members. Differences in personality traits and thinking styles can also create diversity of cognitive attributes within a team (Harrison et al., 2002; Neuman et al., 1999; Triandis, 1995). Thus, a demographically homogeneous team can achieve diverse cognitive attributes important to making novel and creative entrepreneurial decisions.

Therefore, it is appropriate to be skeptical about the benefits of demographic diversity for entrepreneurial team effectiveness. Accordingly, the current study addresses this issue by proposing that demographic diversity in terms of age, gender, and functional background may not be as important in predicting entrepreneurial team effectiveness as team-level cognitive comprehensiveness and team commitment. Hypotheses developed in this study were tested using data from 174 individual entrepreneurs representing 79 high-tech entrepreneurial teams.

3. Theory development

An entrepreneurial team is often characterized as two or more individuals with equity interest jointly launching and actively participating in a business (Kamm et al., 1990; Watson et al., 1995). Western economies are dominated by entrepreneurial teams and this dominance is particularly common in high-tech industry. Since the majority of high-tech start-ups are founded by teams of entrepreneurs, entrepreneurship research should examine this phenomenon in more detail (Lechler, 2001).

Research on entrepreneurial start-ups suggests that firms founded by entrepreneurial teams generally outperformed those founded by individual entrepreneurs (Bird, 1989; Kamm et al.,

S. Chowdhury / Journal of Business Venturing 20 (2005) 727–746 731

1990). The success of high-tech entrepreneurial teams can be attributed to the logic that "high technology industries might require more skills than an individual would be likely to have, necessitating that individuals combine their abilities in teams in order to start an organization successfully" (Gartner, 1985, p. 703). Consequently, entrepreneurship scholars have suggested that the advantage of start-up teams comes from the diversity of characteristics, knowledge, skills, etc. (Timmons, 1990; Vesper, 1990). In addition, research also suggests that team heterogeneity is an important factor for firm performance (Ensley et al., 1998). However, research on demographic diversity in entrepreneurial teams is very limited (Lyon et al., 2000).

Diversity is an important topic in both academic research and practice (Cox, 1993; Knouse and Dansby, 1999; Pelled et al., 1999). Demographic diversity refers to the degree of heterogeneity with respect to demographic "immutable characteristics such as age, gender and ethnicity; attributes that describe individuals' relationships with organizations, such as organizational tenure or functional areas; and attributes that identify individuals' positions within society, such as marital status" (Lawrence, 1997, p. 11).

The importance of demographic diversity in academic research and practice arises from the assumption that diversity enhances team effectiveness. One of the key factors in this line of research is the amount of diversity present in teams (Knouse and Dansby, 1999). However, the literature appears to be divided into two contradictory schools of thoughts on this issue: one suggests diversity in team members would lead to team-level diversity of perspectives and, thereby, team effectiveness; the other suggests diverse teams are less cohesive and, therefore, ineffective (Yu, 2002). Several examples from the diversity literature demonstrate such divergent and inconclusive findings. Studies by Bantel and Jackson (1989) and by Murnighan and Conlon (1991) have found positive and negative relationships between the amount of demographic diversity and cognitive task performance in teams. Moreover, Watson et al. (1993) have found both positive and negative influence of team demographic heterogeneity on task performance.

Many researchers have suggested that diversity in a team improves team effectiveness because diversity enhances team decision-making by bringing broader perspectives and a greater pool of alternative solutions and innovative ideas together (Knouse and Chretien, 1996; Milliken and Martins, 1996). This logic can be traced back to an argument originally proposed by Hoffman and Maier (1961) that diversity enhances a team's breadth of perspective, cognitive resources and overall problem-solving capacity.

However, for increasing cognitive breadth, teams with diversity should create synergistic processes (Barry and Stewart, 1997; Campion et al., 1993). A synergistic process is characterized by flexibility and open communication that encourages members to share, and build on one another's divergent ideas and perspectives (Stewart and Barrick, 2000). Accordingly, this synergy builds a broad, team-level cognitive capability, which is defined as a team's ability to utilize broad perspectives, alternatives and ideas in solving complex problems and formulate plans.

Previous research has found teams with diverse cognitive capabilities in terms of skills, knowledge, abilities and perspectives made more innovative and higher quality decisions compared to those with less diverse cognitive capabilities (Bantel and Jackson, 1989; Murray, 1989). In addition, for achieving team-level diverse cognitive capabilities, the team interaction process is at least as important as having members with a variety of cognitive attributes. Extensive research exists on such techniques as devil's advocacy and dialectical inquiry that enhance critical and analytical interactions designed to formulate a strategy using a variety of diverse skills, ideas and perspectives (Schwenk and Cosier, 1980).

A team's diverse cognitive resources are captured in a team-level capability through the team-interaction process that not only exhibits divergent belief structure and dissimilar priorities and assumptions, but also leads to contrasting views of what is important. Accordingly, this process introduces the team to many opposing points of view that might enable members to develop a broader understanding of the issues and the variety of alternatives the team faces (Amason, 1996; Jehn, 1995). The team interaction process that brings together contrasting points of view is also important for developing a broader team level understanding in that it provides constructive criticism and minimizes "groupthink" (Janis, 1982).

Additionally, entrepreneurship research has found that such team process variables as team comprehension and deftness are important contributors to team competency and ultimately new venture performance (McGrath et al., 1994, 1995, 1996). Team comprehension is defined as a team's collective understanding of the important drivers of its venture and deftness is defined as the "emergence of a collective mind" that creates effective relationships among teammates and that allows effective execution of interrelated activities. Accordingly, a team with high comprehension and deftness would have a diverse team-level cognitive capability in terms of the team's ability to understand and utilize a variety of perspectives, ideas and alternatives in solving complex problems and executing plans.

The team-level diverse cognitive capability is conceptualized here as the team-level cognitive comprehensiveness. According to Fredrickson (1984), decision comprehensiveness is regarded as "exhaustive" and "inclusive" in making strategic decision. Team-level cognitive comprehensiveness is a team process that examines critical issues with a wide lens and formulates strategies by considering diverse approaches, decision criteria and courses of actions (Miller et al., 1998; Simons et al., 1999). Hence, a team enhances its cognitive comprehensiveness with an interaction process that systematically analyzes the diverse cognitive attributes presented by its members.

Cognitive comprehensiveness is suggested as a highly influential team process variable (Miller and Cardinal, 1994; Miller et al., 1998) and has been found to have a positive influence on sales growth and profit growth (Simons et al., 1999). Research has found strong relationship between cognitive ability and performance of novel and complex tasks (Hunter and Hunter, 1984). Additionally, West and Meyer's (1997) empirical study concluded that the interaction processes within technology-based ventures should substantially emphasize identifying, embracing and widely communicating a variety of ideas. Thus, team-level cognitive comprehensiveness, by ensuring such a process that embraces diverse cognitive abilities and ideas, is likely to improve entrepreneurial team effectiveness. Accordingly, the above discussion can be used to develop the following hypothesis:

Hypothesis 1. Team-level cognitive comprehensiveness will be positively related to the entrepreneurial team effectiveness.

S. Chowdhury / Journal of Business Venturing 20 (2005) 727–746   733

Idiosyncratic dynamics within heterogeneous teams may divergently influence team synergy building. This may result in high level of cognitive comprehensiveness in some teams but not in others. Hence, demographic diversity merely brings people with diverse background but does not ensure team-level cognitive comprehensiveness.

In addition, the diversity of perspectives and ideas so important to the breadth of team-level cognitive comprehensiveness may also arise from factors other than demographic attributes. Diversity of personality traits within a team is also likely to contribute to the variety of perspectives and ideas available to the team just as people with different personality characteristics differ in their styles and abilities to do different things (Hackman, 1987; Shaw, 1981). Hence, each member in a team with high personality diversity brings unique cognitive attributes (Muchinsky and de Monahan, 1987; Neuman et al., 1999).

Demographically similar people may differ in their thinking style as well (Abraham, 1997; Sternberg, 1988). Thinking style differs from personality characteristics (Johnson, 2002); hence, people with similar personalities may have different ways of thinking about problems and possible solutions. Therefore, it can be argued that a team lacking demographic diversity may have access to a diverse scope of cognitive attributes.

Furthermore, demographic diversity may also create dissonance that makes the team interaction process difficult (Ancona and Caldwell, 1992). Occasionally, heterogeneity may create distrust and acrimony, as dissimilar team members may have divergent vocabularies, priorities and paradigms. Thus, their aggregate cognitive contribution has the potential to become a liability instead of building team-level cognitive comprehensiveness and negatively influence organizational innovation resulting in a poor entrepreneurial performance.

Research suggests that demographic diversity has the potential to create emotional conflicts within teams (Ancona and Caldwell, 1992; Eisenhardt et al., 1997), which is found to negatively influence team effectiveness (Pelled et al., 1999). Emotional conflicts arise from the subconscious tendency of people to place individuals into social categories based on demographic characteristics (Tajfel, 1982). People then perceive their own category as superior and tend to stereotype members of other categories. This, in turn, creates resentment in members of other categories, resulting in hostile interactions between social categories within teams. The hostile interactions from these emotional conflicts within teams are likely to produce anxiety, non-cooperation and ineffective communication resulting in a negative influence on team effectiveness (Eisenhardt et al., 1997).

In summary, demographic diversity is not the only source of diverse cognitive attributes and neither does it guarantee a high team-level cognitive comprehensiveness. Although an entrepreneurial team with high demographic diversity brings entrepreneurs with a variety of cognitive attributes together as members, it may also produce distrust, acrimony and emotional conflict among team members, which may in a lack of innovation, creativity, team effectiveness and overall performance.

Innovation, creativity and overall performance are essential elements of success for an entrepreneurial team. As a result of demographic diversity's ability to enrich a team with diverse cognitive endowment as well as to weaken a team with emotional conflicts, such diversity has the potential to both aid and impair innovation, creativity and overall performance. Therefore, this study does not expect to find a positive relationship between demographic diversity and entrepreneurial team effectiveness.

Additionally, entrepreneurship research on personality suggests that demographic diversity may not positively influence entrepreneurial team effectiveness. Entrepreneurship literature has extensively studied the personality characteristics of successful entrepreneurs (Brockhaus, 1980; Hornaday and Aboud, 1971; Kickul and Gundry, 2002). Such traits as autonomy, dominance and low need for difference are among many personality character-istics proposed in the literature as common to most successful entrepreneurs (Caird, 1993). Occasionally, entrepreneurs have also been branded as mildly sociopath (Winslow and Solomon, 1987). These characteristics make an entrepreneur unlikely to work effectively with people that have different demographic characteristics. Additionally, previous research has found that entrepreneurs engaged in high-tech businesses are similar in terms of such demographic characteristics as age, experience level and education level (Colombo and Delmastro, 2001). Accordingly, demographic diversity might not increase entrepreneurial team effectiveness. Hence, the above argument can be summarized as the following null hypothesis:

Hypothesis 2. Demographic diversity in terms of age, gender and functional background will not be positively related to entrepreneurial team effectiveness.

Furthermore, whenever a group of people works on a challenging project, emotional conflict is possible. This is particularly true for entrepreneurial teams, whose tasks are challenging, novel and innovative, and involve a high level of risk and potential return (Drucker, 1985; Gartner, 1990; Hornaday, 1992). Therefore, entrepreneurs must pay serious attention when forming a team, as the possibility of emotional conflict in such a team is very high. The team process variable that minimizes emotional conflict and enhances cooperation among team members should play an important role in improving team effectiveness. Team commitment is such an important team process variable (Pettigrew, 1998). Team commitment is suggested to enhance cohesion, loyalty and synergy, and minimize emotional conflicts between team members; therefore, it should increase entrepreneurial team effectiveness. Thus, the following hypothesis can be developed from the above discussion:

Hypothesis 3. Team commitment will be positively related to entrepreneurial team effectiveness.

Although team commitment and team-level cognitive comprehensiveness may be related, they are different constructs. Team commitment is a process in which team members feel loyalty and trust towards one another. In contrast, team cognitive comprehensiveness is a process in which team members consider multiple decision criteria, multiple courses of action and multiple perceptions in making decisions. While trust and loyalty within team members may sometimes encourage members to consider each member's ideas and perceptions in a decision-making process, it is also possible that team commitment may be present without cognitive comprehensiveness. A high level of trust and loyalty within a team may cause members to reduce debate and not weigh ideas of different members against one another. Similarly, it is possible to have cognitive comprehensiveness without team commitment.

S. Chowdhury / Journal of Business Venturing 20 (2005) 727–746   735

Teams may have a well-established system that requires members to brainstorm and systematically weigh pros and cons of one another's ideas.

4. Methodology

4.1. Sample and data collection

The study employed a structured field-interview method to collect data. Subjects were high-tech venture owners, whose businesses were registered with a major Midwestern statewide association for information technology economic development. Most of these ventures were in the computer related industry (software development, computer peripherals, website development, internet providers, etc.). To ensure that the findings are relevant to entrepreneurship, the following characteristics were considered in selecting firms for this study: sample firms are between 2 and 5 years old, sample firms must have multiple founders, founders must be participants in decision making, and founders must hold equity shares.

Some of these characteristics were derived from the definition of an entrepreneurial team. Following other empirical studies on entrepreneurial teams, subjects for this study were restricted to firms that are at the most 5 years old (Hansen and Bird, 1997). Less than 2-year-old firms were not considered for this study as the study intended to collect data on sales growth based on the previous 2 years of sales.

Since the study was based on a team-level unit of analysis, data had to be collected from every member of the teams used in this study. To ensure participation of all members of a venture team, it was necessary to get prior permission from each of the members and conduct interviews on the business premises.

Finally, data gathered from 79 ventures with multiple founders were used for this research. All members from these venture teams participated in this study. Altogether 174 individual entrepreneurs participated in the interview process. In addition to the interviews, data came from company publications (business plans and other company reports) to confirm some of the interview information.

4.2. Measurement

The study collected data on independent (three demographic characteristics, team commitment, and team-level cognitive comprehensiveness), control (team size) and dependent (team effectiveness) variables. Demographic data were collected on age, gender, and functional background. Data on ethnic background were collected but not used as they produced negligible variability within teams.

Once interview data were collected on demographic variables, they were then cross-checked with information from the firms' publications (business plans and/or company reports). Next, specific calculations were performed to convert the demographic data into team heterogeneities. Data on two other independent variables—team commitment and team-level cognitive comprehensiveness—were collected using two specific measurement instruments. Finally, data on the dependent variable were collected from interviews using a team-effectiveness questionnaire.

4.2.1. Demographic heterogeneity

Functional background was measured as the field in which the person had the *most* experience (e.g., see Bantel, 1993; Bantel and Jackson, 1989). From an extensive list of categories (e.g., finance, accounting, MIS, engineering, legal, medicine, etc.), the respondents chose the category in which they had the most experience. Data on age were collected as a categorical variable and respondents were grouped based on these age categories. Finally, respondents were categorized as 0 and 1 for male and female, respectively.

Although heterogeneity can be measured in a number of ways (Blau, 1977; Taagepera and Ray, 1977; Teachman, 1980), heterogeneities of the demographic variables for this study were calculated using Blau's index (1977). Blau's index has been cited as reliable and consistent with other acceptable indices of heterogeneity (Bantel and Jackson, 1989). It is calculated as: $1 - \sum p i^2$. Where p is the proportion or percent of team members in a category and i is the number of different categories represented in the team. The demographic variables of age heterogeneity (five categories) and functional background heterogeneity (eight categories) were each measured using Blau's (1977) index described above. For instance, if a team has three members and each member has a different functional background, the team received a score of $[1-(1/9+1/9+1/9)]0.67$, whereas a team that has three members with the same functional background received a score of 0. Gender heterogeneity was measured as the percentage of the smaller gender representation. For example, an entrepreneurial team with two females and one male received a score of 0.33.

4.2.2. Team commitment

Team commitment is measured using an existing instrument (Shapiro and Kirkman, 1999; Mowday et al., 1979). Items of the instrument were adjusted to make them suitable for the purpose of the current study. The team commitment instrument for the current study used three items to measure: the extent to which members felt loyal, felt that they expected to stay with the same team for a long time, and felt that they trusted the team. Each entrepreneur rated his/her team on each of these items based on a five-point, very high/very low scale. This instrument has produced a good reliability with an α of 0.87.

4.2.3. Team-level cognitive comprehensiveness

A team's cognitive comprehensiveness is a team-level variable and proposed to be important for complex and innovative decision-making. The measurement instrument developed for this study used existing literature on team effectiveness (Miller et al., 1998; Simons et al., 1999). The four items used to collect data on the team-level cognitive comprehensiveness measured a team's breadth of perspectives on the problem at hand, the size of the pool of potential solutions to examine, the extent of innovative ideas and the variety of criteria for evaluating a possible solution. A five-point agree/disagree scale was used to collect data on these four items. This instrument has produced a good reliability with an α of 0.82.

S. Chowdhury / Journal of Business Venturing 20 (2005) 727–746 737

A factor analysis with "varimax" rotation suggested that team commitment and cognitive comprehensiveness were separate constructs as proposed earlier. Table 1 presents the results of the factor analysis. Eigenvalues of both the principal components were more than one and they accounted for 74% of the variance in responses.

4.2.4. Control variable

Team size served as a control variable for this study. Venture team size was measured as the total number of active partners having an equity interest in the venture. Respondents provided the number of individuals who were active partners in their venture. These numbers were cross-checked with the data gathered from company reports.

4.2.5. Dependent variable

The study used team effectiveness as the dependent variable. An instrument was adapted from existing research to measure this variable (Cardy and Dobbins, 1994; Stewart and Barrick, 2000). Individual items of this instrument were adjusted to fit the specific requirements of this study. Team outcomes and team behaviors representing team performance were both included as items for this instrument. Altogether seven items measured a team's knowledge of tasks, quality of work, quantity of work, initiative, interpersonal skills, planning and allocation, and overall performance. Each entrepreneur rated his/her team on each of these items based on a five-point behavior-anchored scale (1=consistently exceeds expectations, 5=consistently below expectations). A confirmatory factor analysis resulted in only one factor with eigenvalue more than one. This instrument also showed a high degree of reliability with an α of 0.86.

This study initially planned to use sales growth as an additional dependent measure; however, only 29 out of 79 firms that participated in the interview agreed to share their actual sales information for the last 2 years. As a result, this information was not used for the final data analysis. However, a bivariate correlation between sales growth rate and team effectiveness as measured here for those 29 firms that shared data showed a statistically significant correlation of

Table 1
Results of rotated (varimax) components analysis of team commitment and cognitive comprehensiveness items

Items	Component[a]	
	Cognitive comprehensiveness	Team commitment
Variety of perspectives on the problem at hand	**0.769**	0.228
The size of the pool of potential solutions to examine	**0.922**	0.186
Extent of innovative ideas	**0.905**	0.228
Variety of criteria used to evaluate possible solution	**0.637**	−0.201
I feel very loyal to the existing team of entrepreneurs	0.117	**0.819**
I expect to stay with this team for an extended period of time	0.205	**0.886**
I feel this team of entrepreneurs is very trustworthy	0.296	**0.845**
Eigenvalue	3.80	2.39
Percentage of variance explained	40.1	34.2
Cumulative percentage of variance explained	40.1	74.3

[a] Values in bold define a component.

0.87 ($p<0.001$). This finding, although not definitely, suggests predictive validity of the team effectiveness measure used in this study.

A composite score per team was calculated for all multiple-item, team-level variables (team commitment, team-level cognitive comprehensiveness, team effectiveness). First, for each team an average score on each measurement item was calculated, since multiple responses (each entrepreneur was a respondent) were collected from each team on these items. Finally, the response averages on all items were averaged to create a single score representing each team-level variable.

5. Data analysis and results

5.1. Descriptive statistics and correlations

Table 2 presents descriptive statistics and bivariate correlation coefficients for all studied variables. Team effectiveness correlated negatively with team size and age heterogeneity and positively with team commitment and team-level cognitive comprehensiveness. Team commitment and team-level cognitive comprehensiveness also showed significant correlation. Concern for a multicolinearity (a violation of regression assumption) problem exits as the data show significant correlations between the independent variables. Therefore, variance inflation factor (VIF) was computed for all independent variables to test the existence of multicolinearity. Results show VIF values for all independent variables to be well below the multicolinearity level.

5.2. Hypotheses testing

Hypothesized relationships were tested using the hierarchical regression analysis. To compute the extent of additional variance explained by study variables, the regression

Table 2
Descriptive statistics and bivariate correlations

Study variables	Reliability	Mean	S.D.	1	2	3	4	5	6
1. Team effectiveness	0.86	4.29	0.383						
2. Team size		2.22	0.505	−0.50**					
3. Age heterogeneity		0.765	0.635	−0.31**	0.49**				
4. Gender heterogeneity		0.469	0.554	−0.02	0.15	0.17			
5. Functional background heterogeneity		0.723	0.627	−0.13	0.24*	−0.03	0.09		
6. Team commitment	0.87	3.055	0.989	0.68**	−0.60**	−0.30**	−0.12	−0.22*	
7. Team-level cognitive comprehensiveness	0.81	3.208	0.898	0.61**	−0.58**	−0.38**	−0.17	−0.31**	0.67**

* $p<.05$.
** $p<0.01$.

S. Chowdhury / Journal of Business Venturing 20 (2005) 727–746 739

analysis was performed by entering the control variable (team size) in step1, demographic heterogeneity variables (age heterogeneity, gender heterogeneity, and functional background heterogeneity) in step 2, and finally team commitment and of team-level cognitive comprehensiveness in step 3. Importance of a specific set of variables can be demonstrated by examining the changes in R^2 from step to step (Table 3).

Hypothesis 1 predicted that team-level cognitive comprehensiveness is positively related to team effectiveness. The data analysis results presented in step 3 of Table 3 show a significant positive β (β=0.24, α<0.05), suggesting that team-level cognitive comprehensiveness contributes positively to the team effectiveness. Hence, Hypothesis 1 was supported.

Hypotheses 2 proposed that demographic diversity in terms of gender, age and functional background does not positively influence team effectiveness. As presented in step 2 of Table 3, the change in R^2 is statistically not significant (ΔR^2=0.01, p>0.05). Moreover, the β coefficients for all of the three demographic heterogeneity variables are not statistically significant (p>0.05). Although not finding a statistically significant result does not mean an absence of relationship, this result failed to reject Hypothesis 2. Therefore, the data obtained for this study suggest that, while the team-level cognitive comprehensiveness contributed positively to the team effectiveness, demographic heterogeneities did not.

Hypothesis 3 stated that team commitment is positively related to team effectiveness. Regression results presented in step 3 of Table 3 show that the β coefficient for team commitment is positive and statistically significant (β=0.74, p<0.01). Accordingly, the data for this study indicate that team commitment contributes positively to team effectiveness. Hence, Hypothesis 3 was supported.

Table 3
Hierarchical regression analysis results

Model	Predictor	Team effectiveness		
		β	R^2	ΔR^2
1			0.36**	0.36**
	Team size	−0.60**		
2			0.37**	0.01
	Team size	−0.65**		
	Age heterogeneity	0.06		
	Gender heterogeneity	0.06		
	Functional background heterogeneity	0.02		
3			0.81**	0.44**
	Team size	0.08		
	Age heterogeneity	−0.05		
	Gender heterogeneity	0.09		
	Functional background heterogeneity	0.08		
	Team commitment	0.74**		
	Team-level cognitive comprehensiveness	0.24*		

* p<0.05.
** p<0.01.

Furthermore, the results of the hierarchical regression models presented in Table 3 show how much additional variance in team effectiveness was explained by team-level cognitive comprehensiveness and team commitment. As shown in step 3 of Table 3, addition of these two variables to the regression model resulted in a significant increase in the multiple square correlation coefficient ($\Delta R^2 = 0.44$, $p < 0.01$). Thus, the addition of team-level cognitive comprehensiveness and team commitment significantly explained 44% of the team effectiveness beyond what the control variable and demographic heterogeneity variables explained.

6. Discussion

Results show that team-level cognitive comprehensiveness and team commitment produced significant positive influence on entrepreneurial team effectiveness. However, demographic heterogeneity variables did not significantly influence team effectiveness. It is evident from the results of regression analyses with or without the team-level variables in the model that the data clearly suggest that demographic diversity variables do not have any direct influence on team effectiveness. Additionally, to check if they have any indirect relationship, an examination of the influence of the studied diversity variables on the team-level process variables (team-level cognitive comprehensiveness and team commitment) is important (Baron and Kenney, 1986).

Accordingly, a post-hoc data analysis was performed with two regression models using two dependent variables: team-level cognitive comprehensiveness and team commitment. Results showed that diversity variables did not produce any significant influence on either of the team-level variables. Hence, these results indicate that diversity in terms of gender, age and functional background did not contribute either to the breadth of cognitive comprehensiveness or to the commitment of an entrepreneurial team (Table 4).

Table 4
Post-hoc regression analysis

Model	Predictor	Team commitment			Team-level cognitive comprehensiveness		
		β	R^2	ΔR^2	β	R^2	ΔR^2
1			0.49**	0.49**		0.47**	0.47**
	Team size	−0.70**			−0.68**		
2			0.51*	0.02		0.49**	0.02
	Team size	−0.78**			−0.64**		
	Age heterogeneity	0.16			−0.001		
	Gender heterogeneity	−0.02			−0.06		
	Functional background heterogeneity	−0.03			−0.14		

* $p < 0.05$.
** $p < 0.01$.

S. Chowdhury / Journal of Business Venturing 20 (2005) 727–746   741

The finding that failed to reject the absence of relationships between the studied demographic heterogeneity variables and entrepreneurial team effectiveness is not surprising. In fact, this was a prediction of this research, and several theoretically grounded arguments were made in support of these findings. Accordingly, these results seem to support the argument that demographic diversity may not necessarily contribute positively to entrepreneurial team effectiveness.

Overall, while demographic diversity appears to be unimportant for entrepreneurial team effectiveness, such team-level variables as the cognitive comprehensiveness and the team commitment show positive influence. Moreover, the results suggest that team diversity in terms of age, gender and functional background does not influence the team-level cognitive comprehensiveness and the team commitment. These findings are important; as they suggest that having team-level cognitive comprehensiveness and team commitment are independent of and more important than having members with different demographic characteristics. Hence, the study suggests that while it is important for entrepreneurial teams to consider developing team-level cognitive comprehensiveness and team commitment, it is not so important for entrepreneurs to team up with people that have differing demographic characteristics.

Like most other empirical studies, this study has limitations. First, this study did not include ethnic diversity as a part of demographic diversity. Known as one of the important demographic characteristics, ethnic diversity could have important influence on team effectiveness. However, the study of 79 teams resulted in a negligible variance in terms of ethnic background within teams. Most entrepreneurs formed teams with others from their own ethnic backgrounds. Only three teams showed some diversity in terms of ethnic characteristics. This scarcity may be due to the lack of ethnic diversity within entrepreneurial firms in general. Strong memberships of associations for Hispanic entrepreneurs, African American entrepreneurs and Asian Entrepreneurs, suggest that ethnic minorities tend to team up with members of their own ethnic group to start new businesses.

The next limitation is the use of self-reported data from the same source. Although company publications were used to cross-check interview data on team size and demographic variables, statistical analysis were performed using mainly the interview data provided by the same respondent on dependent and independent variables. This raises the possibility that common response bias might have inflated the findings of this study. Also, the use of perceptual data on team-effectiveness is a weakness. However, entrepreneurs are skeptical about revealing financial performance information. For instance, only 29 out of 79 firms have provided last 2 years' sales information for this study. Dess and Robins (1984, p. 271) proposed that perceptual measures of performance are good substitutes of objective measures whenever "(a) accurate objective measures are unavailable and (b) the alternative is to remove the consideration of performance from the research design". Additionally, prior research has found self-reported measures of performance correlate highly with secondary data on performance (Venkatraman and Ramanujam, 1986).

Another limitation of this study is the use of cross-sectional data. Researchers found that effects of diversity on team effectiveness could have a temporal element (Harrison et al., 1998). Harris and his associates have found that, with time, the effects of demographic diversity decreased and the effects of diversity based on attitude increased. Hence, a control for team tenure could have refined the current findings.

A further limitation is the relatively small sample size. Although 174 entrepreneurs have provided interview data for this study, they represent only 79 high-tech entrepreneurial teams. As the study required team-level analysis, 79 data points were used for performing statistical tests. Even though most team-level studies have used comparatively smaller number of teams (Stewart and Barrick, 2000), the statistical power of this study was limited. However, the relatively strong effects produced by the statistical tests provide evidence for strong influences of team commitment and team-level cognitive comprehensiveness on entrepreneurial team effectiveness.

Despite these limitations; the findings have important implications for practice and future research. This study sought to fill an important gap in entrepreneurship literature as demographic heterogeneity is seldom examined in the context of entrepreneurial teams. Also, studying demographic heterogeneity in entrepreneurial teams and its influence on team effectiveness may help overcome the rather ambiguous results of most previous studies on this topic as they are based on large companies (Priem et al., 1999).

From a practical point of view, the findings begin to address an important issue: How important is it to build an entrepreneurial team with demographic diversity? The current study suggests that demographic diversity in terms of age, gender and functional background does not improve entrepreneurial team effectiveness, but team commitment and team-level cognitive comprehensiveness do. Hence, entrepreneurs should build teams focusing more on highly committed members who will value every member's cognitive styles, perceptions and abilities than on members' demographic diversity.

Members of an entrepreneurial team must focus on developing trust and loyalty toward the team. This might create team commitment and lower emotional conflict and consequently improve team effectiveness. Additionally, entrepreneurs should collectively formulate an agreed-upon system of team interaction that not only would ensure that each member proposed different approaches, points of views, alternatives etc., but would also encourage members to compare the diverse alternatives and approaches and weigh them against each other. This would ensure an entrepreneurial team process in which members will evaluate an issue with a wider lens resulting in cognitive comprehensiveness and ultimately entrepreneurial team effectiveness.

This study opens several avenues for related research. First, future studies on entrepreneurial teams should consider minimizing the limitations identified in this study. One way to reduce common-response bias would be to collect team effectiveness or performance data using an objective measure instead of the perceptual measure used in this study. A multi-method data collection technique could also alleviate this problem.

Moreover, future studies should examine diversity in terms of personality traits and thinking style in conjunction with demographic diversity. Entrepreneurs with different personality characteristics bring different cognitive attributes. For example, extroverts will differ in their abilities and styles when compared with introverts. Although extensive research on entrepreneurship is dedicated to finding an ideal entrepreneur based on personality

S. Chowdhury / Journal of Business Venturing 20 (2005) 727–746   743

characteristics, studies on entrepreneurial team diversity based on personality characteristics are almost nonexistent.

Consequently, entrepreneurship research focusing on studying team diversity in terms of demographic, personality, and thinking style would be important as the effect of diversity seems to be a complex function of demographic and other individual traits (Tolbert et al., 1995). Hence, a comprehensive study of diversity and its influence on both entrepreneurial team dynamics and team effectiveness would be a promising direction for future research.

References

Abraham, R., 1997. Thinking styles as moderators of role stressor–job satisfaction relationships. Leadersh. Organ. Dev. J. 18 (5), 236–243.

Amason, A., 1996. Distinguishing the effects of functional and dysfunctional conflict on strategic decision making: resolving a paradox for top management teams. Acad. Manage. J. 39, 123–148.

Ancona, D.G., Caldwell, D.F., 1992. Bridging the boundary: external activity and performance in organizational teams. Adm. Sci. Q. 37 (4), 634–666.

Bantel, K.A., 1993. Top team, environment, and performance effects on strategic planning formality. Group Organ. Manage. 18, 436–458.

Bantel, K.A., Jackson, S.E., 1989. Top management and innovations in banking: does the composition of the top team make a difference? Strateg. Manage. J. 10, 107–124.

Baron, R.M., Kenney, D.A., 1986. The moderator–mediator variable distinction in social psychological research: conceptual, strategic, and statistical considerations. J. Pers. Soc. Psychol. 51, 1173–1182.

Barry, B., Stewart, G.L., 1997. Composition, process, and performance in self-managed groups: the role of personality. J. Appl. Psychol. 82, 62–78.

Bird, B.J., 1989. Entrepreneurial Behavior. Scott, Foresman and Company, Glenview, IL.

Blau, P.M., 1977. Inequality and Heterogeneity. Free Press, New York.

Brockhaus Sr., R.H., 1980. Risk taking propensity of entrepreneurs. Acad. Manage. J. 23, 509–520.

Caird, S.P., 1993. What do psychological tests suggest about entrepreneurs? J. Manag. Psychol. 8 (6), 11–21.

Campion, M.A., Medsker, G.J., Higgs, A.C., 1993. Relations between work group characteristics and effectiveness: implications for designing effective work groups. Pers. Psychol. 46, 823–850.

Cardy, R.L., Dobbins, G.H., 1994. Performance Appraisal: Alternative Perspectives. Southwest, Cincinnati.

Colombo, M.G., Delmastro, M., 2001. Technology-based entrepreneurs: does internet make a difference? Small Bus. Econ. 16 (3), 177–190.

Cooper, A.C., Dunkelberg, W.C., Woo, C.Y., Dennis, W.J., 1990. New Business in America: the Firms and their Owners. National Foundation of Independent Businesses, Washington, DC.

Cox, T., 1993. Cultural Diversity in Organizations: Theory Research, and Practice. Berrett-Koehler, San Francisco.

Davidsson, P., 2001. Levels of analysis in entrepreneurship research: current research practice and suggestions for the future. Entrep. Theory Pract. 25 (4), 18–37.

Dess, G.G., Robinson, R.B., 1984. Measuring organizational performance in the absence of objective performance measures. Strateg. Manage. J. 5, 265–274.

Drucker, P.F., 1985. Innovation and Entrepreneurship. HarperCollins Publishers, New York.

Eisenhardt, K.M., Schoonhoven, C.B., 1990. Organizational growth: linking founding team strategy, environment, and growth among U.S. semiconductor ventures, 1978–1988. Admin. Sci. Q. 35, 504–529.

Eisenhardt, K.M., Kahwajy, Jean L., Bourgeois, L.J., 1997. Conflict and strategic choice: low top management teams disagree. Calif. Manage. Rev. 39 (2), 42–62.

Ensley, M.D., Carland, J.W., Carland, J.A., 1998. The effect of entrepreneurial team skill heterogeneity and functional diversity on new venture performance. J. Bus. Entrep. 10 (1), 1–14.

Ensley, M.D., Pearson, A.W., Amason, A.C., 2002. Understanding the dynamics of new venture top management teams: cohesion, conflict, and new venture performance. J. Bus. Venturing 17 (4), 365–386.

Frances, D.H., Sandberg, W.R., 2000. Friendship within entrepreneurial teams and its association with team and venture performance. Entrep. Theory Pract. 25 (2), 5–26.

Fredrickson, J.W., 1984. The comprehensiveness of strategic decision processes: extension, observations, future directions. Acad. Manage. J. 27, 445–466.

Gartner, W.B., 1985. A conceptual framework for describing the phenomenon of new venture creation. Acad. Manage. Rev. 10 (4), 696–706.

Gartner, W.B., 1990. What are we talking about when we talk about entrepreneurship? J. Bus. Venturing 5 (1), 15–29.

Gladstein, D.L., 1984. Groups in context: a model of task group effectiveness. Admin. Sci. Q. 29, 499–517.

Hackman, J.R., 1987. The design of work teams. In: Lorsch, J.W. (Ed.), Handbook of Organizational Behavior. Prentice-Hall, Englewood Cliffs, NJ, pp. 315–342.

Hansen, E.L., Bird, B.J., 1997. The stages model of high-tech venture founding: tried but true? Entrep. Theory Pract. 22 (2), 111–122.

Harrison, D.A., Price, K.H., Bell, M.P., 1998. Beyond relational demography: time and the effects of surface- and deep-level diversity on work group cohesion. Acad. Manage. J. 41, 96–107.

Harrison, D.A., Price, K.H., Gavin, J.H., Florey, A.T., 2002. Time, teams, and task performance: changing effects of surface- and deep-level diversity on group functioning. Acad. Manage. J. 45 (5), 1029–1045.

Higashide, H., Birley, S., 2002. The consequences of conflict between the venture capitalist and the entrepreneurial team in the United Kingdom from the perspective of the venture capitalist. J. Bus. Venturing 17 (1), 59–78.

Hoffman, L.R., Maier, N.R.F., 1961. Quality and acceptance of problem solutions by members of homogeneous and heterogeneous groups. J. Abnorm. Soc. Psychol. 62 (2), 401–407.

Hornaday, R.W., 1992. Thinking about entrepreneurship: a fuzzy set approach. J. Small Bus. Manage. 30 (4), 12–24.

Hornaday, J., Aboud, J., 1971. Characteristics of successful entrepreneurs. Pers. Psychol. 24, 141–153.

Hunter, J.E., Hunter, R.F., 1984. Validity and utility of alternative predictors of job performance. Psychol. Bull. 96, 72–98.

Jackson, S.E., Brett, J.F., Sessa, VI., Cooper, D.M., Julin, J.A., Peyronnin, K., 1991. Some differences make a difference: individual dissimilarity and group heterogeneity as correlates of recruitment, promotions, and turnover. J. Appl. Psychol. 76, 675–689.

Janis, I.L., 1982. Victims of Groupthink. Houghton Mifflin, Boston.

Jehn, K.A., 1995. A multimethod examination of the benefits and detriments of intragroup conflict. Admin. Sci. Q. 40, 256–282.

Johannisson, B. 1998, Entrepreneurship as a collective phenomenon. Paper presented at RENT XII, Lyon, France.

Johnson, L.K., 2002. Thinking styles of IT executives. MIT Sloan Manag. Rev. 43 (4), 13–21.

Kamm, J.B., Shuman, J.C., Seeger, J.A., Nurick, A.J., 1990. Entrepreneurial teams in new venture creation: a research agenda. Entrep. Theory Pract., 7–17.

Kickul, J., Gundry, L.K., 2002. Prospecting for strategic advantage: the proactive entrepreneurial personality and small firm innovation. J. Small Bus. Manage. 40 (2), 85–98.

Kisfalvi, V., 2002. The entrepreneur's character, life issues, and strategy making: a field study. J. Bus. Venturing 17 (5), 489–518.

Knouse, S.B., Chretien, D., 1996. Workforce diversity and TQM. In: Knouse, S.B. (Ed.), Human Resources Management Perspectives on TQM: Concepts and Practices. American Society for Quality Control Press, Milwaukee, WI.

Knouse, S.B., Dansby, M.R., 1999. Percentage of work-group diversity and work-group effectiveness. J. Psychol. 133 (5), 486–494.

Lau, D., 2000. Incubators bound in the land of internet deals. Venture Cap. J. 1, 1.

Lawrence, B.S., 1997. The black box of organizational demography. Organ. Sci. 8, 1–22.

Lechler, T., 2001. Social interaction: a determinant of entrepreneurial team venture success. Small Bus. Econ. 16, 263–278.

Lee, D.Y., 2001. The effects of entrepreneurial personality, background and network activities on venture growth. J. Manag. Stud. 38 (4), 583–597.

Low, M., MacMillan, I., 1988. Entrepreneurship: past research and future challenges. J. Manage. 35, 139–161.

Lyon, D.W., Lumpkin, G.T., Dess, G.G., 2000. Enhancing entrepreneurial orientation research: operationalizing and measuring a key strategic decision making process. J. Manage. 26, 1055–1085.

McGrath, R.G., Venkataraman, S., MacMillan, I.C., 1994. The advantage chain: antecedents to rents from internal corporate ventures. J. Bus. Venturing 9 (5), 351–3370.

McGrath, R.G., MacMillan, I.C., Venkataraman, S., 1995. Defining and developing competence: a strategic process paradigm. Strateg. Manage. J. 16 (4), 251–275.

McGrath, R.G., Tsai, M., Venkataraman, S., MacMillan, I.C., 1996. Innovation, competitive advantage and rent: a model and test. Manage. Sci. 42 (3), 389–403.

Metzemaekers, D., 2000. Critical success factors in technology management. Int. J. Technol. Manag. 19 (6), 583.

Miller, C.C., Cardinal, L.B., 1994. Understanding the linkage between strategic planning and firm performance: a synthesis of more than two decades of research. Acad. Manage. J. 37, 1649–1665.

Miller, C.C., Burke, L., Glick, W., 1998. Cognitive diversity among upper echelon executive: implications for strategic decision processes. Strateg. Manage. J. 19, 39–58.

Milliken, F.J., Martins, L.L., 1996. Searching for common threads: understanding the multiple effects of diversity in organizational groups. Acad. Manage. Rev. 21 (2), 402–433.

Mowday, R.T., Steers, R.M., Porter, L.W., 1979. The measurement of organizational commitment. J. Vocat. Behav. 14, 224–247.

Muchinsky, PM., dc Monahan, C.J., 1987. What is person-environment congruence? Supplementary versus complementary model of fit. J. Vocat. Behav. 31, 268–277.

Murnighan, J.K., Conlon, D.E., 1991. The dynamics of intense work groups: a study of British string quartets. Admin. Sci. Q. 36 (2), 165–187.

Murray, A.I., 1989. Top management group heterogeneity and firm performance. Strateg. Manage. J. 10, 125–141.

Neuman, G.A., Wagner, S.H., Christiansen, N.D., 1999. The relationship between work-team personality composition and the job performance of teams. Group Organ. Manage. 24 (1), 28–45.

Pearce, J.A., Ravlin, E.C., 1987. The design and activation of self-regulating work groups. Human Relat. 40, 751–782.

Pelled, H.L., Eisenhardt, K.M., Xin, K.R., 1999. Exploring the black box: an analysis of work group diversity, conflict, and performance. Admin. Sci. Q. 44 (1), 1–28.

Pettigrew, T.F., 1998. Intergroup contact theory. Annu. Rev. Psychol. 49, 65–85.

Priem, R., Lyon, D.W., Dess, G.G., 1999. Inherent limitations of demographic proxies in top management team heterogeneity research. J. Manage. 25, 935–953.

Schwenk, C.R., Cosier, R.A., 1980. Effects of the expert, devil's advocate, and dialectical inquiry methods on prediction performance. Organ. Behav. Hum. Perform. 26, 409–424.

Sethi, R., Simith, D.C., Park, C.W., 2002. How to kill a team's creativity. Harvard Bus. Rev. 80 (8), 16–17.

Shapiro, D.L., Kirkman, B.L., 1999. Employees' reaction to the change to work teams: the influence of "anticipatory" injustice. J. Organ. Change Manag. 12 (1), 51–66.

Shaw, M.E., 1981. Group Dynamics: the Psychology of Small Group Behavior. McGraw-Hill, New York.

Simons, T., Pelled, L.H., Smith, K.A., 1999. Making use of difference: diversity, debate, and decision comprehensiveness in top management teams. Acad. Manage. J. 42 (6), 662–673.

Sternberg, R., 1988. Mental self government: a theory of intellectual styles and their development. Hum. Dev. 31, 197–224.

Stewart, G.L., Barrick, M.R., 2000. Team structure and performance: assessing the mediating role of intrateam process and the moderating role of task type. Acad. Manage. J. 43 (2), 135–148.

Taagepera, R., Ray, J.L., 1977. A Generalized index of concentration. Sociol. Methods Res. 5, 367–384.

Tajfel, H., 1982. Social Identity and Intergroup Relations. Cambridge University Press, Cambridge.

Teachman, J.D., 1980. Analysis of population diversity. Sociol. Methods Res. 8, 341–362.

Timmons, J.A., 1990. New Venture Creation: Entrepreneurship in the 1990s. Irwin, Boston, MA.

Tolbert, P.S., Andrews, A.O., Simons, T., 1995. The effect of group proportions on group dynamics. In: Jackson, S.E., Ruderman, M.N. (Eds.), Diversity in Work Teams: Research Paradigms for a Changing Workplace. American Psychological Association, Washington, DC.

Triandis, H.C., 1995. A theoretical framework for the study of diversity. In: Chemers, M.M., Oskamp, S., Costanzo, M.A. (Eds.), Diversity in Organizations. Sage, Thousand Oaks, CA.

Venkatraman, N., Ramanujam, V., 1986. Measurement of business performance in strategy research: a comparison of approaches. Acad. Manage. Rev. 11 (4), 801–814.

Vesper, K., 1990. New Venture Strategies. Prentice Hall, Englewood Cliffs, NJ.

Wanous, J.P., Youtz, M.A., 1986. Solution diversity and the quality of group decisions. Acad. Manage. J. 29, 149–158.

Watson, W.E., Kumar, K., Michaelson, L.K., 1993. Cultural diversity's impact on interaction process and performance: comparing homogeneous and diverse task groups. Acad. Manage. J. 36, 996–1025.

Watson, W.E., Ponthieu, L., Critelli, J.W., 1995. Team interpersonal process effectiveness in venture partnerships and its connection to perceived success. J. Bus. Venturing 10, 393–411.

West, G.P., Meyer, G.D., 1997. Temporal dimensions of opportunistic change in technology-based ventures. Entrep. Theory Pract. 22 (2), 31–53.

Williams, K.L., O'Reilly, C., 1998. The complexity of diversity: a review of forty years of research. In: Gruenfeld, D., Neale, M. (Eds.), Research on Managing in Groups and Teams, vol. 20. JAI Press, Greenwich, CT, pp. 77–140.

Winslow, E., Solomon, G., 1987. Entrepreneurs are more than nonconformists: they are mildly sociopathic. J. Creat. Behav. 21 (3), 149–161.

Yu, L., 2002. Does diversity drive productivity? MIT Sloan Manag. Rev. 43 (2), 17.

[7]

Friendship Within Entrepreneurial Teams and its Association with Team and Venture Performance

Deborah H. Francis
William R. Sandberg

This article explores friendship within the entrepreneurial team with particular attention to its association with the team's behavior and the performance of the venture. Building on a foundation in the literatures on friendship, entrepreneurial teams, and strategic decisions, we propose 13 such relationships.

Friendship facilitates the formation of management teams for new ventures, thereby improving their early performance. As the entrepreneurial team continues to function, friendship is conducive to decision-making processes that enhance the team's effectiveness in solving "wicked" problems and ultimately improve the venture's performance. Friendships, under different circumstances, may exert either positive or negative influences on turnover within the entrepreneurial team, and those influences may improve or impair the venture's performance. (At the same time, behavior within the team or events in the venture's development may affect friendships within the team.)

Finally we develop and discuss several implications of our propositions for research and practice in entrepreneurship. We point out methodological considerations and directions for future research that would address these implications.

For years researchers who sought to explain the performance of new ventures probed the characteristics of the firm's founder. Then the "traits vs. behavior" debate (Carland, Hoy, Boulton, & Carland, 1984; Carland, Hoy, & Carland, 1988; Gartner, 1988) broadened the inquiry to encompass the entire venture-founding process (Sandberg, 1992). Even so, the idea of focusing on the *entrepreneurial team* rather than the *solo entrepreneur* was late in coming to researchers.

A shift of research attention from the individual to the entrepreneurial team gained impetus from outside the field of entrepreneurship. Top management teams had become the object of interest in strategic management research following the demographic approach of Hambrick and Mason (1984). Advocating "collective entrepreneurship" as a solution to problems of national competitiveness, Robert Reich (1987) cast "the team as hero" and argued that "economic success comes through the talent, energy, and commitment of a team" (p. 77) rather than through the solo efforts encouraged by "the myth of the entrepreneurial hero" (p. 82). Even the inventions and innovations of so heroic a figure as Thomas A. Edison now were understood by an historian as the product of the teams that Edison nurtured in his machine shop and laboratories (Millard, 1990).

Increased scholarly attention to entrepreneurial teams trailed the practice of major start-ups, which by the end of the 1980s frequently were launched by teams rather than solo founders (*Venture*, 1989). Despite greater attention, the literature on entrepreneurial teams remained sparse and inconsistent (Sapienza, Herron, & Menendez, 1991). Laying out a research agenda on the subject, Kamm, Schuman, Seeger, and Nurick (1990, p. 13) called for studies to understand the impact of "group dynamic issues," including "interpersonal relationships among team members," on the teams and their companies. This article is a step in that direction. It explores the relationship between friendships within an entrepreneurial team and the team's behavior.

Friendship clearly is an interpersonal relation that may affect a group's dynamics. It figured in the capacity of plant workers and their managers to "run hot" in a demanding competitive environment (Stewart, 1989). Friendship's effects also were noted in *The Soul of a New Machine*, Tracy Kidder's (1981) study of the team whose development of a new computer was credited with saving Data General Corporation.[1] In the aftermath of that team's subsequent dissolution, its leader "eventually ... [found] for himself a workable attitude toward the departure of his friends and the team's demise" (Kidder, 1981, p. 287). Several years later one of the former project managers described the former team members as "like Army buddies—you've been through the war together" (Bulkeley, 1985, p. 1). By then six of them were working together for a new company.

Friendships, then, may hold teams together and stimulate heroic efforts during difficult times. They also may serve as the basis for forming new teams. Our premise is that by understanding these friendships in their organizational setting, researchers may gain insight into the dynamics and performance of entrepreneurial teams. To that end we lay a foundation by discussing first friendship, and particularly its existence within management teams, and then the special case of entrepreneurial teams. Building on that foundation, we propose 13 relationships between friendship and the formation and performance of entrepreneurial teams and the organizations they lead. Finally we discuss the implications of these relationships for further research in entrepreneurship and identify methodological considerations that bear on that research.

FRIENDSHIP AND ORGANIZATIONS

Researchers who study friendship confront the term's many different meanings (Fischer, 1982). To some extent this situation stems from distinctions of type and degree among friendships and the many elements involved in these distinctions.[2] Management literature generally has treated friendship as a dichotomous variable—someone either is or is not a friend of another—that requires reciprocity from the other (Francis, 1995). Yet friendship is more than a mere friendly relation, itself a preliminary stage in friendship's development (Kurth, 1970), and friendships vary in their degree of solidarity (Hallinan & Williams, 1990).

Departing from their field's traditional practice, some management researchers (e.g. Boyd, 1991; Boyd & Taylor, 1992) have treated friendship as a continuous variable. Friendship, as one of several possible close relationships, is characterized by "strong, frequent, and diverse interdependence that lasts over a considerable period of time" (Kelley et al., 1983, p. 38). In addition, it includes symmetry and high mutual facilitation between friends. The notion of interdependence offers a framework for understanding interpersonal processes (Thibaut & Kelley, 1959). As an element of close relationships, interdependence brings experiences between interacting persons that influence one another's motives, preferences, behavior, and outcomes. In the case of friendships, the

---

1. Kidder's inside account evidently influenced Reich (1987, p. 77), who opened his article by positioning it as a counterpoint to the "traditional ... tale of triumphant individuals."

2. Qualitative distinctions of type among friendships date at least to the ancient Greek philosophers (Snyder & Smith, 1986).

persons' interactions are generally positive and result in greater trust, self-disclosure, and commitment between them (Rusbult & Van Lange, 1996).

Friendship's potential effects within a management team rest on its affective outcomes. A personal relationship is based on knowledge of the person that extends beyond formal roles (Simmel, 1950). Greater knowledge of the other person increases the predictability of his actions in various situations and thus enables greater trust (Gabarro, 1978). Although the most voluntary and least institutionalized of social relations (Bliezner & Adams, 1992), friendship is governed by rules that guide behavior (Argyle & Henderson, 1985). For example, the depth and breadth of self-disclosure between friends and the level of their mutual trust are positively related to the closeness and stability of their relationship (Altman & Taylor, 1973; Bliezner & Adams, 1992; Morton & Douglas, 1981). The degrees of cooperation and expected interaction also increase with higher levels of friendship (Argyle & Henderson, 1985).

Consistent with the foregoing discussion, in this article friendship is understood as "a relationship involving voluntary or unconstrained interaction in which the participants respond to one another personally, that is, as unique individuals rather than as packages of discrete attributes or mere role occupants" (Wright, 1985, p. 119). Each friendship involves a pair of people, but their relationship is embedded in a social milieu (Rusbult & Van Lange, 1996). When a group constitutes the social milieu, dyadic relationships may be aggregated to represent a characteristic of the group. For example, Krackhardt (1995) operationalized the pattern of friendships within an organizational unit as a group characteristic. He recognized that the strength of a friendship affects one's ability to influence the other party but chose "for simplicity" (p. 57) to treat friendship dichotomously.

In thinking about friendship we have in mind both the pattern and the strength of this relationship within a team.[3] Thus we would follow Krackhardt's (1995) concept of friendship rather than his operationalization with its dichotomous simplification. A preferable approach would capture both pattern and strength, but many network analysis techniques commonly employed to that end require groups or networks far larger than the typical venture management team (Francis, 1995).[4] It is possible to measure the *density* of friendships within a team as the ratio of actual friendships to possible friendships (after a conventional measure of network density (Tichy, Tushman, & Fombrun, 1979) and to measure their *intensity* as the average of individual intensities. Recalling that friendship may be treated as a continuous variable, the assignment of a zero value to non-friendship relations allows the average of friendship intensity within a team to represent the proportion of a potential maximum for the team rather than a measure applicable only to the friends within the team. Whether to treat the pattern and strength of friendship as two variables or one is beyond the scope of our discussion in this article. Francis (1995) found that an average based on an additive combination of intensities across friendship pairs better explained teams' behaviors than did density and intensity measures employed separately.

As an informal relationship that is distinct from formal roles, friendship would seem to fall within the purview of research that showed the effects of informal relations in the workplace (e.g. Homans, 1950; Roethlisberger & Dickson, 1939). Even so, until recently very little research had examined friendships within organizations (Fine, 1986). There is evidence, however, that friendships between supervisors and subordinates may underlie

---

3. Other measurable dimensions of the relationships among team members include their social proximity (Alba & Kadushin, 1976), structural equivalence (i.e. the degree to which two members are linked similarly to the same others) (Scott, 1991), and centrality (Scott, 1991).

4. For example, no management team exceeded eight members in the studies by Chandler and Hanks (1998), Francis (1995), or Roure (1986). Francis (1995) discusses the limitations of network analyses in measuring characteristics of small teams.

intraorganizational cooperation (Boyd & Taylor, 1992). More generally, one can build on the relative safety of transactions "with a friend" to suggest that "close, durable relationships [in organizations] force people to be accountable for their actions, discourage negative opportunism, and promote an open and honest exchange of information" (Griesinger, 1990, p. 486). This implies that friendship facilitates group processes that would improve the performance of a management team, and ultimately of the organization.

In sum, friendship's effects may be expected to manifest themselves in the friends' behavior, and specifically in the degrees of trust, candor, cooperation, and interaction they display. There is reason to believe that friendships, like other close relationships featuring interdependence, will exist within organizations. There also is reason to treat the pattern and strength of friendships as a group characteristic. Before considering the consequences for the organization of friendships within its top management team, however, it is necessary to consider the applicability of friendship to such a setting. Does friendship take root in so purposive and task-oriented a group?

Personal Relations and Communities Within Task-Based Groups

Personal relations within an organization often are viewed as causing friction, and emotion is viewed as a universally disruptive force (Hochschild, 1983). Researchers' relative neglect of an affective component of organizational relationships may have stemmed from the belief (see Gabarro, 1987) that it is less important than the nonaffective component of task-based, formal relationships because people satisfy their affective needs in other settings. On the other hand, studies of communities and their interpersonal relationships suggest that the affective component may not always be less important.

A communitarian or *gemeinschaft* perspective views people in a group as being bound by ties of feelings, reacting to one another in social relationships as personalities and not merely as role incumbents (Katz & Kahn, 1978, p. 258). By contrast the *gesellschaft* perspective features rationally conceived social relationships or roles that exist to achieve instrumental objectives (Tonnies, 1971). Entrepreneurial teams presumably have a task-oriented purpose in establishing and managing a firm and therefore may be considered illustrations of *gesellschaft*. Yet the possibility exists that they also illustrate *gemeinschaft*. This dual nature of an organization was evident in German military units during the latter days of World War II (Shils & Janowitz, 1948). In units that continued to fight effectively even under the most difficult circumstances, soldiers reported high levels of solidarity and comradeship. Soldiers' ability to resist and their military unit's ability to avoid social disintegration were a function of the unit's ability to satisfy soldiers' primary needs such as affection, esteem, or power. Shils and Janowitz (1948, p. 285) suggested that the soldiers, isolated from any civilian primary groups, had come to rely on their military unit for these needs. Here an archetypically rational, task-oriented *gesellschaft* was also a *gemeinschaft*, or community. Such dire conditions as mortal combat are not necessary; community may exist in organizations whenever personal and collective goals are blended (Scherer, 1972).

Affective Relations Irrespective of Community

Even when conditions do not transform a task-based organization into a community, people may form affective relationships within their organization. Multiple bonding (comprising both affective and task bonds) occurs in a complex society (Scherer, 1972) as the weakening of kinship ties causes people to look elsewhere to satisfy their primary needs (Bell, 1981). One indication of multiple bonding within the organization is the finding that professionals frequently maintain social relations on and off the job with their co-workers (Weiss & Jacobson, 1955). Economical search explains some of these choices: people who lack the time to pursue outside relationships may instead take advantage of those at hand (Kurth, 1970, p. 148). This explanation may underlie Parker's (1964) finding that 26% of his subjects made friends at work.

Friendships made at work may develop from similar interests that arise from common affiliation, but they are not free of organizational context. The workplace structures a person's meetings with others (Duck, 1991) and may also constrain whom one chooses and maintains as friends (Milardo, 1986). For example, friendships develop more readily among peers than across hierarchical lines (Fine, 1986). People also may become friends through their membership in a highly interdependent network (Milardo, 1986). Each explanation is consistent with evidence that the formation of friendships within small groups is influenced by similarity, propinquity, and interaction (Shaw, 1981).

Summary of Friendship's Prospects and Effects in Top Management Teams

The argument to this point has addressed the potential for friendships' formation within groups such as top management teams and their effects. Numerous reasons—e.g., common interests and experiences, peer status, propinquity, economical search in the face of limited alternatives—exist for people to form workplace friendships. Positive experiences in an interdependent setting may also lead to friendships, and both the potential to establish friendships and their impact are heightened under conditions of great difficulty and isolation from other, customary sources of primary relationships.

The close contact, peer status, and high interdependence that characterize many entrepreneurial teams suggest that friendships could readily develop among members of the team. The pressure, difficulty, and high personal and professional stakes associated with a start-up venture lend themselves to *gemeinschaft* as well as *gesellschaft*. Therefore our attention turns to the special case of the entrepreneurial team.

ENTREPRENEURIAL TEAMS AND THEIR CONTEXT

We define an entrepreneurial team as "two or more individuals who jointly establish a business in which they have an equity (financial) interest" (Kamm et al., 1990, p. 7). This definition focuses on founding and ownership as essential characteristics of entrepreneurial teams but avoids the controversy attending possible distinctions between entrepreneurship and small businesses (see Carland et al., 1984; Carland et al., 1988; Gartner, 1988).[5] Because teams are not always complete at the time of founding, we follow Chandler and Hanks (1998) in including as founders those who join the team within the company's first two years of operation. As will be noted below, some of our propositions are logically restricted to teams of *three* or more. Most research on entrepreneurial teams include two-person teams in their definition, although larger teams appear to be prevalent in their samples (e.g., Roure [1986], with 31 of 36 ventures

---

5. This definition fits comfortably within the domain of entrepreneurship outlined by a Delphi panel as reported by Gartner (1990). In it common themes from Gartner's study are either explicit (organization creation, presence of an owner-manager), implicit (the entrepreneur [here a team], profit-seeking, value creation), or uncontradicted (innovation, growth, uniqueness). Other research on "entrepreneurial teams" has defined the term more broadly, to a significantly different effect. For example, Stewart (1989, p. 11) defined entrepreneurship as "people following up on opportunities for creating new wealth" and explicitly contrasted his definition to others that focused on "top management teams" that start ventures (Stewart, 1989, p. 15).

founded by teams of three or more) or are implied in their terminology (e.g., the interchangeable use of "team" and "group").

Entrepreneurial Teams' Prevalence and Their Impact on Ventures

The importance of entrepreneurial teams stems from both their prevalence and their impact. The evidence suggests "that regardless of the geographic location, type of industry, or gender of founders, a significant number of new ventures are started by teams" (Kamm et al., 1990, p. 8). Even so, the prevalence of teams apparently depends on the type of business being started. A review of research suggests a 30% partnership rate in a large sample of members of the National Federation of Independent Business but a typical rate of 70% in several studies of high-tech start-ups (Cooper & Daily, 1997).

For our purposes in examining the dynamics of teams, however, their impact is of greater interest. Surveying research in entrepreneurship, Kamm and associates (1990) found evidence that team-founded ventures are more likely to achieve high sales, that venture capitalists ascribe great importance to the venture team's capabilities, and that strong and weak minicomputer firms can be distinguished in their first twelve years of operation by various characteristics of their top management teams. Analyzing the *Venture* (1989) study of the 100 best-performing IPOs (initial public offerings of stock), they also found that team ventures were significantly more successful than others in terms of the stock market's capitalization of the firms, although not in revenues or net income (Kamm et al., 1990, p. 8). Following his own review of various studies, Vesper (1990) concluded that team ventures are not desirable in all types of ventures but are preferred when substantial capital must be raised. Recent research in India yielded evidence of superior growth by team-founded ventures relative to solo or two-person ventures, although the difference may also have been attributable to "a healthier capital base" (Thakur, 1999, p. 292n).[6]

The arguments against venture teams often begin with the problem of dilution. The solo founder avoids sharing ownership or control (Vesper, 1990). In terms of the venture's value as distinct from personal preferences, however, adherence to a go-it-alone policy may be destructive through its limiting of human resources. From the same perspective, dilution of ownership or control is irrelevant unless it brings team dynamics that harm rather than enhance the venture's performance.[7]

Formation and Functioning of Entrepreneurial Teams

In thinking about the critical issues and events in the life of an entrepreneurial team, it is useful to adopt a framework comprising three categories: the team's formation, its functioning, and the effects of both on the team's stability and the venture's performance (Cooper & Daily, 1997). The entrepreneurship literature provides insight into both the team's formation and its functioning, although it will be seen that most of that literature is atheoretical and the exceptions lack empirical validation.[8] Rarely are the underlying dynamics of the entrepreneurial team explored in depth in the empirical studies.

---

6. One must not leap to discern a pattern in the findings of Thakur (1999) and Kamm et al. (1990) regarding teams and capitalization. It is possible that larger teams raise more funds, but the two studies examine different aspects of capitalization. Thakur's "healthier capital base" apparently refers to capital employed at founding whereas Kamm and associates measured the market capitalization of publicly traded companies, essentially capturing the value of these more mature and larger firms.

7. The value of the venture is of concern here, not the value of any one person's ownership interest or career. Indeed the dismissal of a poorly performing member of the management team may increase the venture's value to its financial backers (Fiet, Busenitz, Moesel, & Barney, 1997).

8. Cooper and Daily (1997) thoroughly summarize this literature.

Team formation. Even though the formation of a new venture team often seems to be a chance occurrence, two patterns of origination have been described as the "lead entrepreneur" and "group" approaches (Kamm & Nurick, 1993). In the first, one person has a business idea or desires to start a venture and enlists others to join the effort. In the second, a team forms from the outset and together seeks a business opportunity, sometimes with no particular business idea in mind. Such a team may emerge from a shared idea, experience, or friendship (Timmons, 1990). Indeed, "the relationship may take top priority in the beginning, at least" (Kamm & Nurick, 1993, p. 18).

The venture team's formation involves several factors and carries several consequences. Many teams emerge (or are recruited) from among friends, relatives, and former associates (Kamm et al., 1990). These and other contacts within a social network may be sources of resources in addition to their own participation in establishing the venture; their involvement may stem from either affective or instrumental motives (Larson & Starr, 1993). Although affective motives may produce resources or team memberships that could not otherwise be attained, friendship as a basis for team selection is deemed inferior to selection based on filling gaps in the team's capabilities (Timmons, 1979). Among a dozen new venture teams studied by Chandler and Hanks (1998, p. 323), though, technical or functional skills were much less frequently the basis for inclusion in a team than was "a common interest in the [venture's] technology or service." In most cases, they noted, team members "knew each other as coworkers or as family members" (p. 323). This reliance on personal ties more than technical or functional completeness may affect the venture's eventual performance because the venture's prospects are improved if the team can align their needs, values, beliefs, and goals (Bird, 1988).

Team functioning. A team must continue to function effectively after its formation. Issues that threaten the team's continuity may arise even before the venture begins operation (Kamm & Nurick, 1993). The frequency of dissolution or partial breakup among venture teams soon after start-up is not documented, but informed opinion suggests these outcomes are common (Timmons, 1990). Only two of 12 venture teams studied by Chandler and Hanks (1998) remained intact five years after founding. As the venture develops, a "falling out" among team members—"when partners grow to dislike, distrust, and even hate one another"—may threaten the company's survival (Thurston, 1986, p. 24). As Thurston makes clear, the falling out may begin with a concern about one partner's performance but "in deep disagreements it is overshadowed by bad personal relationships" (p. 24). The quality of interpersonal processes (specifically, factors identified as leadership and team commitment) within venture partnerships has been associated with the perceived success of the venture (Watson, Ponthieu, & Critelli, 1995).

The interpersonal problems of entrepreneurial teams have many potential causes, including a lack of heterogeneous experience and skills, the absence of leadership on account of a desire for equitable influence, and conflicting goals and values (Timmons, 1979). Some of these causes (e.g. the lack of heterogeneity) appear to be traceable to the team's formation and others (e.g. conflicting goals and values) may also have been addressable at that time, but all manifest themselves as the team functions.

Kamm and Nurick (1993, p. 23) assumed that the locus of decision-making authority "is a major team maintenance issue" and that a successful team resolves decision-making conflicts through consistent reference to its principal goals. Research has found that conflict within teams making strategic decisions is beneficial to decision quality but may be detrimental to the team's willingness to continue working together (Schweiger, Sandberg, & Ragan, 1986). The key to capturing conflict's benefits without its apparent costs is to encourage the give-and-take of cognitive conflict while avoiding the affective conflict that personalizes disagreement and corrodes relations within the team (Amason, 1996). The identification of mutually agreeable options is easier in an atmosphere of trust that facilitates the honest discussion of decision makers' needs and priorities (Pruitt,

1991), described as a team culture that "discourage[s] political behavior and promote[s] candor, cooperation, and a clear sense of purpose" (Schweiger & Sandberg, 1991, p. 19).

Effects on team and venture. The potential impact of friendship within an entrepreneurial team is suggested by the convergence of two factors: (1) the effects of friendship, notably self-disclosure and mutual trust (Altman & Taylor, 1973; Bliezner & Adams, 1992) and greater expected interaction and cooperation (Argyle & Henderson, 1985); and (2) the culture that makes top management teams more effective in difficult, conflictive decisions by promoting candor and cooperation and discouraging political behavior. Apparently friendships within an entrepreneurial team promote such a culture, and thus the team's effectiveness.

A clue to the theoretical link between friendship and effective entrepreneurial teams may lie in the metaphoric use of warfare. The Data General manager who said of his teammates, "[Y]ou've been through the war together," evoked (whether intentionally or not) not only the conditions but also the solidarity and comradeship cited by Shils and Janowitz (1948) to explain the effectiveness of some German army units late in World War II. The shared goals, high stress, close contact, peer status, and high interdependence that characterize many entrepreneurial teams suggest that friendships could readily develop. Thus friendships may affect the entrepreneurial team even if its members initially came together as strangers or mere acquaintances.

FRIENDSHIP AND ENTREPRENEURIAL TEAMS

The preceding discussion provides a foundation for propositions regarding the role and effects of friendship in entrepreneurial teams. Adhering to Cooper and Daily's (1997) framework, we organize the propositions according to their bearing on the team's formation, its functioning, and its stability. From these propositions we further propose effects of friendship on venture performance.

Consideration of friendship's *effects* on the venture team must be tempered by the recognition that friendship itself comes to reflect the team's experiences with one another as well as its members' reaction to the venture's performance and to exogenous events. That is, the variables of interest (friendship, elements of team functioning, and venture performance) will display reciprocal influences over time. Our focus in this article is on friendship's influence rather than its origins, but we readily acknowledge that the state of friendship at one moment (which we believe will affect subsequent conditions and events) is in part the product of prior conditions and events.

Friendship and Team Formation

The functional completeness of a venture's top management team—the degree to which the company's presidency and key positions in marketing, finance, production, etc., are filled at the time of founding—is a significant predictor of venture success (Roure & Keeley, 1990). Friendships are a source of founding team members (Kamm et al., 1990) and sometimes are the basis for coming together in search of a business opportunity (Timmons, 1990). Thus the friendship may induce involvement by people who would not be attracted by the business opportunity alone (Kamm & Nurick, 1993), or who would price their services beyond the reach of a start-up venture were friendship not involved.

Proposition 1: Venture teams achieve completeness more rapidly to the degree that their formation is based on friendships that predate the venture.

The establishment of a venture and its top management team may raise numerous legal issues. Those related to the team and its members include employment terms (e.g., employment at will or under an employment agreement, the commitment to provide services, the level and types of compensation, any extension of fiduciary duties to partners), the disposition of equity held by owners (e.g., by transfer to third parties, on the death of an owner, on termination of employment) (Mandel, 1997). Such thorny issues may be addressed through explicit, legally enforceable contracts or through implicit, unwritten agreements rooted in mutual trust and the value of one's reputation (Barney & Ouchi, 1986).[9] Friendship's heightened levels of self-disclosure and trust (Bliezner & Adams, 1992) and of cooperation (Argyle & Henderson, 1985) lead us to propose:

> Proposition 2: Higher levels of friendship lead a founding team to rely more on implicit agreements and less on explicit, written contracts in establishing their venture.

The first investment in virtually any venture will be equity capital, in part as a consequence of the extreme riskiness of start-up financing but also as a proof of the founders' seriousness. The founders typically must provide the initial capital from their personal resources in order "to demonstrate commitment on the part of the entrepreneur. Investors perceive, and rightly so, that the individual entrepreneur will be more committed to the venture if she or he has a substantial portion of personal assets invested in the venture" (Stevenson, Roberts, & Grousbeck, 1994, p. 234). In addition to this pressure, which is common to virtually all new ventures, however, comes investment as a manifestation of the solidarity associated with friendship (or perhaps as a demonstration of solidarity in response to the expectations of friends). A similar effect may be expected from the founders' own valuations of the venture as not only a business enterprise (*gesellschaft*) but also a social relationship (*gemeinschaft*).

> Proposition 3: Higher levels of friendship lead members of a founding team to invest a higher proportion of their personal assets in starting the venture.

Friendship and Team Functioning

Among the most crucial of a top management team's roles is the making of strategic decisions. In doing so, the team draws on its cognitive resources through its own processes of interaction. The quality of the team's decisions, and thus of the company's strategy and performance, depends on those processes. In his study of top management teams in small and mid-sized companies, Amason (1996) showed that the immediate results of strategic decisions (decision quality, commitment to decisions, understanding of decisions, and team members' affective acceptance of the process) affected the companies' performance. Moreover, those immediate results were themselves the products of two types of conflict, cognitive and affective. *Cognitive conflict* is "task oriented and focused on judgmental differences about how best to achieve common objectives" whereas *affective conflict* is "emotional and focused on personal incompatibilities or disputes" (Amason, 1996, pp. 127, 129). Cognitive conflict increases the desirable results of decision making but affective conflict depresses them.

Amason identified the team's interaction processes as antecedent to decisions and the two types of conflict. As we noted earlier, the promotion of desirable, cognitive conflict and the minimization of destructive, affective conflict are encouraged by a supportive team culture that discourages political behavior and promotes candor and

---

9. Similar issues and solutions associated with transactions between organizations engaged in innovation are detailed by Ring and Van de Ven (1989).

cooperation (Schweiger & Sandberg, 1991). We believe that friendship creates such a culture through its emphasis on self-disclosure, communication, trust, and cooperation (Argyle & Henderson, 1985).

Corroboration of this anticipated link between a team culture characteristic of friendship and the constructive use of cognitive conflict appears in recent research by Dooley and Fryxell (1999). In a sample of strategic decision-making teams in U.S. hospitals, they found that cognitive dissent reduced the team's perceived decision quality when *loyalty* (measured as an aspect of trustworthiness, namely the disinclination toward opportunism) was *low* but increased it when *loyalty was high.*

There is little research linking friendship and decision making, but much fragmentary evidence of an association. Shah and Jehn (1993) found that groups of friends communicated more and made better decisions than groups of acquaintances. Norms of cooperation and openness associated with successful top management teams (Eisenhardt, 1989; Eisenhardt & Schoonhoven, 1990) are more common in groups of strong, intimate friends than in groups of acquaintances (Argyle & Henderson, 1985; Jehn & Shah, 1997). Friendship fosters a safe environment for discussing concerns, which facilitates the generation of alternative views and promotes understanding (Bliezner & Adams, 1992). It also is conducive to cooperation (Krackhardt & Stern, 1988) and greater influence among team members (Bliezner & Adams, 1992; Lopata, 1981). A more cooperative team is more tolerant of disagreement among members (Torrance, 1957), and therefore less likely to suffer disaffection as a consequence of cognitive conflict.

On the basis of these effects of friendship and its behavioral outcomes, we expect that friendship would promote the interpersonal processes associated with desirable decision-making outcomes. We recognize that friendship (like other close relationships) at any moment reflects affective responses to past contact with another person, and that in the context of entrepreneurial teams the past contact is likely to include precisely the decision-making experiences at issue here. Over time the association between friendship and the outcomes of interest to us therefore is likely to be reciprocal rather than unidirectional.[10] Following our primary interest in friendship's effects on the team's functioning, and consistent with strategic management's research on these phenomena (e.g., Amason, 1996; Dooley & Fryxell, 1999; Schweiger, Sandberg, & Ragan, 1986; Schweiger, Sandberg, & Rechner, 1989), we treat the team's friendship as antecedent to a given decision and therefore its effects on decision-making as distinctly identifiable. Therefore, addressing the results identified by Amason (1996) and others, we propose that:

Proposition 4: Higher levels of friendship within a venture team at the outset of a strategic decision will promote a more effective decision-making process, thus resulting in a higher quality decision, greater commitment to it, greater understanding of it, and greater affective acceptance of fellow team members and the team's processes.

Proposition 5: Higher levels of friendship within a venture team at the outset of a strategic decision will result in greater participation by individual team members in that decision.

Proposition 6: Venture teams characterized by higher levels of friendship at the outset of a strategic decision will experience more cognitive conflict and less affective conflict during the process than will other teams.

---

10. Capturing both causal directions over time would require a cross-lagged panel research design whereby the same team's processes, outcomes, and friendship could be remeasured through a series of decisions. We thank a reviewer for reminding us of this reciprocal relationship and of the research design required to test it.

The effects of cohesion on a team's decisions may not always be positive. Janis (1972) argued that cohesive groups may fall victim to "groupthink," unwittingly failing to examine their own assumptions or consider alternative courses of action and thus making poor decisions. Other research has shown that "groupthink" does not necessarily threaten highly cohesive groups, and that leadership style (Shaw, 1981) and cooperation within the group (Gaenslen, 1980) may diminish the threat. In addition, Janis (1972) noted that groupthink is preventable when teams establish norms of critical evaluation of their proposals.

Schweiger and his colleagues (1986, 1989) found that teams made better strategic decisions through the use of formal techniques to encourage cognitive conflict, but at the risk of incurring affective conflict. Levels and effects of affective conflict decreased, however, as members became more accustomed to their team and to the conflict-inducing techniques (Schweiger et al., 1989). Amason has urged researchers to focus on "the influence of team norms, CEO behavior, and team reward systems on the occurrences of cognitive and affective conflict." He warned that teams may harm themselves by encouraging cognitive conflict "before they are prepared to deal with its consequences" (1996, p. 144). We argue that friendship's heightened cooperation, candor, and trust are desirable preconditions for the use of cognitive conflict-inducing techniques.

> Proposition 7: Among venture teams newly employing cognitive conflict-inducing decision techniques, higher levels of friendship will result in more rapid achievement of the benefits and reduction of the affective conflict associated with such techniques.

Friendship and Team Stability

Stability of a venture's founding team over time is thought to contribute to its success (Kamm & Nurick 1993). Even so, turnover is common. Among the 25 fastest-growing small companies identified by *Inc.* magazine in 1983, almost half of the founding teams had not survived their companies' first five years (*Inc.*, 1983). Cooper and Daily (1997) summarize other studies of turnover among founding teams; all showed similarly high turnover.

Affective conflict arising from strategic decisions is but one possible cause of turnover among venture teams. Other causes include the company's adjustments to a changing environment and the need to obtain different skills in the top management team (Virany & Tushman, 1986). Conflicting values and goals also are a source of divisiveness and possible turnover among venture teams (Timmons, 1979).

Little is known about the effects of friendship on the stability of entrepreneurial teams. Indeed, Cooper and Daily (1997) recently identified those effects as a possible question for research. We believe that friendship can be expected to reduce the rate of turnover arising from the sources identified above. Its palliative effect on affective conflict has already been discussed. It is reasonable to expect that when friendship is strong within a team, its members will be less quick to dismiss others whose skills are not suited to changing conditions, but will attempt instead to develop the needed skills in them. It also is reasonable to expect that friendship, which apparently increases the similarity of friends' views of the world (Kilduff, 1990), reduces the likelihood of disparate values and goals among team members. In addition, friendship increases social integration and cohesion, which are associated with lower turnover (O'Reilly, Caldwell, & Barnett, 1989; Wagner, Pfeffer, & O'Reilly, 1984).

Turnover also may occur as attractive opportunities lure members of the entrepreneurial team away from the company. These opportunities may include employment or the opportunity to found another venture. In deciding whether to depart in pursuit of another opportunity, a member of the team presumably weighs the costs of departing. In the case of a team characterized by a high level of friendship, these costs will include the psychic costs of leaving friends as well as the usual economic costs and considerations of personal risk. By imposing additional costs on departure, friendship will reduce turnover among the entrepreneurial team.

> Proposition 8: Friendship within an entrepreneurial team is negatively related to subsequent turnover among the team.

Bonds of friendship may contribute to *higher* turnover under certain conditions. For example, the founding teams of high-performing minicomputer manufacturers were less stable over time if the founding CEO left the company (Virany & Tushman, 1986). One explanation for this result may be friendship: in the face of other opportunities, changes in their personal circumstances, or disappointment in their prospects within the company, team members may remain from a sense of loyalty or commitment to the founder. His or her departure frees them from that bond and may cause an immediate exodus. Some members of the entrepreneurial team may even follow the founder to another venture; others who remain may discover that their ostensible commitment to the company had been a commitment to its founder, and therefore leave the organization at a later time.

This reasoning suggests a moderated relationship between friendship and the subsequent stability of the entrepreneurial team. The moderator reflects the removal of a potentially key element of the team's friendship (remembering that we conceive of friendship as a *group* characteristic), namely the person around whom the founding team was formed. Our reasoning regarding the founding CEO's departure should also apply to the departure of other members of the entrepreneurial team, including both founders and those who joined later.[11] Following that event, we propose, turnover increases because friendship's restraint on departure has been weakened and its bonds to departing members heightens the allure of following them. In shifting consideration from the founding CEO to other members of the founding team and then to later members of the entrepreneurial team, one allows that effects may be weaker, but the same dynamics of friendship would be expected to operate.[12]

> Proposition 9: Higher levels of friendship within an entrepreneurial team increase the likelihood of turnover following the departure of (a) the founding CEO or (b) another founder.
> Proposition 10: Higher levels of friendship within an entrepreneurial team increase the likelihood of turnover following a departure from the team.

Friendship and Venture Performance

The impact of friendship within the venture team on the venture's performance will reflect the contributions of many distinct influences. In this section we take up relationships between friendship and performance that may be mediated by another variable. (Evidence of a mediating effect is found if friendship and the mediating variable are related and the relationship between friendship and performance changes substantially when the mediator is included in the model [James & Brett, 1984].)

Following Cooper and Daily (1997), we have separated these relationships according

---

11. Recall that we follow Chandler and Hanks (1998) in regarding as founders people who join the team within two years of the venture's creation.

12. Propositions 8-10 are logically restricted to teams of three or more. A team of two is dissolved upon one member's departure, leaving a solo entrepreneur if the company survives. Turnover takes on a different meaning for a "team of one" that we do not attempt to address in this article.

to whether they primarily involve the team's formation, its functioning, or its stability. Not every influence of friendship will lead to improved venture performance under all likely conditions, but we believe an overall pattern can be discerned.

Friendship during formation. We have argued that friendship facilitates the formation of a complete venture team (Proposition 1) and stimulates a greater commitment of the founders' financial resources to the venture (Proposition 3). Both effects should lead to better venture performance through quicker readiness to exploit the perceived opportunity and improved access to resources, both managerial and financial. This reasoning is consistent with evidence that first-year growth is higher for businesses when founders know each other very well and communicate frequently (Hansen, 1995). The other proposed effect on team formation was a greater reliance on implicit agreements and a reduced reliance on explicit, written contracts in establishing the venture (Proposition 2). Here the potential effects on performance are more ambiguous: what is gained in speed or saved in legal costs at the outset may come at the cost of future misunderstanding, strife, and litigation. On balance, though, we believe that this situation will not be identical to that facing a team of strangers or acquaintances who proceed without explicit contracts. The team characterized by friendship will have based its implicit understandings on a firmer foundation than would another team, and may still possess those friendships to use in resolving future misunderstandings.

> Proposition 11: Higher levels of friendship during the formation of a venture team will be positively related to the subsequent performance of the venture.

Friendship while a functioning team. The effects on performance of top management friendship during later stages in a venture's life seem generally positive. We have proposed that friendship affects the team's strategic decision-making effectiveness (Propositions 4-7). Following Amason (1996) and other researchers, we focused on how friendship influences the process of decision, with emphasis on its facilitation of constructive, cognitive conflict and avoidance of destructive, affective conflict. In each instance we proposed effects on strategic decisions as well as on the team's subsequent ability to work together. Inasmuch as strategic decisions are crucial to the subsequent performance of new ventures (McDougall, Robinson, & DeNisi, 1992; Sandberg, 1986), we expect these influences of friendship to yield only positive effects on venture performance.

The impact on performance of friendship's effects on team stability are less straightforward. Greater stability of the top management team (Proposition 8) would be expected to improve the performance of ventures that are faring well because it reduces untimely losses of talent, discontinuity in planning and execution, and the risk of losing proprietary information. On the other hand, team stability may be dysfunctional for ventures that are performing poorly or that need different management skills to accomplish a change in strategy. Turnaround strategies, for example, commonly require the replacement of top management (Hofer, 1980): would friendship deter involuntary but necessary turnover?

We also proposed that friendship may lead to *increased* turnover within a venture team following the departure of founders (Proposition 9) or other members of the team (Proposition 10). In both situations the initial instance of turnover was thought to trigger other, voluntary departures. These could prove detrimental to the venture's performance, perhaps even to the point of jump-starting a new rival.

In weighing the positive effects of friendship on strategic decisions (and thereby on performance) against its mixed effects on team stability (and thereby on performance), we conclude that for most ventures the positive effects will prevail. The need for a turnaround strategy, or for sudden and widespread change in the venture's managerial skills, is minimized by consistently effective strategic decisions over a period of years. Those same decisions also enhance the venture's prospects, and thus the career opportunities available within the organization. Improved strategic decisions arising from the influences of friendship within the entrepreneurial team thus reduce the likelihood of the venture's facing situations in which friendship's influences on team stability would impair venture performance.

> Proposition 12: Higher levels of friendship within the entrepreneurial team during its "functioning" phase will be positively related to the venture's subsequent performance.

While exercising a positive effect on the performance of most ventures, friendship within the entrepreneurial team may have a counterintuitive, negative effect on the performance of *a segment of the population* of ventures. This possibility could stem from friendship's effect on the venture's threshold level of performance, or the minimum performance necessary to motivate continued effort in the venture. "The persistence of underperforming firms" in a sample of 1,547 entrepreneurs of new businesses stemmed in part from the entrepreneur's "psychic income from entrepreneurship" (Gimeno, Folta, Cooper, & Woo, 1997). Greater psychic income lowered the threshold of economic performance that an entrepreneur required to justify remaining in business. The researchers did not consider psychic income from the *specific* venture,[13] which we believe would be enhanced by any feelings of friendship within the entrepreneurial team. We would expect the threshold of performance thus to be lowered, thereby increasing the venture's persistence. Among ventures that perform well this effect would be unnoticed because performance exceeds even the "non-friendship" threshold, but the effect could become pronounced among ventures performing marginally or poorly. It is possible, then, that the population of ventures characterized by high levels of friendship within their entrepreneurial teams will include a larger than normal share of persisting, poor performers.

> Proposition 13: Among ventures experiencing poor performance, a higher level of friendship within the entrepreneurial team increases the likelihood of survival.

The sense in which these ventures "survive" may imply a subsequent improvement in their performance, but that is not our expectation. One might argue that through persistence the ventures remain alive and therefore may benefit from remotely possible windfalls or new opportunities. Even allowing for this effect, we remain skeptical. We believe that the net benefits of such future returns, if substantial, would have encouraged persistence in *any* venture team; our concern is with increased persistence owing to bonds of friendship rather than to a team's perception of the venture's prospects.

IMPLICATIONS

In considering the effects of friendship within an entrepreneurial team on the performance of the venture they found and lead, we have organized our thoughts around three categories devised by Cooper and Daily (1997): the team's formation, its subsequent functioning, and its stability. From those categories came links to the founding and subsequent performance of an entrepreneurial venture. Our approach has been to identify aspects of the team that have been demonstrated to affect the performance of ventures, and to probe for likely influences of friendship on those aspects of the team. We have

---

13. Gimeno and his colleagues operationalized psychic income in terms of the entrepreneur's intrinsic need to be self-employed and whether his or her parents were entrepreneurs.

sought to identify the immediate behavioral consequences of friendship and the specific means by which they would affect the team and the venture.

Direct Implications for Research and Management

The proposed effects of friendship within an entrepreneurial team point to several potential streams of research. In general, potential research agendae could comprise the behavioral consequences in each aspect of the team and their effect on the venture. Thus the propositions regarding the formation of the venture team (Propositions 1-3) suggest research on the speed of completing the team, the reliance on implicit versus explicit agreements in establishing the venture, and the commitment of individual founders' resources to the venture—all observable behavioral outcomes. In turn, we have proposed that friendship's influences on these aspects of the team will positively affect the venture's performance (Proposition 11).

Similarly, the propositions regarding the team's functioning (Propositions 4-7) concentrate on observable behavioral outcomes of friendship in terms of improved decisions and desirable affective responses to the decision-making process and in terms of both individual participation in decisions and the entrepreneurial team's ability to learn conflict-inducing decision techniques. In turn, we have extended this reasoning to propose a positive effect on venture performance (Proposition 12). In addition, we have proposed that friendship encourages the persistence of ventures that are performing poorly (Proposition 13); whether that outcome would have a net positive or negative effect on venture performance over the long run is itself a matter for investigation.

Propositions 8 through 10 together imply a moderated relationship between friendship and turnover within the entrepreneurial team. That is, a negative relationship is proposed (Proposition 8) except following the departure of a founder (Proposition 9) or other member (Proposition 10), whereupon a positive relationship is proposed. In testing these propositions, researchers may wish to consider alternative operationalizations of turnover. For example, a dichotomous treatment of turnover (i.e. the team either experienced turnover or did not) would suffice for the latter propositions provided that a period of time is specified and team size is controlled. Another approach would measure the *rate* of turnover during a specified period, as implied by Proposition 8. Researchers interested in the removal of restraints on team members' departure might wish to measure the *time until next departure,* again controlling for team size.

Further Implications

Further ideas for research arise from aspects of friendship and the entrepreneurial team that we have not addressed. To the extent that friendship proves to affect the team and its venture, researchers and managers may wish to broaden their consideration of it.

For instance, the antecedents of friendship are beyond the scope of this article yet could produce variations in friendship that would affect the relationships discussed here. Consider what John D. Rockefeller wrote of his friendship with fellow tycoon Henry M. Flagler: "It was a friendship founded on business, which Mr. Flagler used to say was a good deal better than a business founded on friendship" (Gordon, 1996, p. 44). Flagler, fresh from financial disaster as partner in a failed salt company, moved to Cleveland and worked for a former partner of Rockefeller. He prospered and rented a house near Rockefeller's. Soon the two became friends through discussions of their business affairs over lunch or while walking to and from work. In time Rockefeller asked Flagler to become his partner in his new venture into oil refining, through which Flagler played a key role in the development of Standard Oil (Gordon, 1996). How a friendship was formed may deserve attention in attempting to assemble a venture team and in research on the team's subsequent performance.

Our discussion has not explored the development of friendships following the establishment of an entrepreneurial team. We have proposed effects of given levels of friendship at particular moments but have not proposed direct or moderating effects of *changes* in the level of friendship, or of how those changes occurred, on the team or the venture. Among the antecedents of friendship are propinquity, interaction, and individual psychological characteristics (Francis, 1995). Interaction enables people to learn of the characteristics of others that make them attractive (Shaw, 1981),[14] which implies that entrepreneurial teams should seek to know one another beyond their organizational roles. Because friendships are embedded in a social context—here the organizational culture of the entrepreneurial team—their importance may warrant both research and managerial attention to the development and manipulation of that culture. Associated with the latter point is the possible impact of the *pattern* or structure of friendships within the entrepreneurial team. One might draw on network theory to explore this topic (Krackhardt, 1995).

CONCLUSION

Relationships among the entrepreneurial team are an underexplored subject in entrepreneurship research. We believe that its status is similar to that of strategic management's work on the top management team. For years researchers explained organizational outcomes in terms of the team's demographics, neglecting the intermediate behavioral processes (Jackson, 1992) and the context in which human action occurs (Pettigrew, 1992). More recent research confirms the indispensability of team processes in modeling the effect of team demography on organizational performance (Smith et al., 1994). Management is fundamentally a social activity (Walsh, 1995) and "organizational members are feeling, emotive, affective human beings ... [whose] ... decisions are often based on an *emotional understanding of issues*" (Shrivastava & Alvesson, 1987, p. 102; italics in original).

We believe that by taking account of the friendships within the entrepreneurial team, researchers who explore the impact of top management within ventures and other entrepreneurial firms will improve the explanatory power of their models and achieve new insights. Considerable development and testing remain en route to a comprehensive theory of friendship in entrepreneurial teams. This article is only a beginning.

REFERENCES

Alba, R. D., & Kadushin, C. (1976). The intersection of social circles: A new measure of social proximity in networks. *Sociological Methods and Research, 5*(1), 77-102.

Altman, I., & Taylor, D. (1973). *Social penetration: The development of interpersonal relationships.* New York: Rhinhart & Winston.

Amason, A. C. (1996). Distinguishing the effects of functional and dysfunctional conflict on strategic decision making: Resolving a paradox for top management teams. *Academy of Management Journal, 39,* 123-148.

---

14. For example, "[Henry] Flagler admired Rockefeller's attention to detail, careful habits, and insistence on thorough investigation. Rockefeller liked Flagler's 'vim and push' and his creative solutions to legal and administrative problems" (Gordon, 1996, p. 43).

Argyle, M., & Henderson, M. (1985). The rules of friendship. In S. Duck (Ed.), *Understanding personal relationships: An interdisciplinary approach*, pp. 63-84. Beverly Hills, CA: Sage.

Barney, J. B., & Ouchi, W. G. (1986). *Organization economics*. San Francisco: Jossey-Bass.

Bell, R. R. (1981). *Worlds of friendship*. Beverly Hills, CA: Sage.

Bird, B. (1988). Implementing entrepreneurial ideas: The case for intention. *Academy of Management Review, 13,* 442-453.

Bliezner, R., & Adams, R. G. (1992). *Adult friendship*. Newbury Park, CA: Sage.

Boyd, N. G. (1991). *Should leaders and subordinates be friends? An examination of some behavioral implications of leader-subordinate friendship*. Unpublished doctoral dissertation, Memphis State University, Memphis, TN.

Boyd, N. G., & Taylor, R. R. (1992). The influence of leader-subordinate friendship on the evaluation of subordinate performance. Paper presented at the annual meeting of the Southern Management Association, New Orleans, LA.

Bulkeley, W. M. (1985). Venturing out: Computer engineers memorialized in book seek new challenges. *Wall Street Journal,* September 20, pp. 1, 13.

Carland, J. W., Hoy, F., Boulton, W., & Carland, J. A. C. (1984). Differentiating entrepreneurs from small business owners: A conceptualization, *Academy of Management Review, 9,* 354-359.

Carland, J. W., Hoy, F., & Carland, J. A. C. (1988). "Who is an entrepreneur?" is a question worth asking. *American Journal of Small Business,* Spring, 33-39.

Chandler, G. N., & Hanks, S. H. (1998). An investigation of new venture teams in emerging businesses. In: P. D. Reynolds, W. D. Bygrave, N. M. Carter, S Manigart, C. M. Mason, G. D. Meyer, and K. G. Shaver (Eds.), *Frontiers of entrepreneurship research*, pp. 318-330. Wellesley, MA: Babson College.

Cooper, A. C., & Daily, C. M. (1997). Entrepreneurial teams. In D. L. Sexton & R. W. Smilor (Eds.), *Entrepreneurship 2000*, chapter 6. Chicago: Upstart Publishing Company.

Dooley, R. S., & Fryxell, G. E. (1999). Attaining decision quality and commitment from dissent: The moderating effects of loyalty and competence in strategic decision-making teams. *Academy of Management Journal, 42,* 389-402.

Duck, S. (1991). *Understanding relationships*. New York: Guilford Press.

Eisenhardt, K. M. (1989). Making fast strategic decisions in high-velocity environments. *Academy of Management Journal, 32,* 543-576.

Eisenhardt, K. M., & Schoonhoven, C. B. (1990). Organizational growth: Linking founding team, strategy, environment, and growth among U.S. semiconductor ventures, 1978-1988. *Administrative Science Quarterly, 35,* 504-529.

Fiet, J. O., Busenitz, L. W., Moesel, D. D. & Barney, J. B. (1997). Complementary theoretical perspectives on the dismissal of new venture team members. *Journal of Business Venturing, 12*(5), 347-366.

Fine, G. A. (1986). Friendships in the work place. In V. J. Derlega & B. A. Winstead (Eds.), *Friendship and social interaction*, pp. 185-206. New York: Springer-Verlag.

Fischer, C. S. (1982). What do we mean by 'friend'? An inductive study. *Social Networks, 3,* 287-306.

Francis, D. H. (1995). *The influence of the friendships within the top management team on the team's decision-making processes and outcomes*. Unpublished doctoral dissertation, University of South Carolina, Columbia, SC.

Gabarro, J. J. (1978). The development of trust, influence and expectations. In A. G. Athos & J. J. Gabarro (Eds.), *Interpersonal behavior: Communication and understanding in relationships,* pp. 290-303. Englewood Cliffs, NJ: Prentice Hall.

Gabarro, J. J. (1987). The development of working relationships. In J. W. Lorsch (Ed.), *Handbook of organizational behavior,* pp. 172-189. Englewood Cliffs, NJ: Prentice Hall.

Gaenslen, F. (1980). Democracy vs. efficiency: Some arguments from the small group. *Political Psychology,* Spring, 15-29.

Gartner, W. B. (1988). "Who is an entrepreneur?" is the wrong question. *American Journal of Small Business,* Spring, 11-32.

Gartner, W. B. 1990. What are we talking about when we talk about entrepreneurship? *Journal of Business Venturing, 5,* 15-28.

Gimeno, J., Folta, T. B., Cooper, A. C., & Woo, C. Y. (1997). Survival of the fittest? Entrepreneurial human capital and the persistence of underperforming firms. *Administrative Science Quarterly 42*(4), 750-783.

Gordon, J. S. (1996). The master builder. *Audacity, 4*(2), 40-53.

Griesinger, D. W. (1990). The human side of economic organization. *Academy of Management Review, 15,* 478-499.

Hallinan, M. T., & Williams, R. A. (1990). Students' characteristics and the peer-influence process. *Sociology of Education, 63,* 122-132.

Hambrick, D. C., & Mason, P. A. (1984). Upper echelons: The organization as a reflection of its top managers. *Academy of Management Review, 9,* 193-206.

Hansen, E. L. (1995). Entrepreneurial networks and new organization growth. *Entrepreneurship Theory and Practice, 19*(4), 7-19.

Hochschild, A. R. (1983). *The managed heart: Commercialization of human feeling.* Berkeley. University of California Press.

Hofer, C. W. (1980). Turnaround strategies. *The Journal of Business Strategy, 1*(1), 19-31.

Homans, G. C. (1950). *The human group.* New York: Harcourt, Brace & World.

Inc. (1983). Inside the Inc. 500, December, 67-76.

Jackson, S. E. (1992). Consequences of group composition for the interpersonal dynamics of strategic issue processing. In P. Shrivastava, A. Huff, & J. Dutton (Eds.), *Advances in strategic management,* vol. 8, pp. 345-382. Greenwich, CT: JAI Press.

James, L. R., & Brett, J. M. (1984). Mediators, moderators, and tests for mediation. *Journal of Applied Psychology, 69*(2), 307-321.

Janis, I. (1972). *Victims of groupthink.* Boston, MA: Houghton Mifflin.

Jehn, K. A., & Shah, P. P. (1997). Interpersonal relationships and task performance: An examination of mediating processes in friendship and acquaintance groups. *Journal of Personality and Social Psychology, 72*(4), 775-790.

Kamm, J. B., & Nurick, A. J. (1993). The stages of team venture formation: A decision-making model. *Entrepreneurship Theory and Practice, 17*(2), 17-27.

Kamm, J. B., Shuman, J. C., Seeger, J. A., & Nurick, A. J. (1990). Entrepreneurial teams in new venture creation: A research agenda. *Entrepreneurship Theory and Practice, 14*(4), 7-17.

Kanter, R. M. (1980). How the top is different. In H. J. Leavitt, L. R. Pondy, & D. M. Boje (Eds.), *Readings in managerial psychology,* 3rd ed., pp. 522-534. Chicago: University of Chicago Press.

Katz, D., & Kahn, R. L. (1978). *The social psychology of organizations,* 2d ed. New York: John Wiley & Sons.

Kelley, H. H., Berscheid, E., Christensen, A., Harvey, J. H., Huston, T. L., Levinger, G., McClintock, E., Peplau, L. A., & Peterson, D. R. (1983). *Close relationships.* New York: W. H. Freeman & Co.

Kidder, T. (1981). *The soul of a new machine.* New York: Avon Books.

Kilduff, M. (1990). The interpersonal structure of decision making: A social comparison approach to organizational choice. *Organizational Behavior and Human Decision Processes, 47,* 270-288.

Krackhardt, D. (1995). Entrepreneurial opportunities in an entrepreneurial firm: A structural approach. *Entrepreneurship Theory and Practice, 19*(3), 53-69.

Krackhardt, D., & Stern, R. N. (1988). Informal networks and organizational crises: An experimental simulation. *Social Psychology Quarterly, 51*(2), 123-140.

Kurth, S. B. (1970). Friendship and friendly relations. In G. McCall, M. McCall, N. Denzin, G. Suttles, & S. B. Kurth, (Eds.), *Social relationships,* pp. 136-170. Chicago: Aldine.

Larson, A., & Starr, J. A. (1993). A network model of organization formation. *Entrepreneurship Theory and Practice, 17*(2), 5-15.

Lopata, H. Z. (1981). Friendship: Historical and theoretical introduction. In H. Z. Lopata, & D. Maines, (Eds.), *Research in the interweave of social roles: Friendship,* pp. 1-22. Greenwich, CT: JAI Press.

Mandel, R. P. (1997). Legal and tax issues. In W. D. Bygrave (Ed.), *The portable MBA in entrepreneurship,* 2nd ed., chapter 10. New York: John Wiley & Sons.

McDougall, P. P., Robinson, R. B. Jr., & DeNisi, A. S. (1992). Modeling new venture performance: An analysis of new venture strategy, industry structure, and venture origin, *Journal of Business Venturing, 7*(4), 267-289.

Milardo, R. M. (1986). Personal choice and social constraint in close relationships: Applications of network analysis. In V. J. Derlega & B. A. Winstead (Eds.), *Friendship and social interaction,* pp. 145-166. New York: Springer-Verlag.

Millard, A. (1990). *Edison and the business of innovation.* Baltimore, MD: Johns Hopkins University Press.

Morton, T. L., & Douglas, M. A. (1981). Growth of relationships. In S. Duck & R. Gilmore (Eds.), *Personal relationships, vol. 2: Developing relationships,* pp. 3-26. London: Academic Press.

O'Reilly III, C. A., Caldwell, D. F., & Barnett, W. P. (1989). Work group demography, social integration, and turnover. *Administrative Science Quarterly, 34,* 21-37.

Parker, S. R. 1964. Type of work, friendship patterns and leisure. *Human Relations, 17,* 215-219.

Pettigrew, A. M. (1992). On studying managerial elites. *Strategic Management Journal, 13,* 163-182.

Pruitt, D. G. (1991). Strategy in negotiation. In V. A. Kremenyuk (Ed.), *International negotiation: Analysis, approaches, issues,* pp. 78-89. San Francisco: Jossey-Bass.

Reich, R. B. (1987). Entrepreneurship reconsidered: The team as hero. *Harvard Business Review, 65*(3), 77-83.

Ring, P. S., & Van de Ven, A. H. (1989). Formal and informal dimensions of transactions. In A. H. Van de Ven, H. L. Angle, & M. S. Poole (Eds.), *Research on the management of innovation,* ch. 6. New York: Harper & Row.

Roethlisberger, F. J., & Dickson, W. J. (1939). *Management and the worker.* Cambridge, MA: Harvard University Press.

Roure, J. B. (1986). *Success and failure of high-growth technological ventures: The influence of pre-funding factors.* Unpublished doctoral dissertation, Stanford University, Palo Alto, CA.

Roure, J. B., & Keeley, R. H. (1990). Predictors of success in new technology based ventures. *Journal of Business Venturing, 5,* 201-220.

Rusbult, C. E., & Van Lange, P. A. M. (1996). Interdependence processes. In E. T. Higgins & A. W. Kruglanski (Eds.), *Social psychology: Handbook of basic principles,* pp. 564-596. New York: Guilford Press.

Sandberg, W. R. (1986). *New venture performance.* Lexington, MA: D.C. Heath.

Sandberg, W. R. (1992). Strategic management's potential contributions to a theory of entrepreneurship. *Entrepreneurship Theory and Practice, 16*(3), 73-90.

Sapienza, H. J., Herron, L., & Menendez, J. (1991). The founder and the firm: A qualitative analysis of the entrepreneurial process. presented at the Babson Conference on Entrepreneurship Research.

Scherer, J. (1972). *Contemporary community: Sociological illusion or reality?* London: Tavistock Publications.

Scott, J. (1991). *Social networks analysis: A handbook.* Newbury Park, CA: Sage.

Schweiger, D. M. & Sandberg, W. R. (1991). The team approach to making strategic decisions. In H. E. Glass (Ed.), *Handbook of business strategy,* 2nd ed. Boston, MA: Warren, Gorham & Lamont.

Schweiger, D. M., Sandberg, W. R., & Ragan, J. W. (1986). Group approaches for improving strategic decision making: A comparative analysis of dialectical inquiry, devil's advocacy, and consensus. *Academy of Management Journal, 29,* 51-71.

Schweiger, D. M., Sandberg, W. R., & Rechner, P. L. (1989). Experimental effects of dialectical inquiry, devil's advocacy, and consensus approaches to strategic decision making. *Academy of Management Journal, 32,* 745-772.

Shah, P. P., & Jehn, K. A. (1993). Do friends perform better than acquaintances? The interaction of friendship, conflict and task. *Group Decision Making and Negotiation, 2,* 149-165.

Shaw, M. E. (1981). *Group dynamics: The psychology of small group behavior,* 3rd ed. New York: McGraw-Hill.

Shils, E. A., & Janowitz, M. (1948). Cohesion and disintegration in the Wehrmacht in WWII. *Public Opinion Quarterly, 12*(3), 280-315.

Shrivastava, P., & Alvesson, M. (1987). Nonrationality in organizational actions. *International Studies of Management and Organizations, 17,* 90-109.

Simmel, G. (1950). *The sociology of Georg Simmel.* Kurt Wolff, tr. New York: Free Press.

Smith, K. G., Smith, K. A., Olian, J. D., Sims, H. P., Jr., O'Bannon, D. P., & Scully, J. (1994). Top management team demography and process: The role of social integration and communication. *Administrative Science Quarterly 39*(3), 412-438.

Snyder, M. & Smith, D. (1986). Personality and friendship: The friendship worlds of self-monitoring. In V. J. Derlega & B. A. Winstead (Eds.), *Friendship and social interaction,* pp. 63-80, New York: Springer-Verlag.

Stevenson, H. H., Roberts, M. J., & Grousbeck, H. I. (1994). *New business ventures and the entrepreneur.* Burr Ridge, IL: Richard D. Irwin.

Stewart, A. (1989). *Team entrepreneurship.* Newbury Park, CA: Sage.

Thakur, P. T. (1999). Size of investment, opportunity choice and human resources in new venture growth: Some typologies. *Journal of Business Venturing, 14*(3), 283-309.

Thibaut, J. W., & Kelley, H. H. (1959). *The social psychology of groups.* New York: John Wiley & Sons.

Thurston, P. H. (1986). When partners fall out. *Harvard Business Review, 64*(6), 24-34.

Tichy, N. M., Tushman, M. L., & Fombrun, C. (1979). Social network analysis for organizations. *Academy of Management Review, 4,* 507-519.

Timmons, J. A. (1979). Careful self-analysis and team assessment can aid entrepreneurs. *Harvard Business Review,* Nov-Dec, 198-206.

Timmons, J. A. (1990). *New venture creation: Entrepreneurship in the 1990s,* 3rd ed. Homewood, IL: Irwin.

Tonnies, F. (1971). *Ferdinand Tonnies on sociology: Pure, applied, and empirical. Selected Writings,* J. Cahnman & R. Heberle (Eds.), Chicago: University of Chicago Press.

Torrance, P. E. (1957). Group decision making and disagreement. *Social Forces, 35,* 314-318.

Venture. (1989). The IPO fast-track. *Venture, 11*(4), 25-39.

Vesper, K. H. (1990). *New venture strategies,* revised ed. Englewood Cliffs, NJ: Prentice Hall.

Virany, B., & Tushman, M. L. (1986). Top management teams and corporate success in an emerging industry. *Journal of Business Venturing, 1,* 261-274.

Wagner, W. G., Pfeffer, J., & O'Reilly, C. A. (1984). Organizational demography and turnover in top-management groups. *Administrative Science Quarterly, 29,* 74-92.

Walsh, J. P. (1995). Managerial and organizational cognition: Notes from a trip down memory lane. *Organization Science, 6*(3), 280-321.

Watson, W. E., Ponthieu, L. D., & Critelli, J. W. (1995). Team interpersonal process effectiveness in venture partnerships and its connection to perceived success. *Journal of Business Venturing, 10,* 393-411.

Weiss, R., & Jacobson, E. (1955). A method for the analysis of the structure of complex organizations. *American Sociological Review, 20,* 661-668.

Wright, P. H. (1985). The acquaintance description form. In S. Duck & D. Perlman (Eds.), *Understanding personal relationships: An interdisciplinary approach,* pp. 39-62. Beverly Hills, CA: Sage.

Deborah H. Francis is assistant professor of management at Auburn University at Montgomery.

William R. Sandberg is associate professor of management at the University of South Carolina.

[8]

ELSEVIER   Journal of Business Venturing 17 (2002) 365–386

JOURNAL
of BUSINESS
VENTURING

Understanding the dynamics of new venture top management teams
Cohesion, conflict, and new venture performance

Michael D. Ensley[a,1], Allison W. Pearson[b,*], Allen C. Amason[c,2]

[a]*Belk College of Business Administration, University of North Carolina-Charlotte, Charlotte, NC 28223, USA*
[b]*College of Business and Industry, Mississippi State University, PO Box 9581, Mississippi, MS 39762, USA*
[c]*Terry College of Business, The University of Georgia, Athens, GA 30602, USA*

Received 3 February 1999; received in revised form 1 March 2000; accepted 1 May 2000

Abstract

Research conducted under the upper echelon perspective has produced consistent evidence of a relationship between top management team (TMT) interaction and firm performance. We draw upon and extend this research in an effort to explain new venture performance as a function of cohesion and conflict within the top management team. Based upon data collected from a sample of 70 new ventures, we find that TMT cohesion is negatively related to affective conflict and positively related to cognitive conflict. As expected then, we also find that TMT cohesion is positively related to new venture growth. © 2001 Elsevier Science Inc. All rights reserved.

Keywords: New ventures; Top management teams; Performance; Conflict; Cohesion

1. Executive summary

Despite popular legends about individual entrepreneurs, the creation and successful management of new ventures is often a team effort, shared among individuals representing a diversity of skills and experiences. As such, the success of a venture is often a reflection of

---

* Corresponding author. Tel.: +1-662-325-7015.
E-mail address: apearson@cobilan.msstate.edu (A.W. Pearson).
[1] Tel.: +1-704-547-4343. *E-mail address:* mdensley@email.uncc.edu (M.D. Ensley).
[2] Tel.: +1-706-542-3702. *E-mail address:* aamason@terry.cba.uga.edu (A.C. Amason).

0883-9026/02/$ – see front matter © 2001 Elsevier Science Inc. All rights reserved.
PII: S0883-9026(00)00065-3

its team's ability to meld talent and ability in a creative and coordinated fashion. As teams utilize their diversity to produce insightful yet workable strategies, while also promoting satisfaction and commitment among their members, superior venture performance will follow.

Central to the effort to meld talent and ability is the use of conflict. Paradoxically, conflict can be a catalyst for creativity and understanding as well as for animosity and resentment. The open exchange of ideas, the objective assessment of alternatives, and the rigorous contrasting of perspectives produces conflicts out of which creative ideas and solutions emerge. At the same time, such interactions may also produce anger and alienation, which can lead to disaffection and departure by the offended team members. Thus, effective teams embrace the benefits of conflict, while also avoiding its costs. Research has shown that to do this requires encouraging the cognitive dimension of conflict, while simultaneously discouraging the affective dimension.

Unfortunately, cognitive and affective conflict most often occur together, spurred on by good intentions and a lack of understanding. Thus, the dilemma for researchers and managers alike is to understand the antecedents of cognitive and affective conflict, as well as the conditions that lead one to trigger the other.

To address the issue, we offer this study of 70 new venture management teams. We examine the effects of cohesion on cognitive and affective conflict. We reason that cohesion increases constructive cognitive conflicts while simultaneously decreasing destructive affective conflicts. Because of the familiarity and comfort among their members, cohesive teams should experience lower levels of affective conflict and higher levels of cognitive conflict than their less cohesive counterparts. As a result, cohesiveness should relate positively to superior new venture performance.

Although not without some variation, the data we report support this reasoning. Thus, we conclude that cohesion is an important characteristic of successful new venture management teams and suggest that cohesion, when combined with efforts to promote free and open interaction, will lead to more effective teams and better performing ventures.

2. Introduction

Central to the upper echelon perspective is the belief that firm outcomes are a "reflection" of the characteristics and actions of a small group of managers at the top of the organization (Finkelstein and Hambrick, 1996; Hambrick and Mason, 1984). As such, an increasing number of researchers have sought to understand the inner workings of the top management team (TMT). Indeed, a rich stream of literature has developed examining TMT demography and interaction and attempting to relate specific team attributes to firm performance.

Although not as well established, a similar stream has emerged in the entrepreneurship literature. Like the earlier work, central to this line of research is the premise that, despite popular and romantic notions about individual entrepreneurs, the management of new ventures is generally a shared effort (Gartner et al., 1994). However, unlike the earlier work, this research assumes that new venture management is a special type of task and so warrants specific study of the relationships between TMTs and new venture performance (Amason et al., 1997).

M.D. Ensley et al. / Journal of Business Venturing 17 (2002) 365–386 367

We contribute to this emerging stream with the present study addressing the question: How are cohesion and decision making conflict within the TMT related to one another and, ultimately, to new venture performance? In so doing, we integrate further constructs from group theory (McGrath, 1964) and the upper echelon perspective (Finkelstein and Hambrick, 1996) into the literatures of entrepreneurship and new venture management.

3. Theoretical development

The earliest studies of new venture performance were largely anecdotal and focused on characteristics of the venture founders (Hornaday and Aboud, 1971; Palmer, 1971). More recently, researchers have examined constructs like industry structure and strategy in an effort to understand more fully the determinants of new venture success (Lambkin, 1988; McDougall, 1987; Sandberg and Hofer, 1987). From this, we have gathered that strategies are critically important. However, because of their limited resources, new ventures have a narrow range of strategies from which to choose. For example, Chaganti et al. (1989) found that new ventures had great difficulty competing on price against more established competitors. Consequently, new venture strategies often emphasize the need to be somehow unique and different from the other firms in the marketplace.

This need to differentiate creates a difficult situation for new venture TMTs who must learn to manage firms that are themselves new while simultaneously learning to manage firms that are also in some way different (Kimberly, 1979). The resulting ambiguity produces liabilities, which surpass those faced in more established firms. Stinchcombe (1965) refers to these as the liabilities of newness. While touching a variety of issues, the liabilities of newness all derive in some way from the fact that new ventures are unfamiliar and without precedent. Consequently, new venture managers must learn to rely largely upon themselves for information and for the generation of ideas and solutions.

If new ventures are to survive, they must quickly overcome these liabilities and establish for themselves the legitimacy and reduced uncertainty enjoyed by more established firms (Singh et al., 1986). As a practical matter, this means that new venture managers must learn their new jobs, learn the specifics of their new environments, and learn to deal with their new stakeholders while on the job and while utilizing new and untested social ties (Dewar and Dutton, 1986; Galbraith, 1973; McGee et al., 1995). Moreover, they must learn all this quickly and with minimal losses in efficiency and motivation. Thus, the task of the new venture TMT is largely one of creativity and learning, where the ability to produce novel and integrated solutions is an important attribute that can distinguish high performing TMTs from others.

Amidst this demanding environment, the performance of the top management team is key to success. Studies have shown that human capital is an important determinant of new venture performance (Thakur, 1999; Cooper et al., 1994; Herron and Robinson, 1993). Moreover, because new ventures lack the legitimacy, precedent, and inertia of incumbents, the performance of the top management team is especially critical (Thakur, 1999; Kamm et al., 1990). As such, researchers have argued that, in the future, the highest performing entrepreneurial firms will be those with the most outstanding top management teams

368   *M.D. Ensley et al. / Journal of Business Venturing 17 (2002) 365–386*

(Timmons, 1999). Of course, this is consistent with the upper echelon view that the performance of the TMT is reflected in the performance of the firm itself (Hambrick and Mason, 1984). High-performing TMTs should lead to high-performing ventures. In this paper then, we argue that because cohesion and the effective use of conflict by the TMT can facilitate better TMT performance, they may also lead to superior new venture performance.

3.1. Cohesion and conflict within the TMT

Cohesion is viewed by many as a strong predictor of group behavior (Goodman et al., 1987; Barnard et al., 1993; Bettenhusem, 1991; Festinger, 1950; Harrison, 1993; Lott and Lott, 1965) and denotes a state of social relationship among a team defined as "the degree to which members of the group are attracted to each other" (Shaw, 1981, p. 213). The members of cohesive teams exhibit higher levels of affinity and trust for one another as well as higher levels of satisfaction with and affective attraction to the group as a whole (O'Reilly et al., 1989).

Studies linking cohesion and performance are abundant. Mullen and Copper (1994), in a meta-analysis of 49 studies, found "the cohesiveness–performance effect was highly significant" (p. 210). Other examples include Keller's (1986) study of 32 project groups in large R&D organizations. He found that group cohesiveness predicted performance criteria of the group both contemporaneously and one year later, including technical quality, value to the company, and budget and schedule performance. Pelz and Andrews (1976) found project groups that were highly cohesive generated an intellectual competitiveness needed to maintain high performance.

Within new venture TMTs, cohesiveness is especially important because of the complex and ambiguous nature of the team's task. Research has shown that teams that perform well under uncertain and ambiguous conditions are highly coordinated and flexible (Daft and Lengel, 1986; Eisenhardt, 1989; Eisenhardt and Bourgeois, 1988). As Smith et al. (1994) explain, "top management teams that work well together react faster, are more flexible, use superior problem solving techniques, and are more productive and efficient than less integrative teams" (p. 432). The sort of integration that is necessary for this flexibility and efficiency is more likely to be a function of affective, interpersonal relationships than of formal, role-defined relationships (Katz and Kahn, 1978).

Cohesive teams are likely to have a stable and solid foundation of interpersonal relationships that allows them to interact in a flexible and efficient manner. Indeed, as Smith et al. (1994) explain, cohesive teams "operate as efficient clans, not needing to expend extra energy or resources on group maintenance" (p. 432). Cohesive teams are more likely to share tacit understandings and values and so move quickly in the consideration of multiple issues without having to revisit underlying assumptions and goals. All of which suggest that cohesive teams are likely to produce the synergy necessary for superior group performance while also experiencing relatively few process losses (Steiner, 1972).

In view of this, it is not surprising that research has found team tenure to be an important antecedent of high performing new venture TMTs (Eisenhardt and Schoonhoven, 1990). Cohesive teams tend to experience less turnover (O'Reilly et al., 1989). Thus, cohesive teams tend to have longer tenures. It seems likely then that the positive

M.D. Ensley et al. / Journal of Business Venturing 17 (2002) 365–386   369

relationship between team tenure and TMT performance is at least partially attributable to the fact that cohesive teams have certain interactive advantages that allow them to perform better than their less cohesive counterparts.

One area where such an interactive advantage is likely is in the use of conflict. Research has provided evidence that teams engaging in functional, task-oriented conflict tend to outperform those in which conflict is dysfunctional and personally oriented (Schweiger et al., 1989; Amason, 1996; Jehn, 1995; Schwenk, 1989). Of course, given the complex and ambiguous nature of new venture management, some amount of disagreement is inevitable. However, those teams that are able to take advantage of this disagreement by keeping it task focused and constructive should outperform those for whom the disagreement becomes personally focused and destructive.

Recent research has shown conflict to be multidimensional (Pinkley, 1990; Jehn, 1994, 1995). The cognitive dimension of conflict is considered to be generally functional and is defined as "task oriented and focused on judgmental differences about how best to achieve common objectives" (Amason, 1996, p. 127). Cognitive conflict occurs when top management team members consider a number of strategic alternatives from a variety of diverse perspectives. Because that sort of task-focused disagreement improves overall decision quality and understanding, cognitive conflict is seen as a necessary and beneficial component of effective strategic decision making (Mason and Mitroff, 1981; Schwenk, 1989). This is especially true for new ventures where ambiguity is high and where creativity is important (Amason et al., 1997).

On the other hand is the affective dimension of conflict, which is defined as personally oriented disagreement focusing on interpersonal dislikes and disaffections. Jehn (1994, 1995) concludes that it is the affective dimension of conflict that causes problems in decision making. Affective conflict causes problems not only by undermining decision quality and understanding but also by reducing satisfaction and team member affect, which leaves residual consequences that can further reduce TMT effectiveness in the future. Thus, while cognitive conflict is generally functional, affective conflict is generally dysfunctional (Jehn, 1994). Consequently, TMTs that perform well are often those that can encourage the former while discouraging the latter (Amason, 1996; Amason and Sapienza, 1997; Amason et al., 1995; Amason, 1998; Eisenhardt and Zbaracki, 1992; Eisenhardt et al., 1997, 1998).

Of course, the problem is that cognitive conflict can arouse interpersonal disagreements and so trigger affective conflict. Indeed, the evidence points to a strong association between cognitive and affective conflict (Brehmer, 1976; Cosier and Rose, 1977; Baron, 1988; Pelled, 1996; Pelled et al., 1999; Tjosvold, 1985). At the root of this relationship is the fact that no one really likes to be criticized or contradicted. As Pelled et al. (1999) explain "members whose ideas are disputed may feel that others in the group do not respect their judgement" (p. 7). Supporting this view is research in the area of social judgement theory showing that people are generally unable to fully articulate the rationale for their positions (Brehmer, 1976). As a result, there is a natural tendency to suspect the worst when faced with any conflict, whether cognitive or affective, and so, to respond to all conflicts as if they were personal attacks. Consequently, even when teams try to promote task-oriented, cognitive conflict, their efforts often result in personal disaffection (Schweiger et al., 1986). Moreover, once initiated, the increasing levels of affective conflict contribute to a downward spiral that can undermine the whole decision process (Kabanoff, 1991). Most studies of cognitive and affective conflict have found the two to be highly correlated. We expect a similar pattern to emerge in new venture TMTs and so offer our first hypothesis:

Hypothesis 1: In new venture TMTs, the levels of cognitive and affective conflict experienced during decision making will be positively related.

Although we expect cognitive and affective conflict to be positively related, each will likely relate differently to cohesion. The members of cohesive teams are more likely to link satisfaction of their own needs to those of the group (Katz and Kahn, 1978). Moreover, cohesive groups are likely to share common work related values which can facilitate coordination and communication (Jehn, 1994; Smith et al., 1994). As a result, the members of cohesive teams should have greater trust and agreement about interaction norms and group processes (Nemeth and Staw, 1989). An effect of this may be that cohesion will minimize the sorts of misunderstandings and misinterpretations that can cause cognitive disagreements to degenerate into affective conflict.

The mutation of conflict from its cognitive to its affective dimension has been linked to such things as value dissimilarity (Jehn, 1994) and the absence of open and mutual interaction norms (Amason and Sapienza, 1997). Team members whose values differ at a fundamental level are more likely to have different belief structures, understandings, and priorities. As such, they may be less understanding of disagreement and dissent. Likewise, team members who are suspicious of one another's motivations and who do not trust one another to act in the best interests of the team, are likely to respond less well to disagreement. In contrast, cohesive teams are likely to be less distrustful and suspicious and so may be more tolerant of disagreement and dissent. Indeed, a sense of belonging and familiarity should promote mutual and trusting relationships, which should lead to more open and cooperative group norms. Moreover, inasmuch as cohesive team members link their own satisfaction to that of the group, they are less likely to be competitive. Research has shown that competitive norms can promote suspicion and mistrust and so reduce open and mutual interaction norms (Tjosvold and Deemer, 1980).

The presence of open and cooperative norms is essential for cognitive conflict. Recall that the ambiguity of managing a new venture provides abundant opportunity for divergent perspectives and conflicting ideas (Autio et al., 2000; Daft and Lengel, 1986; Kimberly, 1979). As such, there is significant impetus for cognitive conflict in all new venture TMTs. In the presence of such opportunity, group norms become a strong determinant of the actual level of conflict. For example, Amason and Sapienza (1997) found openness to be strongly related to cognitive conflict. They reasoned that norms encouraging frank and open discussion promoted a full airing of the substantive differences within the group. The result of such open disclosure was cognitive conflict. Thus, because cohesive teams are likely to be more open to discussion and dissent, we expect them to experience more cognitive conflict, which leads to our second hypothesis:

Hypothesis 2: In new venture TMTs, cohesion will relate positively to the level of cognitive conflict experienced during decision making.

M.D. Ensley et al. / Journal of Business Venturing 17 (2002) 365–386   371

As mentioned, the sense of familiarity and tolerance that facilitates cognitive conflict should reduce affective conflict. Indeed, many affective conflicts arise because cognitive conflicts are misinterpreted and inflamed (Brehmer, 1976; Pelled, 1996). Suspicion and mistrust can undermine cognitive conflict because they cause substantive issues to be mistaken for personal attacks (Baron, 1988). Similarly, dissimilar values and perspectives can lead to misinterpretation of reasonable criticisms, resulting in disproportionate responses. In such cases, cohesion may act as an influence to reduce affective conflict.

In essence, cohesion would serve as a strong centripetal force binding a team together in the presence of a strong centrifugal force like conflict (Hambrick, 1994). As team members disagree, the chances that misunderstanding and misinterpretation will inadvertently trigger an affective response increases. However, cohesion raises the threshold for such responses. The members of cohesive teams disagree but are less apt to take their disagreements personally. The members of cohesive teams criticize but are less apt to view that criticism with suspicion. Cohesive teams then should be more effective in embracing conflict than teams that are less cohesive because their tendency for cognitive conflict to trigger affective conflict should be substantially reduced. As such, we offer our third hypothesis:

Hypothesis 3: In new venture TMTs, cohesion will relate negatively to the level of affective conflict experienced during decision making.

Finally, those top management teams that make better use of conflict should outperform those that do not. Evidence of this has been provided through a variety of studies of cognitive and affective conflict (Amason, 1996; Cosier and Rose, 1977; Eisenhardt et al., 1997; Guetzkow and Gyr, 1954; Jehn, 1994, 1995). For example, Cosier and Dalton (1990) argue that cognitive conflict allows decision makers to see multiple perspectives, avoid hazardous decisions, and promote innovative thinking. Van de Vliert and de Dreu (1994) argue that increased conflict enhances group performance when the group focuses on task issues, when interpersonal tensions are low, and when members of the group have interdependent goals. Likewise, Amason and Schweiger (1994) provide a model of conflict in strategic decision making showing that cognitive conflict increases strategic decision quality, team consensus, and affective acceptance among team members. In a study of 48 TMTs, Amason (1996) found support for this model. Thus, there is strong evidence that cognitive conflict leads to better top management decision making and better top management decision making should, over time, lead to better organizational performance.

At the same time, affective conflict is thought to negatively impact performance. Again, both theory and evidence provide support. Amason and Schweiger (1994) argue that affective conflict decreases strategic decision quality, team consensus, and affective acceptance of team members. Again, Amason (1996) found empirical support for these relationships. In addition, in an experiment with 88 teams, Jehn (1994) found that affective conflict reduced group performance, where performance was measured by the group's accuracy of problem identification, financial analysis, and recommendations to the firm. Similarly, Pelled (1996) argued that affective conflict reduces group performance because "... the hostility that characterizes affective conflict may make individuals in the group more resistant to the task-related ideas expressed by other group members" (p. 625). Thus, there is strong evidence that affective conflict leads to dysfunctional top management decision making. Over time, such dysfunctional decision making should lead to diminished organizational performance.

Thus, the effective use of conflict, which involves the accentuation of cognitive disagreement and the attenuation of affective disagreement, leads to better decision making by the team. In turn, better decision making by the team should lead to better new venture performance. Inasmuch as we have argued that cohesion is an antecedent to the effective use of conflict, we believe that cohesion should relate positively to venture performance. Other studies too have shown the benefits of cohesion to the performance of TMTs. Cohesion in new venture TMTs is critical due to the complex and ambiguous nature of the team's task. Research has demonstrated that teams performing well under uncertain and ambiguous conditions are highly coordinated and flexible (Daft and Lengel, 1986; Eisenhardt, 1989; Eisenhardt and Bourgeois, 1988). Smith et al. (1994) found that cohesion in the TMT related directly to ROI and sales growth. Similarly, Elron (1997) finds cohesion of the TMT contributes to TMT performance on issues such as implementation of decisions and strategies, comprehensive vision, and goals. Taken together, these findings all point to a complex web of effects whereby cohesive teams interact more efficiently and disagree more effectively, without arousing the sorts of negative affections that can so undermine top management team performance. Thus, we offer our full model,[3] as shown in Figure 1, and our final hypothesis:

Hypothesis 4: Cohesion within new venture TMTs will be positively related to new venture performance.

4. Methodology

To test our hypotheses, we gathered data from the TMTs of 70 new ventures, all of which were members of the 1995 Inc. 500. The names of the TMT members and contact information were obtained from the Dun and Bradstreet Market Identifiers Database. The firms in the Inc. 500 are privately held and are not required to report information on themselves in any standardized way. Thus, we chose to define the members of the top management team as being those individuals who met at least two of three conditions. They either were founders (Kamm et al., 1990), currently held an equity stake of at least 10% (Kamm et al., 1990; Roure and Maidique, 1986; Carland et al., 1984), or were identified in some way as being actively involved in strategic decision making (Cachon, 1990; Stewart et al., 1999). In addition, Roure and Madique (1986) argued that the new venture TMT consisted of those people identified as

---

[3] The linkages in the model correspond to the hypotheses tested. However, the linkages between cognitive and affective conflict and new venture performance are implied, based upon previous research, and are not tested directly. As such, they are depicted with dotted lines.

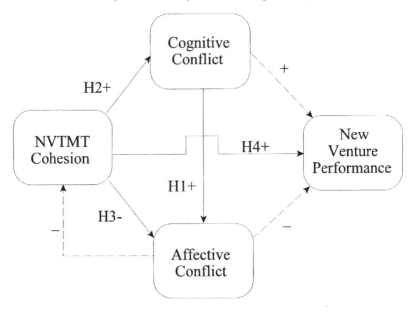

Fig. 1. Theoretical model of the effect of entrepreneurial team cohesion and conflict on new venture performance.

the CEO, President, and critical line or staff function executives. In using the Dun and Bradstreet Market Identifiers Database to identify the Inc. 500 executives, only those executives listed as either the CEO, President, or Vice President of a critical function, such as marketing, were utilized in the sample.

To crosscheck our operationalization of the TMT, the CEO or President of each firm was called and asked to identify those executives involved in TMT activities. All of the team members identified by our criteria were identified by the CEOs/Presidents as members of the firm's core strategic decision making group. Thus, we have considerable confidence in our definition of the TMT.

Firms that had been merged, acquired, gone out of business or for which the top management team could not be identified were excluded. As such, 1156 surveys were sent to the managers of 392 firms. A total of 316 surveys were returned, an initial response rate of 27.3%. However, because the unit of analysis in this study was the TMT, only those firms that provided multiple responses were retained. The final sample then included a total of 192 managers from 70 new ventures, a usable response rate of 18%. The responses per team ranged from 2 to 6 with an average of 2.74, which represents a within-team response rate of nearly 93%. Each of the 70 teams provided responses from at least 50% of their members.

Approximately 90% of the individuals in the sample were male and the average age was 38.4 years. Eighty percent were founders and 84% held equity stakes of at least 10%. Almost 90% considered themselves entrepreneurs and 40% had been involved previously in other new ventures. In all, the firms represented a total of 42 industries. Average firm age at the time of the study was 7.75 years and ranged from 5 to 11 years. Firm size ranged from a low of 10 to a high of 900 employees, with an average of 641. However, only one firm had over 500 employees, therefore, the median number of employees was 95. The median revenue figure was US$14,500,000 and revenues ranged from a low of US$1,500,000 to a high of US$457,000,000 in the year the study was conducted. The 5-year average growth rate ranged from 516% to 25,302%, with an average growth rate of 2084%.

4.1. Measures

Cohesion was measured with a scale developed by Bollen and Hoyle (1990). We employed Bollen and Hoyle's (1990) Perceived Cohesion Scale containing six items, three of which assess the individual's sense of belonging and three of which assess the individual's feelings of morale. Responses are recorded using a five-point Likert scale. Several studies have found psychometric support for their conceptualization and measurement of perceived cohesion using these six items (e.g., Chin et al., 1999). In this study, the Cronbach's alpha coefficient for the subscales was 0.83 for morale and 0.85 for the sense of belonging.

Conflict was measured with six items adapted from Jehn's (1994) Interpersonal Conflict Scale (ICS). The ICS has been employed in a variety of settings including work groups (Jehn, 1995) and top management teams (Amason, 1996) and has been shown to effectively measure affective and cognitive conflict. Each respondent was asked to think of the most recent major strategic decision his or her firm had made and then answer questions about the level of conflict experienced during the making of that decision. Linking the responses to a common incident in this way reduces recollection bias (Podsakoff and Organ, 1986) and facilitates the combining of individual responses into team-level variables. We asked specifically for "the most recent strategic decision" so as to enhance randomization of the referenced decisions and to facilitate accurate and consistent recollections on the part of the managers within each team (Amason, 1996; Amason and Sapienza, 1997; Flanagan, 1954). Three items were used to measure cognitive conflict and three items were used to measure affective conflict. As with the measure of cohesion, factor analysis confirmed the results of previous research, and the subscale reliability coefficients were 0.79 for cognitive conflict and 0.85 for affective conflict.

For both cohesion and conflict, the mean of the individual responses within each team was used as the team-level variable. However, for both cohesion and conflict, the level of within-team agreement was assessed before the individual measures were combined to form the team-level variables (Amason, 1996; Smith et al., 1994). We assessed within-team agreement in two ways. We first used the reliability Within Groups on j number of items procedure, known as the $r_{WG(j)}$. Originally developed as a measure of within team reliability, James et al. (1993) noted that it was really a measure of within team agreement. The $r_{WG(j)}$ produces a value between 0 and 1.0, with scores above .70 denoting acceptable agreement. We also used ANOVA to test the degree of variance between the teams relative to that within the teams. A significant ANOVA would show that between-team variance was significantly greater than within-team variance, again denoting acceptable agreement.

To assess within-team agreement for cohesion, we used both the $r_{WG(j)}$ and ANOVA procedures. For feelings of morale, the $r_{WG(j)}$ was .87 and the ANOVA F statistic was 2.443

M.D. Ensley et al. / Journal of Business Venturing 17 (2002) 365–386   375

($P \leq .01$). Thus, there was acceptable agreement within the teams on the level of morale. For sense of belonging, the $r_{WG(j)}$ was .83 and the ANOVA F statistic was 2.57 ($P \leq .01$). Thus, there was acceptable agreement within the teams on the sense of belonging. For affective conflict, the $r_{WG(j)}$ was .89 and the ANOVA F statistic was 1.771 ($P \leq .01$). Thus, there was acceptable agreement within the teams on the level of affective conflict. Finally, for cognitive conflict, the $r_{WG(j)}$ was .92 and the ANOVA F statistic was 1.528 ($P \leq .05$). Thus, there was acceptable agreement within the teams on the level of cognitive conflict.

Performance was measured in two ways. Sales growth was calculated as the cumulative growth experienced by the firm during the past 5 years. Sales growth is arguably the single most important indicator of new venture performance (Chandler and Hanks, 1993; Brush and Vanderwerf, 1992) and has been included consistently in new venture performance research (Kunkel, 1991; Sandberg, 1986; Zahra, 1993). While financial reporting concerns with privately held firms have resulted in attempts to develop alternative measures of performance, even those alternative measures utilize the concept of growth (Chandler and Hanks, 1993).

We also measured profitability. However, because the firms in the sample were closely held, our ability to gather profitability data was limited to that available through Magazine Inc. However, to be included in the Inc. 500, a firm must submit 5 years of audited financial information. The sales growth measure was taken directly from this data. Information about venture profit was provided in the form of a six-level ordinal scale developed by the Inc. compilation team. The levels reflect profitability in six ranges. The scale reflects profit as a percent of sales that is (1) less than zero, (2) zero, (3) 1–5%, (4) 5–10%, (5) 11–15%, and (6) greater than or equal to 16%.

In addition to these variables, we also collected information on firm size and age. Size was measured as the number of employees. To correct for large variations, we used the natural log of the actual values. We also included TMT size. These variables were used as control measures in our analysis of firm performance.

Because our measures of cohesion and conflict were perceptual and were collected using a single survey, we first performed a procedure to control for common method variation. This procedure, described by Amason (1996), Amason and Sapienza (1997) and Smith et al. (1983) involves randomly splitting each TMT into two groups. In teams with an even number of members the randomly split subgroups are equal in size. In teams with an odd number of members, the extra member is assigned randomly to one subgroup or the other. Then, the independent variables, morale and sense of belonging in our case, are taken from one subgroup while the dependent variables, cognitive and affective conflict in our case, are taken from the other subgroup. The actual variables are still the mean of the subgroup responses and the analysis is still performed at the team level. However, because the independent and dependent variables responses are provided by different individuals from within each team, the relationships between them are free of response–response biases such as common method variation (Podsakoff and Organ, 1986).

The actual hypothesis tests were conducted in a variety of ways. Hypothesis 1, proposing a relationship between affective and cognitive conflict was examined using the zero order correlation. The hypotheses linking cohesion and conflict (Hypotheses 2 and 3) were tested simultaneously using structural equations modeling (SEM). SEM was utilized to capture the simultaneous effects of belonging and morale cohesion as they relate to cognitive and affective conflict. Hypothesis 4 examining new venture performance was tested using hierarchical regression. We chose to use regression to test the final hypothesis because our dependent variables, sales growth and profitability, are not constructs measured by reflective indicators, as required by SEM.

5. Results

Table 1 presents the zero-order correlations and descriptive statistics for the variables. Among the several interesting relationships represented in the table is the positive relationship between cognitive and affective conflict (r=.56). This is consistent with the findings of others and offers support for Hypothesis 1. Also of interest is the relationship between the dimensions of cohesion (r=.53). This finding, too, is consistent with the findings of Bollen and Hoyle (1990) and suggests the presence of two related constructs. The belonging dimension of cohesion is negatively related to both cognitive ($r = -.23$) and affective conflict ($r = -.42$) and the morale dimension is negatively related to affective conflict ($r = -.24$). While preliminarily, these results offer some initial support for our general proposition that cohesion and conflict within the TMT are related to one another and, ultimately, to new venture performance.

Fig. 2 provides an illustration of the structural paths described in Hypotheses 2 and 3 and the corresponding t values for the coefficients for those paths. In addition, Table 2 contains the SEM statistics designed to assess the overall degree of fit between the model and the data. These statistics suggest that the model fits the data quite well. The χ^2 statistic is 10.97, with a P value of .43 suggesting no significant difference between the data and the model. The goodness of fit (GFI), adjusted goodness of fit (AGFI), and normed fit (NFI) indices are 0.90, 0.86, and 0.88, respectively, and the root mean square residual (RMSR) is 0.08. In addition, as evidenced by the significant R^2's for each set of indicators, presented in Table 2, a substantial portion of the variation in the indicators is accounted for by the latent variables. Thus, when taken together, these indices provide solid support for our model.

Given the global acceptability of the model, we used it to test the next two hypotheses. Hypothesis 2 stated that, in new venture TMTs, the level of cohesion would be positively related to the level of cognitive conflict experienced during decision making. Similarly, Hypothesis 3 stated that, in new venture TMTs, the level of cohesion would be negatively related to the level of affective conflict experienced during decision making. An examination of the structural path coefficients, depicted in Fig. 2, shows that both dimensions of perceived cohesion were significantly related to cognitive conflict. However, contrary to our expectations, the relationship between cognitive conflict and sense of belonging was negative. Thus, Hypothesis 2 received only partial support. As predicted, feelings of morale was negatively related to the level of affective conflict. However, sense of belonging was unrelated to affective conflict. Thus, Hypothesis 3 also received partial support.

M.D. Ensley et al. / Journal of Business Venturing 17 (2002) 365–386   377

Table 1
Correlation matrix of the team level variables

	Mean	Std	Growth	Sales	Profit	Age	Employees	Size	Cognitive	Affective	Belong	Morale
Growth	2416	3483	1.00									
Sales	50619	84158	.29	1.00								
Profit	3.38	1.40	-.04	-.20	1.00							
Firm Age	7.75	2.74	-.03	.23	-.10	1.00						
Employees	641	3463	.04	.24	-.22	.08	1.00					
Team Size	5.02	2.27	.13	.39	-.18	.14	.55	1.00				
Cognitive	2.78	0.47	.08	.27	.13	-.04	.03	.12	1.00			
Affective	2.37	0.58	-.04	-.10	.02	.01	-.09	.02	.56	1.00		
Belong	4.48	0.51	-.30	-.06	.17	-.24	-.11	-.17	-.23	-.42	1.00	
Morale	4.07	0.84	.01	.10	.17	-.23	.06	.10	-.12	-.24	.53	1.00

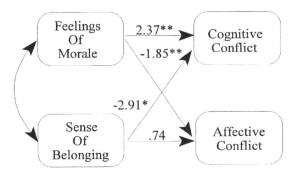

*p<.01; **p<.05; ***p<.10

Fig. 2. Structural equation model of entrepreneurial team dynamics, empirical relationships, and *t* values for LISREL path coefficients.

Our final hypothesis stated that cohesion would be positively related to new venture performance. We tested this hypothesis with hierarchical regression, the results of which are provided in Table 3. In the first step of the analysis, we developed models predicting sales growth and profitability from the control variables. In the second step, the conflict variables were entered into the model to test the direct effects of cognitive and affective conflict on the performance variables. While we did not specify hypotheses regarding these relationships, the model shown in Fig. 1 indicated implied relationships. We then developed a third model, including the two cohesion variables. This was done to assess the effects of cohesion on performance while controlling for these other influences. We tested both dimensions of cohesion together inasmuch as they occur together. This also allows us to test each, while controlling the effects of the other. While the correlation among our predictors may introduce some multicollinearity, the effect of that multicollinearity is to inflate the standard error of our predictors. As such, the presence of any multicollinearity

Table 2
LISREL model of cohesion and conflict relationship

Measures		Incremental fit		Parsimonious fit	
df	Absolute fit (chi-square)	GFI	RMSR	NFI	AGFI
50	10.97 (*P*<.43)	0.90	0.08	0.88	0.86
Dependent variable	R^2				
Affective conflict	0.35				
Cognitive conflict	0.28				

Estimated using a covariance matrix and maximum likelihood estimation.

M.D. Ensley et al. / Journal of Business Venturing 17 (2002) 365–386　　　　　379

Table 3
Hierarchical regression analysis predicting new venture performance

Dependent variable (variables entered per step)	Sales growth (β)	Profit (β)
Step 1: control variables		
Firm age	− 147.10	− 0.03
No. of employees (LOG)	1862.89**	− 0.09
Team size	− 69.40	− 0.09
Control model F ratio	2.03	0.88
Control model R^2	0.08	0.04
Step 2: conflict effects		
Firm age	− 139.91	− 0.02
No. of employees (LOG)	1862.89**	− 0.24
Team size	− 64.10	− 0.09
Cognitive conflict	306.25	0.67
Affective conflict	− 303.18	− 0.25
Conflict effects F ratio	1.21	0.96
R^2	0.08	0.07
R^2 change	0.00	0.03
Step 3: cohesion effects		
Firm age	− 223.38	− 0.02
No. of employees (LOG)	1574.46**	− 0.38
Team size	− 163.66	− 0.08
Cognitive conflict	445.41	0.71
Affective conflict	− 1406.86**	− 0.11
Sense of belonging	3284.33*	0.18
Feelings of morale	816.41	0.35
Main Effects F ratio	2.62**	1.21
R^2	0.23	0.12
R^2 change	0.15*	0.05

* $P<.01$.
** $P<.05$.

would not bias our significance tests (Belsey et al., 1980). In addition, a scan of the correlation matrix provides little evidence of multicollinearity (Hair et al., 1995). Given that the direction of the relationship is consistent with our expectations, the actual test of the hypothesis is the significance of the increase in R^2 between the two models, which is the proportion of variation in performance attributable to cohesion.

As can be seen in Table 3, the control models produced R^2's of .08 for growth and .04 for profitability. Neither model was significant. In the second step of this analysis, cognitive and affective conflict were added to the sales growth model and the profit model. The addition of the conflict variables did not produce a significant change in the explained variance in either model. We then added cohesion in the third step of the analysis. The R^2 for profitability changed to .12, a nonsignificant change. However, the R^2 for the sales growth model improved a total of .15 to .23, a significant change ($P<.05$). Tests of the individual coefficients showed that the bulk of this relationship was attributable to the sense of belonging, which, as expected, was positively related to sales growth ($P < .01$). Thus, Hypothesis 4 was partially supported in the case of sales growth.

In light of these results, it is also worth noting that there was a strong negative relationship between affective conflict and sales growth ($P < .05$). While this finding confirms earlier work, it also provides support for our general supposition that affective conflict is negatively related to performance and that cohesion is negatively related to affective conflict. As a result, cohesion among the TMT is positively related to new venture performance.

6. Discussion

Our intent with this study was to better understand the relationship between TMT cohesion, conflict, and new venture performance. Research adopting an upper echelon perspective has shown consistent and strong linkages between TMT characteristics, TMT dynamics, and organizational performance (Amason, 1996; Bantel and Jackson, 1989; Hambrick and D'Aveni, 1992; Keck, 1997; Judge and Miller, 1991; Michel and Hambrick, 1992; Murray, 1989; Weirsema and Bantel, 1992). Although typically performed on larger and older organizations, this work has direct implications for the study of new ventures. Indeed, it is altogether likely that new venture managers are disproportionately more important to the success of their firms than are the managers of existing firms because of the unique threats associated with trying to be simultaneously both new and different (Kimberly, 1979; Singh et al., 1986) and because of the absence of any precedent or inertia upon which new ventures can rely. Thus, new venture TMTs are important subjects for study.

As expected, we confirmed what others have reported, that cognitive and affective conflict during decision making are positively related. This seems to further support the contention that attempts to stimulate cognitive conflict may backfire and produce interpersonal disagreement and disaffection (Amason and Sapienza, 1997; Schwieger et al., 1986). However, we also found that cohesion (feelings of morale) was negatively related to affective conflict. When taken together, this suggests that cohesion may increase cognitive conflict while minimizing affective conflict. Indeed, this would place cohesion the same category as other centripetal forces like group norms of openness and mutuality, which Amason and Sapienza (1997) found efficacious in reducing affective conflict.

To illustrate this effect more directly, we performed a median split using the two dimensions of cohesion. We divided the sample into high and low groups for belonging and for morale. In each of these groups we then examined the correlation between cognitive and affective conflict. While the high- and low-morale groups displayed similar correlations (high morale = .54; low morale = .59), the high and low belonging groups were quite different. The correlation between cognitive and affective conflict in the low belonging group was .69, while the correlation in the high belonging group was .44. Using Fisher's z transformation (Cohen and Cohen, 1983), we determined that this difference was significant ($P < .067$). Of course, this suggests that the belonging dimension of cohesion acts to prevent the tendency of cognitive conflict to arouse affective conflict. Thus, teams whose members experience a high sense of belonging should be better able to manage conflict than teams with a lower sense of

M.D. Ensley et al. / Journal of Business Venturing 17 (2002) 365–386 381

belonging. Moreover, as depicted in our regression results, that ability to manage conflict effectively is related to superior new venture performance.

Of course, this seems to support research emphasizing the value of TMT tenure in new ventures (Eisenhardt and Schoonhoven, 1990; Roure and Maidique, 1986). It does so because there is strong evidence that longevity and tenure are positively related to cohesiveness (Katz, 1982; Pfeffer, 1983; O'Rielly et al., 1989; Smith et al., 1994). Indeed, this seems to suggest that, as teams continue to work together, they grow closer and gain greater knowledge of each others' skills, abilities, and personal idiosyncrasies. This closeness facilitates venture performance by providing operational efficiencies and trust which insulate the team from the sort of process losses that often occur in teams performing complex tasks (Steiner, 1972).

Thus, we believe we add two new pieces to the growing body of knowledge on new venture TMTs. First, we provide some additional theoretical detail to the existing explanations of how experience and tenure may improve TMT dynamics. The strong and negative relationship between cohesion and affective conflict suggests that teams that experience affective conflict may be less cohesive. As we know, less cohesive teams experience higher turnover. Thus, it may be that affective conflict incites team members to leave or at least withdraw from meaningful TMT interactions. The result of this avoidance is less effective decision making and a less effective TMT. However, in the absence of affective conflict, teams interact more effectively and so stay together longer, during which time they tend to exhibit higher levels of decision making effectiveness.

Our second contribution is in extending upper echelon theory into the study of new ventures. The upper echelon perspective fits best into the arena of new ventures, which are themselves crucibles where managerial choice drives organizational performance most directly. New ventures are little affected by history, inertia, and precedent. Indeed, while the bulk of TMT research has been conducted on existing large firms, primarily because of the ready availability of secondary data, the richest and most interesting studies of TMTs are likely to involve new ventures.

Despite its strengths and these contributions, however, we should be cautiously mindful in our interpretations and in the inferences we draw. Like all studies, this work has limitations. For instance, our sample, while adequate, is small. Seventy firms is but a fraction of the thousands of new firms that spring to life each year. Moreover, our sampling frame of the Inc. 500 all but insured that our 70 firms would be unlike the majority of new firms in terms of success. Clearly, we have sampled only from the top of the distribution. Yet, we must weigh these limitations against the benefits they provide. Studies of team dynamics require the collection of rich primary data. Such data is hard to gather from very large samples of firms. By looking at a smaller group, we were able to perhaps gather more detailed information. In addition, less successful firms are often less willing to provide information and so often exclude themselves from consideration. By focusing on successful firms, we again increased the amount of information we could collect and use. Thus, while not without limitations, this work represents a fair tradeoff in terms of the data gathered and presented.

We also recognize that the relationship between cohesion and conflict is, in all likelihood, a reciprocal one. As we have shown, cohesion relates negatively to affective conflict. However, over time, the presence of affective conflict will likely produce lingering resentment and avoidance, one result of which would be reduced cohesion. Indeed, we illustrate such reciprocation in our theoretical model (see Fig. 1). However, because of the specific temporal sequence implied by our measures, we were able to test only the relationship of cohesion to affective conflict. The cohesion measure is fully retrospective, while the measure of conflict is specific to a recent decision. Thus, we relate cohesion in a general and historical sense, to conflict in a specific and recent event, which suggests a specific causal ordering. For this reason also, it is the retrospective measure of cohesion that we relate to organizational performance.

Regarding performance, we clearly expect it to be affected by conflict. This too we illustrate in our theoretical model. However, we did not specifically hypothesize or test a relationship between conflict and performance, again due to our measures. Our conflict scales relate specifically to a single, recent decision. However, our performance measures are financial and so incorporate past actions up to the point where the measures were recorded. While we expect conflict to relate to financial performance, the conflict experienced during a recent decision episode would likely have little impact on retrospective financial data. Moreover, inasmuch as it is the cumulative effect of conflict over time that affects performance, the relationship between the conflict in any one specific decision and historical financial performance would likely be a weak one. Thus, so as not to mislead, we chose not to hypothesize a direct relationship between conflict and performance. Nevertheless, we did test the relationship in our regression analysis and did, in fact, find that with cohesion controlled, there is a significant negative relationship between affective conflict and sales growth. Thus, as we would expect, the relationship between conflict and performance appears to be robust.

We are mindful of results that did not support our model. In our structural equations analysis, the sense of belonging dimension of cohesion produced a negative, significant relationship with cognitive conflict. These results are somewhat counterintuitive, raising the question: How would a form of cohesion work to decrease cognitive conflict? One possible explanation lies within the groupthink (Janis, 1982) literature. As groups become highly cohesive, and in the presence of a dominant leader, group members, may in fact, withhold useful ideas that may contradict popular opinion in order to maintain their positive status in the group. This suggests that entrepreneurs may need to actively encourage cognitive conflict among the entrepreneurial team members to create a norm of acceptance for new ideas.

Finally, we would like to conclude by inviting other scholars to join us in our efforts to extend the upper echelon perspective further into the study of new ventures. Indeed, if we are correct in reasoning that new ventures are an especially appropriate and interesting venue for the study of top management teams, then it would stand to reason that some of the most interesting work in the study of upper echelons is yet to be conducted.

References

Amason, A., 1996. Distinguishing the effects of functional and dysfunctional conflict on strategic decision making: resolving a paradox for top management teams. Acad. Manage. J. 39 (1), 123–148.

Amason, A.C., 1998. Good and bad conflict in decision making. In: Papadakis, V., Barwise, P. (Eds.), Strategic Decisions, Kluwer, Norwell, MA, pp. 51–63.

Amason, A.C., Sapienza, H.J., 1997. The effects of top management team size and interaction norms on cognitive and affective conflict. J. Manage. 23, 495–516.

Amason, A.C., Shrader, R.C., Tompson, G.H., 1997. Newness and novelty: relating top management team characteristics to new venture performance. Paper presented at the Annual Meeting of the Academy of Management, Boston, MA.

Amason, A.C., Schweiger, D.M., 1994. Resolving the paradox of conflict, strategic decision making and organizational performance. Int. J. Conflict Manage. 5, 239–253.

Amason, A.C., Thompson, K.R., Hochwarter, W.A., Harrison, A.W., 1995. Conflict: An important dimension in successful management teams. Organ. Dyn. 23 (2), 20–35.

Autio, E., Sapienza, H.J., Almeida, J.G., 2000. Effects of age at entry, knowledge intensity, and imitability on international growth. Acad. Manage. J. 43, 900–924.

Bantel, K.A., Jackson, S.E., 1989. Top management and innovations in banking: does the composition of the top team make a difference? Strategic Manage. J. 10, 107–124.

Barnard, W.A., Baird, C., Greenwalt, M., Karl, R., 1993. Intragroup cohesiveness and reciprocal social influence in male and female discussion groups. J. Soc. Psychol. 132 (2), 179–188.

Baron, R.A., 1988. Attributions and organizational conflict: the mediating role of apparent sincerity. Organ. Behav. Hum. Decision Processes 41, 111–127.

Belsey, D.A., Kuh, E., Welsch, R.E., 1980. Regression Diagnostics: Identifying Influential Data and Sources of Collinearity. Wiley, New York, NY.

Bettenhusem, K., 1991. Five years of groups research: what have we learned?. J. Manage. 17 (2), 315–336.

Bollen, K.A., Hoyle, R.H., 1990. Perceived cohesion: a conceptual and empirical examination. Soc. Forces 69, 479–504.

Brehmer, B., 1976. Social judgment theory and the analysis of interpersonal conflict. Psychol. Bull. 83, 985–1003.

Brush, C.G., Vanderwerf, P.A., 1992. A comparison of methods and sources for obtaining estimates of new venture performance. J. Bus. Venturing 7, 157–170.

Cachon, J.C., 1990. A longitudinal investigation of entrepreneurial teams: Part 1. Who is involved and what makes them succeed. In: Churchill, N.C., Bygrave, W.D., Hornaday, J.A., Muzyka, D.F., Vesper, K.H., Wetzel, W.E. (Eds.), Frontiers of Entrepreneurship Research, Center for Entrepreneurial Studies, Babson College, Wellesley, MA, pp. 100–102.

Carland, J.C., Hoy, F., Boulton, W.R., Carland, J.C., 1984. Differentiating entrepreneurs from small business owners: a conceptualization. Acad. Manage. Rev. 9 (2), 354–359.

Chaganti, R., Chaganti, R., Mahajan, V., 1989. Profitable small business strategies under different types. Entrepreneurship: Theory Pract 13 (3), 21–37.

Chandler, G.N., Hanks, S.H., 1993. Market attractiveness, resource-based capabilities, venture strategies, and venture performance. Entrepreneurship: Theory Pract. 9, 331–349.

Chin, W.W., Salisbury, W.D., Pearson, A.W., Stollak, M.J., 1999. Perceived cohesion in small groups: adapting and testing the perceived cohesion scale in a small group setting. Small Groups Res. 30 (6), 751–766.

Cohen, J., Cohen, P., 1983. Applied Multiple Regression/Correlation Analysis for the Behavioral Sciences. Lawrence Erlbaum Associates Publishers, Hillsdale, NJ.

Cooper, A.C., Gimeno-Gascon, F.J., Woo, C.Y., 1994. Initial human and financial capital as predictors of new venture performance. J. Bus. Venturing 9 (5), 371–396.

Cosier, R.A., Dalton, D.R., 1990. Positive effects of conflict: a field assessment. Int. J. Conflict Manage. 1 (1), 81–92.

Cosier, R.A., Rose, G.L., 1977. Cognitive conflict and goal conflict effects on task performance. Organ. Behav. Hum. Perform. 19, 378–391.

Daft, R.L., Lengel, R.H., 1986. Organizational information requirements, media richness and structural design. Manage. Sci. 32 (5), 554–572.

Dewar, R.D., Dutton, J.E., 1986. The adoption of radical and incremental innovations: an empirical analysis. Manage. Sci. 32 (11), 1422–1434.

Eisenhardt, K.M., 1989. Making fast strategic decisions in high-velocity environments. Acad. Manage. J. 32 (3), 543–576.

384   *M.D. Ensley et al. / Journal of Business Venturing 17 (2002) 365–386*

Eisenhardt, K.M., Bourgeois, L.J., 1988. Politics of strategic decision making in high-velocity environments: toward a midrange theory. Acad. Manage. J. 31, 737–770.

Eisenhardt, K., Schoonhoven, C.B., 1990. Organizational growth: linking founding team, strategy, environment, and growth among U.S. semiconductor ventures, 1978–1988. Adm. Science Quarterly 35, 504–529.

Eisenhardt, K.M., Zbaracki, M.J., 1992. Strategic decision making. Strategic Manage. J. 13, 17–38 (Special).

Eisenhardt, K.M., Kahwajy, J.L., Bourgeois, L.J., 1997. Conflict and strategic choice: how top management teams disagree. Calif. Manage. Rev. 39 (2), 42–62.

Eisenhardt, K.M., Kahwajy, J.L., Bourgeois, L.J., 1998. Taming interpersonal conflict in strategic choice: how top management teams argue but still get along. In: Papadakis, V., Barwise, P. (Eds.), Strategic Decisions, Kluwer, Norwell, MA, pp. 65–83.

Elron, E., 1997. Top management teams within multinational corporations: effects of cultural heterogeneity. Leadership Q. 4 (8), 393–413.

Festinger, L., 1950. Informal social communication. Psychol. Rev. 57, 271–292.

Finkelstein, S., Hambrick, D., 1996. Strategic Leadership: Top Executives and their Effects on Organizations. West, Minneapolis.

Flanagan, J.C., 1954. The critical incident technique. Psychol. Bull. 51, 327–358.

Galbraith, J.R., 1973. Designing Complex Organizations. Addison-Wesley, Reading, MA.

Gartner, W.B., Shaver, K.G., Gatewood, E., Katz, J.A., 1994. Finding the entrepreneur in entrepreneurship. Entrepreneurship: Theory Practice 18 (3), 5–10.

Goodman, P.S., Ravlin, E., Schminke, M., 1987. Understanding groups in organizations. In: Cummings, L.L., Staw, B.M. (Eds.), Research in Organizational Behavior, vol. 9 (pp. 121–173).

Guetzkow, H., Gyr, J., 1954. An analysis of conflict in decision making groups. Hum. Relat. 7, 313–327.

Hair, J.F. Jr., Anderson, R.E., Tatham, R.L., Black, W.C., 1995. Multivariate Data Analysis, fourth ed. Prentice-Hall, Englewood Cliffs, NJ.

Hambrick, D.C., 1994. Top management groups. A conceptual integration and reconsideration of the "team" label. In: Cummings, L.L., Staw, B.M. (Eds.), Research in Organizational Behavior (vol. 16, pp. 171–213).

Hambrick, D.C., D'Aveni, R.A., 1992. Top team deterioration as part of the downward spiral of large corporate bankruptcies. Manage. Sci. 38, 1445–1466.

Hambrick, D.C., Mason, P.A., 1984. Upper echelons: the organization as a reflection of its top managers. Acad. Manage. Rev. 9 (2), 193–207.

Harrison, A.W., 1993. Work-group effectiveness: a structural equations analysis of the effects of individual differences. Unpublished doctoral dissertation, Auburn University, Auburn.

Herron, L., Robinson, R.B. Jr., 1993. A structural model of the effects of entrepreneurial characteristics on venture performance. J. Bus. Venturing 8 (3), 281–294.

Hornaday, J.A., Aboud, J., 1971. Characteristics of successful entrepreneurs. Pers. Psychol. 24, 141–153.

James, L.R., Demaree, R.G., Wolf, G., 1993. R/sub wg/: an assessment of within-group interrater agreement. J. Appl. Psychol. 78 (2), 306–310.

Janis, I.L., 1982. Groupthink, second ed. Houghton Mifflin, Boston, MA.

Jehn, K.A., 1994. Enhancing effectiveness: an investigation of advantages and disadvantages of value-based intragroup conflict. Int. J. Conflict Manage. 5, 223–238.

Jehn, K.A., 1995. A multi-method examination of the benefits and detriments of intragroup conflict. Adm. Sci. Q. 40, 256–282.

Judge, W.O., Miller, A., 1991. Antecedents and outcomes of decision speed in different environments. Acad. Manage. J. 34 (2), 449–464.

Kabanoff, B., 1991. Equity, equality, power, and conflict. Acad. Manage. Rev. 16 (2), 416–441.

Kamm, J.B., Shuman, J.C., Seeger, J.A., Nurick, A.J., 1990. Entrepreneurial teams in new venture creation: a research agenda. Entrepreneurship: Theory Pract. 14 (4), 7–17.

Katz, R., 1982. Project communication and performance: an investigation into the effects of group longevity. Adm. Sci. Q. 27, 81–104.

Katz, D., Kahn, R., 1978. The Social Psychology of Organizations, second ed. Wiley, New York.

Keck, S.L., 1997. Top management team structure: differential effects by environmental context. Organ. Sci. 8 (2), 143–156.

Keller, R.T., 1986. Predictors of the performance of project groups in R&D organizations. Acad. Manage. J. 29 (4), 715–726.

Kimberly, J.R., 1979. Issues in the creation of organizations: initiation, innovation, and institutionalization. Acad. Manage. J. 22 (3), 437–445.

Kunkel, S.W., 1991. The impact of strategy and industry structure on new venture performance. Unpublished doctoral dissertation, University of Georgia, Athens.

Lambkin, M., 1988. Order of entry and performance in new markets. Strategic Manage. J. 9, 127–141 (Special).

Lott, A.J., Lott, B.E., 1965. Group cohesiveness as interpersonal attraction: a review of relationships with antecedents and consequent variables. Psychol. Bull. 64, 259–309.

Mason, R.O., Mitroff, I.I., 1981. Challenging Strategic Planning Assumptions. Wiley, New York.

McDougall, P., 1987. An analysis of new venture business level strategy, entry barriers, and new venture origin as factors explaining new venture performance. Unpublished doctoral dissertation, University of South Carolina, Columbia.

McGee, J.E., Dowling, M.J., Megginson, M.J., 1995. Cooperative strategy and new venture performance: the role of business strategy and management experience. Strategic Manage. J. 16 (7), 565–581.

McGrath, J.E., 1964. Social Psychology: A Brief Introduction. Holt, Rinehart, and Winston, New York.

Michel, J., Hambrick, D.C., 1992. Diversification posture and top management team characteristics. Acad. Manage. J. 35, 9–37.

Mullen, B., Copper, C., 1994. The relation between group cohesiveness and performance: an integration. Psychol. Bull. 115 (2), 210–227.

Murray, A.I., 1989. Top management group heterogeneity and firm performance. Strategic Manage. J. 10, 125–141.

Nemeth, C.J., Staw, B.M., 1989. The tradeoffs of social control in groups and organizations. Adv. Exp. Soc. Psychol. 22, 175–210.

O'Reilly C.A. III, Caldwell, D.F., Barnett, W.P., 1989. Work group demography, social integration and turnover. Adm. Sci. Q. 34 (1), 21–38.

Palmer, M., 1971. The application of psychological testing to entrepreneurial potential. Calif. Manage. Rev. 13 (3), 38.

Pelled, L.H., 1996. Demographic diversity, conflict, and work group outcomes: an intervening process theory. Organ. Sci. 7 (6), 615–631.

Pelled, L.H., Eisenhardt, K.M., Xin, K.R., 1999. Exploring the black box: an analysis of work group diversity, conflict, and performance. Adm. Sci. Q. 44, 1–28.

Pelz, D.C., Andrews, F.M., 1976. Scientists in Organizations. Institute for Social Research, Ann Arbor, Michigan.

Pfeffer, J., 1983. Organizational demography. In: Cummings, L.L., Staw, B. (Eds.), Research in Organizational Behavior, vol. 5 (pp. 299–357).

Pinkley, R.L., 1990. Dimensions of conflict frame: disputant interpretations of conflict. J. Appl. Psychol. 75, 117–126.

Podsakoff, P.M., Organ, D.W., 1986. Self-reports in organizational research: problems and prospects. J. Manage. 12, 531–544.

Roure, J.B., Maidique, M.A., 1986. Linking prefunding factors and high-technology venture success: an exploratory study. J. Bus. Venturing 1 (3), 295–306.

Sandberg, W.R., Hofer, C.W., 1987. Improving new venture performance: the role of strategy, industry structure, and the entrepreneur. J. Bus. Venturing 2 (1), 5–29.

Sandberg, W.R., 1986. New Venture Performance: the Role of Strategy and Industry Structure. D.C. Heath and Company, Lexington, MA.

Schweiger, D.M., Sandberg, W.R., Ragan, J.W., 1986. Group approaches for improving strategic decision making: a comparative analysis of dialectical inquiry, devil's advocacy, and consensus. Acad. Manage. J. 29, 51–71.

Schweiger, D.M., Sandberg, W.R., Rechner, P.L., 1989. Experiential effects of dialectical inquiry, devil's advocacy, and consensus approaches to strategic decision making. Acad. Manage. J. 32, 745–772.

Schwenk, C.R., 1989. A meta-analysis on the cooperative effectiveness of devil's advocacy and dialectical inquiry. Strategic Manage. J. 10, 303–306.

Shaw, M.E., 1981. Group Dynamics: the Psychology of Small Group Behavior. McGraw-Hill, New York.

Singh, J.V., Tucker, D.J., House, R.J., 1986. Organizational legitimacy and the liability of newness. Adm. Sci. Q. 31 (2), 171–194.

Smith, C.A., Organ, D.W., Near, J.P., 1983. Organizational citizenship behavior: its nature and antecedents. J. Appl. Psychol. 68, 653–663.

Smith, K.G., Smith, K.A., Olian, J.D., Sims, H.P., O'Bannon, D.P., Scully, J.A., 1994. Top management team demography and process: the role of social integration and communication. Adm. Sci. Q. 39, 412–438.

Steiner, G.A., 1972. Tomorrow's corporate planning and planners. Managerial Plann. 20 (5), 1–11.

Stewart W.H. Jr., Watson, W.E., Carland, J.C., Carland J.W. Jr., 1999. A proclivity for entrepreneurship: a comparison of entrepreneurs, small business owners, and corporate managers. J. Bus. Venturing 14 (2), 189–214.

Stinchcombe, A., 1965. Social structure and organizations. In: March, J.G. (Ed.), Handbook of Organizations, 142–193.

Thakur, S.P., 1999. Size of investment, opportunity choice, and human resources in new venture growth: some typologies. J. Bus. Venturing 14 (3), 283–309.

Timmons, J.A., 1999. New Venture Creation: Entrepreneurship for the 21st Century. Irwin-McGraw-Hill, Boston, MA.

Tjosvold, D., 1985. Implications of controversy research for management. J. Manage. 11, 21–37.

Tjosvold, D., Deemer, D.K., 1980. Effects of controversy within a cooperative or competitive context on organizational decision making. J. Appl. Psychol. 65, 590–595.

van de Vliert, E., de Dreu, C.K.W., 1994. Optimizing performance by conflict stimulations. Int. J. Conflict Manage. 5 (3), 211–222.

Weirsema, M.F., Bantel, K.A., 1992. Top management team demography and corporate strategic change. Acad. Manage. J. 35 (1), 91–121.

Zahra, S.A., 1993. Environment, corporate entrepreneurship, and financial performance: a taxonomic approach. J. Bus. Venturing 8 (4), 319–341.

[9]

Social Interaction:
A Determinant of Entrepreneurial
Team Venture Success

Thomas Lechler

ABSTRACT. An important issue to explain the success of new ventures is mostly ignored by the research of entrepreneurship: the social interaction within entrepreneurial teams. The purpose of this paper is to introduce the concept of social interaction, which was originally developed for innovation teams in the field of entrepreneurship research and theory.

The theoretical discussion proves if an adoption of the social interaction to the field of entrepreneurship is theoretically possible. Using the data of 159 German entrepreneurial teams, the effects of social interaction on new business success are empirically proven. The introduced measurement model, which consists of six dimensions, shows a high quality in the empirical test. The quality of the social interaction within entrepreneurial teams is crucial for the new venture success. An empirical comparison with the frequently used team conflicts confirm that the measurement of conflicts is not a sufficient substitute measurement for social interaction. Overall, the social interaction in entrepreneurial teams could be seen as an important but not only factor of business success.

1. Introduction

People who are founding and developing new ventures are confronted with a great variety of challenges deriving mainly from business and technological uncertainty. In this context entrepreneurs have to solve technological, managerial, jurist as well as human related problems. Moreover, the transformation of an idea into saleable products can take years and requires financial resources and leadership in business and technology. Existing theoretical and empirical studies reflect the great variety of influences on entrepreneurial success. Despite the magnitude of research on new ventures and small businesses, researchers still cannot explain theoretically the

Stevens Institute of Technology
Castle Point on Hudson
Hoboken, NJ 07030
U.S.A.
E-mail: tlechler@stevens-tech.edu

growth of firms adequately (Tuck and Hamilton, 1993). As the entrepreneur is the focus and plays a key role in the firm's activities, various studies analyse the characteristics and behaviours of these key people. However, most of these studies see the entrepreneur as a single person. This traditional view is strikingly paraphrased by Cooney and Bygrave (1997): "*For a long time it has been a great myth that entrepreneurship implicitly describes the battle of a lonely hero against economic, governmental and social forces.*"

In contrast to these research efforts, multiple entrepreneurs have been well documented since the beginning of the industrial revolution. For example, Werner von Siemens and Georg Halske founded in 1847 the Siemens AG of today, and in 1863, Dr. Eugen Lucius, Carl Meister and Ludwig M‚ller founded the Hoechst AG, demonstrating impressively that even at the beginning of the 20th century entrepreneurial teams could be very successful. Analysing the industry, entrepreneurial teams appear to be more common than the entrepreneurship literature suggests (Cooper, 1986; Teach et al., 1986; Vyakarnam et al., 1997). Hunsdiek (1987) reports for Germany a median of 2.2 entrepreneurs per new high-tech venture. Based on a sample of 340 very promising East German new high-tech ventures which get substantial financial support from the German government, Pleschak and Werner (1998) report that 68% of these firms are founded by two or more persons. Cooper et al. (1990) cite a study of 2994 entrepreneurs and members of the National Federation of Independent Business who reported that they had only 30% full-time partners at the time of start-up. Entrepreneurial teams are a part of the economic reality.

The variation of occurrence rates of venture

teams depends on the kind of businesses (Cooper and Daily, 1996). In high-tech industries, entrepreneurial teams are the dominating form of start-ups, shown by the median percentage of 70% calculated across ten different studies (Cooper et al., 1990). To conclude the brief analysis, entrepreneurial teams are an omnipresent phenomenon in western economies and entrepreneurial research should analyse the phenomenon of entrepreneurial teams and their success factors in more depth.

2. Entrepreneurial teams as a determinant for venture success

In times of enormous knowledge growth the tendency towards entrepreneurial teams is getting stronger (Hunsdiek, 1987) and is often seen as the superior entrepreneurial start-up concept. Besides, many high-tech start-ups require substantial time and capital until they reach a market. Last but not least, teams can establish more powerful networks in different environments. These relations lead to the basic assumption of our research: *In knowledge-intensive dynamic industries entrepreneurial teams outperform single entrepreneurs.*

A number of empirical studies already document that firms founded by teams are on average more successful than those founded by individuals (Cooper and Bruno, 1977; Mayer et al., 1989; Bird, 1989; Timmons, 1990; Kamm et al., 1990; Vyakarnam et al., 1997). The next table summarises the empirical results of those studies which analyse the effects of entrepreneurial teams and their characteristics on the venture success in comparison to single entrepreneurs.

The present empirical studies (Table I) confirm the hypothesis that entrepreneurial teams are more successful than individuals. All studies, independent of the country or industry, indicate more or less a positive influence of the entrepreneurial teams on venture success. Reviewing the empirical studies, we find a preference for analysing high technology industries. In this regard Gartner (1985, p. 703) wrote: "*High technology industries might require more skills than an individual would be likely to have, necessitating that individuals combine their abilities in teams in order to start an organisation successfully.*" The contextual influence of the industry might have an effect on the success rate of entrepreneurial teams.

Overall the main argument for the advantages of teams is based on the positive effects of a combination of people with diverse personalities, characteristics, knowledge, skills and abilities (Vesper, 1990; Vyakarnam et al., 1997). Significant empirical research has been done explaining the formation of entrepreneurial teams, their functioning and their influence on the success of new ventures (Cooper and Daily, 1996; Cooney and Bygrave, 1997; Vyakarnam et al., 1997). Others show that the heterogeneity of team member characteristics within the teams plays a key role (Klandt and Kirschbaum, 1985; Teach et al., 1986; Picot et al., 1989; Doutriaux, 1992; Ensley, 1997).

Some argue that if a business is less dependent upon a single person, illness or the loss of an entrepreneur is less likely to cripple the whole venture (Cooper and Daily, 1996). In addition, positive psychological effects were identified. Working together in a team lowers entrepreneurial stress caused by the entrepreneurial situation. The team members are also more likely to trust and support each other (Boyd and Gumpert, 1983). Theoretically, the statistically proven positive relationships between multiple founders and venture success are implicitly or explicitly attributed to the resource based theory of the firm.

This approach is too narrow to explain both the performance differences between teams and the question of team design within a process, because it implies that differences in the performance between entrepreneurial teams could be explained by the characteristics of their members. However, such a simple input-performance-explanation ignores many research findings and theories which have been generated in team studies. In these studies, an input-process-output explanation is preferred, i.e. the input-performance relation is mediated by the interaction process of the team members. This interaction process is not only determined by the skills reflected in a team-composition, but from other variables of team-design. Therefore, it is interesting to take a closer look at team-interaction and its determinants.

TABLE I
Relevance of entrepreneurial teams

Year	Authors	Type of study	Sample size and industry	Success measurements	Country	Results
1977	Cooper, Bruno	Survey	250 High tech	Sales/year	U.S.A.	Portion of venture teams in the successful group of successors 76% Portion of single founders in the successful group 24%
1980	Obermayer	Case studies	33 Div. companies	Sales/year	U.S.A.	3 out of 10 single founders reach sales > $6 mio. 16 out of 23 team ventures reach sales > $6 mio.
1985	Klandt, Kirschbaum	Case studies	25 Software	Sales/year #Employees/year	Germany	Successful venture teams 38% Successful single founders 18%
1986	Teach, Tarpley, Schwartz	Survey	237 Software	Sales/year	U.S.A.	Successful venture teams 46% Successful single founders 16%
1987	Albach, Hunsdiek	Survey	180	Sales/year	Germany	Successful Venture Teams 43% Successful single founders 20%
1989	Picot, Laub, Schneider	Survey	52 Tech. Ventures Div. industries	Sales/year #Employees/year # offene Aufträge	Germany	Successful Venture Teams 63% Successful single founders 38%
1989	Feeser, Willard	Survey	42 Computer hardware	Sales/year #Employees/year	U.S.A.	Venture teams are more successful (not quantified)
1989	Mayer, Heinzel, Müller	Survey	45 High tech	Sales/year #Employees/year Level of innovation	Germany	Teams reach higher growth rates (not quantified)
1992	Doutriaux	Longitudinal 8 Jahre	73 High tech	Sales/year Over 8 years	Canada	Significant influence of the team size on sales after 3–4 years
1993	Kulicke u.a.	Survey	93 Tech. ventures Div. industries	Sales/year	Germany	Significant influence on success Successful Venture Teams 76% Unsuccessful single founders 60%
1996	Brüderl, Preisendörfer, Ziegler	Survey	1710 All industries	Survival Sales growth Employees growth	Germany	No clear result Bivariate analysis teams are more successful, but in multivariate analysis no significant influence
1999	Pleschak, Werner	Survey	124 Tech. ventures Div. industries	Survival Sales growth Employees growth	Germany	Tendency that teams are more successful Not significant

3. Social interaction irrelevant or essential for entrepreneurial theory?

Analyzing the present comparisons between teams and single founders more critically, we see that none of these studies (Table I) takes the disadvantages of teams into account. Personal interviews by the author with bankers and venture capitalists reveal both the advantages of multiple founders and their potential risks. Teams carry the potential of inefficient communication, complex long lasting decision processes and personal conflicts. Dysfunctions, like group losses, social loafing, group think, risk-shifting are well documented in the research literature on teams (Latané et al., 1979; Janis and Mann, 1977; Janis, 1982). Why should they not exist in entrepreneurial teams?

Within the entrepreneurial research area only a few authors discuss the disadvantages of entrepreneurial teams (Doutriaux, 1992; Eisenhardt and Schoonhoven, 1990). Cooper and Bruno (1977, p. 21) mention the problem ". . . *that a firm with multiple founders typically has more overhead . . .*". Also, Kamm et al. (1989) note that with the growing size of the firm, the possibility of combining the complementary skills increases, which leads on the one hand to positive effects in team performance; but on the other hand the increase of team size limits the efficiency caused by too much expertise and management styles. Beneath the great successes of teams we also find many examples of failures (Kamm et al., 1990). The disadvantages suggest that teams might also have some limitations. We have to admit that the performance of the team can be less than the sum of the performance of its team members. However, it can also be more! But which theory gives an answer to this question? Can this theory be applied to the situation of a new venture – which differs in many respects from the situation of teams within large organisations? Why does the performance of entrepreneurial teams vary and why do some teams fail? The discussions in the field of entrepreneurial research mostly focus on the characteristics of teams. To answer the questions on a theoretical basis we leave the field of entrepreneurial research for a moment and take a look at the body of organisational theory.

Today, analyses of teams within organisations are fashionable, and the body of knowledge is growing fast. Teams as an organisational concept are discussed in different functions and contexts (Hackman, 1987; Gladstein, 1984; Cohen and Bailey, 1997; Hoegl, 1998; Helfert, 1998). One major area of research investigates top management teams and their decision-making processes. The second major research field studies the role of teams in the innovation processes. In the theoretical literature the importance of teams for innovation is prevalent. Empirical studies suggest strong influences of teams on innovation success (Johne and Snelson, 1990; Clark and Fujimoto, 1991; Coopers, 1993; Pinto et al., 1993; Mohrman et al., 1995; Lechler, 1997; Hoegl, 1998). These authors consider teamwork as a crucial factor for high team performance resulting in product, project or innovation success (Hackman, 1987; Gladstein, 1984; McGrath, 1964; Ancona and Caldwell, 1990; Shea and Guzzo, 1987). In his comprehensive empirical work, Hoegl (1998) transfers the theoretical concepts of teamwork into a measurement model to measure the quality of teamwork. Analyzing 147 software teams in software development laboratories within four large international companies, he proves a significant influence of teamwork quality on the project success. In this context, the quality of teamwork is defined as the collaboration within teams. In our further analysis we call it the quality of social interaction within the teams.

Even though the results on social interaction in other research areas are definitely clear, we only find a few studies analysing various aspects of social interaction within entrepreneurial teams. Watson et al. (1995) examined the influence of team interpersonal process effectiveness on new venture success, conceptualising and operationalising leadership, interpersonal flexibility, team commitment and helpfulness as independent predictor variables. From these variables team commitment and leadership show a significant and strong influence on venture success (Watson et al., 1995). Whereas Cooper and Daily (1996) found that consensus of entrepreneurial teams in decision-making is not necessarily good, a "*lack of consensus may lead to a greater variety of approaches to problem-solving*" (Cooper and Daily, 1996, p. 139). Beyond this they looked at team heterogeneity, psychological variables of the team and consensus in decision-making. In his empirical study, Ensley (1997) analyses the effects of entrepreneurial team skill heterogeneity and conflict on strategic orientation and performance of new ventures. He reports a negative influence of affective conflict on strategic orientation; whereas a direct link between affective conflict and performance could not be supported by his research.

To summarise the discussion, we see that the analysis of team characteristics (Table I) is dominant. Only some aspects of the social interaction within entrepreneurial teams are investigated – mainly conflicts within the teams (Ensley, 1997). But until now we do not find any approach examining the social interaction as a whole. The quality of social interaction might play an important role for entrepreneurial teams as it does for innovation success. Dealing with the two questions we have raised in this section we can summarise our discussion with the main hypothesis: *The quality of the social interaction within entrepreneurial teams is positively related with the new venture success.*

The purpose of this paper is to introduce within the field of entrepreneurship research the concept of social interaction, which was originally developed in the field of innovation teams. It is the goal to develop a model to measure the quality of social interaction within the entrepreneurial team and to prove empirically the importance of the social interaction for the venture success.

4. The conceptual framework

Theoretical discussions identify weaknesses in the theoretical foundation of entrepreneurship by transferring concepts of organisational theory which are intentionally focused on large complex organisations (Dandridge, 1979). For a sustained extension of entrepreneurial theory we have to check if a transfer of the teamwork model from innovation teams is permitted in a theoretical sense. The subject of the analysis is the team. For our problem a transfer is valid if the characteristics of innovation teams roughly coincide with the entrepreneurial teams.

According to the common literature (Alderfeld, 1987; Hackman, 1987; Wiendieck, 1992; Guzzo and Shea, 1992), Hoegl (1998) defines a team as

"a social system of three or more people, which is embedded in an organization (context), whose members perceive themselves as such and are perceived as members by others (identity), and who collaborate on a common task (teamwork)." Innovation teams also have to create and implement new products or services within a given schedule and budget.

An entrepreneurial team is defined by Vyakarnam et al. (1997, p. 2) as *"the 'top team' of individuals who is responsible for the establishment and management of the business"* whereas Watson et al. (1995, p. 394) go further, including the financial interest of the team members and the minimal size in their definition: *"A venture team is two or more individuals who jointly establish and actively participate in a business in which they have an equity (financial) interest"* (also Cooney and Bygrave, 1997). In addition Kamm et al. (1990) complete the characteristics with the number of team members and that the team members are present during the pre-start-up phase and that they hold equity in the firm.

Innovation teams and entrepreneurial teams in high-tech firms have similar characteristics (Table II). Both are confronted with a highly dynamic context in which they have to perform. Entrepreneurial as well as innovation teams have to implement innovative tasks. In Schumpeter's words: "They have to perceive profit opportunities to carry out and implement new factor combinations" (Schumpeter, 1952; Vyakarnam et al., 1997). At the beginning the time frames are nearly the same, whereas in the long run some differences may occur. Both are more or less responsible for the results and they have to expect nearly the same consequences. Also, the relations between the team members are characterised by equality. The similarities indicate a high validation for the introduction of the social interaction model and suggest the concepts of social interaction can be applied to entrepreneurial theory.

To measure the social interaction in venture teams we have chosen and modified the model of Hoegl (1998), who conceptualised and empirically tested the social interaction of innovation teams. It contains 6 components: (1) communication, (2) cohesion, (3) work norms, (4) mutual support (5) coordination and (6) the balance of member con-

TABLE II
Comparison of team characteristics

Characteristics	Innovation teams	Entrepreneurial teams in high-tech ventures
Task characteristics	Innovative task Creating a new product	Innovative task Creating a new business
Common goals	Successful innovation	Successful business
Tenure	2 or more years, defined end	open end
Common responsibility	Responsible for technical results	Responsible for business results
Common risks	Career risks	Personal and career risks

tributions. These components are defined in the following section.

Components of Social Interaction within Entrepreneurial Teams:

(1) *Communication:* The communication within a team provides the means for information exchange among team members (Pinto and Pinto, 1990). The quality of communication depends on frequency, formalization, structure and openness of the information exchange (Hoegl, 1998). *Frequency* refers to how often and extensively team members communicate; *formalisation* relates to how much preparation is required before communication among the team members can occur (Katz, 1982); *the structure of communication* depends on whether direct communication between team members is possible or if the information exchange occurs through mediators (e.g. team leader); *openness* refers to how openly and sincerely team members share information with each other.

(2) *Cohesion:* Group or team cohesion describes the degree to which team members desire to remain in the team. Mullen and Copper (1994) explain three pivotal aspects of cohesion: interpersonal attraction of team members, commitment to the team task and group pride/team spirit. Several authors agree that it is unlikely to achieve high team performance without an adequate level of team cohesion (Hoegl, 1998; Mullen and Copper, 1994; Guzzo and Shea 1992; Helfert, 1998).

(3) *Work norms:* Norms are defined as shared expectations within a team regarding the behaviour of team members (Levine and Moreland, 1990; Goodman et al., 1987).

Norms regarding effort of team members are particularly important for successful teamwork.

(4) *Mutual support:* Mutual support is considered essential for teamwork (Tjosvold, 1995). The collaboration of the team members depends on cooperation rather than competition (Hoegl, 1998).

(5) *Coordination:* Within the process of the task fulfillment many activities are delegated within the team. Mostly the members are working parallel on different subtasks. These contributions have to be harmonised and synchronised by defining time frames, budget lines and deliverables. The way in which the team is controlling these activities influences the quality of social interaction.

Hoegl (1998) also defines the balance of member contributions as the sixth dimension of teamwork, but the results show some problems of content validity. By definition this concept is too close to the technical task performance. On the other hand many authors in the field of entrepreneurial research are taking conflicts and their influences on the performance into account (Ensley, 1997).

(6) *Conflict resolution:* The style with which the team members handle rising conflicts is important for their perception of the social interaction. Conflicts in situations of high pressure and dynamic contexts in which entrepreneurs are acting are inevitable. What is in question is how the team resolves upcoming conflicts before they unfold their destructive effects on performance.

To estimate the importance of the social interaction we also have to define the dependent variable.

The definition of the success is linked to many problems. Some are the dependence on the time, the perspective and the settled goals. Because success is multi-dimensional we define new venture success by five dimensions:

1. *Economic success:* The authors of different studies of new venture performance agree that the success of these ventures can be measured in terms of economic growth (Eisenhardt and Bird, 1990; Bantel, 1998; Cooper and Gimeno Gascón, 1992; Teal, 1998). Thus, we define economic success by growth rates of sales per year, ROI and the number of full-time employees as well as the company image.

2. *Competitive position:* The achieved competitive position depends on the technological and market position. The technological position of a new venture is defined by the level of technical innovations and the level of technological position in comparison to the competition. The market position is defined by the market success and the strength of the market position in comparison to the competition.

3. *Efficiency:* The efficiency describes the level of cost and time performance in comparison to the competition.

4. *Client satisfaction:* Client satisfaction is defined by the quality of image and the satisfaction of the customers with the performance of the products or services.

5. *Personal success:* This dimension refers to the personal satisfaction of the team members with the business performance as well as with teamwork. Cooper and Gimeno Gascón (1992) mention the need for achievement, internal locus of control and risk taking as pivotal personal characteristics of entrepreneurs and they are likely to have influence on the perceived personal success of new ventures. We define personal success by the development of the founder's personal income, personal satisfaction with the business results and the satisfaction with entrepreneurial teamwork.

The measurement model of Hoegl (1998) was adopted and modified in order to investigate entrepreneurial teams. The dimensions of the social interaction refer to the team as the unit of analysis. Accordingly, all items measuring the social interaction were specified on the team-level of

analysis. The dimensions of the social interaction were measured with Likert scales including 3 to 6 items. All items used were measured on seven point rating scales ranging from strong disagreement (1) to strong agreement (7).

With this model we can now specify our main hypothesis: *The quality of the social interaction within entrepreneurial teams is positively linked to the venture success.* According to Hoegl (1998), we propose that each of the six components of social interaction has a positive relation to the five success dimensions. In other words: The higher the value of each dimension the higher the new venture success should be.

5. Research design and sample characteristics

The analysis of social interaction in entrepreneurial teams is part of a larger ongoing empirical study to identify the success factors of entrepreneurial teams in Germany. The goal is to build up a large database which allows us to empirically prove our hypothesis.

Firms with the following characteristics were preferred for the sample:

- Technology-driven companies;
- Companies aged 6 years or less;
- Multiple founders;
- Founders work part- or full-time within the firm since formation; and
- Founders hold equity shares.

In order to identify new technology-based firms founded by entrepreneurial teams, databases of two German banks were used. All of the identified firms were first contacted by phone. Phone contact was initially made to confirm fulfilment of the requirements while convincing entrepreneurs to participate in our study.

The data was gathered in individual interviews using a fully standardised questionnaire with open questions at the end of each section. In each company at least two members of the entrepreneurial team were interviewed. With this multiple respondents approach it is possible to avoid the common method variance problems of a single key informant. Also, the control of the interview situation was important in order to prevent the team members from answering the questionnaire together.

The questionnaire itself is divided in two parts.

270   *Thomas Lechler*

The first part contains only quantitative measures of the firm, the structure of the team and the quantitative business results. This information is free from personal bias, and therefore we asked only one respondent for this kind of data. The interview for this part took an average of 45 minutes.

The second part of the questionnaire contains items only measuring the social interaction within the entrepreneurial team and the personal evaluation of the business results. This kind of data was gathered separately from two members of the entrepreneurial team. For the second part of the questionnaire the interview took approximately 60 minutes.

The actual sample included 183 firms founded in Germany. Because of higher ages and different business models, 24 cases were eliminated from the analysis. In sum, we analysed the data of 159 teams, comprising 322 different interviews with at least two members from each team.

All of the firms operate in technology-intensive services and in high- and low-tech industries. The main fields of the industrial firms are machinery construction, electronics, chemicals, construction and plant and engineering.

The average age of the firms is 3.5 years. Overall, 53% of the firms are younger than 3 years old. All of the firms were founded by teams, with two (58.5%), three (27.6%) or more members (13.9%). The median team size is two and the mean is three founders per team. Most of the companies are small in size. 80% have less than 10 employees and 60% reach yearly sales under DM 2 million.

TABLE III
Industries

	Proportion	Number
Industrial	23%	36
Software	66%	106
Hardware	11%	17

6. Empirical findings

6.1. *Measurement model of social interaction*

The following table shows the statistical coefficients describing the quality of the used scales to measure the six components of social interaction defined above.

Table IV contains the results of both the present study and Hoegl's study (shown in parentheses) from which the measurement scales were developed.

The results reach a high quality level for the used measurement scales. Each component was assessed using three to six items. All components were first separately tested for uni-dimensionality by a confirmatory factor analysis and for reliability analysis estimating Cronbach's Alpha. After these tests, only the coordination component had to be modified by eliminating one item. All developed scales attain explained variances between 60% (communication) and 81% (work norms) and high Cronbach's Alphas. These values indicate high reliability and also construct validity of the developed measurement model.

In the next step, scores for the components were calculated by summarising and weighting the

TABLE IV
Quality of measurement models of the social interaction (in parenthesis: Values of Hoegl's study)

Components of social interaction	No. of items	Cronbach's Alpha	Communality	Factor loadings
Communication	6 (10)	0.86 (0.89)	4.17	0.88 (0.89)
Coordination	3 (4)	0.78 (0.75)	2.12	0.80 (0.73)
Mutual support	5 (7)	0.89 (0.94)	4.01	0.93 (0.91)
Work norms (effort)	4 (4)	0.91 (0.86)	3.34	0.84 (0.82)
Cohesion	6 (10)	0.87 (0.91)	3.53	0.90 (0.88)
Conflict resolution	5	0.87	3.23	0.80

Eigenvalue 4.44 (4.35).
Variance explained (Factor Social Interaction) 74.10% (72.60%).
Cronbach's Alpha of the Social Interaction Scale 0.93.

scores of the single items. With these scores a factor analysis was calculated with the six sum-scales of the social interaction components. The high factor loadings and communalities document (Table IV) that, the six dimensions represent a homogeneous construct to measure the quality of social interaction. The whole scale of the six components explains 76% of the variance and attains a Cronbach's Alpha of 0.92 (Table IV).

The comparison with the original measurement model which has been developed to measure the quality of teamwork within innovation teams could be seen as another validation test for the used scale. The high agreement with the results from the original sample of 581 members of innovation teams is striking. Thus the validity and reliability of the used measurement model are high enough to apply it for observation of the social interaction of entrepreneurial teams.

After constructing and proving the scales of social interaction we are now able to describe the characteristics of the social interaction within the entrepreneurial teams. How do the entrepreneurs rate the quality of social interaction within their teams?

To describe the characteristics, we first averaged the ratings of the interviewed team members for each team separately. These averages are used for all of the following analyses.

The results are surprising. Most of the teams reach a high quality level of social interaction. The means lie over 5.8 on a seven-point-scale and the medians reach even higher ratings. Only a few teams indicated a low rating for the social inter-action. Even the lowest rating reaches just 2.81. Also the ratings of the team members do not differ. The reasons for the high ratings lie in the team foundation. The members of only six teams did not know each other before the foundation of the firm. All others were friends, relatives or former colleagues. It seems that the social relationship is most important for the choice of the partners.

6.2. *New venture success*

In this section we first examine the scales developed to measure new venture success from the qualitative perspective. In the second part the success of the assessed companies will be analysed. New venture success was measured using four different scales as qualitative measures and the annual sales and profits over the last five business years as quantitative measures.

Table VI summarises the details on the

TABLE V

Characteristics of the Social Interaction Scale and its components

		Social Interaction	Commun-ication	Coordina-tion	Mutual support	Cohesion	Work norms	Conflict resolution
N	Valid	155	157	158	158	157	158	158
	Missing	4	2	1	1	2	1	1
Mean		5.80	5.87	5.42	6.01	6.07	6.00	5.42
Median		5.95	6.08	5.66	6.30	6.25	6.38	5.60
Standard deviation		0.81	0.91	0.98	0.90	0.84	1.08	0.98
Minimum		2.81	2.92	2.17	2.70	3.00	2.00	2.10
Maximum		7.00	7.00	7.00	7.00	7.00	7.00	7.00

TABLE VI

Quality of measurement models of the subjective success dimensions

Dimensions of new venture success	No. of items	Cronbach's Alpha	Eigenvalue	Variance explained
Economic success	4	0.76	2.38	59%
Competitive position	4	0.78	2.52	63%
Efficiency	2	0.82	1.71	85%
Client satisfaction	2	0.89	1.81	90%

measurement scales for Economic Success, Competitive Position, Efficiency and Client Satisfaction. The outcomes were evaluated by each of the interviewed team members separately. The items were rated on 7-point rating scales. Each success dimension was measured by two to four items. Using a confirmatory factor analysis the four dimensions were separately tested for unidimensionality and the reliability was tested by estimating Cronbach's Alpha. Each scale reached a satisfactory level of scale quality.

To measure the quantitative side of new venture success we used the sales and profits of the companies from the last five years of business. The profits or losses were measured within six different classes:

1. Losses more than DM −100,000;
2. Losses between DM −30,000 and DM −100,000;
3. Losses or profits between DM −30,000 and DM +30,000;
4. Profits between DM +30,000 and DM +100,000;
5. Profits between DM +100,000 and DM +500,000;
6. Profits above DM +500,000.

Due to the fact that the quantitative data was sampled for the last five business years, we have no data from the first business year of the six-year-old firms. Therefore, the sample size differs between the first and the second business year. In the start-up phase many new ventures and especially high-tech-ventures show losses. But overall many of the young companies were successful within the first years. Within the third year of business more than 50% of the firms have profits

above DM 30,000. The sales and profit measures show high deviations, caused by differences in firm age, and therefore as measures of success have only limited predictive quality.

6.3. *The importance of the social interaction*

With these success measurements we can now prove the main hypothesis: *The quality of the social interaction within entrepreneurial teams is positively linked to the venture success.*

Most of the used variables did not meet the condition of normality, therefore Spearmans's rank correlations were used. The correlations shown in Table VIII between the quality of social interaction and the dimensions of new venture success are significant at the 1%-level, except the economic success and the quantitative success indicators. Social interaction is a construct that measures a specific type of team process. In this sense, the correlation with efficiency is not surprising.

More surprising is the strong relationship between the social interaction and the client satisfaction. We can only speculate about this correlation, but it seems that within a team of high social interaction, mistakes are compensated for by members taking over the responsibilities of other team members. This supportive culture for solving problems or correcting mistakes by others results in satisfied clients. On the other hand, there is no correlation to the economic results. It seems that problems in the social interaction are compensated by other processes like the task orientation.

In comparison to the results of Hoegl (1998), who investigated the impact of teamwork quality

TABLE VII
The development of profits and sales over time

	Profits/Losses				Sales Mio. DM			
	Mean	Median	Std. Dev.	N	Mean	Median	Std. Dev.	N
1st year	3.27	3.00	1.11	130	0.96	0.3	2.90	131
2nd year	3.52	3.00	1.19	139	1.74	0.7	4.14	141
3rd year	3.79	4.00	1.19	116	2.36	1.0	7.08	118
4th year	4.20	4.00	1.03	70	3.33	1.6	9.65	69
5th year	4.16	4.00	1.15	38	2.91	2.2	2.93	40
6th year	4.36	5.00	1.36	16	3.21	2.1	2.91	16

TABLE VIII
Correlations between the social interaction and the new venture success

Components of social interaction	Dimensions of new venture success						
	Economic success	Competitive position	Efficiency	Client satisfaction	Sales	Profits	Satisfaction
communication	n.s.	0.31**	0.26**	0.38**	n.s.	n.s.	0.46**
Coordination	n.s.	0.24**	0.32**	0.31**	n.s.	0.21**	0.50**
Mutual support	n.s.	0.32**	0.22**	0.43**	n.s.	0.17*	0.55**
Work norms (effort)	n.s.	0.29**	n.s.	0.25**	n.s.	n.s.	0.38*
Cohesion	0.21**	0.30**	0.27**	0.41**	n.s.	n.s.	0.64**
Conflict resolution	n.s.	0.29**	0.18*	0.27**	n.s.	n.s.	0.55**
Social interaction	n.s.	0.31**	0.27**	0.40**	n.s.	n.s.	0.55**

Spearman Rank correlations; * $p < 0.05$, ** $p < 0.01$; two tailed.

TABLE IX
Quality of measurement models of the conflict types

Alternative measure	No. of Items	Cronbach's Alpha	Eigenvalue	Variance explained
Affective conflicts	3	0.82	2.22	74%
Cognitive conflicts	3	0.85	2.33	78%

on project success, there are similarities in the level of the correlations between the interaction and the success dimensions, thus supporting the validity of our results.

Overall, the results indicate that the quality of the social interaction within entrepreneurial teams is crucial for the new venture success and they support our hypothesis.

6.4. *Alternative measurement of social interaction*

Some empirical studies investigate single variables of social interaction. But do we need to take the social interaction as a whole into account or are single variables sufficient for predicting success? Research often focuses on conflicts, which could be seen as the negative results of failures in the social interaction. The role of conflicts in decision processes has been investigated for top management teams. In this area it is believed that two types of conflicts exist: Affective and cognitive conflicts. This concept and the measurement scales used were introduced to the entrepreneurial area by Ensley (1997) who overtook the concept of Amason et al. (1995).

On the other hand, we propose conflicts as a complementary measure for the quality of social interaction. Do our concepts of social interaction and the management of conflicts relate to the conflicts?

Ensley (1997, p. 104) proposed and verified a causal relationship between cognitive and affective conflicts. The correlation (0.73) he found approximately matches the present results. This may also be interpreted as a validation test. The correlations indicate a strong relationship between the conflicts and the activities for conflict resolution. Nevertheless, the insignificant and low

TABLE X
Correlations between the types of conflicts and conflict resolution mechanisms

	Affective conflicts	Cognitive conflicts
Affective conflicts	–	0.71**
Cognitive conflicts	0.71**	–
Conflict resolution	–0.48**	–0.55**
Social interaction	–0.44**	–0.53*

* $p < 0.05$, ** $p < 0.01$.

TABLE XI
Correlations between the types of conflicts and the new venture success

	Economic success	Competitive position	Efficiency	Client satisfaction	Sales growth	Profits	Satisfaction
Affective conflicts	n.s.	n.s.	n.s.	n.s.	n.s.	n.s.	n.s.
Cognitive conflicts	n.s.	−0.19*	n.s.	n.s.	n.s.	n.s.	n.s.

* $p < 0.05$, ** $p < 0.01$.

correlation between the social interaction and the affective conflicts once more confirm that the measurement of conflicts is not a sufficient substitute measurement for social interaction.

The quality of the used measurement scales for the two conflict types (Table VI) is high enough to use them for further analysis. The next step investigates the impact of the two types of conflict on the new venture success.

The correlations between the dimensions of new venture success and the two types of conflicts show only punctuated influences. It is interesting that the affective conflicts are correlated significantly with the economic success and efficiency. These results are contradictary to Ensley (1997) who could not find any significant influence of the conflicts on new venture success at all. Ensley (1997, p. 106) states that in the field of top management team research there is: ". . . *significant disagreement about the role of affective conflict in top management groups.*" The weak relationship to the venture success also documents that the use of conflicts does not sufficiently represent the social interaction.

7. Integration of the results in a theoretical framework

Our analysis of diverse empirical studies shows that entrepreneurial teams are more successful than single founders. The existence and economic importance of entrepreneurial teams are uncontested, but we could not find any empirical study analysing the risks of entrepreneurial teams. In our discussion we identified a lack of theoretical and empirical work for the team phenomenon in the field of entrepreneurial research. Until now most of the empirical studies focus on the characteristics of the teams. With this approach it is not possible to explain accurately the differences in

the performance of entrepreneurial teams. This is empirically shown by the weak linkages between the team characteristics and the new venture success.

We decided therefore, to change the level of analysis from this input-oriented approach, to the process-oriented approach. Risks of entrepreneurial teams could be better explained by analysing the process level. The influence of team processes on the new venture success are shown by some empirical studies. They used only isolated variables but none of the present studies conceptualised the team process within the entrepreneurial team. The main goal of our study was to close this theoretical gap by introducing the social interaction as a description of the team process to the entrepreneurial research.

The research of top management teams and innovation teams offers some theoretical concepts describing the social interaction more precisely. In the first step we proved the relevance of the social interaction within innovation teams. In the next step we compared the characteristics of innovation and entrepreneurial teams. The strong similarities allowed us to adopt the concept of social interaction for the entrepreneurial team research. In the last step we tested empirically the validity of the social interaction within entrepreneurial teams. The high similarities to other empirical studies justify our introduction of social interaction into the field of entrepreneurial research.

Our hypothesis that the social interaction influences the new venture success is supported. For a more precise and broader understanding, the present results suggest a need for an integration of the social interaction in existing frameworks like the ones of Slevin and Covin (1995, p. 181), Cooper and Daily (1997, p. 130) or Ensley (1997, p. 155).

Social interaction is important for the new

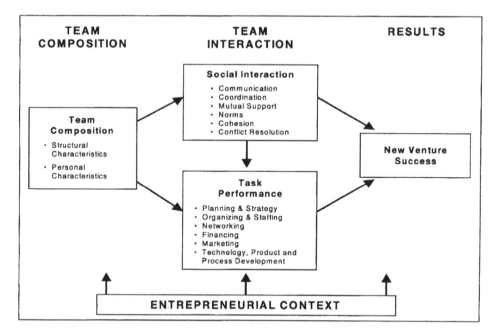

Figure 1. Extended framework for the success factors of entrepreneurial teams.

venture success, but this raises the question, how is it influenced and which other factors does it influence? The concept of social interaction of entrepreneurial teams is a part of an empirical study to investigate the success factors of venture teams. Thus, the concept is an integrated part of the broader theoretical framework (figure) underlying this study. Figure 1 shows the causal relations we want to investigate further.

Some of the causal relations have already been empirically tested, but our analyses will go a step further and test the entire causal structure of the success factors of new high-tech ventures.

List of items used in the study: Dimension scales of social interaction

Communication

1. The entrepreneurial team members communicate frequently with each other.
2. The entrepreneurial team members communicate intensively with each other.

3. Team members share ideas and information frankly.
4. I'm completely content with the accuracy of information interchange within the entrepreneurial team.
5. I'm completely content with the exactness of information provided by other team members.
6. The founders share opinions and information spontaneously.

Coordination

7. The founders adjust closely the processing of their tasks.
8. Within the entrepreneurial team job's aren't done twice.
9. Within the entrepreneurial team related tasks are well coordinated.
10. Within the entrepreneurial team every task is assigned to specific team members.

Mutual support

11. The founders support and complement each other as well as they can.
12. Discussions among the founders are always constructive and beneficial.
13. Proposals and contributions of the founders are always respected.
14. Proposals and contributions of the founders will be discussed and developed.

15. The entrepreneurial team works within a cooperative ambience.
16. The founders reach consensus in every important issue.

Work norms (effort)

17. Every founder perceives herself/himself as responsible for the entrepreneurial team's goals.
18. The founders share the workload of the entrepreneurial team equally.
19. Every founder works as best as she/he can in order to achieve the entrepreneurial team's goals.
20. Every founder is involved equally in reaching the common goals of the entrepreneurial team.

Cohesion

21. Every founder is completely integrated in the entrepreneurial team.
22. Working in the entrepreneurial team has the highest priority for every team member (in comparison with other jobs and private life).
23. Mutual sympathy is a characteristic of the entrepreneurial team.
24. Strong cohesion is a characteristic of the entrepreneurial team.
25. I'm proud to be part of the entrepreneurial team.
26. The entrepreneurial team is convinced of his capacity to perform well.

Conflict resolution

27. Disagreements between the founders are frankly discussed.
28. Disagreements between the founders are objectively discussed.
29. The founders normally come easily to an agreement.
30. Disagreements between the founders are solved rapidly.
31. The founders solve conflicts and disagreements within the entrepreneurial team completely.

Affective conflicts

32. The decision-making process provokes frequently personal conflicts between the founders.
33. Within the entrepreneurial team affective conflicts occur often.
34. The decision-making process causes often emotional reactions of the team members.

Cognitive conflicts

35. Referring to basic decisions entrepreneurial team members often disagree.
36. In discussions the founder's points of view often differ greatly.
37. The founders often hold different views in the decision-making process.

References

Alderfer, C. P., 1987 'An Intergroup Perspective on Group Dynamics', in J. W. Lorsch (ed.), *Handbook of Organizational Behavior*, Englewood Cliffs: Prentice-Hall, pp. 190–222.

Amason, Allen C., Kenneth R. Thompson, Wayne A. Hochwarter and Allison W. Harrison, 1995, 'Conflict: An Important Dimension in Successful Management Teams', *Organizational Dynamics* **2**, 20–35.

Ancona, Deborah G. and David F. Caldwell, 1990, 'Beyond Boundary Spanning: Managing External Dependence in Product Development Teams', *Journal of High Technology Management Research* **1**(2), 119–135.

Bantel, Karen A., 1998, 'Technology-Based, Adolescent Firm Configurations: Strategy Identification, Context, and Performance', *Journal of Business Venturing* **13**(3), 205–230.

Bird, Barbara J., 1989, *Entrepreneurial Behavior*, Glenview, IL: Scott Foresman and Company.

Boyd, David P. and David E. Gumpert, 1983, 'Coping with Entrepreneurial Stress', *Harvard Business Review* **61**(2), 44–59.

Clark, K. B. and T. Fujimoto, 1991, *Product Development Performance*, Boston: Harvard Business School Press.

Cohen, Susan G. and Diane E. Bailey, 1997, 'What Makes Teams Work: Group Effectiveness Research from the Shop Floor to the Executive Suite', *Journal of Management* **23**(3), 239–290.

Cooney, T. M. and W. D. Bygrave, 1997, *The Evolution of Structure and Strategy in Fast-Growth Firms Founded by Entrepreneurial Teams*, Working Paper presented at the Babson Entrepreneurship Conference 1997.

Cooper, A. C., W. C. Dunkelberg, C. Y. Woo and W. J. Dennis, 1990, *New Business in America: The Firms and their Owners*, Washington, DC: National Foundation of Independent Businesses.

Cooper, Arnold C., 1986 'Entrepreneurship and High Technology', in Donald L. Sexton and Raymond W. Smilor (eds.), *The Art and Science of Entrepreneurship*, Cambridge, MA: Ballinger, pp. 153–168.

Cooper, Arnold C. and Albert V. Bruno, 1977, 'Success among High-Technology Firms', *Business Horizons* **20**(2), 16–22.

Cooper, Arnold C. and Catherine M. Daily, 1996, *Entrepreneurial Teams*, Working Paper.

Cooper, Arnold C. and Catherine M. Daily, 1997, 'Entrepreneurial Teams', in Don Sexton and Ray Smilor (eds.), *Entrepreneurship 2000*, Chicago, IL: Upstart Publishing Company, pp. 127–150.

Cooper, Arnold C. and F. Javier Gimeno Gascón, 1992, 'Entrepreneurs, Processes of Founding, and New Firm Performance', in Donald L. Sexton and John D. Kasarda (eds.), *The State of the Art of Entrepreneurship*, Boston: PWS-Kent Publishing Co., pp. 301–340.

Cooper, R. G., 1993, *Winning at New Products: Accelerating the Process from Idea to Launch*, Reading, MA: Addsion Wesley.

Dandridge, T., 1979, 'Children are not Little "Grown-Ups":

Small Business Needs Its Own Organizational Theory', *Journal of Small Business Management*, 53–57.

Doutriaux, Jerome, 1992, 'Emerging High-Tech Firms: How Durable Are Their Comparative Start-Up Advantages?', *Journal of Business Venturing* **7**(4), 303–322.

Eisenhardt, Kathleen M. and Claudia Bird Schoonhoven, 1990, 'Organizational Growth: Linking Founding Team, Strategy, Environment, and Growth among U.S. Semiconductor Ventures, 1978–1988', *Administrative Science Quarterly* **35**(3), 504–529.

Ensley, Michael Dean, 1997, *The Effect of Entrepreneurial Team Skill Heterogeneity and Conflict on New Venture Strategic Orientation and Performance: A Study of the INC. 500*, Dissertation Submitted To The Faculty of Mississippi State University.

Feeser, Henry R. and Gary E. Willard, 1989, 'Incubators and Performance: A Comparison of High- and Low-Growth High-Tech Firms', *Journal of Business Venturing* **4**, 429–443.

Gartner, William B., 1985, 'A Conceptual Framework for Describing the Phenomenon of New Venture Creation', *Academy of Management Review* **10**(4), 696–706

Gladstein, Deborah L., 1984, 'Groups in Context: A Model of Task Group Effectiveness', *Administrative Science Quarterly* **29**, 499–517.

Goodman, Paul S., Elizabeth Ravlin and Marshall Schminke, 1987, 'Understanding Groups in Organizations', *Research in Organizational Behavior* **9**, 121–173.

Guzzo, Richard A. and Gregory P. Shea, 1992, 'Group Performance and Intergroup Relations in Organizations', in Marvin D. Dunnette and Leaetta M. Hough (eds.), *Handbook of Industrial and Organizational Psychology*, Palo Alto: Consulting Psychologists Press, pp. 269–313.

Hackman, J. Richard, 1987, 'The Design of Work Teams', in Jay W. Lorsch (ed.), *Handbook of Organizational Behavior*, Englewood Cliffs: Prentice-Hall, pp. 315–342.

Helfert, Gabriele, 1998, *Teams im Relationship Marketing – Design effektiver Kundenbeziehungsteams*, Wiesbaden: Gabler Verlag.

Hoegl, Martin, 1998, *Teamarbeit in innovativen Projekten – Einfluflgrößen und Wirkungen*, Wiesbaden: Gabler Verlag.

Hunsdiek, Detlef, 1987, *Unternehmensgründung als Folgeinnovation – Struktur, Hemmnisse und Erfolgsbedingungen der Gründung industrieller innovativer Unternehmen*, Stuttgart: Poeschel Verlag.

Janis, Irving L., 1982, *Groupthink* (2nd ed.); Boston, MA: Houghton Mifflin Company.

Janis, Irving L. and Leon Mann, 1977, *Decision Making: A Psychological Analysis of Conflict, Choice and Commitment*, New York: The Free Press.

Johne, Axel and Patricia Snelson, 1990, *Successful Product Development: Lessons from American and British Firms*, Oxford: Blackwell.

Kamm, Judith B., Jeffrey C. Shuman, John A. Seeger and Aaron J. Nurick, 1990, 'Entrepreneurial Teams in New Venture Creation: A Research Agenda', *Entrepreneurship Theory and Practice* **14**(4), 7–17.

Kamm, Judith B., Jeffrey C. Shuman John A. Seeger and Aaron J. Nurick, 1989, 'Are Well-Balanced Entrepreneurial Teams More Successful?', in R. H. Brockhaus, N. C. Churchill, J. A. Katz, B. A. Kirchhoff, K. H. Vesper and W. E. Wetzel (eds.), *Frontiers of Entrepreneurship Research*, Wellesley, MA: Babson College.

Katz, Ralph, 1982, 'The Effects of Group Longevity on Project Communication and Performance', *Administrative Science Quarterly* **27**, 81–104.

Klandt, Heinz and G. Kirschbaum, 1985, *Software- und Systemhäuser: Strategien in der Gründungs- und Frühentwicklungsphase*, Sankt Augustin: Gesellschaft für Mathematik und Datenverarbeitung.

Latané, Bibb, Kipling Williams and Stephen Harkins, 1979, 'Many Hands Make Light the Work: The Causes and Consequences of Social Loafing', *Journal of Personality and Social Psychology* **37**(6), 822–832.

Lechler, T., 1997, *Erfolgsfaktoren des Projektmanagements*, Frankfurt a.M.: Peter Lang.

Levine, John M. and Richard L. Moreland, 1990, 'Progress in Small Group Research', *Annual Review of Psychology* **41**, 585–634.

Mayer, Michael, Walter Heinzel and Raymund Müller, 1989, 'Performance of New Technology-Based Firms in the Federal Republic of Germany at the Stage of Market Entry', in R. H. Brockhaus, N. C. Churchill, J. A. Katz, B. A. Kirchhoff, K. H. Vesper and W. E. Wetzel (eds.), *Frontiers of Entrepreneurship Research 1989 – Proceedings of the 1989 Babson College Entrepreneurship Research Conference*, Wellesley MA: Babson College, pp. 200–215.

McGrath, Joseph E., 1964, *Social Psychology: A Brief Introduction*, New York: Holt Rinehart and Winston, Inc.

Mohrman, S. A., S. G. Cohen and A. M. Mohrman, 1995, *Designing Team-Based Organizations: New Forms for Knowledge Work*, San Francisco: Jossey-Bass Verlag.

Mullen, Brian and Carolyn Copper, 1994, 'The Relationship Between Group Cohesiveness and Performance: An Integration', *Psychological Bulletin* **115**(2), 210–227.

Picot, Arnold, Ulf-Dieter Laub and Dietram Schneider, 1989, *Innovative Unternehmensgründungen – Eine ökonomische empirische Analyse*, Berlin: Springer Verlag.

Pinto, M. B., J. K. Pinto and J. E. Prescott, 1993, 'Antecedents and Consequences of Project Team Cross-functional Cooperation', *Management Science* **39**(10), 1281–1297.

Pinto, Mary Beth and Jeffrey K. Pinto, 1990, 'Project Team Communication and Cross-Functional Cooperation in New Program Development', *Journal of Product Innovation Management* **7**, 200–212.

Pleschak, Franz and Henning Werner, 1998, *Technologieorientierte Unternehmensgründungen in den neuen Bundesländern – Wissenschaftliche Analyse und Begleitung de BMBF-Modellversuchs*, Physika Verlag, Heidelberg.

Schumpeter, Joseph, 1952, *Theorie der wirtschaftlichen Entwicklung – Eine Untersuchung über Unternehmergewinn, Kapital, Kredit, Zins und den Konjunkturzyklus*, Berlin: 5. Auflage, Duncker & Humblot Verlag.

Shea, Gregory and Richard A. Guzzo, 1987, 'Group

Effectiveness: What Really Matters', *Sloan Management Review* (Spring 1987), 25–31.

Slevin, Dennis P. and Jeffrey G. Covin, 1995, 'Entrepreneurship as Firm Behavior: A Research Model', in Gerome A. Katz and Robert H. Brockhaus Sr. (eds.), *Advances in Entrepreneurship, Firm Emergence, and Growth*, pp. 175–224.

Teach, Richard D., Fred A. Tarpley and Robert G. Schwartz, 1986, 'Software Venture Teams', in Robert Ronstadt, John A. Hornaday, Rein Peterson and Karl H. Vesper (eds.), *Frontiers of Entrepreneurship Research 1986 – Proceedings of the 1986 Babson College Entrepreneurship Research Conference*, Wellesley, MA: Babson College, pp. 546–562.

Teal, Elisabeth Jane, 1998, *The Determinants of New Venture Success: Strategy, Industry Structure, and the Founding Entrepreneurial Team*, Dissertation, University of Georgia.

Timmons, Jeffrey A., 1990, *New Venture Creation: Entrepreneurship in the 1990s*, 3rd ed., Homewood: Irwin.

Tjosvold, Dean, 1995, 'Cooperation Theory, Constructive Controversy, and Effectiveness: Learning from Crisis', in Richard A. Guzzo and Salas Eduardo and Associates, *Team Effectiveness and Decision Making in Organizations*, San Francisco: Jossey-Bass, pp. 79–112.

Tuck, A. C. and W. C. Hamilton, 1993, 'The Evolution of Structure and Strategy in Fast-Growth Firms Founded by Entrepreneurial Teams', *International Small Business Journal* 12, 12–22.

Vesper, Karl H., 1990, *New Venture Strategies*, Revised Edition, Prentice Hall, Englewood Cliffs, NJ.

Vyakarnam, Shailendra, R. C. Jacobs and Jari Handelberg, 1997, *Formation and Development of Entrepreneurial Teams in Rapid Growth Businesses*, Working Paper.

Watson, Warren E., Louis D. Ponthieu and Joseph W. Critelli, 1995, 'Team Interpersonal Process Effectiveness in Venture Partnerships and its Connection to Perceived Success', *Journal of Business Venturing* 10(5), 393–411.

Wiendieck, G., 1992, 'Teamarbeit', in Erich Frese (ed.), *Handwörterbuch der Organisation*, Stuttgart: C. E. Poeschel.

[10]

1042-2587
© 2007 by
Baylor University

Collective Cognition: When Entrepreneurial Teams, Not Individuals, Make Decisions

G. Page West, III

New venture success often depends on how the founding team collectively understands its world, estimates effects of possible actions, makes decisions, and allocates appropriate resources. Drawing on recent work in managerial cognition and entrepreneurship, this article argues for the importance of examining cognition at the team level. New venture strategy is used as a springboard to discuss collective cognition, although other important critical decision domains in new ventures may also be used to illustrate the arguments. In this and other such decision domains, collective cognition mediates between individual cognitions and firm actions and performance. A method for assessing entrepreneurial top management team cognition is developed and then tested in an exploratory study of technology-based new ventures. Two structural characteristics of collective cognition (differentiation and integration) are strongly related to firm performance, suggesting interesting opportunities for future entrepreneurship research in cognition.

Introduction

Gartner, Shaver, Gatewood, and Katz (1994, p. 6) observe that the field of entrepreneurship needs to account for the reality that "the entrepreneur in entrepreneurship is more likely to be plural," and that "those individuals who might have a significant involvement in the venture" be included in theory development and research. On a practical level, academics who teach entrepreneurship often stress the importance of the team in the start-up process (Timmons, 1994), an emphasis that is also prominent in venture capitalists' assessments of a new venture's potential (Cyr, Johnson, & Welbourne, 2000; Zacharakis & Meyer, 1998). For these reasons, a growing body of research is examining the influence of the founding or top management team on a new venture's survival and performance.

Research on founding teams often examines whether and how such teams understand the nature of the venture opportunity, spot new or emerging opportunities, and come to agreement on what to do. Other research on founding teams proposes frameworks linking the size and composition of the team to the presence of the different types of knowledge that will help the new venture succeed, and to the integration of perspectives among team members that will lead to consistency of actions in the marketplace (Eisenhardt &

Please send correspondence to: G. Page West, III, tel.: (336) 758-4260; e-mail: westgp@wfu.edu.

Schoonhoven, 1990; Ucbasaran, Lockett, Wright, & Westhead, 2003). The results indicate that the presence of idea and knowledge diversity within such teams contributes to team learning (Clarysse & Moray, 2004) and the venture's ability to acquire additional resources necessary for its growth (Brush, Greene, & Hart, 2001; Hayton & Zahra, 2005). Furthermore, members of these teams appear to differ behaviorally in their propensities for external networking (Neergaard, 2005); such networking serves to gather useful new information about markets and customers, making it more likely that the new venture will start up successfully (Grandi & Grimaldi, 2003). These and other studies support the premise that there are synergistic gains to be developed from a *team* of founders that enhances the potential of the new venture (Colombo & Grilli, 2005) through its collective efforts.

Although valuable and desirable, it appears that team synergy is not naturally occurring or effortless; research points to a significant tension that exists between the presence of multiple perspectives in a founding team and the development of a cohesive point of view across the team. On the one hand, founder team composition often results in a relatively homogeneous group that can limit the fresh perspectives and new ideas brought to the founding process (Ruef, Aldrich, & Carter, 2003). Thus, Boeker (1989) concludes that conditions at founding—including the size of the team and the extent to which a firm is owned by its founding managers—can imprint an initial strategy on the new venture that resists change, and can limit the range of options subsequently considered by the team. On the other hand, founding teams do not remain static over time. While departures from founding teams often reflect the difficulty teams have in coming to agreement when differing points of view are present (Ucbasaran et al., 2003), the addition of team members can inject novel experience and new understandings into the team's collective deliberations.

The tension between the propensity to surface new ideas in order to adapt the venture to changing circumstances and the inertia of the venture's initial direction also characterizes the thrust of much research on top management teams in new ventures after the founding event. This body of research often examines entrepreneurial firm performance based upon top management team characteristics that can affect team understanding and decisions (Busenitz et al., 2003), using dimensions such as previous experience (Eisenhardt & Schoonhoven, 1990), networking activity (West & Meyer, 1997) and entrepreneurial orientation (Covin & Slevin, 1991; Lumpkin & Dess, 1996), or based upon differences among team members such as consensus and conflict (Ensley, Pearson, & Amason, 2002; West & Meyer, 1998).

Thus, in many new ventures, the key decisions affecting the venture's ability to embrace present opportunity and to persist over time are made by a team, not by an individual. The tensions that exist in team deliberations—new possibilities versus existing direction, cohesion versus conflict—demonstrate that similarities and differences of opinion often exist among members of a founder team. These similarities and differences of opinion reflect similarities and differences in team members' underlying belief structures about the nature of emerging opportunities and about the relationship between present actions and sustainable performance in the marketplace.

While the founders and each top manager will have individual perspectives and cognitions about their new venture, it is a collective perspective or a collective knowledge structure at the team level that guides the direction of the venture. Collective cognition in new ventures is therefore an important domain to explore, and it is fundamentally different from individual cognition or from the aggregation of individual cognitions. There is a strong parallel between team-level collective perspective and cognition at the individual level of analysis. As a collective cause–effect understanding of the venture in the marketplace, team-level perspective (like a schema) may facilitate or impede organizational alertness, intentions, transactions, and other dimensions important in successfully carrying out the work of the venture, or may instantiate scripts and other automatic behaviors. For this reason, we refer to the collective perspective as entrepreneurial team collective cognition (ETCC).

The attention to ETCC is uncommon in the field of entrepreneurship research. Previous entrepreneurship research has largely explored cognition at the individual level, for example, examining opportunity recognition (Gaglio, 2004; McMullen & Shepherd, 2003), fit with the entrepreneurship role (Markman & Baron, 2002), the propensity to start new ventures (Busenitz & Barney, 1997; Gatewood, Shaver, & Gartner, 1995; Shaver & Scott, 1991), biases and heuristics in individual decision making (Busenitz & Barney, 1997; Simon & Houghton, 2002), and individuals' decision policies (Shepherd & Zacharakis, 1997). While important in understanding the antecedents to individual entrepreneurial behavior, these studies shed no light on the nature, measurement, or impact of beliefs and representations at the team level of analysis, which is where decisions are made and actions are taken. Nor can a focus on individual cognition account for the cognitive variety or interpretations apparent at a team level. And the methodologies used to examine individual-level cognition have significant limitations when applied to teams.

A review of the founding team literature reveals that only two published studies have dealt with the cognitive characteristics of the collection of top managers who run new ventures. Shepherd and Krueger (2002) researched intentions and desirability with respect to engaging in corporate entrepreneurship, while Ensley and Pearce (2001) included a "shared cognition" variable in a study relating group process to new venture performance. The shared cognition variable used in this study served as an imperfect proxy for strategy content. It was based on a simplistic measure of variation across managers, a method which is problematic for capturing the richness of ideas and the variation among top managers (West & Meyer, 1998). Neither of these studies truly address what Weick and Roberts (1993) term the "collective mind," i.e., the comprehension of unfolding events by teams of interacting individuals. In addition, no research has examined the collective top management team cognitive *structure* of cause–effect knowledge that manifests itself in the kinds of decisions and outcomes associated with new venture strategy.

This article concentrates on collective cognition in entrepreneurial teams and its important structural characteristics. New venture strategy is used as a springboard to discuss collective cognition, although other important critical decision domains in new ventures (e.g., alliance partner selection, venture capital firm or underwriter selection, and manufacturing decisions) may also be used to illustrate the arguments. The focus on strategy is appropriate because strategy is essentially perspective, a cause–effect knowledge structure of the new venture's relationship with the environment in which it operates. Furthermore, strategy is collective because it involves the consideration of multiple issues by multiple top managers, and because critical decisions and practices result from that collective consideration. Strategy is thus an example of a decision domain of teams that invokes ETCC as a sociocognitive concept involving the simultaneous relations between different people and between different ideas. Two important structural properties of ETCC are identified (differentiation and integration) that parallel the dual strategic challenges confronted by new ventures, as noted earlier, of surfacing new ideas versus staying the course and of balancing cohesion versus conflict.

The next section briefly draws parallels between traditional individual level cognition and cognition at a team level of analysis. A brief review of other methods for examining cognitions reveals limitations when extended to the collective level. The use of sociocognitive grid analysis is proposed and described as an approach that overcomes such limitations. An exploratory field study example is presented, and the results suggest interesting new directions for future cognition research in entrepreneurship.

Cognitive Parallels at the Team Level

New venture teams confront the same kinds of strategic decision dynamics that individual founders face. This is because the strategy issues facing teams "rarely present themselves as tidy, discrete bundles . . . and executives are not confronted with decisions so much as they create decision opportunities through their insight or ingenuity" (Hambrick, Finkelstein, & Mooney, 2005, p. 504).

Both venture teams and individual venture founders need information to make strategic decisions, so one would expect both to engage in the same information-seeking behavior in order to better define future direction and generate enhanced firm performance (West & Meyer, 1997). Both use the knowledge gleaned from information seeking to create mental models or schema, which organize beliefs and rules in ways that allow the entrepreneur to make sense out of an uncertain landscape (Busenitz & Lau, 1996) and help identify new commercial opportunities (Shane & Venkataraman, 2000). This mental model can guide attention to new information and emerging trends, invoke memory of other similar past events and conditions, and specify cause–effect and means–ends relationships in the physical and social worlds. It serves as a basis for making predictions and inferences about how to act, the likely probability of success, and how best to allocate resources (Busenitz & Lau, 1996; Gaglio & Katz, 2001), or in other words, what strategy to pursue and how to implement that strategy. This notion of interpretation system at the firm level parallels the enactment perspective at the individual level (Gartner, Carter, & Hills, 2003), through which new opportunities become a reality. Finally, venture teams are not immune from the problems caused by uncertainty, information overload, high novelty, time pressure, and strong emotions (Baron, 1998; Busenitz & Lau, 1996; Shaver & Scott, 1991) as also found with individual venture founders. So one would expect teams, like individuals, to rely on mental models or schema as a heuristic aid to interpretation and decision making.

Given the number of similarities, it is tempting to assume that, although a team does not think or cognize *per se*, the cognitive dynamics driving individual processes are immediately transferable to teams. In this view, the team is simply an aggregation of individual team member schema. However, Bougon (1992) rather convincingly demonstrates that a team perspective represents considerably more than the compilation of individual perspectives. He finds that while an aggregate cognitive map can be seen as the merger of ideas and concepts from a group of individuals, it really reflects the researchers' assumptions about "similarity of meaning" and whether concepts "ought to have been linked"(Bougon 1992, p. 371). Congregate maps, on the other hand, include only the concepts and relationships that have relevance for *all* individuals in a team. Thus, each individual has his or her own cognitive map, but what actually informs and motivates the strategy of the team is the congregate or collective map (Cossette & Audet, 1992).

Cognitive Nature of New Venture Strategy

A variety of critical new venture team decisions can illustrate properties of collective cognition, but perhaps venture strategy is the most illustrative and most compelling because of the significant body of work amassed over the years about the importance of strategy in entrepreneurial firms. These studies examine the usefulness of various strategic approaches (Feeser & Willard, 1990; McDougall & Robinson, 1990; Sandberg & Hofer, 1987) and the influence of industry structure (McDougall, Robsinson, & DeNisi, 1992), as well as broader perspectives that describe the essential nature and characteristics of strategy in new ventures (Gartner, 1985; Slevin & Covin, 1995). Studies have also concluded that new ventures must often change strategically in order to achieve continued growth and success after the start-up (Moore, 1995). As the interface between the firm and the market, strategy thus takes on a central role in the growth and survival of new ventures.

Perspective

In order to delineate and examine the cognitive nature of new venture strategy, it is important to distinguish between strategy as *position* and strategy as *perspective* (Ginsberg, 1988; Mintzberg, 1987). Whereas position conceptualizes strategy as a location in a product/market domain, perspective conceptualizes strategy as "reflected in the integrated sets of ideas through which problems are spotted and interpreted and from which streams of decisions flow" (Ginsberg, 1988, p. 561). Perspective speaks to the sensemaking which new ventures make of their internal and external environments (Daft & Weick, 1984), as they seek to develop an understanding of new means–ends relationships for pursuing opportunities. A venture's strategy—its recognition of opportunities, its decisions and resource allocations, its activities, and its performance—reflects perspective.

Perspective arises from the information seeking and knowledge structuring behaviors of entrepreneurs. Neoclassical economists do not allow the existence of entrepreneurs in an economic system, in large part, because informational asymmetries are assumed away in their economic models. Others argue that the fragmentation of knowledge in society (Hayek, 1945) enables entrepreneurs to accrue different stocks of experience-based knowledge, which leads to different abilities to recognize new opportunities (Shane, 2000). In addition, the idiosyncratic nature of information seeking and knowledge building behaviors enables entrepreneurs to define new opportunities where none had existed before (Gartner et al., 2003; West, 2003). Entrepreneurial insights thus depend on the development of cognitive structure that captures new information and creates meaning in novel ways.

Strategy as perspective explains why different strategies can emerge from ventures facing identical circumstances. The schema-like structure of team cognition will produce this result for a number of reasons. For example, differences in the team cognitive structure among two competing ventures may prompt one team to notice and attend to certain industry information while the other does not. In 1980, Celestial Seasonings discontinued a line of bottled juice beverages because the management team believed there was a relatively small market opportunity for those types of products. At the same time, the Snapple company, with substantially similar channels of distribution, viewed the market opportunity as significant. Celestial Seasonings increased to $75 million in annual revenue by the early 1990s, while Snapple's business skyrocketed to $674 million during the same period. Although confronting the same market, the two firms noticed different information, made different inferential projections, and engaged in very different responses.

On the other hand, teams may receive identical new information, but will interpret that information in different ways reflecting either differences in attributes of the teams' schemas or differences in relationships among attributes of the schemas. Despite possessing the exact same information about the business, different venture capital (VC) firms had widely divergent views of the market potential for Vermeer Technologies, whose algorithms for webpage creation have since become an industry standard. The differing perceptions led some VC firms, but not others, to want to invest. The same type of perceptual differences also led Microsoft to consider acquiring Vermeer, while Netscape passed on the opportunity (Ferguson, 1999). Different responses, or even similar responses executed on different timetables, result from the fact that organizations interpret the same stimuli in a different fashion and then draw different conclusions about the proper direction and pace to take in the future. Strategic perspective thus plays an important mediating role between the competitive environment and strategic actions initiated by a new venture.

Multidimensional

Research on strategy in new ventures tends to emphasize competitive strategy concepts originating from industrial/organization economics. These include industry conditions that encourage or forestall new entry such as barriers to entry and industry rivalry dynamics (Dean, Meyer, & DeCastro, 1993), type of strategy such as pursuing a low-cost or differentiated approach (Shepherd & Shanley, 1999), speed of strategy such as first-mover or rapid-follower approach, and scope of strategy such as whether a new venture should be broad or narrow (Jelinek & Schoonhoven, 1990).

But strategy for new ventures is significantly more complex than the customary array of competitive strategy dimensions. This is true for two reasons. First, new venture strategy is significantly more fine grained in the short term than the traditional broad strategy ideas might suggest. Teams in new ventures are as concerned with the translation of overall direction to practical, day-to-day implementation as they are with direction itself. This involves tactical thinking and attention to a myriad of details and minutiae. Teams focus on building customer, supplier, and financial relationships, and in organizing operations carefully as they start up to be consistent with an overall strategic approach. To accomplish this, they seek to build a resource base that effectively translates strategy to action (Brush et al., 2001) while conferring sustainable advantage (Alvarez & Busenitz, 2001).

Second, strategy for new ventures involves constant evolution and change. The progression through organizational life cycle stages ensures that new strategic challenges continually confront new ventures (Kazanjian, 1988). At the same time, teams must learn how to refine their existing approach and also seek new opportunities for the future (Lumpkin & Lichtenstein, 2005). Thus, at any given time, top managers in new ventures must be considering an array of problems, opportunities, threats, changes, and other substantive strategic issues (Dutton & Jackson, 1987), an agenda that continues to evolve as the venture evolves.

Collective

Differences in perspective within top management teams may have a profound effect on a new venture's strategy and in changes to a venture's strategy. Hambrick and Mason (1984) propose that cognitive properties of top managers affect the extent to which strategic issues are identified within teams and the interpretation of those issues by team members. An empirical analysis by Markoczy and Goldberg (1995) of causal maps, which are constructed to depict individual cognitive structure (see methodology section), finds that significant variance exists among managers at the same level within

the same organization. Cognitive diversity, defined as differences in beliefs and preferences, is likewise found to exist among CEOs and members of their top management
teams (Miller, Burke, & Glick, 1998). The result of such differences can affect the way
an issue is interpreted or a problem is formulated. For example, in a study on team
decision making based upon cognitive-based team composition, Volkema and Gorman
(1998, p. 109) surmised that a problem "described or formulated in one way (e.g., as a
personnel problem) when in fact another formulation is preferable (e.g., as a technology
problem) is likely to obscure important dimensions of the problem and lead to an
ineffective solution." This study found support for an effect on performance of the
interaction of cognitive team composition and problem formulation. The type of
problem or issue that is identified can then affect organizational process that kicks in as
a response, the method used or type of information gathered to inform the team further,
and ultimately, the decisions made by the team. Team decisions, in turn, can affect the
direction and performance of the venture. Team members might differ considerably in
the way in which new information invokes memory or instantiates a schema, resulting
in very different decisions and directions than if left up to an individual (Mohammed,
Klimoski, & Rentsch, 2000).

However, in new ventures formed by teams decisions are not left up to the individual.
Therefore, it is important to understand how the varying individual top manager perspectives about the range of strategic issues within a new venture translate into the new
venture's collective understanding of strategic issues and opportunities. Cognitive variance among top managers may result in a variety of competing or incompatible dominant
logics within the same team (Ginsberg, 1989; Prahalad & Bettis, 1986). The collective
level becomes especially important if a new venture is to be consistent and focused in its
sets of activities, allocate limited resources without incurring waste, and be proactive to
effectively meet the challenge of the changing circumstances it will continue to encounter.
Although individuals regularly enter group settings with varying viewpoints, teams
develop shared and idiosyncratic understandings (Eden, Jones, Sims, & Simthin, 1981;
Mohammed & Ringseis, 2001) from which key decisions and actions flow. The collective
perspective represents a bridge between individuals in a team and actions taken in respect
of team decisions.

Because strategy is perspective, multidimensional, and collective, it is proposed that
ETCC is a mediating variable between firm performance and both the environment and
individual top managers (see Figure 1). In this view, ETCC is an antecedent to new
venture performance because performance will be a byproduct of the cause–effect

Figure 1

Model of Entrepreneurial Collective Cognition

strategic understandings and actions embraced by the team. Antecedent to ETCC are not only the various individual cognitions of the founder and top management team members, but also other sources impacting collective perspective, such as the competitive external environment, the addition of new top managers to the team, and organizational process that serves to bring information and new perspectives to light at the team level.

The preceding discussion emphasizes that new venture strategy is a sociocognitive concept. It concerns itself with the social relations among top managers and with the cognitive relations of their individual, multidimensional perspectives about the competitive environment (Dunn & Ginsberg, 1986). This approach accounts for the set of individuals involved in strategic deliberations, as well as the set of strategy constructs that are in the "range of convenience" of these individuals. The sociocognitive frame of reference exhibits properties of communality and sociality, which provide a critical link between the content of individual and collective reference frames (Dunn & Ginsberg, 1986, p. 959). Thus, the collective perspective may provide evidence of a "dominant logic" used by the team.

Dimensions of Sociocognitive Structure

Properties of ETCC

Just as components of knowledge are believed to be organized in ways such as categories, schemas, and scripts at the individual level (Fiske & Taylor, 1991), the *organization* of cause–effect knowledge emanating from multiple individual perspectives to the team level has its own unique characteristics. Thus, the term "collective cognition" refers to the content of the combination of individual perspectives and the structural characteristics of that combination. Although content is mentioned briefly, this article focuses more on the structural dimensions of ETCC that specifically relate to entrepreneurial strategy and performance.

The content of ETCC refers to strategy constructs that guide the venture's conduct and performance. These dimensions should reflect specific cause–effect understandings that top management teams collectively hold about the connections between new venture activity and new venture survival or performance. For example, the team managing a new venture in the PC software industry might collectively value "focused differentiation" (Porter, 1985) as a strategic rule that will produce superior performance. On the other hand, a team managing a new venture in the fragmented dry cleaning industry might collectively value "low cost" as a route to survival (Bhide, Rayzman, & Hackett, 1999). Or a new venture team may collectively embrace the strategy construct of "new product development" as a route to generate sales revenue growth in new markets (Wetlaufer, 1997).

The structure of ETCC will function for the team in much the same way as a structure of knowledge functions for an individual. An individual's cognitive architecture for a particular domain will determine how new information is stored and evaluated, may bias interpretations and be used as a heuristic for decision making, and may contain stereotypes or scripts that precipitate automatic responses to received stimuli. Similarly, at the team level, the set of strategy constructs represents cause-and-effect knowledge about operating in the competitive environment, will serve to influence how new information is treated, may be resistant to change without significant unlearning, and like scripts or schemas would trigger a portfolio of organization actions.

Two structural dimensions of ETCC are particularly important: differentiation and integration of strategic perspectives in the top management team. Differentiation represents the extent to which each strategic construct is construed as different from every other strategic construct. It suggests what Ginsberg (1989) characterizes as the opposite of "frame uniformity." Frame uniformity means that potentially viable strategic alternatives are not being identified or distinguished by top managers, whereas a deficit of uniform thinking connotes that top managers evaluate alternatives as being very different.

Integration represents the degree to which top managers think in a similar fashion about a set of strategy constructs. Integration within a new venture team suggests that members individually view both the relevance of strategic constructs and their relative importance in ways that are similar to other managers on their team. Ginsberg (1989) refers to this as sociocognitive integration, meaning that there is cognitive similarity across a social setting. In contrast, fragmented thinking among members of a new venture team would be evidenced by the use of different constructs by team members or by different levels of importance ascribed to a set of identified constructs.

Figure 2 graphically illustrates the dimensions of differentiation and integration. The data points in each box represent the hypothetical "ratings" of four top managers in a new venture on each of five important strategy constructs that have been identified. Reading up and down the chart in the top box, each strategy construct is rated at different levels from other constructs with construct 3 as the highest and construct 4 as the lowest. The wide

Figure 2

Illustration of Differentiation and Integration

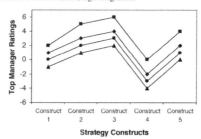

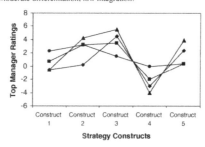

range of ratings across the strategy constructs suggests that the top managers do effectively differentiate among the available strategy constructs. Reading across this same chart, it is apparent that the top managers are fairly uniform in their relative ratings of the five constructs, i.e., each manager tends to view the relationship among the set of constructs similarly. Collectively, therefore, they exhibit a fairly high level of integration. In the lower half of Figure 2, a different picture emerges. Here, the level of differentiation appears to be about the same as in the top chart. However, the top managers do not exhibit integration at the collective level since by reading across the same chart, it is apparent that the relative relationships among the set of constructs is not the same for each top manager.

Hypotheses

As described at the outset, strategy is a critical dimension in determining the success of new ventures. The presence of dynamic markets, evolving competitive threats, changing life cycle dynamics, and the basic nature of entrepreneurial orientation and proactive behavior all suggest that new ventures are constantly confronting evolving strategy issues and possible modifications to their strategies. On the one hand, where strategies and strategy change alternatives are not substantively considered by top managers, new venture performance or sustainability may suffer. Under these circumstances, new opportunities may not be surfaced, new competitive threats may not be appreciated, and changing organizational needs may not be identified. On the other hand, when top managers do effectively differentiate among strategic options, the team is presented with a greater probability of evaluating, selecting, and prioritizing among alternatives that will serve the venture well in the emerging competitive environment. The ability to differentiate alternatives thus increases adaptive generalization and improves survival potential (Chakravarthy, 1982). Previous research in entrepreneurship provides evidence that heterogeneity of ideas and information flow enhances performance (Ensley et al., 2002; West & Meyer, 1998).

The potential and the need for integration follow on the heels of differentiation (Bartunek, Gordon, & Weathersby, 1983; Chakravarthy, 1982; Gersick, 1991; Ginsberg, 1990; Hurst, Rush, & White, 1989). To the extent that top managers have very different sets of beliefs about the relative importance of considered strategic constructs, one wonders whether or not strategy implementation would be internally consistent. Although top managers may give their consent to certain strategic initiatives or direction in public forums, those who still fundamentally disagree at the basic level of cause–effect belief may use a different set of priorities in managing their own functional areas of the venture. On the one hand, where new opportunities have been identified, for example, poor integration across managers may relegate the pursuit of such opportunities to back-burner priority by some and precipitate the incremental (or even destructive) evolution of the venture as a result of fragmented attention and uncoordinated, unsupported actions across the firm. Meyer and Dean (1990) discovered precisely this dynamic in their study of founder CEOs who could not appreciate the strategic necessities recommended by the experienced top managers they had hired. On the other hand, the arrival of strategic decision makers on a shared perspective or area of mutual understanding enables the firm to move forward in a more focused and unified fashion with consistently applied strategic intentions and actions.

New venture performance, however, should depend on moderate levels of differentiation. On the one hand, in some new ventures, top management teams may be particularly facile in scanning the environment, gathering information, creating multiple new perspectives, and communicating these throughout for consideration. This may result in

Figure 3

Relationship between Performance and Differentiation or Integration

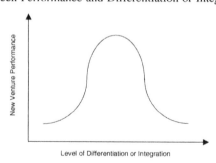

such a flow of new ideas that the team finds it difficult to coalesce around a subset for long enough, because the palette of available ideas is constantly shifting. On the other hand, too little differentiation would suggest too few strategic alternatives considered. This may have disastrous consequences in competitive environments that are constantly shifting.

New venture teams must also cultivate moderate levels of integration. Some teams may be particularly adept at synthesizing new perspectives developed and communicated throughout, and in expeditiously implementing actionable next steps arising out of a synthesis. Firms in these cases may then coalesce too quickly around new perspectives, without allowing for additional new interpretations and perspectives to be substantively considered. Similarly, firms which lack real integration capabilities at all might never be able to coalesce effectively around a subset of developed strategic alternatives. Too little integration suggests fragmented strategic thinking across team members, while too much integration suggests potential agreement on strategic alternatives without ample consideration of all alternatives.

Together, these ideas portray an inverted U-shaped relationship between new venture performance and both differentiation and integration. Greater differentiation and greater integration within founder teams or new venture top management teams are helpful, up to a point. However, higher levels of either differentiation or integration may be detrimental to the performance of the venture (see Figure 3).

Hypothesis 1: There is an inverted U-shaped relationship between the new venture performance and the degree of differentiation and integration of strategic constructs within the top management team.

Hypothesis 1a: New venture performance will be positively associated with moderate levels of differentiation and integration of strategic constructs within the top management team; however,

Hypothesis 1b: New venture performance will be negatively associated with low levels or high levels of differentiation and integration of strategic constructs within the top management team.

The previous discussion suggests that differentiation and integration are fundamentally related with one another, and that their interaction is also a critical variable. While both may exist within a new venture, the strength or weakness of one may overcome the benefit inherent in the other. Strong differentiation abilities create difficulty for the integration component because there is simply more that is new and more to pull together by the team into a unified view across managers. While these teams may possess integration capabilities, the information load (Daft & Lengel, 1984) on these capabilities may be too great such that effective integration does not occur. Weak integrating capabilities in the face of only average differentiating capabilities would produce a similar problem for teams. In contrast, integration capabilities that are better developed than differentiating capabilities may create a different set of problems for new venture teams. Strong integration in the face of relatively weaker differentiation would result in the more rapid arrival on frame uniformity and suggest that top managers may not have adequately discussed the issues and ideas. Streufert and Swezey (1986), in fact, hold that there can be no effective integration without an accommodating level of differentiation.

Top management skills in both differentiation and integration, therefore, become critically important, especially in the type of dynamic environments faced by new ventures. Here, top management teams are challenged to not only surface a manageable set of new strategic options responding to shifting strategic demands, but also to achieve an appropriate level of integration in order to move forward with internal consistency.

Hypothesis 2: New venture performance will be positively associated with the interaction between differentiation and integration of strategic constructs within the top management team.

Methodological Considerations

In order to understand the basis upon which new venture management teams make important decisions impacting the future of their firms, one must confront research challenges in examining properties of collective cognition.

Methods for Examining Collective Cognition

The meaning of a representation of thought is not only a function of the representation itself, but also of the way in which the representation is developed (Markoczy & Goldberg, 1995). The method for developing any representation, therefore, is critical. With the advent of interest in exploring strategy as perspective, several research methods have been used recently to explore and measure aspects of strategic thought.

One method is the repertory grid technique (Fransella & Bannister, 1977; Kelly, 1955; Reger, 1990; Reger & Huff, 1993). Because interviews with managers reveal inconsistently used strategic dimensions, the method does not lend itself to aggregation to a collective level across managers within the same organization (Dunn, Cahill, Dukes, & Ginsberg, 1986) without unjustifiable assumptions made by the researcher. "Clearly the non-presence of a [dimension] in the causal map cannot be taken to mean that the subject believes the construct to be irrelevant, it only means that it is not [there]" (Markoczy & Goldberg, 1995, p. 311). The researcher must then either arbitrarily assign some value to the dimension for that manager in order to make comparisons with other managers who do identify it, treat it as a missing piece of data that results in loss of information and lowers statistical power, or refrain from using the manager at all in team compilations and cross-firm comparisons. Any decision the researcher makes among these alternatives will affect the resulting variable measurements and the final representation of thought used for analysis. The time-consuming nature of the interview technique makes this method difficult to administer to a broad set of managers across many organizations.

Cognitive mapping (Barr, Stimpert, & Huff, 1992; Eden, 1992; Huff, 1990) aims to identify the cause–effect beliefs of individual managers. The method often relies on linguistic analysis of archival documents, such as letters to shareholders in annual reports. Whether these are *post hoc* explanations of corporate strategic actions, impression management (Salancik & Meindl, 1984), or truly underlying managers' cause–effect beliefs is unclear. The method also generally relies on one map as a representation of the entire organization. Integrating multiple cognitive maps into a collective organizational map would be difficult because of inconsistent dimensions surfaced and the overall complexity of individual maps.

Markoczy and Goldberg (1995) suggest a causal mapping method which is sort of a hybrid and an extension of repertory grid and cognitive mapping. In order to make interviews manageable, respondents must select a limited number of strategic dimensions they believe to be important. Inconsistencies among managers also make comparisons and aggregations problematic, for which there is no readily available solution without assumptions by the researcher regarding values to assign to such inconsistencies (Markoczy & Goldberg, 1995). The recommendation to limit managers to 10 elements may result in the exclusion of elements that some managers believe are still important. This method also requires lengthy interviews with managers, who must sort through many elements and then make 90 comparisons between selected elements.

Policy capturing (Hobson & Gibson, 1983; Ireland, Hitt, Bettis, & De Porras, 1987) seeks to identify managers' theories-in-use by using their individual judgments on hypothesized case scenarios to create decision models. Aggregate predictive models may be developed by entering all of the individual judgments into one overall regression model. However, as noted earlier, combining all managers' individual judgments into one regression model is not representative of how a team actually makes important strategic decisions. In fact, regression models adopting this approach explain less variance than do individual models (Hitt, Ireland, Keats, & Vianna, 1983). In any case, the dependent variable in such models is the individual's overall assessment, not a group's decision or a firm's actions. The use of cases created by the researcher is a step removed from the real situations confronting top managers in their firms, and the use of direct item ratings by managers is also a step removed from the underlying cognitive structure that manifests itself in those ratings (Schneider & Angelmar, 1993).

Metric conjoint analysis (Louviere, 1988; Priem, 1992) also captures decision policies used by individual managers through a rating task. The conjoint task method involves "trade-offs concerning the number and levels of variables used versus the willingness of the subjects to participate and the sustained interest of the subjects in the task" (Priem, 1992, p. 146). Consequently, the nature of the conjoint method seems to require the researcher to *ex ante* identify "parsimonious, conceptually rich typologies" in lieu of allowing respondents to utilize their own underlying constructs. Aggregations of individual responses (e.g., Shepherd & Zacharakis, 1997) using regression models are still only predictive of individual judgments.

In summation, there are several issues that present themselves to researchers interested in measuring collective cognition in entrepreneurial top management teams. These include (1) the need to collect consistent data across managers within the same organization such that it can be coalesced in some fashion and evaluated at a collective level, thus facilitating comparisons between organizations; (2) the need to allow managers' own responses to both generate and indicate the importance of constructs each uses in considering firm strategy and related issues, avoiding researcher interpretation of the relevance of any given dimension; (3) the desire to capture current strategic thinking, versus *ex ante* projections or *ex post* explanations; and (4) the ability to easily collect data from multiple managers in a broad set of companies. The combination of these objectives is designed to enhance both reliability and validity in research encompassing collective cognition.

Sociocognitive Grid Analysis

In order to meet the objectives of research wherein strategic perspective is a key variable, a sociocognitive grid approach builds upon and extends previous work in policy grid analysis. The policy grid evolved out of attempts in the public policy sciences to understand the underlying structure and content of systems of interpretation (Heclo, 1976). The approach is used to identify and measure the dimensions of frames of reference used by policy makers to interpret the meaning of events in a particular context and through which such "meanings are attached to policy choices" (Dunn et al., 1986, p. 355). Thus, the goal of policy grid is to understand aspects of perspective on issues or situations facing an organization that may necessitate actions or changes.

Sociocognitive grid involves both method and analysis. The goal of the data collection method is to create a matrix for subsequent analysis that captures dimensions considered relevant by individuals and the team to which the individuals belong. Seeking to overcome one limitation of the repertory grid (that of inconsistently identified dimensions), an enhancement is the inference of a collective frame of reference of an organization. Dunn and Ginsberg (1986) assume that managers are familiar with a set of dimensions related to their particular firm and industry, and then have each manager evaluate the importance of each dimension. Thus, the sociocognitive grid seeks to use a "frame of reference that incorporates the constructs of others within its range of convenience" (Dunn et al., 1986, p. 358). Figure 4 illustrates the result of such an approach, a sociocognitive grid that combines top managers and salient strategy constructs. What is captured in such a grid is a rating by each top manager of each important underlying strategic construct. Having made such an inference, the grid may be analyzed using measures that capture important properties of structure (see Figure 4).

Determination of the appropriate strategic constructs to use is a critical task. One limitation of other methods previously discussed, and of the original policy grid approach as outlined, is that the researcher cannot ensure that the selected dimensions reflect the full range of all managers' underlying construct systems for thinking about

Figure 4

Example of Sociocognitive Grid

Strategic Construct	Construct A	Construct B	Construct C	Construct D	Construct E	Construct F
Manager 1	-0.2	2.1	0.4	0.0	-0.9	0.7
Manager 2	0.1	0.4	0.0	0.4	0.2	0.5
Manager 3	-1.8	0.0	-1.7	-1.1	-1.3	-0.9
Manager 4	-0.7	-0.6	0.4	-0.3	-1.1	0.4
Manager 5	-0.2	-1.9	0.5	2.9	-0.4	2.7
Manager 6	-0.4	1.1	-0.5	0.9	0.7	1.1

strategy and strategic issues. The issue for researchers is to describe individual data in a format that is consistent across all individuals, while still allowing for the variation between individuals in construct use and importance to be represented within that format.

Two theoretical approaches may be used to identify underlying construct systems: decomposition or composition methods (Arkes & Hammond, 1986). Decomposition methods, on the one hand, begin with a limited set of dimensions and observe respondents' use of those dimensions to identify systematic decision rules or approaches they use in confronting issues. Methods that rely on the use of an *a priori* limited set of dimensions assumed to be the relevant set for all managers fall into this category, such as conjoint analysis, causal mapping, and policy grid analysis as described earlier. These methods may identify decision rules, but such rules may not be fully reflective of the complexity of strategic thinking because they may exclude constructs believed to be important by some respondents. Composition methods, on the other hand, identify important constructs used by respondents built up out of a broader base of related item measures. A sample of managers might be asked to evaluate a comprehensive list of strategy-related items such as strategic goals and means (Bourgeois, 1980; West & Meyer, 1998), with a subsequent factor analysis performed in order to uncover the key strategic dimensions which best explain the observed variance. Such an approach questions managers on cause–effect elements and reveals underlying patterns connecting and explaining their responses. Rather than selecting a limited set of conceptually rich typologies to expose to managers, it is more reflective of reality to let managers speak for themselves. Factor analysis has been used in such a way to better identify underlying strategy-related belief structures of individuals (Bowman & Ambrosini, 1997; Houghton, Zeithaml, & Bateman, 1994; Miller et al., 1998). Factor scores may then be used as seeds into a sociocognitive grid. Positive scores for key constructs suggest that they are regarded as more important, while negative scores for key constructs imply that they are regarded as less important (Hair, Anderson, Tatham, & Black, 1990). Thus, a complete set of strategic constructs explaining variance across all managers is captured, as are individual managers' ratings of each construct whether important or unimportant.

Field Study Illustration

Sample

The present study utilizes a sample of new ventures in three technology-based SIC codes (computers, microelectronics, and software). These industries were selected because the presumed rapid pace of change would result in the inclusion of companies in various stages of development and encountering strategic issues frequently. Longitudinal data were collected from CEOs and top managers in new ventures in one geographic area with a developed technology-based entrepreneurial community. CEOs in each of these firms were contacted personally by mail and were asked if they wished to participate in a research study on strategy. Interested CEOs designated the names of top managers in their companies who participate in strategy discussions and decisions. Surveys were sent to the CEOs and top managers at the inception of the study, and then again 2 years later. After 2 years, 22 sets of surveys from intact top management teams were available for analysis. At the beginning of the study, the median age of the responding firms was 3.3 years. The average firm size in the final year of the study was approximately $40 million revenue with 165 employees; an average of 4.9 top managers per firm participated in this study.

Strategy Constructs and Ratings

The structure of top management strategic thinking is inductively identified using quantitative factor analysis of managers' ratings of a series of strategic goals and means gathered during both years. In each survey, the importance of strategic goals and competitive means was measured by two separate questions. Respondents were presented with a list of 20 possible strategic goals and 21 possible means. The list contains items originally used by Bourgeois (1980), and was supplemented with items based on a review of recent work on strategic goals and means that has sought to understand dimensions of strategic cause-and-effect used by top managers. For each item, respondents were asked to rate its importance on a "scale of importance" ranging from 0 to 100, where 100 represented "critically important" and 0 represented "not at all important."

Factor analysis was performed on the goals and means ratings data collected in both years. The same six key factors were identified from the factor analysis in each year; these were named after reviewing and interpreting rotated factor matrices. They include: (1) new products/growth, (2) innovative/differentiation, (3) low cost/competitive price, (4) customer relationship, (5) marketing/image, and (6) human resources. Factor scores for the key strategic constructs were calculated for every respondent. Sociocognitive grids for each company were created using the factors as strategy constructs and the factor scores as managers' construct ratings.

Differentiation and Integration

An index of differentiation is a modified version of the measure suggested by Ginsberg (1989), and is given by the expression:

$$1 - \frac{\sum\limits_{1}^{n} \sum\limits_{j=1}^{m-1} \sum\limits_{k=j+1}^{m} r_{jk}^2}{m^2}$$

where r_{jk}^2 is the coefficient of determination for a manager on the jth pairs of strategic constructs; m is the number of strategic constructs; n is the number of managers. The higher this index as indicated by weak or zero correlations among all pairs of strategic constructs, the higher the level of differentiation among strategic constructs; the lower the index, the more the strategic constructs are not distinguishable from each other. The mean for all companies in this study is .622 within the 0–1 scale range, suggesting a moderate level of differentiation.

An index of integration is a slight modification to Ginsberg (1989) and is given by the expression:

$$\frac{\sum\limits_{1}^{m} \sum\limits_{x=1}^{n-1} \sum\limits_{y=x+1}^{n} r_{xy}^2}{n^2}$$

where r_{xy}^2 is the coefficient of determination for a strategic factor on the xth pairs of managers; m is the number of strategic constructs; n is the number of managers. The lower this index as indicated by weak or zero correlations among all pairs of top managers, the less the management team views the entire set of strategic constructs similarly. The higher this index, the more the management team holds a shared view of the strategic constructs.

The mean for all companies in this study is .232 within the 0–1 scale range, suggesting a low level of integration occurring.

The earlier discussion regarding differentiation and integration proposes that they may bear an inverted U-shaped relationship to new venture performance. Differentiation and integration are therefore both operationalized as deviations from the mean indices of differentiation and integration across all companies in this sample. It is reasonable to expect that performance changes observed over the 2-year study period are related to the structure of collective cognition discovered at the beginning of the study. Therefore, the differentiation and integration variables are derived from the first year of the study.

New Venture Performance

Most participating companies were privately held; hence, detailed objective measures of financial performance are not available. Therefore, firm performance is derived from an average rating of perceived performance by managers in each company. A composite 3-item scale serves as the basis for the perceived performance measure. One item, based on Dess and Robinson (1984), asked for an assessment of the percent of ideal performance being achieved, where ideal performance equated to 100%. Two other items build on the tradition of strategy as competitive advantage leading to enhanced performance (Porter, 1980). These items, assessing growth relative to competitors and overall performance relative to competitors on 7-point agreement scales, were then interpolated into a 0–100 range equivalent. This method is similar to that used by Lumpkin and Dess (1995). The composite measure in the first-year study has a Cronbach alpha coefficient of .87; the composite measure in the second-year study has a Cronbach alpha coefficient of .78. The performance variable is operationalized as relative performance changes between the first and final years, using the composite scale measures. The mean level of relative performance change across the two years is +1.1% with a range of −37.2 to +35.6%.

Control Variable

Performance goals and levels may vary depending upon the stage of its life cycle that a new venture is in (Quinn & Cameron, 1983). Life cycle stage was measured by an average rating of responding managers in each company from the first survey, using Kazanjian's (1988) descriptions of five stages that firms experience. This scale is particularly appropriate for this sample of firms because it was developed using technology-based companies. The mean for all companies responding in the second-year survey was 3.1, which essentially represents the "growth" stage of Kazanjian's model.

Results

Hypothesis 1a predicted that new venture performance would be positively associated with differentiation and integration within top management teams. Table 1 presents three models regressing performance on these measures, while controlling for company life cycle stage. In model 1, differentiation of strategy constructs among top managers is significantly related to new venture performance ($p < .05$), and the overall regression model is significant ($F = 3.85$, $p < .05$). In model 2, integration of perspective among top managers is also significantly related to new venture performance ($p < .10$), and the overall regression model is also significant ($F = 3.24$, $p < .10$).

Table 1

Regression of Performance on
Differentiation and Integration

	Model 1	Model 2	Model 3
Control variable			
Life cycle stage	−.315	−.377	−.253
	(−1.567)	(−1.809)*	(−1.263)
Independent variables			
Differentiation	−.459		
	(−2.281)**		
Integration		−.423	
		(−2.029)*	
Differentiation × integration			−.482
			(−2.403)**
Adjusted R^2	.231	.191	.250
F (2, 18)	3.846**	3.243*	4.163**

*$p < .10.$ ** $p < .05.$
Note: t-values in parentheses.

Hypothesis 1b predicted that either low levels or high levels of differentiation and integration will be negatively associated with firm performance. In each of the models presented in Table 1, the relationship between performance and the independent variable differentiation and integration is significant but negative. Recall that the differentiation and integration variables were operationalized as deviations from medium levels of differentiation and integration indices observed across the entire sample of companies. The results indicate that deviations from average levels of differentiation and integration are, in fact, associated with poorer performance, while improved performance is associated with midrange levels of differentiation, integration, and their interaction. The combination of these results provides strong support for Hypothesis 1b.

Hypothesis 2 predicted that the interaction of differentiation and integration will be associated with new venture performance. In model 3, the interaction of differentiation and integration is significant ($p < .05$), and the overall model is also significant ($F = 4.16$, $p < .05$). Since the interaction variable is also operationalized using deviations from the sample's mean levels of differentiation and integration, the results also demonstrate that moderate levels of the interacting individual variables are associated with improved performance while deviations from moderate levels are associated with performance declines.

Discussion and Implications

This article has developed the argument that ETCC represents a critical, but poorly understood, link between individual cognitions and team decisions leading to new venture survival and growth. We have focused here on strategy as an example of a collective cognitive domain because it represents the cause–effect understanding or knowledge about how the new venture can or should operate in its competitive environment. ETCC about strategy exhibits content properties and structural characteristics. Two structural characteristics—differentiation and integration—are particularly important in new ventures. This is because these characteristics describe the extent to which entrepreneurial top management teams consider new strategic alternatives in an environment where strategic demands are continually shifting, and the extent to which these teams share a unified view of the relative importance of available strategy choices.

An exploratory field study identifies these characteristics in a sample of technology-based new venture top management teams. The study finds that performance improvements are significantly associated with both differentiation and integration. Moreover, the significance found between performance and these measures provides strong support for the argument that an inverted U-shaped relationship exists. Among team members, too much integration (highly consistent views) or too much differentiation (constantly identifying different options and alternatives) adversely affects new venture performance; performance improvement is enhanced where new ventures deviate much less from midrange levels of each of these variables. That more complex new ventures—those where top management teams both differentiate and integrate at midrange levels—achieve higher levels of performance is also indicated by the significance of the regression containing the interaction term between differentiation and integration. Previous research has stressed the theoretical importance of the combination of differentiation and integration as elements of sociocognitive complexity in organizations (Driver & Streufert, 1969; Streufert & Swezey, 1986). The present study provides empirical support. The sample size of respondent new venture across 2 years is reasonably small in this exploratory study ($n = 22$), resulting in a loss of statistical power. Thus the significant results observed are quite likely very strong, practically.

The examination of ETCC holds exciting possibilities for future entrepreneurship research. ETCC can be used as a dependent variable in studies of new ventures. As suggested by Figure 1, ETCC mediates between new venture performance and several other variables of interest to entrepreneurship researchers. Cognition research in entrepreneurship, some of which is referenced earlier, tends to focus on the individual level of analysis. And yet, it remains unclear how individual level cognitions become, or at least impact, organizational level activities and performance. In fact, the varying levels of analysis in entrepreneurship research and theory development remains a significant challenge (Davidsson & Wiklund, 2001; West, 2003). The concept of ETCC presents an opportunity to better understand how the two levels are related.

The apparent interaction between differentiation and integration is one of the more interesting results of this study, and bears further examination. Given a level of integration capability within a team, what are the boundaries of effective differentiation effort or capability, above which and below which the team's effort and decision making becomes suboptimal? A goal for future research would be to identify the ranges of effective levels of each structural component of team cognition. It is possible that such ranges vary by industry and competitive context, reflecting variance in the dynamism and flows of information that new ventures may face.

New venture strategy can be viewed as a function of the composition of the top management team, and changes in new venture strategy may also result from changes in the team composition. Significant attention has always been paid to the role of the new venture's founder or CEO in determining overall direction or changes in direction (e.g., Brush et al., 2001; Johnson & Bishop, 2002; Meyer & Dean, 1990; Willard, Krueger, & Feeser, 1992). The approach outlined here implies that other individuals' perspectives also factor into what the venture does as an organization. Moreover, new individuals may inject new content into strategic discussions and may view existing content differently from others in the team, resulting in changing collective cognition of the team itself. New top management team members may also forestall change. While CEOs in technology firms often value new colleagues with whom they have previously worked or who have significant within-industry experience (Eisenhardt & Schoonhoven, 1990), such new entrants to the top management team may serve to homogenize points of view rather than challenge conventional thinking. In dynamically changing environments where new ideas about strategy are important, this may diminish new venture performance (Ensley et al., 2002).

The sociocognitive grid, as a methodology to assess ETCC, may also be used to assess the efficacy of process within top management teams. Modifications in the organization of the team and in communication methods used by the team may enhance or diminish content of the grid and precipitate changes in the structure of the collective grid. Differentiation measures collected over time, for example, could be used as a metric to assess whether or not new venture top management teams are increasing the flow of new ideas and potential opportunities into strategic consideration. Integration measures collected over time could provide insight on the time it takes for teams to coalesce around new options previously proposed. To the extent that top management is aware of the trends within their own teams, they may wish to take actions to make adjustments in the desired direction (such as structuring new subcommittees to generate options or scheduling special meetings to focus on new ideas and future opportunities).

Focusing on collective cognition could also enhance the team's understanding of its position in the competitive environment. If an index of differentiation is significantly below an industry average, for example, it may suggest that the new venture should enhance its external scanning activity and develop internal communication processes which promote the expression of alternatives and new opportunities. If an index of integration is significantly lower than the industry average, it might suggest that top management concentrate increasingly on its collective understanding of its fundamental value proposition or organizational identity (Dutton & Dukerich, 1991). Industry metrics may be difficult for individual firms to develop, so the extension of this method and the development and validation of indices across industries might be fertile ground for future entrepreneurship research.

These latter ideas suggest that ETCC may also serve as an independent variable, in ways that are valuable other than as a variable leading to new venture performance. Here, we are suggesting an iterative relationship between ETCC as dependent variable and the kinds of variables that contribute to ETCC. While individual cognitions contribute to collective cognition, collective cognition can also serve as a stimulus to change in individual cognitions (Schneider & Angelmar, 1993). ETCC may thus serve as a stimulus to change in top management team process, as the recursive nature of this relationship is similar to that explored in learning models in entrepreneurial firms (Dess et al., 2003; Lant & Mezias, 1990; Lichtenstein, Lumpkin, & Shrader, 2003; Lumpkin & Lichtenstein, 2005). Further research focused on this relationship will help explicate how the individual and organization levels of analysis may be related.

REFERENCES

Alvarez, S.A. & Busenitz, L.W. (2001). The entrepreneurship of resource-based theory. *Journal of Management, 27*(6), 755–775.

Arkes, H.R. & Hammond, K.R. (Eds.) (1986). *Judgment and decision making: An interdisciplinary reader.* Cambridge, U.K.: Cambridge University Press.

Baron, R.A. (1998). Cognitive mechanisms in entrepreneurship: Why and when entrepreneurs think differently than other people. *Journal of Business Venturing, 13*(4), 275–294.

Barr, P.S., Stimpert, J.L., & Huff, A.S. (1992). Cognitive change, strategic action, and organization renewal. *Strategic Management Journal, 13*(Special), 15–36.

Bartunek, J.M., Gordon, J.R., & Weathersby, R.P. (1983). Developing "complicated" understanding in administrators. *Academy of Management Review, 8*(2), 273–284.

Bhide, A.V., Rayzman, V., & Hackett, C.J. (1999). *DAG group*. Cambridge, MA: Harvard Business School Publishing.

Boeker, W. (1989). Strategic change: The effects of founding and history. *Academy of Management Journal, 32*(3), 489–515.

Bougon, M.G. (1992). Congregate cognitive maps: A unified dynamic theory of organization and strategy. *Journal of Management Studies, 29*(3), 369–389.

Bourgeois, L.J., III. (1980). Performance and consensus. *Strategic Management Journal, 1*, 227–248.

Bowman, C. & Ambrosini, V. (1997). Perceptions of strategic priorities, consensus and firm performance. *Journal of Management Studies, 34*(2), 241–258.

Brush, C.G., Greene, P.G., & Hart, M.M. (2001). From initial idea to unique advantage: The entrepreneurial challenge of constructing a resource base. *Academy of Management Executive, 15*(1), 64–78.

Busenitz, L.W. & Barney, J.B. (1997). Differences between entrepreneurs and managers in large organizations: Biases and heuristics in strategic decision-making. *Journal of Business Venturing, 12*(1), 9–30.

Busenitz, L.W. & Lau, C.-M. (1996). A cross-cultural cognitive model of new venture creation. *Entrepreneurship Theory and Practice, 20*(4), 25–39.

Busenitz, L., West, G.P., III, Shepherd, D.A., Nelson, T., Chandler, G.N., & Zacharakis, A.L. (2003). Entrepreneurship research in emergence: Fifteen years of entrepreneurship research in management journals. *Journal of Management, 29*(3), 285–308.

Chakravarthy, B.S. (1982). Adaptation: A promising metaphor for strategic management. *Academy of Management Review, 7*(1), 35–44.

Clarysse, B. & Moray, N. (2004). A process study of entrepreneurial team formation: The case of a research-based spinoff. *Journal of Business Venturing, 19*(1), 55–76.

Colombo, M.G. & Grilli, L. (2005). Founders' human capital and the growth of new technology-based firms: A competence-based view. *Research Policy, 34*(6), 795–818.

Cossette, P. & Audet, M. (1992). Mapping of idiosyncratic schema. *Journal of Management Studies, 29*(3), 325–347.

Covin, J.G. & Slevin, D.P. (1991). A conceptual model of entrepreneurship as firm behavior. *Entrepreneurship Theory and Practice, 16*(1), 7–25.

Cyr, L., Johnson, D.E., & Welbourne, T.M. (2000). Human resources in initial public offering firms: Do venture capitalists make a difference? *Entrepreneurship Theory and Practice, 25*(1), 77–91.

Daft, R.L. & Lengel, R.H. (1984). Information richness: A new approach to managerial behavior and organization design. In B.M. Staw & L.L. Cummings (Eds.), *Research in organizational behavior* (Vol. 6, pp. 191–233). Greenwich, CT: JAI Press.

Daft, R.L. & Weick, K.E. (1984). Toward a model of organizations as interpretation systems. *Academy of Management Review, 9*, 284–295.

Davidsson, P. & Wiklund, J. (2001). Levels of analysis in entrepreneurship research: Current research practice and suggestions for the future. *Entrepreneurship Theory and Practice, 25*(4), 81–100.

Dean, T.J., Meyer, G.D., & DeCastro, J. (1993). Determinants of new-firm formations in manufacturing industries: Industry dynamics, entry barriers, and organizational inertia. *Entrepreneurship Theory and Practice, 18*, 49–60.

Dess, G.G., Ireland, R.D., Zahra, S.A., Floyd, S.W., Janney, J.J., & Lane, P.J. (2003). Emerging issues in corporate entrepreneurship. *Journal of Management, 29*(3), 351.

Dess, G.G. & Robinson, R.B. (1984). Measuring organizational performance in the absence of objective measures: The case of the privately-held firm and conglomerate business unit. *Strategic Management Journal, 5*(3), 263–273.

Driver, M.J. & Streufert, S. (1969). Integrative complexity: An approach to individuals and groups as information-processing systems. *Administrative Science Quarterly, 14*, 272–285.

Dunn, W.N., Cahill, A.G., Dukes, M.J., & Ginsberg, A. (1986). The policy grid: A cognitive methodology for assessing policy dynamics. In W.N. Dunn (Ed.), *Policy analysis: Perspectives, concepts, and methods,* (pp. 355–375). Greenwich, CT: JAI Press.

Dunn, W.N. & Ginsberg, A. (1986). A sociocognitive network approach to organizational analysis. *Human Relations, 40*(11), 955–976.

Dutton, J.E. & Dukerich, J.M. (1991). Keeping an eye on the mirror: Image and identity in organizational adaptation. *Academy of Management Journal, 34*(3), 517–554.

Dutton, J.E. & Jackson, S.E. (1987). Categorizing strategic issues: Links to organizational action. *Academy of Management Review, 12*, 76–90.

Eden, C. (1992). On the nature of cognitive maps. *Journal of Management Studies, 29*(3), 261–265.

Eden, C., Jones, S., Sims, D., & Simthin, T. (1981). The intersubjectivity of issues and issues of intersubjectivity. *Journal of Management Studies, 18*, 37–47.

Eisenhardt, K.M. & Schoonhoven, C.B. (1990). Organizational growth: Linking founding team, strategy, environment, and growth among US semiconductor ventures, 1978–1988. *Administrative Science Quarterly, 35*(3), 504–529.

Ensley, M.D. & Pearce, C.L. (2001). Shared cognition in top management teams: Implications for new venture performance. *Journal of Organizational Behavior, 22*, 145–160.

Ensley, M.D., Pearson, A.W., & Amason, A.C. (2002). Understanding the dynamics of new venture top management teams: Cohesion, conflict, and new venture performance. *Journal of Business Venturing, 17*(4), 365–386.

Feeser, H.R. & Willard, G.E. (1990). Founding strategy and performance: A comparison of high and low growth high tech firms. *Strategic Management Journal, 11*, 87–98.

Ferguson, C.H. (1999). *High st@kes, no prisoners: A winner's tale of greed and glory in the internet wars.* New York: Three Rivers Press.

Fiske, S.T. & Taylor, S.E. (1991). *Social cognition.* New York: McGraw-Hill.

Fransella, F. & Bannister, D. (1977). *A manual for repertory grid technique.* New York: Academic Press.

Gaglio, C.M. (2004). The role of mental simulations and counterfactual thinking in the opportunity identification process. *Entrepreneurship Theory and Practice*, *28*(6), 533–552.

Gaglio, C.M. & Katz, J.A. (2001). The psychological basis of opportunity identification: Entrepreneurial alertness. *Small Business Economics*, *16*, 95–111.

Gartner, W.B. (1985). A conceptual framework for describing the phenomenon of new venture creation. *Academy of Management Review*, *10*(4), 696–706.

Gartner, W.B., Carter, N.M., & Hills, G.E. (2003). The language of opportunity. In C. Steyaert & D. Hjorth (Eds.), *New movements in entrepreneurship* (pp. 103–124). Northampton, MA: Edward Elgar.

Gatewood, E., Shaver, K.G., & Gartner, W.B. (1995). A longitudinal study of cognitive factors influencing start-up behaviors and success at venture creation. *Journal of Business Venturing*, *10*(5), 371–391.

Gartner, W.B., Shaver. K.G., Gatewood, E., & Katz, J.A. (1994). Finding the entrepreneur in entrepreneurship. *Entrepreneurship Theory and Practice*, *18*(3), 5–9.

Gersick, C.G. (1991). Revolutionary change theories: A multilevel exploration of the punctuated equilibrium paradigm. *Academy of Management Review*, *16*(3), 10–36.

Ginsberg, A. (1988). Measuring and modeling changes in strategy: Theoretical foundations and empirical directions. *Strategic Management Journal*, *9*, 559–575.

Ginsberg, A. (1989). Construing the business portfolio: A cognitive model of diversification. *Journal of Management Studies*, *26*(4), 417–438.

Ginsberg, A. (1990). Connecting diversification to performance: A sociocognitive approach. *Academy of Management Review*, *15*, 514–535.

Grandi, A. & Grimaldi, R. (2003). Exploring the networking characteristics of new venture founding teams. *Small Business Economics*, *21*(4), 329–347.

Hair, J.F., Jr., Anderson. R.E., Tatham, R.L., & Black, W.C. (1990). *Multivariate data analysis*. New York: Macmillan.

Hambrick, D.C., Finkelstein, S., & Mooney, A.C. (2005). Executives sometimes lose it, just like the rest of us. *Academy of Management Review*, *30*(3), 503–508.

Hambrick, D.C. & Mason, P.A. (1984). Upper echelons: The organization as a reflection of its top managers. *Academy of Management Review*, *9*, 193–206.

Hayek, F.A. (1945). The use of knowledge in society. *American Economic Review*, *35*(4), 519–530.

Hayton, J.C. & Zahra, S.A. (2005). Venture team human capital and absorptive capacity in high technology new ventures. *International Journal of Technology Management*, *31*(3), 256–277.

Heclo, H. (1976). Policy dynamics. In R. Rose (Ed.), *The dynamics of public policy: A comparative analysis* (pp. 236–266). Beverly Hills, CA: Sage.

Hitt, M.A., Ireland. R.D., Keats, B.W., & Vianna, A. (1983). Measuring subunit effectiveness. *Decision Sciences*, *14*(1), 87–102.

Hobson, C.J. & Gibson, F.W. (1983). Policy capturing as an approach to understanding and improving performance appraisal: A review of the literature. *Academy of Management Review*, *8*(4), 640–649.

Houghton, S., Zeithaml, C.P., & Bateman, T.S. (1994). Cognition and strategic issues in top management teams. In D.P. Moore (Ed.), *Academy of Management best papers proceedings*, (pp. 372–376). Dallas, TX: Academy of Management.

Huff, A.S. (Ed.) (1990). *Mapping strategic thought.* New York: John Wiley & Sons.

Hurst, D.K., Rush, J.C., & White, R.E. (1989). Top management teams and organizational renewal. *Strategic Management Journal, 10*(Special), 87–105.

Ireland, R.D., Hitt, M.A., Bettis, R.A., & De Porras, D.A. (1987). Strategy formulation processes: Differences in perceptions of strength and weaknesses indicators and environmental uncertainty by managerial level. *Strategic Management Journal, 8,* 469–485.

Jelinek, M. & Schoonhoven, C.B. (1990). *The innovation marathon.* Cambridge, MA: Basil Blackwell.

Johnson, D.E. & Bishop, K. (2002). Performance in fast-growth firms: The behavior and role demands of the founder throughout the firm's development. In J.A. Katz & T.M. Welbourne (Eds.), *Advances in entrepreneurship, firm emergence and growth* (Vol. 5, pp. 1–22). New York: Elsevier.

Kazanjian, R.K. (1988). Relation of dominant problems to stages of growth in technology-based new ventures. *Academy of Management Journal, 31*(2), 257–279.

Kelly, G.A. (1955). *A theory of personality: The psychology of personal constructs.* New York: Norton.

Lant, T.K. & Mezias, S.J. (1990). Managing discontinuous change: A simulation study of organizational learning and entrepreneurship. *Strategic Management Journal, 11,* 147–179.

Lichtenstein, B.M.B., Lumpkin, G.T., & Shrader, R.C. (2003). Organizational learning by new ventures: Concepts, strategies, and applications. In J.A. Katz & D.A. Shepherd (Eds.), *Advances in entrepreneurship, firm emergence and growth* (Vol. 6, pp. 11–36). New York: Elsevier.

Louviere, J.J. (1988). *Analyzing decision making: Metric conjoint analysis.* Newbury Park, CA: Sage.

Lumpkin, G.T. & Dess, G.G. (1995). Simplicity as a strategy-making process: The effects of stage of organizational development and environment on performance. *Academy of Management Journal, 38*(5), 1386–1407.

Lumpkin, G.T. & Dess, G.G. (1996). Clarifying the entrepreneurial orientation construct and linking it to performance. *Academy of Management Review, 21*(1), 135–172.

Lumpkin, G.T. & Lichtenstein, B.M.B. (2005). The role of organizational learning in the opportunity recognition process. *Entrepreneurship Theory and Practice, 29*(4), 451–472.

Markman, G.D. & Baron, R.A. (2002). Individual differences and the pursuit of new ventures: A model of person-entrepreneurship fit. In J.A. Katz & T.M. Welbourne (Eds.), *Advances in entrepreneurship, firm emergence and growth* (Vol. 5, pp. 23–54). New York: Elsevier.

Markoczy, L. & Goldberg, J. (1995). A method for eliciting and comparing causal maps. *Journal of Management, 21*(2), 305–333.

McDougall, P.P. & Robinson, R.B., Jr. (1990). New venture strategies: An empirical identification of eight "archetypes" of competitive strategies for entry. *Strategic Management Journal, 11*(6), 447–467.

McDougall, P.P., Robsinson, R.B., & DeNisi, A.S. (1992). Modeling new venture performance: An analysis of new venture strategy, industry structure, and venture origin. *Journal of Business Venturing, 7*(4), 267–289.

McMullen, J.S. & Shepherd, D.A. (2003). Extending the theory of the entrepreneur using a signal detection framework. In J.A. Katz & D.A. Shepherd (Eds.), *Advances in entrepreneurship, firm emergence and growth* (Vol. 6, pp. 139–180). New York: Elsevier.

Meyer, G.D. & Dean, T.J. (1990). An upper echelons perspective on transformational leadership problems in high technology firms. *Journal of High Technology Management, 1,* 223–242.

Miller, C.C., Burke, L.M., & Glick, W.H. (1998). Cognitive diversity among upper-echelon executives: Implications for strategic decision processes. *Strategic Management Journal, 19*(1), 39–58.

Mintzberg, H. (1987). The strategy concept I: Five p's for strategy. *California Management Review, 30*(1), 11–24.

Mohammed, S., Klimoski, R., & Rentsch, J.R. (2000). The measurement of team mental models: We have no shared schema. *Organizational Research Methods, 3*(2), 123–165.

Mohammed, S. & Ringseis, E. (2001). Cognitive diversity and consensus in group decision making: The role of inputs, processes, and outcomes. *Organizational Behavior and Human Decision Processes, 85*(2), 310–335.

Moore, G.A. (1995). *Inside the tornado: Marketing strategies from Silicon Valley's cutting edge.* New York: HarperCollins.

Neergaard, H. (2005). Networking activities in technology-based entrepreneurial teams. *International Small Business Journal, 23*(3), 257–274.

Porter, M.E. (1980). *Competitive strategy.* New York: Free Press.

Porter, M.E. (1985). *Competitive advantage.* New York: Free Press.

Prahalad, C.K. & Bettis, R.A. (1986). The dominant logic: A new linkage between diversity and performance. *Strategic Management Journal, 7*, 485–501.

Priem, R.L. (1992). An application of metric conjoint analysis for the evaluation of top managers' individual strategic decision making processes. *Strategic Management Journal, 13*(Special), 143–151.

Quinn, R.E. & Cameron, K. (1983). Organizational life cycles and shifting criteria of effectiveness: Some preliminary evidence. *Management Science, 29*, 33–51.

Reger, R.K. (1990). The repertory grid technique for eliciting the content and structure of cognitive construction systems. In A.S. Huff (Ed.), *Mapping strategic thought* (pp. 301–310). New York: John Wiley and Sons.

Reger, R.K. & Huff, A.S. (1993). Strategic groups: A cognitive perspective. *Strategic Management Journal, 14*(2), 103–124.

Ruef, M., Aldrich, H.E., & Carter, N.M. (2003). The structure of founding teams: Homophily, strong ties, and isolation among U.S. entrepreneurs. *American Sociological Review, 68*(2), 195–222.

Salancik, G.R. & Meindl, J.R. (1984). Corporate attributions as strategic illusions of management control. *Administrative Science Quarterly, 29*, 238–254.

Sandberg, W.R. & Hofer, C.W. (1987). Improving new venture performance: The role of strategy, industry, structure, and the entrepreneur. *Journal of Business Venturing, 2*, 5–28.

Schneider, S.C. & Angelmar, R. (1993). Cognition in organizational analysis: Who's minding the store? *Organization Studies, 14*(3), 347–374.

Shane, S. (2000). Prior knowledge and the discovery of entrepreneurial opportunities. *Organization Science, 11*(4), 448–469.

Shane, S. & Venkataraman, S. (2000). The promise of entrepreneurship as a field of research. *Academy of Management Review, 25*(1), 217–226.

Shaver, K.G. & Scott, L. (1991). Person, process, choice: The psychology of new venture creation. *Entrepreneurship Theory and Practice, 16*(2), 23–45.

Shepherd, D. & Shanley, M.T. (1999). *New venture strategy: Timing, environmental uncertainty, and performance.* Newbury Park, CA: Sage.

Shepherd, D.A. & Krueger, N.F. (2002). An intentions-based model of entrepreneurial teams' social cognition. *Entrepreneurship Theory and Practice, 27*(2), 167–185.

Shepherd, D.A. & Zacharakis, A. (1997). Conjoint analysis: A window of opportunity for entrepreneurship research. In J.A. Katz (Ed.), *Advances in entrepreneurship, firm emergence and growth* (Vol. 3, pp. 203–248). Greenwich, CT: JAI Press.

Simon, M. & Houghton, S.M. (2002). The relationship among biases, misperceptions and introducing pioneering new products: Examining differences in venture decision contexts. *Entrepreneurship Theory and Practice, 27*(2), 105–124.

Slevin, D.P. & Covin, J.G. (1995). Entrepreneurship as firm behavior: A research model. In J.A. Katz & R.H. Brockhaus, Sr., (Eds.), *Advances in entrepreneurship, firm emergence and growth* (Vol. 2, pp. 175–224). Greenwich, CT: JAI Press.

Streufert, S. & Swezey, R.W. (1986). *Complexity, managers, and organizations.* Orlando, FL: Academic Press.

Timmons, J.A. (1994). *New venture creation.* Boston: Irwin.

Ucbasaran, D., Lockett, A., Wright, M., & Westhead, P. (2003). Entrepreneurial founder teams: Factors associated with member entry and exit. *Entrepreneurship Theory and Practice, 28*(1), 107–127.

Volkema, R.J. & Gorman, R.H. (1998). The influence of cognitive-based group composition on decision-making process and outcome. *Journal of Management Studies, 35*(1), 105–121.

Weick, K.E. & Roberts, K.H. (1993). Collective mind in organizations: Heedful interrelating on flight decks. *Administrative Science Quarterly, 38*(3), 357–381.

West, G.P., III (2003). Connecting levels of analysis in entrepreneurship research: A focus on information processing, asymmetric knowledge and networks. In C. Steyaert & D. Hjorth (Eds.), *New movements in entrepreneurship* (pp. 51–70). Northampton, MA: Edward Elgar.

West, G.P., III & Meyer, G.D. (1997). Temporal dimensions of opportunistic change in technology-based ventures. *Entrepreneurship Theory and Practice, 22*(2), 31–52.

West, G.P., III & Meyer, G.D. (1998). To agree or not to agree: Consensus and performance in new ventures. *Journal of Business Venturing, 13*(5), 395–422.

Wetlaufer, S. (1997, September–October). What's stifling the creativity at Coolburst? *Harvard Business Review, 75*(5), 36–40.

Willard, G.E., Krueger, D.A., & Feeser, H.R. (1992). In order to grow, must the founder go: A comparison of performance between founder and non-founder managed high-growth manufacturing firms. *Journal of Business Venturing, 7*, 181–194.

Zacharakis, A.L. & Meyer, G.D. (1998). A lack of insight: Do venture capitalists really understand their own decision process? *Journal of Business Venturing, 13*(1), 57–76.

G. Page West, III, is professor of strategy and entrepreneurship in the Wayne Calloway School of Business and Accountancy at Wake Forest University.

The author would like to thank Charles Bamford, Candida Brush, Connie Marie Gaglio, Elizabeth Gatewood, and two anonymous reviewers for helpful comments on earlier drafts of this article.

Part III
Team Turnover

[11]

Available online at www.sciencedirect.com

ELSEVIER

Journal of Business Venturing 21 (2006) 664–686

The use of networks in human resource acquisition for entrepreneurial firms: Multiple "fit" considerations

Aegean Leung [a,*], Jing Zhang [b], Poh Kam Wong [c], Maw Der Foo [a]

[a] *Department of Management and Organization, National University of Singapore, Singapore 117592, Singapore*
[b] *Cass Business School, City University, 106 Bunhill Row, London EC1Y 8TZ, United Kingdom*
[c] *NUS Entrepreneurship Center, National University of Singapore, Singapore 118412, Singapore*

Received 1 October 2003; received in revised form 1 March 2005; accepted 1 April 2005

Abstract

This study proposes a multi-dimension, multi-contingent "fit" perspective for examining different practices adapted by entrepreneurial firms in acquiring human resources. We posit that while environmental constraints are important considerations for adapting recruitment practices through networks, strategic needs and interpersonal dynamics are the key drivers behind the evolution of such practices. As they transit from the startup to the growth phase, entrepreneurial firms utilize different network pools in search of diversity, yet cling to strong ties to find talents with common values and goals. Our findings carry important implications for future research in human resource management by integrating the macro- and micro-perspective, and at the same time, enhance the understanding of network effects and their strategic bearings in the entrepreneurial process, specifically in the acquisition of human resources.
© 2005 Elsevier Inc. All rights reserved.

Keywords: Human resource acquisition; Entrepreneurship; Developmental phase; Fit; Network effect

1. Executive summary

People are the key to organization competitiveness and the quality of core human resources in a firm impacts organizational growth and well-being. Understanding how

---

* Corresponding author.
   E-mail addresses: aegeanleung@yahoo.com (A. Leung), j.zhang@city.ac.uk (J. Zhang), bizwpk@nus.edu.sg (P.K. Wong), mawder@nus.edu.sg (M.D. Foo).

0883-9026/$ - see front matter © 2005 Elsevier Inc. All rights reserved.
doi:10.1016/j.jbusvent.2005.04.010

A. Leung et al. / Journal of Business Venturing 21 (2006) 664–686   665

organizations can acquire the right type of talents is therefore of prominent interest to organizational scholars and practitioners alike, which is why the notion of "fit" is a dominant theme in human resource literature. Yet what is "fit" is under constant debate. Integrating and extending extant literature on HRM and entrepreneurship, this paper proposes a multi-dimensional, multi-contingent fit model in examining how the practices adapted by entrepreneurial firms in acquiring their core talents may change during different developmental phases of the firm. The general proposition is that entrepreneurial firms adapt different network strategies in acquiring their core human resources at different stages due to multiple considerations of fit.

The overarching theoretical framework of our model is based on the "system approach" of contingency theory, stressing the interactions among multiple contingencies and structural characteristics in the organization system. Due to the lack of internal resources, including a well-structured HR system, entrepreneurial firms may not have the luxury of choosing a "buy" or "make" employment mode in accordance with their business strategies, as suggested in the mainstream HRM literature. Saddled with the liabilities of newness and smallness, the more relevant questions to entrepreneurial firms are "what to buy" and "how to buy", taking into account their needs and constraints.

Through examining how environmental constraints, strategic needs and interpersonal dynamics in entrepreneurial firms interact during different developmental phases, our study highlights some unique features in human resource acquisition in those firms. While recruitment through networks seems to be the predominant practice, the type of networks entrepreneurs tap in to acquire their core talents vary from a mixed pattern during the startup phase to an overwhelming reliance on business networks during the growth phase. Yet the use of strong ties in acquiring talents persisted during both phases. Our analysis of the contingents indicated that the change in the network pattern may be attributed to the need for different types of talents due to the changing environmental conditions and strategic needs of the firm; whereas the stability in tie strength may reflect the persistent emphasis on value and goal congruence when entrepreneurs choose their core team members.

Our findings carry important implications for future research in human resource management by integrating inter-personal, strategic and environmental considerations into the "fit" picture, thus bridging the invisible barrier between macro- and micro-HRM research. Our examination of the recruitment practices through networks, and how they change over time, enhances the understanding of network effects and their strategic bearings in the entrepreneurial process, specifically in the acquisition of human resources. Understanding the various factors affecting the "fit" dynamics of organizational practices may help entrepreneurs and managers in formulating strategies and making decisions in human resource acquisition.

2. Introduction

Literature on human resource practices in entrepreneurial firms is still relatively under-developed (Baron, 2003; Katz and Welbourne, 2002). This is unfortunate considering the significant contribution entrepreneurial firms make to our economy, and the importance of human resource in determining those firms' success or failure (Katz et al., 2000; Katz and Welbourne, 2002). Due to generally sparse human resource practices, recruitment and selection are considered as prominent HR functions (Hornsby and Kuratko, 1990) and the key components of overall effective management of a firm's human resources in entrepreneurial firms (Cardon, 2003). While several studies have examined recruiting and staffing issues in entrepreneurial firms (see Cardon and Stevens, 2004 for a comprehensive review), little has been done to examine the "fit" between the hiring practices and the changing contextual factors of the firm over different developmental stages (Heneman et al., 2000; Leung, 2003).

Addressing the research gap, this paper proposes a multi-dimensional, multi-contingent fit model in examining how changing contextual factors during different developmental phases of the firm may lead to changes of practices in acquiring core talents. Our overarching theoretical framework is the "system approach" of contingency theory which stresses the interactions among multiple contingencies and structural characteristics in the organization (Drazin and Van de Ven, 1985; Van de Ven and Drazin, 1985). Since we are venturing into a relatively unexplored field, the nature of this study is exploratory, focusing more on building a new theoretical perspective than on theory testing. Instead of trying to find additional evidence of the well-debated theme of "fit" and performance, we try to bring out the various factors organizations have to consider in trying to acquire talents with the right "fit".

3. Theoretical background and proposed conceptual framework

3.1. Extant "fit" literature in HRM research

The most frequently applied theory in the human resource literature addressing the "fit" issue in talent acquisition is the person–environment (P–E) fit (or P–O fit when applied to organizations) theory. The P–O fit framework argues that organizational behavior and effectiveness are ultimately a joint function of characteristics of the organizational environment and the individual (Kristof, 1996; Schneider et al., 2001). Empirical research for over a decade has provided strong support for the positive effects of P–O fit on individual work attitudes such as job satisfaction, organizational commitment, organizational citizenship behavior (OCB), task performance and turnover; and individual well-being (Schneider et al., 2001). Such findings are mainly based on bivariate or highly circumscribed multivariate relationships. For example, Chatman and colleagues focus on value and goal congruence in predicting job satisfaction and organizational commitment of individuals (Chatman, 1991; O'Reilly et al., 1991). Using the same measurements, Vandenberghe (1999) suggests that the congruence of individual values with organizational culture predicts turnover. However, in most of the P–O fit literature, the organizational context is very often represented by a set of static organizational characteristics for individuals to fit in, rather than dynamic factors which change with time. Organizational dynamics such as changes in institutional environment and strategic needs over time are rarely taken into consideration (Schneider et al., 1997; Schneider, 2001).

A. Leung et al. / Journal of Business Venturing 21 (2006) 664–686   667

Strategic human resource management (SHRM) literature, on the other hand, focuses almost exclusively on how human resource practices can "fit" organizational strategies in generating the necessary human capital pool to sustain superior performance (Barney and Wreight, 1998; Wright et al., 2001). The key argument under this stream of literature is that a "fit" between strategy and HRM system of the organization will result in sustainable competitive advantage based on its unique human capital, thus resulting in superior organizational performance. The "make" or "buy" employment modes are mapped with different types of organizational strategies based on Miles and Snow's typologies, from prospectors to defenders (Miles and Snow, 1978, 1984). "Make" oriented organizations primarily hire at entry level, and develop employees within the internal labor market, while "buy" oriented organizations acquire needed skills from the open market (Delery and Doty, 1996; Heneman et al., 1994). Amidst the contradictory empirical findings of the type of strategy to map with each employment mode, Lepak and Snell (1999, 2002) proposed that there can be multiple employment modes within the same organization, depending on the type of employees and their roles in the organization. However, both the strategy–practice fit and the human capital–practice fit approaches argue at a broad conceptual level that a certain set of HR practices will suit a specific strategic orientation of the firm. How organizations may have to take into consideration factors other than competitive strategies in formulating their HR practices is seldom touched.

3.2. Unique challenges on human resource acquisition for entrepreneurial firms

Defined as young, small, and growing (Baker and Aldrich, 2000; Markman and Baron, 2002), *entrepreneurial firms* in general are saddled with the "liabilities of newness and smallness" (Aldrich and Auster, 1986; Ranger-Moore, 1997; Stinchcombe, 1965). They may not have the abundant resources at their disposal as in large, established firms. The organizational practices they adapt are more often than not the result of "improvisation" (Baker and Aldrich, 2000) and "effectuation" (Sarasvathy, 2001). Instead of having the choice of various means to achieve a specific goal, entrepreneurial firms usually have to "make do" with the limited resources they have in hand to attain the best outcomes they can get (Sarasvathy, 2001). With regard to hiring practices, the mainstream "make" or "buy" option in the HRM literature may not be applicable to these firms. Since entrepreneurial firms, in general, do not have the HRM system and the organizational resources to provide internal training and career development (Katz et al., 2000), adapting the "internal system" of staffing is seldom an option. The "market system" is deemed to be more appropriate (Cardon, 2003; Delery and Doty, 1996; Heneman and Tansky, 2002). However, recruiting "strangers" from the market is an enormous challenge to entrepreneurial firms with their highly uncertain future, and a general lack of resources and organizational reputation (Williamson, 2000; Williamson et al., 2002). Entrepreneurial firms may have to enact unique strategies and practices to overcome such environmental constraints (Williamson et al., 2002). Therefore, in considering the overall "fit" picture in human resources acquisition in entrepreneurial firms, we need to incorporate these environmental contingents into the equation.

3.3. Towards a "system approach" of fit

Each stream of the literature reviewed above represents one dimension of fit consideration in the process of human resource acquisition: how different individual characteristics may fit into different organizational settings (P–O fit); how different business strategies may need different HRM systems (strategic fit); and how different HRM practices may be an outcome of the environmental constraints firms face (environmental fit). While each stream of the extant literature provides a unique angle for our understanding of the rationales for a specific set of human resource practices, a holistic integration of such dimensions is yet to be developed.

Underlying the contingency approach is the proposition that performance is a consequence of the "fit", or congruence, between several factors: structure, people, technology, strategy, and culture (Nightingale and Toulouse, 1977; Tosi and Slocum, 1984; Van de Ven and Drazin, 1985); although the traditional contingency approach applied in strategic management, organizational theory and organizational behavior studies rarely examine "fit" at such a "system" level (Drazin and Van de Ven, 1985). However, the "system approach" of contingency theory is arguably a more realistic representation of organizational reality (Drazin and Van de Ven, 1985; Miller, 1981). Under this approach, fit is defined as "the internal consistency of multiple contingencies and multiple structural characteristics" (Drazin and Van de Ven, 1985, p. 515). Such an approach advocates the simultaneous consideration of the interaction among environmental, strategic and people variables within a certain structure (Miller, 1981; Van de Ven and Drazin, 1985).

Adapting the "system approach", we propose a multi-dimensional, multi-contingent model of "fit" to examine why recruitment through networks (RTN) becomes the most commonly adapted practice among entrepreneurial firms. Our model suggests that environmental, strategic and inter-personal considerations all play a part in influencing the hiring practices for core talents in entrepreneurial firms. The contingents in these multiple dimensions change as firms evolve from their startup to their growth phase. As a result, although firms may persistently rely on network ties to recruit talents, the network ties utilized may vary with changing organizational context represented by the two different developmental phases. In this study, the *startup phase* is defined as the inception and survival stages of the firm, and the transition to the *growth phase* is signified by the emergence of a clear growth strategy, followed by consecutive years of rapid growth (Churchill and Lewis, 1983; Hanks et al., 1993; Hite and Hesterly, 2001). Fig. 1 summarizes our conceptual framework.

3.3.1. Environmental fit — hiring practice as a response to environmental constraints

Liabilities of newness and smallness are generally quoted as the main constraining factors for entrepreneurial firms to compete in the talent market (Cardon and Stevens, 2004; Williamson, 2000; Williamson et al., 2002). Such liabilities are manifested in the lack of financial and material resources (Hannan and Freeman, 1984), the lack of organizational legitimacy (Williamson, 2000) and a high level of uncertainty (Gartner et al., 1992). The lack of financial resources may hamper entrepreneurial firms' ability to offer attractive remuneration packages. Resource constraints also cause them

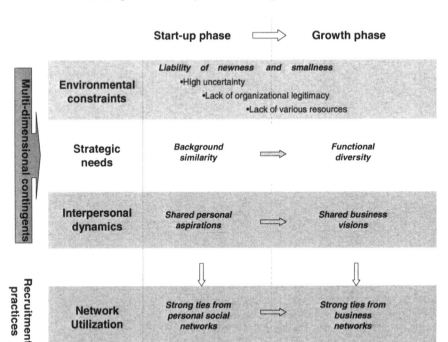

Fig. 1. A multi-dimensional framework of fit considerations in hiring.

to shy away from investment-intensive methods such as college recruitment (Barber et al., 1999). Unlike established firms, entrepreneurial firms often cannot rely on their name, their reputation, or their market share to attract talents (Aldrich, 1999). The HR function is also limited in smaller firms. In addition to their other roles, owners or line management have to recruit staff and they are less likely to employ sophisticated recruitment and selection programs (Barber et al., 1999; Heneman and Berkley, 1999). The deviation from institutionalized recruitment practices, together with the general absence of well-defined job descriptions for positions, reduce entrepreneurial firms' legitimacy as employers-of-choice (Williamson, 2000). From the potential recruit's perspective, committing one's career to a relatively young and small firm can be a high-risk undertaking due to the relatively high mortality rate of firms at their early and adolescence stages (Bruderl and Schussler, 1990; Hannan and Freeman, 1989).

Proposition 1a. *Liabilities of newness and smallness are the key environmental constraints faced by entrepreneurial firms in human resource acquisition.*

Extant literature on staffing practices in entrepreneurial firms suggests that informal recruitment practices through networks generally prevail in such firms (Aldrich, 1999; Aldrich and Langton, 1997; Barber et al., 1999). RTN provide a "convenient and inexpensive" way of acquiring talents (Barber et al., 1999). Network recruitment may also help to address the issue of organizational legitimacy. Through networks, potential employees can obtain private information on the firm (Shane and Cable, 2002), thus becoming more open to consider joining the firm. Similarly, individuals with existing ties to entrepreneurs are more likely than strangers to join ventures operating in highly uncertain conditions (Hite and Hesterly, 2001; Uzzi, 1996). More importantly, in the absence of sophisticated selection processes, using networks in recruitment and selection will help achieve better "fit", be it personality, ability or attitude (Brass, 1995, p. 52 and 62–63). Therefore, we can see the pragmatic as well as strategic rationales in entrepreneurial firms adapting recruitment practices through networks.

As entrepreneurial firms transit from the startup phase to the growth phase, however, we can expect an improvement in resource availability as their businesses grew to a sustainable size. The establishment of a certain track record also improves their organizational legitimacy. At this stage, there should also be a reduction in the degree of uncertainty since the firms have moved beyond survival to growth (Hite and Hesterly, 2001). Such improvements, together with the need for expanding the core team to cope with the growth pace, may steer entrepreneurial firms to turn more to the market for talents (Cardon, 2003; Williamson, 2000), reducing the reliance on RTN.

Proposition 1b. *Recruitment through networks is the predominant practice in acquiring human resource in entrepreneurial firms, although the extent of its predominance will decrease during the growth phase.*

3.3.2. Strategic fit — meeting strategic needs through hiring practices

During the startup phase, organizational structure is relatively simple, and the owner/manager is synonymous with the business, with highly centralized decision-making authority. The focus of the firm at this phase is to turn identified opportunities into viable business, and to survive with limited resources. Fast decision making and actions are imperative. Schneider et al. (1997), quoting from Miller's work (1991) suggested that homogeneity in the management team at this early phase can bring about the cohesiveness and cooperation required to achieve those short-term goals. In their study of new venture teams, Chandler and Hanks (1998) also found that shared background and interests, rather than functional diversity, tend to be the predominant selection criteria for team members at this stage.

As the firm transits to the growth phase, its strategic focus shifts from short term survival to longer term growth and sustainability. As business size grows, and business demands become more intense and diversified, entrepreneurs need to decide what tasks they focus on to bring about maximum benefits for the organization, and delegate other roles (Johnson and Bishop, 2002). Gradually, as the organizational structure shifts from an owner-run firm to professional management with increased specialization, diversity of skills becomes necessary (Churchill and Lewis, 1983; Hanks et al., 1993). Chandler and Hanks (1998) found that the development of distinctive functional area competencies by team members is associated with sales growth performance as firms go beyond their founding years. Management heterogeneity facilitates growth and organizational

A. Leung et al. / Journal of Business Venturing 21 (2006) 664–686   671

transition, in that it increases the knowledge and perspectives available to the core team, enabling the team to go into issues more deeply and develop a more complete understanding of problems, and develop alternative solutions to these problems (Foo et al., 2005; Pelled et al., 1999). Debates among team members based on their different perspectives lead to increased decision comprehensiveness, and are particularly important in situations characterized by change and uncertainty (Eisenhardt, 1989b; Simons et al., 1999).

Proposition 2a. *Contingent on the strategic needs of the firm, entrepreneurs stress background similarity during the startup phase and functional diversity during the growth phase in acquiring their core team members.*

Personal social networks, in general, comprise families, kin, friends and other affiliations through various social interactions (Dubini and Aldrich, 1991). Apart from family members, individuals are also more likely to affiliate themselves and share similar values with people from similar socioeconomic backgrounds (Aldrich, 1999; Schneider et al., 1998). Therefore, a focus on background similarity may be achieved through hiring from the personal social networks of the entrepreneurs. To tap into more diverse talents during the growth phase, however, entrepreneurs may need to reach beyond their own social circles (Aldrich, 1999) and seek people who are dissimilar to themselves. *Business networks* established during the process of building up the firm, be that with suppliers, customers or service providers, form a rich pool for entrepreneurial firms to search for people with diverse backgrounds and perspectives (Leung, 2003). For example, professional managers from larger corporations may possess very different backgrounds and perspectives from entrepreneurs (Busenitz and Barney, 1997), and such people can become the source of diversity for entrepreneurial firms at the growth phase.

Proposition 2b. *The network ties utilized in acquiring core team members evolve from personal social ties during the startup phase to business related ties during the growth phase of the firm.*

3.3.3. Inter-personal fit — screening for the right "type" of people with hiring practices

Utilizing different network pools to search for talents in accordance with varying strategic needs does not automatically translate into getting people with the "right fit". The essence of person–organization fit lies in value and goal congruence between the person and the organization (Chatman, 1989; Kristof, 1996), within which the "fit" content may also change over time (Schneider et al., 1997). Empirical studies have found that during the startup phase of new firms, entrepreneurs make recruitment decisions based mainly on the mutual compelling interests among team members or their common aspirations to start a venture (Chandler and Hanks, 1998; Kamm and Nurick, 1993). Rather than just having a clear business vision as a common ground, entrepreneurs and their team members are being drawn to each other based on similar beliefs, interests, and personal chemistry (Bird, 1988). As firms move to the growth phase, business vision and strategic goals become more well-defined and stable (Churchill and Lewis, 1983). From the P–O fit perspective, during this phase entrepreneurial firms need to have members with diverse perspectives and complementary competencies and also members who share the vision of the organization. This mix of complementary competencies and shared vision facilitate effective communications and execution of organizational tasks (Schneider et al., 1997).

Proposition 3a. *For value and goal congruence, entrepreneurs tend to seek talents with shared personal aspirations in the startup phase and with shared business visions during the growth phase of the firm.*

To identify people who share similar values requires a prolonged period of repeated interactions between the parties concerned (Jones and George, 1998). The key elements during the process are the exchanges of knowledge and information. Values are manifested through strings of consistent attitudes and behaviors over time, and the information used in the judgment is tacit rather than explicit. Uzzi (1996) suggested that embedded ties are more effective in transferring fine-grained, tacit information. Therefore, in the context of hiring core team members, we expect the preference for direct, strong ties to persist through the startup phase to the growth phase of entrepreneurial firms.

Relying on strong ties does not necessarily limit the diversity of information and competencies entrepreneurial firms need, especially for their growth phase. It is probable that, if we consider only personal networks, strong ties tend to breed homogeneity, since such ties tend to link people with similar background and perspectives together (Aldrich, 1999, p. 82). However, during the course of building up their businesses, entrepreneurs are likely to come across business counterparts who are different from themselves. For example, professional managers from larger corporations are very different from entrepreneurs (Busenitz and Barney, 1997). They come into contact with entrepreneurial firms mainly through business relationships as customers, suppliers, and resource or service providers. Entrepreneurs may form strong ties with some of these business associates through repeated interactions over a prolonged period of time. These business associates may also come to understand and share the firms' business visions. Having them on board provides the diversity of perspectives and competencies entrepreneurial firms need for facilitating growth. The networks of such people may in turn bring in diverse information which is not obtainable through the entrepreneurs' personal networks, performing the structural-hole function for entrepreneurial firms (Bian and Ang, 1997; Burt, 1992).

Proposition 3b. *The network ties utilized in recruiting core team members are likely to be strong ties at both the startup phase and the growth phase of the firm.*

4. Methodology

4.1. Samples and data collection

Since this was an exploratory study on why and how entrepreneurial firms might come to adapt different types of networks in acquiring their human resources, a case study approach was used (Yin, 1984). A multiple-case study approach and a "theory-based" sampling design (Chandler and Hanks, 1998; Yin, 1984) were adopted to allow replication within the same group and comparison across groups. Data were collected from two cohorts of 10 entrepreneurial firms each, through interviews with the owner-managers. The first cohort consisted of firms between 2 and 3 years old at the time of the interview. The second cohort consisted of firms between 6 and 30 years old, with an average age of 16.7 years. With the first group, we captured the recruitment of initial team members other than the founders. With the second group, we captured data on how they recruited their core team members during both the startup and the growth phases. Data from the first group acted as a validity check on the retrospective data collected from the second group on their recruitment practices during the startup phase, since entrepreneurs from older firms might be recollecting events that happened 10 to 20 years ago. The second group of firms allowed us to collect data that captured the transition from the startup phase to the growth phase. Our sample firms came from a wide range of industries including manufacturers of food products, printed products, mechanical tooling, and electronic components; internet service providers, software developers, trading companies, and pet stores (services and products).

The bulk of the interviews were conducted between the periods of mid-2002 to mid-2003, with some follow-up interviews conducted in 2004. A combination of open-ended and structured questions was used. The length of the interviews ranged from 45 min to 90 min. Before the questionnaires were administered, the concepts of core team members (for both cohorts) and the differentiation between the startup and the growth phases (for the second cohort only) were explained to the entrepreneurs. With reference to the definitions of top management team and core talents (Hambrick and Mason, 1984; Lepak and Snell, 1999), we defined *core team members* as people who hold key positions in the company and are involved in the company's management and strategic decision process. For the *transition from the startup to the growth phase*, we used four contingents from the stage-model literature (Churchill and Lewis, 1983; Hanks et al., 1993; Smith et al., 1985) to identify the dividing line between the startup and the growth phases: the formation of a clearly articulated growth strategy, additional capital injection, expansion of the general work force and the core team, rapid positive growth for the 3 years after transition. Entrepreneurs made their own decisions on the transition point based on one or more of the dimensions.

The open-ended questions aimed to capture the contingents leading to the adaptation of the recruitment practices through networks, and the structured questions helped trace the channels the owner–manager used to recruit their core team members, and the characteristics of the ties used. A total of 71 hires were captured from the two cohorts of firms, 33 from the startup phase and 38 from the growth phase.

4.2. Measures of key concepts and data analysis

Our study adopted the strategy of building pre-defined constructs and propositions based on existing literature, as recommended by Yin (1984, p. 100–101) and Eisenhardt (1989a, p. 536). Such an approach provides a well-defined focus when we go into organizations, facilitating the systematic collection of specific kind of data. The constructs and propositions also serve as guides for data analysis along clearly defined theoretical ground.

In line with the definitions for core concepts used in this paper, various contingents affecting the choice of recruitment practices were categorized through theme coding of the transcripts for testing Propositions 1a, 2a and 3a. *Liabilities of newness and smallness* was coded when entrepreneurs referred to uncertainty (or risky, unpredictable environment), the lack of organizational legitimacy (e.g., reputation, recognition, and track record), and the lack of financial, organizational and material resources. *Similarity in background* or *functional diversity* were coded with reference to the demographics of the recruits, and *shared personal aspirations* or *shared business vision* were coded when entrepreneurs referred to dreams and passion or shared view point on business and identification with firm's goals as reasons for choosing a certain member.

For data analysis, we took the steps recommended by Yin (1984) and Eisenhardt (1989a) to conduct both within-case analysis and cross-case pattern searching. The transcript from each single firm was analyzed, noting all the contingents related to the use of different recruitment channels, and then sorted by the pre-defined themes. Repeat occurrences of any emergent themes, as in the case of trust and attitude, were also noted and categorized. Coupled with within-case analysis, we searched for repeated patterns among the same group of firms, and for similarities and/or differences across groups (startup firms versus growth firms) based on the dimensions we established from existing literature. Themes were considered established only if there were multiple occurrences within and across cases, reducing to a certain extent the danger of reaching false conclusions based on isolated evidence and information process biases (Eisenhardt, 1989a, p. 540). Quotations that were representative of the generated themes were then selected to "add voice" to our text (Wolcott, 1990), as reported in our findings. The matching of proposed themes at the proposed developmental phase (startup or growth) was the basis for supporting our propositions.

For coding, data analysis and testing of Propositions 1b, 2b and 3b, we relied mainly on numerical tabulation based on pre-defined variables and measures to capture patterns and relationships between variables, combining qualitative coding and quantitative analyses (Bettenhausen and Murnighan, 1985). Hires in the startup phase and hires in the growth phase were grouped into two separate groups. Recruitment channels were coded into four categories, i.e., recruitment through social ties, recruitment through business ties, internal promotion, and recruitment from the open market. Recruitment through social ties was coded when the recruit was (or was introduced by) a family member or a friend; a schoolmate or an acquaintance from social activities. Recruitment through business ties was coded when the recruit was (or was introduced by) a business associate (e.g., supplier, customer, service provider of the firm, or former colleague). Internal promotion was coded when the position was filled by an existing employee. Recruitment from the open market was coded when the person was a stranger recruited through job advertisement, employment agency, etc. Three commonly used measures for tie strength are duration of the relationship, intimacy of the relationship, and frequency of interaction (Brass, 1995; Burt and Knez, 1995). In this paper, the strength of ties was coded into dichotomies of strong (coded as 1) and weak ties (coded as 0) utilizing two of the three measures developed by Burt and Knez (1995). The two items capturing the duration of the relationship (How many years have you known each other before the recruitment?) and intimacy level of the relationship (To what extent do you agree that you keep a close relationship with each other prior to the recruitment?) were used as guidelines to code tie strength. The third item concerning meeting frequency was dropped due to the high possibility of recall error for such a detail. Prior studies have revealed a high correlation between frequency and closeness (Hansen, 1999), hence we do not expect the omission to affect the assessment of tie strength. Following Granovetter's (1973) definition, indirect ties were classified as weak ties. Some examples coded as indirect weak ties are:

> *He was a former acquaintance introduced by a friend — weak social tie* (G2-250503); *He came to sell us leased lines — weak business tie. (G1-090402)*

Multi-dimensional χ^2 tests were used to test Propositions 1b, 2b and 3b. The first χ^2 test differentiated RTN (social and business ties) and other recruitment channels. The second differentiated the types of networks used among the positions recruited through networks, and the third tested the strength of ties used in the two groups of positions hired during the startup and the growth phase.

5. Findings

As predicted in Proposition 1a, the "liability of newness and smallness" was mentioned as a key constraint in attracting people by entrepreneurs from both groups:

> *Most of the good technical resources (talents) who are home grown in Singapore don't really want to work for small companies like ours (young and small with high risk of failure). They prefer MNCs or large local companies. (G1-200602)[1]*

> *In competing with more established employers for talents, we sometimes can't afford to match their salaries. (G2-050602)*

> *The point is that you also have to build your company to a certain size to be able to attract people to join you. When the company is very small, people look at the company, they don't see a career path. They will never come. But when your company starts to grow, and you've got a good vision, they get to know you, then they will say, "hey this company will grow, and I want to be part of this growth". (G2-250703)*

The results of the multi-dimensional χ^2 test (Table 1) conducted on the two groups of positions with regard to their recruitment channels supported Proposition 1b. Of the total number of hires in both the startup and the growth phases, 76.1% were through networks. While there was a significant difference between the two groups of hires in the different phases ($\chi^2 = 4.732$, $p = 0.015$), RTN was the predominant trend in both (87.9% during the

---

[1] The reference code for the quotations are created as follows: G1 or G2 represent the two cohorts of firms at the startup and the growth phase, followed by the interview date.

Table 1
Multi-dimensional χ^2 test for recruitment channels for positions

Growth phases * recruitment channels cross-tabulation

			Recruitment channels		Total
			Other recruitment channels	Recruitment through networks	
Growth phases	Startup phase	Count	4	29	33
		Expected count	7.9	25.1	33.0
		% Within growth phases	12.1%	87.9%	100.0%
		% Within recruitment channels	23.5%	53.7%	46.5%
		% of Total	5.6%	40.8%	46.5%
	Growth phase	Count	13	25	38
		Expected count	9.1	28.9	38.0
		% Within growth phases	34.2%	65.8%	100.0%
		% Within recruitment channels	76.5%	46.3%	53.5%
		% of Total	18.3%	35.2%	53.5%
Total		Count	17	54	71
		Expected count	17.0	54.0	71.0
		% Within growth phases	23.9%	76.1%	100.0%
		% Within recruitment channels	100.0%	100.0%	100.0%
		% of Total	23.9%	76.1%	100.0%

$N = 71$, $\chi^2 = 4.73$, $df = 1$, $p = 0.015$.

startup phase, and 65.8% during the growth phase). However, the reliance on RTN decreased in the growth phase relative to the startup phase.

Propositions 2a and 3a were closely related and were often mentioned together during our conversations with the entrepreneurs. Consistent with our predictions, firms at the startup phase focussed more on similarity in background for team members, than on functional qualifications. This was closely linked to a preference for people who had shared personal aspirations and values with the entrepreneurs:

> *Either they are friends that I know for many years or a friend's friend who have known one another for many years. So, there is (a) certain bond and confidence in one another. (G1-090902)*

> *... even if the person has very good qualifications or lots of experience, it doesn't mean that the person can work with me. I think the chemistry is very important, whether they can work with me, whether they can work with their colleagues, whether they find that the office is right for them, I think that is very important. I choose my partners from previous colleagues. They know me very well — my management skill and my background. Me too. We need a cohesive team to work together and overcome the difficulties together, not blame each other. (G2-140703)*

> *Of course they don't know the technology in detail, so I have to train them up. That's why I put them at the middle (level). ... So, last three years we trained them up, they are the best persons. ... (In contrast) those guys who are looking at the money,*

A. Leung et al. / Journal of Business Venturing 21 (2006) 664–686   677

although they have a strong technology background, are not welcomed. (This is) because those startup (members) have to suffer together in the process of the company growth. (G2-120602)

At the growth phase, however, entrepreneurs tended to make their recruitment choices based more on complementary competencies than on a common background:

We have to ask ourselves why this person will benefit the organization. . . . So it's not just because he's a friend or that we have known each other for 10 years. No, it's more than that. It's more because we knew him or her, we knew that he has the particular knowledge or function that we want him or her to fill. That's why we offered to do this job together. (G2-310502)

I needed him because he was from a multinational company. . . . As a company moving into the international market, we needed someone with multinational experience to help us manage the firm. Without that, we could not go to another level. I had only worked as an employee for seven months. It was quite difficult for me to spearhead the company's internationalization. (G2-140703)

He had over 20 years with an American MNC. I take him in because he has certain ideas and certain expertise that I think he can share with us — what he had learned from the MNC. One of the weaknesses of (a) smaller company is that we do not have proper procedures and systems. This director has some ideas how we can go about to do (doing) that. I feel that it is the right time to bring in some people who give you some new ideas to organize the company, experienced people rather than young people. He was being laid off, and I brought him in to give the company some new ideas. (G2-210307)

Competency match alone is not sufficient. The core people who joined the firm during the growth phase also need to identify with the company's vision. Professional managers joined the firm because they could see where the company was going, not just because they believed in the entrepreneur:

These people have worked with me before. They have a feel for what the company is like. They know the direction of the company. They know the vision. And I believe because of all these, they stay very motivated. And they are confident in how things will be done. (G2-250703)

Before they join your company, they already obtained an understanding of your product, not just based on knowing me. They do not join the company because they have faith on (in) me. They know my character, they also know the recognition of the company and its products in the market, then, they join. (G2–140703)

Propositions 2a and 3a were therefore generally supported.

The results of the multi-dimensional χ^2 test (Table 2) conducted on the positions hired through networks during the startup and the growth phase revealed that while there was a distinctive difference in the patterns of network ties used in hiring during the two phases ($\chi^2 = 11.653$, $p < 0.001$), there was not a clear trend that social networks were the preferred

Table 2
Multi-dimensional χ^2 test for types of networks used in hiring

Growth phases * types of network cross-tabulation

			Types of networks		Total
			Social networks	Business networks	
Growth phases	Startup phase	Count	13	16	29
		Expected count	7.5	21.5	29.0
		% Within growth phases	44.8%	55.2%	100.0%
		% Within types of networks	92.9%	40.0%	53.7%
		% of Total	24.1%	29.6%	53.7%
	Growth phase	Count	1	24	25
		Expected count	6.5	18.5	25.0
		% Within growth phases	4.0%	96.0%	100.0%
		% Within types of networks	7.1%	60.0%	46.3%
		% of Total	1.9%	44.4%	46.3%
Total		Count	14	40	54
		Expected count	14.0	40.0	54.0
		% Within growth phases	25.9%	74.1%	100.0%
		% Within types of networks	100.0%	100.0%	100.0%
		% of Total	25.9%	74.1%	100.0%

$N=54$, $\chi^2=11.653$, $df=1$, $p<0.001$.

channels of recruitment during the startup phase. Rather, in absolute numbers, business ties seemed to be more frequently used than social ties (16 vs. 13). However, a separate χ^2 test on the positions recruited through networks during the startup phase showed no distinctive preference between social and business networks ($\chi^2=0.310$, $p=0.577$). A validity check on positions hired during the startup phase in the first and second cohort of firms showed no significant difference in recruitment channels used between the two groups of firms ($\chi^2=0.214$, $p=0.519$).

The mixed network pattern used during the startup phase may be interpreted from the angles of availability and preference. In many cases, family members or friends might not be available, or were unwilling to take up positions in the startups (Aldrich and Langton, 1997). They might be holding positions with more established firms and were reluctant to make the move:

> *When my account manager resigned, I asked if she (my niece) can do the account. She worked for HL (an established financial company). She said HL is better.... I even talked to my classmates, university classmates ...at least four or five of them: "please come and join me, I need someone to help". He came (a university classmate), he came alone. (G1-120602)*

In such cases, entrepreneurs may have no choice but to utilize whatever other channels available to them in line with the "improvisation" and "effectuation" theory of the entrepreneurial process (Baker and Aldrich, 2000; Sarasvathy, 2001). On the other hand, some entrepreneurs might not want to hire from their social circle when they had a choice:

> *I do not believe in running the business with family members. I believe in getting outsiders. (G2-250503)*

A. Leung et al. / Journal of Business Venturing 21 (2006) 664–686   679

> *I seldom take friends' recommendations. I try to avoid (that because) there will be a lot of power and politics problems. If you want to fire him, (someone hired) based on a friend's recommendation, (it) can be a lot of problems. No family members. Also, staff's family members cannot be here. (G2-140703)*

> *It is difficult to do business with family members — emotions tend to get in the way. A lot of people run the company with family management. It does not work. Having close friends working with you is the same thing. Better remain as good friends (than mixing friendship and business together). (G2-250703)*

During the growth phase, the network utilization pattern was much clearer. Of the 25 hired through networks, 24 (96%) were from business networks. Proposition 2b was partially supported.

The multi-dimensional χ^2 test on positions recruited through networks and tie strength (Table 3) showed no significant difference between the startup and the growth phase ($\chi^2 = 0.207$, $p = 0.325$). There seemed to be a tendency towards strong ties for both phase (62.1% of the hires during the startup phase, and 68% of the hires during the growth phase were strong ties). A separate χ^2 test on hires through strong ties showed no significant difference between the two phases ($\chi^2 = 0.029$, $p = 0.866$). Proposition 3b, with regard to the strength of ties utilized in RTN, was supported.

On top of the themes of shared personal values or business vision, additional themes captured from dialogues with the entrepreneurs provided further explanation as to why strong ties were generally preferred. One emerging theme was the issue of trust. From firms at the startup phase, we hear repeated references to the importance of trust:

> *For those people we know, we know what we can expect and what they can deliver. (G1-080402)*

> *I think that (trust) is the most important. . . . You must at least get people who are competent. But he may not be aligned with you. He may not have the commitment, and ask why he must work so hard. (G1-110902)*

From firms at the growth phase, emphasis on trust is apparent:

> *So, there is trust, you can trust him. We knew each other (through working as counterparts for 10 years). (There was) no need to go through the process of building up trust. . . . Trusting the person means trusting him to manage for the company. . . (If) you believe the person has the sense of responsibility to do the job well, has the ability, then you give him the job. (G2-140703)*

> *When I talk to people in the interview, I must feel that I am confident in the person, and can trust him. I believe that if you cannot trust a person, do not hire him. (G2-210703)*

Another emerging theme closely related to trust was the stress on attitude:

> *In business, I still think the attitude is more important than qualification(s). (G1-110902)*

Table 3
Multi-dimensional χ^2 test on strength of ties used in hiring

Growth phases*tie strength cross-tabulation

			Tie strength		Total
			Weak	Strong	
Growth phases	Startup phase	Count	11	18	29
		Expected count	10.2	18.8	29.0
		% Within growth phases	37.9%	62.1%	100.0%
		% Within tie strength	57.9%	51.4%	53.7%
		% of Total	20.4%	33.3%	53.7%
	Growth phase	Count	8	17	25
		Expected count	8.8	16.2	25.0
		% Within growth phases	32.0%	68.0%	100.0%
		% Within tie strength	42.1%	48.6%	46.3%
		% of Total	14.8%	31.5%	46.3%
Total		Count	19	35	54
		Expected count	19.0	35.0	54.0
		% Within growth phases	35.2%	64.8%	100.0%
		% Within tie strength	100.0%	100.0%	100.0%
		% of Total	35.2%	64.8%	100.0%

$N=54$, $\chi^2=0.207$, $df=1$, $p=0.325$.

Experience is not important.... If the basic attitude of the person is right, can be trusted, keen to learn, he can overcome the handicaps. (G2-210703)

Judgment of both trustworthiness and attitude required fine-grained information transfer, which is best achieved through the utilization of strong ties (Krackhardt, 1992; Uzzi, 1996). Therefore, entrepreneurs who are looking for such qualities in their core team members will lean towards strong ties.

6. Discussion

In this study, we explored multiple "fit" considerations linking RTN practices, and their evolution over different phases of organizational development, to the changing environmental, organizational and interpersonal dynamics of entrepreneurial firms. Our findings support our general proposition that entrepreneurial firms adapt different network strategies in acquiring their core human resources at different developmental phases due to multiple considerations of fit. Our effort represents an initial attempt to adapt a "system approach" of contingency theory (Miller, 1981; Van de Ven and Drazin, 1985) to understand the underlying dynamics of HR practices.

6.1. Implications

Mainstream HRM literature suggests that organizations should choose between "buy" (market system) or "make" (internal system) for their HRM practices contingent on the type of business strategies adopted (e.g., Delery and Doty, 1996; Miles and Snow, 1984).

Our study suggests that, due to their specific needs and constraints, the strategic choices entrepreneurial firms need to make with regard to their HRM practices is "how to buy" the right types of talents they need at different developmental phases of the firm with the means available to them. Specifically, they "buy" from social and business networks during the startup phase, and "buy" almost exclusively from business networks during the growth phase. Such an understanding highlights the need to study human resource practices in entrepreneurial firms in their specific context.

Our examination of the recruitment practices through networks, and how they change over time, enhances the understanding of network effects in the entrepreneurial process, specifically in the acquisition of human resources. Extant studies on the utilization of networks in resource acquisition by entrepreneurial firms seem to suggest that strong ties contribute more to firm survival, and weak ties are more important in facilitating growth (Bruderl and Preisendorfre, 1998; Hite and Hesterly, 2001; Stearns, 1996). While such studies have solid theoretical ground in the strength of weak ties theory (Granovetter, 1973) and structure-holes theory (Burt, 1992), our findings suggest that the use of strong ties in acquiring core team members persists throughout the startup and the growth phases of the firm. We bring additional insights to the debate on the effects of strong/weak ties by showing that, instead of switching from strong ties to weak ties to achieve diversity in perspectives and competencies, entrepreneurial firms shift from personal social networks to business networks. This is consistent with the concept of stability versus change when studying network effects and organizational transition (Burkhardt and Brass, 1990). While shifting their network pool in search of talents with diverse competencies, entrepreneurs cling to strong ties to find talents who are different from themselves, and yet still share certain common ground and values.

On the practical front, our study broadens the understanding of recruitment practices of entrepreneurial firms. The limited literature on the topic thus far focuses more on what the practices are, rather than on why such practices are employed. By taking a "system approach" in examining how network recruitment practices of entrepreneurial firms emerge and evolve, this study highlights the importance of strategic alignments among multiple contexts and practices. Such an understanding is of reference value for strategic decisions of entrepreneurial firms on human resource acquisition. Decision-makers need to be conscious of the multiple fit dynamics in considering what type of people they need and how they are going to get them.

Specifically, our study suggests that entrepreneurs, in seeking people to join their firms, may utilize strong ties during both the startup and growth phases. These strong ties could come from a mix of business and social networks in the startup phase and from business networks in the growth phase. Such findings may have certain implications for job seekers as well. While Granovetter's study (1974) suggests that weak ties lead to better job prospects for managers, professionals and technical positions, our findings suggest that to become a core member in an entrepreneurial firm, more direct relationships (either in a business or social context) may have to be established before one will be considered for the job.

6.2. Limitations and future research

Given that this is an exploratory study done on a small sample of entrepreneurial firms, we need to be cautious in generalizing the findings. While the main purpose of this study is to build new theoretical perspectives, further studies with more robust research designs are needed to validate our propositions. The retrospective longitudinal approach employed in this study also has its limitations. Entrepreneurs may have cognitive and perceptual limitations that reduce the validity and reliability of their retrospective accounts (Chandler and Lyon, 2001). We have taken measures to improve validity by comparing the retrospective data from firms at the growth phase with those collected from a separate cohort of startup firms. Nevertheless, longitudinal panel studies should be conducted in the future to validate our findings.

Collecting multi-dimensional data from a single informant also has its inherent weaknesses, although there is little dispute that owner–managers are the most appropriate people to provide data on the firm and the team. Given time and accessibility, collecting a separate set of data from team members of the respective firms can certainly further enhance our understanding of the fit dynamics, and increase the validity of the findings.

Of the two general types of network studies highlighted by Brass (1995), the ego-centric network approach focuses on the networks of a focal individual, and the whole network approach captures the comprehensive structure linking all members together. In this study, we focused on the egocentric networks of the entrepreneurs. To generate a more comprehensive understanding of the network effect recruitment and selection of talents in entrepreneurial firms, capturing the dynamics of the whole network structure among core team members of the firm should be an important agenda for future studies.

There is also the possibility of country specific bias in our findings, since all the firms in our study are Singaporean local enterprises. Singapore is a predominantly Chinese society, and there will inevitably be a strong influence of the Chinese business culture. The preference for direct, strong ties even in business settings, for example, may be related to the specific Chinese perspectives on relationships (guanxi) and trust. According to Brunner et al. (1989), "the reliability of a guanxi varies directly with its closeness: the closer the guanxi, the more reliable it is; the more distant, the less reliable". Nonetheless, network recruitment practices can also be found in Western societies. For example, Inc., a magazine on fast-growing entrepreneurial firms (Caggiano, 1998; Fenn, 1997) reported similar network strategies used in the recruitment practices of entrepreneurial firms in the US. Hence, the implications of our findings may reach beyond the Chinese cultural context. Comparative studies across cultures should be done in future to test the generalizability of the findings from this study.

Acknowledgements

We would like to thank Ron Rodgers, Dan McAllister, S. Venkataraman and the two anonymous reviewers for their comments and contributions on the earlier versions of this paper. We would also like to express our appreciation for the financial support from the NUS Entrepreneurship Center and from the NUS Business School on new venture teams.

References

Aldrich, H.E., 1999. Organization Evolving. Sage, London.

Aldrich, H., Auster, E.R., 1986. Even dwarfs started small. In: Staw, B.M., Cummings, J.L. (Eds.), Research in Organizational Behavior, vol. 8. JAI Press, Greenwich, CT, pp. 165–198.

Aldrich, H., Langton, N., 1997. Human resource management practices and organizational life cycles. In: Reynolds, P., et al., (Eds.), Frontiers of Entrepreneurship Research. Babson College, Babson Park, MA.

Baker, T., Aldrich, H.E., 2000. Bricolage and Resource-seeking: improvisational responses to dependence in entrepreneurial firms. Unpublished paper.

Barber, A.E., Wesson, M.J., Robertson, Q.M., Taylor, M.S., 1999. A tale of two job markets: organizational size and its effects on hiring practices and job search behavior. Personnel Psychology 52, 841–867.

Barney, J., Wreight, P.M., 1998. On becoming a strategic partner: the role of human resources in gaining competitive advantage. Human Resource Management 37, 31–46.

Baron, R., 2003. Human resource management and entrepreneurship: some reciprocal benefits of closer links. Human Resource Management Review 13 (2), 253–256.

Bettenhausen, K., Murnighan, J.K., 1985. The emergence of norms in competitive decision-making groups. Administrative Science Quarterly 30, 350–372.

Bian, Y., Ang, S., 1997. Guanxi networks and job mobility in China and Singapore. Social Forces 75, 981–1005.

Bird, B., 1988. Implementing entrepreneurial ideas: the case for intention. Academy of Management Review 13, 442–453.

Brass, D.J., 1995. A social network perspective on human resources management. Research in Personnel and Human Resources Management 13, 39–79.

Bruderl, J., Preisendorfre, P., 1998. Network support and the success of newly founded businesses. Small Business Economics 10, 213–225.

Bruderl, J., Schussler, R., 1990. Organizational mortality: the liability of newness and adolescence. Administrative Quarterly 35, 530–547.

Brunner, J.A., Chen, J., Sun, C., Zhou, N., 1989. The role of guanxi in negotiations in the Pacific basin. Journal of Global Marketing 3 (2), 7–23.

Burkhardt, M.E., Brass, D.J., 1990. Changing patterns or patterns of change: the effect of a change in technology on social network structure and power. Administrative Science Quarterly 35, 104–127.

Burt, R., 1992. Structural Holes: The Social Structure of Competition. Harvard University Press, Cambridge.

Burt, R., Knez, M., 1995. Kinds of third-party effects on trust. Rationality and Society 7, 255–292.

Busenitz, L.W., Barney, J.B., 1997. Differences between entrepreneurs and managers in large organizations: biases and heuristics in strategic decision-making. Journal of Business Venturing 12, 9–30.

Caggiano, C., 1998. Recruiting secrets of the smartest companies around. Inc. October 01, 1998.

Cardon, M.S., 2003. Contingent labor as an enabler of entrepreneurial growth. Human Resource Management 42 (4), 357–373.

Cardon, M.S., Stevens, C.E., 2004. Managing human resources in small organizations: what do we know? Human Resource Management Review 14 (3), 295–324.

Chandler, G.N., Hanks, S.H., 1998. An investigation of new venture teams in emerging business. In: Reynolds, P., et al., (Eds.), Frontiers of Entrepreneurship Research. Babson Colleage, Babson Park, MA.

Chandler, G.N., Lyon, D.W., 2001. Issues of research design and construct measurement in entrepreneurship research: the past decade. Entrepreneurship Theory and Practice, 101–113 (summer).

Chatman, J.A., 1989. Improving interactional organizational research: a model of person–organization fit. Academy of Management Review 14 (3), 333–349.

Chatman, J.A., 1991. Matching people and organizations: selection and socialization in public accounting firms. Administrative Science Quarterly 36, 459–484.

Churchill, N.C., Lewis, V.L., 1983. The five stages of small business growth. Harvard Business Review, 30 (May/June 1983).

Delery, J.E., Doty, D.H., 1996. Modes of theorizing in strategic human resource management: test of universalistic, contingency, and configurational performance predictions. Academy of Management Journal 39, 802–835.

Drazin, R., Van de Ven, A.H., 1985. Alternative forms of fit in contingency theory. Administrative Science Quarterly 30, 514–539.

Dubini, P., Aldrich, H., 1991. Personal and extended networks are central to the entrepreneurial process. Journal of Business Venturing 6, 305–313.

Eisenhardt, K.M., 1989a. Building theories from case study research. Academy of Management Review 14 (4), 532–550.

Eisenhardt, K.M., 1989b. Making fast strategic decisions in high-velocity environments. Academy of Management Journal 32 (3), 543–576.

Fenn, D. Rules of Engagement. Inc. January 01, 1997.

Foo, M.D., Wong, P.K., Ong, A., 2005. Do others think you have a viable business idea? Team diversity and judges' evaluation of ideas in a business plan competition. Journal of Business Venturing 20 (3), 385–402.

Gartner, W.B., Bird, B.J., Starr, J.A., 1992. Acting as if: differentiating entrepreneurial from organizational behavior. Entrepreneurship Theory and Practice 16 (3), 13–31.

Granovetter, M.S., 1973. The strength of weak ties. American Journal of Sociology 78 (6), 1360–1380.

Granovetter, M.S., 1974. Getting a Job — A Study of Contacts and Careers. The University of Chicago Press.

Hambrick, D.C., Mason, P.A., 1984. Upper echelons: the organization as a reflection of its top managers. Academy of Management Review 9, 193–206.

Hanks, S.H., Watson, C.J., Jansen, E., Chandler, G.N., 1993. Tightening the life-cycle construct: a taxonomic study of growth stage configurations in high-technology organizations. Entrepreneurship Theory and Practice, 5–29 (Winter).

Hannan, M.T., Freeman, J., 1984. Structural inertia and organizational change. American Sociological Review 49, 149–164.

Hannan, M.T., Freeman, J., 1989. Organizational Ecology. Harvard University Press, Cambridge, MA.

Hansen, M.T., 1999. The search-transfer problem: the role of weak ties in sharing knowledge across organization subunits. Administrative Science Quarterly 44 (1), 82–111.

Heneman III, H.G., Berkley, R.A., 1999. Applicant attraction practices and outcomes among small businesses. Journal of Small Business Management 37, 53–74.

Heneman, R.L., Tansky, J.W., 2002. Human resource management models for entrepreneurial opportunity: existing knowledge and new directions. In: Katz, J., Welbourne, T.M. (Eds.), Managing People in Entrepreneurial Organizations, Advances in Entrepreneurship, Firm Emergence and Growth, vol. 5. JAI Press Inc., Greenwich, CT, pp. 55–82.

Heneman III, H.G., Judge, T.A., Heneman, R.L., 1994. Staffing Organization. McGraw-Hill, WI.

Heneman, R.L., Tansky, J.W., Camp, S.M., 2000. Human Resource management practices in small and medium-sized enterprises: unanswered questions and future research perspectives. Entrepreneurship Theory and Practice 25 (1), 11–26.

Hite, J.M., Hesterly, W.S., 2001. The evolution of firm networks: from emergence to early growth of the firm. Strategic Management Journal 22, 275–286.

Hornsby, J.S., Kuratko, D.F., 1990. Human resource management in small business: critical issues for the 1990s. Journal of Small Business Management 28 (3), 9–18.

Johnson, D.E., Bishop, K., 2002. Performance in fast-growth firms: the behavioral and role demands of the founder throughout the firm's development. In: Katz, J.A., Welbourne, T.M. (Eds.), Managing People in Entrepreneurial Organizations, Advances in Entrepreneurship, Firm Emergence and Growth, vol. 5. JAI Press Inc., Greenwich, CT, pp. 1–22.

Jones, G.R., George, J.M., 1998. The experience and evolution of trust: implications for cooperation and teamwork. Academy of Management Review 23 (3), 531–546.

Kamm, J.B., Nurick, A.J., 1993. The stages of team venture formation: a decision-making model. Entrepreneurship Theory and Practice, 17–27 (Winter).

Katz, J.A., Welbourne, T.M. (Eds.), 2002. Managing People in Entrepreneurial Organizations, Introduction, Advances in Entrepreneurship, Firm Emergence and Growth, vol. 5. JAI Press Inc., Greenwich, CT.

Katz, J.A., Aldrich, H.E., Welbourne, T.M., Williams, P.M., 2000. Guest editor's comments: special issue on human resource management and the SME: toward a new synthesis. Entrepreneurship Theory and Practice 25 (1), 7–10.

Krackhardt, D., 1992. The strength of strong ties: the importance of philos in organizations. In: Nohria, N., Ecckes, R.G. (Eds.), Networks and Organizations: Structure, Form, and Action. Harvard Business School Press, Boston, MA, pp. 216–239.

Kristof, A.L., 1996. Person–organization fit: an integrative review of its conceptualization, measurement, and implications. Personnel Psychology 49 (1), 1–49.

Lepak, D.P., Snell, S.A., 1999. The human resource architecture: toward a theory of human capital allocation and development. Academy of Management Review 24 (1), 31–48.

Lepak, D.P., Snell, S.A., 2002. Examining the human resource architecture: the relationships among human capital, employment, and human resource configurations. Journal of Management 28 (4), 517–543.

Leung, A., 2003. Different ties for different needs — recruitment practices of entrepreneurial firms at different developmental phases. Human Resource Management 42 (4), 303–320.

Markman, G.D., Baron, R.A., 2002. Individual differences and the pursuit of new ventures: a model of person–entrepreneurship fit. In: Katz, J.A., Welbourne, T.M. (Eds.), Managing People in Entrepreneurial Organizations, Advances in Entrepreneurship, Firm Emergence and Growth, vol. 5. JAI Press Inc., Greenwich, CT, pp. 23–54.

Miles, R.E., Snow, C.C., 1978. Organizational Structure, Strategy, and Process. McGraw-Hill, New York.

Miles, R.E., Snow, C.C., 1984. Designing strategic human resources systems. Organizational Dynamics 13, 36–52.

Miller, D., 1981. Toward a new contingency approach: the search for organizational gestalts. Journal of Management Studies 18 (1), 1–26.

Miller, D., 1991. The Icarus Paradox: How Exceptional Companies Bring About Their Own Downfall. Harper, New York.

Nightingale, D.V., Toulouse, J.M., 1977. Toward a multilevel congruence theory of organization. Administrative Science Quarterly 22, 264–280.

O'Reilly, C.A., Chatman, J., Caldwell, D.E., 1991. People and organizational culture: a profile comparison approach to assessing person–organization fit. Academy of Management Journal 34, 487–516.

Pelled, L.H., Eisenhardt, K.M., Xin, K.R., 1999. Exploring the black box: an analysis of work group diversity conflict, and performance. Administrative Science Quarterly 44 (1), 1–28.

Ranger-Moore, J., 1997. Bigger may be better, but is older wiser? Organizational age and size in the New York life insurance industry. American Sociological Review 62, 903–920.

Sarasvathy, S.D., 2001. Causation and effectuation: toward a theoretical shift from economic inevitability to entrepreneurial contingency. Academy of Management Review 26 (2), 243–263.

Schneider, B., 2001. Fit about fit. Applied Psychology: An International Review 50 (1), 141–152.

Schneider, B., Kristof-Brown, A., Goldstein, H.W., Smith, D.B., 1997. What is this thing called fit? In: Aderson, N., Herriot, P. (Eds.), International Handbook of Selection and Assessment, pp. 393–412.

Schneider, B., Smith, D.B., Taylor, S., Fleenor, J., 1998. Personality and organization: a test of the homogeneity of personality hypothesis. Journal of Applied Psychology 83 (3), 462–470.

Schneider, B., Smith, D.B., Paul, M.C., 2001. P–E fit and the attraction–selection–attrition model of organizational functioning: introduction and overview. In: Erez, M., Kleinbeck, U., Thierry, H. (Eds.), Work Motivation in the Context of a Globalizing Economic. , pp. 231–246.

Shane, S., Cable, D., 2002. Network ties, reputation, and the financing of new ventures. Management Science 48 (3), 364–381.

Simons, T., Pelled, L.H., Smith, K.A., 1999. Making use of differences: diversity, debate, and decision comprehensiveness in top management teams. Academy of Management Journal 42 (6), 662–673.

Smith, K.G., Mitchell, T.R., Summer, C.E., 1985. Top level management priorities in different stages of the organizational life cycle. Academy of Management Journal 28 (4), 799–820.

Stearns, T.M., 1996. Strategic alliances and performance of high technology new firms. Frontiers of Entrepreneurship Research, 268–281.

Stinchcombe, A.L., 1965. Social structure and organizations. In: March, J.G. (Ed.), Handbook of Organizations. Rand McNally, Chicago, pp. 142–193.

Tosi, H.L., Slocum, J.W., 1984. Contingency theory: some suggested directions. Journal of Management 10 (1), 9–26

Uzzi, B., 1996. The sources and consequences of embeddedness for the economic performance of organizations: the network effect. American Sociological Review 61, 498–674.

Vandenberghe, C., 1999. Organizational culture, person–organization fit, and turnover: a replication in the health care industry. Journal of Organizational Behavior 20, 175–184.

Van de Ven, A.H., Drazin, R., 1985. The concept of fit in contingency theory. In: Staw, B.M., Cummings, L.L. (Eds.), Research in Organizational Behavior, vol. 7. JAI Press, Greenwich, CT, pp. 333–365.

Williamson, I.O., 2000. Employer legitimacy and recruitment success in small businesses. Entrepreneurship Theory and Practice 25 (1), 27–42.

Williamson, I.O., Cable, D.M., Aldrich, H.E., 2002. Smaller but not necessarily weaker: how small business can overcome barriers to recruitment. In: Katz, J.A., Welbourne, T.M. (Eds.), Managing People in Entrepreneurial Organizations, Advances in Entrepreneurship, Firm Emergence and Growth, vol. 5, pp. 83–106.

Wolcott, H.F., 1990. Writing up qualitative research. Qualitative Research Methods Series, vol. 20. Sage Publications.

Wright, P.M., Dunford, B.B., Snell, S.A., 2001. Human resources and the resource based view of the firm. Journal of Management 27, 701–721.

Yin, R.K., 1984. Case Study Research: Design and Methods. Sage Publications.

[12]

° *Academy of Management Journal*
2002, Vol. 45, No. 3, 818–826.

ENTREPRENEURIAL TRANSITIONS:
FACTORS INFLUENCING FOUNDER DEPARTURE

WARREN BOEKER
RUSHI KARICHALIL
University of Washington

Research in entrepreneurship and life cycle theories of the firm have both suggested that new ventures may outgrow the managerial capabilities of their founding teams, at which point the founders may be replaced by professional managers. This study explored factors affecting founder departure. Results indicate that founder departure increases with firm size, decreases with founder ownership and board membership, and has a U-shaped relationship with firm growth. Founders who work in research and development or who are chief executives are also less likely to leave.

Organizational researchers studying new ventures have noted a critical difference between starting a successful firm and managing a successful firm. New ventures are often founded by entrepreneurs who are interested in the initial development of a product or a market but have very limited managerial interests or capacities (Willard, Krueger, & Feeser, 1992). As the ventures become more established, these entrepreneurs may be forced to focus closely on general management tasks—tasks for which they may have no natural proclivity. Theorists studying the life cycle of start-up firms have maintained that management styles and capabilities must change as a firm evolves from an entrepreneurial focus on creating a market opportunity to operation as an established business (Rubenson & Gupta, 1992).

The phenomenon of an entrepreneurial founder being replaced by a "professional" manager has also been widely cited in the business and popular press. Auletta (1998) pointed to several examples of entrepreneurial start-ups in which founders resigned from their firms to be replaced by more experienced managers when it appeared that the skills of the founders did not meet the evolving needs of the firms (examples include Internet start-ups such as Pointcast, Razorfish, and eBay). Despite the wealth of anecdotal descriptions of new ventures in which the original founders have been replaced, there have not been theoretically grounded, empirically rigorous studies of the specific factors influencing founder departure.

In this study, we explored the causes of founder departure among semiconductor start-ups from 1983 through 1999 to better understand the process by which new ventures manage the transition to established firms. Although it is well documented that founders often have difficulty handing over control of their companies to professional managers (Adizes, 1999), it is often difficult to sort out the degree to which founders may have been "encouraged" to leave by boards and investors rather than leaving voluntarily. Our study investigated firm and individual characteristics that influence the likelihood of departure among founders rather than the specific motivations (voluntary or not) of each founder. In this study, we first examine how founder departure is influenced by the size and growth of a firm and then examine the effects of firm governance, including the influence of ownership and board composition. We conclude by focusing on individual differences among founders that may increase their likelihood of departure.

THEORY

Past research has demonstrated that many founders of companies have difficulty managing new ventures beyond their start-up stage. Hambrick and Crozier (1985) found that firms that had successfully evolved from start-up ventures to established firms had replaced at least some founders, whereas firms that had left their initial founding teams in place had much greater difficulty managing the transition. As these authors noted, "The finance vice-president who was adept at establishing controls and reports [in a new venture] may not be proficient at the very different tasks of cultivating the financial community, managing currency fluctuations, or dealing with complex tax problems" (1985: 35). As Daily and Dalton (1992) ob-

Thanks to Eric Abrahamson, Jerry Goodstein, Anil Gupta, and Donald Hambrick for help, ideas, and insights. Much thanks to Michael Song and the Center for Technology Entrepreneurship at the University of Washington, and to a Dempsey Faculty Fellowship to the first author, for funding of this project.

served, the transition from an entrepreneurial management style to a professional management style almost inevitably occurs as a firm outgrows the expertise of the entrepreneur or founder. This transition may lead to the "leadership crisis" described by Greiner (1972) and other life cycle theorists (Cetro, Covin, Daily, & Dalton, 2001; Hanks, 1990) that occurs when a firm moves from its earliest start-up stage to a growth stage requiring professional management and delegation.

Life cycle theorists have been less clear in identifying the specific causal factors that influence when new ventures will undergo this transition. Reflecting work on human development, some have viewed organizations as progressing through specific developmental stages and challenges as they grow older and have argued, from this perspective, that 'new ventures make transitions as they age (Adizes, 1999; Greiner, 1972; Hanks, 1990). Other theorists have seen firm size and growth as requiring new ventures to replace their entrepreneurial founders with professional managers (Hanks, 1990; Wasserman, 2001). Flamholtz (1990), for example, argued that once a size threshold is reached, the value of the founders to a new venture is severely limited, and firm control should generally pass to professional managers. Following these two sets of causal arguments, we first account for the effects of firm size and age on founder departure before including other covariates:

Hypothesis 1a. There is a positive relationship between new venture size and founder departure.

Hypothesis 1b. There is a positive relationship between new venture age and founder departure.

Beyond the absolute effects of size, the effects of change in size—firm growth—are also critically important determinants of founder departure. In past work on top management change, researchers have argued that the primary motivation for managerial change is the inability of a current top management team to meet expectations related to firm growth (Finkelstein & Hambrick, 1996). In new ventures, which are typically focused on growth more than on earnings or profitability (Boeker, 1992; Eisenhardt & Schoonhoven, 1990), low growth may serve as an indication that the founders do not have the correct set of skills to manage the firms. Low growth or decline is seen as equating with (or resulting from) poor performance, and past research has contained the argument that poor performance in new ventures may lead to founder departure (Blair, 2001).

Although lack of growth may lead stakeholders and other of a firm's constituencies to question the managerial abilities of the company's founders, rapid growth may create a greater need for new managers with different capabilities, a need that may also lead to founder replacement (Wasserman, 2001). Firms that are growing at a more rapid rate may need to more proactively add new sets of managerial competencies and capabilities (Flamholtz, 1990), making the skills and capabilities of the founders more rapidly obsolete. Thus, the likelihood of founder departure may be significantly higher in rapidly growing firms.

Taken together, these two sets of ideas present something of a paradox. Is founder departure more likely when a firm is growing rapidly and the need for professional management is most urgent, or when the firm is growing more slowly or declining and there is pressure for founder replacement? Given the different dynamics involved in the two cases, we posit that both perspectives may be correct and argue that both fast growth and slow growth may lead to founder departure, a situation resulting in a U-shaped relationship between new venture growth and the departure of founders.

Hypothesis 2. The relationship between new venture growth and founder departure is U-shaped. New ventures are more likely to experience founder departure under conditions of high firm growth and under conditions of low firm growth.

The Role of Power and Influence

Life cycle perspectives focus predominant attention on the influences of age, size, and firm growth on the need for a new set of managerial and leadership skills in new ventures. Beyond these factors, the control and governance of the new ventures critically influence whether founders stay or leave. Given the important role that a firm's founders play in its initial conceptualization and start-up, they are often more entrenched and less likely to leave than are the top managers in established firms (Cetro et al., 2001; Flamholtz, 1990). Daily and Dalton (1992) noted that the personal stakes of founders in the businesses that they created can be much stronger than those of professional managers. Rubenson (1989) argued that the importance of its founders to a new venture and their stronger attachment to the firm makes them less likely to cede control. This may be especially true if founders can maintain influence through ownership or control over the firm's board (Rubenson & Gupta, 1996). We investigated these specific dimensions in our study.

Founder ownership. Agency theorists have argued that managerial ownership tends to insulate managers and protect their positions within firms (Jensen & Meckling, 1976). Ownership can permit managers to act opportunistically and safeguard them from possible encroachment by new managers who might usurp their power or position (Williamson, 1975). Frederickson, Hambrick, and Baumrin similarly noted that "as an executive's stockholdings increase, it becomes less likely that he or she will be replaced" (1988: 265).

If the founders hold a significant ownership stake in a new venture, the influence derived from their ownership position may protect their ability to remain in place and lower the likelihood of their departure. Founders may feel strongly that they are quite competent at running the new venture and may resist any suggestion that they should step aside (Flamholtz, 1990). Nonfounder owners (particularly outside owners) may have fewer qualms about founder departure and may be more willing to replace founders with new managers who have a better set of professional management skills. Outside owners are likely to have fewer personal or relational ties to founders than inside owners and may be more focused on optimizing firm performance (Useem, 1984).

Hypothesis 3. New ventures with a higher proportion of founder ownership have lower founder turnover.

Ownership concentration. In addition to founder ownership, the extent to which ownership is dispersed or concentrated may affect the influence of the owners. An organization in which one owner controls 80 percent of shares may be significantly different from one in which four owners each owns 20 percent or from one in which one owner holds 50 percent of shares and three other owners each hold 10 percent. When the ownership of a new venture is fairly concentrated, owners often exert a tighter and more proactive control over decisions around top management staffing (Flamholtz, 1990). This critical role played by owners means that they are likely to be very involved in decisions involving changes to the top management team, especially the founders. Founder departure may be lower in firms with more dispersed ownership, since concentrated ownership may lead to more centralized, less participative, decision making and increase the likelihood that founders will leave.

Hypothesis 4. New ventures with more concentrated ownership will have more founder departures.

Board of directors. The composition of a firm's board of directors, particularly the extent to which it is composed of outsiders (people who are not employed by the firm), has an important influence on its ability to carry out its governance responsibilities effectively (Ocasio, 1993). Agency theorists agree that a board can only govern and monitor effectively if it is independent (Fama, 1980). Outsiders can fulfill this governance role more effectively since inside directors' objectivity may be impaired by their dual roles as full-time managers and directors (Mizruchi, 1983). Managers in firms with insider-dominated boards may compromise the best interests of the firms to serve their own interests, such as preserving their own positions in the organization or playing a more powerful role in succession decisions (Zajac & Westphal, 1996). Similarly, founders of firms with higher proportions of inside directors may maintain more power and be less likely to depart.

Hypothesis 5. New ventures with higher proportions of inside board members will have fewer founder departures.

Individual Differences among Founders

Individual differences among founders may have an important influence on the likelihood that they remain in top management positions. Founders from specific functional backgrounds, those with greater industry experience, and those who are more influential may be less likely to leave the new ventures they started.

Functional responsibility. The functional responsibility of founders to a large degree determines how well situated they are to provide input into organizational decisions. It is likely that different functional areas within new ventures will vary in the extent to which they are involved in critical decisions affecting the early growth of the firms. Hambrick (1981) argued that top managers in research and development are especially critical in technologically intensive industries (such as the semiconductor industry examined here) since innovative products provide an important and sustainable competitive advantage to such firms. Because of the continued importance of research and development to the future success of new ventures, founders with these responsibilities are predicted to be less likely to leave.

Hypothesis 6. Founders working in research and development functions are less likely to leave new ventures than founders from other functional backgrounds.

Industry experience. Past work on entrepreneurship suggests that new ventures develop problems as they grow because founders have a limited ability to adapt to the increasingly complex needs of the organizations (Rubenson & Gupta, 1992). Founders who have little industry experience may be more limited in the range of expertise and competence they can draw upon as their firms continue to expand (Wasserman, 2001). As a result, they may be less able to spot trends or generate a range of possible alternatives from which to make the best possible business decisions. Executives with long experience in an industry bring detailed knowledge about how that industry operates (Eisenhardt & Schoonhoven, 1990) and may be more likely to have worked at firms that were larger or have faced issues pertinent to older or larger organizations, and thus they possess more valuable experience.

Hypothesis 7. Founders with more industry experience are less likely to leave new ventures than founders with less industry experience.

Chief executive. Formal hierarchical position is an indication of authority and power and may be a useful indicator of how much authority managers have in their current firms (Finkelstein, 1992). Other things being equal, higher-ranking executives are likely to have more influence in decision making than lower-ranking managers and will be more critical to the successful running of the business. In this study of founding teams, we could only differentiate between two levels of founders, the chief executive and the founders reporting to the chief executive. Given this simple dichotomy, we would expect founding chief executives to have more influence and be less likely to depart. This notion is supported by past work on chief executives and top management teams that has demonstrated that chief executive turnover occurs less frequently than top management turnover (Finkelstein & Hambrick, 1996). Alternatively, in cases of poor performance, owners may decide to replace a firm's chief executive as the firm's figurehead, hoping that this change will signal the seriousness of their efforts to restore the firm's performance. However, for most new ventures, we believe that the chief executive will have more power and influence than other founders and will be less likely to depart.

Hypothesis 8. A founding chief executive is less likely to leave than other founders.

METHODS

The hypotheses were tested on 78 semiconductor producers founded between 1983 and 1991 and located in the Santa Clara–San Jose area of California (Silicon Valley). Data on these firms were collected from three of the four largest market research firms serving the semiconductor industry. The sample of 78 firms includes most of the semiconductor firms started in the Silicon Valley area during this time period (Schoonhoven, Eisenhardt, & Lyman, 1990) and all of the firms that were followed by the market research firms over the period. Information was also obtained from articles in the electronics and business press and from other public documents. When we could not get particular information from publicly available sources, we interviewed top executives at the firms with missing information.

We studied these firms for the first seven years after their foundings; as in other studies of firm founding, founding was defined as the date of incorporation. This seven-year period was chosen after consulting with industry analysts and venture capitalists who argued that after three to five years, a new venture is no longer considered a start-up and that after seven years, it is thought of as an established company. Four of the 78 firms in the sample failed within the first seven years; information on these firms was included for as long as they survived. The failed firms did not vary significantly from the remainder of the sample along any independent variables except firm growth.

We chose to study a single industry to control for potentially confounding interindustry effects and because the longitudinal data available on these firms were comprehensive, particularly for the variables of interest in the study. The data used to examine the hypotheses were available quarterly; we used the quarterly observations to better represent the assumption of continuous time in estimating our longitudinal models.

Measures and Model

Independent and dependent variables. For the measure of *founder turnover*, founders were identified as the set of top managers reporting to the firm's chief executive (and including the chief executive) at the time of a firm's founding. For the 78 semiconductor firms, there were a total of 431 founders at risk of departure.

Firm size was measured quarterly as: (1) sales (using a logarithm) and (2) number of employees.

Earlier studies of top management turnover in established firms suggest founder turnover declines over time (Miller, 1991). *Firm age* was measured as the number of quarters since a company's incorporation.

Firm growth was measured as both employee

822   *Academy of Management Journal*   June

growth and sales growth. Employee growth was the proportionate increase in employees in the two quarters preceding data collection. Sales growth was measured by comparing a firm's revenue growth to revenue growth for other firms in the semiconductor industry competing in the same product categories over the prior two quarters.[1] Using data from the market research firms, we identified 20 specific segments that comprised the product-markets within the semiconductor industry (following Eisenhardt and Schoonhoven [1990]) and identified the proportion of sales in each product category for each firm. We then weighted revenue growth for the firm by the specific product categories the firm competed in and compared it to the average revenue growth rate in that category for other firms in the sample. Firm growth was then measured as change in revenues over the prior two quarters.[2] *Founder ownership* was assessed as the proportion of total firm ownership held by the founders of a company. *Ownership concentration* was the proportion of ownership held by the top four owners of a firm. *Board insiders* was the proportion of board members on who were employed by the firm. *Research and development* was coded as a dummy variable if the founder's primary responsibilities in the new venture were in research and development. *Industry experience* was a founder's number of years of employment in the semiconductor industry prior to founding the new venture. *Chief executive* was a dummy variable coded 1 for each founder who was the chief executive.

Control variables. Organizations were differentiated on the basis of whether they were publicly or privately held. Given the varied findings of past research on the effects of public ownership on succession (Useem, 1984), no specific predictions were made regarding the likelihood of founder departure in public versus private firms. *Public ownership* was coded as 1 if a firm was publicly held and 0 if the firm was privately held.

We included *top management team size* in the analysis of founder departure to control for any variation in turnover that was the result of the

overall size of a team (Boeker, 1992). For example, larger teams may have more individuals with a wider variety of backgrounds and expertise, so that the departure of an individual manager has less effect on a new venture and, thereby, size increases the likelihood of founder departure. Top management team size was measured as the number of managers reporting directly to the chief executive.

The growth and decline of a top management team may have different effects on the likelihood that founders depart (Finkelstein & Hambrick, 1996). New ventures may expand their top teams to bring in individuals with different managerial capabilities. This growth may, in turn, lead to greater turnover, when founders' talents do not match the requirements of the firms as they grow and newly hired managers replace the founders. Alternatively, firms with shrinking top management teams may be more likely to experience founder departure. Given these potentially contradictory effects, we make no predictions for the effects of *top management team growth* on founder departure; it was measured as the proportionate change in the size of the top management team reporting to the chief executive over the two quarters prior to data collection.

Firms competing in periods of rapid industry growth may need to update and adjust the capabilities of their top management teams more frequently, (Virany, Tushman, & Romanelli, 1992), a process that would lead to greater turnover of founders. *Industry growth* was measured as change in sales of the overall (semiconductor) market over the prior two quarters.

We included *board size* to control for any governance issues that might arise from the size and the relative cohesiveness of a board. Past research has shown that larger boards may be more heterogeneous and less likely to take action against incumbent managers (Mizruchi, 1983). Board size was measured as number of directors.

Modeling procedures. We tested our dependent variable, the likelihood of a founder leaving a new venture, by using a hazard rate model to specify continuous-time event history analysis for all founders. The models were estimated using maximum likelihood as implemented in the statistical program TDA (Blossfeld & Rohwer, 1995). TDA (transition data analysis) allows estimation of models with time-varying coefficients and takes "right-censoring" of data (owing, for example, to firm failure) into account. We used the "piecewise" exponential specification with our quarterly observations because we made no assumptions about duration dependence that would require a specific parametric distribution.

---

[1] We also examined three- and four-quarter periods of revenue growth, which showed the same results.

[2] Because all firms start with no sales, we began our measure of sales growth four quarters after incorporation. Therefore, the first two quarters of performance we examined would occur in the fifth and sixth quarters after founding. Because practically all of the founders stayed with their firms for six quarters (only 17 of the 431 founders left sooner), performance information was available for practically all of the founders in our sample.

2002   *Boeker and Karichalil*   823

TABLE 1
Descriptive Statistics and Correlations[a]

Variable[b]	Means	s.d.	1	2	3	4	5	6	7	8	9	10	11	12	13	14	15	16
1. Founder departure	0.01	0.01																
2. Sales	15.82	9.88	.05															
3. Employees	1.53	0.57	.14	.35														
4. Firm age	18.80	9.23	−.05	.26	.23													
5. Sales growth	0.13	0.11	−.13	−.09	−.06	−.12												
6. Employee growth	0.11	0.05	−.10	−.06	−.05	−.16	.21											
7. Founder ownership	0.32	0.11	−.20	−.08	−.10	−.13	−.07	.11										
8. Ownership concentration	0.15	0.06	−.03	−.04	−.05	−.16	.09	.08	.15									
9. Board insiders	0.43	0.08	−.16	−.17	−.12	−.10	.07	.02	.36	.22								
10. Research & development	0.28	0.10	−.21	−.04	−.03	−.06	.02	.05	.05	.03	.03							
11. Industry experience	9.27	4.18	−.10	.11	.13	.13	.12	−.09	−.07	−.07	.10	.03						
12. Chief executive	0.19	0.05	−.26	−.03	−.05	−.07	.01	.09	.04	.05	−.08	.02	.24					
13. Public ownership	0.52	0.39	.13	.31	.28	.13	−.21	−.18	−.07	−.11	−.12	−.05	.10	.00				
14. Top management team size	5.38	1.10	.10	.22	.20	.18	.11	−.08	−.07	−.09	−.09	−.06	.07	−.02	.15			
15. Top management team growth	0.02	0.00	−.12	.07	.08	−.09	.14	.12	.06	.03	.06	.03	−.01	.04	−.08	−.09		
16. Industry growth	0.11	0.07	.09	.10	.08	−.01	.27	.20	−.08	.01	−.07	.02	.09	−.04	−.08	.05	.08	
17. Board size	7.26	2.33	−.08	.17	.13	−.07	.11	−.13	−.10	−.18	−.19	.01	.05	−.02	.12	.15	.05	.13

[a] All correlations above .12 are significant at $p < .05$.
[b] Sales is a logarithm. Employees is measured in thousands; firm age, in quarters.

RESULTS

Table 1 shows means, standard deviations, and correlations among the variables, and Table 2 presents the results of our longitudinal models. Model 1 in Table 2 shows the effects of the control variables on the likelihood of founder departure. The effects of both public ownership and top management team size were significant and positive, and the effect of top management growth was significant and negative. Public firms may face greater outside scrutiny and may be more willing to replace founders or encourage them to leave than privately held firms (Useem, 1984). A larger top management team may have more individuals with a wider variety of backgrounds and expertise, so that the departure of an individual founder may be more likely since it may have less effect on the overall organization. Finally, new ventures that are increasing the size of their top management teams may be less likely to have current top managers (including the founders) leave.[3] The effects of the other controls were not significant.

The results of our hypotheses can be divided into the effects of three sets of variables on founder

departure: (1) firm size, age, and growth, (2) ownership and board characteristics, and (3) individual differences among founders. In regard to the effects of size, age, and firm growth, Hypothesis 1a argues that as new ventures increase in size, the skills of the original founders may become less appropriate than they were when they founded their ventures, leading to a greater level of founder departure. We captured firm size both as sales (logged) and as the number of employees. As is shown in model 2 of Table 2, Hypothesis 1a was supported when size was measured as the number of employees, but not when size was measured as sales. Hypothesis 1b, which draws from life cycle theory to argue that firm age will influence founder departure, was not supported in model 2. Hypothesis 2 predicts that both fast-growing and slow-growing new ventures will have the most founder departures, a pattern resulting in a U-shaped relationship between growth and founder departure. As in Hypothesis 1, growth was measured separately as sales growth and employee growth. The predicted U-shaped relationship was confirmed using both measures, as indicated in model 2 of Table 2, where the direct effect of growth is negative, and the effect of the quadratic term (growth squared) is positive for both sales growth and employee growth.

We next added the effects of governance and control on founder departure in model 3 of Table 2. Hypothesis 3 includes the effects of founders' ownership on the likelihood of their exit; results in

---

[3] We also ran a separate model, including all of our hypothesized and control variables, for the departure of nonfounding managers. Our results showed no significant effects of firm size or high growth, two of the specific variables argued to influence the need for different types of managers in new ventures.

824 *Academy of Management Journal* June

TABLE 2
Maximum-Likelihood Estimates of Founder Departure[a]

Variable	Model 2	Model 3	Model 4
Independent sales[b]		.23 (.15)	.22 (.16)	.22 (.15)
Employees		.38* (.16)	.38* (.17)	.37* (.16)
Firm age		.09 (.08)	.09 (.08)	.09 (.08)
Sales growth		−.85* (.41)	−.83* (.41)	−.84* (.41)
Sales growth squared		.30** (.12)	.30** (.12)	.29** (.12)
Employee growth		−.60* (.28)	−.59* (.28)	.58* (.28)
Employee growth squared		.40* (.20)	.39* (.20)	.38* (.19)
Founder ownership			−.27* (.12)	−.24* (.12)
Ownership concentration			.09 (.06)	.08 (.05)
Board insiders			−.22* (.11)	−.21* (.11)
Research & development				−.46* (.20)
Industry experience				.12 (.16)
Chief executive				−.93* (.40)
Control				
Public ownership	.36* (.16)	.34* (.15)	.32* (.15)	.30* (.15)
Top management team size	.31* (.13)	.29* (.12)	.27* (.12)	.27* (.12)
Top management team growth	.11* (.05)	−.09* (.04)	−.09* (.04)	−.09* (.04)
Industry growth	−.07 (.05)	−.06 (.05)	−.05 (.04)	−.05 (.04)
Board size	.03 (.02)	.02 (.01)	.02 (.02)	.02 (.02)
Log-likelihood	−376.14	−348.78	−338.65	−334.26

[a] Standard errors are in parentheses.
[b] Logarithm.
 * $p < .05$
 ** $p < .01$

model 3 support our argument for lower levels of departure in firms where founders retain a greater share of ownership. The results for Hypothesis 4, which examines the effect of ownership concentration, show no effect on founder exits. Finally, Hypothesis 5 tests the influence of board composition on founder turnover, demonstrating that companies whose boards had higher proportions of insiders were less likely to have founders depart and confirming the hypothesis.

Finally, we investigated whether individual differences among founders affected the likelihood of their departure. Hypothesis 6 predicts that founders working in research or development functions would be less likely to leave new ventures. This hypothesis is confirmed in model 4 of Table 2, which indicates that founders with research and development responsibilities were less likely to depart. Hypothesis 7 argues that founders with greater industry experience might be less likely to depart since they are likely to have a broader and more comprehensive set of relevant skills that may be more valuable as firms grow larger. Results in model 4, however, demonstrate no support for this hypothesis. Finally, Hypothesis 8 predicts that the founder who was the original chief executive of a new venture will be less likely to leave than other founders, a prediction that was supported in model 4 of Table 2.

DISCUSSION

This study links concepts from life cycle models of firm development to the need for changes in managerial capabilities as new ventures evolve. Our findings point to two sets of causal factors that affect founder departure in opposite ways: The size and growth (very high and very low, respectively) of a new venture accelerate the rate of founder departure. These pressures, in turn, appear to be ameliorated by the participation of founders as owners and board members, as well as by their individual positions and functional responsibilities.

One of the most interesting findings of our study concerns the relationship between new venture growth and founder turnover. Firms growing very rapidly appear to have a greater need for new sets of managerial and professional skills that the founders may not possess, resulting in a greater likelihood founders will exit. These findings present an interesting contrast to studies of top management succession in established firms, which have generally viewed rapid firm growth as an affirmation of the approaches taken by the firms' top managers, an affirmation that in turn lowers top management turnover (Finkelstein & Hambrick, 1996). We also found stronger effects for both size and growth when they were measured in terms of employees rather than sales. These results

2002 _Boeker and Karichalil_ 825

may indicate that the complexity of leadership increases more directly with growth in the number of employees than with growth in sales.

Our findings on the role of founder ownership and board participation provide an interesting extension to agency theorizing. According to agency theory, given separation of a firm's ownership and control, an effective monitoring mechanism (such as a vigilant board) is required to control managers' opportunism, an assertion that is consistent with our hypotheses. The higher levels of insider ownership observed in our sample of new ventures may represent a situation in which ownership and control are not separate, and agency perspectives may not apply in the same way to new ventures as to established firms. Participation by founders on a board and through equity ownership appear to be important sources of power and influence that permit founders to better protect their own positions as a new venture evolves.

Finally, our results demonstrate that some founders (those with R&D backgrounds and/or the chief executive) may be more critical for a new venture to retain. These findings have interesting potential implications for work from a resource-based perspective; previous researchers taking this perspective have argued for the view that the specialization of management skills to the critical challenges of a firm are a source of sustainable competitive advantage (Castanias & Helfat, 1991).

An important limitation of this study is that we could not verify the specific motivation leading individual founders to leave the firms they helped start. Our theoretical assumption, borne out by the empirical findings of our study, is that founders appear to leave when a new venture has outgrown the managerial capabilities of its founding team. However, we cannot definitively determine from our data the precise, individual-level processes that result in a specific founder's decision to leave. Uncertainty about founders' intentions should not diminish the importance of the findings on founder turnover, which are not empirically dependent on the motivations of specific founders. The perspective of this study is that specific firm and individual characteristics influence the likelihood that founders remain with new ventures, and our results demonstrate that the relationship between firm and individual characteristics and founder tenure is not random.

Given that semiconductor producers compete in riskier technologies, there may be greater uncertainty concerning the future direction of these firms, which may in turn provide greater impetus for founding team turnover than exists in less technologically intense industries and may limit the generalizability of our findings. Furthermore, the ability to generalize our findings across global markets presents an important potential limitation. Other countries may not have as well-developed a market or infrastructure for new ventures, or a tradition of governing board and ownership independence, both of which may influence founder departure.

A better understanding of appropriate managerial profiles as new ventures grow and develop could serve to more closely integrate current work in entrepreneurship, strategy, and human resources. Future research should investigate in more detail the interplay between the departure of founding managers and the addition of new managers to the new ventures that the founders exit, including the types of new managers brought in and the skills and competencies they appear to bring to the companies. Studying the factors leading to founder departure, especially under varying levels of organizational performance, can provide important insights into the roles of firm control and individual differences in limiting or encouraging change in the top management of new ventures.

REFERENCES

Adizes, I. 1999. _Managing corporate life cycles._ Englewood Cliffs, NJ: Prentice-Hall.

Auletta, K. 1998. The last sure thing. _New Yorker,_ November 9: 52.

Blair, J. 2001. Razorfish's founders are expected to step down. _New York Times,_ May 3: D1.

Blossfeld, H.-P., & Rohwer, G. 1995. _Techniques of event history modeling._ Hillsdale, NJ: Erlbaum.

Boeker, W. 1992. Power and managerial dismissal: Scapegoating at the top. _Administrative Science Quarterly,_ 37: 400–421.

Castanias, R. P. & Helfat, C. E. 1991. Managerial resources and rents. _Journal of Management,_ 17: 155–171.

Cetro, S. T., Covin, J. G., Daily, C. M., & Dalton, D. R. 2001. Wealth and the effects of founder management among IPO-stage new ventures. _Strategic Management Journal,_ 22: 641–658.

Daily, C. M., & Dalton, D. R. 1992. Financial performance of founder-managed versus professionally-managed corporations. _Journal of Small Business Management,_ 30(2): 25–34.

Eisenhardt, K. M., & Schoonhoven, C. 1990. Organizational growth: Linking founding team, strategy, and growth among U.S. semiconductor ventures, 1978–1988. _Administrative Science Quarterly,_ 35: 504–529.

Fama, E. 1980. Agency problems and the theory of the firm. _Journal of Political Economy,_ 88: 288–307.

826 *Academy of Management Journal* June

Finkelstein, S. 1992. Power in top management teams: Dimensions, measurement, and validation. *Academy of Management Journal*, 35: 505–538.

Finkelstein, S., & Hambrick, D. C. 1996. *Strategic leadership: Top executives and their effect on organizations*. St. Paul: West.

Flamholtz, E. 1990. *Growing pains.* Greenwich, CT: JAI Press.

Frederickson, J. W., Hambrick, D. C., & Baumrin, S. 1988. A model of CEO dismissal. *Academy of Management Review*, 13: 255–270.

Greiner, L. E. 1972. Evolution and revolution as organizations grow. *Harvard Business Review*, 50(4): 37–46.

Hambrick, D. C. 1981. Environment, strategy, and power within top-management teams. *Administrative Science Quarterly*, 26: 253–276.

Hambrick, D. C., & Crozier, L. M. 1985. Stumblers and stars in the management of rapid growth. *Journal of Business Venturing*, 1: 31–45.

Hanks, S. H. 1990. The organization life cycle: Integrating content and process. *Journal of Small Business Strategy*, 1(1): 1–12.

Jensen, M. C., & Meckling, W. H. 1976. Theory of the firm: Managerial behavior, agency costs and ownership structure. *Journal of Financial Economics*, 3: 305–360.

Mizruchi, M. 1983. Who controls whom? An examination of the relations between management and boards of directors in large American corporations. *Academy of Management Review*, 8: 426–435.

Ocasio, W. 1995. The enactment of economic adversity—A reconciliation of theories of failure-induced change and threat-rigidity. In L. L. Cummings & B. M. Staw (Eds.), *Research in organizational behavior*, vol. 17: 287–331. Greenwich, CT: JAI Press.

Rubenson, G. C. 1989. *Departure of organizational founders: Explaining variance in founder tenure, successor characteristics, successor power and future firm performance.* Doctoral dissertation, University of Maryland, College Park.

Rubenson, G. C., & Gupta, A. K. 1992. Replacing the founder: Exploding the myth of the entrepreneur's disease. *Business Horizons*, 35(6): 53–59.

Rubenson, G. C., & Gupta, A. K. 1996. The initial succession: A contingency model of founder tenure. *Entrepreneurship Theory and Practice*, 21(2): 21–35.

Schoonhoven, C. B., Eisenhardt, K., & Lyman, K. 1990. Speeding products to market: Waiting time to first product introduction in new firms. *Administrative Science Quarterly*, 35: 177–207.

Useem, M. 1984. *The inner circle.* New York: Oxford University Press.

Virany, B. Tushman, M., & Romanelli, E. 1992: Executive succession and organization outcomes in turbulent environments: An organizational learning approach. *Organization Science*, 3: 72–91.

Wasserman, N. 2001. *Founder-CEO succession and the paradox of entrepreneurial success.* Paper presented at the annual meeting of the Academy of Management, Washington, DC.

Willard, G. E., Krueger, D. A., & Feeser, H. R. 1992. In order to grow must the founder go: A comparison of performance between founder and non-founder managed high-growth manufacturing firms. *Journal of Business Venturing*, 7: 181–194.

Williamson, O. 1975. *Markets and hierarchies: Analysis and antitrust implications.* New York: Free Press.

Zajac, E., & Westphal, J. 1996. Who shall succeed? How CEO/board preferences and power affect the choice of new CEOs. *Academy of Management Journal*, 39: 64–90.

Warren Boeker *(wboeker@u.washington.edu)* is a professor of management at the University of Washington Business School. He received his Ph.D. degree from the University of California, Berkeley. His research interests are focused on the evolution of entrepreneurial organizations and effects of founder and top management power and influence on new venture strategies.

Rushi Karichalil is a doctoral student majoring in strategic management at the University of Washington Business School. His research interests include new venture strategies, corporate governance, and strategic management in transitional economies.

———Μ———

[13]

1042-2587
Copyright 2003 by
Baylor University

Entrepreneurial Founder Teams: Factors Associated with Member Entry and Exit

Deniz Ucbasaran
Andy Lockett
Mike Wright
Paul Westhead

This exploratory study provides a review of the neglected area of entrepreneurial founder team turnover. A novel distinction is made between entrepreneurial founder team member entry and team member exit. Ninety owner-managed ventures were monitored between 1990 and 2000. Presented hypotheses relating to a team's human capital were explored using multivariate logistic regression analysis. Variables associated with entry were found not to be the same as those associated with exit. The size of the founding team was significantly negatively associated with subsequent team member entry. The link between team turnover and entrepreneurial team heterogeneity was mixed. Functional heterogeneity was weakly significantly positively associated with team member entry. Heterogeneity of prior entrepreneurial experience was significantly positively associated with team member exit. In addition, family firms were significantly negatively associated with team member exit. The average age of the team was not significantly associated with team member entry or exit. Additional insights in future research may be gathered if a broader definition of team turnover (i.e., considering team member entry and exit) is considered. Practitioner awareness of the different factors associated with team member entry and exit may encourage them to provide assistance, which facilitates the team building process over time in developing firms. Promising areas for additional research are highlighted.

Introduction

Gartner et al. (1994) argued that the "entrepreneur in entrepreneurship" is typically plural, not singular. Only recently has the entrepreneurial team phenomenon received explicit attention (Ensley, Carland, & Carland, 1998, 2000; Ensley et al., 1999). Entrepreneurial founder teams (EFTs) may provide a venture with access to an array of valuable financial, social, and human capital resources (Kor & Mahoney, 2000). Each team member adds to the diversity of views and skills, and can enable the completion of complex tasks. The presence of an EFT can play a pivotal role facilitating busi-

---

Please send all correspondence to: Deniz Ucbasaran at the Nottingham University Business School, Jubilee Campus. Her e-mail address is deniz.ucbasaran@nottingham.ac.uk.

ness development and superior business performance (Roure & Madique, 1986; Kamm & Shuman, 1990; Westhead, 1995). Subsequent changes in the EFTs have been noted (Cooper & Daily, 1997). Cooper and Bruno (1977) detected that 48% of suveyed high-technology firms reported that at least one founder had left the surveyed ventures. Boyd and Gumpert (1983) found that more than two-thirds of founders starting with partners eventually dissolved ties. Further, Timmons (1990) focusing upon high-potential ventures noted that almost every new firm had lost at least one founder over a five-year period.

Changes in senior managers have been explored in studies focusing upon top management team (TMT) turnover. These studies have focused on large established firms and have explored turnover with regard to organizational strategy and performance (Hambrick & Mason, 1984; O'Reilly, Cardwell, & Barnett, 1989; Jackson et al., 1991). TMT turnover can be viewed as a strategy of adaptation linked to changing external environmental conditions (Furtado & Karan, 1990; Wiersema & Bantel, 1992, 1993). Also, TMT turnover may encourage the successful turnaround of a business (Kesner & Dalton, 1994). For example, poor business performance can preempt TMT turnover in large corporations. In addition, the announcement of changes to a company's TMT can impact its share price (Furtado & Karan, 1990).

In sharp contrast to larger established firms, the issue of management turnover has been neglected in the context of independent private firms owned by EFTs. The relationships found with regard to TMTs in larger established firms may not necessarily hold for EFTs in independent private firms. Two features of EFTs suggest that their turnover will be distinctive. First, there are important differences in ownership and control between larger established firms and newer independent private firms. Fama and Jensen (1983) argue that classic entrepreneurial firms are associated with owners (i.e., principals) that combine residual risk bearing (i.e., ownership) and decision making (i.e., control). Indeed, Hawley (1927) argued that ownership rights are crucial for undertaking entrepreneurship, because they allow the entrepreneur to make decisions about the coordination of resources to gain entrepreneurial rents, in return for absorbing the uncertainty of owning those resources. The majority equity stake generally held by EFTs brings power that can imprint on the formulation and execution of strategy (Boeker, 1989). Studies focusing on entrepreneurial teams generally define team members as those who hold ownership and control positions (Kamm & Shuman, 1990; Gartner et al., 1994; Watson, Ponthieu, & Critelli, 1995; Cooney, & Bygrave, 1997; Chandler & Hanks, 1998a; Ensley, Carland & Carland, 2000).[1] In large complex organizations, there are benefits from separating decision-making functions (i.e., control) from residual risk bearing (i.e., ownership). Managers in most large organizations are unlikely to hold substantial amounts of equity. We can speculate that the link between adverse performance and team departures may be relatively weaker in the context of EFTs (Furtado & Karan, 1990). In contrast to TMTs in larger established organizations, EFTs do not have the external pressures to leave imposed by a board of directors, or the market for corporate control.

A second issue concerns the nature of team turnover itself. Team turnover may be attributed to the departure of existing team members (i.e., exit) and/or the introduction of members to the team (i.e., entry). Studies have tended to focus on team turnover either in terms of the extent to which members were no longer with the team after a specified period (i.e., exit) (Jackson et al., 1991; Walsh & Ellwood, 1991; Wiersema & Bantel, 1993; Krug & Hegarty, 1997), or the extent to which there were changes in the TMT over a specified period (Daily & Dalton, 1995; Krishnan, Miller, & Judge, 1997). The

---

1. Having previously focused on control as the key element, Ensley and colleagues in their latest work now focus upon the requirement for both ownership and control.

latter group of studies do not distinguish between entry and exit. These studies predominantly relate to large established firms, where arguably the necessary range of managerial skills are already present in the TMT so that team member entry is less of an issue. Team member entry is likely to be important for new private ventures, because venture owners need to fill skills gaps to facilitate the development and implementation of their strategies. As the firm develops beyond the start-up phase, the competencies and behaviors required are likely to change, necessitating augmentation and transition in the initial founding team (Gartner, Bird, & Starr, 1992). New team members will need to be equity holders in order to have the incentives and the power to enhance organizational performance. In contrast, exit from a team has been widely researched in large established firms, with under-performing managers being replaced due to conflicts and reduced cohesion (O'Reilly et al., 1989; Ensley et al., 2002).

This study aims to make the following contributions to knowledge. First, the study explores the neglected area of team turnover in EFTs. In particular, we suggest that greater clarity is needed when discussing turnover with regard to team member entry as well as exit. Second, guided by the human capital perspective, we suggest that the variables associated with team member entry may not necessarily be the same as those associated with team member exit.

The article is structured as follows. In the following section, we discuss the conceptual framework underpinning the study. The second section develops the hypotheses and, in particular, explores in turn whether entrepreneurial team member entry and exit are associated with the initial amount and nature of human capital embodied in the team itself. In the third section, the sample and methodology utilized are discussed. The fourth section provides definitions of the selected dependent, independent, and control variables. Results are then presented in the fifth section. The final section discusses conclusions, limitations, and areas for further research.

Conceptual Framework

Venture development may be shaped by the ability of an entrepreneur to efficiently utilize accumulated tangible and intangible resource stocks (Bloodgood, Sapienza, & Almeida, 1996). A venture with an EFT will generally have a larger and a more diverse array of human capital than a venture associated with a solo entrepreneur. Becker (1975) argued that human capital resources consist of achieved attributes, which are linked to increased levels of productivity. The EFT may use the human capital of its members to leverage social (Adler & Kwan, 2002), financial, and other forms of capital. However, we acknowledge that some solo entrepreneurs may be able to access human capital from their pool of employees. Due to their ownership stake in the firm, EFT members may have a clearer incentive to leverage their human capital to enhance organizational performance. In this study, EFT members are individuals with an equity stake in the business, and who have a key role in the strategic decision making of the venture at the time of founding. The firm thus possesses a supply of human capital resources inextricably linked to the team members who founded the venture. These initial resources, may impact upon the strategic alternatives at the entrepreneurs' disposal, which in turn bear upon the capabilities developed in younger firms (Boeker, 1989). These resources are not necessarily fixed. Rather, team members can manage the resources at their disposal through the entry of new members, as well as the exit of team members.

The overall level of human capital in an EFT is a function of the quantity and quality of the human capital embodied in each member of the team. One proxy for the quantity of human capital is the size of the team. The larger the EFT, the greater the absolute level of human capital at its disposal. If the size of the team remains stable in the short to medium term, its level of human capital can only be increased through learning and training. A quicker means of increasing the absolute level of human capital may be through the introduction of new team members.

The size of a team does not necessarily equate with the quality of human capital accumulated. One means of assessing the quality of human capital of the team as a whole is to examine the extent to which the human capital of individual team members is complementary or not. The heterogeneity of human capital can be particularly important for new ventures, because as the venture evolves, certain human capital attributes may be more essential than others. EFTs associated with small firms, and confronting financial constraints, can draw upon the heterogeneous human capital of individual team members, and use their resources and legitimacy to enhance the survival chances of the firm (Zimmerman & Zeitz, 2002). Mismatches between the competencies required by the venture and those possessed by the team may emerge over time (Virany & Tushman, 1986; Birley & Stockley, 2000). Individuals with human capital not currently possessed by the EFT may be encouraged to join the team. It can be reasonably speculated that homogeneous EFTs will be more likely to introduce new team members.

The downside of expanding the EFT is the greater potential costs associated with coordination and integration of team members. Difficulties with the coordination and integration of team members can have serious implications for the cohesion of the team. The lower the level of cohesion, the higher will be the costs of coordination and integration of team members. If cohesion is not ensured, the stability of the team may be compromised, resulting in team member exit. Evidence suggests that cohesive teams with close social relationships (Ensley, Pearson, & Amason, 2002) exhibit higher levels of trust and affinity towards one another, as well as higher levels of satisfaction with the team as a whole (O'Reilly et al., 1989). Ensley et al. (2002) found that team cohesion increased cognitive conflict, which is considered desirable, while minimizing affective conflict, which is considered to be dysfunctional. They concluded that team cohesion may enhance firm performance, as well as reduce the incidence of team member exit (O'Reilly et al., 1989).

The cohesion of an EFT can be linked to the size of the team and the heterogeneity of the team's human capital. Higher levels of team member heterogeneity may be associated with higher costs of coordination and integration of team members. Heterogeneity of various aspects of human capital has been linked to conflict and strategic consensus (Knight et al., 1999; Pelled, Eisenhardt & Xin, 1999). These problems are presumed to be associated with team member exit.

Derivation of Hypotheses

Our argument, as outlined above, is that as the firm develops it typically requires an evolving set of human capital. Where the firm's stock of human capital is limited in terms of EFT size, or the quality of the human capital possessed by each team member, we would expect the firm to add members to the EFT. Some firms may be associated with homogeneity with regard to the stock of human capital, as well as a duplication of expertise. For the latter firms, we would expect that the EFT would seek to augment its array of human capital. In contrast, heterogeneous EFTs are likely to be associated with higher costs of coordination and integration of team members. The latter firms would be expected to be associated with EFT member exit. In the following sections, hypotheses are presented relating to team member entry and exit. Where possible we substantiate our conceptual arguments with existing studies of private founder-owned ventures (i.e., where there is limited separation of ownership and control). Due to the sparsity of research specifically focusing upon EFTs, we use evidence relating to TMTs to guide the formulation of hypotheses relating to team member entry and exit in private firms. Separate hypotheses relating to team member entry and exit are discussed below in relation to several team dimensions.

Team Member Entry

EFT member entry may be associated with a team that does not have the necessary human capital to carry out its productive activities. In this section, three aspects of the level of human capital are explored in relation to a firm's propensity to add EFT members: the size of the team, the average age of the team, and whether or not the firm is a family firm. In addition, we discuss the implications of the heterogeneity of human capital in the team for member entry.

The Level of Human Capital in a Team

The overall level of human capital in an EFT can be linked to the quantity and quality of human capital embodied in each member of the team. Many owner-managed ventures are established by relatively small entrepreneurial teams with limited resource pools (Kor & Mahoney, 2000). EFT members seeking venture development may subsequently seek and recruit new team members to cover the broadening scope of managerial resource requirements. This discussion suggests the following hypothesis:

H1: The size of the founding team is negatively associated with subsequent team member entry.

As intimated above, the total human capital available to the firm may be associated with the quality and quantity of its EFT members. The average age of a team can be taken as a proxy for the accumulated human capital of the team. Teams composed, on average, of younger individuals may possess fewer experience-related human capital resources, provoking a need to bring in new team members who can fill such gaps. This discussion leads to the following hypothesis:

H2: The average age of founding team members is negatively associated with subsequent team member entry.

An overriding concern for the owners of family firms is to provide employment (i.e., managerial) opportunities for family members (Westhead, 1997). Owners of family firms seeking to ensure family ownership and control of their ventures are generally reluctant to employ "outsiders" (i.e., non-family members). The EFT in family firms can be expanded in two ways. First, if available, additional family members may be added to the EFT. Family members may have already accumulated idiosyncratic knowledge relating to their family venture (Bjuggren & Sund, 2002). The costs of adding new family members associated with ex-ante informational uncertainty may be less than the costs of adding non-family members, because the EFT already knows the new team members. Second, non-family members may be promoted to key managerial positions, or "outsiders" with managerial or specific expertise may be recruited. Several studies have suggested that family firms should recruit more "outsiders" on to their boards to obtain more varied and objective advice (Hoy & Verser, 1994; Fiegener et al., 2000; Westhead, Cowling, & Howorth, 2001). This discussion leads to the following hypothesis:

H3: Family firm teams will be positively associated with subsequent team member entry.

Team Heterogeneity

Heterogeneity may be indicative of a broad range of human capital within the team, facilitating the gathering of information from a variety of sources, and inducing alternative interpretations and perspectives (Smith et al., 1994; Hambrick, Cho, & Chen, 1996; Ensley et al., 2000). Higher levels of heterogeneity within a team are expected to be associated with less duplication of specific skills and human capital. Studies exploring heterogeneity have generally tended to focus on demographic heterogeneity as a proxy for cognitive characteristics (Hambrick & Mason, 1984; Wiersema & Bantel, 1992). There is, however, some debate surrounding the extent to which demographic characteristics (e.g., ethnicity and gender) are representative of underlying cognitive processes (Kilduff, Angelmar, & Mehra, 2000). Studies focusing upon TMTs in larger organizations (Eisenhardt & Schoonhoven, 1990; Pelled et al., 1999; Ensley et al., 2000) have generally focused upon demographic measures. The functional background of team members can be viewed as a more appropriate surrogate indicator of the heterogeneity of the human capital necessary for venture development. Owners of private firms with a small pool and array of resources may, therefore, seek to increase the human capital of the firm to ensure business development.

Resource-based theorists suggest that developing firms require an increasingly diverse range of human capital (Kor & Mahoney, 2000). A firm associated with the liabilities of "newness" and "small size" may have limited access to a broad array of resources. EFTs associated with low functional heterogeneity may be associated with skill shortages. Also, an EFT characterized by a low degree of functional heterogeneity may have a duplication of functions skills within the team. This discussion suggests the following hypothesis:

H4: The functional heterogeneity of a founding team is negatively associated with subsequent team member entry.

Team Member Exit

In this section we relate the likelihood of exit to the alternatives faced by team members, their emotional attachment to the team, and conflicts between team members. The more attractive the perceived alternatives, the lower the emotional attachment to a team, and the higher the levels of conflict within a team, the greater the likely incidence of team member exit. In this section, three aspects of the level of human capital are explored in relation to the exit of EFT members: the size of the team, the average age of the team, and whether or not the firm is a family firm. In addition, we examine the implications of the heterogeneity of human capital in the EFT for member exit.

The Level of Human Capital in a Team

Firms with larger and more heterogeneous EFTs have to deal with coordination issues, which can be linked to the subsequently higher probability of team member exit. EFTs with numerous members may meet less frequently, which may lead to problems in decision making and implementation (Hambrick et al., 1996). Also, larger teams may be associated with higher levels of dysfunctional affective (emotional) conflict (Amason & Sapienza, 1997), which may lead to team member exit. Smaller teams that are closely knit may be less likely to experience team member departure because members will have to consider both the economic and psychic costs associated with leaving the team (Francis & Sandberg, 2000). This discussion suggests the following hypothesis:

> **H5:** The size of a founding team is positively associated with subsequent team member exit.

The probability of EFT member exit from a business may be negatively related to the psychic income derived from business ownership, and the costs of switching to alternative occupations (Gimeno et al., 1997). Flexibility may decline and rigidity and resistance to change increase as people age (Wiersema & Bantel, 1993). Older team members may be more risk averse in their behavior, more emotionally attached to the business, and reluctant to transfer their human capital by quitting the venture in order to move to an alternative organization (Morin & Suarez, 1983; Palsson, 1996; Levesque, Shepherd, & Douglas, 2002). This discussion leads to the following hypothesis:

> **H6:** The average age of team members is negatively associated with subsequent team member exit.

The extent to which EFT members know each other may be associated with team member exit. Further, the degree of prior joint experience between members of a team may impact upon the team's knowledge of the skills and abilities at its disposal (Birley & Stockley, 2000). Prior joint experience might be associated with more efficient decision making (Eisenhardt & Schoonhoven, 1990). Most notably, team members can show more awareness of each other, and do not have to deploy efforts toward team building and eradicating emotional conflict. A team comprising family members may resemble the characteristics of a team with prior joint experience. When considering exit from the team, a member is likely to consider the costs and benefits associated with this decision (Francis & Sandberg, 2000). In closely knit teams, the costs of departure may include the psychic costs of leaving friends and family, as well as the economic costs and considerations of personal risk. By imposing additional costs on departure, family ties may reduce exit-related turnover among EFTs. This discussion suggests the following hypothesis:

> **H7:** Family firm teams will be negatively associated with subsequent team member exit.

Team Heterogeneity

EFT heterogeneity may be associated with less duplication of human capital and improved decision making (Bantel & Jackson, 1989; Murray, 1989). However, heterogeneity creates the potential for increased conflict within the team. Functional heterogeneity, which we believe is a more appropriate indicator of human capital than demographic factors, may create the potential for increased conflict. Greater potential for disagreement may encourage the exit of team members (Amason, 1996; Jehn, 1997). This discussion leads to the following hypothesis:

> **H8:** The functional heterogeneity of a founding team will be positively associated with subsequent team member exit.

EFT members may differ according to their prior levels of entrepreneurial experience. As with functional heterogeneity, prior entrepreneurial experience may be associated with assets as well as liabilities (Starr, Bygrave, & Tercanli, 1993; Wright, Robbie,

& Ennew, 1997). On the asset side, entrepreneurial experience may considerably enhance an EFT member's human capital (Gimeno et al., 1997; Chandler & Hanks, 1998b; Ucbasaran, Wright, & Westhead, 2003), and the overall human capital of the team. Conversely, EFT members associated with the liabilities of prior entrepreneurial experience may exhibit "irrational," or sub-optimal behavior. Heterogeneity of prior entrepreneurial experience may create conflict between non-experienced and experienced team members, particularly, if the latter have a dominating role. As a result, cohesion may be undermined and team members may exit. This discussion suggests the following hypothesis:

H9: The entrepreneurial experience heterogeneity of a founding team will be positively associated with subsequent team member exit.

Methods

The Sample

This study draws upon a longitudinal data set of small and medium-sized private enterprises. Principal founders of independent businesses located in 12 environments in Great Britain were originally surveyed in 1990/91 (Birley & Westhead, 1992). In total, the study in 1990/91 yielded a sample of 744 valid responses, 621 of which represented businesses between the age of 1 and 50 years. In 1997, attempts were made to contact the 621 independent firms interviewed in 1990/91. Data were collected over a two-month period using structured telephone interviews. After detailed and extensive searching, we noted that 138 businesses (22.2%) had survived in 1997 at the original 1990/91 address, and a further 75 businesses had survived at a new address (12.1%). Thirteen businesses had survived but had been taken over by another business (2.1%). Forty-seven businesses were confirmed as having closed (7.6%), whilst a further 348 businesses (56.0%) did not appear to be trading in any identifiable form. Following previous studies (Garnsey & Cannon-Brookes, 1993; Westhead, 1995), businesses that could not be traced through this process were regarded as business closures.

Over the period July 2000 and August 2000, attempts were made to contact the 213 confirmed surviving businesses in 1997. In order to ascertain their status in 2000, and to update the addresses of these businesses, a four-stage process was used. First, a search on the UK Info Disk 2000 CD-Rom service was conducted. Second, a search on the BT (British Telecom) On-Line service was conducted. Third, the value-added tax (VAT) de-registration directory was searched. Fourth, Kompass and Kelly's Trade Directors were searched. This process revealed that 29 firms were confirmed to have closed by 2000. One firm was confirmed to have been taken over. In total, 183 surviving firms were identified.

Attempts were made to contact the owners of the 183 surviving firms by telephone. Ninety-eight firms agreed to be interviewed; though six were eliminated due to our inability to speak with the principal owner. An effective response rate of 50% was achieved. Mann-Whitney "U" tests were conducted to test for response bias. These tests revealed no statistically significant differences (at the 0.01% level) between respondents (92 firms) and non-respondents (91 firms) in terms of the age of the business, the employment size of the business, industry and sales turnover with regard to data collected in 1997. This evidence does not eliminate the concern relating to non-response bias, but it does indicate some representativeness. Due to the inevitable problem of sample attrition, the follow-on sample cannot be regarded as a representative sample of the total private business population in the U.K. Responses relate to private firms that have been able to address business survival and development obstacles.

Of the 92 private firms in the follow-on sample, 58 (63%) respondents indicated the firm had been established as a team start, and the remaining 34 (37%) respondents reported solo entrepreneur start-ups. This finding is consistent with the notion that entrepreneurial teams form a sizeable proportion of new ventures. In 39 out of the 58 team founder cases (67%), there were two members in the team, while in 13 cases (22.4%) the team consisted of three members, and in the remaining 6 cases (10.4%) between three and six members were involved in the team.

EFT members were defined as individuals who owned at least 10% of the equity in the venture. They also hold a key role in the strategic decision making of the venture at the time of its founding. In order to analyze changes in team member entry and exit, three data points were selected: number of EFT members at founding, number of team members in 1990, and the number of team members in 2000. These three points in time enabled the research team to explore whether the increase (or decrease) in the number of team members between founding and 2000 cancelled each other out. Some respondents reported the same number of team members at founding and 2000. Additional analysis revealed that some of these respondents had actually recorded changes in team member composition over this period. The "hidden" dynamics of team member entry and exit were, therefore, monitored over the selected time periods. If team member entry or exit was recorded in either, or both of these two periods, the dependent variables were allocated a value of one, whilst no change was allocated a value of zero (see discussion on definition of the dependent variables in next section).

The team member entry analysis focused upon the full sample of 92 firms relating to firms where new human capital was introduced. Further, the sub-sample of firms that began with a founding team was explored with regard to team member exit. Ninety of the firms in the full sample provided data on entry, of which 38 firms reported that they had experienced new team member entry. Twenty-two of these firms introduced one new member, 11 firms introduced two new members, and 5 firms introduced three or more new members. Only 5 out of the 38 firms reporting team member entry also reported team member exit. Of the 56 valid team founder firms providing data, 22 firms reported team member exit. Fourteen of the firms experienced the exit of one member, five firms experienced the exit of two members, and three firms experienced the exit of three or more members. Only one out of the 22 firms reporting team member exit indicated that they had introduced a new team member.

This study focuses on information provided by one of the individuals meeting our criteria for a team member. Reliance on one respondent is not expected to be a problem in relation to the variables explored. It is not uncommon for studies of teams to rely on the information provided by key respondents, such as the chief executive officer (CEO) (Eisenhardt & Schoonhoven, 1990; Knight et al., 1999). Given that most of the teams examined in this study are associated with two or three individuals (mean size was 2.49), we would expect team members to know each other well enough to provide some basic background information.

Definition and Measurement of Variables

Dependent Variables

The team member entry and exit dependent variables were defined as follows:

Team Member Entry: Three points in time (i.e., founding, 1990/91 and 2000) were used to determine whether a firm reported EFT member entry between founding and 1990/91 and/or between 1990/91 and 2000. If a respondent reported that the firm had introduced at least one new team member over *either* of the two periods, the firm was allocated a value of one. Conversely, if no team member had been introduced over *either* of the two periods, the firm was allocated a value of zero.

Team Member Exit: Three points in time (i.e., founding, 1990/91 and 2000) were used to determine whether a firm reported EFT member exit between founding and 1990/91 and/or between 1990/91 and 2000. If a respondent reported that the firm had experienced the departure of at least one team member over *either* of the two periods, the firm was allocated a value of one. Conversely, if no team member had left the team over *either* of the two periods, the firm was allocated a value of zero.

Independent Variables

The level of human capital in a team was measured with regard to the size of the team, average age of the team, and whether or not the venture was a family firm. These independent variables are discussed, in turn, below.

Entrepreneurial Team Size: Team size was measured in 1990/91 in terms of the number of members in the founding team (i.e., founders who owned at least 10% equity in the venture, and they played a key role in the strategic decision-making of the venture at founding).

Average age of the team: In 2000, we ascertained the average age of the team at time of founding. The average age of the team variable was based on the following categories: 16–24 years (1); 25–34 years (2); 35–44 years (3); 45–54 years (4); and over 55 years (5).

Family Firm: In 2000, we ascertained whether the firm was perceived to be a family firm. Respondents perceiving a family firm were allocated a value of one, whilst those perceiving a non-family firm were allocated a value of zero.

Functional and Entrepreneurial Heterogeneity: The telephone interviews conducted in 2000 gathered demographic and functional background data for each member of the initial team. In the case of categorical variables, Teachman's (1980) heterogeneity scale was used to measure heterogeneity $(H) = -\Sigma P_i (\ln P_i)$. This index takes into account how team members are distributed among the possible categories of a variable. The total number of categories of a variable equals n, and P_i is the fraction of team members falling into each category of the variable (Pelled et al., 1999). For functional heterogeneity, the following categories were used: general management (1); sales/marketing (2); production (3); and finance (4). For heterogeneity of entrepreneurial experience, yes (1) and no (0) categories were used.

Control Variables

Organizational characteristics were considered by Jackson et al. (1991) as control variables in their study of TMTs'. In this study, four control variables were selected and are discussed below.

Venture Firm Size and Age: The skills required by a team may vary between younger and older ventures (Hambrick & Mason, 1984). Firm size and age were ascertained relating to data collected in 1990/91. The total number of employees employed in the business when it received its first order was log transformed. Further, the age of the firm was calculated with regard to the number of years since the business received its first order, and was log transformed.

Industry: The propensity to introduce (and remove) team members may be associated with a firm's industrial activities (Wiersema & Bantel, 1993). In 1990/91, the main industrial activity of each firm was ascertained. Manufacturing firms were coded with a value of one, while service-based firms were coded with a value of zero. All firms in the sample were either manufacturing or services firms.

The External Environment: Respondents were asked to indicate in 1990/91 the extent to which they agreed with five statements relating to their perception of the firm's external environmental conditions when the businesses were founded. A five point scoring system was employed, where a value of 1 suggested "strongly disagree," a value of 3 suggested "neutral," whilst a value of 5 suggested "strongly agree." These statements were derived from the original Society for Associated Research on International Entrepreneurship (SARIE) questionnaire (Birley & Westhead, 1993). Environmental hostility was measured with regard to the following statements: there was a large number of businesses in the area that I live; there was a large number of businesses in my industry; there was a large number of business failures in the area that I live; there was a large number of business failures in my industry; and there was political uncertainty in the country. With reference to these statements, a summated average scale was calculated (Cronbach's Alpha = 0.81).

Results

Descriptive statistics and Pearson correlation coefficients relating to the selected control and independent variables are reported in Table 1. As expected, the size of the team was significantly positively ($p < .01$) associated with whether or not the team was a family firm ($r = .269$), functional heterogeneity ($r = .686$), and entrepreneurial experience heterogeneity ($r = .535$). Family firms were significantly positively ($p < .01$) associated with functional heterogeneity ($r = .324$). In addition, heterogeneity of entrepreneurial experience was significantly positively ($p < .05$) associated with functional heterogeneity ($r = .232$), but significantly negatively ($p < .05$) associated with manufacturing firms ($r = -.262$). The Variance Inflation Factor (VIF) scores were all low apart for the measures relating to team size and functional heterogeneity. Results from the regression models may be distorted by the problem of multicollinearity, particularly, the links between team size and the measures for heterogeneity. This issue needs to be considered when interpreting the results from the presented regression models.

Logistic regression analysis is an appropriate technique to explore the combination of variables associated with a binary dependent variable. This technique does not have limiting assumptions surrounding data normality. The combination of control and independent variables associated with the entry of new members to the founding team are summarized in Table 2, whilst variables associated with the exit of members from the founding team are reported in Table 3. With regard to each dependent variable two models are presented. The first model focuses upon all the control and independent variables excluding the variable(s) relating to heterogeneity. However, the second model includes control and independent variables as well as the variable(s) relating to heterogeneity. Following the precedent of previous exploratory studies, we sought to avoid Type II errors (i.e., accepting the null hypothesis when it should be rejected). The 0.1 level of significance was, therefore, selected to discuss significant relationships highlighted by significant models.

Team Member Entry

Both models in Table 2 are significant at the 0.05 level. Model 1 relates to team member entry and excludes the functional heterogeneity independent variable. Two

Table 1

Pearson Correlation Matrix and Descriptive Statistics of Control and Independent Variables

	Mean	S.D.	VIF[a]	1.	2.	3.	4.	5.	6.	7.	8.	9.
1. Age[1]	2.71	0.34	1.320	1.000								
2. Size[2]	0.47	0.82	1.057	−.025	1.000							
3. Manufacturing[3]	0.37	0.49	1.118	−.094	.072	1.000						
4. Team Size[4,5]	1.95	1.00	3.035	.081	−.109	−.183	1.000					
5. Family[6]	0.33	0.47	1.336	.172	.104	.044	.269 **	1.000				
6. Hostility[7]	2.59	0.75	1.293	.132	.052	−.153	.012	−.188	1.000			
7. Founder(s) age[8]	3.29	0.91	1.137	−.186	.016	.032	.045	.082	.140	1.000		
8. Hfunc[9]	0.33	0.37	2.487	−.075	−.036	−.013	.686 **	.324 **	.124	.015	1.000	
9. Hentexp[10]	0.01	0.23	1.669	−.086	−.128	−.262 *	.535 **	.028	.095	−.010	.232 *	1.000

*Correlation is significant at 0.05 level (2-tailed); **Correlation is significant at 0.01 level (2-tailed).
[a] Variance Inflation Factor.
[1] Age = Natural log of age of firm in 2000 (years).
[2] Size = Natural log of number of employees in the business at time of founding (full-time employees = 1; part-time employees = 0.5; and casual employees = 0.25).
[3] Manufacturing = Whether the firm was engaged in manufacturing (1 = yes; 0 = no) (alternative category represents services activities).
[4] Team Size = Number of team members who had a least 10% equity and were involved in the strategic decision-making at the founding stages of the business.
[5] The average team size was 2.48 (standard deviation of 0.88) for the team only sample.
[6] Family = Whether the firm was a family firm (1 = yes; 0 = no).
[7] Hostility = Environmental hostility.
[8] Founder(s) Age = Average age of the entrepreneurial founder team members, or age of founder (years).
[9] Hfunc = Heterogeneity of functional background.
[10] Hentexp = Heterogeneity of prior entrepreneurial experience.

variables are individually significantly associated with the dependent variable. Subsequent team member entry is significantly positively associated with the average age of the team ($p < .01$), and weakly negatively associated with the size of the founding team ($p < .10$).

Model 2 relates to team member entry and includes the functional heterogeneity independent variable. This latter model is associated with a higher level of "explanation" than Model 1 (see Cox & Snell R square, Nagelkerke R square, and R square logit). Three variables are individually significantly associated with the dependent variable. As found in Model 1, subsequent team member entry is positively associated with the age of the team ($p < .001$), and negatively associated with the size of the founding team ($p < .01$). Contrary to expectation, the level of functional heterogeneity in a founding team is weakly positively (rather than negatively) associated with member entry ($p < .10$). In part, this detected relationship may be due to the problem of multicollinearity highlighted above. We can infer from the evidence presented in Models 1 and 2 that firms with smaller EFTs are more likely to add new team members. H1 is, therefore, supported. In contrast, H2, H3 and H4 are not supported.

Table 2

Logistic Regression Models of Variables Associated with the Entry of New Members to the Founding Team[a]

Control and Independent Variables	Hypothesized Direction of Association	Dependent Variable: MEMBER ENTRY (Yes/No) Model 1 β	Dependent Variable: MEMBER ENTRY (Yes/No) Model 2 β
CONTROLS			
Age		2.406 **	2.869 ***
Size		−.134	−1.49
Manufacturing		.475	.416
Environmental Hostility		−.161	−0.410
TEAM LEVEL			
Team Size	−	−.473 †	−.868 **
Average Team Age	−	−.066	.041
Family	+	.956	.614
Hfunc	−		1.764 †
Model χ^2		15.583	18.512
Model χ^2 significance		.029	.018
−2 log likelihood		95.951	93.021
Overall predictive accuracy		63.5%	72.9%
Cox & Snell R square		.168	.196
Nagelkerke R square		.229	.268
R square logit		.146	.172
Number of businesses		85	85

† $p < .10$
* $p < .05$
** $p < .01$
*** $p < .001$
[a] When the model was run including only those businesses that started as a team, the same variables were found to be significant except for the age of the business variable.

Team Member Exit

Models relating to the exit of members from the founding team are presented in Table 3. Model 3, which excludes the variables relating to functional and entrepreneurial heterogeneity, is not significant at the 0.1 level of significance. Consequently, this model is not discussed further. In contrast, Model 4, which includes the variables relating to functional and entrepreneurial heterogeneity, is significant at the 0.001 level of significance. None of the control variables is significantly associated with the dependent variable. However, two independent variables are significantly associated with the exit of members from the founding team. As hypothesized, family firms are negatively associated with the

Table 3

Logistic Regression Models of Variables Associated
with the Exit of Members from the Founding Team

Control and Independent Variables	Hypothesized Direction of Association	Dependent Variable: *MEMBER EXIT* (Yes/No) Model 3 β	Dependent Variable: *MEMBER EXIT* (Yes/No) Model 4 β
CONTROLS			
Age		−1.780	−.856
Size		.057	.273
Manufacturing		−.720	−.104
Environmental Hostility		−0.065	−.297
TEAM LEVEL			
Team Size	+	.486	−.410
Average Team Age	−	1.059	1.355
Family	−	−2.346	−2.756
		*	**
Hfunc	+		−.040
Hentexp	+		5.780
			***
Model χ²		11.941	22.853
Model χ² significance		.103	.007
−2 log likelihood		49.850	38.939
Overall predictive accuracy		74.5%	82.4%
Cox & Snell R square		.209	.361
Nagelkerke R square		.297	.514
R square logit		.216	.387
Number of businesses		51	51

†p < .10
*p < .05
**p < .01
***p < .001

dependent variable ($p < .01$). Also, as hypothesized, the entrepreneurial experience heterogeneity of a founding team was strongly positively associated with subsequent team member exit ($p < .001$). Evidence reported in Model 4 supports H7 and H9, but fails to support H5, H6 and H8.

Conclusion

Limited research has been conducted surrounding the dynamics of team development in new and developing independent private firms. Studies focusing on TMTs in larger and established firms have failed to explore whether the factors associated with team

Table 4

Summary of Results

Team Member Entry Dependent Variable

H1: The size of the founding team is negatively associated with subsequent team member entry.   Supported

H2: The average age of founding team members is negatively associated with subsequent team member entry.   Not Supported

H3: Family firm teams will be positively associated with subsequent team member entry.   Not Supported

H4: The functional heterogeneity of a founding team is negatively associated with subsequent team member entry.   Not Supported

---

Team Member Exit Dependent Variable

H5: The size of a founding team is positively associated with subsequent team member exit.   Not Supported

H6: The average of team members is negatively associated with subsequent team member exit.   Not Supported

H7: Family firm teams will be negatively associated with subsequent team member exit.   Supported

H8: The functional heterogeneity of a founding team will be positively associated subsequent team member exit.   Not Supported

H9: The entrepreneurial experience heterogeneity of a founding team will be positively associated with subsequent team member exit.   Supported

---

member entry are the same as those associated with team member exit. Variables associated with new team member introductions, for example, have received limited attention in TMT studies. The novel contribution of this study has been the exploration of team member entry as well as team member exit reported by independent private firms. A unique comparative static longitudinal database of independent private firms was utilized to ascertain the entry and exit of team members at three points in time (i.e., founding, 1990/91 and 2000). A conceptual framework has been presented that emphasizes the importance of both human capital and team cohesion in private owner-managed firms. Linked to the conceptual framework, hypotheses have been presented. Several independent (and control variables) were identified and presumed to be associated with the two selected binary dependent variables. Multivariate logistic regression analysis was utilized to identify the combination of control and independent variables associated with EFT entry, or exit. Two models were presented with regard to each dependent variable. The first model included all the control and independent variables excluding the measure(s) relating to heterogeneity. The second model included control and independent variables as well as the variable(s) relating to heterogeneity.

A summary of the key findings from the multivariate regression models is presented in Table 4. Three out of the nine presented hypotheses were supported. One hypothesis relating to team member entry, and a further two hypotheses relating to team member exit were supported.

Supporting H1, we detected that private firms with smaller EFTs were more likely to report the entry of new team members. An important motive for the need to bring in new team members is to add to the total amount of human capital within a team. We can infer here that EFTs in private firms may be constrained by the amount of human capital at their disposal. This constraint can be overcome be recruiting appropriate additional team members.

In line with expectations (H7), family firm teams concerned with maintaining cohesion (i.e., protecting the interests of the family members that own the majority of ordinary voting shares in the business) are less likely to be associated with the exit of members from the EFT. When considering whether to leave the family firm, team members may reflect upon the potential non-pecuniary costs associated with affecting the family relationship. Although not in a statistically significant direction, we detected that family firms were positively associated with new member entry (Models 1 and 2 in Table 2), either from other family members or from outside, consistent with the need to augment human capital.

Supporting H9, firms exhibiting heterogeneity with regard to a team's entrepreneurial experience were more likely to be associated with the exit of team members. This suggests that where one or more entrepreneurs have prior entrepreneurial experience, these individuals may try to dominate those who are inexperienced entrepreneurially, thus reducing cohesion and creating conflict-induced team turnover. We can infer here that teams introducing members who have had prior entrepreneurial experience should be aware of both the assets and potential liabilities associated with this experience. The fact that one or more team members have been through the process before does not necessarily mean they can replicate previous contributions (and strategies) with the same success in the future.

Results from this study will interest practitioners (both entrepreneurs and venture capitalists). Most notably, we detected that EFTs in private firms do not remain static over time. For example, an EFT considered to be well balanced at the initiation of the venture may not be regarded as well balanced as the venture develops over time. If practitioners become more aware of the dynamic nature of entrepreneurial teams, they may be better able to provide assistance that facilitates the more appropriate management of the process of team member entry, as well as the process of team member exit. This more appropriate assistance may enhance the performance of assisted private firms. Practitioners should also assess the nature of human capital brought by individual members to the team. This study suggests diversity, in terms of entrepreneurial experience, which may increase the incidence of team member exit due to the problems associated with cohesion.

This study is associated with two main limitations. First, the sample size is relatively small, restricting the nature of multivariate statistical analysis, and the generalizability of the findings. Second, the study was unable to distinguish between voluntary and involuntary departure, and hence motives for bringing in new team members or motives for departure.

Table 4 highlights that the variables associated with team member entry are not the same as those associated with team member exit. Future studies focusing upon private firms need to consider, and distinguish between, team member entry as well as exit. Studies conducted in a variety of industrial, locational, and cultural settings, need to be conducted to ascertain whether the findings reported in this study can be generalized to other contexts.

Additional research is warranted relating to several issues. First, studies need to explore the processes leading to EFT turnover. For example, how does conflict (affective and functional) between team members impact on EFT turnover? To what extent do different levels of power of different equityholders affect their ability to enforce exit of partners? Second, the cognitive behavior of team members needs to be monitored to highlight the issue of diversity within teams. For example, does cognitive diversity within a team inhibit comprehensive examination of current opportunities and threats, as well as extensive long-range planning (Miller, Burke, & Glick, 1998)? Also, can a team member's mindset (e.g., managerial versus entrepreneurial) impact on EFT turnover? Third, studies need to explore the differing motives for team member entry and departure. For example, to what extent is bringing in new team members proactive and an indication that the team is aware of its limitations? To what extent is the team simply bringing in new members to replace those who have exited, or in the case of family firms, bringing in other family members for non-profit motives? How does the presence, or absence, of a formal board of directors affect the composition of an EFT over time? Fourth, how do these aspects of team turnover vary between different types of ventures, such as family versus non-family firms; start-up teams versus teams in entrepreneurial established businesses (e.g., some management buyouts and buy-ins); and start-up teams versus teams in established organizations? Fifth, there is potential for exploring definitional issues, and potentially distinguishing between a venture's management team and entrepreneurial team. Though there may be some overlap between a venture's management and entrepreneurial team, there is scope for exploring the extent to which all team members contribute to the key entrepreneurial functions of opportunity identification and exploitation, as opposed to only managerial functions. The distinction between the managerial and entrepreneurial team may, in addition, be pertinent in relation to individuals who are only promised equity at a later stage. In this study, such individuals were viewed as not being part of the entrepreneurial team on the grounds that they did not fulfil the joint ownership and control criterion. The latter individuals are viewed as agents rather than principals. Consequently, they are not in a position to decide on the entrepreneurial coordination of resources until such time as they become residual risk-bearing equity holders. The changing team behavior of managers as they move from having been promised equity to obtaining equity is an area that requires further exploration. Finally, additional studies might usefully involve data collection covering the perspectives of different team members in order to extend the examination of the rationale for team turnover.

REFERENCES

Adler, P.S. & Kwan, S.-K. (2002). Social Capital: Prospects for a New Concept. *Academy of Management Review*, 27(1), 17–40.

Amason, A. (1996). Distinguishing the Effects of Functional and Dysfunctional Conflict on Strategic Decision Making: Resolving a Paradox for Top Management Teams. *Academy of Management Journal*, 39(1), 123–148.

Amason, A. & Sapienza, H. (1997). The Effects of Top Management Team Size and Interaction Norms on Cognitive and Affective Conflict, *Journal of Management*, 23(4), 495–516.

Bantel, K.A. & Jackson, S.E. (1989). Top Management and Innovations in Banking: Does the Composition of the Top Team Make a Difference? *Strategic Management Journal*, 10, Summer Special Issue, 107–112

Becker, G.S. (1975). *Human Capital*. New York: National Bureau of Economic Research.

Birley, S. & Stockley, S. (2000). Entrepreneurial Teams and Venture Growth. In D.L. Sexton and H. Landstöm (eds.), *The Blackwell Handbook of Entrepreneurship*, Oxford: UK: Blackwell.

Birley, S. & Westhead, P. (1992). A Comparison of New Firms in 'Assisted' and 'Non-Assisted' Areas in Great Britain. *Entrepreneurship and Regional Development*, 4(3), 299–338.

Birley, S. & Westhead, P. (1993). New Venture Environments. In S. Birley and I.C. Macmillan (eds.), *Entrepreneurship Research: Global Perspectives*, 207–247. Amsterdam: Elsevier Science.

Bjuggren, P.-O. & Sund, L.-G. (2002). A Transaction Cost Rationale for Transition of the Firm within the Family. *Small Business Economics*, 19(2), 123–133.

Bloodgood, J.M., Sapienza, H.J., & Almeida, J.G. (1996). The Internationalization of New High-Potential U.S. Ventures: Antecedents and Outcomes. *Entrepreneurship Theory and Practice*, 20(4), 61–76.

Boeker, W. (1989). Strategic Change: The Effects of Founding and History. *Academy of Management Journal*, 32(3), 489–515.

Boyd, D.P. & Gumpert, D.E. (1983). Coping with Entrepreneurial Stress. *Harvard Business Review*, March–April, 46–56.

Chandler, G.N. & Hanks, S.H. (1998a). An Investigation of New Venture Teams in Emerging Business. *Frontiers of Entrepreneurship Research*, Wellesley, MA: Babson College, 318–330.

Chandler, G.N. & Hanks, S.H. (1998b). An Examination of the Substitutability of Founders Human and Financial Capital in Emerging Business Ventures. *Journal of Business Venturing*, 13(5), 353–369.

Cooney, T.M. & Bygrave, W.B. (1997). The Evolution of the Structure and Strategy in Fast Growth Firms Founded by Entrepreneurial Teams. *Frontiers of Entrepreneurship Research*, Wellesley, MA: Babson College, 428–429.

Cooper, A.C. & Daily, C.M. (1997). Entrepreneurial Teams. In D.L. Sexton and R.W. Smilor (eds.), *Entrepreneurship 2000*, 127–150. Chicago: Upstart Publishing Company.

Cooper, A.C. & Bruno, A. (1977). Success Among High Technology Firms. *Business Horizons*, April 20, 16–22.

Daily, C.M. & Dalton, D.R. (1995). CEO and Director Turnover in Failing Firms: An Illusion of Change? *Strategic Management Journal*, 16(5), 393–400.

Eisenhardt, K.M. & Schoonhoven, C.B. (1990). Organizational Growth: Linking Founding Team, Strategy, Environment, and Growth among US semiconductor Ventures, 1978–1988. *Administrative Science Quarterly*, 35(3), 504–537.

Ensley, M.D., Pearson, A.W., & Amason, A.C. (2002). Understanding the Dynamics of New Venture Top Management Teams: Cohesion, Conflict and New Venture Performance. *Journal of Business Venturing*, 17(4), 365–386.

Ensley, M.D., Carland, J.C., & Carland, J.W. (2000). Investigating the Existence of the Lead Entrepreneur. *Journal of Small Business Management*, 38(4), 59–77.

Ensley, M.D., Carland, J.C., Carland, J.W., Banks, M. (1999). Exploring the Existence of Entrepreneurial Teams. *International Journal of Management*, 16(2), 276–286.

Ensley, M.D., Carland, J.C., & Carland, J.W. (1998). The Effects of Entrepreneurial Team Skill Heterogeneity and Functional Diversity on New Venture Performance. *Journal of Business and Entrepreneurship*, 10(1), 1–11.

Fama, E. & Jensen, M. (1983). Separation of Ownership and Control. *Journal of Law and Economics*, 26(2), 301–25.

Fiegener, M.K., Brown, B.M., Dreux, D.R., IV, & Dennis, W.J., Jr. (2000). The Adoption of Outside Boards by Small Private U.S. Firms. *Entrepreneurship and Regional Development*, 12(4), 291–309.

Francis, D.H. & Sandberg, W.R. (2000). Friendship Within Entrepreneurial Teams and its Association with Team and Venture Performance. *Entrepreneurship Theory and Practice*, 25(2), 5–26.

Furtado, E.P.H. & Karan, V. (1990). Causes, Consequences, and Shareholder Wealth Effects of Management Turnover: A Review of Empirical Evidence. *Financial Management*, 19(2), 60–75.

Garnsey, E. & Cannon-Brookes, A. (1993). The 'Cambridge Phenomenon' Revisited: Aggregate Change among Cambridge High-Technology Companies Since 1985. *Entrepreneurship and Regional Development*, 5, 179–207.

Gartner, W.B., Bird, B.J., & Starr, J.A. (1992). Acting as If: Differentiating Entrepreneurial from Organizational Behavior, *Entrepreneurship Theory and Practice*, 16(3), 13–31.

Gartner, W.B., Shaver, K.G., Gatewood, E., & Katz, J.A. (1994). Finding the Entrepreneur in Entrepreneurship. *Entrepreneurship Theory and Practice*, 18(3), 5–10.

Gimeno, J., Folta, T.B., Cooper, A.C., & Woo, C.Y. (1997). Survival of the Fittest? Entrepreneurial Human Capital and the Persistence of Underperforming Firms. *Administrative Science Quarterly*, 42(4), 750–783.

Hambrick, D.C., Cho, T.S., & Chen, M. (1996). The Influence of Top Management Team Heterogeneity on Firm's Competitive Moves, *Administrative Science Quarterly*, 41(4), 659–684.

Hambrick, D.C. & Mason, P.A. (1984). Upper Echelons: The Organization as a Reflection of its Top Managers. *Academy of Management Review*, 9(2), 193–206.

Hawley, F. (1927). The Orientation of Economics on Enterprise. *American Economic Review*, 17, 409–428.

Hoy, F. & Verser, T. (1994). Emerging Business, Emerging Field: Entrepreneurship and the Family Firm. *Entrepreneurship Theory and Practice*, 19(1), 9–24.

Jackson, S.E., Brett, J.F., Sessa, V.I., Cooper, D.M., Julin, J.A., & Peyronnin, K. (1991). Some Differences Make a Difference: Individual Dissimilarity and Group Heterogeneity as Correlates of Recruitment, Promotion and Turnover, *Journal of Applied Psychology*, 79(5), 675–689.

Jehn, K.A. (1997). A Qualitative Analysis of Conflict Types and Dimensions in Organizational Groups. *Administrative Science Quarterly*, 42(3), 530–557.

Kamm, J.B. & Shuman, J.C. (1990). Entrepreneurial Teams in New Venture Creation: A Research Agenda. *Entrepreneurship Theory and Practice*, 14(4), 7–17.

Keck, S.L. (1991). Top Management Team Structure: Does it Matter Anyway? Paper presented at the Academy of Management Meeting, Miami, FL.

Kesner, I.F. & Dalton, D.R. (1994). Top Management Turnover and CEO Succession: An Investigation of the Effects of Turnover on Performance. *Journal of Management Studies*, 31(5), 701–713.

Kilduff, M., Angelmar, R., & Mehra, A. (2000). Top Management Team Diversity and Firm Performance: Examining the Role of Cognitions. *Organization Science*, 11(1), 21–34.

Knight, D., Pearce, C.L., Smith, K.G., Olian, J.D., Sims, P.H., Smith, K.A., & Flood, P. (1999). Top Management Team Diversity, Group Process and Strategic Consensus. *Strategic Management Journal*, 20(5), 445–465.

Kor, Y.Y. & Mahoney, J.T. (2000). Penrose's Resource-Based Approach: the Process and Product of Research Creativity. *Journal of Management Studies*, 37(1), 109–139.

Krishnan, H.A., Miller, A., & Judge, W.Q. (1997). Diversification and Top Management Team Complementarity: Is Performance Improved by Merging Similar or Dissimilar Teams? *Strategic Management Journal*, 18(5), 361–374.

Krug, J.A. & Hegarty, W.H. (1997). Post Acquisition Takeover among US Top Management Teams: An Analysis of the Effects of Foreign versus Domestic Acquisitions of US Targets. *Strategic Management Journal*, 18(8), 667–675.

Levesque, M., Shepherd, D.A., & Douglas, E.J. (2002). Employment or Self-Employment: A Dynamic Utility-Maximizing Model. *Journal of Business Venturing,* 17 (3), 189–210.

Miller, C.C., Burke, L.M., & Glick, W.H. (1998). Cognitive Diversity Among Upper-Echelon Executives: Implications for Strategic Decision Processes. *Strategic Management Journal,* 19(1), 39–58.

Morin, R.A. & Suarez, F. (1983). Risk Aversion Revisited, *Journal of Finance,* 38(4), 1201–1216.

Murray, A.I. (1989) Top Management Group Heterogeneity and Firm Performance. *Strategic Management Journal,* Summer Special Issue, 10, 125–141.

Norburn, D. & Birley, S. (1988). The Top Management Team and Corporate Performance. *Strategic Management Journal,* 9(3), 225–237.

O'Reilly, C.A., III, Caldwell, C., and Barnatt, D. (1989). Work Group Demography, Social Integration and Turnover, *ASQ,* 34(1), 21–37.

Palsson, A.M. (1996). Does the Degree of Relative Risk Aversion Vary With Household Characteristics? *Journal of Economic Psychology,* 17(6), 771–787.

Pelled, L.H., Eisenhardt, K.M., & Xin, K.R. (1999). Exploring the Black Box: An Analysis of Work Group Diversity, Conflict, and Performance, *Administrative Science Quarterly,* 44(1), 1–28.

Roure, J.B. & Madique, M.A. (1986). Linking Pre-Funding Factors and High-Technology Venture Success: An Exploratory Study. *Journal of Business Venturing,* 1(3), 295–306.

Smith, K.G., Smith, K.A., Olian, J.D., Sims, H.P., O'Bannon, D.P., & Scully, J.A. (1994). Top Management Team Demography and Process: The Role of Social Integration and Communication. *Administrative Science Quarterly,* 39(3), 412–443.

Starr, J., Bygrave, W.B., & Tercanli, D. (1993). Does Experience Pay?: Methodological Issues in the Study of Entrepreneurial Experience. In S. Birley and I.C. Macmillan (eds.), *Entrepreneurship Research: Global Perspectives,* 125–155. Amsterdam: Elsevier Science.

Teachman, J.D. (1980). Analysis of Population Diversity. *Sociological Methods and Research,* 1, 149–177.

Timmons, J.A. (1990). *New Venture Creation.* Homewood, IL: Irwin.

Ucbasaran, D., Wright, M., & Westhead, P. (2003). A Longitudinal Study of Habitual Entrepreneurs: Starters and Acquirers. *Entrepreneurship and Regional Development,* 15(3), 207–228.

Virany, B. & Tushman, M.L. (1986). Top Management Teams and Corporate Success in an Emerging Industry. *Journal of Business Venturing,* 1(3), 261–274.

Walsh, J.P. & Ellwood, J.W. (1991). Mergers, Acquisitions and the Pruning of Managerial Deadwood. *Strategic Management Journal,* 12(3), 201–218.

Watson, W.E., Ponthieu, L.D., & Critelli, J.W. (1995). Team Interpersonal Effectiveness in Venture Partnerships and Its Connection to Perceived Success. *Journal of Business Venturing,* 10(5), 393–411.

Westhead, P. (1995). Survival and Employment Growth Contrasts between Types of Owner-Managed High-Technology Firms. *Entrepreneurship Theory and Practice,* 20(1), 5–27.

Westhead, P. (1997). Ambitions, 'External' Environment and Strategic Factor Differences between Family and Non-Family Companies. *Entrepreneurship and Regional Development,* 9(2), 127–157.

Westhead, P., Cowling, M., & Howorth, C. (2001). The Development of Family Companies: Management and Ownership Issues. *Family Business Review,* 14(4), 369–385.

Wiersema, M.F. & Bantel, K.A. (1992). Top Management Team Demography and Corporate Strategic Change. *Academy of Management Journal,* 35(1), 91–121.

Wiersema, M.F. & Bantel, K.A. (1993). Top Management Team Turnover as an Adaptation Mechanism: The Role of the Environment. *Strategic Management Journal*, 14(7), 485–504.

Wright, M., Robbie, K., & Ennew, C. (1997). Venture Capitalists and Serial Entrepreneurs. *Journal of Business Venturing*, 12(3), 227–249.

Zimmerman, M.A. & Zeitz, G.J. (2002). Beyond Survival: Achieving New Venture Growth by Building Legitimacy. *Academy of Management Review*, 27(3), 414–431.

Deniz Ucbasaran is lecturer in Economics of Enterprise, Nottingham University Business School, UK.

Andy Lockett is lecturer in strategy, Nottingham University Business School, UK.

Mike Wright is professor of financial studies and director of the Centre for Management Buyout Research at Nottingham University Business School. He is also a visiting professor at Erasmus University and INSEAD, and an editor of the Journal of Management Studies.

Acknowledgments: We thank the participants at the Global Entrepreneurship Conference, 2001, Lyon, France, and the Babson-Kauffman Entrepreneurship Research Conference, 2001, Jönköping, Sweden, for their valuable comments. The 1990/91 SARIE database was collected in association with Sue Birley. We would also like to thank Ada Karman Lei for her assistance in collecting the data in 2000. The insightful comments of Ray Bagby and two anonymous reviewers are appreciated. Opinions (and the potential errors) expressed in this articles are, of course, the authors' alone.

[14]

Organization Science

Vol. 16, No. 2, March–April 2005, pp. 123–133
ISSN 1047-7039 | EISSN 1526-5455 | 05 | 1602 | 0123

inf**orms**®

DOI 10.1287/orsc.1050.0115
© 2005 INFORMS

New Venture Evolution and Managerial Capabilities

Warren Boeker
University of Washington, Box 353200, Seattle, Washington 98110, wboeker@u.washington.edu

Robert Wiltbank
Willamette University, 900 State Street, Salem, Oregon 97301, wiltbank@willamette.edu

This study examines factors influencing changes in the top management of start-up firms. Whereas a significant amount of research has examined top management transitions in established firms, we know much less about the factors influencing the evolution of top management capabilities in a new firm. Our research examines these issues in a sample of new ventures founded from 1983 through 1995, examining each firm for seven years after its founding to evaluate the conditions that influence a firm's changes in top management. Results indicate that top management team changes occur in cases of very low or very high firm growth, but are mitigated by a functionally diverse top management team. Power and control of inside and outside constituencies also affect changes in top management, with venture capital ownership and board representation increasing change in top management, and managerial ownership decreasing changes.

Key words: entrepreneurship; top management teams; governance and control; organizational evolution and change

A critical factor in the success of a new venture is the ability of its initial leadership to continue to meet new challenges as the business evolves. New ventures are often begun by an entrepreneur who has a very specific marketable product or idea, who then brings together other founders and funding to create the new business. What conditions motivate changes in the leadership of such a firm? Research focused on managerial changes in start-up firms is framed by approaches from an entrepreneurial perspective on the one hand, and by studies of large firm executive succession on the other. The entrepreneurial perspective tends to emphasize the life cycle aspect of venture development and the possibility that founding entrepreneurs become less adept at managing the firm's evolution beyond their initial focus and across an expanding operation (Boeker and Karichalil 2002, Jayaraman et al. 2000). Research on larger firms has focused on the ability of firms to adapt to environmental change, the consequences of promoting insiders rather than outsiders to the position of chief executive, and the effects of entrenchment and power dynamics on the actual execution of leadership change (Hambrick et al., forthcoming).

Despite arguments that start-up firms need to augment their managerial capabilities as they grow, there have been few theoretically grounded, empirically rigorous studies of whether and how new ventures add these capabilities (Rubenson and Gupta 1996). Willard et al. (1992) argue against the importance of changing CEOs as new ventures evolve by showing no mean performance differences in a sample of 110 founder-run firms, compared with 45 "professional CEO"-run firms. Much of the interest in chief executive change in new ventures

stems from anecdotal studies of firms that have faltered soon after founding because the founding team was unable to manage the established firm (Auletta 1998). In many cases, these new ventures were subsequently revived when a new executive with more managerial experience was brought in (Flamholtz 1990). To better understand the critical role that change in top management can have in a new venture, we bring together life cycle perspectives on new venture evolution and leadership change, and the large firm succession dimensions of power and governance.

This study furthers this line of research by examining two key research questions: (1) How do firm growth, strategic change, and characteristics of the existing top management team influence the extent of top management team change in new ventures? (2) How are these changes affected by the power dynamics and oversight of the team, represented by different levels of ownership and board independence? Our empirical setting is the semiconductor industry from 1983 through 1995, following each firm for seven years after it is founded. Our paper begins by hypothesizing factors in top management team change, then proceeds to a discussion of the ways in which ownership and board oversight might effect the implementation of those changes. We conclude with a discussion of the models and results of our empirical analysis.

Theoretical Development

When an organization begins, founders assume a charismatic role in which the person and his or her position are tightly coupled (Weber 1968, Giddens 1979). As the new venture grows and develops, the job and attention

Boeker and Wiltbank: *New Venture Evolution and Managerial Capabilities*
Organization Science 16(2), pp. 123–133, © 2005 INFORMS

124

of founders shifts from personally directing and controlling many of the activities of the organization to providing direction to others who are responsible for actual operations (Kimberly 1980). Although it is possible for founders to adapt their style and become successful at running a larger business, these founders often have neither the interest nor the skills necessary to do so (Jayaraman et al. 2000). Stevenson and Jarillo (1990) argue that very different sets of skills are needed to effectively manage the entrepreneurial challenges of a start-up versus the administrative challenges of an established firm. As Jayaraman et al. note (2000, p. 1,216): "A founder's ongoing involvement in general management activities may be decreasingly valuable or even detrimental to a company's success as the firm grows."

Many popular press accounts and much of the conventional wisdom surrounding new firm start-ups also argues that new ventures quickly outgrow their founding leaders and require change in the form of professional managers with more managerial- than entrepreneurial-oriented capabilities to successfully lead the firm as it develops (Willard et al. 1992). The recently emerging world of Internet and e-commerce offers several examples of experienced professional managers being brought in to help manage start-ups after founding. Well-publicized examples include James Barksdale (formerly of FedEx) at Netscape, Timothy Koogle (formerly of Motorola) at Yahoo!, and Meg Whitman (formerly of FTD) at eBay. In these examples, professional managers were brought in to help run the start-up because of their broader set of managerial capabilities and experiences (Auletta 1998).

Life Cycle Effects on Firm Development

Life cycle models and the life cycle metaphor has been used to describe human development (Levinson 1987), new venture development (Burgelman and Sayles 1986), industry evolution (Hannan and Carroll 1992), and even the rise and fall of nations (Kennedy 1987). In organizational analyses, theorists have characterized organizations as evolving through life cycle stages as they grow, accompanied by very significant changes in the managerial capabilities needed by the firm (Van de Ven and Poole 1995). In most life cycle models, theorists posit that organizations confront certain generic problems as they age and grow. Managers and members respond by modifying the organization's management, systems, structure, and authority (Pugh et al. 1968). In this process, life cycle models call attention to the common set of challenges faced by the firm as it matures, and attempt to develop broad heuristics that can be applied to firms at specific stages of their development (Aldrich 1999).

The underlying dimensions of life cycle reasoning are the age and growth of the firm. Managerial demands are argued to change as a new venture grows, with organizational tasks and external interfaces typically increasing and becoming more complex (Covin and Slevin

1997). One of the earliest proposed life cycle models, Greiner's (1972) model of organization development, argues that firms proceed through distinguishable phases; at each phase, major changes in the organization need to take place for the firm to be successful in the succeeding period. Greiner (1972) describes the first stage of firm development as "growth through creativity" (p. 41), occurring soon after the firm is founded. During this phase, the nascent organization is driven by the pioneering product and market insight of its founders. This evolutionary stage ends in a "crisis of leadership" (p. 41), in which firm founders realize that they do not possess the necessary skills to manage the firm to its next stage. Among a very broad set of managerial responsibilities, we refer to typical skills demanded of top managers including leadership, delegation, oversight and guidance, creative response to changing opportunities and threats, and interfacing with complex sets of external stakeholders.

A key argument of life cycle theorists studying the earliest founding stages is that the original founding group may not possess the proper skills to manage a larger and more established firm, and may not be able to modify their personal management style to match the evolving firm's needs (Gilmore 1988). One of the significant changes that can arise is the need for extensive delegation and a relinquishment of control and direct involvement in many aspects of the firm, often a very different leadership approach than what initially led to entrepreneurial success (Churchill and Lewis 1983). Under these changing conditions, the top management team may need to change to effectively match the capabilities of the team with the changing needs of the firm.

Given the difficulties of managing these transitions, life cycle theorists have argued that new ventures may need to bring in professional managers who possess capabilities better suited to running an established firm (Adizes 1989, Hanks 1990). In one of the few empirical examinations of this basic notion, Hambrick and Crozier (1985) find that successful start-ups are more proactive in adding managers with more experience, whereas new ventures that are less successful at growing past the founding stage are likely to leave the set of founding managers essentially unchanged. Rubenson and Gupta (1996) outline important factors in this process, explaining key relationships that influence changes in the founder as the firm transitions through development stages. They suggest a model examining three sets of variables: those relating to the changing needs of the organization, those relating to the ability and desire of the founder to adapt to those changing needs, and those related to the ability of the founders to prevent their own succession.

Building on that framework, in this study we examine firm growth and strategic change as drivers of the

Boeker and Wiltbank: *New Venture Evolution and Managerial Capabilities*
Organization Science 16(2), pp. 123–133, © 2005 INFORMS

Figure 1   Top Management Team Change in New Ventures

Changing firm needs
  High growth
  Low growth
  Strategic diversification

Capability to adapt
  Team experience
  Functional diversity

→ TMT change

Ability to execute change
  Manager ownership
  CEO ownership
  Board independence
  VC involvement

Note. VC = venture capitalists; TMT = top management team.

need for changes in the capabilities of top management. The necessity of changing top management may be tempered, however, by the capabilities of the current top management team to adapt to the firm's evolving leadership demands. Following an investigation of these life cycle effects after founding, we turn to an analysis of the power of incumbent top managers to prevent team change, examining the role of ownership and board membership in influencing power dynamics in the upper echelon of the organization (Finkelstein and Hambrick 1996). Figure 1 illustrates our framework and the manner in which these variables influence change in the top management of the new venture.

Firm Growth. Firms that are growing at a more rapid rate may need to more proactively adjust their managerial capabilities, making the need for new top management talent especially acute in faster-growing organizations. As noted by Argote (1999), firm growth may lead to information overload for the individual manager. Processes of delegation, planning and balancing resources needs, and organizing specialized subsystems are aspects of the administrative challenge brought on by firm growth (Lawrence and Lorsch 1967, Chandler 1962). Higher rates of growth also challenge the ability of any individual manager to adapt, leading to an increased need to change the team rather than to rely on adaptation (Rubenson and Gupta 1992). Thus, we expect fast-growing new ventures to institute more changes in their top management teams (Flamholtz 1990).

Although fast growth can create the need for different top managers, a lack of start-up growth may also serve as an indication that new top managers with different skills are needed, in this case to help turn the new venture around. Slow growth may serve as a signal to stakeholders and other firm constituencies that the current management of the new venture is ineffective and that new capabilities may be needed. Past work on top management change has argued that the inability of current

top management team to meet growth expectations is the primary motivation for bringing in new leadership (Finkelstein and Hambrick 1996), and Boeker and Karichalil (2002) demonstrate an increased rate of founder departure under conditions of low growth.

Both fast growth and slow growth are therefore expected to lead to changes in top management. Fast-growing new ventures need different top management talent to successfully exploit the ventures' growth, whereas slow-growing new ventures may need new managers to turn around a potential failure.

HYPOTHESIS 1. *There is a U-shaped relationship between firm growth and change in top management of a new venture. New ventures that are growing more rapidly or more slowly will make more changes to their top management.*

Strategic Diversification. Diversification, broadening the set of products and markets the firm competes in, also impacts the ability of current management to successfully manage the new venture. Start-up firms typically begin with a business plan targeting a specific product or market that parallels the founders' expertise (Cooper and Gimeno 1992, Eisenhardt and Schoonhoven 1990). As the new venture expands, it must decide whether and how rapidly to diversify into new products or services. To the extent that the firm remains strategically focused as it grows, the expertise provided by the founders may be sufficient to continue to compete in the original set of products (Rubenson 1989).

Diversification by the firm into new products, however, often requires different product or market expertise—expertise that may not be available or readily recognizable to the founding managers of the firm (Hambrick and Crozier 1985). As the firm diversifies and modifies its strategy, the skill set of the founding managers may be less well matched to these new markets. If the firm decides to diversify into new product areas, it is likely to require different capabilities from top management (Hofer and Charan 1984).

HYPOTHESIS 2. *New ventures with greater strategic diversification will make more changes to their top management.*

Top Management Experience. Although the nature of managing a new venture changes as it grows and pursues new strategies, some top management teams may be better able than others to adapt their management practices. Founders and teams with more overall industry experience should have greater relevant business, managerial, and industry familiarity, and may be better able to cope with the changing needs of the firm as it expands (Hofer and Charan 1984). Experience has been shown to be a critical factor in studies of the effects of leaders and their organizations. Roberts and Berry (1985, p. 323), for example, find that "familiarity with the technology

Boeker and Wiltbank: *New Venture Evolution and Managerial Capabilities*
Organization Science 16(2), pp. 123–133, © 2005 INFORMS

126

and market being addressed is the critical variable that explains much of the success or failure in new business development."

Founders with less experience in the industry may not have the same capabilities and knowledge to draw on as the firm evolves (Eisenhardt and Schoonhoven 1996). As a result, they may be unable to spot trends or generate a range of possible alternatives from which to make the best possible business decision. Rubenson (1989) demonstrates that managers who have more business and industry experience are likely to better understand how to manage a new venture as it grows and be better positioned to grow revenue and market share. In addition, Eisenhardt and Schoonhoven (1990) point out that top managers with a great deal of industry experience are likely to have more influence in the firm than less experienced managers. Top management teams of new ventures with greater overall levels of industry experience are likely to be better able to accommodate the needs of the firm brought on by their firm's growth and strategic change, thus reducing the need to make changes.

HYPOTHESIS 3. *New ventures having top management teams with greater industry experience will make fewer changes to their top management.*

Functional Diversity of Top Management. The diversity of the team's experience is as important as the absolute level of experience of the top management team. Teams comprising individuals representing only a small number of functions may not have the requisite skills to manage a new venture as it evolves. The diversity in functional representation captured by the entire team represents the expertise and capabilities that can be contributed to the new firm as it develops. Start-up ventures comprising teams representing a narrow set of functions may be limited in the knowledge base that they can access (Cohen and Levinthal 1990, Aldrich 1999).

Research examining diversity of experience has found that as top management teams' functional experience broadens, they avoid overcommitment to the status quo, have a wider range of practices to call on, and tend to be more open to new ways of operating (Geletkanycz and Black 2001). Bunderson and Sutcliffe (2002) show these benefits reach even to the individual level, where intrapersonal diversity of experience has similar positive effects that at times can outweigh the effects attributed to dominant functional experience. In addition to the broader skill set of these top managers, Williams et al. (1995) find that top management teams with greater functional diversity implement organizational changes more quickly. Adaptation to the changing needs of the venture becomes a more realistic option for management teams with more diverse experience. As a result, whereas growth and strategic change may increase the need to adjust the capabilities of the top management team in a new venture, the diversity of experience in the team

may meet these needs without requiring changes in the members of the team.

HYPOTHESIS 4. *New ventures having top management teams with greater functional diversity will make fewer changes to their top management.*

These initial hypotheses provide the context for us to answer the first question of this study: In what ways do firm growth and strategic change affect change in managerial capabilities? Growth and strategic change are predicted to motivate changes in the top management team of the new venture, but these changes may be mitigated through the experience and variety of experience of current top management. Our second question involves the manner in which power and control influence change in top management. Whereas life cycle theories suggest the need to change top management as the firm develops, the balance of power and competing interests among top managers, owners, and the board is likely to play a significant role in the patterns of change we actually observe.

New Venture Ownership
One of the key issues in this balance of power is ownership of the firm. Decisions about top management change are strongly influenced by who controls the firm (Finkelstein and Hambrick 1996), and ownership has an important influence on the amount of power individuals and groups have in the organization (Goodstein and Boeker 1991). This is particularly true in new ventures, where owners often play an active role in managing and advising the firm, and are typically more directly involved in the operation of the firm than are the owners in more established organizations. Ownership of new ventures is also fairly concentrated, leading owners to exert tighter and more proactive control over decisions around top management staffing (Flamholtz 1990).

Prior work on the role of inside ownership has examined how ownership can act to protect top management's power base and position (Berle and Means 1932, Mizruchi 1983). Management ownership may permit managers to act opportunistically, safeguarding their position from possible encroachment by new managers who might usurp their power or position (Williamson 1985). If insiders have a stronger ownership position in the new venture, the importance of protecting their position may manifest itself in less change in top management (Aldrich 1999). Owner-managers may feel that they continue to be competent at running the firm and may be less willing to share power with new top managers brought in after founding. Owner-managers may also identify more strongly with the firm they founded and believe that they know what is best for the new venture because they started it and have a greater ownership interest in it.

Conversely, outsider owners may have fewer reservations about changing top managers, due to reduced

Boeker and Wiltbank: *New Venture Evolution and Managerial Capabilities*
Organization Science 16(2), pp. 123–133, ©2005 INFORMS

personal or relational ties to the existing management group (Useem 1984). Increases in outside ownership also increase the incentives for outside owners to actively monitor and influence the composition of top management, because they have a larger stake in the outcome. Particularly when outside ownership is concentrated within powerful groups, outside owners may act as a credible check on the power and influence of top managers (Boeker 1992).

HYPOTHESIS 5. *New ventures with greater ownership by insiders will make fewer changes to top management.*

We also wish to disentangle the specific effect of chief executive ownership from the effect of inside ownership generally. Past research has argued that strong chief executives are more proactive in making changes to and influencing the top management team (Finkelstein and Hambrick 1996).

Ownership by the chief executive is likely to increase the power of the chief executive to influence management team changes beyond their preeminent role as head of the firm. Although life cycle theory would normally suggest the value of changing the founder or CEO as the firm develops, power derived through ownership may enhance his or her ability to adjust the team's capabilities to meet the changing needs of the firm. As a result, chief executives with greater ownership (likely resulting in greater influence) are predicted to initiate more changes in top management.

HYPOTHESIS 6. *New ventures with greater ownership by the chief executive will make more changes to the top management team.*

A reduction in top management ownership represents an increasing stake for outside owners. Outside owners who are actively involved in the operation and development of new ventures are venture capitalists. Venture capitalists not only provide financial backing for start-up firms, but also often help oversee the operation of the firm, provide management and legal advice, and aid the founders in defining new markets and strategies as the new venture evolves (Gompers and Lerner 2001). One of the main roles for venture capitalists is monitoring the managerial capabilities of the firm. As Hellman and Puri (2002) point out, it is often venture capitalists that are instrumental in initiating changes in the top management of the new venture. Kaplan and Stromberg (2001) find that the majority of venture capitalists expect to make changes to top management as they invest in new ventures. Changing top management may also represent a signal by venture capitalists to their limited partners that they are actively involved in the ventures; it may also signal to potential new investors (particularly the public markets) that the management team is more developed and more capable. Venture capitalists typically have a significant ownership stake in the

new venture and are proactive about advocating changes in managerial talent as the situation warrants (Sapienza and Gupta 1994).

HYPOTHESIS 7. *New ventures with greater ownership by venture capitalists will make more changes to their top management.*

Boards of Directors

Oversight, in addition to ownership, is likely to affect the implementation of change in ventures. A venture's board of directors plays the primary oversight role and is extensively involved with policy decisions made by the management team, including executive compensation and team make up (Lynall et al. 2003). In agency terms, managers are agents of the owners (principals) and as such do not necessarily share in the residual profits of the enterprise. Accordingly, their interests in the firm's goals and resources may diverge substantially from those of the owners. Boards of directors play a central role in addressing these agency problems (Jensen and Meckling 1976).

Past work on firm governance has noted a key distinction between inside and outside board members. Whereas outside board members may fill their monitoring role well, inside board members (board members who are also employees) are likely to exert more influence over decision making in the firm, and are likely to be less independent than outside directors (Rediker and Seth 1995, Boyd 1994). Mizruchi (1983) argues that inside directors, as full-time managers, may be less interested in sharing control with potential new managers, particularly those from outside the firm. Because inside board members are also full-time managers, their objectivity may be limited and diverging interests may undermine the ability of the board to exert control (Westphal and Zajac 1995). Boards composed of a higher proportion of insiders may be more reluctant to welcome changes in top management, be concerned that such changes might disrupt their own positions in the firm, and limit their range of responsibilities and activities, if not remove them entirely. In such cases, we would expect that boards with more insiders would generally be less likely to demand changes in top management.

Conversely, ventures with a greater proportion of outside directors may be more proactive at critically monitoring the performance of the firm and its managers, and be more willing to adjust the management team's capabilities by changing top managers. Agency theorists have long argued that independent boards—those composed of outsiders—more effectively monitor management behavior and firm policy (Fama 1980). Substantial research has argued that outsider-dominated boards help keep management's use of power in check (Monks and Minow 2001), are more likely to replace chief executives following periods of poor performance (Weisbach

Boeker and Wiltbank: *New Venture Evolution and Managerial Capabilities*
Organization Science 16(2), pp. 123–133, © 2005 INFORMS

128

1988), and more effectively enact poison pill policies in favor of shareholder wealth rather than in favor of protecting management (Brickley et al. 1994). The generally accepted perspective is that outside directors are better able to exhibit independence and objectivity.

In this study, we explore this possibility in relation to managerial change in a new venture. In newer ventures, however, the overall independence level of the board is likely lower than in larger firms. Outside board members of new ventures are more likely to consist of close friends and acquaintances of the founding entrepreneur (entrepreneurs). Outsiders in these new ventures may act more as insiders than their counterparts in larger firms, creating a conservative test of our hypothesis:

HYPOTHESIS 8. *New ventures with boards composed of a greater proportion of outside directors will make more changes in top management.*

As with our arguments for ownership, we predict venture capitalists on the board of directors to be more closely involved with the operation of the firm and more proactive in encouraging adjustments to the management team.

HYPOTHESIS 9. *New ventures with boards composed of a greater proportion of venture capitalists will make more changes to top management.*

Addressing our second research question regarding the execution of top management change, these hypotheses argue that because power and oversight is internal to the firm, the execution of change will occur less frequently. When power and oversight reside outside the management team, particularly when they are concentrated (as is the case with venture capital owners and board members), we expect change to significantly increase.

Methods

These hypotheses were tested on a sample of 86 semiconductor firms founded between 1983 and 1995 in the area of the United States known as Silicon Valley. Information on the firms was collected from public data sources and three market research firms. In cases where we could not obtain the information from publicly available sources, we interviewed top executives at firms with missing information.

The data used in the analysis included annual observations on all the variables over the first seven years after the new venture was founded. This seven-year period was chosen to allow for the full effect of the relationships we hypothesize, reaching well past estimates of the start-up phase. Industry analysts and venture capitalists in this industry tend to agree that the start-up period lasts up to approximately five years, after which the firm is no longer considered a start-up. Our data consist of annual panel data for the seven years after the firm was founded

(founding was measured as date of incorporation), helping to ensure coverage of the relevant window for new venture management changes. Because we believe our independent variables will have an influence on subsequent decisions to change or add to the top management team, all independent variables are lagged one year.

Measures: Dependent Variable

Top Management Change. We define the top management team as the chief executive and all top managers reporting to the chief executive. We operationalize this as the sum of the number of additions to the top management team and the number of departures from the top management team.

Measures: Independent Variables

Firm Growth. Firm growth was measured as growth in sales. Sales growth was measured as the proportionate increase in revenue over the year prior to which top management change or addition was measured. To separate out any effects that were due to the size of the firm or the overall growth in the industry, controls for firm size (in terms of sales) and industry growth were also included in the model.

Strategic Diversification. Strategic diversification was operationalized as diversification into new product areas. Using data from the market research firms, we identified 20 comprehensive product groups within the semiconductor industry.[1] Strategic diversification is measured as any increase in the number of product groups in which the firm competed in the prior year.

Top Management Industry Experience. Top management experience was an organization-level variable that measured the average amount of time that current top managers had worked in the semiconductor industry.

Top Management Functional Diversity. Top managers were found to come from four types of primary functional experience: (1) research and development, (2) manufacturing and operations, (3) marketing and sales, and (4) finance, accounting, legal, and administrative. Top management functional diversity was measured using an entropy measure, where Pi is the percentage of top managers in the ith functional area across the four functional areas.

$$Functional\ diversity = \sum Pi \ln(1/Pi).$$

The entropy measure for top management functional diversity assesses whether top managers represent a wide variety of functions. Higher scores indicate a more diverse set of functional experiences for the top management team.

Inside Ownership. Top management ownership measured the proportion of total firm ownership held by individuals who were employees of the firm.

Boeker and Wiltbank: *New Venture Evolution and Managerial Capabilities*
Organization Science 16(2), pp. 123–133, © 2005 INFORMS

Chief Executive Ownership. Chief executive ownership measured the proportion of firm ownership held by the chief executive of the firm.

Venture Capital Ownership. Venture capital ownership measured the proportion of firm ownership held by venture capitalists who were funding the organization.

Outside Directors. Outside directors measured the proportion of board members who were not employed by the firm.

Venture Capital Directors. Venture capital directors measured the proportion of board members who were members of venture capital firms.

Controls
Five controls were added to the effects hypothesized above.

Firm Size. Size was measured as firm sales (using ln Sales).

Firm Age. Based on earlier studies of top management turnover in established firms, top management changes are generally expected to decline over time. Firm age was measured as the number of years since incorporation.

Top Management Team Size. Top management size was measured as a count of the members of the top management team (direct reports to the chief executive). Top management team size was included to control for any effect on additions or departures as the result of the size of the top management team.

Industry Growth. During periods of slower industry growth, firms may see less need for change in the types of top managers needed to successfully run the firm. In contrast, firms competing in periods of rapid industry growth are likely to update and adjust the capabilities of the top management team more frequently (Finkelstein and Hambrick 1996). Industry growth was measured as sales growth of the overall market over the prior year.

Public Ownership. Organizations were differentiated on the basis of whether they were publicly or privately held. No specific predictions were made regarding the extent of top management additions in public versus private firms. Public or private ownership was coded as one if the firm was publicly held and zero if the firm was privately held.

Modeling Procedure
The dependent variables of top management change consists of counts with a lower boundary of zero, making ordered probit estimation preferable for modeling these discrete events (Greene 1997). In all models, we introduced fixed effects for firm and time, as well as controls for heteroscedastic disturbances.

Results
Table 1 shows means, standard deviations, and correlations among the variables. Models exploring the effects of the control variables and the independent variables are shown in Table 2. The first model in Table 2 examines the effects of the control variables by themselves before adding the hypothesized independent variables.

Table 1 Correlation Matrix*

Variables	Mean	Std. dev.	1	2	3	4	5	6	7	8	9	10	11	12	13	14
1. Top mgmt. change	0.19	0.14														
2. Firm growth	0.68	0.44	0.10													
3. Strategic diversification	3.27	1.86	0.14	0.15												
4. Mgmt. industry experience	9.42	4.27	−0.15	0.13	0.08											
5. Mgmt. functional diversity	0.71	0.24	−0.17	0.12	0.21	0.09										
6. Top mgmt. ownership	0.60	0.20	−0.09	0.05	−0.13	0.20	−0.04									
7. Chief exec. ownership	0.12	0.11	−0.04	−0.10	−0.14	0.09	−0.07	0.13								
8. VC ownership	0.34	0.20	0.18	0.14	0.19	−0.12	0.03	−0.34	−0.16							
9. Outside directors	0.57	0.12	0.11	−0.05	0.04	−0.17	−0.13	−0.20	−0.18	0.29						
10. VC directors	0.28	0.21	0.16	0.12	0.19	−0.15	−0.16	−0.16	−0.14	0.37	0.22					
11. TMT size	5.26	1.75	−0.08	−0.11	0.08	0.06	0.09	−0.12	−0.05	0.09	0.13	0.13				
12. Firm size	16.72	10.12	0.16	−0.10	0.23	0.11	0.18	0.08	−0.20	0.23	0.18	0.19	0.12			
13. Firm age (quarters)	18.4	9.22	0.20	−0.18	0.18	0.21	0.23	−0.12	−0.15	0.19	0.24	0.17	0.09	0.40		
14. Industry growth	0.63	0.38	0.03	0.27	0.15	0.08	0.05	0.07	−0.03	0.08	0.06	0.06	0.02	0.11	−0.02	
15. Public ownership	0.59	0.42	0.13	−0.20	−0.04	0.11	0.25	0.05	−0.21	−0.17	0.13	−0.12	0.07	0.27	0.18	−0.07

*All correlations above $r = 0.12$ are significant at $p < 0.05$.

Boeker and Wiltbank: *New Venture Evolution and Managerial Capabilities*
Organization Science 16(2), pp. 123–133, © 2005 INFORMS

130

Table 2   Determinants of Top Management Team Change

	Top management change	Top management change
Controls		
Top management team size	0.072	0.068
	(0.072)	(0.070)
Firm size	0.077†	0.068†
	(0.050)	(0.045)
Firm age	0.162	0.156
	(0.181)	(0.178)
Industry growth	0.015	0.013
	(0.098)	(0.010)
Public ownership	0.546*	0.512*
	(0.241)	(0.226)
Constant	0.685**	0.643**
	(0.291)	(0.282)
Independent variables		
Firm growth		−1.601**
		(0.526)
Firm growth^2		0.386*
		(0.165)
Strategic diversification		0.306
		(0.202)
Top management industry experience		−0.258†
		(0.135)
Top management diversity		−0.365*
		(0.138)
Inside ownership		−0.113*
		(0.047)
Chief executive ownership		0.175*
		(0.080)
Venture capital ownership		0.137**
		(0.039)
Outside directors		0.259
		(0.189)
Venture capital directors		0.676**
		(0.140)
Log likelihood	−258.42	−315.15

*$p < 0.05$, **$p < 0.01$, $^\dagger p < 0.10$, using a two-tailed test.
$N = 516$ firm-years.

Firm size (measured as number of employees) was marginally significant (at the 0.10 level), offering some indication that the demands of managing larger numbers of employees increases change in top management. Public ownership also was significant. Public firms may face greater outside scrutiny (Useem 1984) and fewer internal political constraints, leading to more top management change. The effects of the hypothesized variables were then added to the second model of Table 2.

Effects of Firm Growth. Hypothesis 1 predicted that both fast-growing and slow-growing new ventures would be likely to demonstrate change in top management talent, resulting in a U-shaped relationship between growth and top management change. The predicted U-shaped relationship was confirmed as indicated in Table 2, where the direct effect of growth is negative and the quadratic growth (growth^2) term is positive.[2]

Strategic Diversification. Hypothesis 2 predicted that strategic diversification would increase change in the top management team. Firms changing their strategy by diversifying into new product areas may need to change their top management team by acquiring managers with a wider variety of skills and capabilities. This hypothesis was not supported

Industry Experience and Functional Diversity. We also investigated whether differences in top management industry experience and breadth of functional experience affected team change. Hypothesis 3 argued that top management teams with greater industry experience have a more advanced set of relevant, valuable skills, reducing the need to change managers as the firm evolves from founding; it was marginally supported ($p < 0.10$) in the model. Hypothesis 4 predicted that more functional diversity would also create less need for the new venture to change managers as it developed and was significantly supported in the model. Both experience and functionally diverse top management appear to limit the need to bring on new managers as the new venture develops.

Effects of Ownership and Boards of Directors. Hypotheses 5 through 7 argued that ownership by specific groups would influence top management change in the new venture. Hypothesis 5 examined the effect of inside owners in reducing top management change, arguing that they may be interested in maintaining the status quo within the top management team. Hypothesis 6 posited that ownership by the chief executive will lead to more top management changes, and Hypothesis 7 argued that ownership by active external constituencies such as venture capitalists would increase top management change. Results in Table 2 demonstrate support for each of these hypotheses: Greater inside ownership led to less top management change, whereas chief executive and venture capital ownership led to more change.

Hypotheses 8 and 9 examined the structure of the board of directors and its effect on top management change in new ventures. Hypothesis 8 argued that new ventures with greater outside director participation would make more changes in their top management because insider directors may be more interested in protecting their positions and the stability of the team. The results in Table 2, however, indicated no support for this hypothesis. Hypothesis 9 looked at the effect of venture capitalists on the board, which may be a more direct measure of focused board oversight than differences between inside and outside directors; the hypothesis was supported. Increasing venture capital representation on the board led to significantly more change in top management.

Given the importance of the life cycle of the firm and firm growth on changes in top management, we also evaluated the interactive effects of the independent variables and firm growth. Because we have no strong theoretical

Boeker and Wiltbank: *New Venture Evolution and Managerial Capabilities*
Organization Science 16(2), pp. 123–133, © 2005 INFORMS   131

reasons to make specific a priori predictions, this analysis is exploratory. Results of the analysis (not shown) indicated that the interactive effects of growth with top management team diversity and management ownership were significant. In these cases, the effect of team diversity and management ownership combine with growth to further reduce top management team change beyond the direct effects of those variables.

Discussion

Past work in entrepreneurship has noted the critical difference between starting and managing a successful firm. This study expands on the life cycle arguments that have motivated past studies by including effects of top management characteristics, governance, and ownership. By examining changes in the top management of the new venture we obtain a more comprehensive picture of the factors driving changes in managerial talent. Our study shows what factors motivate new ventures to change their top management, and how the ownership and oversight of the venture can enhance or interfere with that process.

Life cycle perspectives have argued that the complexity of the organization and the required mix of critical skills change as new ventures grow and develop. The results of our study demonstrate support for this perspective, but with the added insight that both low growth and very high growth can lead to pressures for top management change. Our results demonstrate clear differences that exist between new ventures and established firms. In both established firms and new ventures, low growth is seen as leading to top management change. In established firms, growth and success is associated with a lack of change in top management. However, in successful new ventures it is precisely because the new venture has been successful, and is growing so rapidly, that different managerial capabilities are often needed to handle the increased complexity of managerial tasks.

Change in top management occurs through both the addition and departure of executives. Managerial additions are an important theoretical and empirical subset, because many of the notions surrounding the evolution of new ventures and the life cycle of the firm are focused on the types of managerial capabilities that need to be added to the new venture. Aldrich (1999), for example, argues that the expansion of new ventures into other product areas is often accompanied by the introduction of new managers to the focal organization with the capabilities to help the new venture to compete more successfully in the new market. In the case of strategic diversity, although we did not find that direct effects of diversification had a significant effect on top management change, supplementary analysis (not shown) indicates that strategic diversity did have a significant effect on additions to the firm. Further research is needed to understand whether the use of additions (rather than departures) is

affected by product line extensions differently than by product line deletions.

The functional diversity of the top management team appears to mitigate the need for top management change. New ventures with more functionally diverse top management made fewer changes in top managers, supporting our argument that some firms may be able to accommodate the changing needs of their ventures more effectively than others, based on their broader skill set. Whereas some firm characteristics lead to a need for new management talent (firm growth and strategic change), they can be counterbalanced by the ability of top management to meet these needs through their breadth of knowledge, as represented by their functional diversity (Rubenson and Gupta 1996).

In addition to the factors that motivate and mitigate management change, we explore the intervening role of power and control in the actual execution of change. Top managers who are also owners appear less than enthusiastic in making changes to their team; our findings demonstrate that firms with a higher proportion of top management ownership experience less top management change. In addition to managerial ownership, ownership by the chief executive is significantly related to increasing the extent of change in other top managers. Through this process, the chief executive may be able to maintain his or her position if the top management team is adjusted to the changing needs of the venture as it develops through its life cycle.

Other ownership effects were also significant. As ownership by venture capitalists increases, top management change increases. VC representation on the board of directors shows additional effects on top management change, representing formal influence over the company in addition to the implied rights of influence represented by ownership. Additionally, in supplementary analysis of additions and departures as components of team change, venture capital power led to a significant emphasis on departures rather than on additions, indicating a strong bias for replacing members of the team rather than adding new members.

We also examined outside directors as an influence in firm control and increased management change, but did not find significant effects of the hypothesized relationship. Where outside board members in large firms are argued to be more independent of the influence of the chief executive, in new ventures it may be that even directors fitting the definition of *outsiders* are more closely allied with the venture's management through friendships or social ties. The specific subgroup of outside directors that are composed of venture capitalists, rather than the broad notion of outsider, appears to be a better proxy for independence in the case of new ventures.

The combination of concepts from life cycle theory and power in executive succession provide a compelling picture of how new ventures come to make changes

Boeker and Wiltbank: *New Venture Evolution and Managerial Capabilities*
Organization Science 16(2), pp. 123–133, © 2005 INFORMS

132

in their management. The development of the venture presents changing leadership needs and a need for different managerial capabilities. These capabilities may already exist in teams with greater diversity of experience, but the power and influence represented by ownership and boards of directors directly influence the extent to which top management changes actually occur.

Limitations and Future Research

This research offers a broad, macro-level view of some of the antecedents of change in top management team capabilities. Future research should be directed at a more micro-level, and even at a case-based investigation of the specific types of skills and competencies that new managers bring to new ventures. A better understanding of the sorts of managerial profiles that may be more appropriate as a new venture evolves may offer practical insights into venture capitalists, boards, and top managers of new ventures. A practical area for future research is an examination of performance implications of changes in the top management of the new venture. What types or combinations of managerial competencies appear to offer performance advantages to new ventures?

Although our research is explicitly interested in examining the transition from an entrepreneurial firm to a professionally managed firm, a potential limitation of our study is the implication that all entrepreneurial firms necessarily need a new group of professional managers to add skills and capabilities to the founding team. Clearly, inadequate managerial skill and leadership can have a pervasive influence on the firm, but it is unclear whether a wholesale shift in the top management of the new venture will somehow lead to performance improvements. Few observers would argue that Microsoft, Wal-Mart, Hewlett-Packard, FedEx, Southwest Airlines, and other firms would have been better off replacing their founders. Our intents in this paper are to suggest that the team's overall capability does need to meet the changing needs of the venture, and to outline the indicators and moderators of those changing needs. Leaders of new ventures may benefit from proactively dealing with these issues.

Future research in entrepreneurship and firm founding must continue to investigate the evolution of managerial capabilities during the early development of the new venture. The results of this study provide some of the first empirical support for the role of growth, strategy, power, and governance on changes in the top management capabilities of the new venture. Studying the question of how change in a founding team unfolds can provide important insights into the role of firm control and individual differences in limiting or encouraging changes in managerial capabilities.

Acknowledgments

The authors would like to thank Eric Abrahamson, Jerry Goodstein, and Michael Hitt for help, ideas, and insights. They also thank the Center for Technology Entrepreneurship at the University of Washington for helping to fund this project.

Endnotes

[1] Other studies in the semiconductor industry (Eisenhardt and Schoonhoven 1990) have used the same categories.

[2] We examined the inflection point of the curvilinear effect and confirm that it fell within the range of the independent variables in each case.

References

Adizes, I. 1989. *Corporate Life Cycles: How and Why Corporations Grow and Die, and What to Do About It.* Prentice-Hall, Englewood Cliffs, NJ.

Aldrich, H. 1999. *Organizations Evolving.* Sage, Thousand Oaks, CA.

Argote, L. 1999. *Organizational Learning: Creating, Retaining and Transferring Knowledge.* Kluwer, New York.

Auletta, K. 1998. The last sure thing. *The New Yorker* (Nov. 19) 40–47.

Berle, A., Jr., G. C. Means. 1932. *The Modern Corporation and Private Property.* Macmillan, New York.

Boeker, W. 1992. Power and managerial dismissal: Scapegoating at the top. *Admin. Sci. Quart.* **37** 400–421.

Boeker, W. B., R. Karichalil. 2002. Entrepreneurial transitions: Factors influencing founder departure. *Acad. Management J.* **45**(4) 818–826.

Boyd, B. K. 1994. Board control and CEO compensation. *Strategic Management J.* **15** 335–344.

Brickley, J., J. Coles, R. Terry. 1994. Outside direction and the adoption of poison pills. *J. Financial Econom.* **35** 371–390.

Bunderson, J. S., K. M. Sutcliffe. 2002. Comparing alternative conceptualizations of functional diversity in management teams: Process and performance effects. *Acad. Management J.* **45**(4) 875–894.

Burgelman, R., L. Sayles. 1986. *Inside Corporate Innovation: Strategy, Structure, and Managerial Skills.* Free Press, New York.

Chandler, A. D., Jr. 1962. *Strategy and Structure.* MIT Press, Cambridge, MA.

Churchill, N. C., V. Lewis. 1983. The five stages of small business growth. *Harvard Bus. Rev.* **61**(May–June) 30–50.

Cohen, W. M., D. A. Levinthal. 1990. Absorptive capacity: A new perspective on learning and innovation. *Admin. Sci. Quart.* **35**(1) 128–152.

Cooper, A., J. Gimeno. 1992. Entrepreneurs, processes of founding, and new-firm performance. D. Sexton, J. Kasarda, eds. *The State of the Art of Entrepreneurship.* PWS-Kent, Boston, MA.

Covin, J. G., D. P. Slevin. 1997. High growth transitions: Theoretical perspectives and suggested directions. D. L. Sexton, R. W. Smilor, eds. *Entrepreneurship: 2000.* Upstart, Chicago, IL, 96–126.

Eisenhardt, K. M., C. Schoonhoven. 1990. Organizational growth: Linking founding team, strategy, and growth among U.S. semiconductor ventures, 1978–1988. *Admin. Sci. Quart.* **35** 504–529.

Eisenhardt, K. M., C. Schoonhoven. 1996. Resource-based view of strategic alliance formation: Strategic and social effects in entrepreneurial firms. *Organ. Sci.* **7**(2) 136–150.

Fama, E. 1980. Agency problems and the theory of the firm. *J. Political Econom.* **88** 288–307.

Boeker and Wiltbank: *New Venture Evolution and Managerial Capabilities*
Organization Science 16(2), pp. 123–133, © 2005 INFORMS

Finkelstein, S., D. C. Hambrick. 1996. *Strategic Leadership: Top Executives and Their Effect on Organizations.* West, St. Paul, MN.

Flamholtz, E. 1990. *Growing Pains.* JAI Press, Greenwich, CT.

Geletkanycz, M. A., S. S. Black. 2001. Bound by the past? Experience-based effects on commitment to the strategic status quo. *J. Management* **21**(1) 3–21.

Giddens, A. 1979. *Central Problems in Social Theory.* Macmillan, London, UK.

Gilmore, T. 1988. *Making a Leadership Change.* Jossey-Bass, San Francisco, CA.

Gompers, P., J. Lerner. 2001. *The Money of Invention: How Venture Capital Creates New Wealth.* Harvard Business School Press, Boston, MA.

Goodstein, J., W. Boeker. 1991. Turbulence at the top: A new perspective on governance structure. *Acad. Management J.* **34**(2) 306–331.

Greene, W. H. 1997. *Econometric Analysis,* 3rd ed. Prentice-Hall, Englewood Cliffs, NJ.

Greiner, L. E. 1972. Evolution and revolution as organizations grow. *Harvard Bus. Rev.* **50**(4) 37–46.

Grove, A. S. 1999. *Only the Paranoid Survive: How to Exploit the Crisis Points that Challenge Every Company.* Doubleday, New York.

Hambrick, D. C., L. M. Crozier. 1985. Stumblers and stars in the management of rapid growth. *J. Bus. Venturing* **1** 31–45.

Hambrick, D. C., S. Finkelstein, A. Mooney. Executive job demands: New insights for explaining strategic decisions and leader behaviors. *Acad. Management Rev.* Forthcoming.

Hanks, S. H. 1990. The organization life cycle: Integrating content and process. *J. Small Bus. Strategy* **1**(1) 1–12.

Hannan, M. T., G. R. Carroll. 1992. *Dynamics of Organizational Populations: Density, Legitimation, and Competition.* Oxford University Press, New York.

Hellman, T., M. Puri. 2002. Venture capital and the professionalization of start-up firms: Empirical evidence. *J. Finance* **57**(1) 169–197.

Hofer, C., R. Charan. 1984. The transition to professional management: Mission impossible? *Amer. J. Small Bus.* **9**(1) 1–11.

Jayaraman, N., A. Khorana, E. Nelling, J. Covin. 2000. CEO founder status and firm financial performance. *Strategic Management J.* **21** 1215–1224.

Jensen, M., W. Meckling. 1976. Theory of the firm: Managerial behavior, agency costs, and ownership structure. *J. Financial Econom.* **4** 305–360.

Kaplan, S., P. Stromberg. 2001. Venture capitalists as principals: Contracting, screening, and monitoring. *Amer. Econom. Rev.* **91**(2) 426–430.

Kennedy, P. 1987. *Rise and Fall of the Great Powers.* Random House, New York.

Kimberly, J. R. 1980. *The Organizational Life Cycle: Issues in the Creation, Transformation, and Decline of Organizations.* J. R. Kimberly, R. H. Miles, eds. Jossey-Bass Publishers, San Francisco, CA.

Lawrence, P. R., J. W. Lorsch. 1967. *Organization and Environment, Managing Differentiation and Integration.* Harvard Business School Press, Boston, MA.

Levinson, D. 1987. *Seasons of a Man's Life.* Knopf, New York.

Lynall, M. D., B. R. Golden, A. J. Hillman. 2003. Board composition from adolescence to maturity: A multitheoretic view. *Acad. Management Rev.* **28**(3) 416–439.

Mizruchi, M. 1983. Who controls whom? An examination of the relations between management and boards of directors in large American corporations. *Acad. Management Rev.* **8** 426–435.

Monks, R., N. Minow. 2001. *Corporate Governance.* Blackwell Publishers, Oxford, UK.

Pugh, D. S., D. J. Hickson, C. R. Hinings, C. Turner. 1968. Dimensions of organization structure. *Admin. Sci. Quart.* **13** 65–105.

Rediker, K. J., A. Seth. 1995. Boards of directors and substitution effects of alternative governance mechanisms. *Strategic Management J.* **16** 85–99.

Roberts, E., C. Berry. 1985. Entering new businesses: Selecting strategies for success. *Sloan Management Rev.* (Spring) 3–17.

Rubenson, G. C. 1989. Departure of organizational founders: Explaining variance in founder tenure, successor characteristics, successor power and future firm performance. Ph.D. dissertation, University of Maryland, College Park, MD.

Rubenson, G. C., A. K. Gupta. 1992. Replacing the founder: Exploding the myth of the entrepreneur's disease. *Bus. Horizons* **35**(6) 53–59.

Rubenson, G. C., A. K. Gupta. 1996. The initial succession: A contingency model of founder tenure. *Entrepreneurship Theory Practice* **21**(2) 21–35.

Sapienza, H. J., A. K. Gupta. 1994. Impact of agency risks and task uncertainty on venture capitalist-CEO interaction. *Acad. Management J.* **37**(6) 1618–1632.

Stevenson, H. H., J. C. Jarillo. 1990. A paradigm of entrepreneurship: Entrepreneurial management. *Strategic Management J.* **11** (Special Issue) 17–27.

Useem, M. 1984. *The Inner Circle.* Oxford University Press, New York.

Van de Ven, A. H., M. S. Poole. 1995. Explaining development and change in organizations. *Acad. Management Rev.* **20**(3) 510–540.

Weber, M. 1968. *Economy and Society.* Bedminster Press, New York.

Weisbach, M. 1988. Outside directors and CEO turnover. *J. Financial Econom.* **20** 431–460.

Westphal, J., E. Zajac. 1995. Who shall govern? CEO/board power, demographic similarity, and new director selection. *Admin. Sci. Quart.* **40** 60–83.

Willard, G. E., D. A. Krueger, H. R. Feeser. 1992. In order to grow must the founder go: A comparison of performance between founder and non-founder managed high-growth manufacturing firms. *J. Bus. Venturing* **7** 181–194.

Williams, R. J., J. J. Hoffman, B. T. Lamont. 1995. The influence of top management team characteristics on M-form implementation. *J. Managerial Issues* **7**(4) 466–481.

Williamson, O. 1985. *The Economic Institutions of Capitalism: Firms, Markets, and Relational Contracting.* Macmillan, New York.

Part IV
Outcome

[15]

LINKING PREFUNDING

FACTORS AND

HIGH-TECHNOLOGY

VENTURE SUCCESS:

AN EXPLORATORY STUDY

JUAN B. ROURE
Stanford University and IESE-Navarra University

MODESTO A. MAIDIQUE
University of Miami and Stanford University

EXECUTIVE SUMMARY

This study reports on the exploratory phase of a research project on prefunding factors influencing the success of high-technology start-up companies. The study was done in collaboration with two major West Coast venture capital firms that allowed the authors full access to the due diligence files, investment proposals, and closing documents associated with eight ventures. Half of the eight ventures studied are currently public companies with sales that range from $65 million to $500 million and with an after-tax profit of about 10% of sales. The other half have either been dissolved or did not reach $3 million in sales within the five years following their funding.

Information was obtained on those prefunding factors that were available for investor review prior to funding, such as the founders track records, the characteristics of the founding team, the nature of the target market, the technological strategy of the firm, the proposed composition of the board, and the deal structure.

In spite of the small sample size, findings of this research revealed discernible differences between successful and unsuccessful firms. The founders of the successful ventures had more prior experience working together; tended to form larger, more complete teams; and had more extensive experience in the function they performed in the new venture. Successful founders also had experience in rapid growth firms that competed in the same industry as the start-up.

The successful ventures targeted product-market segments with high buyer concentration in which, through technological advantage, their products could attain and sustain a competitive edge.

Address correspondence to J. Roure, IESE–Navarra University, Avola. Pearson 21, 08034 Barcelona, Spain; Or M. Maidique, University of Miami, P.O. Box 249117, Coral Gables, FL 33124.

The authors gratefully acknowledge support from IESE (Navarra University, Spain), where J. Roure is Professor on leave. Additional funding for this study was provided by the Center for Entrepreneurial Studies, New York University and the Department of Industrial Engineering and Engineering Management, Stanford University. The study benefitted from comments on early drafts of B. Dean, K. Eisenhardt, F. Haspeslagh, H. Riggs, R. Sutton, and S. Wheelwright.

Journal of Business Venturing 1, 295–306 (1986)
© 1986 Elsevier Science Publishing Co., Inc., 52 Vanderbilt Ave., New York, NY 10017

0883-9026/86/$03.50

Often this advantage was achieved by careful management of the product-development process, which resulted in early market entry and its corollary, reduced competition.

On the other hand, some factors that the authors had predicted would allow them to distinguish between success and failure were not found to do so. Both successful and unsuccessful ventures targeted high growth markets, anticipated high gross margins, had founders with over five years of relevant experience, had experienced venture capitalists on their boards, and were characterized by a wide range of founder equity shares.

INTRODUCTION

Most new companies fail soon after they are launched (Shapero and Giglierano 1982). High-technology start ups fare better than the average business, but their failures are usually more devastating because of the capital, time, and number of people involved (Cooper 1971; Roberts 1972; Timmons, Smollen, and Dingee 1977). One study following a group of 250 Silicon Valley technology firms founded in the 1960s reports that as of 1980, 36.8% had been discontinued, 32.4% had merged or had been acquired, and only 30.8% had survived as independent companies (Bruno and Cooper 1982). By 1980, each of these remaining independent firms on average had approximately $8.6 million in annual sales, employed 135 people, and had been in business for 14 years.

Despite these substantial initial failure rates, the amount of venture capital committed to high technology startups has increased almost tenfold during the past decade (*Venture Capital Journal* 1985). In 1983 and 1984, venture capitalists, the principal financiers of early-stage high-tech firms, invested over $6 billion in such businesses. The magnitude and trend of such investments suggest the need for a better understanding of those factors that influence early-stage performance of technological companies.

High-tech start-ups have been the subject of numerous case studies that illustrate the many pitfalls to be avoided by entrepreneurs. However, systematic research on the factors that explain the success or failure of new high technology ventures is scarce.

Three major studies that relate different factors of ventures to certain measures of success have been carried out. The first one is Cooper and Bruno's longitudinal study of 250 technological firms (1977). The study concludes that the more successful companies (i.e., those that survived longest) were founded by two or more founders and had one or more founders with prior experience in the markets or technologies they addressed. Furthermore, the authors found that entrepreneurs with prior experience in "large" organizations (those with over 500 employees) were more likely to be successful.

In another study on venture capital investments, Hoban (1976) concluded that the proportion of equity owned by the principals, the stage of development of the product, and the extensiveness of the market evaluation were positively correlated with the rate of return achieved.

Finally, a third study analyzed 13 software firms and found that start-up success was correlated with certain characteristics of the founders: education, experience, and internal locus of control (Van de Ven, Hudson, and Schroeder 1984). This study also concluded that success was positively correlated with one person being in command, active involvement of top management and board members in decision making, and implementation of the start-up on a small scale with incremental expansion over time.

In another group of studies, researchers have explored the criteria used by venture capitalists in evaluating venture proposals (MacMillan, Siegel, and Subba Narasimha 1985; Poindexter 1976; Tyebjee and Bruno 1984; Wells 1974). These studies, however, do not directly relate those factors that are considered critical by the investors to the subsequent success or failure of the company.

Clearly, the success of a high-technology start-up depends on many factors. Like a newborn child, the infant high-technology company requires nurturing and constant attention. But just as with a child, the successful development of a new venture is influenced by factors related to the "genes of the parents" and to the "nature of the gestation cycle." In a similar way, the likelihood of success of a high-technology company is often influenced by certain inherent individual and team characteristics of the firm's founders and by other prefunding factors.

As Maidique (1986) has pointed out, except for the handful of studies mentioned above, the prefunding factors that influence the success or failure of technological start-ups have received little attention by management scientists.

This article is part of an ongoing research project concerning the key prefunding factors that influence the success of high-technology companies funded by venture capital. Here we report on the initial results of our exploratory research. Based on this exploratory study and a review of the literature, we also propose a series of hypotheses that we plan to test with a larger sample.[1]

METHODOLOGY

Our exploratory research was conducted in three stages. First, we reviewed the relevant literature on technological start-ups including related work on entrepreneurship, product development, and venture capital. Second, we arranged semi-structured interviews with eight venture capitalists who collectively have over one hundred years of investment experience with high-tech firms. In these interviews we obtained the venture capitalists' general views on those factors that they believe influence the success or failure of high-tech start-ups. The following criteria were used in selecting the venture capitalists interviewed for our preliminary study: 1) affiliation with a well-known, professionally managed venture capital firm and 2) experience in the venture capital business for at least five years. Finally, in the third stage of our research we analyzed eight venture capital–financed start-ups and identified the factors that differentiate successful ventures from unsuccessful ones.

For the purpose of this study we define a successful venture as a firm that: 1) has been incorporated for more than three years; 2) has reached a sales level of over $20 million; and 3) has achieved after-tax profits greater than 5% of sales. We consider unsuccessful a venture that: 1) has been discontinued within five years of its initial funding or 2) has never reached $3 million in sales during the same period. This set of criteria is similar to the success-failure criteria selected by many institutional venture investors.

We chose our eight ventures by asking two partners of major West Coast venture capital firms to select from their portfolios matched pairs of companies that met our success-failure criteria. By studying companies that were part of professionally managed portfolios, we were ensured of the availability of business plans, closuring documents, and other reference data. All eight high-tech companies were from the electronics industry and were funded after 1974 (see Table 1).

---

[1]A preliminary version of these hypotheses was proposed by one of the authors, Juan Roure, as part of his Ph.D. Research Interest Paper, Stanford University, Department of Industrial Engineering and Engineering Management, October 1984.

298   J.B. ROURE AND M.A. MAIDIQUE

TABLE 1.   Types of Businesses Selected by Venture Capitalists

Company	Business
1	Semi-custom semiconductors
2	Disk drives
3	Computer-aided engineering workstations
4	Fault-tolerant computers
5	Specialized computer terminals and software
6	Computer-aided design workstations
7	Color graphics hardware
8	Marine instruments

All eight companies were located on the West Coast (five in Northern California) and in geographical areas with a supportive local infrastructure.

The four successful firms, all currently public companies, ranged in annual sales from $65 to $500 million, with after-tax profits of about 10% of sales. Of the four failures, two firms were dissolved within five years of their first funding and the other two did not reach sales of $3 million during the first five years after the initial funding.

ANALYSIS OF RESULTS

We focused on five categories of factors that, based on our exploratory interviews and on previous field research discussed earlier, we hypothesized could be important determinants of success in high-tech ventures:

1. Founders' track records;
2. Characteristics of founding team;
3. Target market;
4. Technological strategy; and
5. Deal structure.

In the following sections we report on the preliminary findings in each one of these categories and we propose a series of hypotheses that we will test in a subsequent stage of our project.

Founders' Track Records

We define as founders those members of the original team who, as indicated by the data available before the company was funded, were expected: 1) to play a key role in the development of the firm; 2) to become employees of the company within the first year after the initial funding date; and 3) to share in the ownership of the company in a significant manner. A founders' track record comprises previous positions held, tenure, and the host organization in which he or she had work experience.

Others have previously argued that experience is a characteristics of successful entrepreneurs (MacMillan et al. 1985; Vesper 1980). In our sample, however, virtually all of the founders of both the successful and unsuccessful companies had five or more years of experience in the particular industry in which their firms competed. This result is consistent with the findings of Cooper and Bruno's longitudinal study (1977). What did seem to make a difference between success and failure, however, is the nature of the founders' relevant experience and the characteristics of the organizations in which they obtained their experience. Founders of the successful companies typically had had two or more years of prior experience in the same position that they assumed in the new company. They also had had a successful and fast-rising career in previous organizations and had worked in units of "large" companies (over 500 people) that were characterized by high growth (more than 25% increase in sales or number of employees per year).

In contrast, the founders of the firms that failed had significantly less experience in positions similar to those that they assumed in the new venture. In addition, founders of unsuccessful companies had had a moderate career pace in large or small companies. Moreover, these companies were often characterized by a rate of growth that was much lower than that of companies of their successful counterparts. These results are partially supported by the Van de Ven et al. (1984) study that found that start-up success and company stage of development were positively related to the skills and expertise that the entrepreneurial team brought to the new venture.

Hypothesis 1 The success of a new venture will be positively related to the percentage of founders who have held positions similar to those they assumed in the new company.

Hypothesis 2 The success of a new venture will be positively related to the percentage of founders who have previously worked in high-growth organizations.

Characteristics of Founding Team

Founders of high-technology companies often form groups to start new companies. In three studies carried out in different U.S. regions, the authors found that the percentage of new firms started by two or more founders was 48 in Austin, Texas (Susbauer 1969), 61 in Palo Alto, California (Cooper 1971), and 59 in a study of 955 geographically diversified firms (Shapero 1971). Cooper and Bruno (1977), in their study of Silicon Valley firms, found that groups of two or more founders were involved in 83.3% of high-growth companies but in only 53.8% of discontinued firms, an observation that suggests that groups of founders are more successful than individuals. Venture capitalists also believe that the quality of the management team is one of the most important criteria in predicting new companies' success (Timmons and Gumpert 1982).

Notwithstanding these important findings, a review of the literature did not reveal any research on the characteristics of the original founder team. Our analysis of eight cases of success and failure convinced us that two principal characteristics of the team affect the success of technological start-ups. The first one is the degree of team completeness or percentage of essential functions in the new company that are filled by the founders' team at the time of funding. By a complete team, we mean a group that included as original founders the president and the executives responsible for marketing, engineering, finance, and operations. Occasionally, for a specific company, one of these functional areas was not viewed as critical by the venture capitalists for the start-up phase. In this case, we did not include that function in our completeness analysis. In the same way, if in a certain company both hardware and software experts were considered necessary, then we included both of these functions as requirement for team completeness.

The successful companies had larger and more complete teams at the time of funding. In two of the four successful companies the team was 100% complete and in the other two the team was 80% complete. On the other hand, whereas one of the unsuccessful companies had an 80% complete team and another had a 75% complete team, the other two had teams that included only 50% of the essential functions (see Table 2). In addition, one of these latter companies did not have a president when it was initially funded.

The second important characteristic of the founders' team that we found to be associated with the success of a new firm is the degree of prior joint experience; that is, the extent to which founders had previously worked together in the same organization for at least six months. We measured this variable by determining the actual number of prior relationships among pairs of founders and dividing that number of relationships by the total number of possible relationships among them. For example, if an entrepreneur starts a new company with three additional founders but has worked before in another organization with only two of them, the third one being new to the team, then the number of existing pairwise relationships in this case would be three; the total number possible, however, would be six. Thus, for this hypothetical firm the degree of joint experience would be 50%.

Of the four successful ventures, two had a 100% level of joint experience and the other two had a 50% level. By contrast, only one of the failures had a 50% level, whereas two of them had a 33% level, and the last had no prior joint experience (see Table 2). This result is not surprising. During the start-up period, entrepreneurs have limited time and a limited amount of capital with which to achieve clear results. Therefore, any resources spent developing relationships among the group may significantly reduce what is left for other vital activities.

Hypothesis 3 The degree of completeness of the founders' management team at the time of funding will be positively related to the success of the new firm.

Hypothesis 4 The degree of prior joint experience among the founders will be positively related to the success of the venture.

Target Market

All eight ventures in our sample targeted high-growth markets, ranging from 35% to 50% annually at the time of funding (see Table 3). This finding is consistent with the venture capitalists' usual criteria of evaluating new ventures using the growth rate of the target market

TABLE 2.   Founding Team Characteristics

Company[a]	Number of Members	Completeness	Joint Experience
S1	5	100	50%
S2	4	80	50%
S3	4	100	100%
S4	4	80	100%
Average	4.25	90	75%
U1	3	75	33%
U2	3	50	33%
U3	3	50	0%
U4	4	80	50%
Average	3.25	64	29%

[a] S = Successful; U = Unsuccessful.

TABLE 3. Characteristics of the Target Market

Companies[a]	Growth %	Market Share (%)	Buyer Concentration
S1	50	10	4
S2	40	15	4
S3	50	9	4
S4	45	13	4
Average	46	11.75	4
U1	50	2	1
U2	35	8	2
U3	40	6	4
U4	35	3,4,20[b]	2
Average	40	6.25	2.5

[a] S = Successful; U = Unsuccessful.
[b] The company had three different products addressing three different market segments.

(MacMillan et al. 1985). We, however, could not use rate of market growth as a factor allowing us to discriminate between success and failure.

Another market factor we evaluated was the projected market share targeted by the new firm. We obtained this data by taking it directly from the company business plan if it was explicitly given there, or, in other cases, from the venture capitalists' notes taken when they conducted their due diligence investigation. If this information was not readily available, we divided the company's fifth-year (or latest available year) sales projection by the overall relevant market size for the venture in that year.

We found that the successful companies targeted a significantly higher market share than did the unsuccessful ones (see Table 3). Based on these exploratory results, we speculate that successful companies try to carve out market niches within which they can play an important role. This finding is partially supported by a study done on 177 start-ups of PIMS (Profit Impact of Market Strategy) corporate ventures, in which the level of market share achieved and the level of return on investment were correlated (Hobson and Morrison 1983).

Hypothesis 5 The projected market share targeted by the new company will be positively related to the success of the venture.

If our follow-up statistical study confirms these results regarding market share, then they could serve to refute conventional wisdom concerning the evaluation of new ventures, which holds that the larger the market the better. What do these results imply with regard to optimum target market size? Assuming that the venture capitalist has a goal of participating in ventures that can reach $100 million in sales in five years and can address markets with growth rates of 40%–50%, the size of the relevant market at the time of funding should be in the range of $100 to $200 million, assuming target market shares of 20% and 10%, respectively.

A third market characteristic that we hypothesized as a possibly important one is the level of buyer concentration. We rated the level of buyer concentration from one to five: very low, low, medium, high, and very high. Very low buyer concentration means that the new venture expected to serve a very large number of potential customers with limited buying capacity, whereas very high concentration implies that the venture expected to serve a very small number of potential customers who have a large buying capacity.

All the successful companies in our sample were characterized by high levels of buyer concentration. On the other hand, only one of four failures had a high level of buyer concentration (see Table 3). This result emphasizes the difficulties in building a major distribution system during the start-up period and the complexity of maintaining effective communication with a varied and dispersed set of customers. On the other hand, depending on a very small number of buyers may increase the buyer's bargaining power and therefore may lower the probability of success for the new company (Porter 1980).

Hypothesis 6 The success of a new venture will have an inverted U-shaped curvilinear relationship to the number of potential buyers.

Finally, we analyzed the nature of competition in the venture's targeted market niche. Three of the successful companies targeted markets in which, because of their early entry, no competitor enjoyed a dominant position at the time of founding and in which large companies were supplying only a generic product. The fourth company targeted a market in which two competitors existed, one of them being the leader. The company did not, however, challenge the existing leader. Rather, it adopted a follower strategy by becoming a second source for the leader's products. Clearly, the successful companies targeted market segments relatively uninhabited by strong competitors or avoided head-on competition with firms already established in that market.

In contrast, two of the unsuccessful ventures targeted markets in which a clear leader existed, plus some lesser competitors. In both situations the new companies tried to compete head-on with the leaders. The two other failures targeted markets in which several competitors, including some major firms, were already vying for leadership and into which other major firms clearly were planning to enter.

Hypothesis 7 The level of competition in the new venture's targeted market segment is negatively related to the success of the venture.

Technological Strategy

We measured the level of strategic technological advantage of the product by comparing projected performance and cost reduction to those of competing existing products. Successful companies targeted major or significant improvements in performance and two of them also targeted cost reductions; that is, they aimed at substantially increasing the value of their products to the customer (see Table 4). These results are consistent with the findings of studies done on success and failure of new products (Cooper 1979; Maidique and Zirger 1984).

Hypothesis 8 The success of a new venture will be positively related to its product's projected level of performance improvement.

Another variable we studied was the gross margin targets of the new companies. Gross margin is especially important because it can be viewed as a proxy for the proprietary technological edge of the venture. We found, however, that the gross margin percentages targeted by all eight companies, after their fourth years of operation, ranged from 40 to 60%. This factor, therefore, did not allow discrimination between success and failure.

Last, we analyzed the effort required to complete the product development in our eight

TABLE 4. Level of Strategic Technological Advantage

Companies[a]	Performance Improvement[b]	Cost Reduction[b]
S1	Major	None
S2	Major	Minor
S3	Significant	Significant
S4	Major	Major
U1	Minor	Minor
U2	Significant	None
U3	None	Significant
U4	None	Significant

[a]S = Successful; U = Unsuccessful
[b]Major, Significant, Minor, None.

ventures. Hoban (1976), found that the probability of higher return is improved by investing in ventures in which product development is quite advanced. Our data, however, did not support these findings. The projected remaining product-development time for our start-ups ranged from 12 to 18 months, but this measure did not seem to be a factor in the success or failure of the firms.

On the other hand, we did find a qualitative difference between successes and failures. Successful venture teams, in contrast with unsuccessful ones, had planned the product development in greater detail, identifying the main milestones. This finding coincides with one of the main conclusions of the Stanford Innovation Project (SINPRO) on new product success and failure (Maidique and Zirger 1985).

Hypothesis 9 The level of detail in planning the development of the technology will be positively related to the success of the venture.

Deal Structure

Hoban (1976) found that the percentage of equity owned by venture capitalists was negatively related to the success of the new venture. The results of our interviews with venture capitalists suggest that both entrepreneurs and external investors must be highly motivated in order for a venture to succeed. The equity, therefore, should be structured in such a way that the founders and the venture capitalists will both benefit significantly in the event of the venture's success. From the analysis of our eight cases, however, we were not able to confirm this hypothesis. The range of equity percentage owned by venture capitalist after the first round of financing varied from 15 to 73%, but the actual figure did not appear to promote success or failure.

Hypothesis 10 The share of equity owned by the founders will have an inverted U-shape curvilinear relationship to the success of the venture.

Finally, we analyzed the board of directors' composition after the first round of financing. One of the most efficient ways by which a venture capitalist can influence the direction of a new company is by becoming a member of its board of directors. Thus, we hypothesized that the presence of venture capitalists and entrepreneurs with previous experience on the boards of start-ups could be associated with the success of the venture. All of the firms in our sample, however, had two or three partners from venture capital firms on their boards, and three of the companies had a successful entrepreneur as board member. Hence, we detected no relationship between the composition of the board and the success of the company. In order to obtain useful data on this variable we would have to compare our sample with companies that do not have venture capitalists on their boards; that is, with companies funded by sources other than venture capital.

CONCLUSIONS

Because our study has a limited sample and is exploratory in nature, it must limit itself to the articulation of hypotheses that can later be tested by our own follow-up research or that of others. The most salient of the preliminary hypotheses we have derived from our analysis deal with the characteristics of the entrepreneurs and the founding team, certain key market factors, and the strategic performance and/or cost advantages provided by the product to be introduced by the venture.

Our preliminary study confirms the findings, first by Cooper and Bruno (1977) and lately by Van de Ven et al. (1984), regarding the importance of the founders' prior experience. In addition, our study sheds some further light on the nature of the founding team's experience. Successful entrepreneurs had had prior experience in the same roles that they fulfilled in the new venture and had had fast-rising careers in high-growth units of medium to large companies. We also found that successful companies had a higher percentage of critical functions filled at the time of first financing. But perhaps our most significant finding was that successful companies had a much higher degree of prior joint experience among the members of the founding team than did the unsuccessful companies.

The successful start-ups in our sample targeted market segments uninhabited by strong competitors and with a limited number of potential customers, who had, however, large buying capacity. In addition, as did the researchers of a study on start-ups of PIMS corporate ventures (Hobson and Morrison 1983), we found that successful companies targeted focused product market segments where they could expect higher market shares.

Our successful companies developed technological strategies that resulted in significant performance improvements compared with other companies serving the same markets. The successful ventures also had prepared more detailed technology development plans. These results support the findings of prior studies of success and failure patterns of new products (Cooper 1979; Maidique and Zirger 1984).

Finally, our study examined the deal structure and its effects on the success of the venture. We hypothesized that founders and venture capitalists should both be strongly motivated financially if the venture is to be successful. Unlike Hoban (1976), however who, concluded that the proportion of equity owned by the venture capitalist is negatively related to the success of the new company, we did not find confirmation for this hypothesis in our small sample.

In summary, the most important results of our research suggest that the likelihood of a start-up's success is significantly increased by having a management team with previous joint experience, thus avoiding the waste of resources associated with integrating the different members of the team. In addition, our results suggest that a successful high-growth technological start-up needs from the beginning an experienced, complete team that can manage the company throughout the development process. In contrast with the view that the larger the market the better, we found that in order to capitalize on its limited resource base, the technological venture has to focus on a high-growth market segment in which the company can play an important role. Finally, the successful company not only has to be able to offer a better product, it has to be able to provide a product that represent a major improvement in performance compared with existing substitutes.

The next stage of our research is to test the hypotheses proposed here with a larger sample and to refine our understanding of the process of technological venture formation. By doing so, we hope to develop a model that will substantially increase the predictability of high-technology start-up performance. For the venture capitalist, this model would allow a more effective selection of investments and thus higher returns. And for the entrepreneur, the knowledge would provide a basis for the design of a successful venture business plan and a blueprint for early corrective action.

REFERENCES

Bruno, A.V., and Cooper, A.C. 1982. Patterns of development and acquisitions for Silicon Valley startups. In *Technovation* 1 (1982), pp. 275–290.

Cooper, A.C. 1971. The founding of technologically-based firms. *The Entrepreneur's Handbook, II,* In J.R. Mancuso, ed. Dedham, Mass.: Artech House, pp. 175–233.

Cooper, A.C., and Bruno, A.V. April 1977. Success among high-technology firms. *Business Horizons* 20(2):16–23.

Cooper, R.G. 1979. The dimensions of industrial new product success: Project new prod. *Journal of Marketing* 9(3):93–103.

Hoban, J.P., Jr. 1976. Characteristics of venture capital investments. Unpublished doctoral dissertation, University of Utah.

Hobson, E.L., and Morrison, R.M. 1983. How do corporate start-up ventures fare? In *Frontiers of Entrepreneurship Research*, J.A. Hornaday, J.A. Timmons, and K.H. Vesper, eds. Wellesley, Mass.: Babson Center for Entrepreneurial Studies, pp. 390–410.

MacMillan, I.C., Siegel, R., and Subba Narasimha, P.N.S. 1985. Criteria used by venture capitalists to evaluate new venture proposals. *Journal of Business Venturing* 1(1):119–128.

Maidique, M.A. 1986. Key success factors in high technology ventures. *The Art and Science of Entrepreneurship,* In D.L. Sexton and R.W. Smilor, eds. Cambridge, Mass.: Ballinger Publishing Co., pp. 169–180.

Maidique, M.A., and Zirger, B.J. 1984. A study of success and failure in product innovation: The case of the U.S. electronic industry. *IEEE Transactions on Engineering Management* EM–31(4):192–203.

Maidique, M.A., and Zirger, B.J. 1985. The new product learning cycle. *Research Policy.* 14(6):299–313.

Poindexter, J.B. 1976. The efficiency of financial markets: The venture capital case. Unpublished doctoral dissertation, New York University, New York.

Porter, M.E. 1980. *Competitive Strategy.* New York: The Free Press.

Roberts, E.B. 1972. Influences upon performance of new technical enterprises. In *Technical Entrepreneurship: A Symposium,* A.C. Cooper and J.L. Komives, eds. Milwaukee: The Center for Venture Management.

Shapero, A. 1971. *An Action Program For Entrepreneurship.* Austin, Tex.: Multi-Disciplinary Research, Inc.

Shapero, A.N., and Giglierano, J. 1982. Exits and entries: A study in yellow pages journalism. In *Frontiers of Entrepreneurship Research,* K.H. Vesper, ed. Wellesley, Mass.: Babson Center for Entrepreneurial Studies, pp. 113–141.

Susbauer, J.C. 1969. The technical company formation process: A particular aspect of entrepreneurship. Unpublished doctoral dissertation, Texas University, Austin.

Timmons, J.A., and Gumpert, D.E. Jan.–Feb. 1982. Discard many old rules for raising venture capital. *Harvard Business Review 60(4):152–156.*

Timmons, J.A., Smollen, L.E., and Dingee, A.L. 1977. *New Venture Creation.* Homewood, Il.: Richard D. Irwin.

Tyebjee, T.T., and Bruno, A.V. 1984. A model of venture capitalist investment activity. *Management Science* (9):1051–1066.

Van de Ven, A.H., Hudson, R., and Schroeder, D.M. 1984. Designing new business start ups: Entrepreneurial, organizational, and ecological considerations. *Journal of Management* 10(1):87.

Venture Capital Journal. Jan. 1985 Wellesley, Mass.: Venture Economics, p. 1.

Vesper, K.H. 1980. *New Venture Strategies.* Englewood Cliffs, N.J.: Prentice-Hall.

Wells, W.A. 1974. Venture capital decision-making. Unpublished doctoral dissertation, Carnegie-Mellon University, Pittsburgh.

[16]

Organizational Growth:
Linking Founding Team,
Strategy, Environment,
and Growth among
U.S. Semiconductor
Ventures, 1978–1988

Kathleen M. Eisenhardt
Stanford University
**Claudia Bird
Schoonhoven**
San Jose State University

This study explores organizational growth in technology-based ventures. We relate characteristics of the founding top-management team, strategy, and environment to the sales growth of newly founded U.S. semiconductor firms. The results indicate significant main and interaction effects for the founding top-management team and market stage on firm growth. In contrast, the technical innovation of firm strategy and marketplace competition were not significant. Finally, the founding top-management team and market-stage effects were increasingly large over time. Overall, these results indicate that both environmental determinism and strategic choice operate on young firms. These findings also suggest chaos-theory linkages to positive-feedback models and sensitive dependence of organizational growth on founding conditions.°

In his seminal paper, Stinchcombe (1965) argued that young firms have a high propensity to fail. He noted that new organizations are likely to fail because organization members cannot adjust quickly enough to new roles and working relationships and because these organizations lack a "track record" with outside buyers and suppliers. The validity of this phenomenon, the "liability of newness," has been supported in a number of studies across many types of organizations (e.g., Carroll and Delacroix, 1982; Freeman, Carroll, and Hannan, 1983; Singh, Tucker, and House, 1986).

However, the liability of newness research fails to deal with two common observations. One is that leaders sometimes can and do influence the performance of firms, particularly young and small ones. Second, there are often enormous differences in the quality of life of different surviving ventures. Some young firms become resounding successes. Names such as Apple and Sun come to mind as young firms that have become large and important within the economy. Others languish as small firms, surviving, but barely clinging to life. Why do these differences in organizational growth arise?

Previous research indicates that founding conditions play an important role in shaping young firms. Kimberly (1980) and Mintzberg and Waters (1982) indicated that founding executives influenced the structures and processes of a new medical school and grocery chain, respectively. Carroll and Delacroix (1982) showed that environmental factors at founding influenced the hazards of death among a sample of newspapers. Carroll and Hannan (1989) also showed that population density at founding had a persistent effect on the life chances of organizations across multiple populations. Thus, it seems likely that founding conditions also affect organizational growth.

The purpose of this paper is to link organizational growth with founding conditions, including the top-management team, technical strategy, and competitive environment. The research population is firms in the U.S. semiconductor industry founded between 1978 and 1985. In previous research, we linked an early measure of entrepreneurial performance, first product introduction, to founding conditions (Schoonhoven, Eisenhardt, and Lyman, 1990). This paper extends that work

•

We would like to thank our research assistants, especially Kathy Lyman, who did an outstanding job in data set construction and analysis assistance. We appreciate the advice and support of Dr. David Geddes, U.S. Department of Commerce. We also benefitted from the comments of Howard Aldrich, Phil Anderson, Kim Cameron, John Freeman, Connie Gersick, Jim Jucker, Sara Keck, Mike Lawless, Barbara Lawrence, Jim March, Elaine Mosakowski, Elaine Romanelli, Dick Scott, Bob Sutton, Andy Van de Ven, our three reviewers, and the lively seminar participants at Duke University, University of Minnesota, University of Texas at Austin, University of Michigan, and the 1989 Asilomar Conference. This research was supported by the U.S. Department of Commerce, Grant No. RED-870-G-86-15.

Organizational Growth

and extant research by examining organizational growth and by adding top-management-team and strategic effects to environmental ones in a study of technology-based ventures.

BACKGROUND

Stinchcombe (1965) argued that founding conditions have a disproportionate effect on young firms. Young organizations are set on a course at founding that may be difficult or costly to change (Boeker, 1989). Structures and processes develop quickly (Gersick, 1989), and organization members equally quickly come to see them as the only way to do things (Zucker, 1977). Structures and processes become part of an integrated whole in which it is difficult to change one element without unraveling the whole (Eisenhardt, 1988). Finally, young organizations make investments in people, technology, and assets that they may not be able to change because they are too myopic or resource-poor.

Stinchcombe (1965) emphasized the importance of two sets of founding factors. One is environmental. Young firms face perils because they lack the legitimacy and power of existing suppliers. A second set is organizational. Young organizations typically have key organization members in unfamiliar roles and new work relationships. The result is often delays and inefficiencies that jeopardize the young organization.

More recently, researchers, within and outside of the liability of newness paradigm, have elaborated on these factors. Some of this research has focused on founding environmental factors such as demand. Carroll and Delacroix (1982) found that newspapers born in conditions suggestive of high demand, such as industry maturity and economic expansion, outlived newspapers born in conditions of low demand. Romanelli's (1989) results indicated that minicomputer firms born during times of increasing industry sales had enhanced life chances. Sandberg and Hofer (1987) found that barriers to entry contributed to the success of young firms. Others have concentrated on the role of founders as the critical factor shaping young firms. The bulk of the evidence comes from case studies. Mintzberg and Waters (1982), who studied Steinberg's grocery chain, attributed much of the success of the firm to the unique abilities of its entrepreneur, Sam Steinberg. In his study of a medical school founding, Kimberly (1980: 40) attributed the school's early structure and results to the founder, "his personality, his dreams, his flaws, and his talents." Kazanjian (1988) found that top managers played an important role in solving the problems that allowed young firms to progress into subsequent stages of development.

In more specific research, Cooper and Bruno (1977) found that team size was associated with high growth, and Eisenhardt and Bourgeois (1988, 1989; Eisenhardt, 1989) found linkages between firm performance and the speed, politics, and conflict of entrepreneurial top-management teams. Roure and Maidique (1986) showed empirical support for links between the prior joint experience among top-management team members and venture success. Other researchers have examined organizational strategy. Sandberg and Hofer (1987) found that a differentiation strategy led to young-firm success, while Romanelli (1989) identified various conditions favoring specialist versus generalist strategies among young minicomputer firms.

This research all suggests that the liability of newness arguments may provide a framework for understanding the growth of young firms and that specific environmental, leadership, and strategic factors are likely to be germane. However, with the exception of Cooper and Bruno (1977), there have been no studies within the organization literature examining the growth of young firms, and none linking top-management-team factors to environment, strategy, and growth.

The Growth of Young Firms

Stinchcombe (1965) emphasized that underlying the failure of young organizations is their limited resources. Limited resources make young firms particularly vulnerable to even slight inefficiencies or delays (Van de Ven, Hudson, and Schroeder, 1984) and limit their ability to shift to more favorable circumstances. Using this same line of reasoning, we would expect that if limited resources are associated with organizational failure, then an abundance of resources would be related to the growth of young firms.

Following this argument and those outlined above, our overall premise is that founding environment, strategy, and top-management team have a significant impact on the resource levels and, ultimately, on growth of young firms. Specifically, the founding environment shapes the resource opportunities of young firms. The founding strategy further locks the young firm into a pattern of resource opportunities and consumption. Yet, simultaneously, founding top-management teams are differentially able to enhance and exploit the available opportunities for growth.

Environment. The founding environment plays a crucial role in shaping the resource opportunities of new firms (Carroll and Delacroix, 1982). Particularly germane to technology-based ventures is the role of technical change in creating differentially attractive resource opportunities (Tushman and Anderson, 1986). Waves of innovation stimulate the birth of emergent markets. Some of these markets then become growth markets, in which innovations such as price/performance improvements trigger market upheaval, large market size, and rapid market growth. Then as waves of innovation dampen, markets mature (Anderson and Zeithaml, 1984).

Emergent markets are new markets characterized by low demand and high uncertainty (Anderson and Zeithaml, 1984). Since products and services are often unfamiliar to potential customers, there is no proven market viability. The technology may still be uncertain. Distribution channels and sources of supply may be problematic (Anderson and Zeithaml, 1984). Would-be entrepreneurs in the microcomputer industry, for example, dabbled with various distribution channels and product designs for a number of years before the Apple I established industry standards for distribution and design (Eisenhardt and Bourgeois, 1990).

Emergent markets are a difficult environment for young firms because the timing of commercial takeoff in such markets is difficult to predict. New firms may not have the resources to ride out the emergent period and financial backers may lose

Organizational Growth

interest. When takeoff finally happens, the young firms already in the market may be too drained to take advantage of the growth, and they may be constrained by obsolete technology, skills, and physical plant. Worst of all, the market may never become viable. In emergent markets, the financial muscle of the big and established firms is likely to dominate. In the VCR industry (Rosenbloom and Cusumano, 1987), for example, it was the large firms, not the young and small ones such as Ampex, that prospered in the emergent period.

In contrast, growth markets provide many resource opportunities for new firms. Such markets are large. Products are commercially viable, and customers are aware of the product advantages. Thus, there is ample room for the young firm's entry. Second, by definition, demand is growing rapidly. Such growth increases "the size of the pie," at least potentially, for all competitors. Third, growth markets are characterized by turbulence because the competitive structure is changing (Anderson and Zeithaml, 1984; Tushman and Anderson, 1986). There may be multiple options for how to compete within an overarching dominant technical design (Porter, 1980). Market share is volatile (Hambrick, MacMillan, and Day, 1982). Most importantly, established firms are often locked into old technology and market approaches by their previous investments. Even their vision of the market may be dated. Thus, the size and age advantages of established firms may be less potent in growth markets. In contrast, new firms may be able to take advantage of the turbulence in growth markets, as did Intel in the semiconductor market of the late 1960s and Sun in the engineering work-station market of the 1980s.

Finally, mature markets are large markets with stable or slowly growing demand. Although the absolute size of demand increases may be high, the growth rate of demand is low. Dominant product designs, process technologies, and successful strategies are usually clear (Hambrick, MacMillan, and Day, 1982). Technology is evolutionary, not revolutionary. Mature markets have less change in competition, products, and technology than growth markets (Anderson and Zeithaml, 1984). Customers are familiar with the products and services within the industry. Market shares are stable (Hambrick, MacMillan, and Day, 1982).

Mature markets provide limited opportunities for new firms because new firms have few, if any, advantages over their established competitors. The past investments of established firms are still viable. They may have learning-curve advantages as well as the usual advantages with customers and suppliers that accrue to entrenched competitors (Stinchcombe, 1965). Therefore, while new firms in mature markets may become profitable (Carroll, 1984), they are unlikely to become large. Romanelli (1987) found that no firms founded in the mature minicomputer market became industry leaders. These arguments lead to the following hypothesis:

Hypothesis 1 (H_1): Founding in a growth-stage market is associated with higher growth among new firms than is founding in either an emergent or mature market.

The resource opportunities available to young firms also depend on the competition for those opportunities within the

507/ASQ, September 1990

founding environment (Hannan and Freeman, 1977; Carroll and Hannan, 1989). The existence of established competitors with large market shares makes it particularly difficult for young firms to grow. One reason is that such competitors are difficult to dislodge, given their size and first-mover advantages (Stinchcombe, 1965; Aaker and Day, 1986). In addition, as market concentration rises, the market share locked up by these firms rises. Finally, high competition often leads to price cutting and falling margins. Thus, sales will fall for equivalent product volumes, and the profits needed for investment in future growth are likely to drop. Sahlman and Stevenson (1985: 23) described this dynamic in their study of the disk-drive industry: "The greatest single industrywide problem that arose in 1983 and 1984 was the increased intensity of competition. . . . Price cutting to get 'designed-in' was rampant. Prices fell more rapidly than anyone had predicted. Given high fixed costs, including R&D, margins fell sharply." While established firms with high market share can often ride out these periods, new firms often cannot prosper. Thus, high levels of competition, especially from large and well-established competitors, limit the growth opportunities of young firms. These arguments lead to the following hypothesis:

Hypothesis 2 (H₂): Lower competitive concentration at founding is associated with higher growth among new firms.

Strategy. Founding strategy also influences the resources of young firms (Romanelli, 1989). Founding strategy locks the firm into a particular strategic direction, because firms develop internal consistencies and investments that tend to perpetuate those strategies (Miles and Snow, 1978) such that founding strategies persist decades after the founding of firms (Boeker, 1989).

Although a number of characterizations of strategy have been proposed, several authors have demonstrated that the most relevant difference in strategy across technology-based ventures is the degree of technical innovation within the core technology of the firm (Maidique and Patch, 1982; Boeker, 1989). Some firms compete by using highly innovative technologies that require extensive new knowledge creation and/or technology synthesis. Others compete with a moderate level of technical innovation. Still others compete by offering a less innovative technology, which may permit the firm to offer price and other compensating advantages to customers. This range of technical innovation was evident in the semiconductor memory markets of the mid-1980s. Some firms used 1970s NMOS or PMOS technology, in which the current flowing through a metal-oxide semiconductor (MOS) has either a negative (N) or positive (P) charge. Others used more innovative CMOS technology, in which current can flow in both positive and negative directions. Still others used very innovative wafer-scale integration technology, in which individual circuits are linked together to form very large integrated circuit memories.

Maidique and Patch (1982) described how differences in technical innovation require different levels of resource commitment. Technically innovative strategies demand a high level of competence in basic technology and consume sub-

Organizational Growth

stantial resources. It is rare for innovative technology to work initially, and it often takes a long time to become viable. During this time, the young firm is expending substantial resources. While these expenditures may ultimately pay off in terms of a breakthrough product, this outcome usually has only a modest probability. Thus, engaging in pioneering technology often requires large resources to commercialize the technology, with little assurance of eventual payoff. In contrast, simple technologies consume few resources and usually come to market quickly. However, they also offer few, if any, competitive advantages to the new firm. Even if the technology is unique, it can be readily copied, and it may offer little of interest to buyers. Thus, although less innovative technologies consume few resources, they offer little opportunity for growth.

Moderately innovative technical strategies seem likely to result in the highest firm growth (Schoonhoven and Eisenhardt, 1987). These technologies are new, but they are evolutionary more than revolutionary. Therefore, the development time and resource expenditures are more certain, and yet the technology is innovative enough to ensure some growth opportunities. Thus, moderately innovative technology is likely to balance resource consumption with growth opportunites. In formal terms:

Hypothesis 3 (H₃): Technical innovation has a curvilinear relationship with growth, with moderate levels of technical innovation associated with higher growth among new firms.

Top-management team. Founding top-management teams are also likely to differ in their ability to exploit or enhance resource levels. In a series of case studies on the microcomputer industry, Eisenhardt and Bourgeois (1988, 1989; Eisenhardt, 1989) found that successful executive teams combined high conflict between team members with fast decisions. These authors indicated that successful executives moved quickly to keep pace with the resource opportunities that rapidly appear and disappear in technology-based industries. They also found that conflict among team members was essential to effective top-management-team performance. Conflict was necessary for team members to avoid complacency and mistakes that might drain resources. Thus, fast and conflictual top-management teams seemed better able to husband resources and exploit opportunities (Bourgeois and Eisenhardt, 1988).

Past joint work experience among the founding team is one factor that might lead to speed in decision making. Executives who have a history together have probably learned how to get along and communicate with each other. This is particularly likely given that they have chosen to form a new firm together. They are also likely to have learned performance routines for making decisions quickly and are more likely to understand the idiosyncracies and strengths of their colleagues than are teams formed from strangers. Therefore, founding teams with prior working experience together can save valuable time in building coordination and trust (Stinchcombe, 1965) and can focus quickly on firm problems, rather than on group-process issues. Evidence from Goodstein and O'Reilly's (1988) study in the electronics industry supports this argument. These authors found that executive teams that have worked together previously were likely to be more cohesive and have higher trust than teams without such experience. Similarly, Zenger and Lawrence (1989) found that individuals with previous work experience together communicated more often than people who did not. Roure and Maidique (1986) also indicated empirical support linking joint experience with more successful ventures. In formal terms:

Hypothesis 4 (H_4): Greater previous joint work experience among the founding team is associated with higher growth among new firms.

A larger team size may also accelerate decision making. More founders means that there are more people available to do the enormous job of starting a new firm and that there is more opportunity for specialization in decision making. Kazanjian (1988) has outlined the large number of problems (e.g., fundraising, technology development, production start-up, marketing) that young firms face. If the team is large, one executive can handle manufacturing issues while another grapples with marketing, a third raises funds, and so forth. In contrast, small teams may stumble over some or all of these problems. In addition, team size is likely to affect the level of conflict within the team. Small-group research indicates that larger groups have more diverse opinions (Bales and Borgatta, 1966). Also, they have more opportunities for subgrouping than small teams (George, 1980). This allows conflict to air rather than to be repressed.

There are empirical studies that link team size with firm success. Cooper and Bruno (1977) found that team size was associated with higher sales in a sample of high-technology ventures, while Roure and Keeley (1989) found that team completeness, which may be highly correlated with team size, was a major predictor of the internal rate of return among new ventures. Although there may be diminishing returns to team size, team size ranged only from one to seven in the firms we studied. Therefore, we hypothesize:

Hypothesis 5 (H_5): Greater founding team size is associated with higher growth among new firms.

Team heterogeneity is also likely to affect conflict. As Janis (1982) argued, homogeneity within a group may lead to inferior decision making because of "groupthink" and insufficient airing of conflict. Other research (e.g., Wagner, Pfeffer, and O'Reilly, 1984; Tsui and O'Reilly, 1989) further suggests that heterogeneity is associated with conflict. Heterogeneity in industry experience among the founding team is likely to generate particularly constructive conflict. Teams with individuals who have entered the industry at different times are likely to have different points of view about technology, competitive tactics, and so forth. People with long experience in the industry bring a knowledge of how the industry operates. Those with less experience bring freshness in perspective. These different points of view encourage conflict, which, in turn, counteracts the danger that the team reaches premature closure or has an insufficient airing of alternatives. Combining conflicting views may yield innovative and yet viable ways to compete, giving competitive advantage to the young firm. Conflicting views may also help young firms to avoid costly mistakes. In formal terms:

Organizational Growth

Hypothesis 6 (H_6): Greater variation in the industry experience of the founding team is associated with higher growth among new firms.

METHODS

The research sample is the population of new semiconductor firms that were founded between 1978 and 1985 in the U.S. A new semiconductor firm was defined as a single-business venture founded exclusively to develop, produce, and sell semiconductor devices on the merchant market. Thus, by definition, we excluded captive producers, new divisions of existing corporations, distributors, and design firms, whose sole business is engineering custom circuits for individual customers.

A master list of semiconductor firms founded in the U.S. between 1978 and 1985 was compiled from the industry lists maintained by the Semiconductor Industry Association (SIA), the major industry trade association; Dataquest and Integrated Circuit Engineering (ICE), the two largest market research firms in the U.S. specializing in the semiconductor industry; Semiconductor Equipment and Materials Institute (SEMI), which tracks new and existing semiconductor firms for its members to target for equipment and engineering sales; and *Electronic News,* a weekly newspaper with a specialty section on the semiconductor industry. After eliminating duplicate firms across sources, we wrote to the CEO of each firm to obtain information about the company. Based on this information, nine firms were eliminated because they did not meet the definition of a semiconductor firm given above.

The final population of firms meeting the above definition was 102. The number of firms that participated in the study was 98, and we were able to obtain sales data for 92. The sample includes firms with substantial variation in growth, including ones that failed and others that have become industry success stories. Almost 70 percent of the sample is located in Silicon Valley.

Data Sources

Our research team gathered data on the history of each firm and then tracked firm growth annually, from birth through 1988 (or until the firm failed). All firms began with 0 sales. We identified the founding date by asking the founder(s) or current CEO: "In what year and month was the company founded?" This date corresponds to the initiation of formal operations, the establishment of a regular location of business, and to founders devoting the majority of their time to creation of the organization.

Several data sources were used. Organizational and team data were collected in structured interviews with the CEOs, founders, and other key executives. The researchers usually worked in pairs in conducting these interviews, with one researcher asking questions and the other recording data. Most interviews were tape-recorded and lasted between one and four hours.

We also gathered annual financial performance data from functional specialists within each firm. We supplemented these data with information from 10-K and annual reports, business plans, and market-research reviews. Data on the environment were obtained from SIA, Dataquest, and ICE.

Environmental Measures

We measured the environmental constructs in several steps. First, using data from Dataquest and ICE, we identified six broad product markets: application-specific integrated circuits (ASIC), memory, logic, gallium arsenide, linear, and discrete. ASICs are semi-custom integrated circuits. Memories are digital, integrated circuits used for data storage. Logic devices are digital, integrated circuits used for computation. Gallium arsenide devices are integrated circuits in which the semiconductor material is gallium arsenide, not silicon. Linear devices are integrated circuits in which data can assume a continuous, nondigital value. Discrete devices are semiconductors containing a single active element such as a transistor or diode. Again, using data from these market research firms, we then identified subcategories within markets. These categories gave us a fine-grained view of market segments within the industry. For example, we were able to capture distinctions in the 1983 memory market between the mature read-only-memory (ROM) market, the growth dynamic-random-access-memory (DRAM) market, and the emergent electrically erasable and programmable read-only-memory (EEPROM) market. The markets are listed in the Appendix.

Second, we gathered information on the size of the market, four-firm concentration ratio, and number of competitors in each market for each year from 1978 through 1987. We adjusted the size of the market to 1988 dollars using the producer price index of the Bureau of Labor Statistics. Since most of the data reflects conditions in the 1980s, a period of low inflation, the inflation-adjusted results are quite similar to the unadjusted results.

Third, we assigned each firm in the sample to a market based on the first product shipped by the firm and the founding year, as reported in the interviews.

Market stage. We typed each market as emergent, growth, or mature for each year in the study. Consistent with our theoretical discussion, we defined emergent markets as (1) new and (2) less than $100 million in sales (adjusted to 1988 dollars). We assessed newness by when the first competitor entered each market. All of the emergent markets except two began during the period of our study. These exceptions began several years before our study. Thus, each of the markets designated as emergent was new. In our theoretical discussion, we also described emergent markets as having low demand and uncertain commercial viability. We chose the $100 million figure as the cut-off point for assessing these characteristics. As recommended by Cameron, Kim and Whetten (1987), considerable effort went into establishing this cut-off point. We conducted numerous interviews with semiconductor executives in which they described market characteristics. We also pored over extensive market-research reports for each year of the study to determine at what point industry experts considered a market to be large and its products commercially viable (i.e., when sales shifted from customers buying the product on a test basis to customers buying the product for volume production). We then verified the $100

Organizational Growth

million cut-off point by rereading market-research reports and matching market descriptions with our theoretical description of emergent markets. Finally, we also verified the robustness of this cut-off point by checking its results with those of cut-off points of $80 and $150 million. The results are insensitive to these differences. Examples of emergent markets include the digital gate array market of the late 1970s and the gallium arsenide market throughout the entire period covered by the study.

Growth markets were those with (1) at least $100 million in annual sales, and (2) an average annual growth rate of at least 20 percent. We computed the growth rate for the current year by the percentage increase (decrease) in market size from the previous year.[1] Examples include the explosive digital gate-array market of the 1980s and the DRAM market throughout the period covered by the study. We chose a 20-percent growth rate for several reasons. First, the 20-percent breakpoint is a natural break in the data. Virtually all market-growth rates are either below 15 percent or above 20 percent. Second, our choice of a 20-percent breakpoint is bolstered by Romanelli's (1987) use of the same growth rate to differentiate growth and mature markets in the minicomputer industry. This suggests a common interpretation of growth in high-technology industries. Finally, we verified our choice by extensive rereading of market-research reports to corroborate the consistency of the theoretical description with our typing of these markets as growth markets.

Mature markets were also at least $100 million markets, but their growth rate was less than 20 percent annually. Examples of mature markets include discrete and linear products. Again, we verified our categorizing of markets using market-research reports. For example, the linear market in 1986 was termed "very mature" (Integrated Circuit Engineering, 1987). We also noted that none of the mature markets had important innovations or changes during the period of our study. In contrast, the introduction of CMOS-process technology, the commercialization of semi-custom technologies such as gate arrays, and the microcomputer industry boom all affected one or more of the markets identified as "emergent" and "growth" but none of the markets identified as "mature." We also noted that all of these markets were established before the period under study.

There were several markets that moved from one stage to another. For example, the EEPROM and gate-array markets moved from emergent to growth. Others, such as ROM, went from growth to mature. No firms in this population participated in declining markets.

By using market stages, rather than continuous variables, some variance was lost. However, maximum variance was not as important as was conceptual consistency with the hypotheses. Categorical variables were appropriate, for several theoretical reasons. First, the stages involve a constellation of attributes (Hambrick, MacMillan, and Day, 1982; Anderson and Zeithaml, 1984), not one or two single dimensions or even the same single dimensions. Emergent markets are not just small, but also new and fraught with commercial uncertainty. In contrast, growth-stage markets are large, rapidly

---

1
There was one year of decline in the DRAM market amid a general pattern of growth. In this case, we averaged the growth rates of the current, preceding, and succeeding years to determine the growth rate because this gives a more valid picture of the market.

growing, and include products that have established demand and proven price/performance advantages (Anderson and Zeithaml, 1984). Second, the stages were conceptualized in terms of thresholds, not continuous variables. We argued that one reason why a growth-stage market is attractive is that it is large enough to support growth by a new entrant. However, bigger is not necessarily better. Indeed, from the perspective of the growth of a new firm, a market of several hundred million is not different from a billion-dollar one. Both are large to the new firm. Our theoretical argument is similar for using a growth-rate threshold. Finally, the theoretical conception of market stage includes qualitative elements such as commercial viability (Anderson and Zeithaml, 1984), which are difficult to measure numerically.

We also verified the appropriateness of the market-stage operationalization empirically. We examined organizational growth using several continuous variables that might be associated with market stage: market size, percentage of market growth, and the interaction of market size and growth. The categorical operationalization of market stage provides a better empirical fit with the data than these continuous variables, as shown below.

Competitive concentration. This construct was measured by the four-firm concentration ratio obtained from market-research data. This figure is the ratio of sales of the four largest competitors in the market to the total sales in the market. It reflects the competitive power of the established firms.

Strategy Measures

Technical innovation. We measured technical innovation using an objective measure: micron line width. Micron line width is a physical specification of the degree of miniaturization of the circuit designs created by semiconductor companies. Technically this is referred to as the minimum feature size in microns. Smaller micron sizes represent more innovative technology, since increasing miniaturization to pack more circuits into a smaller area is the heart of semiconductor innovation.

We also measured technical innovation with three questions that were answered by the company respondents. The first question measured innovation resulting from the extension of existing knowledge: "To what extent could you rely on existing knowledge to build the first product?" The second question captured innovation resulting from the synthesis of existing technologies: "To what extent did you synthesize existing knowledge to produce your first product?" The third question captured the overall level of technical innovation: "How difficult was it to produce your first product?" We used a 0 to 10 scale for each question. A three-item index was created by (1) reverse coding the first question, and (2) computing the mean response to the three questions. The Cronbach alpha is .75.

These measures of technical innovation are preferable to others (e.g., expert ratings, actual R&D expenditures, R&D as a percentage of sales), for several reasons. First, company informants were the most knowledgeable people about their own degree of technological innovation. In contrast, industry experts were not sufficiently versed in the broad range of semiconductor technologies represented in this study to give accurate ratings across firms, nor were they aware of the specifics of technology used by the almost 100 new companies in the sample. Thus, while expert ratings may work well for small sample sizes and established firms (e.g., Boeker, 1989), they were inadequate for this sample. Second, these measures are preferable to those using R&D expenditures. Since many of these firms have no sales in their first year or two of life and none had sales at founding, R&D as a percentage of sales cannot be computed. Actual R&D expenditures are also inadequate for measuring technical innovation because, for small firms, they are importantly determined by capital and personnel limits, as well as by the technical considerations of the task.

Top-Management-Team Measures

Most semiconductor start-ups are founded by groups of executives (Boeker, 1989). Founders were identified during the interviews. The founding top-management team was defined as those individuals who were founders of the firm and who worked full time for the firm in executive-level positions at the time of founding.

Joint experience. We measured joint work experience in two steps. First, we determined the number of founding executives who had worked with another founding executive for at least six months prior to founding the company. Second, this number was divided by the total number of founding executives. This variable ranges between 0, for teams in which none of the founders had previously worked together, and 1, for teams in which all of the founders had previous work relationships together. Since most teams have either very high or very low joint experience, the assessment of joint experience is insensitive to the method of calculation.

Team size. The founding team size was measured as the number of individuals who were designated by the company respondents as founders. These individuals founded the firm and worked full time for the firm in executive positions at its inception. The number of founders ranged from one to seven.

Heterogeneity of industry experience. We measured the heterogeneity of industry experience by computing the standard deviation of the number of years of semiconductor-industry experience for all executives on the founding team. Company respondents provided this information for each member of the founding team. We then averaged these experience levels for a team score and computed the standard deviation. The standard deviation is superior to the coefficient of variation because the variable itself and its scale are theoretically meaningful in this study (Allison, 1978).

Dependent Measure

Firm growth. We measured firm growth as the difference in sales in each year of life through 1988 relative to sales at founding. However, since the sales at founding were 0 for all firms, the measure of growth in any year reduced simply to the sales in that year. We obtained these growth data directly from firms and public sources such as public-offering documents and annual reports. We adjusted these sales figures to 1,988 dollars using the annual producer price index of the Bureau of Labor Statistics.

We used this growth measure instead of alternative measures such as percentage growth and growth rate, for several reasons. First, it measures the absolute change in size of each firm from a common starting point, the founding of the firm. This fits with our interest in understanding why some young firms grow more than others. Second, it is computationally tractable. In contrast, percentage growth cannot be computed from founding, since all sales are initially zero and, for many firms, are zero in subsequent years as well. Finally, growth rate is simply our measure of growth divided by the time period. However, since the time period is constant across cases for any point in time, one is simply adjusting all cases by a constant. Thus, there is no difference in the pattern of significant results between the two measures.

Five firms were acquired. Since these firms continued as independent entities (e.g., wholly owned subsidiaries) after acquisition, we used their sales figures both before and after acquisition. Failed firms were those that ceased to operate. We analyzed the data for failed firms in two ways: eliminating the dead firms when they failed and including them with 0 sales for each year in which they could have had sales if they had lived. The results using the former method are presented. However, given the small number of firms in this category (e.g., no firms failed before 1985), there is little difference in results.

Analysis

We used multiple analytic approaches: (1) a regression model using a four-year lag, (2) event-history analysis using $20 million in sales as the predicted event, (3) successive regressions, and (4) pooled cross-section regression. The first approach links founding conditions with firm size at a single point in time, while the latter three reveal dynamic patterns.

We used multiple analyses because there was no one optimal approach. Lagged regression involves an arbitrary specification of the lag. Event-history analysis requires transforming the continuous variable, sales, into a dichotomous one. Successive regressions have no summary statistic. Pooled cross-section analysis blurs longitudinal and cross-sectional effects, and interpretation is difficult without an a priori understanding of evolutionary patterns. Thus, we chose multiple analytic approaches.

RESULTS

Figure 1 is a plot of the U.S. semiconductor foundings studied in this paper. In 1978, there were seven foundings. The number of foundings peaked at 29 in 1983 and declined to 13 in 1985.

Four-Year Lag Analysis

The first analysis uses a lag model that links founding conditions with fourth-year sales. The rationale behind a lag model is that new firms require an initial period in which to perfect their product design, gear up their manufacturing process,

Organizational Growth

Figure 1. U.S. semiconductor firm foundings (1978–1985).

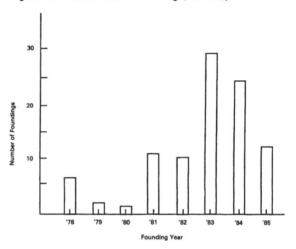

and so on. Differences in performance are neither large nor meaningful in this early period. We chose a four-year lag because meaningful variations in sales growth seemed to emerge at that time. In earlier years there was little difference in sales growth across firms. In later years sample size falls off. We controlled for differences in the economic climate in the fourth year of life using a common measure of the economic health of the semiconductor industry, the book-to-bill ratio, which we obtained from the Semiconductor Industry Association. We also controlled for differences in initial capital by including each firm's capital at founding, which we obtained directly from respondents at each firm.

The first four models in Table 1 indicate multivariate regression results for the four-year lagged analysis. We computed separate regression models for the environment, innovation, and team variables and for the full model, so that the contribution of each set of variables would be apparent. The corresponding correlation matrix is in the Appendix.

The results show that the environment model is significant overall. The growth-stage market (H_1) variable is also significant, but the concentration ratio (H_2) is not.[2] Second, the technical innovation model is not significant, and neither the linear nor squared variables of both measures is significant (H_3). Third, the top-management-team model is significant, but joint experience (H_4) is the only significant predictor among the team variables. Finally, the full model is significant, with the environment and team models contributing significantly and additively to the explained variation.[3]

Since the three top-management-team variables are significantly correlated with fourth-year sales and with each other (see Appendix), multicollinearity among the team variables may be supressing significance within the regression results for individual team variables. In addition, our theory suggested

2

In results not displayed here, we replicated the concentration ratio results with alternative measures of competition: changes in concentration (measured between founding and first year), number of firms in the market, and the competitive density (market size/number of competitors). None of these measures of competition was significant. We also considered whether market stage is more accurately characterized by a continuous, not categorical, construct. We examined three possibilities: founding market size, market growth (percentage increase in market size between founding and year 1), and interaction between market size and market growth. None of these continuous variables was significant.

3

In results not shown here, we produced the same results as the four-year lag analysis by linking the founding variables with 1987 sales while controlling for age and initial capital. The significance patterns of those results are consistent with those presented here.

Table 1

Regression Results for Environment, Technical Innovation, and Top-Management Team on Sales in Year 4 (*N* = 66) (Standardized Beta Weights)

Independent variables	Controls	Environment	Technical innovation	Top-management team	Full model	ANOVA model
H₁: Growth-stage market		.36***			.34***	.33***
H₂: Concentration ratio		.00			.00	
H₃: Technical innovation (micron size)			.05		.02	
Squared			−.12		.00	
Technical innovation (3-item scale)			.16			
Squared			−.18			
H₄: Joint experience				.19*	.16	
H₅: Team size				.17	.18*	
H₆: Heterogeneity of industry experience				.16	.15	
Top-management team*						.39***
Top-management team* × growth-stage market						.69****
Book to bill	.12	.11	.11	.08	.06	.12
Initial capital	−.03	.03	−.03	−.10	−.05	−.03
R²	.02	.14	.02	.16	.27	.46
F	0.48	2.50**	0.23	2.31**	2.19**	10.30****

• *p* < .10; •• *p* < .05; ••• *p* < .01; •••• *p* < .001.
* Strong and weak top-management team categories.

that the combination of size, heterogeneity, and joint experience within the top-management team was most closely associated with firm growth. For these reasons, we collapsed the team variables into "strong" and "weak" team categories and computed the final model in Table 1.

We typed teams as strong when they met three conditions: (1) at least three founders, (2) at least 50 percent joint experience, and (3) at least three years of industry experience variation. We used three founders as the cut-off point because three executives permits functional differentiation within the group (i.e., a CEO plus two functional vice-presidents). Such functional differentiation should contribute to both the pace of decision making through specialization and the level of conflict within the team. Also, three is the median size of the teams in the sample. We chose the 50-percent cut-off point for joint experience because it seems reasonable to assume that at least half of the team should have worked together before for the effects of joint experience to be powerful. However, since the actual distribution of the joint experience variable is bimodal, with only a handful of teams having joint experience between 35 percent and 75 percent, the exact choice of cut-off point is not crucial. Finally, three years of industry variation was the approximate sample median. At the fourth year of life, there were 26 strong teams and 40 weak ones.

We analyzed the effects of strong vs. weak teams and growth vs. nongrowth founding market in the ANOVA model of Table 1. Consistent with the previous models, this model indicates significant team and market-stage main effects. More importantly, it indicates a significant and positive interaction between environment and team. That is, the firms that

Organizational Growth

grew the most, combined synergistically founding in a growth market with a superior top-management team.

Event-History Analysis

We chose the firm's reaching $20 million in sales as the event of interest, for two reasons. First, our conversations with industry executives and investors indicated that $20 million in sales was a widely used "rule of thumb" indicating whether or not a firm had "made it." The $20-million figure seemed to indicate to experienced individuals that the firm had sufficient size to endure. Second, we also observed that $20 million was the minimum figure for firm executives and investors to bring a firm public, the goal of many of these ventures. Thus, approximately $20 million in sales seemed to be a watershed in the life of young semiconductor firms.

We compared the survival curves for firms founded in growth vs. nongrowth markets and for firms founded by strong vs. weak top-management teams. Survival is defined as a firm's *not* having reached $20 million in sales (1988 dollars). There is no left-censoring (i.e., no missing data prior to the study) since the data were collected at the birth of the firms. The discrete-time model controls for right-censoring (i.e., missing data for firms that reach $20 million after the study) (Allison, 1982). We computed survival scores, ranking the firms by survival time, and used a D-statistic to determine significant survival differences across groups (Lee and Desu, 1972).

Figure 2 compares the survival curves for firms founded in growth vs. nongrowth markets. None of the semiconductor ventures reach $20 million in sales in the first two years of life. After that time, firms founded in growth markets are significantly more likely to reach $20 million in sales than are firms founded in nongrowth markets and to do so sooner.

Figure 3 compares firms founded by strong vs. weak teams. Firms founded by strong top-management teams are significantly more likely to reach $20 million in sales and to do so sooner in their lives than are firms founded by less able teams.

Overall, the event-history analysis produces the same results as the four-year lag results for the importance of being founded in a growth-stage market by a strong team. More importantly, the findings add a longitudinal dimension to the results by revealing a lag period, which is then followed by a time during which firms are likely to reach substantial size.

Successive Regressions

In this analysis, we linked the founding conditions with sales in each of the first six years of life. The goal was to observe how relationships between founding conditions and growth changed with time under varying lag periods to see whether these relationships remained constant, decayed, or grew.

Table 2 summarizes the multivariate regression results for R-squared. We did not continue past six years because the sample size drops below 20. For years 3 through 6, this analysis produces the same general pattern of results as the other analyses: founding in a growth-stage market (H_1) and founding top-management-team variables (H_4–H_6) are significant predictors of growth, while founding concentration ratio (H_2) and both measures of technical innovation (H_3) are not.

Figure 2. Event-history results for growth vs. nongrowth markets (*N* = 92).

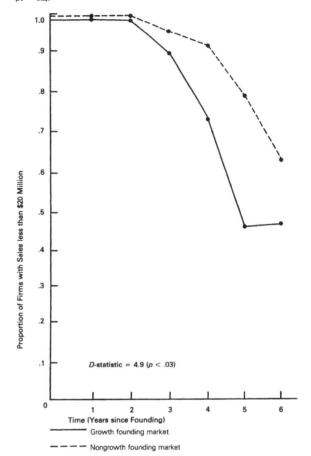

Time (Years since Founding)

——— Growth founding market

– – – – Nongrowth founding market

However, the interesting feature of the analysis is the pattern over time. This pattern is easiest to see in Figure 4, which plots the *R*-squared values for the environment, strategy, and team models from Table 2 against age. As indicated, the effects of the founding environment are negligible in the first two years of life. They become significant in the third year of life and then grow, not fade, with time. In contrast, the technical innovation has an early impact on sales but then decays in time. That is, firms with a simple and well-known technology are apparently able to establish sales early on. However, by the second year, the advantage of well-known technology dissipates and, in later years, is no longer significant, as firms with innovative technologies catch those with simple ones. Finally, the top-management team has a signifi-

Organizational Growth

Figure 3. Event-history results for strong vs. weak top-management teams (*N* = 92).

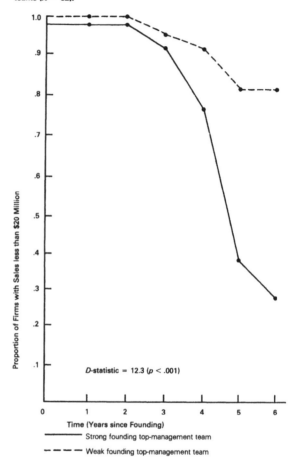

D-statistic = 12.3 (*p* < .001)

Time (Years since Founding)

—————— Strong founding top-management team

— — — Weak founding top-management team

cant impact on sales throughout the period of the study. Superior teams are associated with early sales, and like the environment effect, the size of the top-management team impact increases, not fades, with time. Overall, these results indicate that firm growth has a very sensitive dependence on founding conditions. As firms age, the gap between the small and large widens.[4]

Pooled Cross-Section Regression

In the final analysis, we attempted to confirm the pattern of findings from the successive regression panels by aggregating the data in a pooled cross-section regression to summarize these longitudinal patterns.

4
In results not shown here, we produced the same results as the four-year lag analysis and the successive regressions by including the failed firms with 0 sales for each year in which they could have had sales if they had lived. These analyses adjust for a possible survivor-selection bias. The significance patterns of those results are consistent with those presented here.

Table 2

R-squared Regression Results for Sales by Year

Sales	N	Environment	Technical innovation	Top-management team	Full model
Year 1	89	.01	.08**	.09**	.20***
Year 2	87	.03	.01	.09**	.13
Year 3	78	.08**	.00	.09*	.17*
Year 4	66	.14**	.02	.16**	.28**
Year 5	53	.16**	.00	.17**	.32**
Year 6	27	.21*	.03	.26*	.41

* $p < .10$; ** $p < .05$; *** $p < .01$.

We entered an observation for each firm for every year for which we have data. For example, if a firm has five years of sales data, then it would contribute five observations (one for each year of sales data) to the regression. We used an ordi-

Figure 4. R-squared regression results for sales by year.

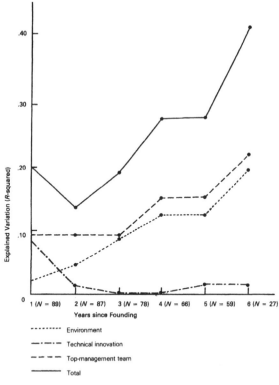

Organizational Growth

nary-least-squares approach because autocorrelation is likely to be minimal given the preponderance of firms to time periods. No firm contributes more than 2.5 percent of the cases. Also, ordinary-least-squares regression permits full utilization of the data. In contrast, while a generalized least squares algorithm would correct for autocorrelation, a substantial sacrifice of observations would occur since a balanced design of years and firms is required.

Table 3 displays the results. The first model is the base case, including the previous control variables. Market size is included to control for the possibility that firms grow simply because their markets grow. The second regression models the founding environment, team, and their interaction without any time effects beyond an age control. The third regression models the findings of the successive-regressions analysis. Founding team and founding growth-market conditions are modelled with age × founding-condition interaction terms for the growth-market founding condition (H_1) and the founding top-management team variables (H_4–H_6). A positive interaction term indicates that the effect of the variable amplifies with age, which is what we observed in the previous analysis. Technical innovation at founding is modelled with a separate coefficient in year 1 and with no coefficients in subsequent years. This models the decay observed in the previous analysis. The final model is a best-estimates model of the results.

These results confirm the previous findings: (1) firms founded in growth-stage markets (H_1) by superior top-management teams (H_4–H_6) achieve greater growth (main effects), and (2) there is a significant interaction effect between founding

Table 3

Regression Results—Pooled Cross Sections (N = 422)

Independent variables	Model 1	Model 2	Model 3	Model 4
Age	.50****	.51****	.25****	.29****
Book to bill	.03	.05	.03	
Initial capital	.00	.03	.03	
Market size	−.01	.00	.03	
Growth-stage market		.12**		
Concentration ratio		−.04		
Joint experience		.08		
Team size		.09*		
Heterogeneity of industry experience		.09*		
Top-management team* × growth-stage market		.21****		
Age × growth-stage market			.15**	.12**
Age × joint experience			.05	
Age × team size			.07	
Age × heterogeneity of industry experience			.12**	
Age × top-management team*				.14***
Age × top-management team × growth-stage market*			.40****	.39****
Year 1 × technical innovation			.11**	.09**
R^2	.24	.37	.54	.51
F	29.5****	21.2****	41.1****	85.3****

* $p < .10$; ** $p < .05$; *** $p < .01$; **** $p < .001$.
* Strong and weak top-management team categories.

market and founding team. These results also confirm that the effects of founding in a growth market and a strong founding top-management team amplify in time. This can be seen by the significant and positive age × founding-conditions terms in models 3 and 4 and the dominance of those models over model 2, which contains no interactions with age. Finally, the results also corroborate that the effects of innovative technical strategies at founding (H_3) are significant only in the early years of life and then decay. The concentration ratio (H_2) is never significant.

DISCUSSION AND CONCLUSIONS

Market Stages, Top-Management Team, and Their Interactions

This paper showed that founding environment affects the growth of young semiconductor firms. Specifically, technology-based firms founded in growth-stage markets are more likely to become large than are those founded in emergent or mature markets. Many of the ventures that became large targeted their first products into growth markets at the time of their birth. As we discussed above, these markets are not simply fast-growing. In fact, mature markets often have greater absolute growth, and emergent markets often have greater percentage growth. Rather, growth-stage markets provide the combination of market size, rapid demand increases, and marketplace upheaval that produce superior resource opportunities for new firms. As Aaker and Day (1986) noted, a growth market is no guarantee of success, and we found that some firms founded in a growth stage did not prosper. However, it does appear that the resource opportunities of such markets do give young firms a substantial advantage.

In contrast, only a few firms founded in emergent markets reached sales of $20 million. Most languished at low sales levels, waiting for their markets to become established. In some cases, the market never did become established. In other cases, emergent markets did blossom into growth markets, but the early entrants were often too weak to take advantage. For example, several of the early foundings in the digital gate-array market lacked the financial and managerial resources to exploit the growth stage when it arrived. Finally, several firms begun in mature markets have reached the $20 million mark, but they are not among the largest firms in the study. Typically these firms have carved out small, often profitable niches within large markets.

The study also showed that the founding top-management team influences the growth of new firms. Specifically, the size of the team, members' past experience together, and members' hetereogeneity in industry experience are linked with higher growth. We also found that founding environment and team variables were uncorrelated: strong teams established ventures in nongrowth markets, weak teams started in growth markets and so on. Entrepreneurs appeared to begin ventures in markets that they knew rather than in markets that industry analysts saw as attractive. What appeared to happen, then, was that founding top-management teams

Organizational Growth

were differentially able to navigate within the constraints of the founding environment. Strong teams appeared to move more quickly, get more done, and make fewer mistakes than other teams.

The findings have implications for the debate within organization theory about whether top executives make a difference (e.g., Meindl, Ehrlich, and Dukerich, 1985). Our findings suggest that they do. Consistent with research by Pfeffer and Davis-Blake (1986) and Smith, Carson, and Alexander (1984), we found that when differences in abilities and fitness of leaders are considered, leaders influence organizational performance.

Finally, we found a strong interaction between founding market stage and strength of the founding top-management team. Superior teams were especially adroit at exploiting growth markets. In contrast, weak teams were generally less successful in growth markets than strong teams and performed particularly poorly in nongrowth markets.

These results have implications for the convergence of environmental determinism and strategic choice explanations for important firm outcomes (e.g., Miles, 1982; Hrebiniak and Joyce, 1985). They show significant environmental effects in that founding environment had an important impact on subsequent growth. It appeared that choice was constrained from the outset, as many entrepreneurs began businesses in markets that they knew rather than surveying all possible venture options. On the other hand, the findings also suggest a role for senior leaders. While founding executives may have been constrained by their markets and technology, they no doubt made choices about many issues such as pricing, advertising, and in-house manufacturing that, together, influenced the course of the firm. Thus, the study suggests that organizational growth is a combination of environmental and leadership processes. Although we did not assess strategic choice directly, presumably, the superior top-management teams were navigating their firms more expertly than were the weaker teams. Thus, consistent with Miles (1982) and Hrebiniak and Joyce (1985), it would appear that environmental determinism and strategic choice are not ends of a continuum but, rather, separate dimensions. Thus, situations, such as young firms in technology-driven industries, exhibit both strong environmental and strong top-management team effects.

Competition and Technical Innovation

Not all of the hypotheses were supported. Contrary to our expectations, we found that competition at founding did not affect firm growth and that this finding was robust across several measures of competition and held across time lags, as well. One reason for this result may be that we measured competition at founding, not over time. However, the plausibility of this explanation is limited by the fact that competition has no significant effect, even in the early years when the lag is small. A second explanation seems more plausible. There may have been insufficient competition in the markets studied to trigger the negative effects of competition. Unlike the market for the disk-drive industry (Sahlman and Stevenson, 1985), none of the markets that we studied was described, by the executives we interviewed or by the market research reports we reviewed, as overcrowded. This threshold interpretation is also consistent with the similarly insignificant competition results reported by Romanelli (1989) in the minicomputer industry and Delacroix, Swaminathan, and Solt (1989) in the wine industry. Perhaps, then, extreme levels of competition are necessary to influence growth.

We also found that innovative technical strategies at founding had no lasting impact on growth. A less innovative technology gave firms an early growth advantage, but in subsequent years, firms with a more innovative technical strategy caught up, and technical innovation was no longer a significant predictor of firm growth. By the third or fourth year of life, there was no difference in firm size based on differences in technical innovation. Thus, while a less innovative technology leads to rapid product introduction (Schoonhoven, Eisenhardt, and Lyman, 1990), the advantage for growth was not sustained. Although contrary to our expectations, this result is consistent with the view that multiple strategies can be equally successful (e.g., Miles and Snow, 1978; Porter, 1980). According to this view, the fit between strategy, structures, and process is more germane to performance than the particular strategy per se.

Time Dependence of Initial Conditions

The final result surprised us. We found that the effects of the founding team and environment grew, not faded, with time.[5] Not only did semiconductor ventures become larger over time, but, also, the gap between the large and the small widened. This result is similar to findings, across many disciplines, in the study of chaos (Gleick, 1987). Chaos findings indicate that the behavior of systems, such as new firms, that can be modelled by simple and nonlinear equations (in our case, by interaction terms between environment and team) are highly sensitive to initial conditions. Gleick (1987: 8) described this phenomenon, popularly known as the "Butterfly Effect": "Tiny differences in input . . . quickly become overwhelming differences in output—a phenomenon given the name 'sensitive dependence on initial conditions'. In weather, for example, this translates into what is only half-jokingly known as the Butterfly Effect—the notion that a butterfly stirring the air today in Peking can transform storm systems next month in New York."

In less colorful terms, what we may have observed was that initial, small, or even chance advantages, such as a large team or a growth-stage market, created new advantages in the future, multiplying advantages in what was apparently a positive-feedback system. For example, large teams initially had more skills to build strategic alliances, raise money, and meet potential customers. Once their firms were modestly successful, other customers, investors, and allies were then attracted to what appeared to be a successful venture. In turn, suppliers became more willing to do business with these apparently successful ventures. Over time, firm growth became a self-fulfilling prophesy for many of these firms, as "the rich got richer while the poor got poorer" and "success bred success." Thus, the effects of initial conditions among this

5
Selection effects due to deaths in the population or differences related to the time of founding (e.g., systematic differences in founding team related to birth year) are potential alternative explanations. In the first case, since we have so few deaths, this explanation seems unlikely. Also, there is no difference in significance patterns between analyses with deaths in the sample (sales = 0) and removed. In the second case, we have observed no founding dependence among our independent variables. That is, the correlations of the independent variables with firm age are not significant. Thus we think that these alternative explanations are ruled out. We appreciate a colleague's pointing out these potential alternatives.

Organizational Growth

cohort of ventures exhibited positive-feedback behavior and were amplified, not diminished, with time.

Admittedly, these results are tentative and our discussion is speculative. However, if the results are valid, they suggest a strong dependence of organizational growth on founding conditions and an underlying similarity in the chaos dynamics of social and physical systems, an intriguing avenue for future research.

We began this paper by observing that the liability of newness research has focused primarily on how environmental factors affect the life chances of organizations. This paper sought to extend that research by examining the "quality of life," using organizational growth and by adding top-management team and strategy factors to environmental ones. What remains to be done are analyses of how founding conditions influence other important outcomes such as the survival and profitability of young firms. This work is underway.

REFERENCES

Aaker, David, and G. Day
1986 "The perils of high growth markets." Strategic Management Journal, 7: 409–421.

Allison, Paul D.
1978 "Measures of inequality." American Sociological Review, 43: 865–880.
1982 Event History Analysis. Beverly Hills, CA: Sage.

Anderson, Carl, and Carl A. Zeithaml
1984 "Stage of the product life cycle, business strategy, and business performance." Academy of Management Journal, 27: 5–24.

Bales, Robert, and Ernest Borgatta
1966 "Size of group as a factor in interaction profile." In A. Hare, E. Borgatta, and R. Bales (eds.), Small Groups: Studies in Social Interaction: 495–512. New York: Knopf.

Boeker, Warren
1989 "Strategic change: The effects of founding and history." Academy of Management Journal, 32: 489–515.

Bourgeois, L. J., and Kathleen M. Eisenhardt
1988 "Strategic decision processes in high velocity environments: Four cases in the microcomputer industry." Management Science, 34: 816–835.

Cameron, Kim S., Myung Kim, and David A. Whetten
1987 "Organizational effects of decline and turbulence." Administrative Science Quarterly, 32: 222–240.

Carroll, Glenn R.
1984 "The specialist strategy." In G. Carroll and D. Vogel (eds.), Strategy and Organization: 117–128. Marshfield, MA: Pitman.

Carroll, Glenn R., and Jacques Delacroix
1982 "Organizational mortality in the newspaper industries of Argentina and Ireland: An ecological approach." Administrative Science Quarterly, 27: 169–198.

Carroll, Glenn R., and Michael T. Hannan
1989 "Density delay in the evolution of organizational populations: A model and five empirical tests." Administrative Science Quarterly, 34: 411–430.

Cooper, Arnold C., and Albert Bruno
1977 "Success among high-technology firms." Business Horizons, 20: 16–22.

Dataquest
1987 "IC start-ups, 1987." Staff report by Dataquest, Inc., San Jose, CA.

Delacroix, Jacques, Anand Swaminathan, and Michael E. Solt
1989 "Density dependence versus population dynamics: An ecological study of failings in the California wine industry." American Sociological Review, 54: 245–262.

Eisenhardt, Kathleen M.
1988 "Agency- and institutional-theory explanations: The case of retail sales compensation." Academy of Management Journal, 31: 488–511.

1989 "Making fast strategic decisions in high velocity environments." Academy of Management Journal, 32: 543–576.

Eisenhardt, Kathleen M., and L. J. Bourgeois III
1988 "Politics of strategic decision making: Towards a mid-range theory." Academy of Management Journal, 31: 737–770.
1989 "Conflict, resolution, and strategic choice in high velocity environments." Working paper, School of Engineering, Stanford University.
1990 "Charting strategic decisions in the microcomputer industry: Profile of an industry star." In M. Von Glinow and S. Mohrman (eds.), Managing Complexity in High Technology Organizations, Systems, and People: 74–89. New York: Oxford University Press.

Freeman, John H., Glenn R. Carroll, and Michael Hannan
1983 "The liability of newness: Age dependence in organization death rates." American Sociological Review, 48: 692–710.

George, Alexander
1980 Presidental Decision Making in Foreign Policy: The Effective Use of Information and Advice. Boulder, CO: Westview.

Gersick, Connie C. G.
1989 "Marking time: Predictable transitions in task groups." Academy of Management Journal, 32: 274–309.

Gleick, James
1987 Chaos. New York: Viking Press.

Goodstein, Jerry, and Charles O'Reilly
1988 "It's what's up top that counts: The role of executive team demography and team dynamics in determining firm success and failure." Working paper, School of Business Administration, University of California, Berkeley.

Hambrick, Donald C., Ian MacMillan, and Diana Day
1982 "Strategic attributes and performance in the BCG matrix—A PIMS-based analysis of industrial product businesses." Academy of Management Journal, 25: 510–531.

Hannan, Michael T., and John H. Freeman
1977 "The population ecology of organizations." American Journal of Sociology, 82: 929–964.

Hrebiniak, Lawrence G., and William F. Joyce
1985 "Organizational adaptation: Strategic choice and environmental determinism." Administrative Science Quarterly, 30: 336–349.

Integrated Circuit Engineering
1987 Status 1986: A Report on the Integrated Circuit Industry. Scottsdale, AZ: Integrated Circuit Engineering.

Janis, Irving L.
1982 Groupthink. Boston: Houghton Mifflin.

Kazanjian, Robert
1988 "Relation of dominant problems to stages of growth in technology-based new ventures." Academy of Management Journal, 31: 257–279.

Kimberly, John
1980 "Initiation, innovation, and institutionalization in the creation process." In J. Kimberly and R. Miles (eds.), Organizational Life Cycle: 134–160. San Francisco: Jossey-Bass.

Lee, E., and M. Desu
1972 "A computer program for comparing K samples with right-censored data." Computer Programs in Biomedicine, 2: 315–321.

Maidique, Modesto A., and Peter Patch
1982 "Corporate strategy and technological policy." In Michael L. Tushman and William L. Moore (eds.), Readings in the Management of Innovation: 273–285. Marshfield, MA: Pitman.

Meindl, James R., Sanford Ehrlich, and Janet Dukerich
1985 "The romance of leadership." Administrative Science Quarterly, 30: 78–102.

Miles, Raymond E., and Charles C. Snow
1978 Organizational Strategy, Structure, and Process. New York: McGraw-Hill.

Miles, Robert
1982 Coffin Nails and Corporate Strategies. Englewood Cliffs, NJ: Prentice-Hall.

Mintzberg, Henry, and James Waters
1982 "Tracking strategy in an entrepreneurial firm." Academy of Management Journal, 25: 465–499.

Pfeffer, Jeffrey, and Alison Davis-Blake
1986 "Administrative succession and organizational performance: How administrator experience mediates the succession effect." Academy of Management Journal, 29: 72–83.

Porter, Michael E.
1980 Competitive Strategy. New York: Free Press.

Romanelli, Elaine
1987 "Contexts and strategies of organization creation: Patterns in performance." Working paper, Fuqua School, Duke University.

1989 "Environments and strategies of organization start-up: Effects on early survival." Administrative Science Quarterly, 34: 369–387.

Rosenbloom, Richard, and Michael Cusumano
1987 "Technological pioneering and competitive advantage: The birth of the VCR industry." California Management Review, 29: 51–76.

Roure, Juan, and Robert H. Keeley
1989 "Predictors of success in new technology based ventures." Working paper, School of Engineering, Stanford University.

Roure, Juan, and Modesto A. Maidique
1986 "Linking prefunding factors and high technology venture success: An exploratory study." Journal of Business Venturing, 1: 295–306.

Sahlman, William, and Howard Stevenson
1985 "Capital market myopia." Journal of Business Venturing, 1: 7–30.

Sandberg, William, and Charles Hofer
1987 "Improving new venture performance: The role of strategy, industry structure, and the entrepreneur." Journal of Business Venturing, 2: 5–28.

Schoonhoven, Claudia B., and Kathleen M. Eisenhardt
1987 A Study of the Influence of Organizational, Entrepreneurial, and Environmental Factors on the Growth and Development of Technology-based Start Up Firms. Washington, DC: U.S. Department of Commerce, National Technical Information Service.

Schoonhoven, Claudia B., Kathleen M. Eisenhardt, and Katherine Lyman
1990 "Speeding products to market: Waiting time to first product introduction in new firms." Administrative Science Quarterly, 35: 177–207.

Singh, Jitendra V., David J. Tucker, and Robert J. House
1986 "Organizational legitimacy and the liability of newness." Administrative Science Quarterly, 31: 171–193.

Smith, J., K. Carson, and R. Alexander
1984 "Leadership: It can make a difference." Academy of Management Journal, 27: 765–776.

Stinchcombe, Arthur
1965 "Social structure and organizations." In James G. March (ed.), Handbook of Organizations: 142–193. Chicago: Rand McNally.

Tsui, Anne, and Charles A. O'Reilly III
1989 "Beyond simple demographic effects: The importance of relational demography in superior-subordinate dyads." Academy of Management Journal, 32: 402–423.

Tushman, Michael L., and Philip Anderson
1986 "Technological discontinuities and organizational environments." Administrative Science Quarterly, 31: 439–465.

Van de Ven, Andrew H., Roger Hudson, and Dean M. Schroeder
1984 "Designing new business startups: Entrepreneurial, organizational, and ecological considerations." Journal of Management, 10: 87–107.

Organizational Growth

Wagner, W. Gary, Jeffrey Pfeffer, and Charles A. O'Reilly III
1984 "Organizational demography and turnover in top-management groups." Administrative Science Quarterly, 29: 74–92.

Zenger, Todd R., and Barbara S. Lawrence
1989 "Organizational demography: The differential effects of age and tenure distributions on technical communication." Academy of Management Journal, 32: 353–376.

Zucker, Lynne
1977 "The role of institutionalization in cultural persistence." American Sociological Review, 42: 726–743.

APPENDIX

Table A.1

Description of Markets (Dataquest, 1987; Integrated Circuit Engineering, 1987)*

Application-specific	
Digital gate arrays	Emergent: 1978–1980; Growth: 1981–1987
Analog gate arrays	Emergent: 1978–1987
Standard cells	Emergent: 1978–1982; Growth: 1983–1987
Programmable logic devices	Emergent: 1978–1982; Growth: 1983–1987
Silicon compilers	Emergent: 1981–1987
Memory	
DRAM	Growth: 1978–1987
SRAM	Growth: 1978–1987
ROM	Growth: 1978–1982; Mature: 1983–1987
EPROM	Growth: 1978–1984; Mature: 1985–1987
EEPROM	Emergent: 1978–1985; Growth: 1986–1987
FERRAM	Emergent: 1985–1987
Discrete	
Optoelectronic components	Mature: 1978–1987
Power field effect transistors	Mature: 1978–1987
Other	Mature: 1978–1987
Linear	Mature: 1978–1987
Gallium arsenide	
Digital	Emergent: 1981–1987
Analog	Emergent: 1982–1987
Logic	
Microprocessors	Growth: 1978–1987
Microperipherals	Mature: 1978–1987
Standard logic	Mature: 1978–1987

---

* Market stage was defined as follows: Emergent: Inflation-adjusted sales <$100 million annually; Growth: Inflation-adjusted sales >$100 million annually and annual growth rate ≥20%; Mature: Inflation-adjusted sales >$100 million annually and annual growth rate <20%.

Table A.2

Correlation Matrix, Year 4 ($N = 66$)

Variable	Mean	S.D.	2	3	4	5	6	7	8	9	10
1. Sales	14187	14376 '	.13	−.03	.36**	.07	.02	.02	.29**	.31**	.24*
2. Book to bill	1.0	0.1		.06	.05	.08	−.06	.23*	.02	.08	.16
3. Initial capital	831	1670			−.18	.04	.24*	.06	−.05	.29	.17
4. Growth-stage market	0.4	0.5				.17	−.13	.01	.09	−.02	.01
5. Concentration ratio	53.4	28.3					−.13	−.01	−.22*	.14	.18
6. Technical innovation (micron size)	1.9	1.1						−.21*	−.15	−.04	−.08
7. Technical innovation (3-item scale)	5.2	2.6							−.18	−.19	−.08
8. Joint experience	.06	.05								.49***	.21*
9. Team size	3.0	1.5									.43***
10. Heterogeneity of industry experience	4.2	3.4									−

*$p < .05$; **$p < .01$; ***$p < .001$.

---

[17]

STRATEGIC ORGANIZATION Vol 4(3): 215–247
DOI: 10.1177/1476127006066596
Copyright ©2006 Sage Publications (London, Thousand Oaks, CA and New Delhi)
http://so.sagepub.com

ARTICLES

Does experience matter? The effect of founding team experience on the survival and sales of newly founded ventures

Frédéric Delmar   Strategy and Organization, EM Lyon, France

Scott Shane   Weatherhead School of Management, Case Western Reserve University, USA

Abstract

While earlier researchers have argued that the founding team's industry and start-up experience should positively affect new venture performance, robust empirical support for these arguments has been lacking. Moreover, theory suggests that the relationship between founding team experience and new venture performance may be more complex than previous empirical research suggests. We test specific hypotheses about the effect of founding team industry and start-up experience on the survival and sales of 223 new ventures initiated by a representative sample of Swedish new ventures, using a methodology that overcomes the limitations to previous research. Our results show that founding team experience enhances both new venture survival and sales, but that the effects are non-linear, and vary with venture age.

Key words • industry experience • new venture creation • sales growth • start-up experience • survival

Does founding team experience enhance the performance of new ventures? Practitioners seem to think so. Investors in new ventures often say that they 'bet on the jockey, not on the horse' when choosing which ventures to back. Arguing that experienced entrepreneurs will do a better job with a mediocre business opportunity than inexperienced entrepreneurs will do with an excellent opportunity, investors hold that entrepreneurs' greater industry and start-up experience will create better-performing ventures than entrepreneurs with less experience. But is it true?

Perhaps surprisingly, the extant literature does not help very much in answering this question. Although several studies have examined the effects of founding team experience on the performance of new ventures, they offer little clear evidence to guide researchers or practitioners. Despite theory to suggest that founding team experience might show increasing or decreasing returns, and might vary with organizational age (Brüderl and Schussler, 1990; Fichman and Levinthal, 1991), prior studies exploring the effect of founding team experience on new venture performance posit a linear relationship that does not vary with venture age or with the amount of founding team experience.

Moreover, as Table 1 summarizes, prior research faces four methodological limitations. First, studies that test the effect of venture team experience on new firm survival (Wicker and King, 1989; Brüderl et al., 1992; Taylor, 1999; Bates and Servon, 2000; Van Praag, 2003) rarely test for convergent validity with other dimensions of new venture performance. The few studies that do examine the effect of founding team experience on firm survival and other measures of new venture performance (Gimeno et al., 1997; Shane and Stuart, 2002; Bosma et al., 2004) do not find consistent effects on multiple measures of performance.

This pattern of empirical results makes it difficult to accept the hypothesis that founding team experience enhances new venture performance. Because venture team start-up and industry experience do not have the same effects on multiple measures of new venture performance, researchers should only accept the more nuanced hypothesis that venture team experience reduces the likelihood of new venture failure. This result raises an important theoretical question: Perhaps founding team endowments offer a buffer that allows new firms to survive, but have no effect on sales or profits (Brüderl and Schussler, 1990; Fichman and Levinthal, 1991) because the benefits of experience that permit survival may not be sufficient to generate positive outcomes (Otani, 1996).

Second, virtually all previous studies that examine the effect of founding team experience on aspects of new venture performance other than survival fail to correct for venture failure, limiting the validity of their findings. [Gimeno et al., 1997 is the only exception we could identify.] Studies that fail to correct for new venture survival face a selection problem because they only examine the performance of new ventures that have managed to survive. The failure to correct for new venture survival in regressions that examine the effect of founding team experience on new venture performance results in systematic downward bias in the estimates for the effect of founding team experience. If founding team experience reduces the failure rate of new ventures, then a selected sample of surviving ventures will have a higher level of founding team experience than a non-selected sample of all new ventures. The reduced variance among the surviving ventures makes it less likely that the effect of founding team experience on measures of new venture performance will be observed. Thus, the examination of the uncorrected effects of founding team experience on measures of new venture performance suggests less convergence between the effects of venture

Table 1 Prior studies looking at venture team industry and start-up experience

Study	Sample	Significant effect of team start up exp. on survival	Significant effect of team industry exp. on survival	Sample representative of population of new firms	Corrects for selection	Measures effect of team exp. on another performance measure	Retrospective surveys or interviews
Bates and Servon (2000)	275 businesses in 1992 Characteristics of Business Owners Database formed 1986–92 who were self-employed because they could not find suitable work elsewhere	Not tested	Positive	No	No	Not tested	No
Bosma et al. (2004)	896 new businesses started in the Netherlands in 1994 and registered in database of Dutch chamber of commerce	No	Positive	No	No	Positive effect of start-up and industry experience on three-year profit and positive effect of industry experience on three-year employment	No
Brüderl et al. (1992)	1849 business founders in Munich area who founded firms during 1985 and 1986	None	Positive	Yes	No	No	Yes
Brüderl and Preisendorfer (1998)	1849 business founders in the Munich area who founded firms during 1985 and 1986	None	Positive	Yes	No	Yes, positive effect of industry experience on sales growth	Yes
Gimeno et al. (1997)	1547 firms from NFIB membership founded in 1983–5 with exit recorded in 1986 and 1987	None	Positive	Yes	No	Yes, positive effect of startup and industry experience on economic performance	Yes

(continued overleaf)

218　　　　STRATEGIC ORGANIZATION 4(3)

Table I Continued

Study	Sample	Significant effect of team start up exp. on survival	Significant effect of team industry exp. on survival	Sample representative of population of new firms	Corrects for selection	Measures effect of team exp. on another performance measure	Retrospective surveys or interviews
Klepper (2001)	Population of entrants in the US automobile industry 1895–1966	Positive	No	No	No	Not tested	No
Pennings et al. (1998)	Dutch accounting firms established 1880–1990	Not tested	Curvilinear	No	No	Not tested	No
Shane and Stuart (2002)	134 firms founded to exploit inventions assigned to MIT 1980–94	None	None	No	No	Yes, positive effect of industry experience on likelihood of IPO	Yes
Taylor (1999)	British household panel survey 1991–5	Positive	Not tested	Yes	No	Not tested	Yes
Van Praag (2003)	271 white males 20–32 years old who become self-employed in unincorporated companies 1985–9	No	Positive	No	No	Not tested	No
Wicker and King (1989)	413 retail and service establishments in five Southern Californian counties in 1985 taken from California State Board of Equalization	Not tested	Positive	No	No	Not tested	No

team experience on firm survival and other performance measures than is actually the case (Greene, 2000).

Third, many of the studies of the effect of venture team experience on new venture survival use retrospective designs (Brüderl et al., 1990; Gimeno et al.,

1997; Brüderl and Preisendorfer, 1998; Taylor, 1999; Shane and Stuart, 2002) to gather data, raising the potential for another type of selection bias. Because the failure rate of new ventures is very high in their early years, studies using retro-spective methods typically examine a selected group of surviving firms. Unless researchers have some archival method for gathering information about the vari-ables of interest, retrospective research designs fail to capture information on failed ventures (because key informants are not available to answer questions about those ventures). As a result, the observed positive association between founding team experience and the survival of new ventures indicates that these studies systematically over-sample new ventures with experienced founders, bias-ing the estimates of the effect of founder industry and start-up experience.

Fourth, even the empirical evidence that shows the positive effect of found-ing team experience on new venture survival has limited generalizability because most previous studies (Wicker and King, 1989; Gimeno et al., 1997; Bates and Servon, 2000; Van Praag, 2003; Bosma et al., 2004) have explored convenience samples that do not represent known populations, or are limited to a single industry or sector (Pennings et al., 1998; Klepper, 2001; Shane and Stuart, 2002). Because previous samples are not representative of the population of newly founded firms, researchers cannot conclude that founding team indus-try and start-up experience enhance the survival of the typical new venture.

The purpose of this study is twofold: First, it examines the effect of found-ing team experience on the survival and sales development of new ventures using a research design that overcomes the four methodological limitations described above. Second, it examines hypotheses which argue that the effect of founding team experience is neither constant over venture age, nor linear across the entire range of experience.

Empirically, we examine the effect of founder industry and start-up experi-ence on new venture survival, together with sales over their first 30 months of life for a sample of 223 new ventures representative of the population of new firms founded in Sweden in 1998. Our results indicate that founding team industry and start-up experience enhance both new venture survival and new venture sales, but the effects are nonlinear, and vary with venture age.

Theoretical background and hypotheses

A wide variety of studies have shown that new firms suffer from a liability of newness (Carroll and Hannan, 2000). As Stinchcombe (1965: 263) explained: 'new organizations, especially new types of organizations, generally involve new roles, which have to be learned.' In addition, new ventures lack routines for coordinating the activity of organization members, as well as for producing and delivering products or services. Furthermore, new ventures lack the social ties to key stakeholders that facilitate economic activity (Arrow, 1974).

Researchers have studied a variety of factors that overcome these liabilities of newness, and positively affect the performance of start-up firms. These factors include aspects of the external environment, including founding conditions (see Carroll and Hannan, 2000 for a review), and industry characteristics (Eisenhardt and Schoonhoven, 1990; Caves, 1998). They also include aspects of firm strategy (Boeker, 1989), including the choice of alliance partners (Stuart et al., 1999), entry timing (Mitchell, 1991), and barriers to entry (Sandberg and Hofer, 1987). Researchers have even examined the effect of the status of the financial backers of new firms (Freeman, 1999), and the prominence of the prior employers of venture founders (Burton et al., 2002).

Many of these factors, such as environmental conditions or firm strategy, operate at a higher level of analysis than the individual level at which we focus. Hence, they are beyond the scope of our study. However, researchers have also examined the effect of a variety of individual factors, including the social capital of founders (Shane and Stuart, 2002), founding team demography (Eisenhardt and Schoonhoven, 1990), the amount of time that the founding team members have worked together (Roure and Maidique, 1986), venture team size (Eisenhardt and Schoonhoven, 1990) and the functional backgrounds of the founders of new ventures (Jones-Evans, 1996).

While these individual factors affect the performance of new ventures and are important for researchers to study, we argue that two other individual attributes, the prior start-up and industry experience of the founding team, are also important and have received less rigorous scholarly attention. Prior founding team industry and start-up experience are important for two reasons. First, theory suggests that founding team experience is likely to be critical to the performance of new ventures. Earlier researchers (Jovanovic, 1982; Otani, 1996) have suggested that both founding team prior industry and start-up experience help a new venture to overcome liabilities of newness (Bates, 1990; Gimeno et al., 1997). Start-up experience, which we define as the previous creation of new organizations, provides information about such activities as opportunity identification and evaluation, resource acquisition and firm organizing. Industry experience, which we define as previous work in the industry in which the new firm will operate, provides information about industry rules and norms, customer and supplier networks, and employment practices.

Both of these forms of experience help entrepreneurs to overcome liabilities of newness and enhance the performance of their new ventures because the activities in which entrepreneurs engage are subject to learning curves. The more that entrepreneurs start firms or work in an industry, the better they become at organizing firms, acquiring resources, attracting customers and suppliers, and hiring employees. Because this learning can be transferred by entrepreneurs from one setting to another, the position of a new venture on the learning curve is determined, at least in part, by the prior industry and start-up experience of the founding team.

Second, practitioners focus their attention on founding team start-up and industry experience, which suggests their importance. Surveys of investors consistently reveal that they consider the industry and start-up experience of new firm founders to be among the most important determinants of new venture success (MacMillan et al., 1985; Hall and Hofer, 1993). We view practitioner attention to these dimensions as suggestive of a lay theory of new venture success that has not received adequate empirical testing.

Theory suggests that founding team experience enhances the performance of new ventures in three different ways. First, it provides information that facilitates the development of the organizing routines and skills in which new ventures are initially disadvantaged. Second, founding team experience provides role familiarity, which is important when founding team members adopt the roles that they play in new ventures. Third, founding team experience links the entrepreneur to a network of employees, suppliers, investors and customers (Campbell, 1992).

Defining venture performance

Researchers have discussed a variety of outcomes that founding team characteristics, such as prior industry and start-up experience, might affect. For example, Schoonhoven et al. (1990) examined the effect of founding team characteristics on the time it takes semiconductor firms to get new products to market, while Burton et al. (2002) and Shane and Stuart (2002) have looked at the effect that founding team characteristics have on the ability of new ventures to raise external capital.

Although previous studies show the effect of founding team experience on a wide variety of outcomes, we believe survival and sales are particularly important measures to study. Many studied outcomes, such as getting new products to market or raising money, are aspects of the organizing process itself (Delmar and Shane, 2003). Because founding team experience might have different effects on aspects of the venture organizing process than on the survival and sales of new ventures, examination of the effect of founding team experience on the latter outcomes is necessary to conclude that founding team experience has implications for new venture outcomes beyond aspects of the organizing process itself.

Hypotheses

Start-up experience
The venture team's start-up experience should enhance the survival and the sales of a new venture for at least three reasons. First, much of the relevant knowledge about creating a new company is learned by doing (Jovanovic, 1982). Start-up experience provides tacit knowledge of organizing routines and skills that have already been learned from their prior activities, and which can be transferred to the new venture (Ripsas, 1998; Shepherd et al., 2000). Experienced firm

founders have often learned what needs to be done to successfully organize a new firm because they have previously encountered the problems associated with hiring new employees, finding financial capital, developing a new product, and establishing contacts with potential customers. Thus, start-up experience provides a particular type of human capital that cannot be acquired easily through other means (Carroll and Mosakowski, 1987).

Second, start-up experience provides knowledge of what roles are necessary in organizations, and who should fill those roles. Knowledge of the appropriate roles and responsibilities for organization members is often difficult to develop without establishing new companies and defining the required new organizational roles and responsibilities (Brüderl et al., 1992). For example, fulfilling the role of gathering information and making decisions as an entrepreneur is likely to require experience in these fields (Duchesneau and Gartner, 1990). Start-up experience may also lead founders to better identify information channels needed to identify and exploit productive opportunities. Alternatively, experienced founders may know what firm organizing activities to focus attention on, and so be better able to set up a new firm than inexperienced founders (Ericsson and Smith, 1991).

Third, start-up experience links the entrepreneur to a network of employees, suppliers, investors and customers (Campbell, 1992). Because social ties are an important lubricant of economic activity (Arrow, 1974), the initial lack of ties to stakeholders hinders new firms relative to established organizations (Stinchcombe, 1965). Start-up experience transfers these social ties from prior settings, facilitating resource acquisition, the implementation of techniques to evaluate customer needs and other organizing activities that enhance new venture sales (Venkataraman, 1997). In addition, start-up experience provides legitimacy in the eyes of important stakeholders of the new venture, which, in turn, facilitates the process of obtaining resources and organizing new firm operations (Aldrich, 1990). Consequently, founders' experience represents a resource that reduces the liability of newness that new ventures face (Shane and Khurana, 2003).

Fourth, start-up experience provides tacit knowledge about how to run a new firm that has been learned from prior mistakes (Ripsas, 1998; Shepherd et al., 2000). For instance, experienced firm founders have often learned what needs to be done to successfully organize a new firm because they have previously encountered the problems associated with hiring new employees, finding financial capital, developing a new product, establishing contacts with potential customers, and attracting and hiring employees (Brüderl et al., 1992; Aldrich, 1999). This also allows them to focus on the task of building a venture, despite competing demands on their time, because they know what activities are important to develop a new business. These arguments lead to the first hypotheses, as follows.

HYPOTHESIS 1A   The founding team's start-up experience will increase a new venture's survival.

HYPOTHESIS 1B   The founding team's start-up experience will increase a new venture's sales.

Industry experience

The venture team's start-up experience should enhance the survival and the sales of a new venture for at least three reasons. First, a founding team with more industry experience has a better understanding of how to satisfy customer demand in that industry because such information is often only available through industry participation (Knight, 1921; Von Mises, 1949; Johnson, 1986). By working with customers and understanding the advantages and disadvantages of various product and service offerings, as well as gaps in existing efforts to satisfy customer needs, a founding team develops a rich understanding of what to offer as a product or a service. This gives them an advantage in being able to more rapidly identify and develop a market entry strategy, and to focus on relevant steps to achieve a positive outcome.

Second, many of the skills and much of the information necessary to effectively exploit an opportunity can only be learned through employment in an industry, because such information is uncodified. This knowledge might be related to production processes, market niches, technological developments, or products or services (Cooper et al., 1994; Klepper, 2001). Because a founding team with industry experience has acquired this knowledge, ventures founded by experienced teams are more likely to survive and achieve greater sales than ventures founded by teams that are novices in an industry.

Third, social ties to suppliers and distributors are created over time through activity in an industry. When people found ventures in the same industry as they have been working in, they can transfer social ties from their prior settings to their new venture. These social ties are valuable in obtaining commitment and support from suppliers, distributors and customers. Moreover, these ties, and the status of the people with whom the ties are created, provide legitimacy in their eyes of important stakeholders in the new venture, which, in turn, facilitates the process of obtaining resources and organizing new firm operations (Aldrich, 1990). As a result, founding teams with more industry experience are likely to have advantages over other founding teams in developing their new businesses. These arguments lead to the following hypotheses.

HYPOTHESIS 2A   The founding team's industry experience will increase a new venture's survival.

HYPOTHESIS 2B   The founding team's industry experience will increase a new venture's sales.

Decreasing marginal returns to experience

Founding team experience is unlikely to have a linear effect on new venture performance as the amount of experience increases. Rather, the effect of start-up and industry experience on new venture performance is likely to decline with the amount of experience because experience effects face diminishing marginal returns.

Experience curves affect the development and performance of new businesses. When people embark on the process of creating new firms, they develop a conception of what the newly formed organization will look like and seek to establish the organization in a way consistent with that vision (Witt, 2000). The specific steps that firm founders take towards the establishment of new organizations are affected by the knowledge that they have about the industry in which the firm will operate and the new firm organizing process. Founders without any experience in the venture's industry or in the start-up process have little knowledge to guide this process. As a result, those firm founders are likely to make more mistakes than the firm founders with industry and start-up experience, hindering the performance of their new ventures.

Each additional amount of experience that firm founders have is likely to have a positive performance effect because this experience provides knowledge that guides the entrepreneurial process and reduces founder error (Witt, 2000). However, the level of performance benefits that founder industry start-up and industry provide is likely to decline with each additional amount of experience. While each additional amount of experience provides additional knowledge to guide future entrepreneurial processes and to reduce error in the process, the additional knowledge that experience provides increases at a decreasing rate (Cyert and March, 1963). As a result, the knowledge gained from industry and start-up experience that allows firm founders to undertake many aspects of new firm activity more effectively – establishing a new company, dealing with suppliers, finding customers, organizing production and so on – is unlikely to be as great for the founding team's second, third or fourth prior start-up as it is for their first prior venture (Witt, 2000). As a result, the performance benefits of the fourth prior start-up will have a lesser effect than the performance benefits of the third prior start-up, which, in turn, will be smaller than the performance benefits for the second prior start-up and so on. These arguments lead to the third set of hypotheses, as follows.

> **HYPOTHESIS 3A**   The effect of the founding team's start-up experience on new venture survival will be a positive, but declining, function of founding team start-up experience.

> **HYPOTHESIS 3B**   The effect of the founding team's industry experience on new venture survival will be a positive, but declining, function of founding team industry experience.

> **HYPOTHESIS 3C**   The effect of the founding team's start-up experience on new venture sales will be a positive, but declining, function of the amount of founding team start-up experience.

> **HYPOTHESIS 3D**   The effect of the founding team's industry experience on new venture sales will be a positive, but declining, function of the amount of founding team industry experience.

Decrease with venture age

The effects of founding team industry and start-up experience will vary over the life of a venture. The beneficial effect of founding team experience will decline as the venture ages. New ventures begin as ideas and are transformed by entrepreneurs into new organizations (Aldrich and Martinez, 2001). The transformation of ventures from ideas into organizations suggests that the relative contribution of founder knowledge to the performance of new ventures will decrease as ventures age. In the initial phases of venture development, when the venture is mostly an idea, founder knowledge accounts for almost all of the factors that affect venture performance. Whether a venture survives or develops depends largely on what founders know about how to get control over resources or how to establish organizational boundaries (Aldrich and Martinez, 2001). In the later stages of venture development, when employees have been hired and assets purchased, characteristics of these factors begin to affect venture performance. As a result, the relative effect of founder industry and start-up experience on venture performance declines with venture age.

Second, the founders of new ventures face steep learning curves in developing new businesses (Gibb, 1994). These steep learning curves mean that, as new ventures develop, the effect of each unit increase in experience on outcomes declines with the amount of experience. As a result, the magnitude of the performance gap between experienced and inexperienced ventures declines as ventures age.

The experience of founders influences where a new venture starts on this learning curve. When a new firm is first founded, it possesses little more than the assets that the founders bring with them to the venture. For the typical new venture, those assets take the form largely of the founders' human capital (Bhide, 2000). In contrast, ventures founded by more experienced entrepreneurs begin their lives further up the learning curve because the human capital that their founders provide is more valuable to the performance of the new ventures than the human capital of inexperienced founders. However, the value of founder human capital decreases as ventures age because the effect of each unit increase in experience on outcomes declines with venture experience. As a result, the performance benefits that experienced new venture founders provide to new ventures will decline as ventures age.

Third, new ventures change as they get older (Churchill and Lewis, 1983). In particular, their activities become more and more complex, making the performance of new ventures less directly linked to the characteristics of the founding team and more the result of other factors.

In addition, as ventures age, labor begins to be divided among organization members and the proportion of labor accounted for by the founder decreases (Witt, 2000). Consequently, founder-specific characteristics influence a smaller portion of venture activities as ventures age.

Furthermore, learning involves the creation of routines that can be used to respond to future circumstances when similar circumstances appear in the future

(Cyert and March, 1963). Examples of these routines in new ventures include routines for invoicing, checking inventory, purchasing, budgeting, evaluating investments, selecting employees and so on (Mathews, 2003). As organizations develop, founder decision making begins to be replaced by organizational routines. The organization ecology literature suggests that these routines become embedded in organizations over time (Carroll and Hannan, 2000). As a result, the role of individuals in ensuring that activities occur in organizations declines as ventures age. These arguments lead to the fourth set of hypotheses, as follows.

HYPOTHESIS 4A   The effect of the founding team's start-up experience will be a positive, but declining, function of venture age.

HYPOTHESIS 4B   The effect of the founding team's industry experience will be a positive, but declining, function of venture age.

HYPOTHESIS 4C   The effect of the founding team's start-up experience on new venture sales will be a positive, but declining, function of venture age.

HYPOTHESIS 4D   The effect of the founding team's industry experience on new venture sales will be a positive, but declining, function of venture age.

Method

Design and sample

In order to test the effect of venture teams on the sales of newly founded firms, we had to overcome two difficult data collection problems. First, to avoid selection bias (which would bias our estimates of the effects of experience on new venture sales), we needed to collect data on firms from the point at which they were started forward in time (Heckman, 1979; Yamaguchi, 1991; Blossfeld and Rohwer, 1995). Second, to generalize our results to a known population, we needed to obtain a sample representative of that population.

Therefore, we first identified members of the Swedish labor force who were starting new ventures at a particular point of time, creating a sample of new ventures that represented the population of all new ventures at risk of formation in Sweden at that point in time. In the first nine months of 1998, we randomly sampled, by telephone, 35,971 Swedes between the ages of 16 and 70 (the definition of the working-age population in Sweden) and asked them to participate in our study. A total of 30,427 individuals (84.6%) agreed to participate.

We then asked the respondents if they were in the process of starting a new business either alone or as a part of a team. We provided the respondents with a definition of a new business in order to minimize problems with perceptual differences in the definition of a new business. The definition we provided was broad, and included a variety of different types of new businesses including farms, consultancies and home-based businesses.

If there was an affirmative answer to the screening question, we subsequently asked the respondent if the new firm was an independent effort or an effort on behalf of an existing organization. We did this to ensure that our sample consisted only of independent new businesses, not divisions of existing corporations.

If there was an affirmative answer to the independent venture question, we then asked if the respondent was a member of the start-up team, rather than an adviser or investor. Because we were interested only in founding team members, we excluded those people who indicated that they were not members of the start-up team.

We were also concerned that many of the respondents might have started their new firms before we began our observation period. Therefore, we asked the respondents to indicate the month and year when work on the new venture first began. We defined work on the new venture as any action taken to exploit the identified opportunity (for example, product development or seeking funds). By focusing on organizing action as our definition of initiating a new venture, we were able to differentiate between ventures whose founders had merely thought about starting a new firm and ventures whose founders had acted to establish new firms.

We discovered that some respondents indicated that they were in the process of starting a new business, but had begun that effort as early as 1947. Therefore, we excluded all respondents who had started businesses before 1998, the start year of our observation period. The problem with including respondents who had started businesses before our observation period is that we had no way to observe the other members of their start-up cohort. We suspected that many people who had started businesses in earlier cohorts (for example, 1947) had long since terminated their efforts. The inclusion of respondents from earlier cohorts who were still in the process of starting their businesses would have resulted in selection bias, because other individuals who had started new ventures in their cohort, but who had already terminated their efforts, would have indicated that they were not in the process of establishing a new firm when surveyed by us in 1998. As a result, our screening questions capture all of the new ventures started in 1998, but only long-in-process entrants from earlier years. Because long-in-process new firms do not represent the population of new firms started in earlier years, their inclusion would bias our sample.

The main objective of our survey was to gather panel data about the new ventures over time. Therefore, we resurveyed the respondents every six months for two years.[1] We obtained high response rates for the successive waves: 90.5 percent at six months, 91.9 percent at 12 months, 98.5 percent at 18 months and 96.1 percent at 24 months. Only 12 of the firms that ceased to participate at one of the waves of data collection never returned to participate. We explored whether the 12 firms that dropped out of participation and 211 firms that continued to participate differed significantly on any of the variables in our study. Because we did not find any statistically significant differences between the two groups, we have included all 223 ventures in this study. That is, the 12 firms that did not return to our data collection were treated as right censored at the point that they ceased participation. We also analyzed the data excluding these 12 cases and found qualitatively the same results.

Our sample provided an interesting snapshot of the development of new ventures in Sweden. Of the 223 new ventures, 17.8 percent were in the manufacturing sector, 21.6 percent were in professional services and the rest were in the non-professional service sector. The most prominent industries in the sample were professional services, retail establishments, and hotels and restaurants. Approximately two-thirds of the ventures, or 63.4 percent, served firms as their main customers. The employment of the average firm in our sample was consistent with the employment of the average new firm in Sweden in the year of observation, which had 1.4 employees.

Analysis

Survival

We examined the influence of founding team start-up and industry experience on the survival of the new ventures across the 30-month observation period of our panel. Over our observation period, 82 of the 223 ventures (36.8 percent) were disbanded. Half of the ventures in our sample that disbanded did so before the tenth month.

We predicted the hazard of the venture being disbanded using event history analysis with standard errors clustered by venture (Blossfeld and Rohwer, 1995; Wooldridge, 2002). We employed a piece-wise constant exponential model, which splits the time axis into time periods, and assumes that the transition rate is constant within these intervals, but can change between them (Blossfeld and Rohwer, 1995).[2] The piece-wise model is useful when researchers cannot make assumptions about the time dependence of the process, which is the case here given the controversies about the time dependence of new venture termination (Brüderl and Schussler, 1990; Fichman and Levinthal, 1991).

Sales

We analyzed how founding team start-up and industry experience influenced the sales of the new ventures across the 30-month observation period of our panel. The ventures in our sample experienced significant changes in their level of sales over their first 30 months of life. We found that only 3.1 percent of the ventures in our sample had achieved any sales at all in their first month, and that the average amount of monthly sales for a one-month-old venture was Skr2580 (Skr is the abbreviation for the Swedish krona or crown) ($290; US$1 equaled approximately Skr9 at the time of observation). However, 52.5 percent of our sample that survived to 30 months had achieved sales by month 30, and the average monthly sales of the ventures that had survived to 30 months was Skr223,030.

Because our sales measure is limited (i.e. it takes the value of zero for a non-trivial fraction of the population, but is roughly continuously distributed over positive values), we used a random effects Tobit model in which we cluster our standard errors by venture.[3]

Dependent variables

Venture failure

We measured venture failure as the termination of the venture by all members of the team pursuing it. We identified termination by asking the respondents at each wave of the survey whether all members of the founding team had ceased their effort to establish the venture, and if so, in what month that effort ended. As we were able to identify the specific month of termination, we were able to create survival models that measured the monthly spells for the new ventures. In the month that all members of the founding team terminated their effort to establish the new venture, we coded the venture with a '1'. Otherwise, we coded this variable as '0'. Those ventures not terminated by the end of our 30-month observation period were treated as censored.[4]

Sales

We measured sales as the log of the level of sales achieved by the venture in the month of observation, plus 1 to correct for zero values. We measured sales by asking the respondents every six months the value of sales that had been made since the last interview. We then predicted the average monthly level of sales for that period of the panel. Sales were measured in thousands of Skr .

Predictor variables

In our models, we invoke the concept of Granger causality and measure changes in the independent variables in the time period prior to changes in the dependent variable (survival or sales). Granger causality holds that an effect in a prior period can lead to an effect in a subsequent period; however, an effect in a subsequent period cannot lead to an effect in a prior period. For example, our results suggested that the venture's employment, which is measured at time (t–1) leads to a change in the level of venture sales which is measured at time (t), not that a change in the level of venture sales, which was measured at time (t) leads to a change in employment, which was measured at time (t–1).

We measured industry experience as the log of the total number of years of experience in the industry across all founding team members. On average, the founding teams had 15.6 years of industry experience, but 24 percent of the ventures had no founding team experience in their industry. We used the log transformation of this variable because the distribution of this variable was heavily skewed, containing several outliers. We corrected for zero years of experience by adding 1 to all values.

We measured start-up experience as the log of the total number of firms previously started by the members of the founding team. On average, the founding teams had started three previous firms, but 52 percent of the teams had no previous start-up experience. We again relied on the log transformation to correct for skewed data and added 1 to all values to allow the log transformation of cases with zero years of experience.

Control variables

Team age

We controlled for the sum of the ages of the team members because age influences industry and start-up experience. We again used log transformation to correct for skewness.

Team size

We controlled for team size because a larger venture team has the opportunity to obtain more human capital and more resources (information, time and money) than a smaller team (Roberts, 1991; Klepper, 2001). Moreover, larger teams can accomplish tasks more quickly because founding team members can specialize their activities. Furthermore, larger teams benefit from variation in experience, which may yield more innovative solutions to problems (Leonard and Sensiper, 1990). We measured team size as the log of number of members of the venture team.

Employment

We measured the venture's employment because a smaller team can compensate for less human capital by hiring employees who contribute their human capital to the new venture. Moreover, hiring employees increases the production capacity of a new venture, increasing the sales that the firm can achieve. We measured the number of employees by asking the respondents every six months how many part-time and full-time employees were working in the new firm. We counted part-time employees as one-half of full-time employees. Once more we corrected for skewness by using the log transformation. We updated this variable at the time of each survey.

Industry

We controlled for several differences in the industries in which the new ventures operate. All firms in Sweden are required by law to register with the government and are captured in the business register, which is updated every two weeks. In addition, questionnaires are sent out to companies to verify that the information in the registry is correct. We used data from this business register to create four industry measures. These variables are coded at the five-digit standard industrial code level, and are updated on a yearly basis, using data from 1998, 1999 and 2000. For example, one industry was 72201, IT consultants; another industry was 55300, restaurants; a third industry was 63330, travel agencies.

To ensure that the industry classification of the new firms in the sample was reliable, we had two industry experts from Statistics Sweden (the managers of the business registry) code the firms to industries based on information received from the respondents at the time of the initial interview. Both experts coded 89.4 percent of the cases as belonging in the same industry. In the remaining 10.4 percent, we used the classification done by the most senior expert. The five measures created using data from Statistics Sweden were as follows.

First, we measured industry entry as the number of new firms that entered the industry in the year of investigation. We measured the number of entries because new firm failure is more likely to occur in industries with a higher rate of entry than in industries with a lower rate of entry (Caves, 1998; Carroll and Hannan, 2000).

Second, we measured industry size as the total value of sales in the industry in the year of investigation. We control for industry size because the total amount of sales possible for a new firm is greater in larger markets than in smaller ones (Eisenhardt and Schoonhoven, 1990).

Third, we measured industry growth as the annual percentage rate of change of sales in the industry in the year of investigation. Industry growth facilitates the sales of new firms because it is easier for new firms to generate sales in environments of increasing demand than in environments of constant or shrinking demand (Audretsch and Mahmood, 1995).

Fourth, we measured the average firm age in the industry in the year of investigation because new firms often grow faster in younger industries than in older ones (Acs and Audretsch, 1989).

Fifth, we measured the average firm size in the industry in the year of investigation because firms have a more difficult time entering and growing in industries dominated by large dominant incumbent firms (Caves, 1998).

Time
Because we expected that new ventures would either drift towards higher sales or be terminated over time, we expected that some of the variance in sales and survival across the new ventures in the sample would be explained by venture age. To mitigate this effect, we included a series of dummy variables for each of the waves of data collection: up to six months, 7–12 months, 13–18 months and 19–24 months. (The final wave was the omitted period.) By including the dummy variables for each of the waves, we parcelled out the portion of the variance that is explained solely by the passage of time.

Correcting for selection

One problem with studying determinants of the sales of new firms is that only those firms that survive are measured, and many new firms do not survive. The coefficients on variables that have a significant effect on both survival and sales will be biased downward in regressions predicting sales if only surviving firms are included in the sample and researchers do not correct for the selection that results from survival, because the firms that fail are more likely to have lower values in the predictor variables (Heckman, 1979; Greene, 2000). To correct for this problem, we used Lee's (1983) generalization of the Heckman selection model (1979) to create a selection correction variable. By introducing this variable into our models predicting firm sales, we could obtain more precise estimates for our independent variables (Greene, 2000; Hamilton and Nickerson, 2003).

We used the hazard of termination during the 30 months of observation calculated from a piecewise exponential model to predict firm exit for our 223 ventures to generate the selection correction variable (lambda):

$$\lambda_{it} = \frac{\phi[\Phi^{-1}(F_i(t))]}{1 - F_i(t)}$$

where $F_i(t)$ is the cumulative hazard function for project i at time t, ϕ is the standard normal density function, and Φ^{-1} the inverse of the standard normal distribution function (Lee, 1983).

The model used to predict the hazard of venture failure and to compute lambda must include at least one covariate that influences the probability of venture failure but not the level of sales the venture achieves (Greene, 2000). Therefore, we include four additional covariates in the failure models: *purchased*, a dummy variable that takes the value of 1 if the new venture was started through the purchase of a business from another party; *need permit*, a dummy variable that takes the value of 1 if the venture needs permits or licenses to operate; *obtained government loan*, a dummy variable that takes the value of 1 if the venture obtained debt from a government agency; and *received equity from the government*, a dummy variable that takes the value of 1 if the venture obtained an equity investment from a government agency.

Controlling for past performance

New venture performance and founding team human capital are both associated with unobserved characteristics of new ventures, such as product quality. For example, founding teams with more industry experience may have higher-performing firms because they develop higher-quality products. As a result, estimates of the effects of human capital may simply proxy for unobserved product quality and not have any real effect on firm performance. To increase the likelihood that our measures of human capital actually measure the effect of human capital and not other things that happen to be correlated with human capital, we included lagged venture performance in our regressions to predict new venture survival and sales. By including lagged performance, we control for unobserved factors that co-determine firm sales and human capital (Wooldridge, 2002; Hamilton and Nickerson, 2003). As a result, our measures of human capital represented only founding team human capital, and allowed us to accurately estimate the effects of the venture team's human capital on firm performance (Heckman and Borjas, 1980). We measured sales in thousands of Skr.

Results

Predicting survival

Table 2 provides the results of our regressions to predict new venture survival. Model 1 is our base model. It reports results from the piece-wise constant model of the hazard of venture termination that includes the control variables: the lagged past performance measure, employment, venture team size and age, the industry variables and the time pieces. Model 2 adds the effect of founding team start-up and industry experience.

Consistent with hypothesis 1a, we found that new ventures whose founding teams have greater start-up experience are more likely to survive ($-1.21, p<.05$). The probability of venture termination is 42.2 percent lower for ventures founded by teams with the mean level of start-up experience (three prior start-ups) than for ventures founded by teams with no previous start-up experience. However, in contrast to hypothesis 2a, we found no significant effect for venture team industry experience on the hazard of venture team survival.

We also hypothesized that the marginal effect of industry and start-up experience on new venture survival would decline with experience (hypotheses 3a and 3b). Our results in support of hypothesis 1a suggest the decreasing marginal effect of start-up experience. Because we examined the effect of the log of start-up experience, our finding of a statistically significant and economically meaningful effect of start-up experience on venture termination implies that start-up experience has a decreasing marginal effect on new venture termination.

In model 3, we examined the effect of having start-up experience of one, two, three or four or more start-ups among members of the venture team (as compared with the null of no start-up experience). We also examined the effect of having 1–5, 6–10, 11–15 or more than 15 years of industry experience (as compared with the null of no industry experience). Consistent with hypothesis 3a, the results in model 3 show that the amount of start-up experience does not have a linear effect on new venture survival. The difference in the effect of having no start-up experience and having one prior start-up was statistically significant, but the difference between having one prior start-up and more than one prior start-up was not statistically significant. However, the results in model 3

Table 2 Piece-wise exponential models to predict the hazard of venture termination

	Model 1			Model 2			Model 3			Model 4		
	β	(s.e.)	p	β	(s.e.)	p	β	(s.e.)	p	β	(s.e.)	p
Start-up experience				-1.208	(0.520)	*				-2.269	(1.514)	
Industry experience				-0.051	(0.266)					2.185	(1.364)	
Team age	-1.560	(0.845)	t	-0.957	(0.954)		-1.534	(0.931)		-1.116	(0.957)	
Team size	1.103	(0.847)		1.942	(0.969)	*	1.736	(1.043)		1.972	(0.956)	*
1 start-up							-1.247	(0.596)	*			
2 start-ups							-0.504	(0.344)				
3 start-ups							-0.381	(0.395)				
4 or more start-ups							-0.210	(0.433)				
1–5 yrs exp.							-0.193	(0.324)				
6–10 yrs exp.							-0.298	(0.372)				
11–15 yrs exp.							0.272	(0.533)				
>15 yrs. exp.							-0.099	(0.397)				
Start-up × 0–6										1.663	(1.613)	
Start-up × 7–12										0.487	(1.573)	
Start-up × 13–18										2.005	(1.751)	
Start-up × 19–24										2.090	(2.287)	
Industry × 0–6										-2.452	(1.435)	t
Industry × 7–12										-1.903	(1.401)	
Industry × 13–18										-2.706	(1.468)	t
Industry × 19–24										-4.326	(1.611)	**

	Model 1		Model 2		Model 3		Model 4	
No. employees	−1.636	(1.003)	−1.537	(0.964)	−1.580	(0.952) †	−1.506	(0.932)
Lagged sales	−79.377	(49.146)	−78.061	(51.135)	−80.764	(54.399)	−78.067	(50.078)
Industry entry	0.007	(0.021)	0.010	(0.021)	0.012	(0.022)	0.010	(0.021)
Industry size	0.006	(0.005)	0.006	(0.005)	0.006	(0.005)	0.006	(0.005)
Industry growth	−0.111	(0.290)	−0.115	(0.296)	−0.125	(0.304)	−0.113	(0.303)
Average firm age	0.026	(0.050)	0.041	(0.049)	0.036	(0.052)	0.041	(0.049)
Average firm size	−0.015	(0.026)	−0.014	(0.026)	−0.016	(0.030)	−0.013	(0.025)
Months 0–6	0.723	(0.479)	0.687	(0.479)	0.672	(0.479)	0.670	(0.845)
Months 7–13	1.492	(0.464) **	1.459	(0.464) **	1.466	(0.465) **	1.744	(0.817) *
Months 14–18	0.698	(0.527)	0.661	(0.526)	0.677	(0.530)	0.581	(0.904)
Months 19–24	0.015	(0.623)	−0.009	(0.623)	−0.006	(0.624)	0.243	(0.968)
Obtained government loan	−0.367	(0.048) ***	−0.374	(0.050) ***	−0.360	(0.052) ***	−0.401	(0.052) ***
Received government inv.	−0.272	(0.031) ***	−0.324	(0.030) ***	−0.285	(0.032) ***	−0.304	(0.032) ***
Need permit	−0.406	(0.260)	−0.435	(0.264) †	−0.389	(0.267) †	−0.444	(0.263) †
Purchased business	−1.259	(0.705) †	−1.294	(0.742) †	−1.219	(0.743) †	−1.391	(0.769) †
Constant	−2.097	(1.458)	−2.830	(1.615)	−1.815	(1.616) †	−4.480	(2.115) *
log likelihood	205.88		203.17		201.91		202.32	
Chi square	434.99		581.02		479.97		593.40	

Key: † = $p < 0.10$; * = $p < 0.05$; ** = $p < 0.01$; *** = $p < 0.001$ in two-tailed tests. The sample consists of 5093 firm-month observations, 223 cases and 82 failures. All models are significant at the $p < 0.0001$ level.

do not support hypothesis 3b. There is no significant diminishing return for the effect of industry experience on new venture survival.

We hypothesized that the effects of founding team industry and start-up experience would decline as the ventures aged. In model 4, we examined the effects of interactions between venture age and start-up experience (hypothesis 4a) and industry experience (hypothesis 4b). As model 4 shows, we do not find support for hypothesis 4a. The magnitude of the effect of start-up experience on reducing the hazard of venture termination does not decline as the ventures age.

We also failed to find support for hypothesis 4b. The magnitude of the effect of industry experience on reducing the hazard of venture termination is not significantly different for most time pieces. Moreover, the magnitude of the effect of industry experience on reducing the hazard of venture termination is significantly higher for ventures between 19 and 24 months old than for the other time pieces.

We tested for the robustness of the effects for founding team industry and start-up experience on new venture survival. In unreported regressions, we explored whether the effects of founding team industry and start-up experience on new venture survival were curvilinear. When we introduced them into the regressions, the quadratic forms for the experience variables were insignificant, suggesting that the founding team experience effects we observed are better expressed as linear functions than as curvilinear ones.

In unreported regressions, we also examined whether founding team industry and start-up experience interacted with each other to affect the survival of new ventures and whether founding team industry and start-up experience interacted with industry characteristics. We did not find significant effects for either of these types of interaction.

Predicting sales

Table 3 presents the results of our regressions explaining new venture sales. Model 1 is the base model that takes into account the effects of the selection correction lambda, the lagged past performance measure, employment, venture team size and age, industry differences and the time period effects. Model 2 adds the effect of founding team start-up and industry experience.

Consistent with hypothesis 1b, we found that new ventures whose founding teams had greater start-up experience have higher levels of logged sales (.21, $p < .10$). Ventures with founding teams that had the mean level of start-up experience (three prior start-ups) had sales that were 11.3 percent higher than ventures with founding teams that had no prior start-up experience. Consistent with hypothesis 2b, we found that new ventures whose founding teams had more industry experience had higher levels of logged sales (.14, $p < .05$). Ventures with founding teams that had the mean level of industry experience (16 years) had sales that were 17 percent higher than ventures with founding teams that had no prior industry experience.

We also hypothesized that the marginal effect of industry and start-up experience on new venture survival would decline with experience (hypotheses 3c and 3d). In model 3, we examined the effect of having start-up experience of one, two, three and four or more start-ups among members of the venture team (as compared with the null of no start-up experience). We also examined the effect of having industry experience of 1–5, 6–10, 11–15 and 16 or more years of industry experience (as compared with the null of no industry experience). In contrast to hypothesis 3c, the results in model 3 show that the amount of founding team start-up experience does not show decreasing marginal effects on ventures sales. Only ventures with founding teams that had four or more prior start-ups had sales significantly higher than ventures with teams that had no prior start-up experience. Similarly, in contrast to hypothesis 3d, the results in model 3 show that the amount of founding team industry experience does not show decreasing marginal effects on venture sales. Only venture teams with 11–15 years of industry experience had sales significantly higher than ventures with teams that had no prior industry experience.

We hypothesized that the effects of founding team industry and start-up experience would decline as ventures age. In model 4, we examined the effects of interactions between venture age and start-up experience (hypothesis 4c) and industry experience (hypothesis 4d), respectively. Model 4 supports hypothesis 4c. While the main effect of start-up experience is positive, the coefficient on the interaction of start-up experience with the time pieces is negative, statistically significant and show a declining magnitude as ventures age, suggesting that the size of the effect of start-up experience on sales gets smaller as the ventures age.

However, model 4 does not provide support for hypothesis 4d. No significant effects of the interactions between the effect of industry experience and venture age on venture sales were observed.

We tested for the robustness of the effects for founding team industry and start-up experience on new venture sales. In unreported regressions, we explored whether the effects of founding team industry and start-up experience on new venture sales were curvilinear. The quadratic forms for the experience variables were insignificant when they were introduced into the regressions, suggesting that the founding team experience effects we observed are better expressed as linear functions than as curvilinear ones.

In unreported regressions, we also examined whether founding team industry and start-up experience interacted with each other to affect the sales of new ventures, and whether founding team industry and start-up experience interacted with industry characteristics. We did not find significant effects for either of these types of interaction.

To ensure that our results were not artifacts of specification errors, we reran our analyses without our controls for past performance and number of employees, which were highly correlated with our selection correction lambda. The

Table 3 Tobit models to predict new venture sales

	Model 1			Model 2			Model 3			Model 4		
	β	(s.e.)	p	β	(s.e.)	p	β	(s.e.)	p	β	(s.e.)	p
Start-up experience	-0.176	(0.227)		0.213	(0.114)	t				0.525	(0.151)	***
Industry experience	0.115	(0.243)		0.135	(0.065)	*				0.168	(0.093)	*
Team age				-0.501	(0.252)	*	-0.374	(0.239)		-0.483	(0.249)	
Team size				0.057	(0.259)		-0.092	(0.283)		0.060	(0.259)	
1 start-up							-0.008	(0.117)				
2 start-ups							-0.017	(0.100)				
3 start-ups							0.030	(0.111)				
4 start-ups							0.266	(0.105)	*			
1–5 yrs ind. exp.							0.083	(0.096)				
6–10 yrs ind. exp.							0.018	(0.106)				
11–15 yrs ind. exp.							0.265	(0.136)	*			
>15 yrs ind. exp.							0.103	(0.104)				
Start-up × 0–6										-0.510	(0.141)	***
Start-up × 7–12										-0.323	(0.142)	*
Start-up × 13–18										-0.362	(0.146)	*
Start-up × 19–24										-0.248	(0.147)	t
Industry × 0–6										-0.093	(0.091)	
Industry × 7–12										-0.013	(0.093)	
Industry × 13–18										0.048	(0.095)	
Industry × 19–24										-0.058	(0.096)	

	Model 1	Model 2	Model 3	Model 4
Lambda	0.334 (0.022) ***	0.328 (0.022) ***	0.324 (0.022) ***	0.322 (0.021) ***
No. employees	0.304 (0.042) ***	0.298 (0.042) ***	0.297 (0.042) ***	0.277 (0.042) ***
Lagged sales	0.057 (0.030) t	0.058 (0.029) *	0.056 (0.029) t	0.057 (0.029) t
Industry entry	-0.002 (0.005)	-0.002 (0.005)	-0.003 (0.005)	-0.001 (0.005)
Industry size	0.003 (0.001) t	0.002 (0.001) *	0.002 (0.001) t	0.002 (0.001)
Industry growth	0.102 (0.047) *	0.103 (0.048) *	0.084 (0.050) t	0.105 (0.050) *
Average firm age	-0.002 (0.014)	-0.005 (0.013)	-0.003 (0.013)	-0.005 (0.013)
Average firm size	0.004 (0.003)	0.004 (0.003)	0.004 (0.003) t	0.005 (0.003) t
Months 0-6	-0.458 (0.052) ***	-0.461 (0.052) ***	-0.465 (0.052) ***	-0.132 (0.097)
Months 7-13	-0.221 (0.053) ***	-0.226 (0.053) ***	-0.231 (0.053) ***	-0.053 (0.100)
Months 14-18	-0.112 (0.052) *	-0.113 (0.052) *	-0.116 (0.052) *	0.027 (0.102)
Months 19-24	-0.090 (0.053) t	-0.090 (0.053) t	-0.090 (0.052) t	0.091 (0.103)
Constant	0.410 (0.370)	0.810 (0.391) *	0.699 (0.386) t	0.590 (0.395)
log likelihood	692.94	688.52	685.86	677.01
Wald Chi square	737.31	773.28	787.43	817.34

Key: t = $p < 0.10$; * = $p < 0.05$; *** = $p < 0.001$ in two-tailed tests. The sample consists of 223 cases and 881 observations. All models are significant at the $p < .00001$ level.

results of this test were qualitatively the same as those for our reported results, suggesting that our results are not artifacts of specification errors.

Finally, we tested the robustness of our sales models to the sensitivity of the Tobit estimator to the distribution of the error terms. We re-estimated our models using a random effect GLS model and a Poisson regression and found qualitatively the same results, suggesting that our results are not artifacts of the use of a Tobit estimator.

Discussion

The purpose of this study was to test the effect of founding team start-up and industry experience on new venture survival and sales in a way that overcomes the methodological limitations of prior research, as well as to explore whether these effects were non-linear and vary with venture age. To do this, we examined the effect of prior start-up and industry experience of the venture team on the survival and sales of a representative sample of 223 new firms founded in Sweden in 1998, using data collected prospectively, and correcting for venture failure when estimating the effects on venture sales. We found that founding team experience enhances both new venture survival and new venture sales, but that the effects are non-linear and vary with venture age.

Implications

Our findings suggest that researchers take a more nuanced view of the effects of founding team industry and start-up experience on the performance of new ventures than is currently expressed in the literature. Unlike much of the prior research, which focuses largely on new venture survival, the results of this study show that venture team start-up and industry experience enhance new venture survival and new venture sales in different ways. Specifically, we observed that founding teams with prior start-up experience are less likely to fail than ventures with no prior start-up experience, but that the effects are driven almost exclusively by the difference between any and no prior start-up experience. In contrast, we found that only ventures whose founding teams had started four or more prior start-ups had significantly higher sales than ventures founded by teams with less experience.

These findings suggest that the effect of founding team start-up experience on new venture survival and new venture sales are not the same. Consequently, the discussion of the effect of founding team experience on new venture performance presented in the research literature should reflect these differences. Perhaps small amounts of start-up experience might offer a buffer that allows new firms to survive, but have no effect on sales (Brüderl and Schussler, 1990; Fichman and Levinthal, 1991), because the benefits of small amounts of experience are enough to enhance survival, but not enough to generate positive sales outcomes (Otani, 1996).

The findings also suggest that researchers should develop more nuanced explanations for the effect of experience than the simple linear effects posited in the literature. Our results indicate that non-linearities exist in the effects of founding team experience on venture survival and sales, as indicated by the significantly higher sales of ventures founded by teams with 11–15 years of industry experience. Researchers need to consider these non-linearities in their explanations for the effect of founding team experience on new venture performance.

Researchers should also refine the argument that founding team experience enhances new venture performance in order to incorporate variation in the effects of industry and start-up experience on new venture survival and sales as ventures age. For example, our results indicate that the effect of start-up experience on venture sales is not constant, but instead decreases as ventures age.

While our findings illustrate the value of time variant explanations for the effect of founding team experience on venture performance, they also indicate the need for the development of additional theoretical explanations. The explanation that we proposed – that the contributions of founding team members are more important early in the life of ventures – can account for the effect of start-up experience on venture sales. However, it cannot explain the effect of industry experience on venture failure, which appears to grow as ventures age. Perhaps industry and start-up experience affect the performance of ventures differently as they age. Or perhaps the effects of experience on venture failure and venture sales are different as ventures age. Either way, lower-level (variable-specific) theoretical explanations for the effect of the interaction between founding team experience and venture age on new venture performance need to be developed.

In sum, our findings are important from a theoretical perspective because they do not support the parsimonious explanation presented in the literature, which holds that founding team experience enhances new venture performance. Rather, they suggest that researchers need to explain the effects of founding team experience on new venture performance in ways that account for the differences in the effects on venture survival and sales, the non-linear form of these effects and their interaction with venture age.

This study also provides a useful methodological contribution by showing how the use of panel data and certain statistical techniques can control for methodological limitations to the results of many studies of entrepreneurial activity (Hamilton and Nickerson, 2003). One limitation that the techniques used in this study overcome is bias from unobserved heterogeneity in opportunities. Although human capital influences the performance of new firms, so do the characteristics of entrepreneurial opportunities. Because the distribution of human capital across entrepreneurs is correlated with the attributes of entrepreneurial opportunities (for example, pharmaceutical company researchers tend to found biotechnology firms, not gas stations), cross-sectional studies of the effect of human capital on new firm performance suffer from bias (Shane, 2000). By using lagged performance variables in our regression analysis, we were able to parcel out the effect of opportunity from the effect of human capital and more accurately measure the effect of human capital on the performance of new firms.

The techniques used in this study also mitigate the problem of selection bias that hinders efforts to estimate the effects of many aspects of entrepreneurial activity. Many new firms fail early in their lives (Aldrich, 1999), making it difficult to draw accurate inferences from samples of surviving firms. This study shows how researchers can design data collection efforts on new firms to avoid the selection bias that comes from using retrospective research designs.

Moreover, failure to correct for the failure of new firms in estimates of the factors that affect the level of sales that they generate leads to biased estimates in regression analysis. This study shows how researchers can more accurately estimate the effect of founding team human capital on new venture sales by correcting for the failure of new ventures.

Limitations

Our study was limited by our inability to measure changes in the human capital of venture teams over time, as members of the founding team enter or exit. Therefore, we cannot determine whether the start-up and industry experience of the founding team has long-lasting effects on new venture sales or can be reversed by changing the composition of the venture team over time.

Our study was also limited by our inability to measure the nature of start-up and industry experience. We know only the amount of prior experience, not its quality. We also lack the data to address whether more recent experience is better than less recent experience, or whether successful experience is better than unsuccessful experience. We have no way of knowing whether founding team members with previous experience in growing firms or industries would have higher sales than founding team members with the same amount of experience in shrinking firms or industries. We lack information about the level of management experience of the members of the team. As a result, we cannot ascertain whether founding teams that have more management experience create ventures with greater sales than founding teams made up primarily of non-managerial employees with the same level of industry experience. Furthermore, we cannot determine whether the value of start-up and industry experience lies in information, the social ties created by experience or another mechanism.

Our effort to overcome methodological limitations in previous research limited the scope of our study. The desire for rigor demanded the collection of data at six occasions over a 30-month period on a representative sample of the Swedish work force. As a consequence, our measures were relatively coarse-grained. However, we believe that the methodological limitations overcome in this study suggest the importance of future studies of the human capital of new venture founding teams that employ more fine-grained measures, using similar longitudinal designs on representative samples of new firms measured from their initiation.

In summary, we have shown that founding team experience enhances both the survival and sales of new ventures, even after the effects of industry, past performance, team size, employment and selection effects are controlled. However, we have found that these effects are non-linear and interact with venture age, suggesting that experience influences new venture performance in ways more complex and nuanced than previous research would suggest.

Acknowledgements

Both authors contributed equally to the writing of this article and are listed alphabetically. The research design owes an intellectual debt to the Panel Study of Business Start-ups undertaken by the Entrepreneurial Research Consortium, a temporary voluntary association of 30+ US and non-US universities. The Knut and Alice Wallenberg Foundation, the Swedish Foundation for Small Business Research, and the Swedish National Board for Industrial and Technical Development funded the study. Arnie Cooper, Per Davidsson, Tim Pollock, three anonymous reviewers and SO! editor Joel Baum provided helpful comments.

Notes

1   Because individual entrepreneurs founded many of the ventures in our sample, it was not possible to obtain information from multiple respondents for all of our ventures. However, for a subset of the ventures founded by two or more people, we interviewed more than one team member. Our interviews revealed a high level of convergence in the responses provided by the venture team members. This convergence adds confidence to our approach of treating respondents as key informants about their ventures.

2   Our results are robust to the specification of the model. We find the same qualitative results for our independent variables after having estimated the models using log-normal; log-logistic, Weibull and Cox models.

3   Our results are robust to the specification of the model. We found qualitatively the same results by estimating the models using random-effect GLS and Poisson regressions. In addition, a probit model to test whether or not sales were achieved produced comparable results.

4   Because termination can be made for either voluntary or involuntary reason, we also tested for these competing events. We find qualitatively the same results in both cases, leading us to conclude that the reason to terminate is not important in this case.

References

Acs, Z. J. and Audretsch, D. B. (1989) 'Births and Firm Size', *Southern Economic Journal* 56(2): 467–76.

Aldrich, H. (1990) 'Using an Ecological Perspective to Study Organizational Founding Rates', *Entrepreneurship Theory and Practice* 14(3): 7–24.

Aldrich, H. (1999) *Organizations Evolving*. London: Sage Publications.

Aldrich, H. and Martinez, M. (2001) 'Many are Called, but Few are Chosen: An Evolutionary Perspective for the Study of Entrepreneurship', *Entrepreneurship Theory and Practice* 25(4): 41–56.

Arrow, K. (1974) *The Limits of Organization*. New York: Norton.

Audretsch, D. B. and Mahmood, T. (1995) 'New Firm Survival: New Results Using a Hazard Function', *The Review of Economics and Statistics* 77(1): 97–103.

Bates, T. (1990) 'Entrepreneur Human Capital and Small Business Longevity', *The Review of Economics and Statistics* 72(4): 551–9.

Bates, T. and Servon, L. (2000) 'Viewing Self-employment as a Response to Lack of Suitable Opportunities for Wage Work', *National Journal of Sociology* 12(2): 23–53.

Bhide, A. (2000) *The Origins and Evolution of New Businesses*. New York: Oxford University Press.

Blossfeld, H. P. and Rohwer, G. (1995) *Techniques of Event History Analysis: New Approaches to Causal Analysis*. Mahwah, NJ: Lawrence Erlbaum Associates.

Boeker, W. (1989) 'Strategic Change: The Effects of Founding and History', *Academy of Management Journal* 32: 489–515.

Bosma, N., Van Praag, M., Thurik, R. and de Wit, G. (2004) 'The Value of Human and Social Capital Investments for the Business Performance of Startups', *Small Business Economics* 23(3): 227–40.

Brüderl, J and Preisendörfer, P. (1998) 'Network Support and the Success of Newly Founded Businesses', *Small Business Economics* 10: 213–25.

Brüderl, J., Preisendörfer, P. and Ziegler, R. (1992) 'Survival Chances of Newly Founded Business Organizations', *American Sociological Review* 57(April): 227–42.

Brüderl, J. and Schussler, R. (1990) 'Organizational Mortality: The Liabilities of Newness and Adolescence', *Administrative Science Quarterly* 35(3): 530–48.

Burton, D., Sorensen, J. and Beckman, C. (2002) 'Coming from Good Stocks', *Research in Sociology of Organizations* 19: 239–62.

Campbell, C. (1992) 'A Decision Theory Model for Entrepreneurial Acts', *Entrepreneurship Theory and Practice* 17(1): 21–7.

Carroll, G. and Hannan, M. (2000) *The Demography of Corporations and Industries*. Princeton, NJ: Princeton University Press.

Carroll, G. and Mosakowski, E. (1987) 'The Career Dynamics of Self-employment', *Administrative Science Quarterly* 32: 570–89.

Caves, R. (1998) 'Industrial Organization and New Findings on the Turnover and Mobility of Firms', *Journal of Economic Literature* 36: 1947–82.

Churchill, N. and Lewis, V. (1983) 'The Five Stages of Small Firm Growth', *Harvard Business Review* 53: 43–54.

Cooper, A. C., Gimeno-Gascon, F. and Woo, C. (1994) 'Initial Human and Financial Capital as Predictors of New Venture Performance', *Journal of Business Venturing* 9: 371–95.

Cyert, R. and March, J. (1963) *A Behavioral Theory of the Firm*. Englewood Cliffs, NJ: Prentice Hall.

Delmar, F. and Shane, S. (2003) 'Does Business Planning Facilitate the Development of New Ventures?', *Strategic Management Journal* 24(12): 1165–85.

Duchesneau, D. and Gartner, W. (1990) 'A Profile of New Venture Success and Failure in an Emerging Industry', *Journal of Business Venturing* 5(5): 297–312.

Eisenhardt, K. M. and Schoonhoven, C. (1990) 'Organizational Growth: Linking Founding Team, Strategy, Environment, and Growth among U.S. semiconductor ventures, 1978–1988', *Administrative Science Quarterly* 36(3): 504–29.

Ericsson, K. and Smith, J. (1991) 'Prospects and Limits of the Empirical Study of Expertise: An Introduction', in K. Ericsson and J. Smith (eds) *Toward a General Theory of Expertise: Prospects and Limits*, pp.1–38. Cambridge: Cambridge University Press.

Fichman, M. and Levinthal, D. (1991) 'Honeymoons and the Liability of Adolescence: A New Perspective on Duration Dependence in Social and Organizational Relationships', *Academy of Management Review* 18(2): 442–68.

Freeman, J. (1999) 'Venture Capital as an Economy of Time', in R. Leenders and S. Gabbay (eds) *Corporate Social Control*, pp. 460–82. Boston, MA: Kluwer.

Gibb, A. (1994) 'Do We Really Teach (Approach) Small Business the Way We Should?', *Journal of Small Business and Entrepreneurship* 11(2): 4–27.

Gimeno, J., Folta, T., Cooper, A. and Woo, C. (1997) 'Survival of the Fittest? Entrepreneurial Human Capital and the Persistence of Underperforming Firms', *Administrative Science Quarterly* 42: 750–83.

Greene, W. (2000) *Econometric Analysis*. Upper Saddle River, NJ: Prentice Hall.

Hall, J. and Hofer, C. (1993) 'Venture Capitalists' Decision Criteria in New Venture Evaluation', *Journal of Business Venturing* 8: 25–42.

Hamilton, B. and Nickerson, J. (2003) 'Correcting for Endogeneity in Strategic Management Research', *Strategic Organization* 1(1): 51–78.

Heckman, J. (1979) 'Sample Selection Bias as a Specification Error', *Econometrica* 47(1): 153–62.

Heckman, J. and Borjas, G. (1980) 'Does Unemployment Cause Future Unemployment? Definitions, Questions and Answers from a Continuous Time Model of Heterogeneity and State Dependence', *Economica* 47(187): 247–84.

Johnson, P. (1986) *New Firms: An Economic Perspective*. London: Allen and Unwin.

Jones-Evans, D. (1996) 'Experience and Entrepreneurship: Technology-based Owner-Managers in the UK', *New Technology, Work, and Employment* 11: 39–54.

Jovanovic, B. (1982) 'Selection and the Evolution of Industry', *Econometrica* 50(3): 649–70.

Klepper, S. (2001) 'Employee Startups in High-tech Industries', *Industrial and Corporate Change* 10(3): 639–74.

Knight, F. (1921) *Risk, Uncertainty, and Profit*. New York: Augustus Kelly.

Lee, L. (1983) 'Generalized Econometric Models with Selectivity', *Econometrica* 51(2): 507–12.

Leonard, D. and Sensiper, S. (1990) 'The Role of Tacit Knowledge in Group Innovation', *California Management Review* 40(3): 112–32.

MacMillan, I., Siegel, R. and Subbanarasimha, P. (1985) 'Criteria Used by Venture Capitalists to Evaluate New Venture Proposals', *Journal of Business Venturing* 1: 119–28.

Mathews, J. (2003) 'Competitive Dynamics and Economic Learning: An Extended Resource-Based View', *Industrial and Corporate Change* 12(1): 115–45.

Mitchell, W. (1991) 'Dual Clocks: Entry Order Influences on Incumbent and Newcomer Market Share and Survival When Specialized Assets Retain Their Value', *Strategic Management Journal* 12: 85–100.

Otani, K. (1996) 'A Human Capital Approach to Entrepreneurial Capacity', *Economica* 63(250): 273–89.

Pennings, J., Lee, K. and Witteloostuijn, A. (1998) 'Human Capital, Social Capital, and Firm Dissolution', *Academy of Management Journal* 41(4): 425–40.

Ripsas, S. (1998) 'Towards an Interdisciplinary Theory of Entrepreneurship', *Small Business Economics* 10: 103–15.

Roberts, E. (1991) *Entrepreneurs in High Technology: Lessons from M.I.T. and Beyond*. New York: Oxford University Press.

Roure, J. and Maidique, M. (1986) 'Linking Refunding Factors and High Technology Venture Success: An Exploratory Study', *Journal of Business Venturing* 1: 295–306.

Sandberg, C. and Hofer, C. (1987) 'Improving New Venture Performance: The Role of Strategy, Industry Structure, and the Entrepreneur', *Journal of Business Venturing* 2: 5–28.

Schoonhoven, C., Eisenhardt, K. and Lyman, K. (1990) 'Speeding Products to Market: Waiting Time to First Product Innovation in New Firms', *Administrative Science Quarterly* 35(1): 177–207.

Shane, S. (2000) 'Prior Knowledge and the Discovery of Entrepreneurial Opportunities', *Organization Science* 11(4): 448–69.

Shane, S. and Khurana, R. (2003) 'Career Experience and Firm Founding', *Industrial and Corporate Change* 12(3): 519–43.

Shane, S. and Stuart, T. (2002) 'Organizational Endowments and the Performance of University Start-Ups', *Management Science* 48(1): 154–70.

Shepherd, D., Douglas, E. and Shanley, M. (2000) 'New Venture Survival: Ignorance, External Shocks and Risk Reduction Strategies', *Journal of Business Venturing* 15: 393–410.

Stinchcombe, A. L. (1965) 'Social Structure and Organizations', in J. G. March (ed.) *Handbook of Organizations*, pp. 142–93. Chicago, IL: Rand McNally.

Stuart, T. E., Huang, H. and Hybels, R. (1999) 'Interorganizational Endorsements and the Performance of Entrepreneurial Ventures', *Administrative Science Quarterly* 44: 315–49.

Taylor, M. (1999) 'The Survival of the Fittest: An Analysis of Self-Employment Duration in Britain', *The Economic Journal* 109: C140–C155.

Van Praag, M. (2003) 'Business Survival and Success of Young Small Business Owners', *Small Business Economics* 21: 1–21.

Venkataraman, S. (1997) 'The Distinctive Domain of Entrepreneurship Research: An Editor's Perspective', in J. Katz and R. H. S. Brockhaus (eds) *Advances in Entrepreneurship, Firm Emergence, and Growth*, pp. 119–38. Greenwich, CT: JAI Press.

Von Mises, L. (1949) *Human Action: A Treatise on Economics.* New Haven, CT: Yale University Press.

Wicker, A. and King, J. (1989) 'Employment, Ownership, and Survival in Microbusinesses: A Study of New Retail and Service Establishments', *Small Business Economics* 1: 137–52.

Witt, U. (2000) 'Changing Cognitive Frames – Changing Organizational Forms: An Entrepreneurial Theory of Organizational Development', *Industrial and Corporate Change* 9(4): 733–45.

Wooldridge, J. M. (2002) *Econometric Analysis of Cross Section and Panel Data.* Cambridge, MA: MIT Press.

Yamaguchi, K. (1991) *Event History Analysis.* Newbury Park, CA: Sage Publications.

Frédéric Delmar is a professor in strategy and organization at EM Lyon in France, and an associate professor at the Stockholm School of Economics in Sweden. His research focuses on new venture development, venture growth, the psychology of the entrepreneur, and on entrepreneurship in the knowledge intensive sector. His research has appeared in *Strategic Management Journal, Journal of Business Venturing* and *Entrepreneurship Theory and Practice,* among other journals. *Address:* Strategy and Organization, EM Lyon, 23 avenue Guy de Collongue, F-69134 Ecully Cedex, France. [e-mail: delmar@em-lyon.com]

Scott Shane is SBC professor of economics at Case Western Reserve University, a visiting professor at Imperial College, and a visiting scholar at the Federal Reserve Bank of Cleveland. His research has appeared in *Management Science, Organization Science, Academy of Management Journal, Academy of Management Review* and *Strategic Management Journal,* among other journals. He has published eight books, among them, *Finding Fertile Ground: Identifying Extraordinary Opportunities for New Ventures; From Ice Cream to the Internet: Using Franchising to Unlock the Potential of Your Business; Academic Entrepreneurship: University Spinoffs and Wealth Creation* and *A General Theory of Entrepreneurship: The Individual-Opportunity Nexus, Foundations* *of Entrepreneurship.* His current research examines how entrepreneurs discover and evaluate opportunities, assemble resources and design organizations; university spin-offs and technology transfer; and business format franchising. *Address:* Weatherhead School of Management, Case Western Reserve University, 11119 Bellflower Rd, Rm 282, Cleveland, OH 44106, USA. [e-mail: sas46@weatherhead.cwru.edu]

[18]

Organization Science

Vol. 19, No. 1, January–February 2008, pp. 3–24
ISSN 1047-7039 | EISSN 1526-5455 | 08 | 1901 | 0003

inf**orms**.

DOI 10.1287/orsc.1070.0311
© 2008 INFORMS

Founding the Future: Path Dependence in the Evolution of Top Management Teams from Founding to IPO

Christine M. Beckman
Paul Merage School of Business, University of California, Irvine, Irvine, California 92697, cbeckman@uci.edu

M. Diane Burton
Sloan School of Management, Massachusetts Institute of Technology, Cambridge, Massachusetts 02142, burton@mit.edu

We contrast life-cycle and path-dependent views of entrepreneurial firms by examining the evolution of top management teams. We show how initial conditions constrain subsequent outcomes by demonstrating that the founding team's prior functional experiences and initial organizational functional structures predict subsequent top manager backgrounds and later functional structures. We find that narrowly experienced teams have trouble adding functional expertise not already embodied in the team. We also find that firms beginning with a limited range of functional positions are less likely to develop complete functional structures. Importantly, we do not find functional structure and functional experience to be interchangeable. We find that firms beginning with more complete functional structures are likely to go public faster, and firms beginning with broadly experienced team members obtain venture capital more quickly regardless of the experience and structural composition of the top management team in place at the time of these outcomes. Further, broadly experienced founding teams that build an early team with a full complement of functional positions achieve important milestones faster than firms that start with neither experience nor structure. This suggests that creating positions as "placeholders" in new ventures, where positions are created and filled with the intent of bringing individuals with more relevant experience onboard later, is not obviously a path by which to succeed. By examining the origins of top management team experience and functional structures, we illustrate the lasting imprint of founders on top management team composition and firm outcomes.

Key words: entrepreneurship; organization and management theory; organizational evolution and change; organizational demography

Introduction

The popular press often portrays successful high-technology firms being launched by specialized technological geniuses: Brilliant scientists found a company (frequently in a garage), then attract more broadly experienced executives and venture capital to bring the firm to the next level (Audia and Rider 2005). A similar view is taken by entrepreneurship scholars who take a life-cycle perspective (e.g., Greiner 1972): Executives are replaced as the firm outgrows their capabilities in a process of "professionalization" (Hellman and Puri 2002, Boeker and Karachalil 2002). Our research examines the extent to which these images reflect reality. There is broad consensus that successful firms are led by seasoned professional managers who bring a full range of skills to the venture (Roberts 1991, Cooper et al. 1994, Burton et al. 2002) and create an organization of functional structure with clear roles and accountability (Ancona and Caldwell 1992, Keck 1997, Roure and Keeley 1990, Jensen and Zajac 2004, Sine et al. 2006). Yet we know relatively little about how teams and firms evolve over time.

Although many pundits explicitly recommend that entrepreneurial firms replace founders with professional managers (Charan et al. 1980, Flamholtz and Randle 2000, Wasserman 2003), it is less clear how a new

firm founded by narrowly experienced technologists in an undifferentiated functional structure is able to attract broadly experienced team members and develop a broad portfolio of functional positions. In fact, much of the extant organizational literature that emphasizes homophily (McPherson et al. 2001, Ruef et al. 2003), imprinting (Boeker 1988, Burton and Beckman 2007), and inertia (Hannan et al. 1996, Phillips 2005) suggests that this kind of professionalization and organizational evolution would be both difficult and unlikely.

In this paper we explore how the breadth of founder prior experiences and early decisions about functional structures influence the types of executives who are attracted and retained and the types of structures that are subsequently put into place. We contrast the life-cycle perspective with a path-dependent view of firm development. We argue that, contrary to the images of the popular press and life-cycle theories of entrepreneurial firm development, homophily and imprinting operate such that subsequent executives and structures bear a strong resemblance to founding executives and structures. Our research extends the idea that founders bring important experiences and make critical choices early in a firm's history that leave a lasting organizational imprint.

Building on established traditions in top management team demography and upper echelon literatures, we

3

4

Beckman and Burton: *Path Dependence in the Evolution of Top Management Teams*
Organization Science 19(1), pp. 3–24, © 2008 INFORMS

examine two facets of the team: the breadth and depth of the position assignments in the new venture and the prior experiences that team members bring to the firm (Bunderson and Sutcliffe 2002). We conceptualize prior functional experience as a measure of the team's human capital (whether someone has prior sales or engineering experience, for example) and functional assignments as a measure of functional structure distinct from the skills and qualifications of any specific incumbent (whether a firm has a vice president of sales or engineering, for example).

Interestingly, although the extant literature recognizes both structural and human capital differences among nascent ventures, they are rarely considered simultaneously. Instead, scholars interested in functional structure tend to ignore the characteristics of the individuals who occupy structural positions (e.g., Roure and Keeley 1990, Sine et al. 2006), and scholars interested in teams and individuals tend to ignore structure (e.g., Cooper et al. 1994). Indeed, in much of the top management team (TMT) demography research, functional structure, and experiences are considered interchangeable (e.g., Ancona and Caldwell 1992, Keck 1997).

Treating structure and experience as conceptual and empirical equivalents may be reasonable in established organizations, where we expect to see team members with relevant experience in a position (e.g., a person with a sales background in a sales job). In entrepreneurial ventures, however, there may or may not be a match between prior functional experience and current functional assignment. Consider the technologist with no management experience who takes on the role of president, the sales person who is responsible for human resource management or customer service, and the recent business school graduate with prior engineering experience who fulfills the business development or marketing function. This potential for a mismatch between prior experience and structural assignment offers a compelling arena in which to compare life-cycle and path-dependent perspectives. Whereas life-cycle models advocate that firms create positions as "placeholders" until executives with the relevant experience can be hired and the firm can be professionalized (Hellmann and Puri 2002, Boeker and Wiltbank 2005), path-dependent models would be more cautionary, given the potential dangers of functional structures filled by individuals with atypical experience (Burton and Beckman 2007). In sum, we argue that functional experience and functional structure are distinct, and we explore their interrelationships and their effects on firm outcomes.

Theory and Hypotheses

Prior experience of the top manager and the functional structure of a firm have long been of interest in the TMT demography (Pfeffer 1983) and upper echelons literatures (Hambrick and Mason 1984). A relatively large body of empirical research confirms the intriguing and sensible possibility that the demographic composition of TMTs has consequences for organizational strategy and performance (see Finkelstein and Hambrick 1996 and Williams and O'Reilly 1998 for reviews).

A large number of studies have focused on functional diversity and demonstrated a relationship among top manager functional diversity and a variety of outcomes including firm performance, reorientation, and external communication (e.g., Eisenhardt and Schoonhoven 1990, Ancona and Caldwell 1992, Lant et al. 1992). When theorists posit a positive main effect of functional diversity, they generally argue that diversity enhances organizational performance because broad functional representation ensures that the TMT has the full range of capabilities needed to manage the organization (e.g., Keck 1997, Randel and Jaussi 2003). Although the mainstream demography literature has advanced to identify a variety of process variables that account for the relationship between diversity and outcomes (e.g., Smith et al. 1994), as well as a host of factors that moderate the relationship between diversity and outcomes (e.g., Jehn et al. 1999), an important conceptual distinction between functional experience and functional structure has been largely ignored. The literature has generally used the same logic to account for diverse functional structures and diverse functional experiences, treating these dimensions as interchangeable and considering the choice of measuring structure or experience a methodological detail (but see Bunderson and Sutcliffe 2002 for an exception).

Functional structure refers to the existence of *functional roles or positions* irrespective of any person who might occupy the role, but functional experience refers to the human capital characteristics of the *individual incumbents*. This distinction is theoretically interesting, as it allows us to consider team evolution from both a structural perspective and a human capital/social psychological perspective. If structure and experience are distinct and separable constructs, each should have a unique effect on firm outcomes. Structure and experience may also evolve through different paths, or one may be antecedent to the other. Our research considers these possibilities and extends the existing empirical and theoretical literatures by distinguishing functional experience from functional structure. Our work contributes to the small but growing number of studies that are longitudinal by design (Boone et al. 2004, Sørensen 2004), and so can also respond to calls to explore the sources of demographic distributions in organizations (Mittman 1992, Lawrence 1997, Carroll and Harrison 1998) and address why TMTs "look the way they do" (Hambrick 2007, p. 338).

We address Hambrick's call by examining the role of the founding team in creating the experiences and structure of the subsequent TMT. If path dependence occurs, then initial functional structures will predict a deepening

Beckman and Burton: *Path Dependence in the Evolution of Top Management Teams*
Organization Science 19(1), pp. 3–24, © 2008 INFORMS   5

of these structures over time. If homophily occurs, then initial functional experiences will predict a deepening of these experiences over time. If functional structure and functional experience are interchangeable, then having either will enable a firm to broaden as it evolves. Furthermore, we examine whether these initial characteristics of the team and firm have lasting consequences. If, as life-cycle theories predict, initial functional structures and experiences are irrelevant to subsequent changes, then there should be little relationship between the founding team experiences and structures and subsequent experiences and structures, particularly as founders are replaced and firms mature. Thus, in stark contrast to a path-dependent perspective, where origins are a source of subsequent constraint, the life-cycle perspective emphasizes opportunity and adaptation.

In summary, we consider five interrelated questions: (1) whether the functional experience of the founders shapes initial decisions about functional structure, (2) whether the initial functional structure constrains future functional structure, (3) whether the initial functional structure shapes the functional experience of executives hired by the firm, (4) whether the functional experience of the founders influences the experiences of executives who join subsequently; and (5) whether the initial functional structure and experiences shape firm outcomes.

To examine these questions, it is important to first distinguish between the founding team and TMT. Founding teams are made up of people who create the firm, irrespective of whether they hold executive titles. For example, a founder may hold a position of "director of engineering" rather than vice president. TMTs are made up of people who hold executive titles, regardless of when they join the firm. Although there is overlap between these teams at founding if all founders hold executive titles, the teams are conceptually and empirically distinct. Founders are not added as the firm grows, and, as TMT members join the firm and founders leave, the teams continue to diverge.

Our first question about the relationship between prior functional background experience and initial functional structural decisions draws on two ideas—that functional background experiences shape a person's world view and that people carry their prior experiences with them across organizational settings. We rely on early statements and recent empirical evidence suggesting that functional training conditions individual cognitions (Dearborn and Simon 1958, Sutcliffe 1994, Tripsas and Gavetti 2000) and an established empirical tradition demonstrating that when employees leave an organization, they carry that organization's routines and ideas with them (Baty et al. 1971, Boeker 1997, Sørensen 1999, Phillips 2002). For example, the functional experience and strategy of the founder's prior firm influences the strategy of the new firm (Boeker 1988), and

founders' experiences in a prior firm shape the routines and practices they put in place in a new firm (Phillips 2005, Beckman 2006). In addition, there is growing evidence that the functional background experiences of a TMT influence how it defines and enacts organizational positions (Fligstein 1990, Phillips 2005). Extending this idea to initial decisions about the allocation of positions and responsibilities, we hypothesize that founders will put functional structures in place that mirror their own experiences (Schein 1992, Burton and Beckman 2007). For example, a founding team with a member from a sales and business planning background may decide to combine the sales and business planning functions under a single executive and build an organization where these functions are closely interrelated and externally (customer) oriented. The background of the initial marketing executive—business development, classical marketing, or sales—leads to different choices about what the marketing function does and with which other functions it is aligned. Thus we hypothesize:

HYPOTHESIS 1 (H1). *Founding team functional experience will shape initial functional structure.*

Once the initial functional structures are put into place in an organization, they are likely to be maintained and strengthened over time. Support for this argument comes from several theoretical traditions. Social theorists have long argued that institutions are self-reinforcing (Michels 1915, Downs 1967). In addition, theories of organizational imprinting suggest that initial decisions about the allocation of responsibility among team members have lasting consequences (Stinchcombe 1965, Baron et al. 1996, Hannan et al. 1996, Burton et al. 2002). For example, Baron et al. (1999) find that founding organizational blueprints, around which employment relations are managed, predict subsequently adopted decisions and structures (including adding new functional positions; creating formal documentation and organizational charts). Finally, arguments of structural inertia suggest that initial structures will be maintained over time (Hannan and Freeman 1984). Thus, a range of work suggests that initial functional structures predict later functional structures. We therefore hypothesize:

HYPOTHESIS 2 (H2). *Founding functional structure will shape the breadth and depth of subsequent functional structure.*

Founding functional structure will also likely shape subsequent management functional experience. Extensive literature on job analysis—which in modern human resource management is the foundation of job descriptions, job design and redesign, performance appraisal, selection, and training—defines jobs as combinations of tasks that require particular knowledge, skills, and abilities that can be generically specified (cf. Fine and Cronshaw 1999). Indeed, the extensive literature on organizational design, formalization, and even internal labor

Beckman and Burton: *Path Dependence in the Evolution of Top Management Teams*
Organization Science 19(1), pp. 3–24, © 2008 INFORMS

markets has a vision of clearly defined and hierarchically ordered positions or roles (see Osterman and Burton 2004 for a recent review). Jobs exist in organizations as "placeholders" against which individuals in the labor market can be matched (e.g., Wanous 1992; see Miner 1987 for a review of this literature and an alternative view). Similarly, these characterizations of roles, jobs, and positions imply that the organizational functional structure shapes the characteristics of subsequent incumbents.

Consider again the firm in which sales and business planning positions are closely aligned. When a new executive is recruited to take over the combined position, the structure of the position will influence the choice of executive for the position. A different founding team might decide to create stand-alone sales and business planning functions, which would lead to different future candidates. Thus, the structural choices made by the founding team have implications for the characteristics of the subsequent executives who would be *capable* of filling the defined positions, *attracted* to the opportunity, and *attractive* to the incumbent team members. Our arguments imply that structural decisions made by firm founders constrain the pool of people who might be willing or able to join the firm. Thus we hypothesize:

HYPOTHESIS 3 (H3). *Founding functional structure will shape the breadth and depth of subsequent functional experience.*

Finally, there are reasons to expect an association between the prior functional experiences of the founding team and subsequent TMT experience. Several mechanisms (which may operate simultaneously) could generate this path dependence. For instance, the attraction-selection-attrition (ASA) cycle described by Schneider (1987) would predict that founding and future TMTs will share similar characteristics. Managers seek organizations where existing personnel have similar characteristics, founders select managers like themselves, and managers who do not fit will leave. For example, Boone et al. (2004) find that even when environmental conditions shifted dramatically, Dutch newspaper executives tended to hire new executives who were demographically similar to those already in place. Thus, founders and managers alike should be attracted to one another when they share common experiences and knowledge.

A large literature on homophily (Rogers and Bhowmik 1971, Ruef et al. 2003) also suggests this relationship. Although research on homophily has generally focused on categories such as race and gender, there is growing evidence that the same processes apply to occupations (McPherson et al. 2001). Founders may privilege and recruit executives with functional experiences similar to their own rather than executives with functional experience that may be more relevant for the position being filled. For example, engineers might prefer a CEO with a technical background over one with a

finance background. It is important to note that these tendencies toward functional homophily within a position may result in team-level functional heterogeneity. Teams will be functionally diverse if, for instance, individual preferences for homophily exist on founding teams where members come from a variety of functional backgrounds. Alternately, founders with diverse functional backgrounds (functional generalists) may value that variety and seek TMT members who themselves have diverse experiences. Thus, at the team level, homophily and similarity-attraction arguments imply similarity between the experiences of the founding team and the experiences of the TMT. We therefore hypothesize:

HYPOTHESIS 4 (H4). *Founding team functional experience will shape the breadth and depth of subsequent TMT functional experience.*

Following a path-dependent logic, our hypotheses suggest a tight linkage between initial team experiences/structures and subsequent TMT experiences/structures. Importantly, this implies there will be relatively little change in functional structure or human capital experience from the founding team to later teams. Thus, in sharp contrast to the dominant image of narrowly experienced engineers in an unstructured nascent venture who are replaced by professionals who evolve the firm into a professional bureaucracy, our hypotheses imply that initial founding team characteristics and structural choices should be a powerful predictor of later experiences and structures—even controlling for compositional changes. Contrary to a life-cycle perspective that would be agnostic about initial conditions, our theoretical arguments imply that initial conditions restrict subsequent firm and team options.

To further understand the lasting consequences of these initial conditions, we also directly link founding experiences and structures to firm outcomes. Both the entrepreneurship and TMT literatures offer ample evidence linking human capital characteristics such as the type and amount of prior experience to firm success (Aldrich and Zimmer 1986, Roberts 1991, Cooper et al. 1994). Other work finds that a range of prior experiences as well as shared experiences benefit the firm (Eisenhardt and Schoonhoven 1990, Beckman et al. 2007). Still other work links the functional structure of the firm to firm outcomes (Ancona and Caldwell 1992, Keck 1997, Roure and Keeley 1990). More recently, Sine et al. (2006) demonstrate that formalized functional positions and functional specialization is positively associated with firm success in a sample of Internet start-ups. Together these studies document that a broad set of *both* team functional experiences and functional structures are predictive of firm outcomes. Thus, we hypothesize:

HYPOTHESIS 5 (H5). *The breadth of founding team functional experiences and functional structures are positively associated with firm success.*

Beckman and Burton: *Path Dependence in the Evolution of Top Management Teams*
Organization Science 19(1), pp. 3–24, © 2008 INFORMS   7

Interestingly, the existing literature is silent as to whether structure might be more important to firm success than experience or vice versa. If the structure and experience are distinct conceptual constructs, then they should have independent effects. If, as the extant demography literature has implied, structure and experience are interchangeable representations of the same underlying construct, then having either broad functional experience represented among the founding team members or a differentiated functional structure should be sufficient to fuel the development of a firm with a broadly experienced TMT and a differentiated functional structure. However, if structure and experience are not interchangeable, then an increase on one dimension cannot compensate for a weakness on another dimension. Our analyses explore these alternatives.

If, as we posit, the founding conditions set teams and firms on a particular path, then cross-sectional studies of TMTs overattribute outcomes to the current team and overestimate the extent to which teams can be reformed. We pursue a research strategy that begins with the founding team and then tracks changes in personnel—both through entrances and exits—and in functional composition to explore exactly how the founding team and initial structures shape the subsequent TMT and later structures.

Data and Methods

This paper begins with a sample of entrepreneurial high-technology firms in California's Silicon Valley that were studied as part of the Stanford Project on Emerging Companies (SPEC) (see Baron et al. 1999 for a detailed description) but includes additional data on individual executives. The focus on firms in a single region allows us to hold constant key labor market and environmental conditions. Within the region, the SPEC study focuses on the high-technology industries of computer hardware and/or software, telecommunications, medical devices and biotechnology, semiconductors, manufacturing, and research. The sampling frame explicitly oversamples young and small firms. The firms in the sample have at least 10 employees and are no more than 10 years old at the time data collection begins in 1994–1996. About half of the firms are founded before 1989, and thus the median age of the firms in 1994 is five years. Our sample is not representative of all start-up firms in that we have fewer solo founders and more teams of three or more founders, but this is typical of high-technology start-ups (Eisenhardt and Schoonhoven 1990, Ruef et al. 2003). Our sampling frame has the disadvantage of biasing the sample toward firms that have survived several years and thus are more likely to be (or become) successful. That said, we sample firms that both do and do not receive venture funding and go public. We see no a priori reason to expect that our hypothesized effects, where TMTs are constrained and shaped by founding teams, will be different for a broader sample of start-up firms.

The key independent and dependent variables for this study are constructed from career histories. We construct a monthly database of every founder and every executive that ever worked for one of the sampled firms from founding through December 2000 or the time of initial public offering (IPO), acquisition, or failure (see below). The founding team was identified in an interview with the founder (the mean founding team has 2.82 members), and all subsequent TMT members are identified as those individuals ranked as vice president or higher (e.g., senior vice president, CTO, CIO, COO). It is important to note that founders do not always hold TMT titles (as evidenced by an average TMT smaller than the founding team at time zero). Our data sources include interviews (conducted in 1994–1995 and 1996–1997), internal company documents (business plans and promotional documents), *Lexis/Nexis* news searches, *Dow Jones Interactive, Edgar Archives* (useful for firms about to go public and for top managers who have been involved with public companies), *The San Jose Mercury News* (the local paper has a regular column on promotions, movements, and resignations in the Silicon Valley), and extensive Web searches. Over a six-year period we completed at least four complete searches for each person and spent thousands of person-hours collecting career data on team members. We confirmed, via interview or telephone, nearly 50% of the career histories collected through 1996–1997 with the person designated by the CEO or the human resources person. This increases the reliability of the earliest team data, the most difficult period to gather consistent data through archival sources.

Despite extensive research, we do not obtain complete career histories on all team members. Often the chronology of careers is correct but the dates unclear. This data problem precludes us from constructing duration variables such as years of experience in a particular function, a method commonly pursued by demography scholars. Because some of our team data may be incomplete, we make a point to control for variables that may impact the completeness of the data (i.e., firm size) as well as the average amount of person data collected by firm.

Our final database contains information on 1,485 executives in 167 firms holding 1,940 positions in our sampled firms. We collect a median of two past positions for each person, including employer identity and job title, with a maximum of 19 positions for a single person, although we limit our analysis to the prior three employers. This includes data for executives (often founders) who we confirm had no prior work experience (at least 38 founders join one of our firms directly from school). For Hypotheses 1–4 and our analysis of team evolution we rely on our full sample (167 firms). For our analysis of outcomes, firms that are not independent (e.g., wholly owned subsidiaries) or at risk of going public (e.g., nonprofit research centers) are excluded (resulting in a sample of 158 firms for our outcome analysis).

Beckman and Burton: *Path Dependence in the Evolution of Top Management Teams*
Organization Science 19(1), pp. 3–24, © 2008 INFORMS

8

Dependent Variables

In this research we examine three types of dependent variables: (1) functional organizational structure, (2) team member functional experience, and (3) firm outcomes. The difference between functional structure and team functional experience mirrors the difference between functional assignment diversity and functional background diversity in the demography literature (Bunderson and Sutcliffe 2002).

Functional organizational structure is measured as whether the firm has defined executive-level positions in each of the following six functional areas: sales and marketing, general administration (including human resources), science/R&D/engineering, operations, business development/strategic planning, and finance/accounting. For each firm, we calculate whether a firm has a given functional position, when it is first established, and how many executive-level positions in a given function simultaneously exist in a team for each month of the firm's life. For example, a technology-intensive firm may be founded with a CTO and a vice president of engineering. The vice president of engineering job is later transformed into the position of senior vice president of engineering, and a vice president of hardware and a vice president of software are hired. This firm clearly has a science/R&D/engineering function. It is established at age 0 and there are ultimately four executive-level positions in this function on the TMT.

We also create a count measure ranging from 0 to 6 that represents the number of functional categories covered each month to predict the breadth of functional structure. Firms with no executive positions are coded 0 for structure; firms with executive positions for all six functions are coded six.

Prior functional experience of TMT members is gathered from career histories. We code up to three prior positions for every individual into one of the six functional areas (see above). From team-level career histories we calculate a variable, updated monthly, indicating how many team members have prior experience in a function to capture the depth of functional experience on a team.

We also create a count measure ranging from 0 to 6 that represents the range of prior functional experience brought by the team in each month and that thus captures the breadth of functional experience. A six indicates that all possible functions are represented in the prior experiences of the team.

We have two firm outcome measures: time to receive venture capital (VC) and time to IPO, and we conduct event-history analyses to examine these outcomes. These firm outcomes represent the most significant milestones in the life of a young start-up (Shane and Stuart 2002), particularly during the time period and in the region that we study. We focus on time to first VC funding rather than cumulative rounds or total funds raised,

because future rounds are based on more direct knowledge about the firm than the first VC financing, and amount is a firm and industry-specific choice (Gompers and Lerner 1999). By modeling time to first VC funding, we examine characteristics of the team that allowed the firm to obtain funding more quickly than other firms, as well as whether they receive VC backing. By choosing IPO as our second dependent variable, we can compare the performance of entrepreneurial firms across multiple industries—a task that is quite difficult using accounting-based measures of profitability. Recent studies have examined IPO as an outcome variable indicating firm success (Stuart et al. 1999, Certo et al. 2001, Gulati and Higgins 2003, Shane and Stuart 2002, Hannan et al. 2006). This IPO measure also allows us to examine a firm outcome that occurs over a longer time horizon than initial VC funding. VC financing and IPO data are collected via public and proprietary databases (such as Venture One and Venture Economics), government filings, annual reports, internal company documents, and a survey instrument sent to the most senior finance executive in the firm (see Hellmann and Puri 2002).

Of our 158 firms at risk of IPO or VC, 26 exit the risk set through IPO, acquisition, merger, or failure without securing VC, and another 14 do not receive VC by the end of 2000. Thus, 118 firms (71%) obtain VC funding and 87 (51%) go public during our sampling period. At first glance these numbers seem unusually high; however, the end of our time period (late 1990s) witnessed an explosion of VC investments and IPOs in entrepreneurial firms in the United States.

Independent and Control Variables

Our key independent variables are the founding team's functional experiences and initial functional structures. These measures are created like the dependent variables but focus on the team and functional structures at founding. That is, we code the breadth and depth of initial functional structure and founding team functional experience in each of the following six functional areas: sales and marketing, general administration (including human resources), science/R&D/engineering, operations, business development/strategic planning, and finance/accounting. At founding the mean number of unique functional positions, our measure of structure, is 1.8, which typically represents a firm with a general administrative position such as president or CEO and a vice president of science or engineering. The mean number of prior functional experiences at founding is 1.5.

Firm-Level Controls. Firm size is the number of employees at the start of a calendar year, lagged by one year. Because of the skewed distribution of this measure, we use a logged measure in our analyses. We control for whether the firm had an innovation strategy, because strategy has been linked to VC financing in prior research (Burton et al 2002). We also control

Beckman and Burton: *Path Dependence in the Evolution of Top Management Teams*
Organization Science 19(1), pp. 3–24, © 2008 INFORMS   9

for whether the firm sought to differentiate itself through its sales, marketing, or service, as this strategy implies a greater need for the sales and marketing function than other strategies. Initial strategy is coded from interviews with the founder and has been empirically validated (see Hellmann and Puri 2000). For example, firms with innovation strategies are those that described themselves as "first movers." In addition, we control for the date the firm shipped its first product, because product shipment may affect the skills and structures required as well as firm outcomes. We also include the cumulative number of rounds of VC funding that the firm had obtained because such firms are more likely to go public (Gompers and Lerner 1999), but we obtain similar results when we use a simple dummy variable (e.g., equal to 1 when the firm obtains VC). Finally, we control for the amount of firm-level team data collected by including the average number of prior positions collected for each person in the firm. This allows us to control for the possibility that we have more data on individuals in successful firms.

Team-Level Controls. We include founding team size and then include measures for the cumulative entrances and exits to the TMT as controls. These variables capture both change and growth in the teams (Tushman and Rosenkopf 1996, Beckman et al. 2007). A life-cycle perspective suggests that growth is the critical determinant of success, and these entrances and exits would be expected to wipe out any effects of origin. Further, these controls ensure that our effects for experience and structure are net effects of turnover. The proportion of TMT positions held by founders is included to control for the extent to which founders with executive titles are counted as part of both teams. All team variables are updated monthly.

Industry-Level Controls. Medical devices and the biotechnology industry (combined as medically related) is the only significantly different industry for our outcomes; thus, we include a dummy variable for this industry in all models. The number of IPOs in each industry by year controls for industry-specific variation in rates of IPO, and the number of VC deals by year controls for available financial resources.

Results

Descriptive statistics and a correlation matrix for the full sample are presented in the appendix. To examine the influence of the founding team's prior functional experience on the initial functional structure (H1), we conduct an event history analysis predicting time to the first executive-level position in a functional area using Cox proportional hazards models with the Huber/White/sandwich estimator of error and clustered by firm to correct for heteroskedasticity and serial correlations. We regress the time to the first position for five

different functions on the prior functional experience of the founding team. The key independent variable is how many members of the founding team had prior experience in the function. (We exclude general administration because almost all firms start with a president and CEO.)

We report these results in Table 1. For each functional area we generate a baseline model that includes control variables only and then a test model that adds a variable indicating the amount of relevant prior functional experience on the founding team. The number of exits indicates the number of firms that ever create an executive-level position in the function reported. During our observation period, 75% of the firms create a position in the science/engineering function (125 of 167); only half ever create an executive position responsible for manufacturing/operations (82 of 167), and fewer than one-fourth create an executive position in business development or strategic planning (42 of 167). Firms that have a function at founding—in other words, a member of the founding team creates the position—are censored immediately. Our models therefore capture the rate of functional position creation for those firms that do and that do not have the relevant prior functional experience.

Table 1 reports hazard ratios and reveals that larger firms with larger founding teams, and those that obtain VC financing, create functional positions at a higher rate. For two of our five functional areas, science/engineering and sales/marketing, we find that having functional experience represented on the founding team significantly increases the rate at which the structural position is added to the TMT. Founding teams with sales experience are 69% more likely to add a sales position. Founding teams with science experience are 44% more likely to add a science position. The coefficients are in the predicted direction for both finance and strategic planning/business development, although they do not achieve statistical significance. Based on these results, we find modest support for H1.

To examine the relationships between initial functional experience and initial functional structure on subsequent team functional experience and later functional structures (H2, H3, and H4), we perform yearly panel-poisson regression analyses predicting counts of experience and structure for each function. We specify an AR1 error structure to account for serial autocorrelation and again report robust standard errors. These results are presented in Table 2.

Table 2 is organized into two panels with yearly team-level observations. The first panel presents our results for TMT functional structure. The second panel presents our results for TMT prior experience. The first six models in each panel represent each of the functional areas of interest and are counts of the depth or number of functional positions or experience in each area. The final model in each panel is a cumulative count variable that

10

Beckman and Burton: *Path Dependence in the Evolution of Top Management Teams*
Organization Science 19(1), pp. 3–24, © 2008 INFORMS

Table 1 Event History Analysis Predicting Time to First Functional Position

	(1) Science/ Engineering	(2) Sales/ Marketing	(3) Mfg./ Operations	(4) Finance/ Acct.	(5) Strategy/ Bus. Dev.
Log firm size	1.20** [0.09]	1.29** [0.13]	1.25* [0.14]	1.08 [0.11]	1.49*** [0.23]
Medical-related industry	0.98 [0.21]	0.28*** [0.11]	0.9 [0.32]	1.21 [0.30]	2.05* [0.85]
Innovation strategy	1.26 [0.22]	1.14 [0.27]	1.23 [0.38]	0.97 [0.22]	1.46 [0.70]
Marketing strategy	0.8 [0.23]	0.84 [0.24]	1.81* [0.62]	0.9 [0.24]	1.59 [0.76]
Cumulative rounds of VC	1.49*** [0.14]	1.29*** [0.10]	1.26*** [0.08]	1.21*** [0.08]	1.19* [0.12]
Prop. founders on TMT	0.92 [0.07]	0.88 [0.12]	0.82 [0.19]	0.59** [0.13]	0.95 [0.28]
Product developed	1.01 [0.23]	0.77 [0.17]	0.50** [0.15]	1.18 [0.27]	0.55* [0.20]
Average number of prior person positions	1.06 [0.08]	0.91 [0.09]	0.97 [0.09]	0.88 [0.09]	1.2 [0.16]
Founding team (FT) size	1.17*** [0.06]	1.16** [0.09]	0.99 [0.09]	1.18* [0.10]	1.1 [0.15]
Cumulative entrances to the TMT	1.12 [0.13]	1.25** [0.14]	1.1 [0.11]	1.02 [0.09]	1.05 [0.17]
Cumulative exits from the TMT	0.82 [0.23]	0.87 [0.20]	0.9 [0.19]	0.79 [0.23]	0.85 [0.17]
FT prior science/engineering exp.	1.44*** [0.11]				
FT prior sales/marketing exp.		1.69*** [0.24]			
FT prior mfg/operations exp.			0.76 [0.31]		
FT prior finance/accounting exp.				1.4 [0.38]	
FT prior strategy/business dev. exp.					1.63 [0.97]
Observations	6,054	7,343	9,762	8,756	12,562
Exits	125	121	82	114	42
Firms	167	167	167	167	167
Log-pseudolikelihood	−558.62	−515.27	−367.73	−498.34	−187.38

Note. Robust standard errors.
*Significant at 10%; **significant at 5%; ***significant at 1%.

ranges from 0 to 6 to capture the breadth of functional positions or experiences.

We test our second hypothesis, that founding functional structure will be associated with subsequent functional structure, in the first panel. Across all specifications, there is a strong positive relationship between the founding structure and the subsequent structure, even controlling for whether the founding team has experience in a given functional area. Model 7 in Panel 1 presents the count variable predicting the number of functional positions eventually covered by the firm. Consistent with the results for each function, firms that begin with more initial structure are likely to cover more functional areas over time. Thus, while the founding team prior experiences shape initial structures (in modest support of H1 in Table 1), it is these initial structures

that shape subsequent structures (in strong support of H2 in Panel 1 of Table 2).

We test the impact of initial structure and founding team prior experience on later TMT prior experience in Panel 2 of Table 2 (H3 and H4). Contrary to H3, initial functional structures do not serve as placeholders to facilitate bringing in later executives with relevant functional experience. Indeed, the only statistically significant finding (for sales/marketing positions) is the opposite of this prediction.

However, the pattern of results revealed in Panel 2 of Table 2 shows support for H4. There is a strong relationship between the functional background experience of the founding team and that of the later TMT prior experience, even controlling for changes in team composition. The relationship is consistently revealed for each of the functional areas (Models 1–6) and in the cumu-

Beckman and Burton: *Path Dependence in the Evolution of Top Management Teams*
Organization Science 19(1), pp. 3–24, © 2008 INFORMS   11

Table 2 Panel Poisson with Robust Standard Errors, with AR1 Error Structure, Predicting TMT Experience and Structure

	Panel 1: TMT functional structure							Panel 2: TMT prior experience						
	(1) Science/ Engin.	(2) Sales/ Mktg.	(3) Mfg./ Ops.	(4) Finance/ Acct.	(5) Admin/ HR	(6) Strategy/ Bus. dev.	(7) Num. of functions	(1) Science/ Engin.	(2) Sales/ Mktg.	(3) Mfg./ Ops.	(4) Finance/ Acct.	(5) Admin/ HR	(6) Strategy/ Bus. dev.	(7) Num.of Prior exp.
FT prior science exp.	0.07 [0.06]							0.43*** [0.06]						
FT science position	0.33*** [0.06]							−0.04 [0.06]						
FT prior sales exp.		0.29*** [0.10]							0.54*** [0.09]					
FT sales/mkt. position		0.15* [0.07]							−0.17** [0.08]					
FT prior mfg./ops. exp.			−0.05 [0.23]							1.49*** [0.21]				
FT mfg./ops. position			0.96*** [0.15]							0.17 [0.20]				
FT prior fin./acct. exp.				−0.03 [0.21]							0.89*** [0.24]			
FT fin./acct. position				0.87*** [0.15]							0.18 [0.21]			
FT prior admin./HR exp.					0.05 [0.06]							0.47*** [0.13]		
FT admin./HR position					0.22*** [0.03]							−0.06 [0.08]		
FT prior business dev. exp.						−0.11 [0.51]							1.24*** [0.31]	
FT business dev. position						0.71*** [0.28]							0.05 [0.57]	
FT prior experience count							−0.00 [0.02]							0.14*** [0.03]
FT structure count							0.11*** [0.02]							0.01 [0.03]
Log-firm size	0.07*** [0.02]	0.07*** [0.03]	0.11*** [0.04]	0.05* [0.03]	0.03* [0.01]	0.15* [0.09]	0.03*** [0.01]	0.01 [0.02]	−0.01 [0.03]	−0.01 [0.05]	0.09* [0.05]	0 [0.02]	0.03 [0.07]	0.01 [0.01]
Medical-related industry	0.53*** [0.14]	−0.37 [0.34]	0.35 [0.25]	0.45*** [0.15]	0.22* [0.10]	1.17*** [0.39]	0.14* [0.07]	0.19 [0.14]	−0.46* [0.27]	0.42 [0.26]	0.27 [0.24]	−0.03 [0.24]	0.56* [0.33]	0.11* [0.07]
Innovation strategy	0.1 [0.13]	−0.24* [0.13]	0.07 [0.19]	−0.25* [0.14]	0.08 [0.07]	0.26 [0.41]	−0.03 [0.05]	0.1 [0.11]	−0.1 [0.13]	0.42* [0.24]	0 [0.18]	0.19 [0.17]	0.22 [0.37]	0.06 [0.06]
Marketing strategy	0.1 [0.16]	−0.17 [0.17]	0.31 [0.20]	−0.03 [0.16]	0.20* [0.09]	0.44 [0.45]	−0.02 [0.05]	0.17 [0.13]	0.09 [0.15]	0.39 [0.31]	0.19 [0.22]	0.13 [0.20]	0.12 [0.48]	0.08 [0.07]

Beckman and Burton: *Path Dependence in the Evolution of Top Management Teams*
Organization Science 19(1), pp. 3–24, © 2008 INFORMS

12

Table 2 (cont'd.)

Panel 1: TMT functional structure

	(1) Science/ Engin.	(2) Sales/ Mktg.	(3) Mfg./ Ops.	(4) Finance/ Acct.	(5) Admin/ HR	(6) Strategy/ Bus. dev.	(7) Num. of functions
Cumulative VC rounds	0.01 [0.02]	0.04** [0.02]	0.03 [0.02]	0.06** [0.02]	0.01 [0.01]	0.04 [0.05]	0.02** [0.01]
Prop. founders on TMT	0.17 [0.23]	−0.72*** [0.20]	−0.64*** [0.27]	−1.31*** [0.30]	0.31*** [0.09]	−0.88 [0.61]	−0.37*** [0.08]
Avg num. prior pers. positions	0.02 [0.07]	−0.25*** [0.06]	−0.1 [0.09]	−0.01 [0.07]	−0.02 [0.03]	−0.02 [0.16]	−0.03 [0.02]
Founding team size	0.08** [0.04]	0.06 [0.05]	−0.09 [0.06]	0.06 [0.05]	0.01 [0.02]	0.04 [0.09]	0.02* [0.01]
Cumulative TMT entrances	0.16*** [0.03]	0.19*** [0.03]	0.17*** [0.03]	0.13*** [0.03]	0.09*** [0.01]	0.20*** [0.06]	0.09*** [0.01]
Cumulative TMT exits	−0.22*** [0.03]	−0.22*** [0.03]	−0.26*** [0.05]	−0.20*** [0.04]	−0.09*** [0.02]	−0.35*** [0.10]	−0.15*** [0.02]
Product developed	−0.29* [0.16]	−0.26 [0.17]	−0.35** [0.17]	−0.19 [0.15]	0.08 [0.07]	−0.46 [0.48]	−0.10* [0.06]
Constant	−1.65*** [0.33]	−0.37 [0.26]	−1.42*** [0.36]	−1.01*** [0.33]	−0.50*** [0.14]	−3.15*** [0.70]	0.86*** [0.10]
Observations	1,256	1,256	1,256	1,256	1,256	1,256	1,256
Number of firms	167	167	167	167	167	167	167
Wald chi-square	359.44	437.37	290.98	170.94	380.4	193.19	502.59
Difference in chi-square from baseline	120.22	12.4	106.78	−18.7	89.59	74.33	23.99

Panel 2: TMT prior experience

	(1) Science/ Engin.	(2) Sales/ Mktg.	(3) Mfg./ Ops.	(4) Finance/ Acct.	(5) Admin/ HR	(6) Strategy/ Bus. dev.	(7) Num. of Prior exp.
Cumulative VC rounds	0.02 [0.01]	0.07*** [0.02]	0.08** [0.04]	0.08*** [0.03]	0.04 [0.03]	0.01 [0.05]	0.04*** [0.01]
Prop. founders on TMT	−0.13 [0.18]	−0.39 [0.25]	−0.91*** [0.33]	−1.49*** [0.36]	−0.66*** [0.25]	−0.49 [0.49]	−0.44*** [0.11]
Avg num. prior pers. positions	0.17*** [0.04]	0.20*** [0.06]	0.28*** [0.09]	0.18** [0.08]	0.08 [0.06]	0.31** [0.12]	0.14*** [0.03]
Founding team size	−0.03 [0.04]	0.08* [0.04]	0.08 [0.09]	0.1 [0.07]	0.1 [0.06]	0.02 [0.16]	0.03 [0.02]
Cumulative TMT entrances	0.15*** [0.02]	0.24*** [0.03]	0.21*** [0.03]	0.16*** [0.04]	0.15*** [0.03]	0.25*** [0.05]	0.13*** [0.02]
Cumulative TMT exits	−0.16*** [0.03]	−0.22*** [0.05]	−0.17*** [0.04]	−0.27*** [0.05]	−0.13*** [0.05]	−0.29*** [0.08]	−0.15*** [0.02]
Product developed	−0.33* [0.14]	−0.11 [0.14]	0.17 [0.27]	−0.53* [0.25]	0.17 [0.16]	0.04 [0.35]	−0.03 [0.06]
Constant	−1.26*** [0.23]	−1.97*** [0.29]	−3.36*** [0.51]	−2.12*** [0.38]	−1.51*** [0.31]	−3.62*** [0.76]	0.00 [0.15]
Observations	1,256	1,256	1,256	1,256	1,256	1,256	1,256
Number of firms	167	167	167	167	167	167	167
Wald chi-square	288.0	352.42	220.31	157.88	152	129.33	507.41
Difference in chi-square from baseline	123.7	75.42	103.99	5.61	−3.87	6.97	111.08

Note. Robust standard errors in brackets.
*Significant at 10%; **significant at 5%; ***significant at 1%.

Beckman and Burton: *Path Dependence in the Evolution of Top Management Teams*
Organization Science 19(1), pp. 3–24, © 2008 INFORMS   13

lative count measure (Model 7). It is important to note that only the parallel structure or experience is predictive. In supplementary analyses we confirmed there were no effects for the noncorresponding functions. In other words, sales experience does not predict the establishment of a science position; it is only science experience that is significantly associated with science functional structures and subsequent science experience. We present the more parsimonious models in the paper for purposes of clarity.

Across most specifications we see that large firms, and firms where teams are growing, have more broadly experienced TMTs and more functional positions. This suggests that firms are growing and becoming more experienced over time, which is consistent with a life-cycle perspective. Further, firms with VC funding often gain TMT experience and functional structures. However, our findings imply that structures and experiences accrue more to those firms that are already advantaged. Overall, our findings for structural precedent (we find support for H2 but not for H3) are weaker than our findings for cognitive framing (H1) and homophily (H4). Yet we see that initial functional structures matter (H2).

Finally, to test H5 regarding firm outcomes, in Table 3 we conduct event history analyses on monthly observations and report Cox proportional hazards models using maximum likelihood estimation and robust estimates of standard error (Lin and Wei 1989). The founding year is represented as age = 0 with all the initial conditions represented as covariates that are updated where appropriate. Firms remain in the sample until they achieve the outcome of interest; until they cease to exist as independent entities through failure, merger, or acquisition; or until the end of the sample period, at which time they are censored.

We present our results in two panels in Table 3 to demonstrate the influence of founding team on the timing of two different outcomes: obtaining VC and completing an IPO. Model 1 is the baseline model that includes controls only. Note that team compositional changes are accounted for by the inclusion of measures of both entrances to and exits from the TMT. Model 2 examines founding team variables and includes count measures for both the amount of initial functional structure in the firm and the amount of prior functional experience possessed by the founders. In Model 3 we also include the interaction of these terms. The main effects are centered prior to calculating the interaction (as suggested by Cronbach 1987) to reduce collinearity between the main effects and the interaction term. Model 4 adds the same count variables and their interaction for the TMT team to assess whether the effects of the founding team are eliminated when the subsequent team is considered. It is in this model that we most strongly assess path dependence against life cycles in determining the relationship between team and firm characteristics and outcomes. As in Table 1, we report hazard ratios, so numbers larger than 1 indicate an increase in the rate, and numbers smaller than 1 indicate a decrease in rate of achieving the firm outcomes.

In the first panel, the VC analysis, we see that firm size and the average amount of data collected for team members are both positively associated with attaining VC financing. In addition, TMT departures are positively related to obtaining financing. This may indicate that firms replace executives to build a team attractive to venture capitalists. In Model 2 we find that each additional functional area represented in the prefounding career history increases the likelihood of attracting VC financing by 14%. The effect of functional structure is also positive but not statistically significant. Interestingly, in Model 3, the interaction of structure and experience is negative and statistically significant. The interaction effect should be interpreted as the effect of experience on the outcome when structure is 0. The influence of founding functional experience on the time to VC financing is weaker for firms that begin with no functional structure; they have a 13% lower likelihood of receiving VC. Not surprisingly, the founding team effects are attenuated when we include characteristics of the subsequent team in Model 4 (although the interaction remains significant) because, as we know from Table 2, founding team experience also predicts TMT experience. The strong correlation between the founding and TMT composition in the early years makes Model 4 difficult to interpret; however, the pattern of results suggest that the range of prior experience held by the founding team is an important correlate of VC financing, and firms that start with both experience and structure reach this milestone faster than other firms.

In Panel 2 of Table 3 we present a similar set of analyses for time to IPO. The control variables have larger effects on the rates of IPO. Firms in medical-related industries go public at least five times more quickly than firms in other industries, and firms in industries with a high number of IPOs go public more quickly than firms in other industries. In addition, we see that the effect of turnover has two countervailing effects on rates of IPO: firms benefit from entrances and are hindered by exits. These effects, while consistent with the life-cycle perspective, do not wipe out the founder effects, as seen in Model 2. Thus, origins do matter for outcomes. In contrast to our VC findings, Model 2 in Panel 2 reveals that functional structure is associated with an increased likelihood of IPO, and prior experience is not. In Model 3 we see that the interaction of structure and experience is negative and statistically significant, suggesting that structure cannot substitute for a lack of experience. The influence of founding functional structure on the time to IPO is weaker for firms that begin with no prior functional experience; they have a 23% lower likelihood of

Beckman and Burton: *Path Dependence in the Evolution of Top Management Teams*
Organization Science 19(1), pp. 3–24, © 2008 INFORMS

14

Table 3 Event History Analysis: Effect of Founding Team on Firm Outcomes

	Panel 1: VC				Panel 2: IPO			
	(1)	(2)	(3)	(4)	(1)	(2)	(3)	(4)
Firm size	1.65***	1.65***	1.70***	1.61***	1.29	1.16	1.19	1.18
	[0.16]	[0.16]	[0.17]	[0.17]	[0.22]	[0.21]	[0.21]	[0.23]
Medical-related industry	1.14	1.3	1.37	1.38	5.46***	6.97***	8.63***	7.10***
	[0.27]	[0.31]	[0.33]	[0.36]	[1.86]	[2.52]	[2.92]	[2.65]
Innovation strategy	1.29	1.33	1.36	1.38	0.74	0.7	0.68	0.77
	[0.30]	[0.31]	[0.32]	[0.34]	[0.20]	[0.19]	[0.19]	[0.23]
Marketing strategy	0.8	0.82	0.78	0.79	1.11	1.03	0.93	0.9
	[0.23]	[0.24]	[0.23]	[0.24]	[0.39]	[0.35]	[0.31]	[0.30]
VC deals/IPOs in industry	1	1	1	1	1.18***	1.19***	1.18***	1.18***
	[0.00]	[0.00]	[0.00]	[0.00]	[0.03]	[0.03]	[0.03]	[0.03]
Cumulative VC					1.12**	1.14***	1.14***	1.08
					[0.06]	[0.06]	[0.05]	[0.06]
Avg. person positions	1.19**	1.19**	1.18**	1.19**	2.21***	2.30***	2.46***	2.58***
	[0.09]	[0.09]	[0.09]	[0.09]	[0.31]	[0.33]	[0.35]	[0.40]
Founding team (FT) size	1.02	0.99	1	1.01	1.13	1.02	1.09	1.03
	[0.05]	[0.05]	[0.05]	[0.05]	[0.09]	[0.09]	[0.10]	[0.10]
Product developed	0.91	0.94	0.89	0.89	0.66	0.69	0.71	0.60*
	[0.20]	[0.21]	[0.20]	[0.21]	[0.18]	[0.19]	[0.20]	[0.18]
Prop. founders on TMT	0.95	0.97	0.94	0.97	0.54	0.59	0.53	0.77
	[0.10]	[0.11]	[0.12]	[0.12]	[0.22]	[0.25]	[0.24]	[0.33]
Cumulative TMT entrances	0.86	0.81	0.83	0.66**	1.63***	1.66***	1.68***	1.43**
	[0.13]	[0.13]	[0.13]	[0.12]	[0.16]	[0.17]	[0.18]	[0.21]
Cumulative TMT exits	1.71*	1.63*	1.80**	2.75***	0.66***	0.65***	0.63***	0.75*
	[0.48]	[0.46]	[0.50]	[1.00]	[0.06]	[0.07]	[0.07]	[0.11]
FT structure count		1.07	1.11	0.87		1.41***	1.50***	1.45***
		[0.13]	[0.13]	[0.18]		[0.21]	[0.21]	[0.20]
FT experience count		1.14*	1.19*	0.95		0.94	1.05	1
		[0.11]	[0.11]	[0.13]		[0.12]	[0.15]	[0.15]
FT structure * experience			0.87*	0.79**			0.77***	0.78***
			[0.07]	[0.09]			[0.07]	[0.07]
TMT structure count				1.4				1.78***
				[0.29]				[0.33]
TMT experience count				1.53***				1.33
				[0.24]				[0.24]
TMT structure * experience				1.05				0.89
				[0.12]				[0.08]
Observations	6,107	6,107	6,107	6,107	13,085	13,085	13,085	13,085
Log-pseudolikelihood	−516.91	−515.43	−513.86	−506.96	−290.02	−287.6	−284.12	−276.69
Exits	118	118	118	118	86	86	86	86
Firms	158	158	158	158	158	158	158	158

Note. Robust standard errors.
*Significant at 10%; **significant at 5%; ***significant at 1%.

going public. The effects of the founding structure persist through the inclusion of contemporary structure (see Model 4). Structure may be an important signal to public investors.

In general, our findings suggest that venture capitalists are more concerned with the prior experience of executives in firms that they fund, whereas the public markets evaluate functional structure. Both milestones are more easily achieved by the firms that start with both structure and experience. A key conclusion from the analyses in

Table 3 is that although the impact of the TMT tends to be stronger than the founding team on these outcomes, founding team effects persist, controlling for changes to the team.

Supplementary Analyses

The above findings begin to establish organizational functional structure and incumbent prior functional experience as distinct constructs and demonstrate support for our main theoretical argument that initial con-

Beckman and Burton: *Path Dependence in the Evolution of Top Management Teams*
Organization Science 19(1), pp. 3–24, © 2008 INFORMS   15

Table 4   Descriptive Statistics for Founding Teams Initial Types

Row	Variable	Full sample	(1) Simple structure (narrow range of functional positions), narrowly experienced team (limited range of prior functional experiences)	(2) Simple structure, broadly experienced team (broad range of prior functional experiences)	(3) Complete structure (broad range of functional positions), narrowly experienced team	(4) Complete structure, broadly experienced team	(4) vs. (1)	(4) vs. (3)	(3) vs. (1)	(2) vs. (1)
1	Number of firms	167	50	14	44	59				
2	Mean founding team size	2.82	2.16	2.71	2.82	3.41	17.57***	3.65**	4.23**	n.s.
3	Cumulative entrances	5.50	4.30	5.64	5.61	6.39	10.32***	n.s.	3.53*	n.s.
4	Cumulative exits	1.68	1.48	1.93	1.73	1.76	n.s.	n.s.	n.s.	n.s.
5	Proportion of founders on TMT	0.55	0.60	0.50	0.56	0.52	n.s.	n.s.	n.s.	n.s.
6	Mean TMT size	4.42	3.24	4.43	4.32	5.49	20.02***	5.06**	3.97**	n.s.
7	TMT experience	2.78	2.12	3.36	2.61	3.32	14.56***	4.71**	n.s.	6.23***
8	TMT functions	3.27	2.56	3.64	3.55	3.58	9.21***	n.s.	7.49***	4.22**
9	Proportion VC backed	0.71	0.58	0.71	0.68	0.83	8.42***	2.76*	n.s.	n.s.
10	Proportion that achieve IPO	0.51	0.42	0.43	0.52	0.61	3.93**	n.s.	n.s.	n.s.
11	Firm age at end of observation period	7.00	9.00	7.50	7.00	6.00	16.58***	n.s.	5.58***	2.94*

Notes. Two-tailed tests for F-statistic. We do not include comparisons between cells 2 and 3 and cells 2 and 4 because there are not significant differences. $*p < 0.10$; $**p < 0.05$; $***p < 0.01$.

ditions constrain subsequent evolution. However, our hypothesis tests do not allow us to fully understand the interrelationships between structure and experience over time. The strong support for the effects of initial experience on subsequent experience and for the effects of initial structure on subsequent structure contrasted with the weaker or nonexistent support for the cross effects. This suggests that structure and experience are not substitutable. Having one does not appear to compensate for the other.

To explore the interrelationships of structure, experience, and outcomes, we first descriptively characterize the team and firm evolutionary patterns revealed in our data (see Table 4). The first column (Full sample) presents overall means for all firms. We then divide our sample, using mean splits on counts of founding team functional experience and counts of initial structural positions, into four subsamples representing each of the archetype cells described in Figure 1. Cell 1 most closely captures the mythical "engineers in a garage" as it describes a firm with a narrow range of functional positions and functional expertise. In contrast, Cell 4 most closely captures the professional team in a functional organization. The off-diagonals, Cells 2 and 3, represent situations where the founding team has either structure or experience, but not both.

Several points are noteworthy. First, Figure 1 and Table 4 demonstrate that experience and structure are clearly distinct concepts, and structure and prior experience do not always go hand-in-hand. The least common starting state is represented by Cell 2—simple structure, but broadly experienced executives—which characterizes 14 of 167 firms; however, firms are relatively

dispersed across the other cells. Firms with neither structure nor experience at founding (50 of 167 firms represented in Cell 1) appear to be disadvantaged on many fronts: They start with smaller teams, do not grow as much, and are less likely to receive VC or to go public than firms with the most broadly experienced teams with complete structures. (See Table 4, Rows 2, 6, 9, and 10.) Table 4 also lends additional support for H5, that the combination of initial background experience and functional structure is important for firm success. Firms in Cell 4 seem to achieve critical milestones more quickly

Figure 1   Archetype Founding Team Types

		Organizational functional structure	
		Low	High
Prior functional experience	High	**Cell 2** Simple structure and broadly experienced team *General partners*	**Cell 4** Complete structure and broadly experienced team *Functional organization*
	Low	**Cell 1** Simple structure and narrowly experienced team *Engineers in a garage*	**Cell 3** Complete structure and narrowly experienced team *Business plan competition entrants*

Beckman and Burton: *Path Dependence in the Evolution of Top Management Teams*
16   Organization Science 19(1), pp. 3–24, © 2008 INFORMS

than firms in Cell 1. In addition, there is suggestive evidence that narrowly experienced teams are not able to accrue needed additional functional expertise as easily as unstructured teams acquire structure. That is, comparing narrowly and broadly experienced teams at each level of structure (Cells 1 and 2; Cells 3 and 4), it appears that, regardless of the starting structure, narrowly experienced founding teams have significantly less broad TMT experience at the end of the sample period (see Table 4, Row 7). In contrast, when firms have broadly experienced teams, the firms that lack initial functional structures (Cell 2) have the same level of structure at the end of the time period as those that started with more complete functional structures (Cell 4) (see Table 4, Row 8). Thus, those teams with early functional experience can develop functional structure, but those teams with early functional structure do not develop functional experience. Finally, it is worth noting that executives exit all types of firms at the same rate (see "Cumulative exits," Row 4 in Table 4). There are no significant differences across the four starting states, suggesting there is not a clear signal about "winning" firms.

In Table 5 we present monthly panel regression models, again correcting for autocorrelation and with robust standard errors, where we attempt to discern the relationship between origin state and ultimate destination. Given the evidence that successful firms have broadly experienced TMTs and complete functional structures, we are particularly interested in understanding the path by which firms end up in this state. Recall our count measures for breadth of experience and structure that range from 0 to 6. If we consider these as interval representations along two continua, then the product of experience and structure, an interaction variable with a theoretical range of 0 to 36, is a linear representation of the combined amount of structure and experience. The larger the product of TMT structure and TMT experience, the closer the firm is to having a complete structure and all functions represented in the prior experiences of the TMT (i.e., Cell 4). We treat this product as our dependent variable in a series of regression models where the key independent variables are initial structure, initial experience, and the interaction of the two.

In Table 5, we report a baseline model, Model 1, with controls only. Models 2 and 3 add founder functional experience and initial functional structure, respectively, to the model. Model 4 includes both key independent variables. Model 5 includes the interaction of these two counts to assess the relative importance of each. This allows us to examine the extent to which experience and structure can serve as substitutes and whether one is more important than the other in influencing firm and team evolution. Consistent with life-cycle predictions of professionalization, firm size, VC, and entrances to the TMT are positively associated with having a broadly experienced team and complete structure, and

TMT entrances is one of the largest effects in the model. Yet net of all of these effects, we see that founding team experience and initial structure are important correlates of the final destination state. Comparing Models 2 and 3, we see that founder functional experience alone improves model fit more than initial functional structure alone. Thus, it appears that initial experience is a more substantial predictor than initial structure. But Model 4 demonstrates a significant joint effect, and Model 5 reveals a slight positive interaction. This is evidence of the advantages associated with starting with both structure and experience (Cell 4) at founding; however, the strength of the experience main effect and the weak statistical significance attached to the interaction imply that Cell 2 is a better origin state than Cell 3.

We explored several alternative explanations of our findings. One additional explanation is that a match between initial and subsequent functional experience is created through preferences for experienced executives. Although all firms may seek to hire broadly experienced executives, it is only firms with broadly experienced founding team members that are able to attract the executive talent necessary for future success. Although similar to homophily, it would be a result of only broadly experienced founders being successful at recruitment. Although it is difficult to empirically disentangle these mechanisms, it is worth noting that all varieties of founding team experiences influence TMT experience, regardless of whether the experience is particularly relevant for the firm's strategy. This gives more credence to the homophily explanation.

Another alternative explanation is that "good" firms attract both broadly experienced founding teams and TMTs rather than founding teams predicting TMTs. This concern of unobserved heterogeneity is a common issue in empirical work, and we have done what we can to explore this possibility—that people are attracted to firms and not to other people. This would imply that rather than initial experience and structure increasing the ability of the firm to reach important milestones, experienced TMT members may be drawn to firms that look like winners. Thus, the causality could go the other way: Good firms attract good people rather than good people creating good firms. Although we cannot rule out this possibility, we do control for several measures of firm quality. In addition to controlling for size and strategy, we are also including whether the firm had a product as a control. Also, recall that the exit rates and proportion of founders on the TMT across our four cells in Table 4 are not significantly different. On average, 1.7 executives leave the firm and founders account for more than 50% of the TMT. This suggests that firm quality is difficult to observe; otherwise, executives and founders would leave low-quality firms at higher rates. Thus, it seems likely that prospective TMT members have an easier time assessing the quality of the existing team than the

Beckman and Burton: *Path Dependence in the Evolution of Top Management Teams*
Organization Science 19(1), pp. 3–24, © 2008 INFORMS

Table 5   Population-Averaged Panel Regression Analysis Predicting TMT Structure * Experience, with Robust Standard Errors and AR1 Error Structure

	(1)	(2)	(3)	(4)	(5)
Log firm size	0.33***	0.34***	0.33***	0.34***	0.34***
	(0.06)	(0.06)	(0.06)	(0.06)	(0.06)
Medical-related industry	−1.03	−0.35	0.14	0.18	−0.03
	(1.11)	(1.05)	(1.10)	(1.07)	(1.03)
Innovation strategy	1.33	1.40	1.44	1.45	1.44
	(0.87)	(0.81)	(0.83)	(0.80)	(0.79)
Marketing strategy	0.39	0.49	0.12	0.32	0.59
	(1.05)	(0.94)	(1.02)	(0.94)	(0.93)
Cumulative rounds of venture capital	0.35***	0.37***	0.36***	0.37***	0.38***
	(0.06)	(0.06)	(0.06)	(0.06)	(0.06)
Prop. founders on TMT	−0.09***	−0.09**	−0.09**	−0.09***	−0.09***
	(0.03)	(0.03)	(0.03)	(0.03)	(0.03)
Product developed	0.21	0.23	0.22	0.23	0.23
	(0.12)	(0.12)	(0.12)	(0.12)	(0.12)
Average number of prior person positions	0.12	0.12	0.13	0.12	0.12
	(0.08)	(0.08)	(0.08)	(0.08)	(0.08)
Founding team (FT) size	0.66**	0.39*	0.28	0.23	0.17
	(0.27)	(0.19)	(0.23)	(0.19)	(0.18)
Cumulative entrances to the TMT	0.16***	0.17***	0.16***	0.17***	0.17***
	(0.05)	(0.05)	(0.05)	(0.05)	(0.05)
Cumulative exits from the TMT	0.08	0.07	0.08	0.07	0.06
	(0.12)	(0.12)	(0.12)	(0.13)	(0.13)
FT prior experience count		1.90***		1.52***	1.29***
		(0.37)		(0.42)	(0.43)
FT structure count			1.80***	1.02**	0.86*
			(0.45)	(0.48)	(0.46)
FT exp. * structure					0.70*
					(0.38)
Constant	2.16**	2.61***	3.02***	3.00***	2.82***
	(0.85)	(0.71)	(0.81)	(0.71)	(0.69)
Observations	14,269	14,269	14,269	14,269	14,269
Chi-square	131.58	183.36	160.08	192.54	192.27

Note. Robust standard errors.

*Significant at 10%; **significant at 5%; ***significant at 1%; two-tailed tests.

firm itself because the quality of the firm (independent of people) is hard to assess. However, there may also be an "escalation of commitment" (Staw 1976), whereby subsequent team members remain with their firm despite lower potential returns. Of course, the entrance rates are significantly different across these cells. The founding teams with both experience and structure grow more rapidly than all other firms, but it appears these changes in composition are driven by founding team composition. Still, understanding how people evaluate prospective employment opportunities in entrepreneurial firms is an important area for future research.

Because we were able to observe firms for a relatively short period of time, we are limited in our ability to assess if and when founder imprints might decay. In supplementary analyses we explore the extent to which our results are driven by having relatively young firms. We first replicated all our time-series analyses, including yearly dummy variables to control for

the main effects of firm age and found results consistent with those reported. We also replicated the analyses in Table 2, Model 7, predicting both TMT functional structure and TMT experience, including interactions with initial experience and structure and firm age. We find statistically significant age interactions; however, the magnitude of the effects is trivial. We thus have some confidence that our results hold for many years post-founding.

We were concerned about several additional factors that could have influenced our results. First, our effects may be skewed by the bubble market of the late 1990s. In supplementary analyses, we examine the possibility that our results arise from period effects rather than our theorized mechanisms. Our results are robust to restricting our VC financing events prior to 1993 (before the market began to heat up) and our IPO events prior to 1996 (the first year that IPO rates jump significantly).

Beckman and Burton: *Path Dependence in the Evolution of Top Management Teams*
Organization Science 19(1), pp. 3–24, © 2008 INFORMS

Firms may add positions to the TMT just prior to receiving external financing or going public to signal readiness to potential investors. We control for this potential "window dressing" by reporting team entrances and exits, and proportion founders on the TMT, lagged 12 months in all outcome analyses. Thus, changes made within a year of the event were not considered. We found substantially the same results with shorter and longer lags, thus we feel comfortable using a conservative one-year window. However, because we have announcement dates and not dates when these discussions commenced, we cannot completely rule out reverse causality.

Finally, we were concerned that the time-series data may overemphasize the within-firm linkage between the founding team and TMT. In addition to using robust standard errors and correcting for autocorrelation in the reported models, we also ran a series of panel regressions. In these models we used founding team experience and structure to predict TMT experience and structure (as in Table 2) at a given firm age (e.g., at year 4 and at year 8), and we found similar results.

Limitations

We have taken a first step in understanding TMT evolution with rich longitudinal data. Of course, our study has several limitations. First, as noted above, we observe firms for a relatively short period of time and are thus limited in our ability to assess the durability of founder effects over long periods. A second weakness is that our data for both executives and firms are somewhat incomplete. We do not have the kind of detailed performance outcomes that are available for established public companies. In addition, we may have been unable to find data on TMT members who were not successful during their career. However, ours is the first study to our knowledge to attempt such a detailed look at the career histories of executives in small firms over time, and such an examination almost by definition involves problems with missing data. Furthermore, we have controlled for the potential problem to the extent possible in all analysis.

A third limitation is that our sample has a success bias because the firms survived on average five years before we contacted them. We believe, however, that in demonstrating an empirical phenomenon in an interesting empirical setting and establishing a new model of longitudinal research, the benefits of the sample far outweigh the concerns. Finally, there are questions of unobserved heterogeneity that cannot be ruled out, although we explore them to the extent possible in the above supplementary analyses.

Discussion

Our research demonstrates that founding teams strongly influence the TMT through path dependence. Consistent with homophily expectations, founding teams that begin with broadly experienced team members are more likely to attract broadly experienced executives. Consistent with ecological research, firms that begin with a range of functional structures are more likely to develop more complete functional structures. Thus, path dependence, where the founding team shapes the subsequent TMT, occurs through both homophily and imprinting.

We see cumulative advantage, as high-quality founding teams become high-quality TMTs and less well-endowed founding teams never catch up. In particular, we see that 26% of our teams begin with broad functional structures but narrowly experienced people (Table 4), and they never catch up in terms of attracting a broad range of functional experience. Firms founded by narrowly experienced founders have difficulty attracting broadly experienced executives. It does not seem to be the case that narrowly experienced founders simply fail to recognize the importance of other types of functional expertise. Instead, even when the firm has created an executive level position for a given function—a strong statement that it needs and values that expertise—the firm is limited in its ability to fill the position with the relevant expertise if it does not already have an executive in place with at least some experience in that function. This suggests that structure is a poor substitute for experience. Thus, our results stand in sharp contrast to the dominant image of engineers in an unstructured nascent venture who are replaced by broadly experienced professionals who then formalize the structures and evolve the firm into a professional bureaucracy. Our results imply that the narrowly experienced "garage" entrepreneur is not likely to succeed (Audia and Rider 2005).

Despite the significant findings, two of our hypotheses receive modest or no support. We find only modest support that initial functional experience predicts the initial functional structure. Given the wealth of other research documenting this transfer (Boeker 1988; Burton and Beckman 2007; Phillips 2002, 2005), it is possible that our measures of functional structure do not adequately capture the nuance of how executives enact organizational positions. In addition, path dependence may operate more strongly through homophily in the cases of race or gender (see Phillips 2005). This would be a useful area for future research, as initial functional structure is an important decision that founders make.

Our lack of support for functional structures predicting experience (H3) is quite relevant for human resource management. At least in entrepreneurial firms, the structure of the position does not predict the experience people bring to the firm, once controlling for initial experience. Instead, it appears that the ASA framework (Schneider 1987) and structural inertia (Hannan and Freeman 1984) together account for the relationship between early structure and experience and later structure and experience. As noted above, establishing positions and filling them with people who are "place-holders" appears to be detrimental to the firm's ability to ultimately attract broadly experienced executives.

Beckman and Burton: *Path Dependence in the Evolution of Top Management Teams*
Organization Science 19(1), pp. 3–24, © 2008 INFORMS   19

Little research has examined changes in teams over time, much less from founding, and a major contribution of this paper is the detailing of the relationship between the founding team and TMT. We demonstrate that the founding team exerts an influence on the firm not only through directly influencing firm outcomes, but also by shaping the very nature of the organization. An ahistorical account of the TMT will overstate the ability of the TMT to change; in fact, future teams may be best understood by a detailed examination of the teams that have come before. This finding limits the role of agency and suggests sharp deviations from the initial path are unlikely (and probably risky, see Hannan et al. 2006). Our research thus further highlights the benefits of an evolutionary perspective on firms and teams (see Aldrich 1999).

We clearly see evidence of path dependence in our analysis, and these effects are net of changes and growth among the firms. The significant influence of team entrances in many of our analyses, however, also offers support for a life-cycle model of entrepreneurial firm development. Growth does allow firms to add both functional experience and structure, and these effects are substantive in our models. However, our intent here is to demonstrate that the initial conditions do matter and not all firms easily professionalize and grow. Particularly in light of our lack of support for H3—initial structure does not predict attracting that functional experience to the firm—firms should be cautious in assumptions of adding experience later. In contrast, our findings suggest deliberate planning into the future is usefully done at founding.

Our results also add to the organizational demography and upper echelon research, which has not to date focused on developing dynamic models or explaining the source of demographic distributions in organizations (Lawrence 1997, Hambrick 2007). Our work begins to address this weakness in the demographic approach by exploring the path-dependent process that results in continued heterogeneity or homogeneity among teams. This is not to say that organizational demography research has not moved in important directions. To the contrary, critical work examines the team processes generated by diversity (Knight et al. 1999, Pelled et al. 1999, Reagans and Zuckerman 2001) and the difficulties of using indirect measures of demographic composition rather than direct measures of social networks to predict firm performance (Reagans et al. 2004). Still, scholars rarely conduct longitudinal studies (see Boone et al. 2004 and Sørensen 2004 for recent exceptions). More importantly, scholars have devoted little attention to the sources of demographic diversity. In addition, we point to a distinction between functional experience and functional structure that has received little attention in this literature; thus, our paper fills several important gaps in the literature.

For the entrepreneurial literature, our research suggests that the relevance of founding teams is more significant than has been acknowledged. Not only do founding teams directly impact firm outcomes, but, through a process of path dependence, the founding team shapes the TMT. Entrepreneurship research often focuses on the individual entrepreneur, but understanding the teams that come together and develop over time is essential to understanding the performance of entrepreneurial firms. We advocate more studies with longitudinal data as well as a focus on functional structure in addition to team human capital. Also important, but largely unexplored in this paper, is the impact of VC in shaping the TMT. Our findings offer suggestive evidence that VC-backed firms are better able to add structure and experience than non-VC-backed firms; however, the precise mechanisms are worthy of additional research.

Much more remains to be understood about entrepreneurial teams. How does a team attract founders with varied experiences when we know diversity is atypical (Ruef et al. 2003)? Given the long-term effects of these initial choices, such an exploration would be very useful. We know founding is not truly the beginning, because entrepreneurs bring experience and networks with them (Burton et al. 2002, Shane and Stuart 2002). A qualitative assessment of how people, ideas, experiences, and structures come together to create a firm would be an important contribution of future work. In addition, delving into individual executive positions in the organization would help us understand in more detail the mechanisms that result in path dependence (Burton and Beckman 2007).

Despite the remaining questions, we are encouraged by the consistency of our results, how they contribute to and reflect current theories, and by the potential rewards of examining teams over time in this rich research setting of entrepreneurial firms. We demonstrate that founding teams matter—both directly and indirectly—largely through a process of path dependence. This sociological and evolutionary approach demonstrates how initial teams have a lasting impact on the firm.

Acknowledgments

Both authors contributed equally to this manuscript. The authors thank Greg Northcraft for his insights and contribution to this manuscript. The authors also thank Roberto Fernandez, Mauro Guillen, Nandini Rajagopalan, Jesper Sørensen, Ezra Zuckerman, seminar participants at University of California, Berkeley, Harvard Business School, Massachusetts Institute of Technology, University of California, Los Angeles, University of California Irvine, Wharton, and attendees at the West Coast Entrepreneurial Research Conference for constructive comments on earlier drafts of this paper. An earlier version of this paper was presented at the Academy of Management Meeting in 2006. This research was supported by Stanford Project on Emerging Companies (SPEC) at the Graduate School of Business, the Harvard Business School Division of Research, UC Irvine, and the MIT Entrepreneurship Center. The authors also thank Jon Reuter, Candice Tulberg, and Stephanie Woerner for helpful research assistance. All errors are the responsibility of the authors.

Beckman and Burton: *Path Dependence in the Evolution of Top Management Teams*
Organization Science 19(1), pp. 3–24, © 2008 INFORMS

20

Appendix

Table A   Descriptive Statistics ($N = 167$)

Variable	Mean	Std. dev.	Min.	Max.
Firm size (logged)	4.07	0.99	0.69	7.47
Medical-related industry	0.14	0.35	0	1
Innovation strategy	0.48	0.50	0	1
Sales/marketing/service strategy	0.23	0.42	0	1
Cumulative rounds of VC	3.10	2.82	0	11
Proportion of founders on TMT	0.67	0.68	0	5
Product developed	0.77	0.42	0	1
Average number of prior person positions (by firm)	2.12	0.85	0	5
Founding team (FT) size	2.82	1.61	1	10
Cumulative entrances to TMT	5.50	3.46	0	18
Cumulative exits from TMT	1.68	2.22	0	15
FT prior experience				
Science/engineering	0.95	0.96	0	3
Sales/marketing	0.31	0.55	0	3
Manufacturing/operations	0.10	0.30	0	1
Finance/accounting	0.11	0.31	0	1
Administration/HR	0.38	0.58	0	3
Business development/ strategic planning	0.07	0.25	0	1
Initial structure				
Science/engineering	0.58	0.80	0	3
Sales/marketing	0.23	0.56	0	3
Manufacturing/operations	0.11	0.35	0	2
Finance/accounting	0.14	0.35	0	1
Administration/HR	1.53	1.11	0	6
Business development/ strategic planning	0.04	0.22	0	2
TMT prior experience				
Science/engineering	1.34	1.24	0	5
Sales/marketing	1.03	1.23	0	5
Manufacturing/operations	0.40	0.64	0	2
Finance/accounting	0.53	0.62	0	2
Administration/HR	0.80	0.99	0	5
Business development/ strategic planning	0.28	0.55	0	3
TMT structure				
Science/engineering	1.23	1.29	0	7
Sales/marketing	1.28	1.51	0	6
Manufacturing/operations	0.56	0.77	0	3
Finance/accounting	0.68	0.67	0	3
Administration/HR	2.32	1.68	0	8
Business development/ strategic planning	0.24	0.54	0	2
FT experience count	1.47	1.03	0	4
TMT experience count	2.78	1.71	0	6
FT structure count	1.77	0.96	0	4
TMT structure count	3.38	1.63	1	6
IPOs in industry	4.51	4.49	0	18
VC deals in industry	1,502.22	1,000.60	567	3,367
Ever VC	0.71	0.46	0	1
Ever IPO	0.51	0.50	0	1

Beckman and Burton: *Path Dependence in the Evolution of Top Management Teams*
Organization Science 19(1), pp. 3–24, © 2008 INFORMS   21

Table B   Correlation Matrix

	1	2	3	4	5	6	7	8	9	10	11	12	13	14	15	16	17	18	19	20	21
1 Firm size (log)	1.00																				
2 Medical industry	-0.15	1.00																			
3 Innovation strategy	-0.08	0.26	1.00																		
4 Marketing strategy	0.08	-0.10	-0.52	1.00																	
5 Venture capital	0.20	0.06	0.20	-0.19	1.00																
6 Prop. founders on TMT	-0.18	0.11	-0.07	0.07	-0.06	1.00															
7 Product development	0.17	-0.27	0.01	0.16	0.13	-0.03	1.00														
8 Average prior positions	0.03	0.04	0.07	0.01	0.07	-0.17	-0.03	1.00													
9 Founding team size	0.13	0.11	0.08	-0.06	0.03	0.40	0.01	-0.17	1.00												
10 Cum. TMT entrances	0.37	-0.16	0.24	0.02	0.31	-0.37	0.22	-0.04	0.24	1.00											
11 Cum. TMT exits	0.21	-0.18	0.12	-0.10	0.14	-0.03	0.19	-0.21	0.18	0.63	1.00										
12 FT exp. science/eng.	0.06	0.08	0.20	-0.04	0.06	-0.14	-0.03	0.01	0.22	0.20	-0.04	1.00									
13 FT exp. sales/mktg.	0.01	-0.17	-0.14	0.19	-0.02	-0.08	0.07	0.11	0.17	0.05	-0.02	0.15	1.00								
14 FT exp. mfg./ops.	-0.02	-0.03	-0.01	0.01	-0.03	0.05	0.04	-0.08	0.14	0.01	0.06	0.04	0.01	1.00							
15 FT exp. fin./acct.	-0.02	-0.03	-0.02	-0.01	-0.06	-0.02	0.09	-0.02	-0.05	0.10	0.11	0.08	0.18	0.01	1.00						
16 FT exp. admin./HR	0.04	-0.09	-0.11	0.19	-0.05	-0.12	-0.04	0.00	0.23	0.17	0.11	-0.16	0.23	0.03	0.04	1.00					
17 FT exp. bus. dev.	-0.05	0.10	0.04	0.09	0.14	-0.07	-0.02	0.08	-0.03	0.01	-0.06	-0.04	0.07	0.04	-0.01	-0.05	1.00				
18 FT struc. science/eng.	0.07	-0.04	0.17	-0.13	0.19	-0.04	0.05	0.05	0.31	0.23	0.08	0.60	0.20	0.00	0.18	0.06	-0.07	1.00			
19 FT struc. sales/mktg.	0.23	-0.17	-0.08	0.03	-0.08	-0.03	0.05	-0.03	0.29	0.21	0.11	0.11	0.09	-0.03	0.19	0.23	0.06	0.22	1.00		
20 FT struc. mfg./ops.	0.18	-0.08	-0.17	0.19	0.01	-0.04	0.10	-0.17	0.13	0.04	-0.06	0.12	0.48	-0.06	0.22	-0.12	-0.09	0.04	0.26	1.00	
21 FT struc. fin./acct.	0.07	-0.12	-0.12	0.02	-0.20	-0.05	0.05	-0.24	0.00	0.03	0.00	0.15	0.16	-0.04	0.03	0.19	-0.09	0.11	0.07	0.16	1.00
22 FT struc. admin./HR	-0.01	-0.01	0.03	0.06	-0.19	0.26	-0.05	-0.14	0.52	0.12	0.14	0.00	0.05	-0.09	0.26	0.18	-0.04	-0.09	0.15	0.01	-0.14
23 FT struc. bus. dev.	-0.04	0.17	0.06	0.04	-0.06	0.08	-0.11	0.04	0.31	0.06	-0.04	0.48	0.03	0.25	0.15	0.04	-0.03	0.34	0.08	0.10	-0.07
24 TMT exp. science/eng.	0.20	0.18	0.25	0.01	0.22	-0.28	0.08	0.17	0.17	0.44	-0.11	0.13	0.06	-0.11	-0.03	0.30	0.09	0.15	0.10	0.06	-0.08
25 TMT exp. sales/mktg.	0.19	-0.16	0.02	0.02	0.30	-0.30	0.15	0.18	0.11	0.52	0.03	0.04	0.00	-0.06	-0.06	0.03	0.10	0.08	0.34	0.10	0.07
26 TMT exp. mfg./ops.	0.15	0.04	0.11	0.06	0.23	-0.18	0.21	0.07	0.06	0.42	0.09	0.24	0.25	-0.04	-0.07	0.10	0.08	0.22	0.10	0.12	-0.12
27 TMT exp. fin./acct.	0.12	0.03	0.03	0.11	0.13	-0.28	0.05	0.23	0.10	0.35	-0.10	0.08	0.19	-0.04	-0.13	0.14	0.04	0.08	0.12	0.06	0.03
28 TMT exp. admin./HR	0.22	0.00	0.14	-0.07	0.12	-0.17	-0.04	0.11	0.12	0.47	0.14	0.05	0.07	-0.06	0.15	-0.02	-0.04	0.12	-0.06	0.11	0.03
29 TMT exp. bus. dev.	0.05	0.17	0.18	-0.06	0.13	-0.27	-0.03	0.08	0.00	0.24	-0.04	0.48	0.00	-0.04	-0.03	0.02	-0.01	0.46	0.18	-0.04	-0.11
30 TMT struc. science/eng.	0.20	0.26	0.27	-0.11	0.23	-0.16	0.21	-0.02	0.35	0.38	-0.09	0.15	0.03	0.20	0.10	0.12	0.27	0.10	0.04	-0.13	-0.01
31 TMT struc. sales/mktg.	0.34	-0.20	0.03	-0.05	0.22	-0.32	0.14	0.05	0.19	0.59	0.08	0.07	0.20	0.12	0.05	0.13	0.01	-0.04	0.11	0.10	0.10
32 TMT struc. mfg./ops.	0.29	0.01	0.05	0.07	0.16	-0.27	0.11	0.13	-0.03	0.30	-0.09	0.11	0.12	-0.04	-0.15	0.37	0.05	0.12	0.39	0.20	-0.01
33 TMT struc. fin./acct.	0.20	0.02	0.06	0.00	0.14	-0.33	0.05	-0.04	0.05	0.44	-0.02	0.09	0.02	-0.11	0.12	0.12	0.06	0.06	0.11	0.29	0.17
34 TMT struc. admin./HR	0.10	0.13	0.16	0.04	0.02	0.19	-0.08	0.04	0.20	0.39	0.10	0.14	0.06	-0.09	0.06	0.15	0.02	0.34	0.09	0.03	-0.09
35 TMT struc. bus. dev.	0.06	0.23	0.11	-0.01	0.06	-0.11	0.04	0.04	0.22	0.20	-0.06	0.43	0.06	0.27	0.46	0.04	-0.05	0.22	0.36	0.17	-0.06
36 FT exp. count	0.00	-0.10	-0.03	0.19	0.04	-0.20	0.14	0.29	0.12	0.19	0.05	0.24	0.58	0.04	0.06	0.05	0.06	0.56	0.14	0.06	0.03
37 TMT exp. count	0.26	0.05	0.19	-0.10	0.35	-0.43	0.06	-0.12	0.33	0.61	-0.01	0.44	0.14	0.04	0.21	0.03	0.28	0.12	0.56	0.52	0.48
38 FT structure count	0.19	-0.22	-0.10	0.10	-0.09	-0.06	0.13	0.14	0.12	0.22	-0.08	0.20	0.38	-0.12	0.03	0.05	0.12	0.07	0.17	0.08	0.06
39 TMT structure count	0.30	0.05	0.13	-0.07	0.30	-0.40	0.02	0.05	0.14	0.54	-0.07	-0.03	0.06	0.13	0.00	0.05	0.10	-0.04	0.04	0.08	-0.05
40 IPOs in ind.	0.07	0.13	0.08	0.08	0.08	-0.05	-0.11	-0.19	-0.07	0.17	0.05	-0.11	0.06	0.13	0.00	0.05	0.03	0.07	-0.02	-0.02	-0.05
41 VC deals in ind.	-0.06	-0.19	-0.14	0.07	-0.17	0.18	0.15	0.22	0.09	-0.30	0.13	0.12	0.01	0.00	-0.03	0.03	-0.07	-0.02	-0.01	0.02	-0.15
42 VC	0.19	0.15	0.22	-0.18	0.71	-0.15	0.15	0.22	0.09	0.28	0.01	0.12	0.07	0.00	-0.03	-0.06	0.12	0.17	-0.01	0.02	-0.15
43 IPO	0.14	0.19	0.16	-0.10	0.27	-0.29	-0.04	0.31	0.12	0.39	-0.17	0.22	0.04	-0.11	-0.09	0.05	-0.03	0.27	0.06	0.04	-0.01

Beckman and Burton: *Path Dependence in the Evolution of Top Management Teams*
Organization Science 19(1), pp. 3–24, © 2008 INFORMS

22

Table B (cont'd.)

	22	23	24	25	26	27	28	29	30	31	32	33	34	35	36	37	38	39	40	41	42
22 FT struc. admin./HR	1.00																				
23 FT struc. bus. dev.	0.20	1.00																			
24 TMT exp. science/eng.	−0.06	0.13	1.00																		
25 TMT exp. sales/mktg.	−0.03	−0.09	0.36	1.00																	
26 TMT exp. mfg./ops.	−0.02	0.11	0.44	0.34	1.00																
27 TMT exp. fin./acct.	0.02	−0.01	0.32	0.40	0.32	1.00															
28 TMT exp. admin./HR	0.03	0.29	0.27	0.16	0.05	0.14	1.00														
29 TMT exp. bus. dev.	0.01	0.12	0.22	0.27	0.04	0.13	0.16	1.00													
30 TMT struc. sci./eng.	0.10	0.27	0.69	0.28	0.18	0.37	0.35	0.13	1.00												
31 TMT struc. sales/mktg.	0.05	0.01	0.34	0.68	0.29	0.44	0.36	0.28	0.29	1.00											
32 TMT struc. mfg./ops.	−0.18	−0.01	0.36	0.38	0.44	0.35	0.11	0.09	0.18	0.38	1.00										
33 TMT struc. fin./acct.	0.00	0.04	0.31	0.38	0.34	0.67	0.25	0.21	0.30	0.45	0.36	1.00									
34 TMT struc. admin./HR	0.40	0.12	0.33	0.22	0.24	0.19	0.24	0.17	0.30	0.24	0.12	0.19	1.00								
35 TMT struc. bus. dev./st. pl	0.16	0.34	0.31	0.21	0.07	0.19	0.18	0.33	0.42	0.18	0.09	0.15	0.12	1.00							
36 FT exp. count	0.11	0.14	0.10	0.19	−0.05	0.31	0.18	0.05	0.23	0.24	0.02	0.09	0.02	0.13	1.00						
37 TMT exp. count	−0.09	0.12	0.61	0.65	0.54	0.63	0.43	0.44	0.49	0.58	0.48	0.61	0.30	0.33	0.22	1.00					
38 FT structure count	0.08	0.22	0.15	0.22	0.02	0.24	0.15	−0.07	0.30	0.31	0.11	0.18	0.04	0.06	0.48	0.13	1.00				
39 TMT structure count	−0.03	0.06	0.54	0.55	0.44	0.61	0.32	0.30	0.47	0.62	0.64	0.71	0.25	0.42	0.13	0.80	0.15	1.00			
40 IPOs in ind	0.09	0.11	0.12	0.13	0.17	0.07	0.15	0.17	0.21	0.18	−0.02	0.08	0.10	0.18	0.08	0.15	0.07	0.13	1.00		
41 VC deals in ind	0.10	−0.10	−0.39	−0.32	−0.37	−0.44	−0.32	−0.15	−0.38	−0.38	−0.31	−0.50	−0.20	−0.17	−0.05	−0.57	−0.06	−0.54	−0.26	1.00	
42 VC	−0.09	0.05	0.24	0.35	0.30	0.26	0.11	0.16	0.29	0.26	0.25	0.30	0.03	0.07	0.09	0.42	0.01	0.39	0.21	−0.35	1.00
43 IPO	−0.07	0.05	0.59	0.46	0.44	0.53	0.28	0.14	0.53	0.39	0.48	0.56	0.28	0.21	0.03	0.66	0.13	0.67	0.27	−0.52	0.45

Beckman and Burton: *Path Dependence in the Evolution of Top Management Teams*
Organization Science 19(1), pp. 3–24, © 2008 INFORMS   23

References

Aldrich, H. E. 1999. *Organizations Evolving*. Sage, London.

Aldrich, H. E., C. Zimmer. 1986. Entrepreneurship through social networks. D. L. Sexton, R. W. Smilor, eds. *The Art and Science of Entrepreneurship*. Ballinger, Cambridge, MA, 3–23.

Ancona, D., D. F. Caldwell. 1992. Demography and design: Predictors of new product team performance. *Organ. Sci.* **3** 321–341.

Audia, P. G., C. I. Rider. 2005. A garage and an idea: What more does an entrepreneur need? *California Management Rev.* **48** 6–28.

Baron, J. N., M. D. Burton, M. T. Hannan. 1996. The road taken: Origins and evolution of employment systems in emerging companies. *Indust. Corporate Change* **5** 239–275.

Baron, J. N., M. D. Burton, M. T. Hannan. 1999. Engineering bureaucracy: The genesis of formal policies, positions, and structures in high-technology firms. *J. Law, Econom. Organ.* **15** 1–41.

Baty, G. B., W. M. Evan, T. W. Rothermel. 1971. Personnel flows as interorganizational relations. *Admin. Sci. Quart.* **16** 430–443.

Beckman, C. M. 2006. The influence of founding team company affiliations on firm behavior. *Acad. Management J.* **49**(4) 741–758.

Beckman, C. M., M. D. Burton, C. O'Reilly III. 2007. Early teams: The impact of team demography on VC financing and going public. *J. Bus. Venturing* **22**(2) 147–173.

Boeker, W. 1988. Organizational origins: Entrepreneurial and environmental imprinting at time of founding. G. R. Carroll, ed. *Ecological Models of Organizations*. Ballinger, Cambridge, MA, 33–51.

Boeker, W. 1997. Executive migration and strategic change: The effect of top manager movement on product entry. *Admin. Sci. Quart.* **42** 213–236.

Boeker, W., R. Karichalil. 2002. Entrepreneurial transitions: Factors influencing founder departure. *Acad. Management J.* **45** 818–826.

Boeker, W., R. Wiltbank. 2005. New venture evolution and managerial capabilities. *Organ. Sci.* **16** 123–133.

Boone, C., W. van Olffen, A. van Witteloostuijn, B. De Brabander. 2004. The genesis of top management team diversity: Selective turnover among top management teams in Dutch newspaper publishing, 1970–94. *Acad. Management J.* **47** 633–656.

Bunderson, J. S., K. M. Sutcliffe. 2002. Comparing alternative conceptualizations of functional diversity in management teams: Process and performance effects. *Acad. Management J.* **45** 875–893.

Burton, M. D., C. M. Beckman. 2007. Leaving a legacy: Position imprints and successor turnover in young firms. *Amer. Sociol. Rev.* **72** 239–266.

Burton, M. D., J. B. Sørensen, C. Beckman. 2002. Coming from good stock: Career histories and new venture formation. M. Lounsbury, M. Ventresca, eds. *Research in the Sociology of Organizations*, Vol. 19. JAI Press, Inc., Greenwich, CT, 229–262.

Carroll, G. R., J. R. Harrison. 1998. Organizational demography and culture: Insights from a formal model and simulation. *Admin. Sci. Quart.* **43** 637–667.

Certo, S. T., J. G. Covin, C. M. Daily, D. R. Dalton. 2001. Wealth and the effects of founder management among IPO-stage new ventures. *Strategic Management J.* **22**(6/7) 641–658.

Charan, R., C. W. Hofer, J. F. Mahon. 1980. From entrepreneurial to professional management: A set of guidelines. *J. Small Bus. Management* **18** 1–10.

Cooper, A. C., F. J. Gimeno-Gascon, C. Y. Woo. 1994. Initial human and financial capital as predictors of new venture performance. *J. Bus. Venturing* **9** 371–395.

Cronbach, L. 1987. Statistical tests for moderator variables: Flaws in analysis recently proposed. *Psych. Bull.* **102** 414–417.

Dearborn, D. W. C., H. A. Simon. 1958. Selective perception: A note on the departmental identification of executives. *Sociometry* **21**(2) 140–144.

Downs, A. 1967. *Inside Bureaucracy*. Little Brown, Inc., Boston, MA.

Eisenhardt, K. M., C. B. Schoonhoven. 1990. Organizational growth: Linking founding teams, strategy, environment and growth among U.S. semi-conductor ventures. *Admin. Sci. Quart.* **28** 274–291.

Fine, S. A., S. F. Cronshaw. 1999. *Functional Job Analysis: A Foundation for Human Resources Management*. Lawrence Erlbaum Associates, Florence, KY.

Finkelstein, S., D. C. Hambrick. 1996. *Strategic Leadership: Top Executives and Their Effects on Organizations*. West Publishing Company, Minneapolis/St. Paul, MN.

Flamholtz, E., Y. Randle. 2000. *Growing Pains*. JAI Press, Greenwich, CT.

Fligstein, N. 1990. *The Transformation of Corporate Control*. Harvard University Press, Cambridge, MA.

Gompers, P. A., J. Lerner. 1999. *The Venture Capital Cycle*. MIT Press, Cambridge, MA.

Greiner, L. E. 1972. Evolution and revolution as organizations grow. *Harvard Bus. Rev.* **50**(4) 37–46.

Gulati, R., M. C. Higgins. 2003. Which ties matter when? The contingent effects of interorganizational partnerships on IPO success. *Strategic Management J.* **24**(2) 127–144.

Hambrick, D. C. 2007. Upper echelons theory: An update. *Acad. Management Rev.* **32** 334–343.

Hambrick, D. C., P. Mason. 1984. Upper echelons: The organization as a reflection of its top managers. *Acad. Management Rev.* **9** 193–206.

Hannan, M. T., J. Freeman. 1984. Structural inertia and organizational change. *Amer. Sociol. Rev.* **49** 149–164.

Hannan, M. T., M. D. Burton, J. N. Baron. 1996. Inertia and change in the early years: Employment relations in young, high technology firms. *Indust. Corporate Change* **5** 503–536.

Hannan, M. T., J. N. Baron, G. Hsu, O. Kocak. 2006. Organizational identities and the hazard of change. *Indust. Corporate Change* **15** 755–784.

Hellmann, T., M. Puri. 2000. The interaction between product market and financing strategy: The role of venture capital. *Rev. Financial Stud.* **13**(4) 959–984.

Hellmann, T., M. Puri. 2002. Venture capital and the professionalization of start-up firms: Empirical evidence. *J. Finance* **57** 169–197.

Jehn, K. A., G. B. Northcraft, M. A. Neale. 1999. Why differences make a difference: A field study of diversity, conflict, and performance in workgroups. *Admin. Sci. Quart.* **44**(4) 741–763.

Jensen, M., E. J. Zajac. 2004. Corporate elites and corporate strategy: How demographic preferences and structural position shape the scope of the firm. *Strategic Management J.* **25**(6) 507–524.

Keck, S. 1997. Top management team structure: Differential effects by environmental context. *Organ. Sci.* **8** 143–156.

Knight, D., C. L. Pearce, K. G. Smith, J. D. Olian, H. Sims, K. A. Smith, P. Flood. 1999. Top management team diversity, group process, and strategic consensus. *Strategic Management J.* **20** 445–465.

Beckman and Burton: *Path Dependence in the Evolution of Top Management Teams*
Organization Science 19(1), pp. 3–24, © 2008 INFORMS

Lant, T. K., F. J. Milliken, B. Batra. 1992. The role of managerial learning and interpretation in strategic persistence and reorientation: An empirical exploration. *Strategic Management J.* **13** 585–608.

Lawrence, B. 1997. The black box of organizational demography. *Organ. Sci.* **8** 1–22.

Lin, D. Y., L. J. Wei. 1989. The robust inference for the Cox proportional hazards model. *J. Amer. Statist. Assoc.* **84** 1074–1078.

McPherson, J. M., L. Smith-Lovin, J. M. Cook. 2001. Birds of a feather: Homophily in social networks. *Annual Rev. Sociol.* **27** 415–444.

Michels, R. 1915. *Political Parties: A Sociological Study of the Oligarchical Tendencies of Modern Democracy.* The Free Press, New York.

Miner, A. S. 1987. Idiosyncratic jobs in formalized organizations. *Admin. Sci. Quart.* **32** 327–351.

Mittman, B. S. 1992. Theoretical and methodological issues in the study of organizational demography and demographic change. P. Tolbert, S. Bacharach, eds. *Research in the Sociology of Organizations,* Vol. 10. JAI Press, Greenwich, CT, 3–53.

Osterman, P., M. D. Burton. 2004. Ports and ladders: The nature and relevance of internal labor markets in a changing world. P. Tolbert, R. Batt, eds. *Oxford Handbook on Work and Organization.* Oxford University Press, Oxford, UK.

Pelled, L. H., K. M. Eisenhardt, K. R. Xin. 1999. Exploring the black box: An analysis of work group diversity, conflict, and performance. *Admin. Sci. Quart.* **44** 1–28.

Pfeffer, J. 1983. Organizational demography. B. Staw, L. Cummings, eds. *Res. in Organ. Behavior,* Vol. 5. JAI Press, Greenwich, CT, 299–357.

Phillips, D. J. 2002. A genealogical approach to organizational life chances: The parent-progeny transfer among Silicon Valley law firms, 1946–1996. *Admin. Sci. Quart.* **47** 474–506.

Phillips, D. J. 2005. Organizational genealogies and the persistence of gender hierarchies: The case of Silicon Valley law firms. *Admin. Sci. Quart.* **50** 440–472.

Randel, A. E., K. S. Jaussi. 2003. Functional background identity, diversity, and individual performance in cross-functional teams. *Acad. Management J.* **46** 763–774.

Reagans, R., E. W. Zuckerman. 2001. Networks, diversity, and productivity: The social capital of corporate R&D teams. *Organ. Sci.* **12** 502–517.

Reagans, R., E. W. Zuckerman, B. McEvily. 2004. How to make the team: Social networks vs. demograhy as criteria for designing effective teams. *Admin. Sci. Quart.* **49** 101–133.

Roberts, E. B. 1991. *Entrepreneurs in High Technology: Lessons from MIT and Beyond.* Oxford University Press, New York.

Rogers, E. M., D. K. Bhowmik. 1971. Homophily-heterophily: Relational concepts for communication research. *Public Opinion Quart.* **34** 523–538.

Roure, J., R. Keeley. 1990. Predictors of success in new technology based ventures. *J. Bus. Venturing* **5** 201–220.

Ruef, M., H. E. Aldrich, N. M. Carter. 2003. The structure of founding teams: Homophily, strong ties, and isolation among U.S. entrepreneurs. *Amer. Sociol. Rev.* **68**(2) 195–222.

Schein, E. H. 1992. *Organizational Culture and Leadership,* 2nd ed. Jossey Bass, San Francisco, CA.

Schneider, B. 1987. The people make the place. *Personnel Psych.* **40** 437–453.

Shane, S., T. Stuart. 2002. Organizational endowments and the performance of university start-ups. *Management Sci.* **48**(1) 154–170.

Sine, W. D., H. Mitsuhashi, D. A. Kirsch. 2006. Revisiting burns and stalker: Formal structure and new venture performance in emerging economic sectors. *Acad. Management J.* **49**(1) 121–132.

Smith, K., K. Smith, J. Olian, H. Sims, D. O'Bannon, J. Scully. 1994. Top management team demography and process: The role of social integration and communication. *Admin. Sci. Quart.* **39** 412–438.

Sørensen, J. B. 1999. Executive migration and interorganizational competition. *Soc. Sci. Res.* **28** 289–315.

Sørensen, J. B. 2004. The organizational demography of racial employment segregation. *Amer. J. Sociol.* **110** 626–671.

Staw, B. M. 1976. Knee-deep in the big muddy—A study of escalating commitment to a chosen course of action. *Organ. Behav. Human Performance* **16**(1) 27–44.

Stinchcombe, A. L. 1965. Social structure and organizations. J. G. March, ed. *Handbook of Organizations.* Rand McNally, Chicago, IL, 142–193.

Stuart, T. E., H. Hoang, R. C. Hybels. 1999. Interorganizational endorsements and the performance of entrepreneurial ventures. *Admin. Sci. Quart.* **44** 315–349.

Sutcliffe, K. M. 1994. What executives notice: Accurate perceptions in top management teams. *Acad. Management J.* **37**(5) 1360–1378.

Tripsas, M., G. Gavetti. 2000. Capabilities, cognition and inertia: Evidence from digital imaging. *Strategic Management J.* **21**(10/11) 1147–1161.

Tushman, M. L., L. Rosenkopf. 1996. Executive succession, strategic reorientation and performance growth: A longitudinal study in the U.S. cement industry. *Management Sci.* **42** 939–953.

Wanous, J. P. 1992. *Organizational Entry: Recruitment, Selection, Orientation, and Socialization of Newcomers.* Addison-Wesley, Reading, MA.

Wasserman, N. 2003. Founder-CEO succession and the paradox of entrepreneurial success. *Organ. Sci.* **14**(2) 149–172.

Williams, K., C. O'Reilly. 1998. Demography and diversity in organizations: A review of 40 years of research. *Res. Organ. Behavior* **20** 77–140.

Name Index

Hansen, E.L. 3, 119, 143
Hansen, M.T. 230
Hargadon, A. 17
Harhoff, D. 60
Harrison, A.W. 155
Harrison, D.A. 114
Harrison, J.R. 357
Hart, M.M. 191
Haunschild, P. 14, 17
Hausman, J. 68
Haveman, H.A. 33
Hawley, A. 40
Hawley, F. 252
Hay, R.K. 7
Hayek, F.A. 194
Hayton, J.C. 191
He, Z.L. 14, 18
Heckman, J. 334, 340–41
Hedberg, B.L.T. 3
Hegarty, W.H. 221
Heirman, A. 86, 93
Helfat, C.E. 249
Helfert, G. 177, 179
Hellman, T. 20, 21, 276, 356–7, 361–2
Henderson, M. 133, 138–40
Heneman, C.E. 221–2
Heneman, H.G. 222, 224
Henkel, J. 60
Herron, L. 132, 154
Herron, M. 15
Hesterly, W.S. 223, 225, 236
Higashide, H. 112–13
Higgins, M.C. 361
Hills, G.E. 193
Hite, J.M. 223, 225, 236
Hitt, M.A. 202
Hoban, J.P. 286, 293–4
Hobson, C.J. 202
Hobson, E.L. 291, 294
Hochschild, A.R. 134
Hoegl, M. 177–9, 181, 183
Hofer, C. 62, 65, 143, 154, 274, 298, 328–9
Hoffman, L.R. 115
Homans, G. 7, 133
Hornaday, J. 118, 154
Hornaday, R.W. 118
Hornsby, J.S. 221
Houghton, S. 192, 204
House, R.J. 297
Howorth, C. 256
Hoy, F. 131, 256
Hoyle, R.H. 161, 163
Hrebiniak, L.G. 318
Hudson, R. 286, 299

Huff, A.S. 201–2
Hunsdiek, D. 174–5
Hunter, J.E. 116
Hunter, R.F. 116
Hurst, D.K. 199

Iammarino, S. 89
Ibarra, H. 36
Ireland, R.D. 202

Jackson, S.E. 113–15, 120, 146, 167, 195, 252, 257, 260
Jacobson, E. 135
James, J. 34, 44, 47
James, L.R. 142, 161
Janis, I.L. 116, 141, 169, 177, 303
Janowitz, M. 134, 138
Jarillo, J.C. 273
Jaussi, K.S. 357
Jayaraman, N. 272–3
Jehn, K.A. 116, 140, 156–8, 161, 257, 357
Jelinek, M. 195
Jensen, M.C. 87, 244, 252, 276, 356
Johannisson, B. 113
Johne, A. 177
Johnson, D.E. 190, 208, 225
Johnson, K.L. 117
Johnson, P. 331
Jones, G.R. 227
Jones, S. 196
Jones-Evans, D. 328
Jovanovic, B. 328–9
Joyce, W.F. 318
Judge, W. 167, 252
Jussim, L. 36

Kabanoff, B. 157
Kahn, R.J. 4, 7, 134, 155, 157
Kahwajy, J. 88
Kalleberg, A, 36
Kamm, J.B. 3, 4, 7, 9, 39, 86–7, 114, 132, 135–8, 141, 154, 159, 175, 177–8, 226, 252
Kanter, R.M. 17
Kaplan, S. 276
Karan, V. 252
Karichalil, R. 272, 274, 356
Katila, R. 14, 17
Katz, D. 4, 7, 134, 155, 157
Katz, J.A. 87, 190, 193, 220–22
Katz, R. 168, 179
Kazanjian, R.K. 4, 195, 206, 298, 303
Keats, B.W. 202
Keck, S.L. 167, 356–7, 359
Keeley, R.H. 138, 303, 356–7, 359